The Complete Book of When and Where

THE COMPLETE  BOOK OF

WHEN &
WHERE

IN THE BIBLE
AND THROUGHOUT HISTORY

E. MICHAEL & SHARON RUSTEN

Tyndale House Publishers, Inc.
WHEATON, ILLINOIS

Visit Tyndale's exciting Web site at www.tyndale.com

The Complete Book of When and Where

Copyright © 2005 by E. Michael and Sharon O. Rusten. All rights reserved.

TYNDALE is a registered trademark of Tyndale House Publishers, Inc.

Tyndale's quill logo is a trademark of Tyndale House Publishers, Inc.

Cover photograph of locomotive © by Colin Garratt; Milepost 92½ /Corbis. All rights reserved.

Cover image of Noah with dove: Veneto-Byzantine School: San Marco, Venice, Italy.

Cover photographs of bridge, hay, uniform, telescope, Big Ben, and stadium © by Photos.com. All rights reserved.

Interior artwork © 1995–2000 by Nova Development Corporation and its licensors. Rights of all parties reserved.

Designed by Ron Kaufmann

The introduction to the Era of the Christian Roman Empire is adapted from Bruce L. Shelley, *Church History in Plain Language* (Dallas: Word, 1995). Used by permission of Thomas Nelson, Inc.

The introductions to the Era of Catholic Christianity, the christian Middle Ages, the Reformation Era, the Age of Reason and Revival, the Age of Progress, and the Age of Ideologies are adapted from Bruce L. Shelley, "Church History in Brief," *Christian History*, copyright Issue 28. Used by permission.

Unless otherwise indicated, all Scripture quotations are taken from the *Holy Bible*, New Living Translation, copyright © 1996. Used by permission of Tyndale House Publishers, Inc., Wheaton, Illinois 60189. All rights reserved.

Library of Congress Cataloging-in-Publication Data

Rusten, E. Michael, date.
   The complete book of when and where / E. Michael and Sharon Rusten.
     p. cm.
   Includes index.
   ISBN 0-8423-5508-1
   1. Church history. 2. Judaism—History. I. Rusten, Sharon O. II. Title.
   BR145.3R87 2005
   270′.02′02—dc22   2004021646

Printed in the United States of America

10   09   08   07   06   05
 7   6   5   4   3   2   1

To Drew and Marta MacDougall
and Mark and Martha Rusten

CONTENTS

The Old Testament Era (2166 BC–7 BC) page 1

The New Testament Era (7 BC–AD 100) page 69

The Era of Catholic Christianity (100–312) page 101

The Era of the Christian Roman Empire (312–590) page 115

The Christian Middle Ages (590–1517) page 139

The Reformation Era (1517–1648) page 215

The Age of Reason and Revival (1648–1789) page 275

The Age of Progress (1789–1914) page 323

The Age of Ideologies (1914–2000) page 413

ACKNOWLEDGMENTS

We want to thank the many who assisted us in this project: our agent and friend, Al Youngren; our editors, Jon Farrar, Erin Keeley Marshall, MaryLynn Layman, and Dave Lindstedt; and those who served as research assistants: Martha Rusten, Chris Bruno, Dana Johnson, Carrie Zeman, Dan Brendsel, Joyce Renick, Matt Wireman, Harold Simmons, David Mathis, Mark Ammerman, Mark Batluck, Andrew Cowan, and Kate Brand.

INTRODUCTION

History is God's story. "All things happen just as he decided long ago" (Ephesians 1:11). God is the author of history in the most literal sense of the word. And the plan of history that he is in the process of working out is the one that brings the maximum glory to him. "For everything comes from him; everything exists by his power and is intended for his glory. To him be glory evermore. Amen" (Romans 11:36).

The purpose of this book is to identify the 1001 most significant events in Judeo-Christian history. They were chosen in light of the effect they had on their generation and succeeding generations, both good and bad. Believing that the Jews continue to be God's chosen people, we have included the most significant Jewish dates of the last two millennia.

Where there is a difference of opinion as to the exact date of an event, we have used a consensus date based on several sources. Each date is preceded by a symbol: + indicating a significance primarily to Christian history, ✡ indicating a significance primarily to Jewish history, or ☪ indicating a significance primarily to Muslim history.

May you come to learn more of the God of history through the unfolding of the events recorded in these pages.

Mike and Sharon Rusten

TIMETABLE OF HISTORY

THE OLD TESTAMENT ERA

2166 BC – 7 BC

	2200 BC	**2000 BC**	**1800 BC**

2200 BC

2200–1950 **Middle Bronze Age I**

2000 BC

2000 City-states emerge in Phoenicia

1950–1750 Middle Bronze Age IIa

1894–1595 First Dynasty rules Babylon

1800 BC

1800 Babylonian astronomers define day from midnight to midnight
1792 Code of Hammurabi issued
1760–1122 Shang Dynasty rules China
1750–1600 Middle Bronze Age IIb

1628 Aegean island of Thira partially destroyed by volcanic eruption

---

Hieroglyphic writing appears in Far East 2200–1700
Seventh and Eighth Dynasties rule Egypt 2181–2173
Ninth and Tenth Dynasties rule Egypt 2160–2040

Eleventh Dynasty rules Egypt 2133–1786

Hittite, Egyptian, and Assyrian Empires Control Major Areas 2000
Ammenemes I reigns in Egypt 1991–1962
Twelfth Dynasty rules Egypt 1991–1786
Sesostris I reigns in Egypt 1971–1928
Ammenemes II reigns in Egypt 1929–1895
Sesostris II reigns in Egypt 1897–1878
Sesostris III reigns in Egypt 1878–1843
Ammenemes III reigns in Egypt 1842–1797

Ammenemes IV reigns in Egypt 1798–1790
Queen Sobkneferu reigns in Egypt 1789–1786
Thirteenth Dynasty rules Egypt from Memphis 1786–1633
Fourteenth Dynasty rules Egypt from Western Delta 1786–1603
Fifteenth Dynasty rules Egypt 1674–1567
Sixteenth Dynasty rules Egypt 1650–1567
Seventeenth Dynasty rules Egypt 1650–1567
Hyksos reigns in New Kingdom of Egypt 1638–1540

1600 BC

- **1600–1550** Middle Bronze Age IIc
- **1595** Hittites conquer Babylon
- **1550–1400** Late Bronze Age I
- **1545–1500** Burnaburiash I of Kassite Dynasty rules Mesopotamia
- **1500** *I Ching* published in China
- **1450** Earliest literature composed in India
- **1450** Brahma worship begins in India

1400 BC

- **1400–1300** Late Bronze Age IIa
- **1400–1100** Phoenicians devise first alphabetic typescript

- **1300–1200** Late Bronze Age IIb
- **1300** First settlers arrive in Fiji, Samoa, and Tonga
- **1274–1245** Shalmaneser I reigns in Assyria
- **1250** Egyptians build temple of Karnak
- **1244–1208** Tukulfi-Ninarta I reigns in Assyria

1200 BC

- **1200–1150** Iron Age Ia

- **1150–1000** Iron Age Ib
- **1124–1103** Nebuchadnezzar I reigns in Babylonia
- **1115–1077** Tiglath-pileser I reigns in Assyria

Amosis reigns in Egypt **1570–1546**
Eighteenth Dynasty rules Egypt **1570–1320**
Ahmose reigns in Egypt **1552–1526**
Amenhotep I reigns in Egypt **1546–1526**
Thutmose I reigns in Egypt **1526–1512**
Thutmose II reigns in Egypt **1512–1504**
Thutmose III reigns in Egypt **1504–1450**
Queen Hatshepsut reigns in Egypt **1503–1483**
Amenhotep II reigns in Egypt **1450–1425**
Thutmose IV reigns in Egypt **1425–1417**
Amenhotep III reigns in Egypt **1417–1379**
Amenhotep IV reigns in Egypt **1379–1362**
Smenkhkare reigns in Egypt **1364–1361**
Tutankhamen reigns in Egypt **1361–1352**
Ay reigns in Egypt **1352–1348**
Horemheb reigns in Egypt **1348–1320**
Ramses I reigns in Egypt **1320–1318**
Nineteenth Dynasty rules Egypt **1320–1200**
Seti I reigns in Egypt **1318–1304**
Ramses II reigns in Egypt **1304–1236**
Merneptah reigns in Egypt **1236–1223**
Twentieth Dynasty rules Egypt **1200–1085**
Dorians destroy Mycenae, ending Mycenaean civilization **1193**
Troy destroyed with Trojan horse 1180
Chou Dynasty succeeds Shang Dynasty in China **1122–480**
Smallpox first recorded in China **1122**

Twenty-first Dynasty rules Egypt **1085–945**

1000-900 Iron Age IIa
994 Teutonic tribes move westward to Rhine River

933 Ashur-dan II reigns in Assyria

900-800 Iron Age IIb
883-859 Ashurnasirpal II reigns in Assyria
859-824 Shalmaneser III reigns in Assyria
853 Assyria victorious at Battle of Qarqar
841 Verified Chinese chronology begins

800-720 Iron Age IIIa
745-727 Tiglath-pileser III reigns in Assyria
727-722 Shalmaneser V reigns in Assyria
722-705 Sargon II reigns in Assyria
720-587 Iron Age IIIb
705-681 Senacherib reigns in Assyria
681-669 Esarhaddon reigns in Assyria
668-627 Ashurbanipal reigns in Assyria
626-605 Nabopolassar reigns in Babylon
609-608 Assyria falls
605-562 Nebuchadnezzar II reigns in Babylon
605 Nebuchadnezzar II defeats Egyptians at Battle of Carchemish
580 Nebuchadnezzar II builds Hanging Gardens of Babylon

562-560 Evil-merodach reigns in Babylon
556-539 Nabonidus reigns in Babylon
556 Rabashi-mardok reigns in Babylon
539-530 Cyrus reigns in Persia
530-522 Cambyses reigns in Persia
521-486 Darius I reigns in Persia
509 **Roman Republic founded**

1000 BC

800 BC

600 BC

Twenty-second Dynasty rules Egypt **945-ca. 730**

Twenty-third Dynasty rules Egypt **817-730**
Phoenicians establish Carthage **813-810**
Homer writes *The Iliad* and *The Odyssey* **800**
First Olympic Games held in Greece 776
Damascus falls **732**
Twenty-fourth Dynasty rules Egypt **720-714**
Twenty-fifth Dynasty rules Egypt **716-656**
Earliest sheet music written on Sumerian clay tablet **700**
Greek musician Terpander completes the octave **673**
Twenty-sixth Dynasty rules Egypt **664-525**
Nineveh falls **612**
Neco II reigns in Egypt **610-595**
Nebuchadnezzar becomes king of Babylon **605**

Siddhartha Gautama, founder of Buddhism, born in India **563-550**
Zoroaster, founder of Zoroastrianism, dies **553**
Confucius born in China **551/552**
Greek philosopher Thales dies **545**
Twenty-seventh Dynasty rules Egypt **525-404**
Buddha preaches first sermon **521**
Democratic reforms sweep Athens **510**

500 Babylonian astronomer determines lunar month
500 Etruscan power reaches height in Italy
490 Athenians defeat Persians at Battle of Marathon
486–464 Xerxes (Ahasuerus) reigns in Persia
480 **Parthenon built in Athens**

464–423 Artaxerxes I reigns in Persia

440 Socrates teaches

430 Aeschylus writes *Prometheus Bound*
424 Herodotus, "father of history," dies
423–404 Darius II Nothus reigns in Persia
415 Hindu mythology codified in the Ramayana
406 Euripides and Sophocles die
404–359 Artaxerxes II Mnemon reigns in Persia

400 Plato and Aristophanes write
399 Socrates dies
390 Northern Italian Gauls capture Rome, then withdraw

377 City walls built around Rome

354 Greek historian Xenephon dies

500 BC

450 BC

400 BC

Indian surgeon performs cataract operations **500**
Greek choral music reaches zenith **500**
Pythagoras, Greek philosopher and mathematician, dies **497**
Tragic dramatist Sophocles born **496**
Athenian shrine at Delphi is first marble building in Greece **490**
Hanno, a Phoenician navigator, is believed to have sailed around Africa **480**
Athens begins to increase domination **477**

Athenian soldiers and judges receive regular salaries **462**
Euripides writes Greek tragedies **455–407**
Acropolis of Athens rebuilt **448–433**

Democritus introduces atomic structure of matter **440**
Parthenon completed and consecrated **438**
Peloponnesian War between Athens and Sparta **431–404**
Plague ravages Athens **430–423**
Pericles of Athens dies **429**
Anaxagoras, Greek philosopher from Asia Minor, dies **428**

Twenty-eighth Dynasty rules Egypt **404–399**
Greeks propose free elementary education **400–250**
Twenty-ninth Dynasty rules Egypt **399–380**
Greek historian Thucydides dies **395**

Thirtieth Dynasty of Egypt is last native dynasty to rule **380–343**

Hippocrates, Greek physician, dies **377**

350 BC

- 350 Phoenician states secede from Persia
- 340 Difference between arteries and veins discovered in Greece
- 340 Aristotle sets foundation for musical theory
- 334 Alexander the Great begins conquests
- 332 Alexander the Great founds Alexandria, Egypt
- 327 Alexander the Great invades India
- 326 Alexander the Great reaches Indus River
- 322 Aristotle dies
- 321 First Imperial Dynasty of India founded
- 311 Seleucid Dynasty begins in Syria

- Plato dies 347
- Thirty-first Dynasty rules Egypt 343-332
- Persia conquers Egypt 343
- First Roman coins minted 338
- Philip II of Macedon assassinated 336
- Ptolemy I Soter reigns in Egypt 323-285
- Euclid writes about geometry 323
- Zeno founds Stoic School 322
- Judea annexed by Ptolemy I Soter of Egypt 320
- Romans finish Appian aqueduct and begin Appian Way 312

300 BC

- 300 *Tao Te Ching*, book of Taoist sayings, published in China
- 275 Colossus of Rhodes completed

- Greek astronomer Aristarchus says sun is center of solar system 300-250
- Ptolemy II Philadelphus reigns in Egypt 285-245
- Greek philosopher Epicurus dies 270

250 BC

- 264-241 First Punic War between Rome and Carthage
- 264 Roman gladiators first compete publically
- 250 First Roman prison erected
- 250 Parchment produced at Pergamum
- 228 Rome first sends ambassadors to Athens and Corinth
- 224 Colossus of Rhodes destroyed by earthquake
- 221 Chin Dynasty founded in China
- 221 All Chinese weights and measures unified
- 211 Denarius, Roman silver coin, minted
- 202 Han Dynasty defeats Chin Dynasty in China

- Greek astronomer makes map of heaven 250-200
- Ptolemy III Evergetes reigns in Egypt 246-222
- Leap year introduced in Egyptian calendar 239
- Oil lamps introduced into Greece 230
- Ptolemy IV Philopator reigns in Egypt 222-205
- Rome conquers northern Italy 222
- Second Punic War between Rome and Carthage 218-202
- Hannibal crosses Alps on march to Rome 218
- **Construction begins on Great Wall of China 215**
- Ptolemy V Epiphanes reigns in Egypt 204-180
- Hannibal reportedly developed compass 203

200 BC

- Ox-driven water wheel invented **200**
- Romans defeat Antiochus at Thermopylae **191**
- Pons Aemilius, first stone bridge, built in Rome **179**
- Earliest known paved streets laid in Rome **170**
- First water clock invented **159**
- Rome destroys Carthage in Third Punic War **149–146**
- Venus de Milo sculpted **140**

- **198** Antiochus defeats Egypt and gains control of Palestine
- **196** Rosetta Stone inscribed
- **183** Hannibal commits suicide to avoid extradition to Rome
- **160** Trigonometry invented
- **147** Romans control Greece
- **140** Crates forms his first great globe of earth

100 BC

- First College of Technology founded in Alexandria **105**
- First cherry trees imported to Rome from Asia Minor **79**

- **100** First Chinese ships reach India
- **66** Florence, Italy, founded
- **55** Lucretius writes fundamental text of Epicureanism

50 BC

- Slaves and gladiators revolt under Spartacus **71**
- Julius Caesar wins major victories in Spain **61**
- Julius Caesar invades Gaul **58**
- Julius Caesar invades Britain **55**
- Julius Caesar crosses Rubicon to start civil war **49**
- Julius Caesar defeats Pompey **48**
- Pompey murdered in Egypt by order of Cleopatra **47**
- Julian calendar of 365.25 days with leap year adopted **46**
- Mark Antony and Cleopatra defeated at Actium **31**
- Roman poet Virgil dies **19**
- Roman poet Horace dies **8**

- **50** Earliest form of oboe invented in Rome
- **47** Fire destroys 40,000 volumes of Great Library of Alexandria
- **43** Roman politician and orator Cicero dies
- **30** Building of Roman Pantheon begins
- **12** Silk Road opens between China and West

THE NEW TESTAMENT ERA

AD 6 – 98

0

Judea becomes Roman province 6
Roman legions annihilated in Germany 9

Roman historian Livy dies 17
Roman poet Ovid dies 17

Caligula assassinated, succeeded by Claudius 41

Romans learn to use soap 50
Claudius assassinated, succeeded by Nero 54

Roman statesman Seneca commits suicide 65
Nero commits suicide 68
Four Caesars reign 69

Emperor Titus reigns 79–81
Arch of Titus built in Rome 81

14 Augustus succeeded by Tiberius
17 **Earthquake destroys much of Ephesus**

37 Tiberius succeeded by Caligula
43 **London founded**

50 **Pyramid built in Teotihuacán, Mexico**

58 **Buddhism introduced into China**
61 British unsuccessfully revolt against Rome

79 **Mount Vesuvius erupts, covering Pompeii**
81–96 **Emperor Domitian reigns**

96–98 Emperor Nerva reigns
98–116 Emperor Trajan reigns

50

75

THE ERA OF CATHOLIC CHRISTIANITY

100 – 312

100

105 **Paper invented in China**

Roman Empire achieves greatest expansion **117**

ca. 117 Tacitus writes *Historiae*

Emperor Hadrian reigns **117–38**

118–25 **Pantheon built in Rome**

Greek historian Plutarch dies **120**

122 Hadrian's Wall constructed in Britain

124 Romans learn to construct domes

Ptolemy says earth is center of universe **127**

132 Seismograph invented in China

150

150 **Earliest Sanskrit inscribed in India**

Political states develop in Peru **150**

150 Korea wins independence from China

164 **Oldest Mayan monuments erected**

166 Syrian merchants arrive in China

Emperor Marcus Aurelius reigns 161–80

Roman Empire ravaged by smallpox **164–80**

Emperor Marcus Aurelius writes *Meditations* **167**

177–84 Plague devastates China

180 Barbarian tribes attack Roman Empire

Romans defeated in Scotland **180**

200 Indonesian sailors settle Madagascar
200 Japan invades Korea
200 Silkworms arrive in China
212 Roman citizenship given to freemen
220 **Chinese Han Dynasty ends**

248 Rome celebrates 1,000th anniversary

257 Franks invade Spain
260 Bantu expand into South Africa
270 Plotinus, founder of Neo-Platonism, dies

300 Asians settle eastern Polynesia

200

250

300

Huns invade Afghanistan **200–540**
Ghana becomes trading nation **200**
Skates invented in Scandinavia **200**
Goths invade Asia Minor **220**
Southern India divides into kingdoms **225**
Goths begin invading Roman Empire 238

Goths invade Black Sea region **257**

Goths sack Athens and Corinth **268**

Roman Empire partitioned **285**

Villages appear in North America 300s

THE ERA OF
THE CHRISTIAN ROMAN EMPIRE

312 – 590

313

375

Oldest bridge built over the Rhine 313

Gupta Dynasty rules Northern India 320

Seat of Roman Empire moved to Constantinople 330

325 Church of the Nativity built in Bethlehem

Books begin to replace scrolls 360

Scots attack Britain 360

Scots driven out of Britain 370

350 Huns invade India and Persia

355 Huns invade Russia

360 Huns invade Europe

Romans conquer Gaul and Spain 383

376 Huns invade Russia

378 Visigoths defeat Roman army

379 Theodius the Great becomes Roman emperor

Roman Empire split into Eastern and Western empires 395

396 Visigoths invade Greece

398 Visigoths plunder Balkans

400

400 Ethiopia and Eritrea flourish
401–3 Visigoths invade Italy
409 Vandals conquer part of Spain
410 Visigoths capture and sack Rome

Teotihuacán, Mexico, flourishes **400–550**
Ecuador and Central Andes flourish **400–550**
Khmer (Cambodia) becomes nation **ca. 400**

Beginnings of alchemy 410
Augustine writes *City of God* 411

Franks settle in Gaul 418

Venice founded 421

425

420 Nanking is capital of Northern China

425 Barbarians settle in Roman Provinces
429 Scots expelled from southern England
433 Attila becomes Hun ruler

Constantinople University founded 425
Vandal kingdom reaches North Africa 429
Last Roman troops leave Britain 436

443 Vandals establish absolute monarchy in North Africa
450 Polynesians reach Hawaiian Islands
450 Maoris arrive in New Zealand

Vandals sack Rome 455
Franks capture Cologne 460

475

470 Huns withdraw from Europe

476 Buddhist cave temples built in northern China
476 Eastern Sicily sold to Visigoths
478 First Shinto shrine built in Japan

Rome struck by earthquake 476
German proclaimed king of Italy 476
Kingdom of Sussex founded 477

Armenian church becomes independent 491

496 British defeat Saxons

Kingdom of Wessex founded 495

THE CHRISTIAN MIDDLE AGES
590 – 1517

500

Indians bring tea to China **500**
Codex Bezae of New Testament written **500**
Corn raised in North America **500s**
Basket making spreads northward from Mexico **500s**
Church of the Nativity burns **529**
King Arthur killed in battle **537**
Plague kills half of Europe **542–94**

500 Chinese and Japanese invent stencils
500 Incense introduced in Christian churches
500 Lombards settle north of Danube
522 Oldest known pagoda built in China
537 Hagia Sophia Cathedral built in Constantinople
550 Pueblo culture begins in Utah

600

Printing press invented in China 593
Barbarian invasions of Europe end **600**
Mayan civilization flourishes in Mexico **600–900**
Horyuji temple built in Japan **607**

Emperor Tai-tsung reigns in China **626**

First reported windmills erected in Persia **650**

594 Buddhism becomes religion of Japan

618 China united under T'ang Dynasty

635 Earliest quill pens used in Spain

655 Arab fleet defeats Byzantine navy

700 First Beijing newspaper printed

740 Woodblock printing begins in Orient

755–63 Rebellion ends Chinese T'ang Dynasty
765 Tibet becomes overwhelmingly Buddhist
771 Arabic numbers enter Arab world
800s Berber Empire rules in Western Sahara
800–1000 Asian plows imported to Europe

868 Illustrated book printed in China
874 Vikings settle Iceland
891 Monks write history of England
ca. 900 Hausa Dynasty of Nigeria founded
900s Chinese invent gunpowder
900s One-thousand-volume encyclopedia written in China

983 Canal locks invented in China

1000 Norman architecture appears in England
1000 Statue Stones quarried on Easter Island
1000 Spinning wheel invented in Asia
1000–1400s Hinduism replaces Buddhism in India
1019 First Japanese novel written

1041 Chinese invent movable type

700 **850** **1000**

Islamic armies invade southern Spain 711
Charles Martel defeats Muslims at the Battle of Tours 732

Carolingian Dynasty of Europe begins 751
Charlemagne becomes king of Franks 771
Vikings invade British Isles 790
First castles built in Europe 800

Algebra developed in Persia 820

Jews settle in Germany 850
Cyrillic alphabet developed in Eastern Europe 863
Treaty pushes Danes north 878

Mayans immigrate to Yucatan Peninsula 900
Romanesque architecture flourishes in Europe 900–1100
Hohokam culture in American Southwest 900–1150

Erik the Red settles Greenland 986
System of musical notation developed 990
Iroquois build log longhouses 1000s
Apache reach southwestern United States 1000s
Navajo reach southwestern United States 1000s
Leif Eriksson reaches Newfoundland 1001

Middle Eastern earthquake kills 50,000 1041

1050

Iron plows used in Europe 1050
Construction of Westminster Abbey begins 1052
Normans conquer Britain 1066
William of Normandy rules England 1066

1050 Polyphonic singing replaces Gregorian chant
1050 Asian astrolabes introduced into Europe
1064–72 Famine results from Nile not flooding

1071 Seljuk Turks capture Asia Minor

Venice trades with Byzantine Empire 1081

1080 Chinese theorize climate changes

El Cid captures Valencia, Spain 1094

1090 Magnetic compass invented in China

1100

Arab traders settle in Africa 1100
European Gothic cathedrals built 1100–1250
Welcher measures latitude and longitude 1120

1100s Cultural advancement sweeps Europe
1100s Indonesians begin converting to Islam

1130 Aimonad Dynasty rules Morocco

Paper first made in Europe 1150
Map shows a round earth 1154

1151 China captures Beijing from Mongols
1155 First map printed in China
1161 Chinese use explosives in warfare
1189 Genghis Khan becomes Mongol leader
1191 Tea introduced in Japan
1192 Shoguns begin rule of Japan

Ptolemy translated into Latin 1175
Rudder invented in Arabia 1180
Saladin unites Egypt and Syria 1187
Magnifying glass invented in England 1200
Arabic numbers introduced into Europe 1202

1200

Magna Carta written 1215

1200 **Genghis Khan begins conquests**
1200 Drought in Africa causes famine
1206 Genghis Khan becomes emperor
1214 Genghis Khan recaptures Beijing

Geographical encyclopedia written in Arabic 1224
Hanseatic League formed in Germany 1230

1240 Kingdom of Mali Established
1242 Mongols withdraw from Europe

1250 Nasir al-Din Tusi develops Shiite theology

1271 Marco Polo travels to Beijing
1277 Genoese traders sail past Gibralter
1280 Cannon invented in China
1286 Eyeglasses invented in Italy

1298 England defeats William Wallace and the Scots
1300–1400 Kashmir converted to Islam
1300–1400 Kingdom of Kongo established

1325 Chinese rebel against Mongol overlords

1337–1453 Hundred Years' War

1363 Tamerlane begins conquest of Asia
1368 Ming Dynasty replaces Mongol Dynasty in China
1368 Chinese reconcile Buddhism, Confuciansim, Taoism

1389 Ottoman Turks defeat Serbs
1397 Denmark, Norway, and Sweden unite
1401 Siam controls Malay Peninsula
1405–33 Chinese sail to Africa
1415 England controls much of France

1438 Inca Empire established in Peru
1438 Incas from Ecuador invade Chile
1440 Cusanos theorizes space is infinite

1250

1300

1375

Longbow developed in Wales **1250–1300**
Tin-plating invented in Bohemia **1250**
Egyptians defeat Mongols **1260**

Planetary charts developed in Spain **1272**
Hapsburgs established in Germany **1273**
Typhoon destroys Mongol fleet **1281**
England conquers Wales **1282–84**

First representative parliament established in England **1295**
Ottoman Empire founded in Turkey **1299**
Renaissance begins in Italy **1300**
Clocks invented in Germany **1300**
Hand cannons invented in Europe **1318**
Tenochtitlan (Mexico City) becomes Aztec capital **1325**

First blast furnace made for smelting **1340**
Plague kills quarter of Europeans **1347–50**
Alarm clocks invented in Germany **1350**

Peasants revolt in England **1381**
Geoffrey Chaucer begins writing *Canterbury Tales* **1387**
Chaucer measures positions of stars **1391**
The Medicis become influential in Florence **1397**
Renaissance spreads throughout Europe **1400–1500s**
Screw invented in Germany **1405**
Trigger invented in Germany **1411**
Portuguese sail African west coast **1419**

First African slaves brought to Europe 1435
Berlin becomes capital of Brandenburg **1448**

1450 Double-entry bookkeeping introduced
1453 Constantinople falls to Ottoman Turks

1467 Civil War begins in Japan

1480s Persian illustrates manuscripts with minatures
1482 Portuguese colonize African Gold Coast
1485 Incas conquer all of Chile
1485–1533 Caitanya begins Hare Krishna movement
1488 Cape of Good Hope circumvented
1492 Spanish drive Muslims from Spain

1497 Cabot reaches North America
1502 Watch invented in Germany
1506 Christopher Columbus dies in poverty
1506-7 First maps of New World created

1513 Niccolo Machiavelli publishes *The Prince*
1516 Thomas More publishes *Utopia*

1450

1475

1500

Concave lenses invented in Germany **1450**

English Wars of the Roses **1455**

Sikh religion founded in India **1467–1539**
Ferdinand and Isabella unite Spain **1469**
Frenchman perfects easy-to-read Roman typeface **1470**
First book printed in English 1475
Oxford University Press established **1478**

Henry Tudor defeats Richard III **1485**
Sir Thomas Malory's *Morte Darthur* published by William Caxton **1485**
Plus and minus signs introduced **1489**
First anatomical text with illustrations **1491**
First globe produced in Nuremberg **1492**

Vasco da Gama sails to India **1498**
Greek and Latin classics printed **1500**

St. Peter's Church built in Rome **1506–1612**

Desiderius Erasmus writes *In Praise of Folly* **1509**
Vasco de Balboa discovers Pacific Ocean **1513**

Ottomans conquer Egypt 1517

THE REFORMATION ERA
1517 – 1648

1519

- **1519** Charles V becomes Holy Roman Emperor
- **1521** **Hernando Cortés conquers Mexico's Aztec Empire**

- **1529** Ottoman Turks reach Vienna
- **1529** Ottoman Turks defeated at Vienna
- **1530** Portuguese organize slave trade
- **1532** François Rabelais writes *Adventures of Gargantua*
- **1533** Juan Pizarro conquers Peru's Inca Empire
- **1536** Advances made in treatment of wounds
- **1539** Mexicans print first American book

- **1543** First great treatise on anatomy written

1535

- **1556** Earthquake in China kills 830,000

1560

- **1562** **English enter slave trade**

- **1564** Spain conquers the Philippians
- **1565** St. Augustine, Florida, first settled

- **1568–1600** Japan unified
- **1570** First complete world atlas published
- **1572** Tycho Brahe's observation of supernova
- **1572** Last of Inca royalty executed

Ferdinand Magellan circumnavigates the earth 1519–21
Ottoman Empire reaches greatest size 1520–66

First book of etiquette published 1528
Grenades invented in France 1528
Diving bell invented in Spain 1528
Bursting Dutch dikes kill 400,000 1530
First stock exchange established in Antwerp 1531
Francisco Coronado explores southwestern United States 1540
Nicolaus Copernicus says Earth circles the sun 1543

Smallpox kills 800,000 Mexican Indians 1545

Emperor Charles V abdicates 1556
Mughal Empire spreads in India 1556–1605

Lead pencil invented 1565

Gerardus Mercator's world map printed 1569
European navies defeat Turks 1571
Francis Drake captures Spanish fleet 1572
Francis Drake sails around world 1577–80

1589

1589 Dredges invented in the Netherlands
1590 **Telescope invented**
1590 Compound microscope invented
1592–98 Japan invades Korea
1594 Logarithms worked out in Scotland

1600 East India Company formed
1600 Freedom of the press begins
1605–15 Miguel de Cervantes publishes *Don Quixote*
1606 Willem Jansz discovers Australia
1607 Claudio Monteverdi writes his first opera
1609 Johannes Kepler develops laws of planetary motion
1610 Flintlock mechanism invented in France
1613 Romanovs rule Russia until 1917
1616 William Harvey discovers circulation of blood

1607

1620 Japan restricts contact with outside
1623 Twelve-man juries in Massachusetts
1624 Dutch settle New Amsterdam (NYC)

1631 Mount Vesuvius erupts, destroying towns

1625

1642 Blaise Pascal invents first digital calculator
1643 Barometer invented
1644 Manchus conquer China

1647 Bayonet invented in Bayonne, France

Flush toilet introduced in Europe **1589**
Knitting machine invented in England **1589**
Thermometer invented **1592**
Golden age of Elizabethan literature begins **1594**
Dafne, first opera, performed **1598**

Dutch and English trade worldwide **1600s**

Francis Bacon teaches inductive reasoning **1605**
English colony established at Jamestown 1607
Samuel de Champlain founds Quebec **1608**
First newspaper regularly published in Germany **1609**
Henry Hudson explores Hudson Bay **1610**
Commercial tobacco farms established in Virginia **1612**

Thirty Years' War **1618–48**
Slide rule invented in England **1622**
Patent law introduced in England **1623**
Calculator invented in Germany **1623**
Submarine invented in England **1624**
Clinical thermometer invented **1626**

Taj Mahal built **1630–40**

René Descartes writes *Discourse on Method* **1637**

English Civil War begins **1642**
France becomes Europe's predominant power **1643–1715**

THE AGE OF REASON AND REVIVAL

1648 – 1789

1649

1650	Modern harmony emerges in music
1650	Slavery depletes Africa's population
1650s	Pascal develops probability theory
1652	Dutch found Cape Town
1655	Rembrandt van Rijn paints *The Polish Rider*
1661	Banknotes issued in Stockholm
1661	Louis XIV becomes absolute ruler
1662	Horse-drawn bus invented in France
1665	**Isaac Newton develops theory of gravity**
1666	Antonio Stradivari begins making violins

1665

1669	Mount Etna erupts in Sicily
1670	Hudson Bay Company founded
1674	Lenses perfected for microscopes
1676	Russo-Turkish wars begin

1675

1688	William Dampier explores Australian North Coast
1690	First American newspaper published in Boston
1693	Earthquake in Sicily kills 60,000

England becomes a Commonwealth	**1649**
Parliament executes Charles I	1649
Tea first served in England	1650
Thomas Hobbes defends royal absolutism	1651
Stockings introduced in Paris	1657
Fountain pens introduced in Paris	1657
English Parliament restores monarchy	1660
Universal joint invented in England	1660
First intravenous injection invented	1665
Great Fire destroys much of London	1666
First blood transfusion performed (sheep to man)	1667
Indian emperor Aurangzeb bans Hinduism	1669
Megaphone invented in England	1670
Jacques Marquette and Louis Joliet explore Mississippi	1673
Speed of light calculated	**1675**
Habeas Corpus Act established in England	1679
Peter the Great westernizes Russia	1689
John Locke writes *Two Treatises of Government*	1690
Calcutta founded by English	1690
Steam pump invented in England	1698

1700

ca. 1700 China gains control of Taiwan

1709–26 Bartolomeo Cristofori invents piano
1710 George Berkeley writes *Principles of Human Knowledge*

1719 Daniel Defoe writes *Robinson Crusoe*
1725 Giambattista Vico publishes *The New Science*
1726 Jonathan Swift publishes *Gulliver's Travels*
1733 Flying shuttle invented in England
1741 Vitus Bering explores Alaska for Russia
1744 Geographic survey produces accurate map
1752 Benjamin Franklin invents lightning rod

1750

1755 Earthquake in Lisbon kills 60,000
1756–63 The Seven Years' War
1757 **British rule begins in India**
1759 Voltaire (Francois-Marie Arouet) publishes *Candide*
1762 Jean-Jacques Rousseau's *Social Contract* published
1763 Chief Pontiac leads Native American rebellion
1765 American colonies protest Stamp Act
1769 Steam carriage invented in France
1770 Boston Massacre

1770

1773 Boston Tea Party
1774 First Continental Congress established

1776 Declaration of Independence written
1776–81 **American Revolution**

1778 La Scala Opera House opens

Industrial coal substituted for charcoal **1700s**
Wars of Spanish succession **1701**
Iron smelting invented in England **1709**

Steam engine invented in England 1712

Johann Sebastian Bach composes Brandenburg Concertos **1721**
Antonio Vivaldi writes *Four Seasons* **1725**
Octant invented in England **1731**
Baby carriage invented in England **1733**
Muslim Wahhabi sect founded **1740s**
France begins publishing *Encyclopedie* **1751**
Citrus fruits become scurvy preventative **1753**

Samuel Johnson's dictionary standardizes English **1755**
Bengalis capture Calcutta from English **1756**
Sextant invented in England **1757**
Marine chronometer invented in England **1759**
Treaty gives Canada to England **1763**
Spinning jenny invented in England **1764**

Mason-Dixon Line established **1767**
Industrial Revolution begins **1770**
Industrial Revolution begins in England 1770s

James Cook crosses Antarctic Circle first **1773**

Battle of Bunker Hill **1775**
Thomas Paine writes *Common Sense* **1776**
Adam Smith writes *Wealth of Nations* **1776**

THE AGE OF PROGRESS
1789 – 1914

1780

1781 Immanuel Kant writes *Critique of Pure Reason*
1781 Jean-Jacques Rousseau's *Confessions* published posthumously

1783 Hot air balloon invented in France
1783 Parachute invented in France

1787 Wolfgang Amadeus Mozart composes *Don Giovanni*
1788 U.S. Constitution ratified
1789 **French Revolution begins**

Factory system of production begins **1781**

Pyrometer invented for furnace temperatures **1782**

Benjamin Franklin invents bifocal glasses **1784**
Power loom invented in England **1785**

First public school established in St. Augustine **1787**
British settle Australia with convicts **1788**
Sierra Leone established as colony **1788**

1790

1791 **U.S. Bill of Rights written**
1792 New York Stock Exchange organized
1794–95 Joseph Haydn performs his London symphonies

1797 Earthquake in Ecuador kills 40,000
1798 Napoleon Bonaparte captures Cairo
1800 Robert Fulton builds submarine
1801 Invention of automated loom
1801-7 Niccolo Paganini revolutionizes violin playing
1803 Louisiana Purchase negotiated

1804 Lewis and Clark embark on expedition

1800

Bank of North America founded **1791**
800,000 Egyptians die of plague **1792**
French king Louis XIV executed **1793**
Reign of Terror in France 1793–94
Vaccination invented for smallpox **1796**
Thomas Malthus publishes essay on population **1798**
Invention of crude battery **1800**
Shoes invented for right and left feet **1800**
John Marshall becomes Supreme Court Chief Justice **1801**
Atomic nature of matter explained **1803**
U.S. Supreme Court first declares a law unconstitutional **1803**
Napoléon Bonaparte becomes emperor **1804**

1805

1816

1822

1807 Georg Hegel defends thesis, antithesis, synthesis
1807 Fulton builds successful steamboat

1810 Canned food processing invented

1812 Grimm's *Fairy Tales* published
1812–14 U.S. wins War of 1812
1815 Congress of Vienna balances European power
1815 Volcano in Indonesia kills 50,000
1816–29 Gioacchino Rossini writes *Barber of Seville*

1818 Zulus form empire

1819 First British settlement established in Singapore

1820 Missouri Compromise negotiated

1821 Electric motor developed
1821 Peru achieves independence
1822 Brazil achieves independence
1822 Ecuador achieves independence
1823 Monroe Doctrine written
1824 Ludwig van Beethoven writes *Symphony no. 9*
1827 First photographic image produced
1828 Steam locomotive inaugurates railroad age

1834 Forerunner of computer invented
1835 Revolving breech pistol invented

England defeats French navy 1805
Holy Roman Empire dissolved 1806

Napoléon Bonaparte controls almost all Europe 1808

Simón Bolívar becomes leader of Latin American revolutions 1810
Napoléon Bonaparte unsuccessfully attacks Russia 1812
Jane Austen's *Pride and Prejudice* published 1813
Napoléon Bonaparte defeated at Waterloo 1815
Industrial Revolution spreads through Europe 1815
Era of Metternich 1815–30

Argentina achieves independence 1816

Table of relative atomic weights developed 1818

Electromagnetism discovered 1820
Romanticism in music 1820–50
Egyptian hieroglyphics deciphered 1821
Freed slaves settle Liberia 1822
Franz Schubert writes compositions 1822–28
Waterproof cloth invented 1823
Mexico becomes a republic 1824
Bolivia achieves independence 1825

Franz Liszt known as leading piano virtuoso 1832–37

Cyrus McCormick patents reaper 1834

1836

- **1836** Mexico defeats Texans at Alamo
- **1837** Seminole Indians travel the Trail of Tears
- **1837** Louis Braille publishes writing system
- **1840s** Firearms with interchangeable parts invented

- **1842–82** Richard Wagner writes operas

- **1846** Rotary press invented
- **1846** **One million Irish starve in Potato Famine**
- **1848** Revolutions sweep through Europe
- **1849** Cholera epidemic kills 16,000 Londoners

1850

- **1850s–1890s** Johannes Brahms leads Neoclassicism in music
- **1850** Krupp produces all steel guns
- **1850** Australia receives limited self-government
- **1850–64** Taiping Rebellion takes place in China
- **1851** Herman Melville's *Moby Dick* published
- **1851** Sojourner Truth delivers anti-slavery speeches
- **1853** Japan liberalizes trade

- **1855** Florence Nightingale reforms military hospitals

1857

- **1857** Dred Scott decision made

- **1859** Spectroscopy reveals composition of stars

- **1860** South Carolina first to secede
- **1861** Telegraph crosses America
- **1861–65** U.S. Civil War

- **1863** Abraham Lincoln delivers Gettysburg Address
- **1864** Indians massacred in Colorado

- Victoria becomes queen of England **1837**
- Morse code invented **1838**
- Adhesive postage stamp invented in England **1840**
- Forerunner of hypodermic syringe patented **1841**

- Anesthetic gases first used **1846**
- Sewing machine invented **1846**
- U.S. issues first postage stamps **1847**
- U.S. wins Mexican American War **1848**
- Public Libraries Act established in England **1850**
- Gustave Courbet paints *The Stone Breakers* **1850**
- Henry Bessemer invents steel mass production **1850s**
- George Boole develops Boolean logic **1850s**
- The Great Exhibition takes place in London **1851**
- Giuseppe Verdi writes *Rigoletto* **1851**

- Charge of the Light Brigade **1854**

- Gregor Mendel begins heredity experiments **1856**
- **Transatlantic cable developed** **1856**
- Louis Pasteur discovers microorganisms cause fermentation **1857**

- Charles Darwin's *Origin of the Species* published **1859**
- John Stuart Mill's *On Liberty* published **1859**
- Giuseppe Garibaldi leads successful Italian rebellion **1860**
- Charles Dickens's *Great Expectations* published **1861**

- Richard Gatling invents Gatling machine gun **1862**

- Red Cross founded **1864**
- Jules Verne writes science fiction **1864**

1865

1865 Lewis Carroll's *Alice's Adventures in Wonderland* published

1868 Shogunate overthrown in Japan
1868 Shinto becomes Japanese state religion
1869 Leo Tolstoy publishes *War and Peace*

1871 P. T. Barnum opens his circus
1871 Thomas Edison invents phonograph

1875 Alexander Graham Bell invents telephone
1876 Successful internal combustion engine invented
1877 Japanese Samurai defeated

1876

1879 Frank Woolworth's first five and dime opened
1880s Open-hearth steel technology develops
1881 Reliable adding machine invented
1881 Czar Alexander II assassinated
1882 Bacteria causing tuberculosis discovered
1883 Volcano in Indonesia kills 36,000

1885

1885 France gives Statue of Liberty to United States
1886 American Federation of Labor founded
1886–89 Eiffel Tower constructed

1888 John Dunlop invents pneumatic tire
1889 Oklahoma opened to settlers

1890 Punch-card data processing machine
1890–1912 William James writes books

Antiseptic surgery begins **1865**
Fyodor Dostoevsky writes *Crime and Punishment* **1866**

Periodic table of elements published **1869**
Egypt opens Suez Canal **1869**
Tchaikovsky first recognized Russian composer **1870s–1890s**
German chancellor Otto Bismarck unites Europe **1871**

Paul Cezanne and others create Impressionism **1874**
Egypt sells England Suez Canal **1875**
General George Custer makes his last stand **1876**
Industrial research laboratories set up **1876**

Thomas Edison invents electric light **1879**
Electric streetlights installed in New York City **1880**
Typhoic bacillus discovered **1881**
Standard Oil founded **1882**
Gottlieb Daimler invents crankshaft engine **1883**

Greenwich established as zero meridian **1884**
Gas-powered car invented **1885**
First hydroelectric plant constructed at Niagara Falls **1886**

Iron discovered in northern Minnesota **1887**
George Eastman develops the box camera **1888**
Johnstown, Pennsylvania, flood kills 2,200 **1889**
Gustav Mahler composes ten symphonies **1889–1912**
Sherman Anti-Trust Act established **1890**
Player piano invented **1891**

1893

1897

1905

1893 Edward Munch's *The Scream* begins Expressionism
1893 Hinduism begins to influence West

1894 Plague in China kills 80,000
1894–95 China loses Sino–Japanese War

1895 Wilhelm Roentgen discovers X-rays
1895 Radio invented by Guglielmo Marconi
1896 Science of radioactivity developed
1896 First modern Olympic Games played in Athens
1896 Tsunami destroys Japanese villages
1897 George Herriman creates daily "Krazy Kat" comic strip
1897 China leases England Hong Kong
1898 Yellow journalism flourishes in America

1900 Boxer Rebellion takes place in China
1900 Commonwealth of Australia established
1900 Sigmund Freud publishes *The Interpretation of Dreams*
1902 Enrico Caruso records first gramograph record
1902 Willis Carrier invents air-conditioning
1903 First World Series played
1904–5 Japan wins Russo–Japanese War

1906 San Francisco earthquake kills 3,000
1907 New Zealand achieves independence

1908 Henry Ford begins mass producing cars

1909 Genetic theory of heredity developed
1909 Frank Lloyd Wright culminates Prairie Style
1910 Japan annexes Korea
1911 Chinese Republic established

New Zealand allows women's suffrage 1893
Giacomo Puccini writes operas 1893–1924

Edward Scripps establishes U.S. newspaper chain 1894
Claude Debussy becomes leading Impressionist 1894
Ottoman Empire massacres Armenians 1894–96
Cuba revolts against Spain 1895

U.S. wins Spanish American War 1896
Discovery of gold in Klondike 1896
Supreme Court rules "separate but equal" 1896
Scientists discover mosquitoes carry malaria 1897
Rudolf Diesel invents his engine 1897
Pierre and Marie Curie discover radium 1898
Arnold Schoenberg writes first atonal work 1899
England and Germany compete in arms race 1900
U.S. establishes gold standard 1900

Hormones discovered 1902
Wright brothers make first flight 1903
Panama declares independence from Colombia 1903
Albert Einstein develops Theory of Relativity 1905
Vacuum tube invented 1906

Pablo Picasso and Georges Braque first Cubists 1907

NAACP founded 1909
England introduces old-age insurance 1909
Robert Peary reaches North Pole 1909
Roald Amundsen reaches South Pole 1911
First Indianapolis 500 race 1911

THE AGE OF IDEOLOGIES

1914 – 2000

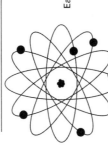

1912

Titanic sinks **1912** — **1912–13** Ottoman Empire loses Balkan Wars

Chemical chain reaction understood **1913**
Theory of atomic structure developed **1913**
Hans Geiger detects subatomic particles **1913**
First traffic lights installed in Cleveland, Ohio **1914**
Panama Canal completed **1914**

1913 U.S. Federal Reserve System established
1913 Igor Stravinsky composes *The Rite of Spring*

1914 Austrian archduke Ferdinand assassinated, triggering WWI
1914 Panama Canal opens

1914

World War I 1914–18
Birth of a Nation filmed **1915**
Easter Uprising occurs in Dublin **1916**

Russian Revolution **1917**

1915 Mohandas Gandhi leads Indian Nationalist movement
1916 First Rose Bowl football game played
1916 First polio epidemic hits U.S.

1918 Russian Imperial family executed

1919

Size of Milky Way determined **1918**
Influenza kills 20 million **1918–20**
Atom first split by Ernest Rutherford **1919**
President Woodrow Wilson supports League of Nations **1919**
Loudspeaker invented **1919**
American companies revolutionize management **1920**
Women's suffrage reaches U.S. **1920**
First radio station broadcasts from Pittsburgh **1920**
Johnson and Johnson introduce Band-Aids **1921**

1919 Gandhi begins Indian passive resistance
1919 Irish Republican Army formed
1919 Nazi Party founded in Germany
1920 Unemployment insurance created in England
1920 American jazz comes to Europe
1920 Earthquake in China kills 200,000
1921 Carl Jung's *Psychological Types* published

Insulin first given to diabetics **1922**	**1922** USSR established
Stock market booms in U.S. **1922**	**1922** Emily Post's *Etiquette* published
Marconi Company broadcasts in England **1922**	**1922** Sinclair Lewis's *Babbitt* published
Louis Armstrong begins his career **1922**	**1923** Japanese earthquake kills nearly 150,000
Transjordan partitioned from Palestine **1923**	
U.S. Army aviators circumvent globe **1924**	**1924** Josef Stalin succeeds Vladimir Lenin as Soviet leader
George Gershwin composes *Rhapsody in Blue* **1924**	**1924** Chinese government includes communists
Television invented **1925**	**1925** Franz Kafka writes *The Trial*

1922

Babe Ruth hits 60 home runs **1927**	**1927** *Jazz Singer* first sound-synchronized movie
Charles Lindbergh flies solo across Atlantic **1927**	**1927** Chiang Kai-shek forms Chinese National Government
Penicillin invented **1928**	**1928** First Mickey Mouse cartoon produced
U.S. stock market crashes 1929	**1929** Edwin Hubble discovers universe is expanding
First incorporation laws established in U.S. **1930s**	**1931** Japan invades Manchuria
Franklin Roosevelt elected U.S. president **1932**	**1932** Nylon invented
Lindbergh baby kidnapped **1932**	**1932** Saudi Arabia becomes nation

1927

U.S. Federal Communications Commission established **1934**	**1934–40** Great Plains become Dust Bowl
Radar developed **1935**	**1935** Electric typewriter introduced
George Gershwin composes *Porgy and Bess* **1935**	**1935** First flight made across South Pole
Jazz becomes "swing" **1935**	**1935** Alcoholics Anonymous begins
John Maynard Keynes writes on economics **1936**	**1936** Oil discovered in Saudi Arabia
Hindenburg dirigible explodes in Lakehurst, N.J. **1937**	**1937** Japan invades China
Germany invades and annexes Austria **1938**	**1938** Yellow River floods kill 900,000
Germany invades Czechoslovakia and Poland **1939**	**1939** Possibility of splitting atom discovered
World War II 1939–45	**1939** Pan American flies to Europe
	1939 Earthquake kills 45,000 in Turkey

1935

1940

1940 Carl Sandburg's *Abraham Lincoln* published
1941 U.S. enters World War II
1941 Japan joins Germany in World War II

1943 Jean-Paul Sartre's *Being and Nothingness* published
1944 G.I. Bill of Rights ratified
1945 U.S. drops atomic bombs on Japan
1945 **United Nations founded**
1946 Nuremburg trials
1946 Ho Chi Minh fights French in Vietnam
1947 *The Diary of Anne Frank* published

1947

1948 *Texaco Star Theater* opens with Milton Berle
1948 Long-playing records invented
1949 Cortisone discovered
1949 Cause of sickle-cell anemia discovered
1949 George Orwell's *1984* published
1949 Chinese Communists defeat Nationalists

1951 Color television developed

1952

1952 Jonas Salk begins polio inoculations

1953 Mapping of DNA begins
1953 Heart-lung machine developed
1954 Discrimination banned in U.S. schools
1954–75 Vietnam War
1955 Warsaw Pact established
1955 Disneyland opens in California
1956 Elvis Presley sings "Blue Suede Shoes"
1957 Fidel Castro begins Cuban communist revolution

Winston Churchill rallies England through radio **1940–45**
Calculating machine breaks German codes **1941**
Manhattan Project develops atomic bomb **1941**

Rodgers and Hammerstein's *Oklahoma!* produced **1943**
First computer tested **1944**
Streptomycin discovered **1944**
Jacques Cousteau begins undersea research **1945**
Jordan becomes nation **1946**

Transistor invented **1947**
Television begins rapid growth **1947**
Korea partitioned into two nations **1948**

North Atlantic Treaty Organization established **1949**
USSR tests its first atomic bomb **1949**
Germany partitioned into two nations **1949**
South Africa adopts apartheid **1949**
Korean War **1950–53**

Hydrogen bomb developed **1952**
Computer predicts election result **1952**
Sir Edmund Hillary climbs Mount Everest **1953**

Silicon-based transistor developed **1954**

DNA and RNA synthesized **1955**
Rosa Parks arrested in boycott **1955**
Soviets crush rebellion in Hungary **1956**
Russians launch Sputnik **1957**

1958

Optical laser invented **1958**
Modem developed **1958**
St. Lawrence Seaway opens **1959**

IBM computer automates businesses **1960**
U.S. presidential debate televised **1960**

South Africa leaves British Commonwealth **1961**
Freedom Riders integrate American South **1961**
Telstar Communications satellite launched **1962**
Rachel Carson writes *Silent Spring* **1962**
President John F. Kennedy assassinated **1963**
Dr. Martin Luther King Jr. delivers "I Have a Dream" speech **1963**
U.S. Civil Rights Act ratified **1964**

First artificial heart transplant performed **1966**

Anti-Vietnam War riots occur in U.S. **1968**
Neil Armstrong walks on moon **1969**
U.S. Defense Department establishes Internet **1969**
Cyclones kill 500,000 in Pakistan **1970**
Andrew Lloyd Webber's *Jesus Christ Superstar* produced **1971**
Yom Kippur War **1973**
President Richard Nixon resigns **1974**

Voyagers I and *II* explore space **1977**
English "test tube" baby born **1979**

IBM introduces first personal computer **1981**
Commercial e-mail service begins **1982**
Global Internet begins **1983**
First Macintosh computer produced **1984**

1963

1958 Computers using transistors introduced
1958 European Common Market established
1959 Commercial copy machine invented
1959 Dalai Lama flees Tibet
1960 Artificial kidney developed
1960s New grains produce higher yields

1961 Yuri Gagarin first to orbit earth

1962 Thalidomide taken off market
1962 James Meredith denied university admittance
1963 Earthquake kills 22,000 in Pakistan
1964 Beatles come to America
1964 Palestinian Liberation Organization founded

1966 Cultural Revolution in China

1968 Pulsars discovered
1969 Woodstock festival attracts 300,000

1970 ATM first used by banks
1971 Pocket calculator invented

1974 Aleksandr Solzhenitsyn's *The Gulag Archipelago* published

1976 Earthquakes kill 780,000 worldwide
1977 Cyclone kills 20,000 in India

1980 Iran-Iraq War splits Arab world
1981 First U.S. cases of AIDS reported
1982 First permanent artificial heart implant performed
1984 CD-ROM invented
1984 AT&T breaks up

1973

1985 — **1991**

1986 Nuclear accident occurs in Chernobyl
1986 *Challenger* space shuttle explodes

1989 **Berlin Wall falls**
1989 Chinese rebellion occurs in Tiananmen Square
1990 Hubble telescope launched
1990s Internet use explodes in popularity
1990–91 Gulf War

1992 North American Free Trade Agreement negotiated
1992 Hurricane Andrew causes $12 billion damage

1994 Blacks win control of South Africa
1995 Media conglomerates form

1997 England returns Hong Kong to China

Mikhail Gorbachev heads Russian Communist Party 1985

Bangladesh floods leave 24 million homeless 1987
Warnings of global warming begin 1988
Salman Rushdie's *The Satanic Verses* published 1989
Hurricane Hugo causes $4 billion damage 1989
Apartheid abolished in South Africa 1990
Germany reunited 1990

Communist government of Russia overthrown 1991
World Wide Web revolutionizes communication 1992

E-commerce begins 1994
Satellite-based Global Positioning System operational 1995

Sheep cloned 1997
Europe adopts Eurocurrency 1999

THE OLD TESTAMENT ERA

2166 BC–7 BC

The Old Testament era includes the story of how God first created heaven and earth and then created his people. This book picks up the thread of history where reliable dating of biblical events begins—with God's choosing of Abraham. God first chose Abraham's family, and after the Exodus, at Sinai, the family became a nation. The nation of Israel later became a monarchy but soon descended into sin, resulting in a period of exile in Babylon. Only a remnant of the nation ever returned from captivity, but God encouraged his people through a series of prophets who foretold a full restoration of God's people and of his coming kingdom.

2166 BC ✡ ABRAM IS BORN

Abram, a descendant of Noah's son Shem (Genesis 11:10-26), was born in the Mesopotamian city of Ur in 2166 BC (Genesis 11:26-28) into a family of idolaters (Joshua 24:2). God chose Abram to be the founder of his people (Genesis 24:7). The name *Abram* probably means "exalted father," but God later changed his name to *Abraham,* meaning "father of many" (Genesis 17:5). While Abram was living in Ur, God called him to leave his country to journey to Canaan, the Promised Land (Acts 7:2-3). Abram/Abraham is described as a man of faith (Genesis 15:6; Hebrews 11:8-19) and "the father of all who believe" (Romans 4:16; Galatians 3:7, 29).

2091 BC ✡ ABRAM DEPARTS FOR CANAAN

On the way to Canaan, Abram and his father, Terah, settled in Haran on the Balih River in northern Mesopotamia (Genesis 11:31; 12:1, 5). When Terah died in 2091 BC, Abram (then seventy-five years old) left Haran with his wife, Sarai, his nephew Lot, and the servants he had acquired in Haran (Genesis 12:5). He settled near Bethel at Beersheba. In his covenant with Abram, God promised to make of

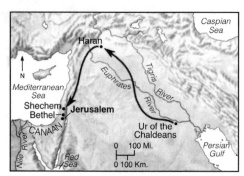

him a great nation, to bless him, to make his name great, and to bless all the families of the earth through him (Genesis 12:1-3). In addition, God gave the land of Canaan to Abram and his descendants (Genesis 12:7). Abram is described as a resident alien without a capital city of his own. He was a wealthy man (Genesis 13:2) with three hundred male servants in his household (Genesis 14:14).

ABRAM'S JOURNEY TO CANAAN Abram, Sarai, and Lot traveled from Ur of the Chaldeans to Canaan by way of Haran. Though indirect, this route followed the rivers rather than attempting to cross the vast desert.

2080 BC ✡ ISHMAEL IS BORN

God promised Abram that he would be the father of a multitude (Genesis 15:4-5). Abram believed God (Genesis 15:6), yet at the age of eighty-five he still was childless. His wife, Sarai, frustrated that she was barren (Genesis 16:1), took things into her own hands. Following the Near Eastern custom, Sarai gave her maidservant Hagar to Abram as an additional wife to ensure that her husband would have a male heir (Genesis 16:2-3). In 2080 BC, Hagar gave birth to Ishmael (Genesis 16:15-16). The apostle Paul states that Ishmael was born according to the flesh, whereas Abram's second son, Isaac, was born through promise (Galatians 4:23). Abram later expelled Hagar and Ishmael (Genesis 21:14). Ishmael is regarded as the progenitor of the Arabs (cf. Genesis 21:18).

2067 BC ✡ ESTABLISHING THE ABRAHAMIC COVENANT

In making a covenant with Abram, God used the same oath rituals used by earthly kings when they made treaties, because his covenant with Abram was in essence a treaty. God commanded Abram to kill a heifer, a goat, and a ram, cut their carcasses in two, and lay each half opposite the other. Then God took an oath by passing between the divided carcasses, thereby stating symbolically, "May I be slain like these animals if I do not keep my oath" (Genesis 15:9-18). Abram performed his covenantal oath of allegiance to God through the act of circumcision (Genesis 17:10-13). Circumcision symbolized the curse of being cut off from God's people (Genesis 17:13-14). Abram, Ishmael, and all the males in his household were circumcised (Genesis 17:23-27). As part of the covenental process, God changed Abram's name to Abraham, and Sarai's name to Sarah (Genesis 17:5, 15).

2066 BC ✡ ISAAC IS BORN

When Abraham was ninety-nine years old and Sarah was eighty-nine, the Lord appeared to Abraham and told him that his wife Sarai would bear him a son (Genesis 17:15-16). Sarah, listening at the nearby tent door, laughed. The Lord asked Abraham why Sarah had laughed, adding "Is anything too hard for the Lord?" (Genesis 18:1-15). The next year, in 2066 BC, Sarah gave birth to Isaac, the heir of God's covenant (Genesis 21:1-5; Romans 4:18-20). The name *Isaac* means "he laughs," because Sarah had laughed at the idea of her giving birth at the age of ninety (Genesis 17:17; 21:6). The great test of Abraham's faith came when God commanded him to sacrifice Isaac on Mount Moriah (Genesis 22:2), the later site of the Jerusalem Temple (2 Chronicles 3:1). Abraham obeyed, but

509 BC	480 BC	215 BC	12 BC
Roman Republic founded	Parthenon built in Athens	Construction begins on Great Wall of China	Silk Road opens between China and West

was spared sacrificing his son when God provided a ram as a substitute (Genesis 22:3-24).

2029 BC ✡ SARAH DIES

Sarah, Abraham's wife, died at the age of 127. The first property Abraham owned in the Promised Land was the burial place he purchased for Sarah (Genesis 23:1-20).

2006 BC ✡ ESAU AND JACOB ARE BORN

Esau and Jacob, fraternal twins, were born to Isaac and Rebekah in 2006 BC (Genesis 25:24-26). God sovereignly chose Jacob over Esau to be the heir of the covenant (Romans 9:10-13). As the two babies struggled with each other in Rebekah's womb, God told her, "The sons in your womb will become two rival nations," and "the descendants of your older son [Esau] will serve the descendants of your younger son [Jacob]" (Genesis 25:23; see also Romans 9:12). With cleverness and deceit, Jacob gained both Esau's birthright (Genesis 25:27-34) and blessing (Genesis 27:1-45), which were Esau's by right as the firstborn of the twins. Jacob was the father of the twelve tribes of Israel, and Esau became the progenitor of the nation of Edom (Genesis 25:30; 32:3; 36:1, 30).

1930 BC ✡ JACOB JOURNEYS TO HARAN

Isaac commanded his son Jacob not to marry a Canaanite woman but to return to Haran in northern Mesopotamia (modern-day Turkey), where his grandfather Abraham had lived and where his uncle Laban was still living (Genesis 28:1-5). On the way, he had a vision of a stairway leading to heaven, known as Jacob's Ladder. Above it stood the Lord, who confirmed the Abrahamic Covenant to Jacob (Genesis 28:11-17). Jacob ratified the covenant by an oath of allegiance to the Lord (Genesis 28:20-22). This experience proved to be Jacob's spiritual conversion. He named the place Bethel, the "house of God" (Genesis 28:19). He continued on to Haran, where he met his uncle Laban and fell in love with his cousin Rachel. He agreed to work for Laban for seven years to earn the right to marry Rachel (Genesis 29:1-19).

2200–1950 BC	2000 BC	1180 BC	776 BC
Middle Bronze Age I	Hittite, Egyptian, and Assyrian Empires control major areas	Troy destroyed with Trojan horse	First Olympic Games held in Greece

1923 BC ✡ JACOB MARRIES LEAH AND RACHEL

Jacob worked seven years for his uncle Laban to fulfill his contract to marry Laban's daughter Rachel. However, on the wedding night, Laban deceived Jacob by substituting Leah, his older daughter, for Rachel. A week later, Laban allowed Jacob to marry Rachel also, but only after Jacob agreed to work for another seven years (Genesis 29:15-30). Jacob the deceiver (Genesis 27:1-38) was himself deceived. Eleven sons and one daughter were born to Jacob during the next thirteen years he was in Haran. Jacob showed particular favor to Joseph, the elder son of Rachel, though he was not the firstborn among his brothers.

1910 BC ✡ JACOB RETURNS TO CANAAN

After Jacob had worked for Laban for twenty years, during which time he had built up his own flocks at the expense of Laban's. God commanded him to return to Canaan. In leaving Haran, Jacob had to deal with his father-in-law, whom he had deceived; in entering Canaan in 1910 BC, he had to deal with his twin brother, Esau, whom he had also deceived (cf. Genesis 27:1-45). But before Jacob arrived in the Promised Land, "a man came and wrestled with him until dawn" (Genesis 32:24). This divine adversary struck Jacob's hip and "knocked it out of joint at the socket" (Genesis 32:25). Because the hip was regarded as the seat of reproductive powers, the smiting of Jacob's hip foreshadowed the smiting of the Messiah, the descendant of Jacob who would be smitten by God (Isaiah 53:4), and who by his sufferings would justify Jacob and all of God's people (Isaiah 53:11). At this time, God gave Jacob a new name: Israel (Genesis 32:28), which means "one who struggles with God."

1899 BC ✡ JOSEPH IS SOLD AS A SLAVE

In 1899 BC, when Joseph was seventeen, his brothers sold him as a slave to merchants, who in turn took him to Egypt and sold him to Potiphar, the captain of the palace guard (Genesis 37:2-36). Joseph's brothers hated him because he was their father's favorite son (Genesis 37:3-4) and the recipient of the family birthright with its double portion of the inheritance. The birthright had initially belonged to Reuben, Jacob's firstborn and the eldest son of Leah, but because Reuben committed adultery with Bilhah, his father's concubine (Genesis 35:22), the birthright was transferred to Joseph, the elder son of Rachel (1 Chronicles 5:1). Selling their brother with his birthright as a slave to Egypt was in direct disregard of their responsibility under the Abrahamic Covenant to possess the royal grant of the Promised Land "as a permanent possession" (Genesis 13:15). God's resulting judgment on the children of Israel was to enslave all of their descendants in Egypt for four hundred years (Genesis 15:13).

1888 BC ✡ JOSEPH IS SENTENCED TO PRISON

While serving in Potiphar's house, Joseph was accused of rape (Genesis 39:6-20) and was sentenced to prison in 1888 BC. During his time there, he correctly interpreted the dreams of Pharaoh's cupbearer and baker, who were also in prison. The baker was later hanged, but the cupbearer was restored to his position in the palace (Genesis 40:1-23). In 1886 BC, when Pharaoh sought to have two of his own dreams interpreted, the cupbearer remembered how Joseph had correctly interpreted his dream two years before and recommended him to Pharaoh (Genesis 41:1-13). Joseph then correctly interpreted Pharaoh's dreams, predicting seven years of abundant crops that would be followed by a seven-year famine (Genesis 41:14-32). As a result, Pharaoh installed Joseph as second-in-command of Egypt (Genesis 41:41-43), making him responsible to store food for the nation during the seven years of abundance so that there would be enough for the seven years of famine (Genesis 41:33-49).

1886–1872 BC ✡ GOD SENDS BUMPER CROPS AND FAMINE

In fulfillment of Joseph's interpretation of Pharaoh's dream, God sent seven years of bumper crops to Egypt, beginning in 1886 BC. Joseph purchased one-fifth of each year's crop and stored it in anticipation of the coming seven years of famine (Genesis 41:46-49). When, as predicted, seven years of worldwide famine followed the years of plenty, only Egypt had stockpiles of grain because Joseph had stored it during the time of abundance. Joseph sold the grain not only to Egyptians but to other nations as well (Genesis 41:54–47:26). The nations of the world were being blessed through the seed of Abraham (Genesis 12:3).

2200–1950 BC	2000 BC	1180 BC	776 BC
Middle Bronze Age I	Hittite, Egyptian, and Assyrian Empires control major areas	Troy destroyed with Trojan horse	First Olympic Games held in Greece

1878 BC ✡ JOSEPH'S BROTHERS SEARCH FOR FOOD IN EGYPT

When the famine extended to Canaan, Jacob sent ten of his sons to Egypt in 1878 BC to purchase food. Jacob held back Benjamin, his remaining son by Rachel. When Joseph saw his brothers, he recognized them but disguised himself so they would not recognize him. Though he sold them grain, he accused them of being spies and kept Simeon as a hostage until they would bring back Benjamin (Genesis 42:1-38). The sons returned to Canaan, and when they had eaten the grain they had purchased in Egypt, Jacob reluctantly let them take Benjamin to Egypt to buy more grain (Genesis 43:1–45:15). On this trip, Joseph revealed himself to his brothers, telling them, "God has sent me here to keep you and your families alive so that you will become a great nation" (Genesis 45:7).

1876 BC ✡ JACOB AND HIS FAMILY MOVE TO EGYPT

After Joseph, the ruler of Egypt under the Pharaoh, revealed himself to his brothers, he commanded them to bring Jacob and the rest of their families to Egypt as quickly as possible (Genesis 45:1-28). As Jacob was leaving Canaan with his family, God appeared to him in a vision, telling him that God would make his descendants into a great nation in Egypt and would bring them back to the Promised Land. Jacob and his sons traveled to Egypt with their families, and Jacob had an emotional reunion with Joseph. The house of Israel, which now numbered seventy people, settled in Goshen, the most fertile part of Egypt (Genesis 46:1–47:12). Seventeen years later, in 1859 BC, after blessing his twelve sons, Jacob died in Egypt at the age of 147 (Genesis 49:1-33).

1526 BC ✡ MOSES IS BORN

Just prior to the birth of Moses in 1526 BC, the Egyptian Pharaoh had decreed that every Hebrew male child was to be thrown into the Nile River to drown. Moses' mother "threw him into the Nile" by placing him in a floating basket. Pharaoh's daughter saw the infant in the river, felt sorry for him, and decided to save him. Moses' sister, who was standing watch over the baby, approached the princess and offered to find someone to nurse the baby for her. When the princess agreed, Moses' sister brought her own mother, and Pharaoh's daughter

509 BC	480 BC	215 BC	12 BC
Roman Republic founded	Parthenon built in Athens	Construction begins on Great Wall of China	Silk Road opens between China and West

offered to pay her to care for him. When Moses grew older, his mother returned him to Pharaoh's daughter and she adopted him (Exodus 1:22–2:10). God thus equipped Moses for leading his people by enabling him to be raised as a member of the royal Egyptian family, where he would receive the best education available at that time.

1486 BC ✡ MOSES FLEES TO MIDIAN

In 1486 BC, when Moses was forty, he witnessed an Egyptian overseer beating a Hebrew. Moses came to the man's defense and killed the Egyptian. Thinking no one had seen him, he buried the body in the sand. But there had been witnesses, and when word of the murder reached the Pharaoh, he ordered that Moses be arrested and killed. Moses escaped by fleeing to Midian, on the eastern side of the Red Sea. There he married Zipporah, the daughter of the priest of Midian, and had a son, Gershom (Exodus 2:11–3:1; Acts 7:23-29). Moses worked as a shepherd in Midian for forty years, thus preparing him to shepherd God's people for another forty years.

1446 BC ✡ PLAGUES STRIKE EGYPT

From the midst of a burning bush, God called Moses to deliver the Israelites from Egypt (Exodus 3:1–4:17). The bush was on Mount Horeb, another name for Mount Sinai (Exodus 19:20; Deuteronomy 5:2). Moses, accompanied by his brother Aaron, who served as his spokesman, asked the Pharaoh to let the Israelites go into the wilderness to worship. When Pharaoh's heart was hardened and he refused to let the people go, God sent ten plagues on Egypt: water turned to blood, frogs, gnats, insects, death of cattle, boils, hail, locusts, darkness, and the death of every firstborn male. The plagues demonstrated the power of the God of Israel and the impotence of the gods of Egypt (Exodus 7:8–12:30).

1446 BC ✡ THE FIRST PASSOVER IS CELEBRATED

Before the tenth and final plague, God warned Pharaoh through Moses that unless Pharaoh would let the children of Israel leave Egypt, God would pass through Egypt and slay every firstborn male: both human and animal. The Jews were instructed to roast a lamb or goat without any defect and to eat it with bitter

THE PLAGUES ON EGYPT

Reference	Plague	What Happened	Result
Exodus 7:14-24	Blood	Fish die, the river smells, the people are without water	Pharaoh's magicians duplicate the miracle by "their magic," and Pharaoh is unmoved
8:1-15	Frogs	Frogs come up from the water and completely cover the land	Again Pharaoh's magicians duplicate the miracle by sorcery, and Pharaoh is unmoved
8:16-19	Gnats	All the dust of Egypt becomes a massive swarm of gnats	Magicians are unable to duplicate this; they say it is the "finger of God," but Pharaoh's heart remains hard
8:20-32	Flies	Swarms of flies cover the land	Pharaoh promises to let the Hebrews go but then hardens his heart and refuses
9:1-7	Livestock	All the Egyptian livestock die—but none of Israel's is even sick	Pharaoh still refuses to let the people go
9:8-12	Boils	Horrible boils break out on everyone in Egypt	Magicians cannot respond because they are struck down with boils as well—Pharaoh refuses to listen
9:13-35	Hail	Hailstorms kill all the slaves and animals left out or unprotected and strip or destroy almost every plant	Pharaoh admits his sin but then changes his mind and refuses to let Israel go
10:1-20	Locusts	Locusts cover Egypt and eat everything left after the hail	Everyone advises Pharaoh to let the Hebrews go, but God hardens Pharaoh's heart and he refuses
10:21-29	Darkness	Total darkness covers Egypt for three days so no one can even move—except the Hebrews, who have light as usual	Pharaoh again promises to let Israel go but again changes his mind
11:1–12:33	Death of Firstborn	The firstborn of all the people and cattle of Egypt die—but Israel is spared	Pharaoh and the Egyptians urge Israel to leave quickly; after they are gone, Pharaoh again changes his mind and chases after them

509 BC	480 BC	215 BC	12 BC
Roman Republic founded	Parthenon built in Athens	Construction begins on Great Wall of China	Silk Road opens between China and West

herbs and bread baked without yeast on the fourteenth day of the first month of 1446 BC. The blood of the lamb was to be put on the sides and tops of the doorframes of their houses. When Pharaoh refused to let the Jews leave, at midnight of the fourteenth day of the first month the Lord slew all the firstborn in Egypt but passed over the houses of the Jews and spared all those who were under the blood of the lamb (Exodus 11:1–12:30).

1446 BC ✡ THE ISRAELITES EXIT EGYPT

After all the firstborn males throughout Egypt were killed, in 1446 BC, Pharaoh gave Moses permission for the children of Israel to leave Egypt (Exodus 12:31-32). But once the people had departed, Pharaoh changed his mind and led his army in pursuit, catching up to the Hebrews at the Red Sea. The situation seemed hopeless to the Jews, but God instructed Moses to stretch out his hand over the sea. When Moses did this, God sent a strong east wind to divide the waters, creating a dry path on which the Jewish people crossed through the sea. When the pursuing army tried to follow, the waters flowed back at Moses' command, drowning the Egyptians (Exodus 14:5-31). God thus vindicated his people by bringing them safely through the ordeal.

1446 BC ✡ GOD CONFIRMS THE SINAITIC COVENANT

In the third month after the Israelites left Egypt in 1446 BC, they arrived at Mount Sinai. There, God made a covenant with them making them his vassal kingdom. The family that had gone down to Egypt had become a nation (Exodus 19:6). The people took an oath of allegiance to God (Exodus 19:8; 24:3, 7). God then gave them his laws to show them how their allegiance was to manifest itself (Exodus 20–23; 25–31). The covenant was confirmed at a meal on Mount Sinai where God—in the person of God the Son (cf. John 1:18)—ate and drank with the elders of Israel (Exodus 24:9-11) in similar fashion to how he instituted the New Covenant with the elders of the church at the Last Supper (Luke 22:20).

1446 BC ✡ THE ISRAELITES WORSHIP A GOLDEN CALF

Immediately after the covenantal meal instituting the Sinaitic covenant in 1446 BC, God invited Moses to the top of Mount Sinai to receive the tablets of stone

2200–1950 BC	2000 BC	1180 BC	776 BC
Middle Bronze Age I	Hittite, Egyptian, and Assyrian Empires control major areas	Troy destroyed with Trojan horse	First Olympic Games held in Greece

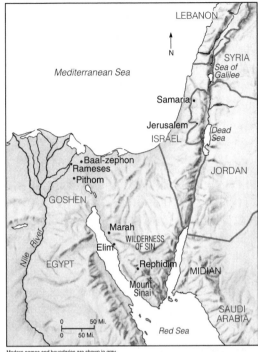

Modern names and boundaries are shown in gray.

planned to deliver his people. After choosing Moses and Aaron to be his spokesmen to Pharaoh, God worked a series of dramatic miracles in the land of Egypt to convince Pharaoh to let the Hebrews go (Exodus 5:1–12:33). When finally freed, the entire nation set out with the riches of Egypt (12:34-36). One of their first stops was at Baal-zephon (14:2), where Pharaoh, who had changed his mind, chased the Hebrews and trapped them against the sea. But God parted the waters and led the people through the sea on dry land. When Pharaoh's army tried to pursue, the waters collapsed around them, and they were drowned (14:5-31).

Marah Moses now led the people southward. The long trek across the desert brought hot tempers and parched throats for this mass of people. At Marah, the water they found was bitter, but God sweetened it (Exodus 15:22-25).

Elim As they continued their journey, the Hebrews (now called Israelites) came to Elim, an oasis with 12 springs (Exodus 15:27).

Sin Desert Leaving Elim, the people headed into the Sin Desert. Here the people became hungry, so God provided them with manna that came from heaven and covered the ground each morning (Exodus 16:1, 13-15). The people ate this manna until they entered the Promised Land.

Rephidim Moses led the people to Rephidim, where they found no water. But God miraculously provided water from a rock (Exodus 17:1, 5-6). Here the Israelites encountered their first test in battle: The Amalekites attacked and were defeated (17:9-13). Moses' father-in-law, Jethro, then arrived on the scene with sound advice on delegating responsibilities (18:1-27).

Mount Sinai God had previously appeared to Moses on this mountain and commissioned him to lead Israel (Exodus 3:1-10). Now Moses returned with the people God had asked him to lead. For almost a year, the people camped at the foot of Mount Sinai. During this time, God gave them his Ten Commandments, as well as other laws for right living. He also provided the blueprint for building the Tabernacle (Exodus 19–40). God was forging a holy nation, prepared to live for and serve him alone.

Goshen This area was given to Jacob and his family when they moved to Egypt (Genesis 47:5-6). It became the Hebrews' homeland for 400 years and remained separate from the main Egyptian centers, because Egyptian culture looked down on shepherds and nomads. As the years passed, Jacob's family grew into a large nation (Exodus 1:7).

Pithom and Rameses During the Israelites' stay in the land of Egypt, a pharaoh came to the throne who had no respect for these descendants of Joseph and feared their large numbers. He forced them into slavery in order to oppress and subdue them. Out of their slave labor, the supply cities of Pithom and Rameses were built (Exodus 1:11).

Midian Moses, an Egyptian prince who was born a Hebrew, killed an Egyptian and fled for his life to Midian. There he became a shepherd and married a woman named Zipporah. It was while Moses was in Midian that God commissioned him for the job of leading the Hebrew people out of Egypt (Exodus 2:15–4:31).

Baal-zephon Slavery was not to last, because God

509 BC	480 BC	215 BC	12 BC
Roman Republic founded	Parthenon built in Athens	Construction begins on Great Wall of China	Silk Road opens between China and West

on which the Ten Commandments were written (Exodus 24:12). During the forty days that Moses was out of sight on the mountaintop, the children of Israel asked Aaron to make them gods that would lead them to the Promised Land, because Moses had disappeared. In response to their request, Aaron made them a golden calf. The people then offered sacrifices to their new idol. When Moses descended from the mountain, he broke the tablets of the covenant in anger, signifying that Israel had broken their covenant with God (Exodus 32:1-35).

1446–1406 BC ✡ MOSES WRITES GENESIS, EXODUS, AND LEVITICUS

Moses wrote the first five books of the Bible between God's giving of the covenant to Israel at Mount Sinai (1446 BC) and the end of the forty years of wandering in the wilderness (1406 BC). The first book, Genesis, details the history of the world from its creation to the call of Abraham (chapters 1–12), and then narrows its focus to Abraham, Isaac, Jacob, and his sons, the twelve patriarchs. At the close of Genesis, the nation of Israel has descended to Egypt. Exodus recounts God's deliverance of Israel from Egypt and begins to introduce the Mosaic Law. Leviticus focuses exclusively on the Law and its priestly functions.

1444 BC ✡ TABERNACLE CONSTRUCTION IS COMPLETED

As part of the Sinaitic covenant, God instructed Israel to build a tabernacle in which he would dwell in the midst of his people. The Tabernacle was a portable sanctuary, fifteen feet wide, forty-five feet long, and fifteen feet high. It was divided into the Holy Place, which was thirty feet by fifteen feet, and the Most Holy Place, which was a fifteen-foot cube. The Tabernacle stood in the western half of a courtyard measuring seventy-five feet by one hundred feet and bordered by linen curtains. God's presence dwelt in the Most Holy Place over the Ark of the covenant (Exodus 25–27; 35–38; 39:32–40:38). The people completed construction of the Tabernacle in 1444 BC at the foot of Mount Sinai.

1444 BC ✡ SPIES SURVEY THE LAND OF CANAAN

After the Tabernacle was constructed in 1444 BC, Moses led the Israelites to Kadesh Barnea, the border of Canaan. There, God commanded Moses to send a leader from each of the twelve tribes to spy out the Promised Land. When the

2200–1950 BC	2000 BC	1180 BC	776 BC
Middle Bronze Age I	Hittite, Egyptian, and Assyrian Empires control major areas	Troy destroyed with Trojan horse	First Olympic Games held in Greece

spies returned, ten of them said that Israel would be unable to conquer Canaan. Only two, Joshua and Caleb, believed God would enable Israel to conquer the land. The people accepted the majority report, saying, "We wish we had died in Egypt, or even here in the wilderness!" (Numbers 14:2). Because of their unbelief, God granted their request. They wandered in the wilderness for a total of forty years until all the unbelievers had died. Of all the men over twenty years of age at the time when they left Egypt, Joshua and Caleb alone entered the Promised Land (Numbers 13–14).

1407 BC ✡ MOSES COMPLETES THE BOOK OF NUMBERS

Moses completed the book of Numbers in about 1407 BC, following the close of the events described in the book. The name of the book is derived from the numberings of the sons of Israel in chapters 1 and 26. The book begins with the hope that the generation that came out of Egypt would enter into the Promised Land (chapters 1–10). After a series of tests and failures (chapters 11–26), however, it becomes clear that this generation will not enter the Promised Land. Even Moses failed to completely obey God. The last section of the book restores hope to the people, as the next generation begins to prepare to enter the Promised Land under the leadership of Joshua (chapters 27–36).

1407 BC ✡ MOSES WRITES THE BOOK OF DEUTERONOMY

Moses wrote the book of Deuteronomy in about 1407 BC. After he died, his death notice was appended to the book (chapter 34). Deuteronomy documents the renewal of the covenant prior to the death of Moses. Deuteronomy was the authoritative covenant document until Jesus instituted the new covenant in the upper room shortly before his death (Luke 22:20).

1406 BC ✡ MOSES DIES

When the Israelites returned to Kadesh Barnea the second time, Moses and Aaron sinned by putting themselves in the role of God: "Listen, you rebels! . . . Must *we* bring you water from this rock?" (Numbers 20:10, emphasis added). For this sin, neither Moses nor Aaron would enter the Promised Land. Before his death, Moses prepared Israel for its conquest of Canaan. Moses had a census

509 BC	480 BC	215 BC	12 BC
Roman Republic founded	Parthenon built in Athens	Construction begins on Great Wall of China	Silk Road opens between China and West

of the people taken, and preparations began for the allotment of the land (Numbers 26; 32). Moses gave his farewell address (Deuteronomy 31:1-13); the people renewed their covenant with God; and Moses had the covenant renewal document—the book of Deuteronomy—placed beside the Ark of the covenant (Deuteronomy 31:24-26). Moses taught the people a song (Deuteronomy 32:1-43) and gave them his final blessing (Deuteronomy 33). Just before he died, Moses ascended Mount Nebo to view the Promised Land he would not enter (Deuteronomy 34:1-4).

1406 BC ✡ CONQUEST OF THE PROMISED LAND BEGINS

After grieving the death of Moses for thirty days, the Israelites crossed the Jordan River in 1406 BC on dry land under the leadership of Joshua, much as they had crossed the Red Sea under the leadership of Moses. They began the conquest of the Promised Land by destroying Jericho using an unorthodox military strategy (Joshua 1:1–6:27). After the sin of one Israelite caused their initial defeat at Ai, a second attack was successful (Joshua 7–8). This was followed by the conquest of southern Palestine and the northern reaches of the country (Joshua 10–11). Joshua then divided the Promised Land among the Twelve Tribes of Israel (Joshua 13–21). Just prior to his death, Joshua led the nation in renewing their covenant with God, as they once again gave him their allegiance (Joshua 23–24).

THE TRIBES WEST OF THE JORDAN
Judah, Ephraim, and half the tribe of Manasseh were the first tribes to receive land west of the Jordan because of their past acts of faith. The remaining seven tribes—Benjamin, Zebulun, Issachar, Asher, Naphtali, Simeon, and Dan—were slow to conquer and possess the land allotted to them.

1399 BC ✡ CANAAN IS DIVIDED BETWEEN THE TRIBES

In approximately 1399 BC, Joshua assigned a specific territory in the Promised Land to each tribe, even though there remained much of the land of Canaan yet to be conquered. The first parcel was given to eighty-five-year-old Caleb, the faithful spy (Numbers 13) to whom Moses had promised the hill country of Hebron for his faithfulness (Joshua 14–22). Two tribes—Reuben and Gad—and half the tribe of Manasseh received land east of the Jordan River (Joshua 13:8-33). In the north, the land was divided between the tribes of Asher, Naphtali, Zebulun, Issachar, Ephraim, Dan, and the other half of Manasseh. The tribes of Judah, Benjamin, and Simeon settled in the south (Joshua 13–19). The Levites (the priestly tribe of Levi) were not allotted a portion of land, but were given forty-eight cities scattered throughout Canaan (Joshua 21).

1367 BC ✡ JUDGESHIP OF OTHNIEL BEGINS

Othniel was the son of Caleb's brother Kenaz. After he distinguished himself by capturing the city of Kiriath-sepher, Caleb rewarded him by giving him his daughter Acsah in marriage (Judges 1:11-15). After the Israelites settled the land, they intermarried with the inhabitants of the land, contrary to God's law, and began to worship foreign gods. In judgment, God sent the king of Aram to rule over them for eight years. When the people finally repented of their sins, God raised up Othniel in about 1367 BC to deliver Israel from the control of Aram. Othniel was the first judge of Israel. (The word *judge* means one who administers justice by punishing the doer of evil and vindicating the righteous.) The peace lasted forty years, until the death of Othniel (Judges 3:1-11).

1309 BC ✡ JUDGESHIP OF EHUD BEGINS

When the Jewish people once again returned to their evil ways, God brought judgment upon them by making Israel a vassal kingdom under Eglon, king of Moab, for eighteen years. When the Jews cried out to God in repentance, God raised up Ehud as the next judge, in about 1309 BC. As he presented Israel's tribute to Eglon, Ehud said to him, "I have a message for you

THE TRIBES EAST OF THE JORDAN
Joshua assigned territory to the tribes of Reuben, Gad, and half the tribe of Manasseh on the east side of the Jordan, where they had chosen to remain because of the wonderful livestock country (Numbers 32:1-5).

from God!" and plunged a sword he had hidden under his clothing into Eglon's stomach, killing him. Ehud then led the Israelites in war against Moab, killing ten thousand men. The balance of power shifted, and Moab became a vassal kingdom of Israel. Peace prevailed for eighty years (Judges 3:12-30).

1230 BC ✡ JUDGESHIP OF SHAMGAR BEGINS

After Ehud had delivered Israel from the oppression of the Moabites, another judge, named Shamgar, arose to save Israel during difficult times. Shamgar killed six hundred Philistines using an unconventional weapon: an ox goad. In so doing, he was a forerunner of Samson, who killed a thousand Philistines with the jawbone of a donkey. Little is known of Shamgar other than his amazing victory over the Philistines. It is unlikely that he was an Israelite, because his title, "son of Anath," indicates that he may have been from Beth-anath, south of Israel. Regardless of Shamgar's ethnic origin, God used him as a judge and a deliverer of Israel (Judges 3:31; 5:6).

1209 BC ✡ JUDGESHIP OF DEBORAH BEGINS

When the Israelites again returned to their sinful ways, God delivered them into the hand of Jabin, the king of Canaan, who oppressed Israel for twenty years. Then, in about 1209 BC, Deborah, the only judge of Israel who was a female prophet, along with Barak, her commander-in-chief, assembled an army of ten thousand to fight Sisera, commander of the Canaanite army. After Barak defeated Sisera's troops and his nine hundred iron chariots, the subsequent peace lasted for forty years (Judges 4:6–5:31). Immediately following the great victory, Deborah composed the song recorded in Judges 5.

1162 BC ✡ JUDGESHIP OF GIDEON BEGINS

As a result of renewed evil among the Israelites, God gave them into the hands of the Midianites for seven devastating years. Then, in about 1162 BC, God called Gideon to deliver Israel. Gideon's first task was to destroy his father's altar to Baal, the god of Canaan. The Israelites of his father's city were so apostate that they wanted to kill Gideon for what he had done. Gideon next defeated the Midianites by obeying God's command to reduce his original army of thirty-

2200–1950 BC	2000 BC	1180 BC	776 BC
Middle Bronze Age I	Hittite, Egyptian, and Assyrian Empires control major areas	Troy destroyed with Trojan horse	First Olympic Games held in Greece

two thousand to a mere three hundred. Gideon's sudden nighttime attack produced a complete victory. After his great victory, Gideon was asked to set up a monarchy, but he refused. Israel lived at peace for the rest of Gideon's life (Judges 6:1–8:32).

1120 BC ✡ KING ABIMELECH ENCOURAGES BAAL WORSHIP

Abimelech was the son of a concubine from Shechem and Gideon, the judge of Israel. After Gideon's death in about 1120 BC, Abimelech, with the help of his mother's family (Judges 9:1-3), murdered all but one of his half-brothers who would have been his rivals for the throne (Judges 9:5). He then tried to set himself up as king of a Canaanite city. Abimelech was subsequently killed as he laid siege on the city of Thebez, when a woman dropped a millstone on his head from a tower (Judges 9:50-57). Abimelech was the very antithesis of the judges God appointed. Whereas his father, Gideon, had attacked the worship of Baal (Judges 6:25-32), Abimelech encouraged Baal worship in Shechem, the very place where Joshua had renewed Israel's allegiance to God (Joshua 24:14-27).

1105 BC ✡ SAMUEL IS BORN

During the latter years of the judges, while Eli was the priest in Shiloh, Hannah, the wife of Elkanah, was in the Tabernacle pleading for God to open her womb and give her a son. She vowed that this son would be dedicated to God. Hannah's prayer was so desperate that Eli at first mistook it for drunken babbling. Soon after this, in about 1105 BC, Hannah conceived and bore a son. When her son Samuel was still very young, Hannah took him to the Tabernacle and left him in the care of Eli the priest. Because of the wickedness of Eli's own sons, when Eli died Samuel succeeded him as priest and judge over Israel (1 Samuel 1–7).

1080 BC ✡ PHILISTINES CAPTURE THE ARK OF THE COVENANT

In approximately 1080 BC, the Philistines defeated Israel at Aphek, a town near Joppa. Thinking the presence of the Ark of the covenant would guarantee them victory, the elders of Israel sent men to Shiloh to bring it into battle (1 Samuel 4:1-9). In the ensuing battle, the Philistines captured the Ark (1 Samuel 4:10-22).

509 BC	480 BC	215 BC	12 BC
Roman Republic founded	Parthenon built in Athens	Construction begins on Great Wall of China	Silk Road opens between China and West

However, when the Philistines placed it in the temple of their god Dagon, the statue of Dagon fell down before the Ark and the people developed tumors. The Philistines sent the ark to Ekron, where more people developed tumors and many died (1 Samuel 5:1-12). After seven months of fallen statues and men, the Philistines sent the Ark back to the Jews of Beth-shemesh. There, unfortunately, seventy men broke God's law by looking into the Ark and as a result were struck dead in judgment (1 Samuel 6:19-20).

1078 BC ✡ JEPHTHAH DEFEATS THE AMMONITES

In about 1078 BC, the Israelites living in Transjordan were threatened by an invasion of the Ammonites. The leaders of Gilead asked Jephthah, the son of an Israelite and a heathen prostitute, if he would be their commander. He agreed only after insisting that after the war he would be judge over them. Before going to battle, Jephthah, influenced by Canaanite custom, ignorantly made a vow that if God would give him victory, he would make a human sacrifice to God of whoever came out of his house first to meet him (Judges 11:30-31). After defeating the Ammonites (Judges 11:32-34), Jephthah came home to a victory celebration led by his only child, a daughter. A man of faith, tainted by heathen customs, Jephthah regretfully fulfilled his misguided vow to God (Judges 11:34-40).

1055 BC ✡ SAMSON DESTROYS THE PHILISTINE TEMPLE

An angel announced the birth of Samson to his previously barren mother, who was told that her son would be a lifelong Nazirite (Numbers 6:1-21). However, the only Nazirite stipulation that Samson took seriously was to let his hair grow. He judged Israel for twenty years (Judges 15:20; 16:31), and they were years of uncontrolled violence and mayhem toward Israel's Philistine oppressors. Samson's final undoing was caused by his obsessive appetite for foreign prostitutes. In approximately 1055 BC, his infatuation with Delilah enabled the Philistines to cut his hair, capture him, and blind him. The only religious act recorded of Samson was his prayer that God would renew his strength as he was paraded as a trophy prisoner at a Philistine temple festival. God answered his prayer and Samson demolished the temple, killing himself and more Philistines than he had slain previously in his life (Judges 13–16).

2200–1950 BC	2000 BC	1180 BC	776 BC
Middle Bronze Age I	Hittite, Egyptian, and Assyrian Empires control major areas	Troy destroyed with Trojan horse	First Olympic Games held in Greece

1050 BC ✡ SAUL IS ANOINTED KING

As a vassal kingdom under the Philistines, the Israelites cried to God for a king who would be able to deliver them. God granted the people their wish in approximately 1050 BC, instructing the prophet Samuel to anoint Saul (r. 1050–1012 BC) as Israel's first king (1 Samuel 9–11). Unfortunately, Saul proved to be unfaithful. As a result of Saul's infringement on the office of priest by offering a sacrifice at Gilgal, Samuel prophesied God's rejection of Saul as king (1 Samuel 10:6-8; 13:8-14). Saul also disobeyed God's command to destroy all the Amalekites (1 Samuel 15:1-35) and he consulted the witch of Endor (1 Samuel 28:1-25). As a result of his unfaithfulness, Saul died in battle (1 Samuel 31:1-13), and God raised up a king after his own heart.

1025 BC ✡ DAVID IS ANOINTED KING

After Samuel told Saul (r. 1050–1012 BC) of God's rejection of him as king (1 Samuel 13:14), God sent the prophet to Bethlehem to anoint the son of Jesse (the son of Obed, who was the son of Boaz and Ruth) that God had selected to be Israel's next king. Jesse brought seven of his sons to Samuel, but Samuel told him that none of them was the one God had chosen. He then asked, "Are these all the sons you have?" Jesse replied that his youngest son was out tending the sheep. Samuel asked to see him, and when David was brought before the prophet, God told Samuel that the young shepherd boy was his choice to be king. Samuel anointed David and the Holy Spirit came upon him mightily (1 Samuel 16:1-13).

1020 BC ✡ DAVID BEGINS COMPOSING PSALMS

Although David had rescued the people of Israel from the threat of Goliath and married the daughter of King Saul (r. 1050–1012 BC), any admiration that Saul had for David was superseded by rage and jealousy (1 Samuel 19). On several occasions, Saul even tried to kill David. Saul's daughter Michal learned of one such plot to kill David in his house and helped him escape from the king. It is against this backdrop that David, during or soon after his escape, composed the first of the seventy-three canonical Psalms directly attributed to him. In Psalm 59 David expresses his hope that God will deliver him from his enemies and announces his faith in the mercy of God toward his people (1 Samuel 19:1-24; Psalm 59).

509 BC	480 BC	215 BC	12 BC
Roman Republic founded	Parthenon built in Athens	Construction begins on Great Wall of China	Silk Road opens between China and West

1012 BC ✡ DAVID BEGINS HIS REIGN IN HEBRON

When David (r. 1012–970 BC) received word that Saul and his son Jonathan had been killed in battle with the Philistines, he was finally free from danger after years of being threatened by Saul. However, David grieved the deaths of both his dear friend Jonathan and of the Lord's anointed king, Saul. When David asked God what he should do next, God told him to go up to the city of Hebron. When he and his family arrived in Hebron, the people of Judah anointed him king. However, the northern tribes continued to follow Saul's son Ishbosheth for the next seven and a half years. David reigned as king over the southern tribe of Judah until Saul's kingdom finally collapsed and David assumed the throne as king over all of Israel (2 Samuel 1:1–2:7; 1 Chronicles 11:1-3).

1005 BC ✡ DAVID BEGINS HIS REIGN IN JERUSALEM

After Saul's death, David (r. 1012–970 BC) reigned for seven and a half years over the tribe of Judah in Hebron. Then around 1005 BC, David was anointed king over the twelve tribes of Israel and made Jerusalem his capital (2 Samuel 3–5). He successfully conquered Israel's enemies, built a royal palace, and secured the material prosperity of his kingdom. Even more importantly, he brought the Ark of the covenant to Jerusalem and placed it in the Tabernacle (2 Samuel 2–6). God made a covenant with David, promising the eternal reign of his descendants (2 Samuel 7). David experienced great successes and committed great sins, including adultery and murder (2 Samuel 11). But because he repented (2 Samuel 12), his descendant the Messiah now sits on David's throne (Acts 2:30-36).

970 BC ✡ SOLOMON'S REIGN BEGINS

Solomon, David and Bathsheba's son, became king in 970 BC (1 Kings 1–2). When God offered to grant Solomon any desire, Solomon chose "an understanding mind" (1 Kings 3:5-9). Because of his wise choice, God promised to give him riches and honor in addition (1 Kings 3:10-15). Solomon demonstrated his wisdom by writing many proverbs, as well as the books of Ecclesiastes and Song of Solomon. Solomon's greatest achievement was building the Temple in Jerusalem, which he began in 966 BC (1 Kings 6:1–9:9). The Temple

2200–1950 BC	2000 BC	1180 BC	776 BC
Middle Bronze Age I	Hittite, Egyptian, and Assyrian Empires control major areas	Troy destroyed with Trojan horse	First Olympic Games held in Greece

was one of the most magnificent edifices of the ancient world. Solomon's greatest mistake was marrying seven hundred foreign wives who turned his heart to their gods (1 Kings 11:1-13). God postponed judgment on Solomon until the next generation because of the faithfulness of his father David.

970 BC ✡ SOLOMON BEGINS WRITING PROVERBS

The wisdom of Solomon (r. 970–930 BC) became legendary in his own day, and many of his insights have been preserved in the book of Proverbs, which he began writing around 970 BC. In it, he expounds on wisdom that begins and ends with the fear of the Lord (1 Kings 3:5–4:34; Proverbs 1:7ff).

966 BC ✡ SOLOMON BEGINS TEMPLE CONSTRUCTION

In 966 BC, the fourth year of his reign, King Solomon (r. 970–930 BC) began to build the Temple for which his father, David (r. 1012–970 BC), had prepared. Four hundred and eighty years had passed since Israel left Egypt, and the Temple's construction marked a fulfillment of God's promises to the people. The Temple was built on Mount Moriah on the very spot where Abraham had almost sacrificed Isaac and where David had built an altar to the Lord. The Temple, which took seven years to build, was ninety feet long, thirty feet wide, and thirty feet high. The ornate details beautified the dwelling place of God on earth. The structure represented God's presence and set the nation of Israel apart as God's representative people for as long as his glory dwelt with them. (1 Kings 6:1–8:66; 2 Chronicles 3:1–7:22).

965 BC ✡ SOLOMON WRITES SONG OF SONGS

Solomon (r. 970–930 BC) wrote this collection of love poetry known as the Song of Songs (or Song of Solomon) somewhere around 965 BC. Because of the erotic nature of the book, both Jews and Christians have had a tendency to allegorize its meaning. Some Jewish interpreters have inferred that the book is a love song between God and Israel, and many Christians see it as referring to Christ and his church. Regardless of other meanings, at face value the book presents the account of a bride and bridegroom and the events surrounding

509 BC	480 BC	215 BC	12 BC
Roman Republic founded	Parthenon built in Athens	Construction begins on Great Wall of China	Silk Road opens between China and West

their wedding celebration. As such, it is an affirmation of God's intention that a married couple should express and enjoy sexual relations.

935 BC ✡ SOLOMON WRITES ECCLESIASTES

The author of Ecclesiastes identified himself as the "Teacher (or Preacher, as some versions translate it), King David's son." The Teacher/Preacher was Solomon (r. 970–930 BC), who likely composed this book later in his life, in approximately 935 BC. The book's theme is the emptiness of temporal pursuits: "Meaningless . . . utterly meaningless!" (1:2). The majority of Ecclesiastes describes Solomon's lament over the failure of temporal pleasures to bring him satisfaction (1:1–12:8). He found that all forms of worldly pleasure—levity, food and drink, power, sexual pleasure, and riches—do not lead to fulfillment. After all his pleasure seeking, Solomon concluded that true joy comes by fearing God and keeping his commandments (12:9-14).

930 BC ✡ REHOBOAM BEGINS HIS REIGN

When Rehoboam (r. 930–913 BC) became king, the repressive measures his father, Solomon (r. 970–930 BC), had initiated to fund his building projects led to a confrontation between the new king and the ten northern tribes of Israel. Rehoboam's arrogance led him to accept his friends' advice to increase the taxes. As a result, the northern ten tribes revolted and chose Jeroboam as their king (1 Kings 12:1-20). Rehoboam ruled the tribes of Judah and Benjamin (1 Kings 12:20-21). Rehoboam's seventeen-year reign saw the flourishing of pagan religions with their high places and Asherim, probably wooden representations of the Canaanite goddess Asherah. Especially abominable was the Canaanite fertility religion with its male cult prostitutes (1 Kings 14:22-24).

930 BC ✡ JEROBOAM I BEGINS HIS REIGN OVER ISRAEL

Solomon (r. 970–930 BC) had placed Jeroboam (r. 930–909 BC) over the forced laborers from the northern tribes, who were working on construction projects in Jerusalem. A prophet had prophesied to him that God would give him a kingdom composed of the ten northern tribes of Israel. Upon learning this, Solomon sought to kill Jeroboam, but Jeroboam escaped to Egypt until Solomon

2200–1950 BC	2000 BC	1180 BC	776 BC
Middle Bronze Age I	Hittite, Egyptian, and Assyrian Empires control major areas	Troy destroyed with Trojan horse	First Olympic Games held in Greece

died. When the ten northern tribes rebelled against Solomon's son Rehoboam (r. 930–913 BC), they made Jeroboam their king (1 Kings 12:20). During his twenty-two-year reign, Jeroboam I incurred God's wrath by building shrines at Dan and Bethel and staffing them with non-Levitical priests to keep his subjects from going to the Temple in Jerusalem (1 Kings 12:26–14:20). His successors were continually evaluated as perpetuating his sins (e.g. 1 Kings 16:26).

913 BC ✡ ABIJAM BECOMES KING OF JUDAH

Abijam (Abijah) succeeded his father, Rehoboam (r. 930–913 BC), as king of Judah and reigned for three years (913–910 BC). Unfortunately, Abijam was not wholly committed to the Lord, as David his great-grandfather had been, and he continued all the sins of his father (1 Kings 15:1-3). Yet in spite of Abijam's incomplete devotion, God still worked through him. As war was beginning between Judah and Israel, Abijam addressed King Jeroboam of Israel (r. 930–909 BC) and his people from a mountaintop, condemning Jeroboam I for his rebellion against God and for driving the priests out of Israel. Even though Jeroboam had the army of Judah trapped and had twice as many warriors, God gave the victory to Judah. Jeroboam's army suffered five hundred thousand casualties, and he never recovered from that defeat.

910 BC ✡ ASA BECOMES KING OF JUDAH

In about 910 BC, Asa succeeded his father, Abijam (r. 913–910 BC), as Judah's king. Asa (r. 910–869 BC) followed the example of his great-grandfather David (r. 1012–970 BC) rather than that of his father and grandfather. Heeding the prophet Azariah's message to him, he abolished male cult prostitution and removed all the idols his predecessors had made. When an Ethiopian army of one million men attacked Judah, God gave Asa the victory because of the king's faith in him. Many true believers in Israel defected to Judah when they realized that God was with Asa. The king and all the people renewed God's covenant by recommitting themselves to him. Unfortunately Asa's life did not end well. Near the conclusion of his forty-one-year reign he depended upon Aram (Syria) instead of on God to defeat Baasha (r. 908–886 BC), king of Israel (1 Kings 15:8-22; 2 Chronicles 14–16).

509 BC	480 BC	215 BC	12 BC
Roman Republic founded	Parthenon built in Athens	Construction begins on Great Wall of China	Silk Road opens between China and West

909 BC ✡ NADAB BECOMES KING OF ISRAEL, FOLLOWED BY BAASHA

Following the death of Jeroboam I (r. 930–909 BC), his son Nadab became king of Israel. Nadab reigned only one year (909–908 BC) until he was assassinated by Baasha (r. 908–886 BC) of the tribe of Issachar. Baasha proceeded to exterminate all the descendants of Jeroboam I, so that he would have no rivals for the throne. In doing so he fulfilled Ahijah's prophecy to Jeroboam that every male descendant of his would be killed and another king raised up in his place (1 Kings 14:10, 14). Because Baasha followed in the sins of Jeroboam I during his twenty-four-year reign, God sent a prophet to announce to him that one day all of his descendants would be killed, just as he had exterminated the house of Jeroboam. This prophecy was fulfilled two years later by his son's servant Zimri (r. 885 BC) (1 Kings 15:25–16:12).

885 BC ✡ ELAH, ZIMRI, AND OMRI REIGN OVER ISRAEL

Elah (r. 886–885 BC) followed his father, Baasha (r. 908–886 BC), as king of Israel, serving only two years. He was assassinated in 885 BC by Zimri, the commander of his chariots, who then became king in his place. Zimri (r. 885 BC) immediately killed all of Baasha's male descendants, thus delivering the punishment prophesied against Baasha (1 Kings 16:6-14). When Israel learned that Zimri had killed King Elah, they made Omri, the commander of the army, king instead. Omri led Israel in besieging Tirzah, where Zimri was in his royal palace. Zimri, realizing he was defeated, committed suicide by setting fire to the palace (1 Kings 16:15-20). Omri reigned for twelve years (885–874 BC) and founded the city of Samaria. Even though he was one of Israel's most powerful kings, he did evil in the sight of the Lord (1 Kings 16:16-28).

874 BC ✡ AHAB BECOMES KING OF ISRAEL

In 874 BC, Ahab succeeded his father, Omri (r. 885–874 BC), as king of Israel and reigned for twenty-two years (874–853 BC). He married Jezebel, daughter of the king of Sidon and a pagan priestess. Influenced by his wife, Ahab built a temple dedicated to Baal in Samaria, his capital city. Jezebel encouraged and supported 450 prophets of Baal and 400 prophets of the Canaanite goddess Asherah. She tore down the altars of the Lord and killed the true prophets

2200–1950 BC	2000 BC	1180 BC	776 BC
Middle Bronze Age I	Hittite, Egyptian, and Assyrian Empires control major areas	Troy destroyed with Trojan horse	First Olympic Games held in Greece

(1 Kings 16:29–18:19). Elijah was the prophet opposing Ahab. In a contest staged between Elijah and the prophets of Baal on Mount Carmel, God made Elijah victorious (1 Kings 18:20-40). Ahab demonstrated his failure to rule justly by his counterfeit trial and subsequent execution of Naboth, so he could annex Naboth's vineyard. Elijah then correctly prophesied the destruction of Ahab, Jezebel, and the dynasty (1 Kings 21:1–22:40).

872 BC ✡ JEHOSHAPHAT BECOMES KING OF JUDAH

In 872 BC, Jehoshaphat (r. 872–848 BC) became co-regent with his father, Asa (r. 910–869 BC), as king of Judah. Following Asa's death in 869 BC, Jehoshaphat reigned alone until his son Jehoram (r. 853–841 BC) joined him as co-regent in 853 BC. During his reign, Jehoshaphat strengthened Judah's military position by placing garrisons of troops throughout the tiny nation. He broke with previous practice by entering into a parity treaty with King Ahab of Israel and arranged for Ahab's daughter Athaliah to marry his son Jehoram (2 Chronicles 17:1–18:1). Jehoshaphat followed the godly example of his father. He did away with heathen worship (1 Kings 22:43, 46) and sent out traveling teachers of the law of Moses (2 Chronicles 17:7-9). He reorganized Judah's system of justice, placing judges in key cities and a court of appeals in Jerusalem (2 Chronicles 19:4-11). Jehoshaphat's alliance with Israel proved to be Judah's undoing after his death, when Athaliah (r. 841-835 BC) later took the throne for herself (2 Kings 11:1-3).

853 BC ✡ AHAZIAH BECOMES KING OF ISRAEL

In 853 BC Ahaziah (r. 853–852 BC) followed his father, Ahab, as king of Israel. He also followed his policies by worshiping Baal (1 Kings 22:51-53). Ahaziah's reign was foreshortened when he fell through the lattice in the upper chamber of his palace in Samaria. Concerned that his injury might be fatal, he sent messengers to inquire of Baal-zebub, the god of the Philistine city Ekron. God commanded the prophet Elijah to meet the messengers and tell them that Ahaziah would die because he tried to consult Baal-zebub instead of God. When the messengers gave Ahaziah Elijah's message, the king twice dispatched a commander and fifty soldiers to capture Elijah to force him to retract his prophecy.

509 BC	480 BC	215 BC	12 BC
Roman Republic founded	Parthenon built in Athens	Construction begins on Great Wall of China	Silk Road opens between China and West

Each time Elijah called down fire from heaven that consumed them. Ahaziah died according to God's word (2 Kings 1).

852 BC ✡ JORAM (JEHORAM) BECOMES KING OF ISRAEL

Joram (r. 852–841 BC), a second son of Ahab and Jezebel, followed his brother Ahaziah as king in 852 BC. He did evil in the sight of God, but not to the extent of his parents, for he removed the sacred pillar of Baal that his father had constructed (2 Kings 3:1-3). Moab, a vassal kingdom of Israel, had rebelled when Ahab died. Joram was determined to end their rebellion, so he asked Jehoshaphat (r. 872–848 BC), king of Judah, to join him in battle. Because of the parity treaty between the two nations, Jehoshaphat agreed. They asked the prophet Elisha about the outcome of the war. Elisha replied that he would answer their request only because of King Jehoshaphat's presence, but the answer was positive. They would be victorious. Joram was later assassinated and succeeded by Jehu (r. 841–814 BC) (2 Kings 9:1-26).

848 BC ✡ JEHORAM BECOMES KING OF JUDAH

Jehoram (r. 848–841 BC), the son of King Jehoshaphat (r. 872–848 BC), became king of Judah in 848 BC following the death of his father. He is not to be confused with Joram, or Jehoram, king of Israel who reigned from 852–841 BC. Jehoram's father had arranged a diplomatic marriage for him with Athaliah, the daughter of Israel's King Ahab. Athaliah was thus the sister of King Joram (Jehoram) of Israel. Jehoram (of Judah) followed the example of his father-in-law Ahab rather than that of his father and introduced the worship of Baal to Judah. In addition, both Edom and Libnah—vassal states of Judah—revolted and became independent nations. Jehoram died to no one's regret and was not buried in the tombs of the kings (2 Kings 8:16-25; 2 Chronicles 21:1-20).

841 BC ✡ AHAZIAH BECOMES KING OF JUDAH; ATHALIAH BECOMES QUEEN

When Jehoram died (r. 848–841 BC), his sole surviving son, Ahaziah, became king of Judah in 841 BC (another Ahaziah had ruled Israel); but he reigned less

2200–1950 BC	2000 BC	1180 BC	776 BC
Middle Bronze Age I	Hittite, Egyptian, and Assyrian Empires control major areas	Troy destroyed with Trojan horse	First Olympic Games held in Greece

than a year. Jehu (r. 841–814 BC), who had been anointed king of Israel by a prophet sent from Elisha, murdered both King Jehoram of Israel and King Ahaziah of Judah (2 Kings 8:24–9:28). To retain power for herself after the death of her son Ahaziah, Athaliah (r. 841–835 BC) killed all the royal family— or so she thought. King Ahaziah's sister hid the king's baby son, Joash, in the Temple for six years with the help of her husband, Jehoiada, the high priest. A few years later, Jehoiada put the seven-year-old Joash (r. 835–796 BC) on the throne, and Athaliah, the child's grandmother, was put to death (2 Kings 11; 2 Chronicles 22:10–23:15).

841 BC ✡ JEHU BECOMES KING OF ISRAEL

During the reign of King Jehoram (r. 852–841 BC) of Israel, Elisha instructed a fellow prophet to anoint Jehu (r. 841–814 BC) king of Israel. As he did so, he prophesied that Jehu would kill every male descendant of Ahab to avenge the blood of the prophets Ahab had slain. Jehu, with the backing of Israel's army, killed both Jehoram, king of Israel, and Ahaziah (r. 841 BC), king of Judah. He then had Ahab's widow Jezebel put to death, as well as seventy male descendants of Ahab and forty-two visiting members of Ahaziah's family (2 Kings 9:1–10:17; 2 Chronicles 22:7-9). Jehu stopped the worship of Baal in Israel by tricking the Baal worshipers into meeting together and then slaughtering them and destroying their Temple. Yet he continued the apostasy of worshiping the golden calves at Bethel and Dan (2 Kings 10:18-36).

835 BC ✡ JOASH BECOMES KING OF JUDAH

In an attempt to put herself in power after the death of her son Ahaziah (r. 841 BC), Queen Athaliah (r. 841–835 BC) killed all his descendants. However, she missed Joash (r. 835–796 BC), Ahaziah's infant son whose aunt, the wife of Jehoiada the high priest, hid him in the Temple (2 Kings 11:1-6). In 835 BC when Joash was seven years old, Jehoiada proclaimed him king and Athaliah was killed (2 Kings 11:4-20). Young Joash began well as king, rebuilding the Temple with the help of his uncle Jehoiada (2 Kings 12:4-20). However, after Jehoiada died, Joash faltered under the influence of officials who abandoned the Temple and reinstituted idol worship (2 Chronicles 24:17-18). When Jehoiada's son Zechariah rebuked him for that, Joash murdered him

(2 Chronicles 24:20-22). Joash was assassinated as part of a plot to replace him (2 Kings 12:20-21).

814 BC ✡ JEHOAHAZ BECOMES KING OF ISRAEL

Jehoahaz (r. 814–798 BC) succeeded his father, Jehu (r. 841–814 BC), as king of Israel in 814 BC. Throughout his seventeen-year reign he followed his predecessors' example of tolerating pagan worship by allowing a statue of the goddess Asherah to stand in Samaria, the capital of Israel. His unfaithfulness to God brought the Lord's judgment upon him and upon the nation in the form of repeated attacks by the kings of Aram (Syria). When Jehoahaz finally turned to God in prayer, God answered by rescuing the Israelites from the tyranny of the Arameans. Although God gave him the victory, Jehoahaz's battles with Aram were costly. Jehoahaz was left with just ten chariots, fifty horsemen, and ten thousand foot soldiers (2 Kings 13:1-9).

798 BC ✡ JEHOASH BECOMES KING OF ISRAEL

In 798 BC, Jehoash (r. 798–782 BC) followed his father, Jehoahaz (r. 814–798 BC), as king of Israel and continued the pattern of sinning against God. In spite of Jehoash's sinful ways, he wept over Elisha when the prophet became fatally ill. Elisha commanded Jehoash to take a bow and some arrows, open a window, and shoot an arrow toward the East in the direction of Transjordan, controlled by the Arameans (Syrians). Then Elisha proclaimed that Jehoash would be victorious over Aram. Elisha next commanded Jehoash to strike the remaining arrows against the ground. Jehoash did so only three times, making Elisha angry by his unenthusiastic response. Elisha rebuked the king, saying, "You should have struck the ground five or six times! Now you will be victorious only three times." Jehoash defeated the Arameans three times but did not completely destroy them (2 Kings 13:10-25).

796 BC ✡ AMAZIAH BECOMES KING OF JUDAH

Amaziah (r. 796–767 BC), the son of Joash (r. 835–796 BC), succeeded his father as king of Judah in about 796 BC. He did what was pleasing in God's sight, yet he did not remove the high places, the pagan shrines where the people still

2200–1950 BC	2000 BC	1180 BC	776 BC
Middle Bronze Age I	Hittite, Egyptian, and Assyrian Empires control major areas	Troy destroyed with Trojan horse	First Olympic Games held in Greece

offered sacrifices and burned incense to pagan gods. Amaziah was victorious in battle over Edom, which had previously won its independence from Judah. Buoyed by this victory, Amaziah next challenged Israel's King Jehoash (r. 798–782 BC) to battle. This decision was Amaziah's undoing. He was captured and his army was overwhelmingly defeated. Jerusalem's defenses were partially destroyed, and the Temple and palace were plundered. After his release, Amaziah was assassinated (2 Kings 14:1-20).

793 BC ✡ JEROBOAM II BECOMES KING OF ISRAEL

In 793 BC Jeroboam II (r. 793–753 BC) became co-regent with his father, Jehoash (r. 798–782 BC), over Israel for ten years, until Jehoash's death. Jeroboam's reign continued for a total of forty-one years. In spite of doing evil in God's sight as did the other kings of Israel, Jeroboam II was one of Israel's most successful rulers. He continued his father's program of aggressive expansion and was able to almost completely restore Israel's borders to where they had been under Solomon. Jeroboam II's management skills, in addition to relative freedom from enemy attacks during his reign, led to unprecedented prosperity (2 Kings 14:16, 23-29). Archaeological excavations in Samaria have revealed the grandeur of his capital city. Yet God was not impressed. The prophet Amos gives God's negative assessment of the reign of Jeroboam II (see the book of Amos).

792 BC ✡ UZZIAH (AZARIAH) BECOMES KING OF JUDAH

In about 792 BC, Uzziah (r. 792–740 BC), whose throne name was Azariah, became co-regent with his father, Amaziah (r. 796–767 BC), from Amaziah's imprisonment by Israel's King Jehoash (r. 798–782 BC) until his later assassination. Uzziah extended the borders of Judah and reestablished control over the port city of Elath on the Gulf of Aqaba, rebuilding the city. He conducted successful military campaigns against the Philistines, Arabs, and Ammonites. Although he did what was pleasing in God's sight, nevertheless as a punishment for intruding into the office of priest and burning incense on the Temple altar, Uzziah was struck with leprosy and his son Jotham (r. 750–735 BC) became co-regent with him (2 Kings 14:21-22; 15:1-7; 2 Chronicles 26:1-23). A first-century AD limestone plaque found in Jerusalem reads, "Hither were brought the bones of Uzziah king of Judah—do not open."

509 BC	480 BC	215 BC	12 BC
Roman Republic founded	Parthenon built in Athens	Construction begins on Great Wall of China	Silk Road opens between China and West

754 BC ✡ AMOS WRITES HIS PROPHECY

Like several other prophets, Amos predicted judgment for the sins of Israel during a time of seeming prosperity. In the 750s BC, during the reign of Jeroboam II (r. 793–753 BC), Amos traveled from his home in Tekoa, about six miles south of Bethlehem in the southern kingdom of Judah, to prophesy in the northern kingdom of Israel. Standing before the royal sanctuary in Bethel, Amos condemned Israel and predicted a series of woes that would befall her. The first section of Amos (chapters 1–2) is a list of nations that the Lord would soon judge. The list culminates with Judah and Israel. The next section (chapters 3–6) contains three sermons of judgment against Israel. This is followed by five more visions of judgment (7:1–9:10). However, the book ends with a promise of future restoration and hope (9:11-15).

753 BC ✝ ROME IS FOUNDED

According to Titus Livius (59 BC–AD 17), Rome was founded on April 21, 753 BC. After several different groups ruled the city, the Romans overcame their Etruscan governors in 509 BC and established a republic. The republic lasted for more than 450 years, until Caesar Augustus (63 BC–AD 14) came to power and established the Roman Empire. The *Pax Romana,* as the first two hundred years of the empire were called, was a time of internal and external stability in the empire. In this atmosphere the New Testament was written. However, as the *Pax Romana* dissolved, persecution of Christians began to increase. After Constantine (285–337) issued the Edict of Milan, the church's power increased as the empire's decreased. In 847, Pope Leo IV (d. 855) consolidated the power of the Rome bishopric. Since then, Rome has been the headquarters of the pope and the Roman Catholic Church.

753–752 BC ✡ FOUR KINGS IN TWO YEARS RULE ISRAEL

In 753 BC, Zechariah, the son of Jeroboam II (r. 793–753 BC), succeeded his father as king of Israel. However, his reign lasted only six months until Shallum assassinated him and took the throne in 752 BC (2 Kings 15:8-12). One month later, Shallum was murdered by Menahem (r. 752–742 BC), who next seized the throne (2 Kings 15:13-16). Under Menahem, Israel became a

2200–1950 BC	2000 BC	1180 BC	776 BC
Middle Bronze Age I	Hittite, Egyptian, and Assyrian Empires control major areas	Troy destroyed with Trojan horse	First Olympic Games held in Greece

ONE THING LEADS TO ANOTHER

Have you ever wondered how Bible scholars are able to assign dates to the events of the Old Testament?

The major breakthrough came with the discovery of tablets containing the Assyrian Eponym lists. (An eponym is a person from whom something gets its name.) They listed all the years from 892 to 648 BC, naming each year after the prime minister or *limmu* of Assyria who was elected that year. In addition to these names, the tablets also recount the major events of each year.

The Eponym lists contain an unbroken chain of events relating not only to Assyria but also to other nations that were interacting with Assyria. Because the tablets give the years of battles between Assyria and Israel, Bible scholars have been able to determine the reigns of the kings of Israel and Judah from these dates.

The Assyrians recorded an eclipse of the sun in a year ruled by a prime minister named Bur-Sagale. Modern astronomers are able to calculate the dates of eclipses with great precision and have determined that the eclipse of the sun described in the tablets occurred on June 15, 763 BC.

In the year 853 BC, ninety years before this eclipse, the lists report the battle of Qarqar in which the Assyrian emperor Shalmaneser III defeated a coalition of Syria and Israel under King Ahab. According to 1 Kings 22:1, the only period when Israel was at peace with Syria was near the end of Ahab's reign, so the battle of Qarqar must have occurred during that time.

While that information was interesting, it did not conclusively link the Eponym lists to the Old Testament until the discovery of the Black Obelisk. The Black Obelisk is a pillar that Shalmaneser III of Assyria erected in 841 BC to commemorate his victory over his enemies, including King Jehu of Israel. Jehu is pictured on the Obelisk as kneeling in subjection to Shalmaneser in the eighteenth year of the Assyrian emperor's reign. The year can then be dated from the Eponym Lists because they give the dates of Shalmaneser's reign. The date of the Black Obelisk is 841 BC, which apparently was the first year of Jehu's reign over Israel. According to 2 Kings 3:1; 9:1-8, 24, twelve years passed between the end of Ahab's reign and the beginning of Jehu's. Thus the date of 853 BC can be established for the end of Ahab's reign over Israel.

Nailing down these two dates made the process of constructing the chronology of the Old Testament relatively easy. The books of 1 and 2 Kings give the lengths of the reigns of the kings of Israel and Judah before and after Ahab and Jehu. By adding the years of these reigns, the accession year of each king can be determined as well as the dates of many associated events.

vassal of Assyria. The annual tribute that Israel had to pay Assyria amounted to a thousand talents of silver, over thirty-seven tons! Meanwhile it appears that when Menahem instituted his coup and became king of Israel, Pekah (r. 740–732 BC) established a rival government in Transjordan. Menahem's evil reign lasted for ten years (2 Kings 15:16-22).

750 BC ✡ JOTHAM REIGNS AS KING OF JUDAH

In 750 BC, when King Uzziah (r. 792–740 BC), also known as Azariah, became a leper, his son Jotham (r. 750–732 BC) began to reign in his father's place. When Uzziah died in 740 BC, Jotham became the sole monarch of Judah. Jotham was a godly king like his father, except that he did not remove the pagan high places where the people still sacrificed and burned incense. Because Jotham was a faithful king, God gave him victory over the Ammonites, who became a vassal kingdom of Judah, paying an annual tribute of one hundred talents of silver (7,500 pounds) and approximately one hundred thousand bushels of both wheat and barley. Jotham reigned until 732 BC, but starting in 735 BC his son Ahaz (r. 735–715 BC) ruled with him (2 Kings 15:32-38; 2 Chronicles 27:1-9).

740 BC ✡ ISAIAH IS COMMISSIONED AS A PROPHET

God commissioned Isaiah as prophet in 740 BC when King Uzziah (r. 792–740 BC) of Judah died of leprosy. Isaiah had a vision of God sitting on a lofty throne in the heavenly Temple throne room. Around him were angelic seraphim singing praises so loudly that the temple shook. Awestruck, Isaiah said, "My destruction is sealed, for I am a sinful man and a member of a sinful race. Yet I have seen the King, the Lord Almighty!" A seraph touched a burning coal to Isaiah's lips, saying, "Now your guilt is removed, and your sins are forgiven." Then the Lord asked, "Whom should I send as a messenger to my people?" Isaiah responded, "Lord, I'll go! Send me." The Lord then commissioned Isaiah as his prophet to his people (Isaiah 6:1-13).

735 BC ✡ AHAZ BECOMES KING OF JUDAH

Ahaz (r. 735–715 BC) became king of Judah in 735 BC. He did not follow the godly example of his father, Jotham (r. 750–732 BC), or his grandfather Uzziah (r.

2200–1950 BC	2000 BC	1180 BC	776 BC
Middle Bronze Age I	Hittite, Egyptian, and Assyrian Empires control major areas	Troy destroyed with Trojan horse	First Olympic Games held in Greece

792–740 BC). Early in Ahaz's reign, Israel's King Pekah (r. 740–732 BC) and the king of Syria asked him to join them in an alliance against Assyria. When he refused, Israel and Syria invaded Judah, inflicting heavy casualties. Isaiah encouraged Ahaz to put his trust in God, but the king turned to Assyria instead. As a result, Judah became a vassal of Assyria for the next century, and the tribute they were forced to pay depleted the country's resources. Ahaz's wickedness consumed him to the point that he burned his own son as a sacrifice to the Assyrian gods, ordered an Assyrian-style altar built in the Temple, and used the bronze altar for divination (2 Kings 16:3-4, 10-16; 2 Chronicles 28:2-4, 23-25; Isaiah 7:1-12).

725 BC ✡ JONAH GOES TO NINEVEH

The book of Jonah is unique among the prophetic books. Instead of focusing on a prophecy, it is rather an extended narrative of an event in the prophet's life that took place around 725 BC. The book opens with Jonah boarding a boat to flee from God's command to preach in Nineveh. The Lord sent a storm that would not subside until Jonah was thrown into the sea (1:1-16). God delivered Jonah by sending a great fish to swallow him. From the fish's belly Jonah repented of his sin and praised God for his salvation (1:17–2:9). After returning to dry land, Jonah went to Nineveh and the people repented (chapter 3). The book ends somewhat ambiguously, with Jonah questioning God's wisdom in saving the Ninevites (chapter 4).

722–721 BC ✡ ISRAELITES ARE CAPTURED AND EXILED

In 732 BC, Hoshea (r. 732–722 BC) assassinated King Pekah (r. 740–732 BC) of Israel and took the throne himself. Hoshea was the last king of Israel, reigning for nine years. At this time Israel became a vassal of Assyria, paying annual tribute. Hoping for support from Egypt, Hoshea stopped the tribute payments. As a result, Assyria invaded Israel and after a three-year siege captured the capital city of Samaria and took the leading citizens of Israel into exile. They were settled in Gozan, a provincial capital along a tributary of the Euphrates River, and in towns south of the Caspian Sea and northeast of the Tigris River. Few ever returned from their exile. This was God's judgment on a nation that refused to give him their allegiance (2 Kings 15:30; 17:1-40).

509 BC	480 BC	215 BC	12 BC
Roman Republic founded	Parthenon built in Athens	Construction begins on Great Wall of China	Silk Road opens between China and West

715–710 BC ✡ HOSEA WRITES HIS PROPHECY

Hosea, whose name means "salvation," wrote the first book of the twelve prophets of the Hebrew Bible, also known as the minor prophets, between approximately 715 to 710 BC. Hosea prophesied in the northern kingdom of Israel during the reign of King Jeroboam II (r. 793–753 BC). Although the nation was outwardly prospering during his ministry, Hosea continually

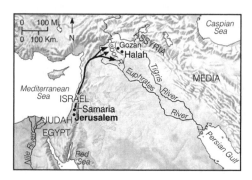

called the people back to genuine covenantal faithfulness and prophesied about the coming judgment. The book of Hosea is an extended allegorical lesson about God and his love toward Israel. In the first part of the book (chapters 1–3), God tells Hosea to marry Gomer, a prostitute. Although Gomer was habitually unfaithful to him, Hosea continued to welcome her back. The last part of the book

ISRAEL TAKEN CAPTIVE Finally, the sins of Israel's people caught up with them. God allowed Assyria to defeat and disperse the people. They were led into captivity, swallowed up by the mighty, evil Assyrian Empire.

(chapters 4–14) is an explanation of God's love for Israel in spite of her unfaithfulness toward him, and the book ends with a prophecy of Israel's coming restoration.

715 BC ✡ HEZEKIAH BECOMES KING OF JUDAH

Hezekiah (r. 715–686 BC) was a godly king of Judah, succeeding his father, Ahaz (r. 735–715 BC). He reinstituted true worship of God in the Temple, which he cleansed and renovated. He renewed the covenant with God, reinstituted the feast of Passover, and destroyed the high places of heathen worship. When Hezekiah became very ill, Isaiah told him he was about to die. In response to Hezekiah's bitter weeping, God informed him through Isaiah that he would add fifteen years to his life. During those fifteen years, Hezekiah unwisely showed off all his treasures to the Babylonians. Through Isaiah God informed Hezekiah that all the treasures of his ancestors someday would be carried off to Babylon. That happened more than a century later during the Babylonian captivity (2 Kings 18–20; 2 Chronicles 29–32; Isaiah 36–39).

700 BC ✡ MICAH WRITES HIS PROPHECY

The prophet Micah was called around 700 BC to proclaim judgment against Jerusalem. Micah's message centered on the exploitation of the poor, unethical merchants, and corrupt civil and religious leaders. Because of the people's lack of covenantal faithfulness, God promised to judge the nation. The book of Micah begins with a promise of judgment, first to surrounding nations and then to Judah and her leaders (chapters 1–3). The middle section is a promise of restoration and a coming kingdom led by the messianic King (chapters 4–5). Because of this hope of future restoration, in the final section of the book (chapters 6–7), Micah pleads with the people to repent of their sin and turn back to the Lord.

700–685 BC ✡ ISAIAH WRITES HIS PROPHECY

Isaiah wrote the prophecies contained in the book bearing his name between 700 and 685 BC. Some of the clearest messianic prophecies come from Isaiah, and the New Testament writers frequently quote them in reference to Christ. The first part of the book (chapters 1–35) is a message of condemnation and judgment for Israel's disobedience. This is followed by a brief historical interlude about Hezekiah's (r. 715–686 BC) deliverance and later sin (chapters 36–39). The final chapters of the book (chapters 40–66), however, are hopeful and center on comfort and future restoration.

697 BC ✡ MANASSEH BECOMES KING OF JUDAH

In about 697 BC, twelve-year-old Manasseh (r. 697–642 BC) became co-regent over Judah with his father, Hezekiah (r. 715–686 BC). After Hezekiah's death in about 686 BC, he became the sole ruler. Manasseh ruled for fifty-five years as the personification of evil. He rebuilt the pagan high places his father had destroyed. He even sacrificed his own son as a burnt offering. In addition, he martyred many godly people who opposed his pagan practices. God's verdict was this: "King Manasseh of Judah has done many detestable things.... So this is what the Lord, the God of Israel says: I will bring such disaster on Jerusalem and Judah

509 BC	480 BC	215 BC	12 BC
Roman Republic founded	Parthenon built in Athens	Construction begins on Great Wall of China	Silk Road opens between China and West

that the ears of those who hear about it will tingle with horror" (2 Kings 21:1-18; 2 Chronicles 33:1-20). These words were fulfilled through the events leading up to the Babylonian captivity.

642 BC ✡ AMON BECOMES KING OF JUDAH

Amon (r. 642–640 BC), the son of Manasseh (r. 697–642 BC), was the fourteenth king of Judah and ruled for two years. During the time of his reign, King Amon ardently supported the idolatrous practices that his father had instituted early in his own reign. As a result, great wickedness prevailed in Judah while Amon was king. Amon, the father of Josiah (r. 640–609 BC), was assassinated by his own servants. Second Kings 21:24 records that the "people of the land killed all those who had conspired against King Amon," indicating that Amon's assassination was not a matter of popular revolt, but rather of royal rebellion.

640 BC ✡ JOSIAH BECOMES KING OF JUDAH

The name *Josiah* (r. 640–609 BC) means, "Yahweh gives" or "Yahweh heals." This godly king began his reign at eight years of age after the assassination of his father, Amon (r. 642–640 BC). Josiah was said to have "turned to the LORD with all his heart." Josiah's reign lasted thirty-one years, during which he led a campaign to annihilate the idolatry instituted by his grandfather Manasseh (r. 697–642 BC) and his father. Josiah's war against Judah's wickedness involved the destruction of all the sanctuaries and relics of idol worship throughout the land. During the eighteenth year of his reign, Josiah began to rebuild the Temple, discovering in it a scroll that was probably the book of Deuteronomy. A public reading of this Book of the Law brought the people of Judah back to the God of their fathers (2 Kings 22–23).

635 BC ✡ ZEPHANIAH WRITES HIS PROPHECY

Zephaniah prophesied in Judah around 635 BC, about ten years before the religious reforms under King Josiah (r. 640–609 BC). Zephaniah preached against the idolatry of Judah and the surrounding nations and proclaimed that a day was coming when all who did not submit to the Lord would be crushed under

2200–1950 BC	2000 BC	1180 BC	776 BC
Middle Bronze Age I	Hittite, Egyptian, and Assyrian Empires control major areas	Troy destroyed with Trojan horse	First Olympic Games held in Greece

his wrath. This coming Day of the Lord is a central theme of Zephaniah. The first part of the book is an extended oracle of judgment (1:1–3:8). Judgment was coming upon the whole earth, the nation of Judah, the surrounding nations, and the city of Jerusalem if they refused to repent. The book ends with a promise of restoration (3:9-20). God promised to turn the hearts of his people back to him and restore Jerusalem.

626 BC ✡ JEREMIAH IS CALLED

Jeremiah was a priest when God called him to be a prophet, in the thirteenth year of King Josiah's reign (626 BC). Jeremiah was primarily a prophet of doom, who prophesied throughout the reigns of Judah's last five kings: Josiah (r. 640–609 BC), Jehoahaz (r. 609 BC), Jehoiakim (r. 609–598 BC), Jehoiachin (r. 598–597 BC), and Zedekiah (r. 597–586 BC). Following the fall of Jerusalem in 586 BC, Jeremiah was taken against his will to Egypt by Jews in rebellion against the Lord (Jeremiah 43:4-7).

626–580 BC ✡ JEREMIAH WRITES HIS PROPHECY

Jeremiah, the "weeping prophet," prophesied in Judah during the years leading up to and at the beginning of its Babylonian captivity. His ministry stretched from approximately 626 to 580 BC. In spite of severe opposition from his countrymen, he faithfully proclaimed God's message of judgment. The book of Jeremiah begins with an account of the prophet's call from God. The next section (chapters 2–45) contains Jeremiah's prophecies of judgment and restoration for Israel from before, during, and after the Babylonian siege of Jerusalem. This is followed by a list of prophecies against the Gentile nations that have wronged Israel (chapters 46–51). The last chapter of the book is a historical narrative of the fulfillment of Jeremiah's prophecies of Jerusalem's fall.

615 BC ✡ NAHUM WRITES HIS PROPHECY

Nahum prophesied around 615 BC, while Judah was constantly under threat from the military might of Assyria. Although a century earlier Nineveh, the capital of Assyria, had repented under the preaching of Jonah, their repentance had long since passed. Consequently, so had their chance for mercy. Therefore, the

509 BC	480 BC	215 BC	12 BC
Roman Republic founded	Parthenon built in Athens	Construction begins on Great Wall of China	Silk Road opens between China and West

book of Nahum proclaims a harsh message of judgment against the Assyrians for their wickedness. The first part of Nahum's prophecy is a declaration and description of Assyria's coming judgment (chapters 1–2). Although it seemed unlikely at the time, its doom was imminent. The second half of the book provides the rationale for the coming judgment (chapter 3). That is, Nineveh's great wickedness was an offense to the Lord, and it would be judged. Just a few years later, in 612 BC, Nineveh fell to the Babylonians.

609 BC ✡ JEHOAHAZ BECOMES KING OF JUDAH

Jehoahaz became the eighteenth ruler of Judah in 609 BC, reigning after his father, Josiah (r. 640–609 BC) was killed at the battle of Megiddo (2 Kings 23:30). His short reign was characterized by idol worship. Jehoahaz had spent only three months in office when Pharaoh Neco (r. 610–595 BC) deposed and deported him to Egypt, where he died in captivity.

609 BC ✡ JEHOIAKIM BECOMES KING OF JUDAH

Jehoiakim (r. 609–598 BC) was the oldest son of King Josiah (r. 640–609 BC) and reigned over Judah following the reign of his younger brother Jehoahaz, who reigned for only three months. Jehoiakim ruled over Judah for eleven years (r. 609–599 BC) after Pharaoh Neco (r. 610–595 BC) of Egypt dethroned Jehoahaz, exiling him to Egypt. In 605 BC Nebuchadnezzar, the crown prince of Babylon, defeated Egypt at the battle of Carchemish and thereby gained control of Palestine. The following year Jehoiakim submitted himself as vassal to Nebuchadnezzar (r. 605–562 BC), who by now had become king of Babylon. In 598 BC King Jehoiakim tried to come out from under the yoke of Babylon, only to die shortly before Jerusalem was captured by Nebuchadnezzar (2 Kings 23:36–24:6; 2 Chronicles 36:5-8).

605 BC ✡ HABAKKUK WRITES HIS PROPHECY

The small book of Habakkuk delivers a mighty message of God's faithfulness and justice in the midst of seemingly dismal circumstances. Written around 605 BC, the book is an account of the prophet's confusion over the Lord's justice and the Lord's answer that he does right and reigns over all the earth. The book

2200–1950 BC	2000 BC	1180 BC	776 BC
Middle Bronze Age I	Hittite, Egyptian, and Assyrian Empires control major areas	Troy destroyed with Trojan horse	First Olympic Games held in Greece

opens with the prophet's questions and God's answers (chapters 1–2). The wicked Babylonians were multiplying in their power, and there seemed to be no way to stop them. How could God allow this? God answers the prophet by saying that he will do right and all the earth will be silent before him (2:20). Habakkuk responds in the third chapter of the book with a prayer of humble submission to God's mercy and trust in God's salvation.

605 BC ✡ JEREMIAH PROPHESIES A 70-YEAR CAPTIVITY

Jeremiah's primary calling from God was to preach a message of judgment to Judah. Judah had set up many high places of worship to idols, engaging in practices that were explicitly forbidden by God. In 605 BC, Jeremiah prophesied that because of Judah's sins, God would send Nebuchadnezzar (r. 605–562 BC), the king of Babylon, to destroy Jerusalem and take the Jews captive to Babylon (modern-day Iraq) for seventy years (Jeremiah 25:1-11).

605 BC ✡ FIRST GROUP OF JEWS ARE DEPORTED TO BABYLON

During Jehoiakim's reign (609–598 BC) and after defeating the Egyptians at the battle of Carchemish in 605 BC, Nebuchadnezzar (r. 605–562 BC) conquered Jerusalem, pillaged Judah, and carried away many of her inhabitants to serve him in Babylon. Daniel, Shadrach, Meshach, and Abednego were among those taken into exile (Daniel 1:1-7).

604 BC ✡ NEBUCHADNEZZAR DREAMS

In 604 BC, the second year of his reign as king of Babylon, Nebuchadnezzar (r. 605–562 BC) assembled his magicians, enchanters, sorcerers, and astrologers to tell him what he had just dreamed and then to interpret the dream. He threatened to kill them if they were unable to do so. When they could not do it, Nebuchadnezzar ordered that all his wise men throughout the land be killed, including Daniel. Daniel and his friends prayed, and the Lord revealed the dream to Daniel that night. Daniel explained to Nebuchadnezzar that in his dream he had seen a great statue representing four successive empires that would rule the earth before a rock, representing the kingdom of God, struck the statue and destroyed it (Daniel 2:1-49).

509 BC	480 BC	215 BC	12 BC
Roman Republic founded	Parthenon built in Athens	Construction begins on Great Wall of China	Silk Road opens between China and West

598 BC ✡ JEHOIACHIN BECOMES KING OF JUDAH

Jehoiachin (r. 598–597 BC) became king of Judah at the age of eighteen after the death of his father, Jehoiakim (r. 609–598 BC). Jehoiachin did evil in the sight of God, returning to much of the idolatry practiced during Manasseh's (r. 697–642 BC) reign. He reigned for only three months and ten days before surrendering to Nebuchadnezzar (r. 605–562 BC), who had laid siege to Jerusalem. The Babylonians carried him away with his mother, servants, and officials as well as the Temple treasures. Jehoiachin died in Babylon.

597 BC ✡ SECOND GROUP OF JEWS IS DEPORTED TO BABYLON

After the first deportation of Jews to Babylon (modern-day Iraq) in 605 BC, the second occurred in 597 BC when King Nebuchadnezzar (r. 605–562 BC) captured Jerusalem and exiled King Jehoiachin (r. 598–597 BC) and his family to Babylon. Also deported were ten thousand Jews, including all the princes and the best of the soldiers. Only the poor were left behind (2 Kings 24:8-16).

597 BC ✡ ZEDEKIAH BECOMES JUDAH'S FINAL KING

In 597 BC, King Nebuchadnezzar (r. 605–562 BC) of Babylon removed Jehoiachin (r. 598–597 BC) from the throne of Judah and took him captive to Babylon. Nebuchadnezzar appointed Mattaniah, Jehoiachin's uncle, as king and changed his name to Zedekiah (r. 597–586 BC). Although the prophet Jeremiah had proclaimed that Babylon's rule over Judah had been ordained by God, Zedekiah rebelled against Babylon with the help of the Egyptian Pharaoh Hophra (r. 589–570 BC). In response, Nebuchadnezzar led an army to Jerusalem in 588 BC, and the city was under siege for many months. In July 586 BC, the Babylonian army broke through the gates and destroyed the city. Zedekiah fled, but was captured by the Babylonian army. He was forced to watch the execution of his sons and then was blinded and taken captive to Babylon (2 Kings 24:14–25:7).

593 BC ✡ EZEKIEL RECEIVES HIS INAUGURAL VISION

Ezekiel was among those exiled to Babylon in 597 BC as part of the Babylonian captivity. He was placed in the village of Telabib. On July 31, 593 BC, as Ezekiel

THE CONSEQUENCES OF NOT TAKING GOD SERIOUSLY

> March 16, 597 BC

The year 605 BC was a decisive one in the history of the ancient Near East. Nebuchadnezzar II, crown prince of Babylon, became commander in chief of the armies of Babylon. In the spring of 605 he marched to Carchemish and defeated the Egyptians and Assyrians. As a result, Babylon assumed control of Syria and Palestine.

From his victory at Carchemish, Nebuchadnezzar led his armies to Judah and besieged Jerusalem. After the fall of Jerusalem, Jehoiakim became a vassal of Babylon (2 Kings 24:1). Nebuchadnezzar took a number of Jewish leaders hostage to Babylon, including Daniel (Daniel 1:1-6).

Jehoiakim, an evil king, remained loyal to Babylon for only three years, so Nebuchadnezzar, now king of Babylon, once again sent his armies to force Jehoiakim to submit. Jehoiakim then remained in subservience to Babylon until his death in 597 BC (2 Kings 24:1-6).

Jehoiakim was succeeded by his eighteen-year-old son Jehoiachin, who likewise did not follow Jehovah (2 Kings 24:8-9). He was so despicable that God said through Jeremiah: "'As surely as I live,' says the Lord, 'I will abandon you, Jehoiachin. . . . I will hand you over to those who seek to kill you, of whom you are so desperately afraid—to King Nebuchadnezzar of Babylon and the mighty Babylonian army. I will expel you and your mother from this land, and you will die in a foreign country'" (Jeremiah 22:24-26).

On March 16, 597 BC, three months into Jehoiachin's reign, this prophesy was fulfilled when Nebuchadnezzar, after besieging the city of Jerusalem accepted the surrender of King Jehoiachin along with those of his mother, advisors, nobles, and officials.

Nebuchadnezzar took ten thousand people captive to Babylon, including the king and all who had surrendered. In addition, Nebuchadnezzar carried away the treasures from the Temple and the royal palace.

Eleven years later, Nebuchadnezzar returned a final time to destroy the city and Temple and to take all but the poorest of the remaining Jews captive to Babylon (2 Kings 25:1-21).

Eight hundred years earlier, God had declared in his covenant with Israel: "If you refuse to listen to the LORD your God and do not obey all the commands and laws I am giving to you today, ... the Lord will scatter you." (Deuteronomy 28:15, 64).

Judah refused to listen to God, and God did just what he had promised.

stood beside the Kebar River, he received his first prophetic vision. An enormous cloud appeared to Ezekiel, and from it four creatures emerged, each with four faces and four wings. Beside each of the faces, brightly shining spinning wheels moved in sequence with the creatures. Above the creatures sat a glorious throne upon an enormous crystal platform. Ezekiel realized that he was beholding the glory of God, and he fell on his face before the throne. God called Ezekiel and commissioned him to go and proclaim the word of the Lord to the rebellious house of Israel (Ezekiel 1:1–2:7).

592 BC ✡ EZEKIEL IS TRANSPORTED TO JERUSALEM

As Ezekiel sat in his house in Babylon on September 17, 592 BC, a messenger from the Lord appeared to him, and in a vision the Spirit transported him into the inner court of Jerusalem's Temple. As Ezekiel toured the Temple, he saw statues and images that represented false gods. In the very place where God had revealed his glory to them, the people of Israel were committing horrific abominations and idolatry! As Ezekiel continued to watch, God's glory moved from the Holy of Holies to the threshold of the building, and then out of the Temple and out of the city. The glory of God departed from Israel because the people had repeatedly broken their covenant with God (Ezekiel 8:1–11:25).

586 BC ✡ JERUSALEM FALLS

Since 605 BC, the kingdom of Judah had been a vassal of Babylon because of its unfaithfulness to God. However, King Zedekiah (r. 597–586 BC) rebelled against Babylon and switched his allegiance to Pharaoh Hophra (r. 589–570 BC) of Egypt. In response, in 588 BC Nebuchadnezzar's (r. 605–562 BC) army began a siege of Jerusalem that continued for many months. After a brief respite during which the Babylonian army left Jerusalem to defeat the Egyptians, the siege continued, and food became scarce. Just as the famine reached its height, the Babylonian army broke through the walls and destroyed Jerusalem in 586 BC. Nebuchadnezzar's army slaughtered many inhabitants of the city, broke down the walls, burned down the Temple, and took its precious vessels. The city lay in ruins until the rebuilding effort led by Nehemiah (2 Kings 24:1–25:21; 2 Chronicles 36:1–21).

2200–1950 BC	2000 BC	1180 BC	776 BC
Middle Bronze Age I	Hittite, Egyptian, and Assyrian Empires control major areas	Troy destroyed with Trojan horse	First Olympic Games held in Greece

586 BC ✡ THIRD GROUP OF JEWS ARE DEPORTED TO BABYLON

The Babylonian army had already taken a group of captives from Jerusalem to Babylon in 605 BC and again in 597 BC. Judah had been a vassal state of King Nebuchadnezzar (r. 605–562 BC), who appointed Zedekiah (r. 597–586 BC) to rule as the king of Judah. Judah rebelled against Babylon in 588 BC, but after a lengthy siege the Babylonians broke through Jerusalem's walls and decimated the city. For a third and final time, the Babylonians deported a large number of Jews, this time taking nearly all of them. Only the poorest of the poor were left in Judah. (2 Kings 24:1–25:21).

JUDAH EXILED Evil permeated Judah, and God's anger flared against his rebellious people. Babylon conquered Assyria and became the new world power. The Babylonian army marched into Jerusalem, burned the Temple, tore down the city's massive walls, and carried off the people into captivity.

580 BC ✡ JEREMIAH WRITES LAMENTATIONS

The book of Lamentations is a prophetic lament over the fallen city of Jerusalem. The prophet Jeremiah composed the book in about 580 BC. A distinguishing mark of the book is its literary craftsmanship. The first, second, and fourth chapters are arranged in Hebrew acrostic poetry—each line begins with one of the twenty-two letters in the Hebrew alphabet in correct order. The fourth chapter includes three consecutive acrostics, and the final chapter contains twenty-two verses as well. The first poem recounts the city's fall (chapter 1). The second poem is a reminder that God's wrath over sin was the reason for the fall (chapter 2). The third poem (chapter 3) is an extended prayer for mercy. The fourth poem (chapter 4) repeats themes about the destruction of the city. The book ends with a prayer for restoration (chapter 5).

573 BC ✡ EZEKIEL RECEIVES A VISION OF A FUTURE TEMPLE

The prophet Ezekiel had been taken captive to Babylon in 597 BC. Once there, the prophet saw a vision of God's glory departing from the Jerusalem Temple.

509 BC	480 BC	215 BC	12 BC
Roman Republic founded	Parthenon built in Athens	Construction begins on Great Wall of China	Silk Road opens between China and West

EXILE IN BABYLON Ezekiel worked for God among the exiles in various colonies near the Kebar River in Babylonia. Jerusalem and its Temple lay more than 500 miles away, but Ezekiel helped the people understand that, although they were far from home, they did not need to be far from God.

In 586 BC, the Babylonian army destroyed that Temple. However, Ezekiel encouraged his fellow exiles with prophecies of restoration, both in the immediate future and in the more distant future to the final restoration and consummation of history. Israel was without a temple for the first time since Solomon's reign. Since the Temple signified God's presence, the people had lost the special privilege of God dwelling in their midst. However, on April 28, 573 BC, Ezekiel received a vision of a glorious Temple to come. That vision represented the hope of the restoration of God's presence among his people (Ezekiel 10:1–22; 33:21–40).

553 BC ✡ DANIEL RECEIVES A VISION OF FOUR BEASTS

In 553 BC, early in Belshazzar's (r. 556–539 BC) Babylonian reign, Daniel had an apocalyptic vision of four beasts coming out of the sea. Each beast was more terrible than the one before it. While Daniel was watching, God the Father took his seat on a throne of fire, and one like a Son of Man came before him. This Son of Man was given a kingdom that will never be destroyed. Daniel was told that the four creatures represented four kingdoms that would be stripped of their power and replaced with an everlasting kingdom. The consummation of this vision was inaugurated more than five hundred years later with the coming of the Son of Man, Jesus Christ (Daniel 7:1–28).

539 BC ✡ BABYLON FALLS

On October 12, 539 BC, while giving a great banquet in his palace, King Belshazzar (r. 556-539 BC) brought out the vessels that King Nebuchadnezzar (r. 605–562 BC) had taken from the Temple of the Lord in Jerusalem. Then his guests drank from the sacred vessels while offering praise to their idol gods. At

2200–1950 BC	2000 BC	1180 BC	776 BC
Middle Bronze Age I	Hittite, Egyptian, and Assyrian Empires control major areas	Troy destroyed with Trojan horse	First Olympic Games held in Greece

MISGUIDED NONCHALANCE

October 12, 539 BC

Arrogance can spell ruin.

The year was 539 BC, and the Babylonian Empire had dominated the Near East for eighty-seven years. King Nebuchadnezzar had taken the Jews captive to Babylon where they still remained. His son-in-law Nabonidus now ruled the empire, together with his son Belshazzar.

Twenty years earlier, Cyrus II had become king of Persia, and now he commanded the combined Medo-Persian forces at war with the Babylonians. Nabonidus was in charge of the Babylonian army in the field, while Belshazzar was in charge of the city of Babylon. The Greek historian Herodotus reported, "A battle was fought at a short distance from the city, in which the Babylonians were defeated by the Persian king, whereupon they withdrew within their defenses. Here they shut themselves up and made light of this siege, having laid in a store of provisions for many years in preparation against this attack."

We see how lightly the Babylonians took this siege by what happened the next day. On October 12, 539 BC, in spite of the siege, Belshazzar held a state banquet in his palace for a thousand of his nobles. The wine was flowing freely when Belshazzar remembered the beautiful gold and silver cups Nebuchadnezzar had taken from the Temple in Jerusalem when he had defeated the Jews. The Temple cups were brought in and distributed to the king and his guests (Daniel 5:1-4).

As they were drinking toasts to their idols, everyone suddenly saw the fingers of a human hand writing on the wall. The king turned pale with fear as terror gripped him (Daniel 5:5-6).

"When the queen mother [Nebuchadnezzar's daughter], heard what was happening, she hurried to the banquet hall. She said to Belshazzar, . . . 'Call for Daniel, and he will tell you what the writing means" (Daniel 5:10-12).

Daniel said, "This is the message that was written: Mene, Mene, Tekel, Parsin. This is what these words mean: Mene means 'numbered'—God has numbered the days of your reign and has brought it to an end. Tekel means 'weighed"—you have been weighed on the balances and have failed the test. Parsin means 'divided'—your kingdom has been divided and given to the Medes and Persians" (Daniel 5:25-28).

Meanwhile, unknown to the celebrating Belshazzar, that very night the Medo-Persian army diverted the waters of the Euphrates River that flowed through the city of Babylon. With the water level in the riverbed lowered, the Medo-Persian army was able to wade into the city under cover of darkness. They captured Babylon and killed Belshazzar that night before his defenders knew what had happened (Daniel 5:30).

the height of their revelry, a hand appeared and wrote a mysterious message on the wall. The king was terrified and called all of his enchanters to interpret the message left by the phantom hand. After all the wise men failed to interpret it, the queen mother directed Belshazzar to Daniel, who was able to interpret the message immediately: Belshazzar's kingdom was going to be overthrown. That very night Darius the Mede conquered Babylon, Belshazzar was killed, and the kingdom fell (Daniel 5:1-31).

539 BC ✡ DANIEL PRAYS FOR THE EXILE TO END

As Daniel read the words of Jeremiah the prophet during the Babylonian captivity, he realized that the seventy-year exile of Israel was nearing its completion. He began to pray, asking God's forgiveness for the sins of his people and pleading for the restoration of Jerusalem. In the midst of Daniel's prayer, the angel Gabriel appeared and gave him a vision. Seventy "sevens" had been decreed for the people of Israel and the holy city Jerusalem. From the decree to rebuild the Temple until the Anointed One comes, there would be sixty-nine "sevens," after which the Anointed One would be cut off, and the last "seven" would come. During this period God would atone for guilt and ring in everlasting righteousness (Daniel 9:1-27).

538 BC ✡ CYRUS REIGNS OVER BABYLON

Cyrus II of Persia (r. 559–530 BC), commonly known as Cyrus the Great, was crowned king of the Persians in 559 BC. In 550 BC, he conquered his own grandfather and took the title "king of the Medes." Then on October 12, 539 BC, Cyrus conquered Babylon, beginning his official reign on March 24, 538. Cyrus's reign was marked by a decidedly different policy than that of the Assyrians and Babylonians who had gone before him. He committed himself to restoring people to their native lands and appointing governors to represent his rule. This policy resulted in the declaration that the Jewish people could return to Palestine and rebuild the Temple, thus fulfilling the prophecies of Isaiah, who named Cyrus as one who would carry out God's purpose for Israel, and of Jeremiah, who prophesied a return to the Promised Land after seventy years (2 Chronicles 36:22-23; Ezra 1:1-4; Isaiah 44:28; 45:1-13; Jeremiah 25:11-12).

2200–1950 BC	2000 BC	1180 BC	776 BC
Middle Bronze Age I	Hittite, Egyptian, and Assyrian Empires control major areas	Troy destroyed with Trojan horse	First Olympic Games held in Greece

537 BC ✡ SHESHBAZZAR LEADS THE RETURN FROM BABYLON

Soon after he had conquered the Babylonian kingdom, Cyrus the Great (r. 559–530 BC) proclaimed that the Jewish people could return to Jerusalem and rebuild the Temple. Cyrus appointed Sheshbazzar as his official representative to lead the people and function as governor when they returned to Judah. With Sheshbazzar taking responsibility for the sacred vessels of the Temple, more than forty thousand Jewish exiles returned to their homeland. Soon after their return, the people took up a collection for the Temple's reconstruction. The Temple was later completed under the leadership of Zerubbabel.

537 BC ✡ DANIEL RECEIVES A VISION OF THE FUTURE

In 537 BC, while serving under King Cyrus of Persia (r. 559–530 BC), Daniel spent twenty-one days fasting and praying. At the end of the three weeks, he had a vision of what the future would hold. He had been given a prophecy that precisely predicted the events from his day to the abomination of desolation in 168 BC, when Antiochus Epiphanes (r. 175–164 BC) desecrated the Jewish Temple, leading to the successful Maccabean revolt (Daniel 11:1-35). Daniel then fast-forwards to the end of the age and summarizes the conclusion of history (Daniel 11:36–12:13).

536 BC ✡ RECONSTRUCTION OF TEMPLE BEGINS

The temple that Solomon (r. 970–930) had built was destroyed by King Nebuchadnezzar (r. 605–562 BC) and his armies. When King Cyrus of Persia (r. 559–530 BC) conquered Babylon, he issued a decree around 538 BC, allowing the Israelites to return to Jerusalem and rebuild the temple. The book of Ezra records that more than forty thousand Jews returned to Jerusalem and began work on the temple in 536 BC. However, they stopped construction when opposition arose from neighboring nations. The work on the temple remained dormant for well over a decade until God used Haggai and Zechariah to enable the Israelites to complete the project in 516 BC (Ezra 1:1–6:15).

509 BC	480 BC	215 BC	12 BC
Roman Republic founded	Parthenon built in Athens	Construction begins on Great Wall of China	Silk Road opens between China and West

520 BC ✡ HAGGAI WRITES HIS PROPHECY

Haggai received a message from the Lord on August 29, 520 BC, for the Israelites who had returned to Jerusalem under Cyrus's (r. 559–530 BC) decree to rebuild the Temple. The message addressed Israel's complacency about the rebuilding. They had not done any work on the Temple since laying the foundation almost fifteen years earlier. Their only concern was with their own houses, finances, and comfort. Haggai's message was a rebuke to the Israelites for being concerned with these things when they should have been giving themselves to the work of rebuilding God's house. Haggai concludes his prophecy by telling the Israelites that the great drought that had come upon the land was a result of their sinful priorities (Haggai 1:1-11; Ezra 1:1-4; 2:1).

520 BC ✡ WORK ON TEMPLE RESUMES UNDER DARIUS

Haggai began preaching in the second year of Darius (r. 550–485 BC), king of Persia, and his preaching motivated the Israelites to resume reconstruction of the Temple. As they began rebuilding, they were confronted by Tattenai, the Persian provincial governor. When Tattenai inquired as to where the Jews got the authority to reconstruct the Temple, they told him of Cyrus's (r. 559–530 BC) decree. Never having heard of it, he made inquiry to Darius. Darius searched the kingdom archives and found Cyrus's decree. Then Darius himself issued a decree to speed the building of the Temple, agreeing to cover whatever expenses they incurred from the royal treasury (Ezra 5–6; Haggai 1:1).

520 BC ✡ ZECHARIAH BEGINS TO PREACH

Zechariah, a contemporary of Haggai, received his first prophetic message in October 520 BC. His prophecy was directed toward the Jews who had returned to Jerusalem under Cyrus's decree to rebuild the Temple. The primary message was for the Jews to return to God so that he would return to them. Zechariah exhorted the Jews to renew their covenant with God. His message, along with Haggai's, was influential in encouraging the Jewish people to continue Temple reconstruction. Zechariah's prophecies were filled with apocalyptic visions that included the declaration of the coming Day of the Lord as a time when God would remove all idols and false prophets from the land, when all those who war against Jerusalem would be defeated, and when the Lord

2200–1950 BC	2000 BC	1180 BC	776 BC
Middle Bronze Age I	Hittite, Egyptian, and Assyrian Empires control major areas	Troy destroyed with Trojan horse	First Olympic Games held in Greece

alone would be worshiped in his house (Ezra 5:1-2; 6:14; Zechariah 1:1-7; 12:1–14:21).

516 BC ✡ TEMPLE IS COMPLETED

The Jews had started rebuilding the Temple in 536 BC, but they experienced so much opposition from their neighbors that they ceased building from 530 to 520 BC. The Lord then raised up Haggai and Zechariah to exhort them to complete the work they had started. The Temple, much simpler and smaller than Solomon's, was finished in 516 BC. However, history records that this Temple remained standing for approximately five hundred years, longer than either Solomon's or Herod's (Ezra 1:1–6:15).

479 BC ✡ ESTHER BECOMES QUEEN OF PERSIA

During the third year of his reign, King Ahasuerus (Xerxes) of Persia gave a banquet for the leaders of his kingdom. On the seventh day of the feast, the king requested that Queen Vashti be brought before him. She refused to come, which infuriated the king. Following the counsel of his wise men, the king decided to replace the queen. As part of his search, all the beautiful, young virgins of the land were brought into the royal harem. Young Esther was in that group. Her family had been taken captive from Jerusalem when Nebuchadnezzar brought the Jews into exile. Esther had been adopted by her older cousin Mordecai. After undergoing an entire year of beautification, Esther was brought before the king. He was so captivated by her that he chose her above all the other women to replace Vashti as his queen (Esther 1–2).

474 BC ✡ XERXES ALLOWS THE JEWS TO DEFEND THEMSELVES

Haman, prime minister to King Xerxes of the Persian Empire, was infuriated by the refusal of Mordecai, a Jew, to bow down to him. In retaliation, Haman plotted to have all Jews in the empire executed. He received permission from the king to set a date for the mass execution of the Jews eleven months later. Mordecai persuaded Queen Esther, his adopted daughter, to risk going before the king and ask him to spare their people. Esther found favor with the king, and he agreed to

509 BC	480 BC	215 BC	12 BC
Roman Republic founded	Parthenon built in Athens	Construction begins on Great Wall of China	Silk Road opens between China and West

THE COST OF INCOMPLETE OBEDIENCE

June 25, 474 BC

It all began with King Saul.

In the fifth century BC, all the Jews in the world lived under the rule of the Persian Empire, which controlled the entire Near East. In 474 BC, the Jews were in a desperate situation. Xerxes was king of the empire, and his prime minister, Haman, hated the Jews. Incensed that a Jew named Mordecai refused to kneel down before him, Haman vindictively plotted to have not only Mordecai put to death, but also all the Jews in the empire. He received permission from Xerxes to issue a decree setting a date for the extermination of the Jews eleven months later (Esther 3:1-15). Because all Jews lived within the Persian Empire, this decree was a direct threat to God's program of redemption.

The key to understanding this confrontation between Haman and Mordecai, and all the Jews, can be found in the name of Haman's father: Hammedatha the Agagite (Esther 3:1). The name indicates that Haman and his father descended from Agag, the king of Amalek (1 Samuel 15:20). Thus Haman was an Amalekite. The Amalekites had been the first nation to attack Israel after the exodus from Egypt. As a result, God commanded Israel, "Never forget what the Amalekites did to you as you came from Egypt. . . . You are to destroy the Amalekites and erase their memory from under heaven. Never forget this!" (Deuteronomy 25:17, 19). Years later, Saul, Israel's first king, disobeyed God and spared Agag, rather than putting him to death as God had commanded. Because of this disobedience, God rejected Saul as king (1 Samuel 15:1-35; cf. 30:1-18).

Mordecai is described as a descendant of Kish (Esther 2:5), who was the father of Saul (1 Samuel 9:1-2). So, five hundred years after King Saul lived, his descendant Mordecai continued to battle the Amalekites.

Mordecai persuaded his cousin, Queen Esther, to risk her life by going uninvited to King Xerxes' court to petition him to spare her people, the Jews, from Haman's decree. She found favor with the king and he granted her an audience. The king listened and agreed to her petition; however, because Persian laws could not be revoked, he had to issue another one. On June 25, 474 BC, King Xerxes issued a decree granting the Jews authority to defend themselves against their enemies when the attack mandated by his first decree commenced (Esther 4:1–8:16).

The book of Esther thus describes the final chapter in God's holy war on the Amalekites.

Haman was hanged on the gallows he had prepared for Mordecai (Esther 7:1-10), and Mordecai replaced him as prime minister (Esther 8:2, 15; 10:3).

When the Jews were attacked the following year, they successfully defended themselves, killing seventy-five thousand of their enemies, including all the sons of Haman (Esther 9:1-17). God's command to exterminate the Amalekites (1 Samuel 15:2-3) was thus fulfilled.

her request. However, since a Persian law could not be changed, the king issued another decree on June 25, 474 BC, granting the Jews the right to defend themselves from attack. Haman was hanged on the gallows that he built for Mordecai, and Mordecai replaced Haman as prime minister (Esther 1–8).

473 BC ✡ FIRST PURIM IS CELEBRATED

The feast of Purim celebrated Esther and Mordecai's prevention of a plot to eradicate the Jewish people. Since 473 BC, the Jewish people have celebrated the annual festival in remembrance of that deliverance (Esther 3:2-7; 9:26). The name *Purim* comes from the word *pur,* the lots that were cast by the Persians to pick the day for the annihilation of the Jews (Esther 3:7; 9:26).

458 BC ✡ EZRA ARRIVES IN JERUSALEM

After the Temple had been completed, King Artaxerxes sent Ezra to Jerusalem in 458 BC, to be in charge of Jewish affairs on behalf of the Persian government. Ezra's main responsibility was to teach the law of God to the Jews of Jerusalem and to set up magistrates and judges to oversee the people. The king sent Ezra with large amounts of silver and gold to buy anything needed for Temple worship. He also gave Ezra authority to take money from the region's treasuries for anything else that was needed. Ezra went to Jerusalem with approximately fifteen hundred men, along with Levites to serve in the Temple. Upon his arrival in Jerusalem, Ezra called the people to return to God and dealt with the problem of Jewish men who had married pagan wives (Ezra 7:1-28; 9–10).

457 BC ✡ JEWS DIVORCE THEIR PAGAN WIVES

In 458 BC, Ezra was commissioned by the Persian government to return to Jerusalem and oversee the Jews to ensure the observance of the Mosaic Law. Soon after Ezra's arrival, the Jewish leaders complained to him that the men were marrying foreign wives. Intermarriage was strictly forbidden to the Jews, for it threatened the survival of their faith. Therefore, Ezra offered a prayer of repentance for people's sin. As he prayed and wept, the people gathered around him and joined in his weeping. They confessed their sin and said they would divorce

509 BC	480 BC	215 BC	12 BC
Roman Republic founded	Parthenon built in Athens	Construction begins on Great Wall of China	Silk Road opens between China and West

their foreign wives. Three days later, Ezra stood in Jerusalem's Temple square and called out for repentance and for the people to put away their foreign wives. They affirmed his call, and by March 27, 457 BC, the divorces were confirmed.

444 BC ✡ NEHEMIAH APPROACHES THE KING

Nehemiah was cupbearer to King Artaxerxes of Persia. He heard news from his brother Hanani, who had returned from Judah, regarding the situation of the Jewish remnant in Jerusalem. When Nehemiah learned about the great distress of his people and how the wall of Jerusalem was still broken down, he was moved to prayer and fasting. A few months later Artaxerxes asked Nehemiah why he looked sad. Nehemiah told the king about the plight of Jerusalem and sought the king's help. God granted Nehemiah favor with Artaxerxes, and the king appointed him governor, sending him to Jerusalem to rebuild the wall and the city (Nehemiah 1:1–2:10).

444 BC ✡ EZRA LEADS A PUBLIC ASSEMBLY

After the Babylonian captivity, many Jews returned to Jerusalem. In 444 BC, on the first day of the Jewish civil calendar, Ezra stood before an assembly of the Jews in Jerusalem. As daybreak came, Ezra unrolled the scroll and all of the people stood up, lifted their hands in the air, and shouted, "Amen! Amen!" Then they bowed and worshiped the Lord. When they stood up again, Ezra began to read the Law. As Ezra read, the people began to realize how they had sinned against God. They began weeping over their disobedience. However, Ezra responded by telling them to rejoice, for God was doing a work of restoration. The people left the assembly and prepared a feast to celebrate their new understanding of what God was saying to them (Nehemiah 8).

444 BC ✡ JERUSALEM WALL IS COMPLETED

The walls of Jerusalem had been in ruin since their destruction by Nebuchadnezzar (r. 605–562 BC) in 586 BC. However, after Nehemiah's return to Jerusalem in 444 BC, the walls were rebuilt in fifty-two days. This was particularly remarkable considering people like Sanballat, governor of Samaria; Tobiah, from a powerful family in Ammon; and Geshem, king of the Arabian tribe

2200–1950 BC	2000 BC	1180 BC	776 BC
Middle Bronze Age I	Hittite, Egyptian, and Assyrian Empires control major areas	Troy destroyed with Trojan horse	First Olympic Games held in Greece

Kedar, were in strong opposition. The key to Nehemiah's success was that he planned his work and then worked his plan, trusting God for the results (Nehemiah 1:1–6:15).

440 BC ✡ 1 AND 2 CHRONICLES ARE WRITTEN

The books of 1 and 2 Chronicles were originally one volume in the Hebrew Bible. *The Words of the Days,* as the book is called in Hebrew, recounts the events that are also recorded in 2 Samuel, 1 Kings, and 2 Kings. This book is the last in the Hebrew canon. Although the author is not definitively known, historical tradition attributes the book to Ezra the priest, who likely wrote it around 440 BC. The book emphasizes the southern kingdom of Judah and the Davidic line. First Chronicles deals exclusively with the ascent of David. Second Chronicles recounts the glory of Solomon's reign, including the construction and dedication of the Temple, the tragic failure of the kings and the kingdom until Judah's exile and return, and the decree of Cyrus (r. 559–530 BC) allowing Jews to return from Babylon.

440 BC ✡ THE BOOK OF EZRA IS WRITTEN

The books of Ezra and Nehemiah originally formed one book in the Hebrew Bible. However, most likely they were written separately and by different men. The book of Ezra, probably written by Ezra around 440 BC, recounts the history of the Jewish people after their return from the Babylonian exile. The first half of the book (chapters 1–6) describes the first return of the people under Zerubbabel's leadership. When they returned to Jerusalem, the people began planning reconstruction of the Temple. Although their enemies opposed their plan, God ultimately allowed them to complete the work. The second part of the book (chapters 7–10) occurs some sixty years after the first and tells of Ezra's journey back to Palestine and his leadership during subsequent reforms after the people began to intermarry with surrounding nations.

430 BC ✡ THE BOOK OF NEHEMIAH IS WRITTEN

The book of Nehemiah was written by Nehemiah (Nehemiah 1:1) in about 430 BC and centers on his return to the Promised Land. The book is essentially a

509 BC	480 BC	215 BC	12 BC
Roman Republic founded	Parthenon built in Athens	Construction begins on Great Wall of China	Silk Road opens between China and West

story of restoration—first of Jerusalem's walls (chapters 1–7) and then of God's covenant people (chapters 8–13). The book opens with Nehemiah, the cupbearer of the king of Persia, hearing a report of Jerusalem's broken walls. He petitions the king for permission to return to his homeland. The king grants Nehemiah's request, and Nehemiah leads the people in rebuilding the walls in spite of foreign opposition. The renewal theme continues in the second part of the book as the people hear the Law read aloud and commit themselves to obeying it and being faithful to the covenant.

430 BC ✡ MALACHI WRITES HIS PROPHECY

Following a long period of captivity, the Jewish nation finally returned to the Promised Land under the leadership of Zerubbabel and rebuilt the Temple (516 BC). Israel waited with renewed loyalty for their Lord to return to his holy Temple and restore the nation to glory. However, more than a century passed while the people grew complacent. The prophet Malachi exhorted them, especially the priesthood, to repent and renew their commitment to God. Malachi warned them that even though God loved them, he was not indifferent to their complacency and would return like a raging furnace on the glorious Day of the Lord, sending his prophet Elijah before him. With these words, written about 430 BC, the prophetic voice in the Old Testament ceased for more than 430 years, until the coming of the Lord Jesus Christ to his Temple (Malachi 1:2; 3:1; 4:1, 5).

332 BC ✡ ALEXANDER THE GREAT CONQUERS PALESTINE

Alexander the Great (356–323 BC), king of Macedonia, was one of history's greatest military leaders. He expanded the Greek Empire as far east as India and was responsible for the Hellenization of the ancient world. In his pursuit of the Persian army led by Darius (d. 330 BC), Alexander and his army of more than thirty thousand soldiers reached the land of Palestine by 332 BC. As Alexander marched down the Mediterranean coast en route to Egypt, most of the cities he encountered gave way to his army. The island city of Tyre, however, refused to surrender. As a result, the Greek army besieged the city for seven months. Eventually Tyre collapsed, and by November 332, Alexander controlled all of Palestine and had reached Egypt. Alexander's conquest of Palestine marked the

2200–1950 BC	2000 BC	1180 BC	776 BC
Middle Bronze Age I	Hittite, Egyptian, and Assyrian Empires control major areas	Troy destroyed with Trojan horse	First Olympic Games held in Greece

HOW GREAT WAS ALEXANDER?

June 10, 323 BC

Some people can never get enough of themselves.

Alexander III of Macedon, whom we know as Alexander the Great, was born in 356 BC. He was such an important figure in world history that chapters 2, 7, 8, and 11 of Daniel all contain prophecies of him and his kingdom. Daniel 11:3-4 prophesies this of Alexander: "Then a mighty king will rise to power who will rule a vast kingdom and accomplish everything he sets out to do. But at the height of his power, his kingdom will be broken apart and divided into four parts. It will not be ruled by the king's descendants, nor will the kingdom hold the authority it once had. For his empire will be uprooted and given to others."

Even as a boy, Alexander was fearless. He tamed Bucephalus, a beautiful, spirited horse that no one else had dared to touch. Bucephalus later carried his master all the way to India.

Tutored by Aristotle, Alexander became co-regent of Macedon at the age of sixteen, along with his father, King Philip of Macedon. When Alexander was twenty, his father died and he became king. He likewise became the leader of the League of Corinth, founded by his father, uniting all of Greece under his authority.

Alexander immediately went on the offensive, conquering Asia Minor, and then the Mediterranean coast all the way to Egypt. There he founded the city of Alexandria, which soon became the greatest city in the Mediterranean. He named it after himself, as he did more than sixty other cities.

Alexander's ambitions next led him east. His greatest career accomplishment was when he defeated the Persians and controlled the splendid capitals of its empire. He reached India on his faithful old horse, Bucephalus, in 327 BC. At that point, his weary soldiers refused to go farther, so Alexander turned back to the west. There he shocked his Greek compatriots by adopting the style of the Persian court, including a harem.

Impressed with his own success, Alexander thought it appropriate that his Greek subjects worship him as a god. However, he didn't have much time to enjoy this worship. Alexander died in Babylon on June 10, 323 BC, at the young age of thirty-three. In thirteen years he had conquered most of the known world, and his military triumphs spread a Greek influence over the Near East that would last for a thousand years. It is because of Alexander the Great that the New Testament was written in Greek.

But after Alexander's death, his Greek generals broke up the mighty kingdom he had amassed and divided it into four parts : Macedon and Greece under Antipater, and later Antigonus and Cassander; Thrace and Asia Minor under Lysimachus; Syria under Seleucus; and Egypt and Palestine under Ptolemy.

God had no tolerance for a world emperor who desired to be worshiped.

beginning of the Greek, and later the Roman, occupation that would last into New Testament times.

331 BC ✝ ALEXANDER THE GREAT DEFEATS DARIUS AT GAUGAMELA

Having successfully made his way along the Mediterranean coast and into Egypt, Alexander (356–323 BC) set his sights on Mesopotamia, seeking to conquer Darius (d. 330 BC) and the Persians once and for all. After July 331 BC, Alexander led his army down the Tigris River in order to enter Babylon. On October 1, 331 BC, he met Darius and the Persian army on the plain of Gaugamela in northern Mesopotamia near Nineveh. Here the decisive battle in the conquest of Greece over Persia was fought, with the Greeks dismantling the Persian army. Darius escaped, but the Persian Empire had fallen, and all of Babylon was under the rule of Alexander the Great.

323 BC ✝ ALEXANDER THE GREAT DIES

Alexander the Great (356–323 BC) spent his final years consolidating the vast empire he had built. The enormity of his accomplishments led to a heightened sense of his own greatness. By 324 BC, he seemed to have become convinced of his own divinity, not at all uncommon amidst the mythological mind-set of ancient Greece. Following a lengthy banquet in early June 323 BC, Alexander came down with a fatal illness, and on June 13 he died. His body was buried in a gold coffin in Alexandria. In the twelve short years of his reign, Alexander's remarkable achievements spread a Greek influence over the near East that would last for a thousand years. Following his death, his kingdom was divided into four parts by his generals.

323 BC ✡ PTOLEMY I SOTER CONTROLS PALESTINE

A close companion of Alexander the Great, Ptolemy I Soter (Savior) (r. 323–285 BC) was a great political and military leader. Following Alexander's unexpected death in 323 BC, Ptolemy gained control of Egypt and Palestine. By 304 BC, Ptolemy assumed the title of king of Egypt and established the Ptolemaic dynasty, which would last for three hundred years. Perhaps the greatest of Ptol-

2200–1950 BC	2000 BC	1180 BC	776 BC
Middle Bronze Age I	Hittite, Egyptian, and Assyrian Empires control major areas	Troy destroyed with Trojan horse	First Olympic Games held in Greece

emy's accomplishments was establishing Alexandria in Egypt as one of the top intellectual centers of the world.

319 BC ✡ PTOLEMY I SOTER CONQUERS JERUSALEM

Ptolemy I Soter (r. 323–285 BC) took control of Egypt in 323 BC. He consolidated his position by hijacking the body of Alexander the Great (356–323 BC) en route to its burial in Macedonia and brought it to Egypt. In 319 BC, he captured Jerusalem on a Sabbath and took many Jews to Egypt as prisoners of war. These prisoners formed the nucleus of what would become the Jewish population of Alexandria, Egypt.

311 BC ✡ SELEUCUS CONQUERS BABYLON AND BEGINS THE SELEUCID DYNASTY

Seleucus I Nicator (358–281 BC), one of Alexander the Great's generals, rose to power in Babylon following Alexander's death in 323 BC. Soon after, Seleucus fled to Egypt when Antigonus I (382–301 BC) forced him to leave the Mesopotamia region. Joining forces with Ptolemy I, the two leaders weakened Antigonus's stronghold, enabling Seleucus to return to Babylon by 311 BC. Regaining control over Babylon, Seleucus established the Seleucid dynasty over the eastern provinces of the former Persian Empire, assuming the title of king in 305 BC. In 301 BC, following the defeat of Antigonus, Seleucus gained control of northern Syria and the following year built the capital city of Antioch. At this time conflicts between the Seleucid and Ptolemaic dynasties arose over the region of Palestine. The Seleucid dynasty would prove to have a major influence on Jewish history.

250 BC ✡ SCRIPTURES ARE TRANSLATED INTO GREEK SEPTUAGINT

According to legend, seventy-two men, six from each of the twelve tribes of Israel, were commissioned to go from Jerusalem to Alexandria to translate the Hebrew and Aramaic Scriptures into the Greek language. There are historical records indicating that Ptolemy II (285-246 BC) requested that the high priest send seventy-two men to Alexandria to work on a Greek translation of the Pentateuch. Their work was entitled the Septuagint (abbreviated LXX), from the

509 BC	480 BC	215 BC	12 BC
Roman Republic founded	Parthenon built in Athens	Construction begins on Great Wall of China	Silk Road opens between China and West

Latin word for *seventy*. Most of the Septuagint, however, seems to be the work of various individuals and groups at different times. The LXX became the official Scriptures for Greek-speaking Jews scattered around the Western Mediterranean. In fact, the New Testament authors writing to Greek-speaking communities, typically quoted from the LXX, and its prevalent usage continued throughout the early church era. It is still the official Old Testament of the Greek Orthodox Church.

218 BC ✡ ANTIOCHUS III TEMPORARILY GAINS CONTROL OF PALESTINE
In the late 220s BC, Antiochus III (r. 223–187 BC) of the Seleucid dynasty of Syria launched a series of campaigns to wrest Palestine from the control of Ptolemaic Egypt. His first attempt in 222 BC proved to be a failure; however, by 218 BC he had gained control of Palestine. Endeavoring to march down into Egypt to further weaken the Ptolemaic Empire, Antiochus met defeat the following year at Raphia, near the Egyptian border. As a result, the Egyptians were able to reclaim Palestine.

198 BC ✡ SELEUCIDS GAIN COMPLETE CONTROL OF PALESTINE
In 203 BC, Antiochus III (r. 223–187 BC) initiated his final and decisive campaign against the Ptolemaic dynasty of Egypt to gain control of Palestine. The final victory came at Paneas in northern Galilee in 198 BC, when his Syrian army defeated the Egyptian army of Ptolemy V (r. 203–181 BC). At first the Jewish community welcomed the new Seleucid rulers. Historian Josephus (AD 37–100) attests to the favor granted early on in Seleucid rule to the Jews who had opened the gates of Jerusalem for Antiochus and his army. However, the good relations were not to endure as Seleucid rulers sought to impose more and more Greek culture on the Jews. Religious quarrels ensued and tension mounted until the Jewish revolt of the Maccabees in the mid-second century BC.

167 BC ✡ FIRST ABOMINATION OF DESOLATION OCCURS
The first abomination of desolation occurred on December 25, 167 BC. On that date, Antiochus IV Epiphanes, Seleucid king from 175 to 164 BC, ordered that an altar to Zeus be built on top of the altar of burnt offering in the Jerusalem

2200–1950 BC	2000 BC	1180 BC	776 BC
Middle Bronze Age I	Hittite, Egyptian, and Assyrian Empires control major areas	Troy destroyed with Trojan horse	First Olympic Games held in Greece

THE MANIFESTATION OF ZEUS

December 16, 167 BC

It happened just as the Bible said it would.

After the death of Alexander the Great in 323 BC, four of his generals divided up his kingdom among themselves, with Seleucus gaining control of Syria and Ptolemy controlling Egypt. Palestine was under the rule of the Ptolemies until 198 BC, when the Seleucids won control.

During the early reign of the Seleucids, the Jews enjoyed a period of brief tranquility. The Seleucid ruler Antiochus III permitted the Jewish people to worship according to their law.

In 187 BC, Antiochus III was succeeded by his eldest son, Seleucus IV Philopater, and then by his youngest son, Antiochus IV Epiphanes, in 175 BC.

The kingdom inherited by Antiochus IV Epiphanes was unstable. Antiochus IV's remedy for this was a vigorous program of Hellenization, introducing Greek culture throughout his kingdom. In his mind one of the unifying factors was religion. Therefore in about 169 BC, he began encouraging his subjects to worship him as the manifestation of Zeus. On coins his image bore the words *Theos Epiphanes*, meaning "the manifest god." However, his enemies changed just one Greek letter in his name, making it *Epimanes*, meaning "madman."

One of the first disputes that Antiochus IV had to settle was between the Jewish high priest Onias III, who supported Egypt, and his brother Jason, who was a supporter of the Seleucids. By out-bribing Onias, Jason secured the high priesthood and made Jerusalem a Greek city (1 Maccabees 1:10-15; 2 Maccabees 4:7-17). In 171 BC, Jason's friend Menelaus bid even more than Jason for the high priesthood, and Antiochus, needing money, gave the position to him, even though Menelaus was not a descendant of Aaron and thus was not qualified for the office. Jason fled as a result (2 Maccabees 4:23-29).

Menelaus then plundered the temple, causing a riot. Jason returned to help the Jerusalemites avenge the mistreatment of their house of worship. Antiochus interpreted the attack on his high priest as a revolt against himself and determined to subdue Jerusalem. Returning there with Menelaus, he robbed the temple of its remaining treasures and left the city in the control of one of his commanders (1 Maccabees 1:20-29; 2 Maccabees 5:11-22).

In his self-appointed role as Zeus manifest, Antiochus ordered the elimination of the Jewish religion. He ordered the destruction of all copies of the Torah and forbade Jews to keep the Sabbath, to offer sacrifices, or to circumcise.

The ultimate desecration of the Jewish Temple occurred on December 16, 167 BC, when Antiochus ordered that an altar of Zeus be built on top of the altar of burnt offering. There swine's flesh was offered to Zeus (1 Maccabees 1:41-64; 2 Maccabees 6:1-11).

Nearly four hundred years earlier, the prophet Daniel had prophesied this exact event in Daniel 11:11-32. Antiochus fulfilled the prophecy precisely when his army took over "the Temple fortress, polluting the sanctuary, putting a stop to the daily sacrifices, and setting up the sacrilegious object that causes desecration" (Daniel 11:31).

Temple. Antiochus IV Epiphanes then offered swine flesh to Zeus on the altar. Daniel 11:31 prophesies of this as "setting up the sacrilegious object that causes desecration." This act led ultimately to the Maccabean revolt.

167 BC ✡ MATTATHIAS AND SONS REBEL

In response to the persecutions instituted by Antiochus IV Epiphanes (r. 175–164 BC), the Maccabean revolt began in 167 BC. In the town of Modein, eighteen miles from Jerusalem, an aged priest named Mattathias (d. 166 BC) killed a Jewish man who had come to sacrifice to the heathen gods as commanded by Antiochus. He also killed the Syrian officer who had come to supervise the sacrifice. Mattathias called on all who were zealous for the Law to follow him and his sons to the mountains to overthrow the Syrians. Mattathias died the next year, but his five sons and their followers carried on guerrilla-type warfare from the mountains against the Syrian forces of Antiochus IV Epiphanes. They tore down pagan altars, attacked at night, and forcibly circumcised children.

166 BC ✡ JUDAS MACCABEUS LEADS A REVOLT

In 166 BC, following the death of the priest Mattathias who started the Maccabean rebellion, his third son, Judas Maccabeus (d. 161 BC), became the leader of the rebel movement. He proved to be a competent military chief and earned the nickname *Maccabee,* which means "the hammerer." The rebels fought the Syrian forces of Antiochus IV Epiphanes (r. 175–164 BC), who also were at war with the Parthians. In 165 BC, the Syrian regent Lysias was forced to make peace with Judas and to withdraw the decrees against Jewish worship practices because he did not have enough soldiers to fight on two fronts. Judas then marched to Jerusalem, and amidst great celebration the Temple was solemnly cleansed and the worship of God restored. This event is commemorated annually at the feast of Hanukkah.

161 BC ✡ JUDAS MACCABEUS DEFEATS NICANOR

In 161 BC, Judas Maccabeus had his final military victory in the Battle of Adasa over the Seleucid general Nicanor. Following the death of Antiochus

2200–1950 BC	2000 BC	1180 BC	776 BC
Middle Bronze Age I	Hittite, Egyptian, and Assyrian Empires control major areas	Troy destroyed with Trojan horse	First Olympic Games held in Greece

WHO WERE THE MACCABEES?

March 9, 161 BC

They won against all odds.

On December 16, 167 BC, the Syrian ruler Antiochus IV Epiphanes had committed the ultimate desecration of the Jewish Temple in Jerusalem. He offered the flesh of a pig as a sacrifice to Zeus on an altar constructed over the altar of burnt offering (1 Maccabees 1:41-64; 2 Maccabees 6:1-11; Daniel 11:31).

The following year, Antiochus commanded everyone in Palestine to sacrifice to the heathen gods under the supervision of an imperial representative. Mattathias, an aged priest, had moved with his family to the village of Modein to try to escape the idolatry of Antiochus. But Antiochus's officers finally came to Modein. Mattathias and his sons were forced to assemble along with the other villagers before an altar the officers had built (1 Maccabees 2:1-18).

When a Jew came forward to offer his sacrifice to the heathen gods, Mattathias ran up and killed him on the altar. He then killed the officer who had commanded them to sacrifice and tore down the altar (1 Maccabees 2:23-26). Then Mattathias and his sons fled into the hills, where many Jews followed them (1 Maccabees 2:27-30).

From the hills they conducted guerilla warfare, with leadership passing to Mattathias's son Judas. Judas was called Maccabeus, which means "hammer," because of the blows he inflicted on the Syrians. The name was applied to Judas's brothers and then to all who took part in the rebellion.

The first battles of the Maccabean Revolt during the 160s BC were against the Syrian army led by Nicanor. In 166 BC, the Syrians were so sure that Nicanor would defeat Judas that they brought traders along to buy Jewish slaves. However, the Maccabees were victorious.

In 164 BC, after three years of fighting, Judas won control of Jerusalem. He cleansed and rededicated the Temple with "songs and harps and lutes, and cymbals" (1 Maccabees 4:54). The eight-day celebration was the beginning of Hanukkah, the Jewish Feast of Dedication, or Lights.

The fight was ongoing. The leaders of Syria changed, but Nicanor continued as commander in chief of the Syrian forces waging war against the Maccabees.

Finally in 161 BC, the Syrian ruler—now Demetrius I Soter, the nephew of Antiochus IV Epiphanes—sent Nicanor and his army one more time against Judas Maccabeus. Before the battle on March 9, 161 BC, Judas prayed, "By the might of thy arm may these blasphemers who come against thy holy people be struck down" (2 Maccabees 15:23-24). God answered. Judas was victorious, and Nicanor was killed. The Jews celebrate this day as Nicanor's Day.

Although as the years passed the Maccabean dynasty became less noble in their purposes, the independent nation they established lasted until 63 BC, when Pompey established a Roman protectorate over Palestine.

IV Epiphanes (r. 175–164 BC), his nephew Demetrius I (r. 162–150 BC) ascended the throne after killing Antiochus's son and his general. Demetrius appointed the pro-Syrian Alcimus as high priest in 161 BC. He then sent a large Syrian force under the leadership of Nicanor to oppose Judas. The two forces met at Kapharsalama, and Judas was victorious. In response, Nicanor vented his wrath on the priests in Jerusalem and threatened to destroy the Temple. Judas then faced Nicanor at the Battle of Adasa in Judea in 161 BC. Nicanor died in the battle, and his army was completely routed by Judas's forces. The Jews celebrate the thirteenth of Adara on the Jewish calendar as Nicanor's Day.

160 BC ✡ JONATHAN BECOMES LEADER OF THE MACCABEES

Following the death of Judas Maccabeus in 161 BC, his youngest brother, Jonathan (d. 143 BC), became the leader of the Maccabean party. For eight years he fought a guerilla war against the Syrian armies of the Seleucid dynasty. Internal strife among the Seleucids distracted their attention from fighting against Jonathan, and he grew in power until he was the effective ruler of all Judea. Rivals attempting to sit on the Seleucid throne then solicited his support, and in 153 BC, Alexander Balas, a contender for the throne, appointed Jonathan as high priest. In 150 BC, Jonathan was also appointed as the official military and civil governor of Judea. Jonathan continued to exploit the weakness of the Seleucid dynasty until he was treacherously killed in 143 BC by a false ally.

154 BC ✡ JEWISH TEMPLE IS BUILT IN LEONTOPOLIS, EGYPT

Having fled the persecution of Antiochus IV Epiphanes (r. 175–164 BC), Onias IV built a Jewish temple at Leontopolis, Egypt, with the permission of Cleopatra (69–30 BC). Onias IV was the son of Onias III (high priest 190–172 BC), the high priest at Jerusalem before the persecution erupted. The temple in Leontopolis imitated the Jerusalem Temple, but was smaller and less elaborate. It was built on an artificial mound and resembled a tower. The temple remained in use until the Roman emperor Vespasian (AD 9-79) shut it down in AD 73, three years after the destruction of the Temple in Jerusalem, fearing that it might become a new center for Jewish rebellion. Vespasian then confiscated the interior furnishings of the Temple for his personal treasury.

142 BC ✡ HIGH PRIEST SIMON MACCABEUS ESTABLISHES HASMONEAN DYNASTY

In approximately 142 BC, Simon Maccabeus succeeded his brother Jonathan (d. 143 BC) as the high priest and ruler of Judea. Simon was a shrewd diplomat and secured Judea's independence from the Seleucid king Demetrius II (r. 145–138 BC), releasing the Jews from their obligation to pay tribute to the Syrian kings. In 140 BC, the Jewish popular assembly decided that in light of the accomplishments of Simon and his brothers, Simon should be appointed as the national governor, the commander in chief of the army, and the hereditary high priest. These titles were passed on to his descendents and successors in what was known as the Hasmonean Dynasty. In approximately 134 BC, Simon was assassinated by the Ptolemies of Egypt, who were trying to gain power in Judea.

134 BC ✡ JOHN HYRCANUS COMES TO POWER

John Hyrcanus (d. 104 BC), the son of Simon Maccabeus (d. 134 BC), came to power in approximately 134 BC, after the death of his father. For the first few years that John Hyrcanus ruled, the Seleucid king Antiochus VII (r. 139–130 BC) imposed taxes on Judea. However, the death of Antiochus VII in approximately 130 BC in a battle with the Parthians proved to be the decisive end of Seleucid power over Judea. Thus, Judea firmly established its national independence under the reign of John Hyrcanus. He reigned until his death in 104 BC, when he was succeeded by his son Aristobulus I.

104 BC ✡ ARISTOBULUS RULES JUDEA

Following John Hyrcanus's death (d. 104 BC), his son Aristobulus I ruled for one year, from 104 to 103 BC. He carried on the conquests his father had begun and forced the Galileans to accept the Jewish religion. According to historian Josephus (AD 37–100), Aristobulus I wore a crown and took the title of "king" rather than "ethnarch," as his father and grandfather had been called.

He hoped that this would cause the neighboring Gentiles to hold him in higher esteem. However, he died in 103 BC and was succeeded by his brother, Alexander Janneus (d. 76 BC).

102 BC ✡ ALEXANDER JANNEUS RULES JUDEA

When Aristobulus I, the high priest and ruler of Judea, died in 102 BC, his brother Alexander Janneus (d. 76 BC) succeeded him as high priest and proclaimed himself king. He also married Salome Alexandra (d. 67 BC), the widow of Aristobulus. Janneus was a ruthless ruler, even killing one of his own brothers. In a six-year civil war with the Pharisees, his mercenaries killed more than fifty thousand Jews. Despite the nation's internal turmoil under his reign, Janneus proved competent militarily and successfully led campaigns both to keep out invaders and to extend the borders of Judea. At the end of his reign, he ruled more territory than any Judean king had since Solomon. When he died in battle in 76 BC, his wife, Alexandra, ascended to the throne.

76 BC ✡ SALOME ALEXANDRA RULES JUDEA

Upon the death of her husband, King Alexander Janneus (d. 76 BC), Salome Alexandra (d. 67 BC) ascended to the throne as queen of Judea. Peace marked her ten-year reign. As enemies kept their distance from Jerusalem, the city enjoyed a season of political, economical, and religious advancement. This season of stability also brought an increased number of pilgrims to Jerusalem and donations from Jews scattered abroad. Alexandra welcomed the Pharisees, who were rising quickly in prominence, to join the Sanhedrin; she stripped privileges and leadership posts from Sadducees who were hostile to the Pharisees. In 67 BC, Alexandra died, and civil war over the throne soon ensued between her sons Aristobulus II (d. 49 BC) and Hyrcanus II (d. 30 BC).

66 BC ✡ ARISTOBULUS II AND HYRCANUS II BATTLE

When Queen Salome Alexandra of Judea, died in 67 BC, her sons Aristobulus II (d. 49 BC) and Hyrcanus II (d. 30 BC) competed for the throne. Meeting in battle near Jericho, Aristobulus was victorious, and Hyrcanus conceded defeat on condition that he be left alone. Hyrcanus's followers, however, refused to

2200–1950 BC	2000 BC	1180 BC	776 BC
Middle Bronze Age I	Hittite, Egyptian, and Assyrian Empires control major areas	Troy destroyed with Trojan horse	First Olympic Games held in Greece

live with defeat and soon convinced him to seek the backing of foreign armies. They stormed Judea, overcame Aristobulus's army, and laid siege to the Temple where Aristobulus took refuge in 65 BC at the time of Passover. Meanwhile, the Roman general Pompey, who was conquering Asia Minor, sent a representative to Syria. Both Aristobulus II and Hyrcanus II sent emissaries offering money for Roman support.

63 BC ✡ POMPEY CONQUERS PALESTINE; ROMAN RULE BEGINS

In 63 BC, Roman general Pompey (106–48 BC), who recently had arrived in the new Roman-controlled territory of Syria, swept into Palestine seeking to settle the dispute between brothers Aristobulus II (d. 49 BC) and Hyrcanus II (d. 30 BC), who both claimed control of Palestine. Pompey conquered Jerusalem after a three-month siege and reinstated Hyrcanus II as high priest. The Roman rule that Pompey subsequently established over Palestine would last more than seven centuries. When civil war erupted between Pompey and Julius Caesar (100–44 BC) in 49 BC, Pompey fled to Egypt, where he was assassinated in 48 BC.

63 BC ✡ HYRCANUS II RULES UNDER ROME

In 63 BC, Roman general Pompey (106–48 BC) conquered Palestine for Rome, thereby settling the civil war between brothers Aristobulus II (d. 49 BC) and Hyrcanus II (d. 30 BC). Pompey initially supported Aristobulus, who had been hiding in the Temple, but the following year he installed Hyrcanus II as high priest and sent Aristobulus away, captive to Rome. Hyrcanus ruled Palestine under Rome along with Antipater, whom Julius Caesar (100–44 BC) appointed regent over Palestine in 48 BC, until 40 BC when Hyrcanus was removed by Aristobulus's son, Antigonus (d. 37 BC), with help from the Parthians.

44 BC ✝ JULIUS CAESAR DIES; CAESAR AUGUSTUS REIGNS

On the eve of March 15, 44 BC, Julius Caesar (100–44 BC) indicated in conversation that he desired his death to be "a sudden one." The next day Caesar was attacked and murdered by a group led by his friend Brutus (85–42 BC). Before his death, Caesar had named his grandnephew, Gaius Octavian (63 BC–AD

14), his heir. After Caesar's death, Octavian eventually defeated the challenge of Mark Antony (83–30 BC) and consolidated his power in 30 BC. Octavian, who later was called "Caesar Augustus" in honor of his accomplishments, referred to his adoptive father, Julius Caesar, as a god and allowed others to call him "the son of god." His accomplishment of bringing peace to the world also brought him the title "savior." However, it was under his reign that the true Son of God and Savior of the world was born, not in a palace in Rome, but in a manger in Bethlehem.

40 BC ✡ PARTHIANS CONQUER JERUSALEM

In 40 BC, Antigonus (d. 37 BC), son of former Judean king Aristobulus II (d. 49 BC), joined with the Parthians and stormed Jerusalem to unseat his uncle Hyrcanus II (d. 30 BC). Fighting in Jerusalem continued until the Parthians tricked Hyrcanus into meeting in Galilee for peace talks. There he was captured and mutilated to disqualify him from serving as high priest in any future regime, and Antigonus was made king. Meanwhile, Herod (73–4 BC), the Judean governor, fled to Rome to seek help from Octavian (63 BC–AD 14) and Mark Antony (83–30 BC). They declared Herod the rightful king. In the spring of 37 BC, Antony's promise of military help came to fruition, and Herod marched into Jerusalem with two legions of Roman soldiers.

37 BC ✡ JERUSALEM SUFFERS A SIX-MONTH SIEGE

In the spring of 37 BC, Herod (73–4 BC) came to the defense of Hyrcanus II (d. 30 BC) and laid siege to Jerusalem with the aid of two legions of Roman soldiers commissioned by Mark Antony (83–30 BC). By the summer of 37 BC, the Roman army proved too strong and Jerusalem fell to Rome. Herod bribed Sossius—the commander of Antony's army—and his Roman soldiers to refrain from laying waste to the Temple, their intended course of action. At Herod's behest, the Romans beheaded Antigonus, and Herod married Hyrcanus's granddaughter, Mariamne, strengthening his right to the throne in the eyes of the Judeans. In 31 BC, Herod charged Hyrcanus with treason and executed him in 30 BC to prevent Roman emperor Augustus from putting any descendants of the Maccabees in charge of Judea.

2200–1950 BC	2000 BC	1180 BC	776 BC
Middle Bronze Age I	Hittite, Egyptian, and Assyrian Empires control major areas	Troy destroyed with Trojan horse	First Olympic Games held in Greece

27 BC ✝ THE TITLE "AUGUSTUS" IS BESTOWED ON OCTAVIAN

Following the assassination of Julius Caesar (100–44 BC), his grandnephew Octavian (63 BC–AD 14) proceeded to Rome to claim the throne. Octavian allied himself with Mark Antony (83–30 BC) and Lepidus to form the triumvirate that ruled the Roman Empire in Caesar's stead. Before long, Octavian won over Lepidus's troops and divided the empire with Antony. When Antony chose to pursue Cleopatra (69–30 BC) over Octavian's sister, Octavian used it as a cause for civil war and narrowly defeated Antony, garnering sole control of the empire in 30 BC. In 27 BC, the senate honored Octavian with the title *Augustus,* meaning "exalted." Stability and technological advancement marked his rule. His census decree in 6 BC brought Joseph and Mary to Bethlehem for Jesus' birth (Luke 2:1), in approximately 5 BC. Augustus died in AD 14, leaving Tiberius as his successor.

19 BC ✡ HEROD'S TEMPLE RESTORATION BEGINS

When Herod (73–4 BC) ascended to the throne of Judea in 37 BC, with the help and protection of Rome, his authority over the region was limited by the regal presence of Mark Antony (83–30 BC). But after Antony's death in 30 BC, Herod discovered much more leeway and soon embarked on a building program of remarkable magnitude throughout Palestine. Among the impressive roads, fortresses, and palaces, the highlight for the Jews was the restoration and renovation of the Temple, which commenced in 19 BC. The Temple grounds were expanded to 36 acres, and the Temple itself reached its culmination of beauty. This unparalleled structure served as the Temple throughout Jesus' life.

509 BC	480 BC	215 BC	12 BC
Roman Republic founded	Parthenon built in Athens	Construction begins on Great Wall of China	Silk Road opens between China and West

THE NEW TESTAMENT ERA

7 BC–AD 100

The New Testament era began with a star in the East leading to a baby in Bethlehem. The babe was Jesus, the Messiah, God incarnate. Jesus proclaimed God's eternal plan to the Jewish people, but the majority rejected him as their Messiah. He was crucified as the Lamb of God who takes away the sins of the world. But death could not hold him, and on the third day he arose, defeating death, and ascended into heaven forty days later.

Because the Jews rejected their Messiah, God sent the Roman armies in AD 70 to destroy Jerusalem and its temple and to take captive the Jewish survivors. God then offered his salvation plan to the Gentiles, and the rest of the first century is the story of the spreading of the Good News from Jerusalem throughout the Roman Empire.

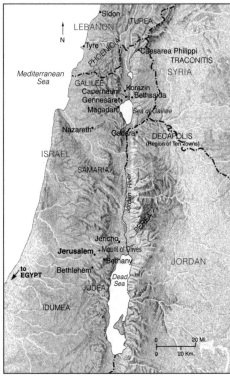

The broken lines (—·—·) indicate modern boundaries.

Jesus' earthly story begins in the town of Bethlehem in the Roman province of Judea (Matthew 2:1). A threat to kill the infant king led Joseph to take his family to Egypt (2:14). When they returned, God led them to settle in Nazareth, in Galilee (2:22-23). At about age 30, Jesus was baptized in the Jordan River and was tempted by Satan in the Judean wilderness (3:13; 4:1). Jesus set up his base of operations in Capernaum (4:12-13), and from there he ministered throughout Israel, telling parables, teaching about the Kingdom, and healing the sick. He traveled to Gadara and healed two demon-possessed men (8:28-34); fed more than 5,000 people with five loaves and two fish on the shores of Galilee near Bethsaida (14:15-21); healed the sick in Gennesaret (14:34-36); ministered to the Gentiles in Tyre and Sidon (15:21-28); visited Caesarea Philippi, where Peter declared him to be the Messiah (16:13-20); and taught in Judea, across the Jordan (19:1). As he set out on his last visit to Jerusalem, he told his disciples what would happen to him there (20:17-19). He spent some time in Jericho (20:29), and then stayed in Bethany at night as he went back and forth to Jerusalem during his last week (21:17). In Jerusalem, he would be crucified, but he would rise again.

7 BC ✝ PLANETS CONJOIN BEFORE JESUS' BIRTH

The Magi, a priestly caste in ancient Persia, were both astronomers and astrologers. The Persian Jews, also interested in astrology, had predicted that when Saturn met Jupiter in the zodiac sign of Pisces, the Messiah would appear. On May 29, 7 BC, Jupiter and Saturn came into conjunction in Pisces for the first time in 853 years and then began moving apart. However, in October and December the two planets met again for the second and third times in Pisces. The Magi were familiar with Jewish prophecy and would have understood this phenomenon to mean that something important was about to happen in Judea. Then in February of 5 BC, a nova appeared in the sky, moving toward Judea. If the Magi left Persia when this appeared, they could have reached Bethlehem

6	17	43	50
Judea becomes Roman province	Earthquake destroys much of Ephesus	London founded	Pyramid built in Teotihuacán, Mexico

THE STAR OF BETHLEHEM

| December 4, 7 BC |

They followed the star.

Ancient Persia had a priestly caste called magi. Astrology was very popular in the ancient Near East, and the magi were both astrologers and astronomers.

Early Jews also were interested in astrology. One of their messianic prophecies said, "A star will rise from Jacob" (Numbers 24:17). To them, Jupiter was "the King's planet" and Saturn was Israel's "defender." An old Jewish proverb said, "God created Saturn to shield Israel."

Early astrologers observed that planets move in a belt in the heavens that they termed the zodiac. They divided the zodiac into twelve equal blocks or signs. According to Chaldean astrology, each sign represented a different nation. Pisces, the sign of the fish, represented Amurru, which included Syria and Palestine. To Jewish astrologers, Pisces represented Judea. They predicted that the Messiah would appear when Saturn, their "defender," would meet Jupiter, "the King's planet," in Pisces. Since many of the Jews did not return from the Babylonian captivity and continued to live in Persia, the magi would have been familiar with Jewish astrological beliefs.

In 7 BC, for the first time in 853 years, Jupiter and Saturn came together in Pisces, with three conjunctions between April and December, the third occurring on December 4, 7 BC. The magi would have tried to understand the significance of what they had seen. Could it be the Jewish Messiah's birth in Judea?

In February of 6 BC, Mars, which had been far away in the sky a few months earlier, joined Jupiter and Saturn in Pisces. Mars was thought to represent war. Could this indicate that the Messiah, the defender of Israel, was about to arise and defeat his enemy? That theory would be in line with the final prophecy of Balaam: "A star will rise from Jacob; a scepter will emerge from Israel. It will crush the foreheads of Moab's people, cracking the skulls of the people of Sheth" (Numbers 24:17).

One year later in late winter, blazing across the sky from the East came a nova, a star that suddenly explodes, becoming ten to one hundred thousand times brighter than it had been. The nova was heading toward Judea, and the magi decided to follow it. The nova was visible for more than ten weeks. If the magi left Persia shortly after it appeared, they would have been able to reach Bethlehem while it was still visible.

When the magi reached Jerusalem, they apparently had lost sight of the star because they asked where the king of the Jews was to be born. This was no doubt because once a month the moon would hide the nova.

When the nova reappeared, at dawn it would have been fifty degrees high due south of Jerusalem—directly over Bethlehem! When the magi saw the star, they were filled with joy and followed it to the house where Jesus and Mary were. There they fell down before him and worshiped him (Matthew 2:1-11).

when it was still visible. In fact, the nova eventually appeared directly over Bethlehem, leading the Magi to Jesus.

5 BC ✝ JESUS IS BORN

Jesus was born in approximately 5 BC in Bethlehem to a young virgin named Mary. The genealogies of Jesus recorded in Matthew and Luke show that he had descended from King David. Herod the Great, the Jewish vassal king under the Romans, learned that Jesus was prophesied as the coming "King of the Jews," and therefore sought to kill all infant boys two years old and younger. However, Jesus' life was saved because an angel of the Lord had told Joseph to escape to Egypt. After Herod died, an angel appeared again to Joseph and told him to return with his family to Israel (Matthew 2 and Luke 2).

AD 9 ✝ JESUS IS LEFT IN THE TEMPLE

When Jesus was twelve, his family went on their annual pilgrimage to Jerusalem to celebrate the feast of Passover. After the feast, Mary and Joseph left Jerusalem as part of a caravan of people returning to their homes. Assuming Jesus was part of the caravan, Jesus' parents inadvertently left him in Jerusalem. When they later realized he was missing, they returned to Jerusalem and finally found him in the Temple listening to the teachers and asking them questions. Everyone, including his parents, was amazed at what he said. Overcoming their astonishment, Mary and Joseph asked him why he had stayed behind rather than going with them. Jesus' reply was, "You should have known that I would be in my Father's house" (Luke 2:41-52).

AD 29 ✝ JOHN THE BAPTIST BEGINS HIS MINISTRY

Born around 6 BC, John the Baptist lived as an ascetic in the wilderness of Judea. Around AD 29, John received the Lord's call to preach repentance and forgiveness of sins to the Jewish people in the Judean desert. John quickly developed a following as his hearers repented and were baptized by him in the Jordan River. As prophesied by Isaiah, John was used by God to prepare the way for the Lord.

6	17	43	50
Judea becomes Roman province	Earthquake destroys much of Ephesus	London founded	Pyramid built in Teotihuacán, Mexico

MESSIAH, KING, AND LAMB

March 30, AD 33

A prophecy fulfilled to the day?

The day was March 30, AD 33, four days before Passover. As Jesus set out for Jerusalem from the village of Bethany, on the eastern slope of the Mount of Olives, he sent two disciples on ahead.

> "Go into the village over there," he said, "and you will see a donkey tied there, with its colt beside it. Untie them and bring them here...." This was done to fulfill the prophecy, "Tell the people of Israel, 'Look, your King is coming to you. He is humble, riding on a donkey—even on a donkey's colt.'" The two disciples did as Jesus said. They brought the animals to him and threw their garments over the colt, and he sat on it. (Matthew 21:2-7)
>
> [As Jesus rode the donkey toward Jerusalem,] the crowds spread out their coats on the road ahead [to honor him]. As they reached the place where the road started down from the Mount of Olives, all of his followers began to shout and sing, ... "Bless the King who comes in the name of the Lord! Peace in heaven and glory in highest heaven!" (Luke 19:36-38)

This was the official entry of the Messiah-King into Jerusalem. Just as David's son Solomon had ridden a donkey at his presentation as king to the cheering crowds of Jerusalem just a little over a millennium earlier (1 Kings 1:33-46), so Jesus entered Jerusalem riding a donkey to claim publicly that he was the greater Son of David, who would sit on David's throne.

More than five hundred years earlier, God had revealed to the prophet Daniel that the Messiah would come four hundred and eighty-three years after the command would be given to rebuild Jerusalem (Daniel 9:25). The command to rebuild Jerusalem was given by King Artaxerxes of Persia, in the month of Nisan in the twentieth year of his reign (Nehemiah 2:1-6). The Jews did not use a solar calendar as we do today, and in biblical prophecies the years are composed of 360 days (e.g., Revelation 11:2-3; 12:6; 13:5). The exact day of the month is not given; but if the command to rebuild Jerusalem was given on the first of Nisan, March 5, 444 BC, it was 483 years of 360 days later—to the day—that Jesus entered Jerusalem on March 30, AD 33, the day of his formal entry into the city as Messiah. The prophecy likely was fulfilled to the day!

Something else also happened on that day. It was the day when the lambs were selected to be slain at Passover. In his triumphal entry, Jesus was presenting himself as *the* Passover Lamb.

AD 29 ✛ JESUS' MINISTRY BEGINS

After being baptized by John the Baptist, Jesus began his ministry in Judea, Samaria, and Galilee. His ministry was characterized by healing the sick, raising the dead, restoring sight to the blind, and preaching about the Kingdom of God. In his three years of ministry, Jesus gathered twelve disciples and prepared them to continue his work after he was gone. Jesus' earthly ministry ended with his crucifixion, resurrection, and ascension.

AD 30 ✛ JESUS CELEBRATES PASSOVER DURING HIS MINISTRY

Jesus was in Jerusalem on April 7, AD 30, celebrating the Passover for the first time since he had begun his public ministry. At the Passover Jesus drove the merchants and money changers out of the Temple and performed miracles, but the Jewish people viewed him only as a miracle worker (John 2:13-25). However, one man did truly believe in him during that festival. Nicodemus, a leader of the Pharisees, came to Jesus one evening seeking to learn more about his message. Jesus told him that to enter the Kingdom of God, he had to be born again. He told Nicodemus of the coming salvation and the coming judgment, and declared that believing in him as Messiah was the only way to obtain salvation (John 3:1-21). Not only did Nicodemus later defend Jesus before the Sanhedrin (John 7:50-51), but he also prepared Jesus' body for burial (John 19:39-40).

AD 33 ✛ JESUS TRIUMPHANTLY ENTERS JERUSALEM

On March 30, AD 33, four days before the Jewish Passover, Jesus directed his disciples to go to a village to find a donkey and a colt, in fulfillment of a prophecy in Zechariah 9:9. Jesus mounted the colt and rode it into Jerusalem as the people waved palm branches and laid down their coats for him, shouting, "Bless the King who comes in the name of the Lord!" To the faithful Jew, this scene brought to mind the occasion when Solomon rode a donkey into Jerusalem to be proclaimed the king of the Jews (1 Kings 1:33-46). This event was the official entry of Jesus the Messiah into Jerusalem. This also was the day when Passover lambs were selected, and Jesus was presenting himself as *the* Passover Lamb.

6	17	43	50
Judea becomes Roman province	Earthquake destroys much of Ephesus	London founded	Pyramid built in Teotihuacán, Mexico

THE LAST SUPPER

April 2, AD 33

It was Jesus' last night before his crucifixion.

On April 2, AD 33, Jesus sent Peter and John to prepare the Passover meal for him to eat with his disciples (Luke 22:7-13).

There at the Last Supper, Jesus instituted the New covenant, replacing the Old covenant of Mount Sinai. At the institution of the Old covenant, Moses, Aaron, Aaron's sons, Nadab and Abihu, and seventy of the elders of Israel had gone up to the top of Mount Sinai where they saw God and shared a meal together with him (Exodus 24:9-11). Which person of the Trinity did they see and eat with? It was God the Son, whose role is to represent the Godhead visibly to humanity (John 1:18). Thus the Old covenant was instituted at a meal between God the Son and the elders of Israel. Now in the upper room, the New covenant was instituted at a meal between God the Son and the disciples, the elders of the church (cf. 1 Peter 5:1; 2 John 1; 3 John 1).

At the Last Supper, when Jesus said, "This is my blood, which seals the covenant" (Matthew 26-28), the words (except for *my*) were identical to the Greek Septuagint's translation of Moses' words at the institution of the Old covenant (Exodus 24:8). Clearly Jesus was instituting a New covenant to replace the Old covenant.

The covenants of the Bible were treaties between God and his people. Thus it is significant that Jesus says, "This wine is the token of God's new covenant to save you—an agreement sealed with the blood I will pour out for you" (Luke 22:20). Since the time of Homer, the pouring out of a cup of wine was the normal way of sealing a treaty between nations. This ritual was so central to treaty making that the Greek word for "libation" became the word for "treaty." Thus Jesus used this contemporary treaty symbolism to make sure everyone understood that he was instituting a New covenant or treaty with his people.

Since the Old covenant contained commandments, one would expect that the New covenant would contain a new commandment. Thus at the Last Supper Jesus says, "Now I am giving you a new commandment: Love each other. Just as I have loved you, you should love each other" (John 13:34).

After Jesus had identified Judas Iscariot as the one who would betray him and Simon Peter as the one who would deny him (John 13:18-38), he and the disciples crossed the Kidron Valley and went to the garden of Gethsemane (John 18:1; Matthew 26:36).

33 ✝ THE FIG TREE WITHERS

On March 31, AD 33, the morning after Jesus' triumphal entry into Jerusalem, Jesus and his disciples left the town of Bethany, where they had spent the night. Being hungry, Jesus approached a fig tree to pick some fruit, but it had no fruit—only leaves. He cursed the tree saying, "May no one ever eat your fruit again!" (Mark 11:12-14). Jesus was giving a visual parable of the Temple in Jerusalem. Like the fruitless fig tree, the Temple was beautiful to look at but produced no spiritual fruit. When Jesus arrived in Jerusalem, he drove out the merchants and their customers from the Temple. Jesus and his disciples passed by the fig tree the next day and saw that it had withered, foretelling the Temple's destruction in AD 70 (Mark 11:12-19).

33 ✝ JESUS GIVES THE OLIVET DISCOURSE

After leaving the Temple on April 1, 33, Jesus and his disciples went to the Mount of Olives where the disciples asked him when the destruction of the Temple would take place. Jesus gave them a foreboding message saying that nations would war against each other, great earthquakes would take place, and famines and epidemics would break out. He told them that his disciples would be dragged into court and thrown into prisons, and many would be killed. Once they saw Jerusalem surrounded by armies, they were to flee before the city and Temple were destroyed. The destruction of the Temple would precede the age of the Gentiles, in which we now live, when the church is made up primarily of Gentiles. Jesus will return at the end of this age (Luke 21:7-24).

33 ✝ JESUS SERVES THE LAST SUPPER

On April 2, 33, at a Jerusalem Passover meal known as the Last Supper, Jesus initiated the New covenant, replacing the Old covenant made with Israel generations before at Mount Sinai. That night Jesus broke the unleavened bread of Passover and passed the wine for the celebration saying, "This is my body, given for you. . . . This wine is the token of God's new covenant to save you—an agreement sealed with the blood I will pour out for you" (Luke 22:19-20). After Jesus identified Judas as the one who would betray him and Peter as the one who would deny him, he led the disciples across the Kidron Valley to the Garden of

6	17	43	50
Judea becomes Roman province	Earthquake destroys much of Ephesus	London founded	Pyramid built in Teotihuacán, Mexico

THE CRUCIFIXION

April 3, AD 33

They crucified their King.

In the early hours of April 3, AD 33, Jesus was taken to Pontius Pilate, the Roman governor.

"Are you the king of the Jews?" he asked him. . . .

Jesus answered, "I am not an earthly king. If I were, my followers would have fought when I was arrested by the Jewish leaders. But my Kingdom is not of this world."

Pilate replied, "You are a king then?"

"You say that I am a king, and you are right," Jesus said. . . .

Then [Pilate] went out again to the people and told them, "He is not guilty of any crime. But you have a custom of asking me to release someone from prison each year at Passover. So if you want me to, I'll release the King of the Jews."

But they shouted back, "No! Not this man, but Barabbas!" (Barabbas was a criminal.)

"But if I release Barabbas," Pilate asked them, "what should I do with Jesus who is called the Messiah?"

And they all shouted, "Crucify him!" . . .

[Pilate] sent for a bowl of water and washed his hands before the crowd, saying, "I am innocent of the blood of this man. The responsibility is yours!"

And all the people yelled back, "We will take responsibility for his death—we and our children!"

So Pilate released Barabbas to them. He ordered Jesus flogged with a lead-tipped whip, then turned him over to the Roman soldiers. (John 18:33-40; Matthew 27:22-26)

The next event was truly remarkable. Though Jesus had been born to be king and had been anointed by the Holy Spirit following his baptism (Acts 10:38), he had never been officially crowned. After the soldiers beat Jesus they coronated him—using all the major features of the coronation of a Caesar.

In the Roman Empire it was frequently the soldiers who chose the next Caesar. Here the soldiers set a crown of thorns on Jesus' head and put a royal purple robe on him (John 19:2). (At this time becoming Caesar was known as "donning the purple.") They placed a stick in his right hand as a scepter and knelt before him in mockery, yelling, "Hail! King of the Jews!" (Matthew 27:29).

Then "Pilate went outside again and said to the people, 'I am going to bring him out to you now, but understand clearly that I find him not guilty.' Then Jesus came out wearing the crown of thorns and the purple robe. And Pilate said, 'Here is the man!'

"When they saw him, the leading priests and Temple guards began shouting, 'Crucify! Crucify!' . . . So they took Jesus and led him away (John 19:4-6, 16).

They crucified him on Skull Hill ("Golgotha" in Hebrew) between two thieves. Pilate had a sign placed over him that said, "Jesus of Nazareth, the King of the Jews." At three in the afternoon an earthquake shook Jerusalem as Jesus died, just as the Passover lambs were being slain all over Jerusalem (John 19:16-30; Matthew 27:33-50).

Gethsemane. There, after Jesus prayed and while the disciples slept, Judas led the Roman soldiers to arrest Jesus (Luke 22:1-54).

33 ✝ JESUS IS CRUCIFIED

After his betrayal, Jesus appeared before the Jewish court, called the Sanhedrin, and then was sent to the governor Pontius Pilate to be tried by the Roman authorities early on the morning of April 3, 33. When Pilate asked Jesus whether he was the King of the Jews, Jesus answered, "Yes, it is as you say." Although Pilate did not find Jesus guilty of any crime, the Jews demanded that he order Jesus' crucifixion. Pilate knew their accusations against Jesus were false, yet he agreed to the crucifixion. Jesus was severely beaten, mocked by the Roman soldiers, spat upon, cursed, and made to carry a heavy wooden cross to a hill named Golgotha where he was crucified. At three in the afternoon, when the lambs were slaughtered for the Passover, an earthquake shook the earth as Jesus died. The Lamb of God had died for the sins of the world (Matthew 27:1-56; John 1:29; 18:33-40).

33 ✝ JESUS LIVES

On Sunday morning, April 5, 33, Mary Magdalene and several other women went to Jesus' tomb to embalm his body, as was customary at that time. When they got there, they saw that the huge stone in front of the tomb had been rolled away and the tomb was empty! Two angels then appeared to the women and told them Jesus had risen from the dead, just as he had said. The women ran to tell Peter and the other disciples what had happened. Jesus then appeared to two of the disciples as they were walking to Emmaus and later to the disciples in an upper room where they were gathered together. Jesus had indeed risen from the dead! (Luke 24:1-49).

33 ✝ JESUS ASCENDS TO HEAVEN

On May 14, 33, forty days after his resurrection from the dead, Jesus again appeared to his disciples and led them up the Mount of Olives. There he blessed them and commissioned them to go to all nations, preaching the gospel. As his disciples stood by watching, Jesus ascended into the sky and soon vanished into

6	17	43	50
Judea becomes Roman province	Earthquake destroys much of Ephesus	London founded	Pyramid built in Teotihuacán, Mexico

heaven in a cloud. As the disciples continued to gaze into the sky, hoping to catch another glimpse of the Lord, two angels clothed in brilliant white robes suddenly appeared among them. The angels promised the disciples that Jesus would return someday, in the same manner they had just witnessed him leave. The disciples then returned to Jerusalem to wait for the Holy Spirit, whom Jesus had promised would come to them (Matthew 28:16-20; Mark 16:9-20; Luke 24:44-53; Acts 1:1-12).

33 ✛ THE HOLY SPIRIT COMES AT PENTECOST

May 24, 33, was Pentecost, the beginning of the Feast of Weeks, and Jewish men from all over the Roman Empire had gathered to offer their firstfruits to God. For the ten days since Jesus' ascension, the disciples had gathered together praying. On this day, as they prayed, they were startled by a loud roaring and tongues of fire that appeared over their heads. This event marked the fulfillment of Jesus' promise of the coming Holy Spirit. As they preached, they found themselves speaking foreign languages that they did not know. Then Peter stepped forward and powerfully proclaimed the gospel of Christ. Peter's message brought deep conviction to many listeners, and three thousand were added to the church that day. This event marked the beginning of the early church's rapid growth (Acts 2:1-42).

35 ✛ STEPHEN IS MARTYRED

After the Day of Pentecost, the Christian church thrived in spite of opposition from the Sanhedrin. Upon hearing Stephen's preaching, the council arrested and falsely accused him of undermining the law of Moses. Stephen's answer to this charge is one of the longest sermons recorded in the Bible. It is a testimony that the gospel of Jesus Christ does not undermine the law of Moses and the history of Israel: in fact, it completes it. Stephen concluded that the history of Israel had climaxed with the coming of Jesus the Messiah, yet the Jewish council had demanded his crucifixion. This charge infuriated the council, so they stoned Stephen, making him the first Christian martyr. This event forced many Christians to flee Jerusalem. In so doing, they spread the gospel of Christ throughout the Roman Empire (Acts 6:8–8:40).

54	58	79	81–96
Claudius assassinated, succeeded by Nero	Buddhism introduced into China	Mount Vesuvius erupts, covering Pompeii	Emperor Domitian reigns

35 + PAUL IS CONVERTED

As Stephen was being stoned, a young Pharisee named Saul of Tarsus stood nearby, holding the attackers' cloaks. He soon became a leading persecutor of the church. After receiving the Sanhedrin's permission to arrest Christians who had escaped from Jerusalem, Saul left for Damascus. Along the way, he was met with a blinding light and the voice of the Lord Jesus, who sent Saul to a believer in Damascus named Ananias. Upon meeting Ananias, Saul's sight was restored and he received the Holy Spirit. The leading persecutor of the Christians had become a Christian. Saul, whose name was changed to Paul, became the greatest missionary and theologian in the history of the Christian church, spreading the gospel throughout the world (Acts 9:1-31; 22:3-16; 26:4-18).

40 + CORNELIUS IS CONVERTED

By AD 40, although thousands had believed the gospel, the converts were virtually all Jews. However, this was about to change. A God-fearing Caesarean Gentile named Cornelius received a message from God to call Peter to his house. Meanwhile, Peter had received a vision from God in which he was commanded to eat animals that were unclean according to the law of Moses. As Peter awoke from his vision and was pondering its meaning, three messengers arrived. The next day, Peter traveled with the men to meet Cornelius. As Peter proclaimed the gospel to Cornelius and his family, he realized the meaning of his vision: God was calling both Jews and Gentiles to Christ. Cornelius and all those who heard and believed received the Holy Spirit and were baptized (Acts 10:1-48).

43 + PAUL JOINS BARNABAS IN ANTIOCH

After Paul's conversion, Barnabas had been one of the first Christians to accept Paul and welcome him as a genuine brother in Christ. Soon after this, the two men went separate ways. Paul spent several years in Arabia and Damascus and then returned to his hometown of Tarsus. While Paul was in Tarsus, the church in Jerusalem sent Barnabas to minister in Antioch. After considering the situation in Antioch, Barnabas went to Tarsus to bring Paul back to Antioch to minister with them there. For the next year, Paul and Barnabas

6	17	43	50
Judea becomes Roman province	Earthquake destroys much of Ephesus	London founded	Pyramid built in Teotihuacán, Mexico

taught the believers in that city. This ministry partnership became the foundation of Christian missions, because later the two men were commissioned as the church's first missionaries (Acts 9:27; 11:22-30).

44 ✛ HEROD MARTYRS JAMES, THE BROTHER OF JOHN

Christ called James and John, the sons of Zebedee, to leave their fishing boat and follow him. Along with Peter and John, James was among the inner circle of Jesus' disciples who witnessed the raising of Jairus's daughter, Jesus' transfiguration, and the agony in the Garden of Gethsemane. After the martyrdom of Stephen and dispersion of the church, James stayed in Jerusalem and continued to minister. However, around 44, King Herod Agrippa I began arresting leading Christians, starting with James. James was executed with a sword. Peter also was arrested, but miraculously delivered from prison. Soon after that, God struck down Herod himself (Matthew 17:1-18; 26:36-46; Mark 1:20, 5:37; Luke 5:10-11; Acts 12:1-2, 21-25).

45 ✛ JAMES WRITES THE FIRST NEW TESTAMENT BOOK

The Epistle of James was written by Jesus' brother James, who was martyred in 62. Its particularly Jewish flavor leads many Bible scholars to date it as the earliest of the New Testament books, written in about 45. James emphasizes that faith apart from works is dead. The epistle is full of practical tests of genuine Christian faith that produces works: overcoming temptation, obeying the Word, controlling the tongue, and patiently enduring until the Lord's return. There are also a number of parallels between this epistle and the Sermon on the Mount (Matthew 5:1–7:29).

48 ✛ PRAYER MEETING LAUNCHES THE MISSIONARY MOVEMENT

During the first several years after Jesus' ascension, thousands of Jews came to Christ and the Word of God spread rapidly throughout Palestine. However, there was no organized effort to reach the uttermost parts of the earth, as Jesus had commanded. In about 48, the leaders of the church in Antioch met together for what became a historic prayer meeting. As they were worshiping and fasting, the Holy Spirit told them to set apart their two prominent

54	58	79	81–96
Claudius assassinated, succeeded by Nero	Buddhism introduced into China	Mount Vesuvius erupts, covering Pompeii	Emperor Domitian reigns

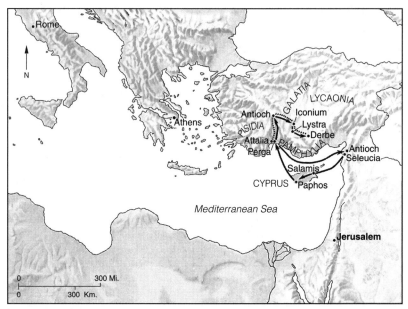

PAUL'S FIRST MISSIONARY JOURNEY (ACTS 13:1—14:28)

leaders—Saul and Barnabas—for an extraordinary work. The church prayed over the men and sent them out, along with John Mark, to proclaim Christ and plant churches. Thus began the missionary movement in the early church (Acts 13:1–14:27).

48 ✝ PAUL EMBARKS ON HIS FIRST MISSIONARY JOURNEY

After the elders of Antioch had laid hands on Paul and Barnabas, they sent them on their first missionary journey in about 48. Accompanied by John Mark, the two missionaries set out to proclaim the gospel in Cyprus. From Cyprus, the team traveled to Perga, where John Mark left to return home against Paul's wishes. However, Paul and Barnabas continued on through the region of Galatia and the cities of Pisidian Antioch, Iconium, Lystra, and Derbe. At the end of their journey, they returned to Antioch and reported to the church that God had opened a door of faith to the Gentiles (Acts 13:1–14:28).

6	17	43	50
Judea becomes Roman province	Earthquake destroys much of Ephesus	London founded	Pyramid built in Teotihuacán, Mexico

49 ✝ JERUSALEM COUNCIL DISCUSSES THE LAW AND GRACE

While many Gentiles became Christians as a result of Paul's missionary journeys, some Hebrew Christians in Jerusalem responded by insisting that circumcision and obedience to the law of Moses were necessary for salvation. In response to this, Paul and Barnabas traveled to Jerusalem from Antioch to meet with the other apostles. Peter, Paul, and Barnabas all testified that both Jews and Gentiles are saved by grace apart from keeping the law. James, the brother of Jesus and a leader of the Jerusalem church, announced the council's decision that Gentiles were free from the law. The council sent its decision to Gentile Christians, asking only that they keep away from meat offered to idols, from blood, from strangled animals, and from fornication. This decision reinforced the inclusion of Gentiles into the church and stimulated future missionary efforts to the rest of the Roman Empire (Acts 15:1-35).

49 ✝ PAUL WRITES GALATIANS

Soon after his first missionary journey, Paul received word that the churches of Galatia had accepted the teachings of certain false teachers. Those "Judaizers," as they were known, taught that—in addition to the gospel of grace—circumcision and obedience to the law of Moses were necessary for salvation. Paul immediately responded to this perversion of the gospel by writing an epistle to the Galatian churches in which he defended his message of justification by faith alone. In the letter, Paul defends his authority as an apostle (chapters 1–2), explains and amplifies justification by faith alone (chapters 3–4), and defends the true nature of obedience and Christian liberty (chapters 5–6).

50–60 ✝ THOMAS TRAVELS TO INDIA

According to the *Acts of Thomas,* a book written in the third century, the apostle Thomas was a missionary to India during the reign of a king named Gundaphorus. Then in 1833, coins were discovered with inscriptions proving Gundaphorus's reign as king in Northwestern India during the first century. In Southwestern India the ancient church of the "Thomas Christians" claims that they were founded by the apostle Thomas; therefore it is likely that Thomas was the one to first bring the gospel to India.

54	58	79	81–96
Claudius assassinated, succeeded by Nero	Buddhism introduced into China	Mount Vesuvius erupts, covering Pompeii	Emperor Domitian reigns

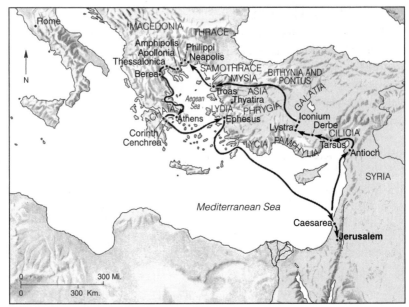

PAUL'S SECOND MISSIONARY JOURNEY (ACTS 15:36—18:22)

50 ✝ HEROD AGRIPPA II BECOMES KING

Several years after his father, Herod Agrippa I (r. 41–44), was struck down by God, Herod Agrippa II (27–100) was appointed by the Roman emperor Claudius to rule Palestine. Following the tradition of many Eastern kings, Agrippa married his sister, Bernice. Acts 26 records Paul giving this couple, along with Porcius Festus (r. 59–62), a defense of his life and ministry. Herod Agrippa II was last in the line of Roman-appointed Herodian kings (Acts 25:23–26:32).

50 ✝ PAUL EMBARKS ON HIS SECOND MISSIONARY JOURNEY

As Paul and Barnabas were making plans to visit and encourage the churches they had established on their first missionary journey, they disagreed over whether or not to bring John Mark, who had abandoned them during the first journey. Unable to agree, Paul set out with Silas instead of Barnabas to visit the churches in Galatia and Asia Minor in 50. When Paul and Silas reached Lystra, Timothy joined their missionary team. After that, Luke joined them in Troas and Paul re-

6	17	43	50
Judea becomes Roman province	Earthquake destroys much of Ephesus	London founded	Pyramid built in Teotihuacán, Mexico

ceived his Macedonian call. Then they entered Europe, traveling through most of modern-day Greece, encountering opposition and miraculous deliverances along the way. In Athens, Paul eloquently debated with the philosophers on Mars Hill, but he saw few results. From Athens, he went to Corinth, where he spent eighteen months of fruitful ministry. From there, Paul traveled with Aquila and Priscilla to Ephesus before returning to Antioch (Acts 15:36–18:22).

51 ✝ PAUL WRITES 1 THESSALONIANS

During his second missionary journey, Paul and his team visited Thessalonica, a city in Macedonia (modern-day Greece). After a successful ministry among the Thessalonian Gentiles, Paul was forced to leave the city. However, he soon sent Timothy back to Thessalonica to continue the ministry there. While Paul was in Corinth, he received word from Timothy that the Thessalonian believers were growing in their faith. Paul responded by writing an epistle to them, thanking God for their faith and good works in Christ. The first section of the epistle (chapters 1–3) is a review of the successful results of the gospel in Thessalonica. The second section (chapters 4–5) is an exhortation to the believers to continue growing and living righteously until the Lord's return.

51 ✝ PAUL WRITES 2 THESSALONIANS

A few months after writing his first epistle to the Thessalonians, Paul received word that some of the believers in Thessalonica were facing persecution, while others had accepted false teaching about Jesus' return. Claiming that the Day of the Lord was already upon them, they had quit working and were living off the rest of the congregation. So Paul wrote another letter to the church, correcting their false teaching and misunderstandings about the Lord's return and also encouraging the persecuted believers. The letter begins with this encouragement (chapter 1), followed by an explanation of the Day of the Lord (chapter 2) and an exhortation to those who were being a burden to the rest of the church (chapter 3).

53 ✝ PAUL EMBARKS ON HIS THIRD MISSIONARY JOURNEY

After recovering his strength in Antioch following his second missionary journey, Paul embarked on a third journey. Once again, he visited and encouraged

54	58	79	81–96
Claudius assassinated, succeeded by Nero	Buddhism introduced into China	Mount Vesuvius erupts, covering Pompeii	Emperor Domitian reigns

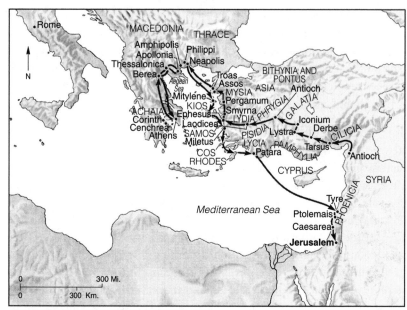

PAUL'S THIRD MISSIONARY JOURNEY (ACTS 18:23–21:16)

the churches in Galatia and Asia Minor. Paul then traveled to Ephesus, where he spent three years ministering. He was forced to leave after an uprising led by Demetrius the silversmith. Paul traveled through Macedonia encouraging the churches while making his way to Corinth, where he spent three winter months. From Corinth, Paul set out for Jerusalem through Macedonia. In his last meeting with the Ephesian elders, they warned him of the persecution he would face in Jerusalem. In about 57, after his final instructions and a tearful parting, Paul continued on to Jerusalem, where the Romans arrested him (Acts 18:23–21:40).

53 ✡ JEWS ARE EXPELLED FROM ROME

The Roman historian Suetonius (69–after 103) wrote that during the mid-fifties the Jewish population of Rome was continually disturbed by a certain "Chrestus." This seems to be a reference to heated debates within the Jewish community in Rome over the person and work of Jesus Christ. The disputes became so frequent and intense by 53 that the Emperor Claudius (10 BC–AD 54) issued a decree expelling the Jews from the city. Priscilla and Aquila were among the Jews forced to

6	17	43	50
Judea becomes Roman province	Earthquake destroys much of Ephesus	London founded	Pyramid built in Teotihuacán, Mexico

leave. Traveling to Corinth, they joined Paul's ministry. When Emperor Claudius was murdered by his wife in 54, the Jews were allowed to return to Rome. This short period of Jewish absence may have contributed to the strength of the Gentile church in Rome, which in turn led to some of the Jewish-Gentile disputes addressed by Paul in his epistle to the Romans (Acts 18:1-3; Romans 14–15).

54 ✝ NERO BECOMES CAESAR

Nero, (37–68), the fifth Roman Caesar, ascended to the throne in 54. During the first five years of his reign, the empire and city of Rome were stable. Soon thereafter, the stability of Nero's reign began to crumble. Influenced by his mistress, Poppaea, Nero had his mother killed, divorced his wife, Octavia, and married Poppaea. It was during this time, approximately 63, that Paul suffered his first imprisonment in Rome. In 64, a great fire devastated the city of Rome. Nero, who was suspected of having some involvement in the disaster, placed the blame on the Christians of Rome and launched a severe persecution of them. Both Paul and Peter were martyred by Nero as part of the persecution. On June 9, 68, as the provinces began to demand his removal, Nero committed suicide.

56 ✝ PAUL WRITES 1 CORINTHIANS

While Paul was in Ephesus during his third missionary journey, he received a report about a division that had arisen over several issues in the Corinthian church. Paul immediately wrote them a letter, and they responded by sending several questions back to him. His response is the epistle now known as 1 Corinthians. The epistle begins with a rebuke over the unnecessary divisions in the church, followed by Paul's instructions on various issues such as immorality, marriage, idols, spiritual gifts, and the Resurrection, among others. The epistle can be divided into two major sections: Paul's rebuke (chapters 1–6) and Paul's response to the church's questions (chapters 7–16). Both sections are dominated by a call for repentance and an emphasis on church unity.

56 ✝ PAUL WRITES 2 CORINTHIANS

After Paul sent his first letter to the church of Corinth, he learned that it had not corrected the problems he had addressed. As a result, he made a brief visit to them and then wrote a painful letter of rebuke (not included in the New Testament). Paul sent Titus to deliver the letter and anxiously awaited their response. To Paul's great delight, the Corinthian believers finally repented of the sins that had been dividing them. Paul responded by writing 2 Corinthians, in which he thanked God for their repentance. However, there was a significant minority within the church that was being led astray by false teachers who were undermining the gospel. The book of 2 Corinthians begins with an explanation of Paul's ministry (chapters 1–9), followed by a strong defense of his apostleship (chapters 10–13).

56 ✝ PAUL WRITES ROMANS

While ministering in Corinth in 56, near the end of his third missionary journey, Paul wrote his epistle to the Roman church. He intended to pass through Rome en route to Spain and desired the Roman church to be a base for his missionary efforts in Spain. This letter is regarded by many as Paul's clearest and most brilliant exposition of the doctrine of justification by grace through faith. In it, Paul touches on some of the most profound and perplexing of all Christian doctrines, such as original sin, justification, sanctification, election, and the sovereignty of God. The first section is an explanation of justification (chapters 1–8), followed by a vindication of God's righteousness in dispensing justification freely to Jews and Gentiles (chapters 9–11), and ending with the implications of this doctrine for life and ministry (chapter 12–16).

57 ✝ PAUL MAKES HIS FINAL VISIT TO JERUSALEM

Paul spent the final part of his third missionary journey in Corinth, ministering among the believers there. The Corinthian church wanted to send an offering to the suffering church in Jerusalem, and Paul was designated to deliver the gift. After being diverted through Asia Minor, Paul finally arrived in Jerusalem, where he was warmly greeted by the church leaders. However, soon after Paul's arrival, a group of Jews from Asia falsely accused him of desecrating the Temple. Although the Romans rescued him from the Jewish mob, Paul was arrested and held by the Romans. After Paul received a series of threats from the Jewish leaders, the Lord appeared to him with the encouragement that he would preach in

FROM PERSECUTOR TO PERSECUTED

June 2, AD 57

God changes lives in unexpected ways!

A group of Jews in Jerusalem in AD 35 made false accusations against a deacon named Stephen. They successfully stirred up the people into an angry mob that dragged Stephen to appear before the Jewish governing council, the Sanhedrin. There, a young Pharisee by the name of Saul witnessed both the false accusations and Stephen's defense of his faith in Jesus the Messiah. Later, when the Jewish mob dragged Stephen out of the city to stone him, they threw their coats at Saul's feet for safekeeping as they picked up stones to throw at Stephen (Acts 6:8–8:1). Saul not only supported Stephen's murder but later became the chief persecutor of Christians.

Twenty-two years later, on June 2, AD 57, the tables were turned, and Saul was in Stephen's shoes. Saul, by then known as Paul, was the one with false accusations brought against him in Jerusalem by a group of Jews from the Roman province of Asia. Finding Paul in the Temple, they shouted, "Men of Israel! Help! This is the man who teaches against our people and tells everybody to disobey the Jewish laws. He speaks against the Temple—and he even defiles it by bringing Gentiles in!" (Acts 21:27-28). This time it was Paul who was attacked by a Jewish mob, and Paul was the one giving his defense (Acts 21:30–22:21).

Paul began his defense with the same words Stephen had used,

> "Brothers and esteemed fathers, listen to me." (Acts 22:1; cf. 7:2). Paul explained, "I am a Jew, born in Tarsus, a city in Cilicia. . . . I persecuted the followers of the Way. . . . The high priest and the whole council of leaders can testify that this is so. For I received letters from them to our Jewish brothers in Damascus, authorizing me to bring the Christians from there to Jerusalem, in chains, to be punished.
>
> "As I was on the road, nearing Damascus, about noon a very bright light from heaven suddenly shone around me. I fell to the ground and heard a voice saying to me, 'Saul, Saul, why are you persecuting me?'
>
> "'Who are you, sir?' I asked. And he replied, 'I am Jesus of Nazareth, the one you are persecuting.' . . .
>
> "I said, 'What shall I do, Lord?' And the Lord told me, 'Get up and go into Damascus, and there you will be told all that you are to do.'" (Acts 22:3-10)

Just as Stephen's defense had caused a riot, so did the words of Paul. "The crowd ... shouted, 'Away with such a fellow! Kill him!'" (Acts 22:22). Just as the men of Jerusalem had thrown off their coats at Paul's feet before stoning Stephen, now they "threw off their coats" in rage against Paul (Acts 22:23). Fortunately for Paul, the Roman soldiers saved him that day from being killed by the angry mob (Acts 22:24-30).

Paul's encounter with the Lord Jesus Christ changed him from Saul the persecutor into Paul the persecuted.

Rome. From Jerusalem, Paul was transferred to Caesarea to avoid further Jewish hostility and eventually on to Rome for an appeal to Caesar (Acts 21:1–23:35).

58 † MARK WRITES HIS GOSPEL

Likely the first of the four Gospels to be written, the Gospel of Mark portrays the life and ministry of Jesus as the perfect servant. Roman Christians probably were the original audience of the book, and tradition suggests that it was written in Rome. Mark, the author, is mentioned in the book of Acts as Paul and Barnabas's companion and later as a beneficial partner to Paul's ministry. Evidence suggests that Mark relied heavily on Peter's testimony in the composition of his gospel. The first section of Mark records many works of Jesus, portraying him as the perfect servant (1:1–8:30). The next section presents teachings of Jesus as the servant (8:31–10). The final section of the book deals with the sufferings of the servant and his subsequent resurrection and exaltation (chapters 11–16).

60 † MATTHEW WRITES HIS GOSPEL

Of the four Gospels, Matthew's is the most Jewish. Matthew presents Jesus as King of the Jews and the long-awaited Messiah. The book was intentionally directed toward a Jewish audience, presenting Jesus as the fulfillment of Old Testament Scriptures. The author of the book was called from his tax-collecting bench to follow Jesus as one of the original twelve disciples. The first part of his narrative can be seen as an offer of the Kingdom to the Jews (1:1–11:1), followed by the rejection and death of the King (11:2–27). The book concludes with the resurrection of the King and the commission of his apostles, who are to spread his Kingdom throughout the world (chapter 28).

60 † LUKE WRITES HIS GOSPEL

In his Gospel account, Luke the physician presents Jesus as the Son of Man who has come to seek and save the lost. Luke was probably a Gentile who traveled and ministered with Paul during his third missionary journey. Written in about 60, his Gospel's stated purpose was to present an accurate account of the events of Jesus' life for a certain "Theophilus." The first part of Luke addresses lineage

6	17	43	50
Judea becomes Roman province	Earthquake destroys much of Ephesus	London founded	Pyramid built in Teotihuacán, Mexico

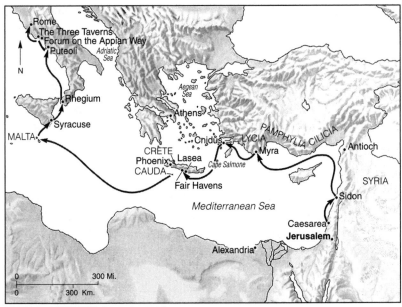

PAUL'S JOURNEY TO ROME (ACTS 21:17—28:31)

and Jesus' early life (1:1–4:13). The next section presents Jesus' ministry as the Son of Man (4:14–9:50). The third part describes the rejection of the Son of Man (9:51–19:27), which leads to a narrative of Jesus' crucifixion and subsequent resurrection and exaltation (19:28–24).

60 ✝ PAUL'S FIRST ROMAN IMPRISONMENT BEGINS

After Paul was arrested in Jerusalem and brought to Caesarea, he stood trial before the Roman governor Felix, but was neither condemned nor released. After two years, Felix was called to Rome and replaced by Festus. With his Jewish accusers pressuring the new governor to convict him, Paul used his right as a Roman citizen to appeal directly to Caesar. He was soon aboard a ship bound for Rome. After sailing to Myra on the southwestern coast of modern Turkey, the ship set out to winter in a harbor at Phoenix on the island of Crete. However, the sailors were caught in a terrible storm for two weeks and shipwrecked on the island of Malta. After wintering there, Paul boarded another Roman ship, arriv-

54	58	79	81–96
Claudius assassinated, succeeded by Nero	Buddhism introduced into China	Mount Vesuvius erupts, covering Pompeii	Emperor Domitian reigns

ing in Rome in 60 without further incident. Under house arrest in Rome for two years, Paul wrote his "prison epistles" of Ephesians, Philippians, Colossians, and Philemon (Acts 25:1–28:31).

60 ✝ PAUL WRITES EPHESIANS

While under house arrest in Rome, beginning in 60, Paul composed several epistles to the various churches he had started and strengthened. The Epistle to the Ephesians is the first of these letters. This letter, which may have been intended to circulate among a number of Asian churches, presents the believer's position in Christ (chapters 1–3) followed by the implications and responsibilities of this position (chapters 4–6). The first part of the book recounts all that believers have been given in Christ, as well as the purpose behind this bestowal, which is to praise God's glorious grace. The book's second part calls the believer to respond rightly to this gift of grace in all areas of life, a response that in turn points back to the glory of God.

60 ✝ PAUL WRITES COLOSSIANS AND PHILEMON

Soon after completing his epistle to the Ephesians, Paul wrote two epistles to the church in Colossae in approximately 60. The first one, known as Colossians, is a testimony to the centrality and supremacy of Christ over his church. The first section of the book deals primarily with Christ's supremacy over creation (chapters 1–2). The second section expounds the implications of his supremacy in the lives of believers (chapters 3–4). The other letter was an appeal to Philemon, a believer in Colossae, to forgive and accept his runaway slave Onesimus. Apparently after escaping from Colossae, Onesimus had traveled to Rome. There he encountered Paul and became a believer. Paul sent Onesimus back to Philemon so that the two could be reconciled as Christian brothers. The book is essentially an application of the principal that forgiven sinners ought to forgive others.

62 ✝ PAUL WRITES PHILIPPIANS

Paul wrote the book of Philippians near the end of his first Roman imprisonment, probably in 62. The Philippian church had helped Paul while he was in prison, so he wrote to thank them for their generosity. Since there was some level of disunity

6	17	43	50
Judea becomes Roman province	Earthquake destroys much of Ephesus	London founded	Pyramid built in Teotihuacán, Mexico

within the Philippian church, he includes an exhortation for those believers to be joyfully united in Christ. After his introduction and thanksgiving for them (chapter 1), Paul addressed their lack of unity by encouraging them to have the mind of Christ (chapter 2), true knowledge of Christ (chapter 3), and the peace of Christ (chapter 4). Paul illustrates the truth and outcome of these three components in his own life, showing how joyful unity in the body of Christ results as these elements are manifested.

62 ✝ LUKE WRITES ACTS

Luke the physician was the author of the New Testament book of Acts. Acts is the second volume that Luke wrote to a man named Theophilus, the first being Luke's Gospel. He met Paul in Troas, the westernmost city on the Mediterranean coast of present-day Turkey. Luke accompanied Paul on some of his missionary journeys, a fact that's identifiable by his use of the pronoun *we* in some sections of Acts. The book's purpose is to present a condensed history of the early church, as seen by an eyewitness to the gospel's rapid spread from Jerusalem to Rome. It also provides an accurate picture of how the early church functioned. Luke probably wrote Acts in 62, shortly after the events described in the book's final chapter.

62 ✝ HIGH PRIEST MARTYRS JAMES, THE LORD'S BROTHER

After the martyrdom of Stephen and the subsequent scattering of the church, Jesus' brother James served as the leader of the remaining church in Jerusalem. James, along with Christ's other brothers, had converted to Christianity after the Resurrection. He appears as a leading figure in Acts, meeting with Paul soon after his conversion, presiding over the Jerusalem council, and counseling Paul about dealing with hostile Jewish elements. James, who was called "the Just," authored the book of James. In about 62, James was beaten and thrown to his death from the roof of the Temple by order of the high priest (Acts 12:17; 15:1-30; 21:18-25).

62 ✝ PAUL WRITES 1 TIMOTHY

Paul wrote the letter we know as 1 Timothy after he was released from his first imprisonment in Rome (probably in 62). The recipient was his beloved disciple Timothy, for whom the book is named. As one of Paul's traveling companions,

54	58	79	81–96
Claudius assassinated, succeeded by Nero	Buddhism introduced into China	Mount Vesuvius erupts, covering Pompeii	Emperor Domitian reigns

Timothy went to various churches to encourage them in their faith. At the time this letter was written to him, Timothy was in Ephesus confronting false teachers who were corrupting the doctrine Paul had taught them. Paul wrote this letter to Timothy both to instruct him in how to lead and govern the church, and to encourage him as he confronted false teaching.

63 ✝ HEBREWS IS WRITTEN

Although the King James Version lists the Epistle to the Hebrews as "The Epistle of Paul the Apostle to the Hebrews," the author of this letter remains unknown. However, early church references to Hebrews and its allusions to the sacrificial system imply that this book most likely was written around 63, prior to the destruction of the Temple in 70. Its early date and clear connections to apostolic sources help to establish the canonicity of Hebrews. The main theme of Hebrews is the superiority and majesty of Jesus Christ. By comparing him to angels (chapters 1–2), Moses (chapters 3–4), and the Aaronic priesthood (chapters 5–10), the author demonstrates Jesus' superiority over the old covenant law. With this in mind, the writer exhorts his audience to cling to the new covenant for salvation through Christ and not to fall back into reliance on the old covenant (chapters 10–13).

63 ✝ PETER WRITES HIS FIRST EPISTLE

The first epistle of Peter is centered on the believer's hope in the promises of God despite suffering. Peter likely was writing to a group of believers in the northern provinces of Asia Minor. Although official Roman persecution of the church had not yet begun at the time this epistle was composed (in 63), localized persecutions of Christians were not uncommon. In this context of suffering Peter exhorts his audience to hope in the salvation they have been promised (1:1–2:12) so that they are able to submit to human authorities (2:13–3:12) and are willing to suffer with Christ (3:13–5:14).

64 ✝ PETER WRITES HIS SECOND EPISTLE

Peter's goal for his second epistle, written from Rome in about 64, was to warn readers about false teachers who would infiltrate the church and to encourage

6	17	43	50
Judea becomes Roman province	Earthquake destroys much of Ephesus	London founded	Pyramid built in Teotihuacán, Mexico

Christians to persevere in the hope of Christ's return. He begins the letter with an encouragement toward Christian maturity (chapter 1). A warning about the character and doctrine of the false teachers follows (chapter 2), and Peter closes the book with an exhortation not to let those teachers sway his audience from their hope in the glorious return of Christ (chapter 3).

64 ✝ FIRE RAVAGES ROME

On the night of July 19, 64, during the reign of Nero (r. 54–68), a disastrous fire broke out in Rome that lasted for six days and destroyed more than half of the city. In response to allegations that he had started the fire to free up space for his megalomaniacal building plans, Nero blamed the Roman Christians, launching the first systematic persecution of Christians in the Roman Empire. They were arrested in great numbers and subjugated to unspeakable atrocities. As reported by the Roman historian Tacitus (55–120), "Some were covered with the skins of wild animals and then torn apart by dogs, some were crucified, some were burned as torches to provide light."

65 ✝ PETER IS MARTYRED

Peter's ministry is difficult to trace after the end of Acts. However, his first epistle most likely was written from Rome. When Peter sends greetings from Babylon in 1 Peter 5:13, *Babylon* is a code word for Rome. Peter indicates that he was in Rome with Mark and had been a source for the writing of Mark's gospel. According to 1 Clement, a letter written around 96 by Bishop Clement (d. 100) in Rome, Peter was martyred by Nero (37–68) in Rome during the persecution of Christians, following the 64 fire in the city.

66 ✝ PAUL WRITES TITUS

The apostle Paul wrote the book of Titus in about 66, between his two imprisonments in Rome. He sent this letter to his trusted companion, Titus. Paul left Titus behind on the island of Crete to look after the church they had planted there. The letter's purpose was to give Titus the qualifications for elders (1:6-9), to warn about false teachers (1:10-16), and to summarize Christian doctrine (chapters 2–3).

54	58	79	81–96
Claudius assassinated, succeeded by Nero	Buddhism introduced into China	Mount Vesuvius erupts, covering Pompeii	Emperor Domitian reigns

66 ✡ A JEWISH REVOLT BEGINS IN JERUSALEM

A Roman official triggered a Jewish revolt in 66, when he stole money from the Temple treasury in Jerusalem. Fighting broke out in the city, and soon a full-scale rebellion raged against Rome. Jewish extremists took control of Jerusalem and massacred the Romans there. The Roman governor in Syria assembled an army and attempted to storm Jerusalem. His plans were thwarted, so he ordered a retreat that developed into a rout. The revolt lasted three more years.

66–67 ✝ CHRISTIANS IN JERUSALEM ESCAPE TO PELLA

When the Jewish revolt against Rome began in 66, there were thousands of Jewish Christians in Jerusalem (Acts 21:20). Eusebius (265–339), the church historian, reported that during the war, "The whole body of the church at Jerusalem, having been commanded by a divine revelation, given to men of approved piety there before the war, removed from the city, and dwelt at a certain town beyond the Jordan, called Pella." The "divine revelation" no doubt was the Gospel of Luke, which records Jesus saying to his disciples, "When you see Jerusalem surrounded by armies, then you will know that the time of its destruction has arrived. Then those in Judea must flee to the hills. Let those in Jerusalem escape" (Luke 21:20-21). Most likely in the winter of 66–67, the Christians in Jerusalem took Jesus at his word and escaped the city's destruction.

67 ✝ PAUL IS ARRESTED AND BROUGHT TO ROME AGAIN

Paul apparently was released from his first imprisonment in Rome in approximately March of 62. It seems that he, after several years of traveling, went to Greece (2 Timothy 4:20) and possibly was arrested when the emperor Nero (37–68) was there in the fall of 67. Paul once again was imprisoned in Rome (2 Timothy 1:8; 2:9), where he wrote his second letter to Timothy.

67 ✝ PAUL WRITES 2 TIMOTHY

Paul wrote this letter to Timothy, his son in the faith, in 67 during his second Roman imprisonment. Knowing that his own death was near, Paul shared his concern for Timothy (1:5-14), described his own situation (1:15-18), exhorted Timothy to endure and to avoid foolish controversies (chapter 2), warned him

6	17	43	50
Judea becomes Roman province	Earthquake destroys much of Ephesus	London founded	Pyramid built in Teotihuacán, Mexico

regarding the last days (chapter 3), and ended the letter by charging Timothy to preach the Word (chapter 4).

68 ✝ PAUL IS MARTYRED

Imprisoned in Rome for a second time by Emperor Nero (37–68), Paul was chained in a cold dungeon like a common criminal. From this Roman prison, Paul wrote his final letter to Timothy. Paul probably was beheaded with a sword, the typical method of execution in 68 for a Roman citizen.

70 ✡ JERUSALEM AND THE TEMPLE ARE DESTROYED

In 66, Jewish zealots led an uprising against Roman rule and successfully drove the Roman army out of Jerusalem. But the peace did not last. The emperor Nero (37–68) sent Vespasian (9–79) to quell the revolt. Accompanied by his son Titus (41–81), Vespasian conquered Galilee in 67. The next year, as Vespasian marched toward Jerusalem, he learned of Nero's death and withdrew to Caesarea. In 69, Vespasian allowed himself to be proclaimed emperor and turned the war over to Titus. Titus conquered almost all of Judea and laid siege against Jerusalem for 143 days before finally breaking through the walls and decimating the city and the Temple. The conquest was completed on September 2, 70, thus fulfilling the prophecy Jesus made to his disciples before his crucifixion that the Temple in Jerusalem would be so completely destroyed that not one stone would be left on another (Matthew 24:2).

73 ✡ MASADA FALLS

After the fall of Jerusalem in 70, the remaining Jewish soldiers fled with their wives and children to the rock fortress on the mountain of Masada, which is in the desert near the Dead Sea. Some 960 men, women, and children found refuge there. Although they had few sources of food and water, they repelled the Roman army for three years. However, in 73, as the Roman army scaled a ramp that they had built on the side of the mountain, the Jews knew they could no longer fend off the enemy. As the fortress burned around them and their attackers were on the brink of breaking through the barricades, the Jews committed mass suicide rather than face punishment and enslavement under the Romans.

54	58	79	81–96
Claudius assassinated, succeeded by Nero	Buddhism introduced into China	Mount Vesuvius erupts, covering Pompeii	Emperor Domitian reigns

81 ✝ DOMITIAN BECOMES CAESAR

General Titus (41–81) succeeded his father, Vespasian (9–79), as the Roman emperor in 79. However, Titus's reign was short-lived, and his brother Domitian (51–96) succeeded him in 81. The early years of Domitian's reign were prosperous, and he was well liked. However, in 87, he began to demand that he be worshiped as lord and god. Christians were unwilling to submit to this decree. As a result, the emperor instituted a great persecution against the church. John's exile to the island of Patmos, where he wrote Revelation, was part of this persecution. Domitian's later conduct became increasingly erratic, and a group led by his wife assassinated him in 96.

90 ✝ THE RISE OF GNOSTICISM BEGINS

In the last part of the first century, a group of false teachers arose in the Christian church who taught that salvation comes through a secret knowledge (*gnosis*). The early church fathers claimed that this teaching originated with Simon Magus, who is mentioned in Acts 8. These "Gnostics," as they came to be known, taught a form of dualism in which spirit is good and material is evil. As a result, Gnostics denied Jesus' humanity. Their understanding of the material world caused them to become either extreme ascetics in order to avoid corruption by matter or extreme hedonists who thought that what happens in the physical world is irrelevant. Some of the later New Testament books— Colossians, 1 and 2 Timothy, Titus, 2 Peter, and 1, 2, and 3 John—combat the earliest forms of Gnosticism.

95 ✝ JOHN WRITES THE BOOK OF REVELATION

As part of Emperor Domitian's (51–96) persecution of the church, the apostle John was exiled to the tiny island of Patmos in the Mediterranean Sea. There, in about 95, he received four visions that he described in the book of Revelation (1:9–3:22; 4:1–16:21; 17:1–21:8 and 21:9–22:17). In the first vision (1:9–3:22), the glorified Son of God sends letters to seven churches in Asia Minor, revealing the blessings that will come to them if they are faithful, and the judgments that will come if they are unfaithful. The rest of the book (visions 2–4) spells out the details of these blessings and judgments.

6	17	43	50
Judea becomes Roman province	Earthquake destroys much of Ephesus	London founded	Pyramid built in Teotihuacán, Mexico

EXILED TO PATMOS

September 18, AD 96

What was the apostle John doing on the island of Patmos?

He was there because of a man named Domitian. Domitian was the second son of Vespasian, who commanded the Roman army sent in February, AD 67, to put down the rebellion in Judea. Vespasian's army was so successful that by June, AD 68, only Jerusalem was left to be conquered. Then on June 9, Emperor Nero committed suicide, and Vespasian halted military operations to see what would happen next in Rome.

The following year, 69, was a year of civil war with a succession of four Caesars. Galba succeeded Nero and then was followed by Otho, Vitellius, and finally Vespasian. Vespasian turned the war against the Jews over to his oldest son, Titus, and concentrated his energy on defeating Vitellius. To stem the revolt of Vespasian's legions, Vitellius tried to take Domitian hostage. However, after two daring escapes, Domitian was able to reach his father's legions. After the death of Vitellius in December, the Roman Senate proclaimed Vespasian as Caesar, and Domitian returned in triumph to Rome.

Vespasian did not come to Rome for ten months, and during that time nineteen-year-old Domitian got a taste of ruling the empire. However, he became embroiled in arguments with a representative of his father, and exercising power became a frustrating experience.

During Vespasian's reign, Domitian was given only minor roles, while his older brother Titus functioned as his father's heir apparent. When Vespasian died in 79, Titus succeeded him. Since Titus was only forty at the time, Domitian again received no positions of authority, as it was assumed that Titus would rule for years to come. However, Titus suddenly died only two years later and Domitian became Caesar. As Caesar, Domitian was autocratic and cruel. He declared himself "lord and god" and demanded to be worshiped. Those refusing to acknowledge his deity were persecuted.

Domitian persecuted all classes of Christians: Roman citizens and noncitizens, male and female, slave and free. It was as part of this persecution that the apostle John, who had been living at Ephesus, was exiled to the island of Patmos. John tells us, "In Jesus we are partners in suffering and in the Kingdom and in patient endurance. I was exiled to the island of Patmos for preaching the word of God and speaking about Jesus" (Revelation 1:9).

In the Roman Empire, prisoners were commonly exiled to islands, and in John's case it was to Patmos, a desolate volanic island ten miles long and six miles wide, thirty-seven miles off the coast of Asia Minor.

In his later years, Domitian's behavior became so intolerable as to drive other pagans, including his wife, to plot a conspiracy against him. He was assassinated on September 18, 96, a few weeks before his forty-fifth birthday.

Nerva, the next caesar, proclaimed a recall of all of Domitian's exiles in 96, and John returned to Ephesus.

95 ✝ JOHN WRITES HIS GOSPEL

John, the son of Zebedee and brother of James, wrote the last of the four Gospels in about 95. His audience was not limited to one nation or people. Rather, he presents Jesus as the Savior and Lord of all nations of the world. John clearly states that his purpose in writing was to persuade his audience that Jesus is the Son of God and that, by believing, they would have life in Christ (20:31). The first part of the book consists of seven signs Jesus performed to prove his deity (chapters 1–12). The second section deals almost exclusively with Christ's final instructions to his disciples (chapters 13–17). The last section is a narrative of the crucifixion and resurrection of Jesus (chapters 18–21).

6	17	43	50
Judea becomes Roman province	Earthquake destroys much of Ephesus	London founded	Pyramid built in Teotihuacán, Mexico

THE ERA OF CATHOLIC CHRISTIANITY

100–312

Catholic Christianity spread rapidly throughout the Mediterranean world. It confronted the alien ideas of Gnosticism, Marcionism, and Montanism and addressed the lies by appealing to the apostolic writings and to the orthodox bishops who guarded them. At the same time, Christians faced the persecuting power of Rome and dared to die heroically as martyrs, becoming examples to other believers to follow in their train. This seed of martyr's blood, as Tertullian called it, eventually bore abundant fruit in the conversion of the Empire.

BRUCE L. SHELLEY

110 ✝ IGNATIUS OF ANTIOCH IS MARTYRED

Ignatius (50–110) was bishop of Antioch and is known for the seven letters he wrote to the churches at Philadelphia, Smyrna, Ephesus, Tralles, Magnesia, Rome, and to Polycarp (69–155), the bishop of Smyrna. He wrote these letters under armed guard on his way to be martyred in Rome. The letter to the church in Rome urges them to refrain from intervening with the authorities to prevent his martyrdom. His letters show a strong commitment to Jesus Christ and to Jesus' physical birth, death, and resurrection, although Ignatius did not clearly understand grace and forgiveness. Ignatius was the first person aside from the New Testament writers to write of Jesus' virgin birth.

110 ✝ PERSECUTION BEGINS UNDER EMPEROR TRAJAN

Trajan (53–117) was the son of the Roman governor of Asia and Syria. Proclaimed emperor in 98, he became the most militarily ambitious Roman ruler of all time. The first organized persecution of Christians by the Roman government began about 110 in Asia Minor. There in 112, Governor Pliny the Younger (61–112) wrote to Emperor Trajan regarding the "contagion of this superstition" of Christianity that was spreading both in cities and rural areas. Pliny reported that whenever he was informed of a Christian he would bring the person before his tribunal. If that person admitted to being a Christian, he or she would be put to death. Trajan replied to Pliny that he was following the proper procedure and added that Christians should not be sought out, but if reported they should be punished unless they recanted and worshiped the Roman gods.

115–117 ✡ JEWS REVOLT IN EGYPT

The Jewish position in Egypt deteriorated under the Roman Empire's rule. After rioting in 41 and 66, they instigated a final rebellion from 115 to 117 during the reign of Emperor Trajan (53–117). This uprising took place not only in Egypt but also in Cyrene (in modern-day Libya) and on Cyprus. The Roman response was the violent suppression of the Alexandrian Jews and the destruction of their historic synagogue. As a result, the Jewish community of Alexandria that had been one of the largest outside of Israel went into permanent decline.

105	118–25	150	161–80
Paper invented in China	Pantheon built in Rome	Earliest Sanskrit inscribed in India	Emperor Marcus Aurelius reigns

132–135 ✡ BAR KOKHBA REVOLTS

In the early second century, the harsh Roman occupation of Palestine led to a second Judean war. The immediate cause was Emperor Hadrian's (76–137) plan to rebuild Jerusalem, making it a Roman city dedicated to Jupiter. This was too much for the Jews. The revolt began in 132, led by Simon ben Kosiba (d. 135), popularly known as Bar Kokhba, "son of the star." Bar Kokhba assumed the role of an ancient Judean king, but neither his personal popularity nor the support of the rabbis was enough to bring victory. He was killed in 135, and his troops were completely decimated. Rome's revenge was swift. The entire Jewish population of Judea was deported and replaced with Gentiles. The province's name was changed from Judea to Syria-Palestine. The revolt was one of the darkest times in Jewish history.

144 ✝ MARCION IS EXCOMMUNICATED

Marcion (75–155), a prominent ship owner from Pontus in Asia Minor, was excommunicated from the church for immorality. He then developed his own unique theology and gained a large following that became a major threat to orthodox Christianity. He established churches throughout the empire, and his views remained influential for nearly two centuries. In Marcion's theology, the God of the Old Testament and the God of the New Testament were completely separate beings. The God of the Old Testament created the world and the evil in it, and his religion revolved around law. In contrast, the God of the New Testament was the true God, the Father of Jesus, and a God of love and grace. Marcion's canon consisted of only ten epistles of Paul and an edited version of Luke. In reaction to Marcion, orthodox Christianity was forced to define the true canon of Scripture.

150 ✝ EASTER CONTROVERSY BEGINS

The date of Easter became a major controversy in the early church. The first discussion of the question occurred about 150 when Polycarp (69–155), bishop of Smyrna, visited the bishop of Rome. Christians in Asia Minor (modern-day Turkey) wanted the Lord's Supper on the same day as the Jewish Passover, with Easter being celebrated two days later, regardless of day of the week. On the other hand, the Roman church believed that Easter should always fall on

Sunday. Twenty years later, the same argument broke out in Laodicea. The controversy came to a head throughout the Christian world between 190 and 194, and was the subject of discussion at many synods. Rome's position finally prevailed and was officially adopted by the Council of Nicea in 325.

150 ✝ JUSTIN BECOMES ONE OF CHRISTIANITY'S FIRST APOLOGISTS

Born to Greek parents in Palestine, Justin (100–165) was converted through contact with an old Christian man who used Old Testament prophecies to convince him of the truth of Christianity. Already an educated philosopher, Justin became a devoted Christian. For the remaining thirty or so years of his life, he traveled, wrote, and evangelized. He became one of the first Christian apologists, explaining Christianity as a reasonable system. For Justin, all truth was God's truth, and he incorporated Greek thought with Jewish prophecy, presenting Christ as the fulfillment of the Hebrew tradition. In his greatest work, his first Apology (his second may not be genuine), he addressed the emperor in a defense of the faith. At Justin's martyrdom in 165, he demonstrated the conviction he had written earlier: "You can kill us, but cannot do us any real harm."

156 ✝ POLYCARP IS MARTYRED

Born in a Christian home, Polycarp (69–155) appears to have been a disciple of the apostle John and to have met other eyewitnesses of Jesus as well. He served the church as bishop of Smyrna. On a trip to Rome, Polycarp met Marcion (75–155), whom he referred to as "firstborn of Satan." At the end of his life when the civil authorities demanded that he deny his faith, Polycarp's response was, "I have served Christ eighty-five years. How can I blaspheme my King? I am a Christian." At his martyrdom he reportedly was miraculously untouched by the flames, so he was killed with a dagger and his body burned. His followers collected his bones as relics.

172 ✝ THE MONTANIST MOVEMENT BEGINS

In 155, the pagan priest Montanus was converted to Christianity. He began prophesying that Jesus and the New Jerusalem would come soon to Pepuza, a

105	118–25	150	161–80
Paper invented in China	Pantheon built in Rome	Earliest Sanskrit inscribed in India	Emperor Marcus Aurelius reigns

city in Asia Minor. The precursor of these events was to be a unique outpouring of the Holy Spirit. Considering his followers to be an elite group of Christians, Montanus instructed them to withdraw from the world. He called for special days of fasting and warned of coming persecution, which would fit the church for Christ's return. During this time two of his prophetesses, Prisca and Maximilla, gave what were considered new revelations from God supplanting Scripture. The most famous convert to Montanism was Tertullian (160–225). The church of Rome initially looked favorably on Montanism but then turned against it. The movement then was forced underground, and it dissipated following Tertullian's death.

175 ✝ MELITO, BISHOP OF SARDIS, PETITIONS THE EMPEROR

Melito was the bishop of Sardis during the reign of Emperor Marcus Aurelius (160–180). At a time when being a Christian was a crime against the state, Melito wrote a petition to the emperor begging him to examine the charges that were being made against those who believed in Christ. Melito proposed to the emperor that Christianity be made the religion of the empire, since church and state were complementary works of God for mankind's benefit. There is no evidence of a response from the emperor. Melito's many visits to historic Christian sites earned him the distinction of the first known Christian pilgrim. Melito also was the first Christian writer to list the books of the Old Testament, distinguishing them from the Apocrypha.

177 ✝ IRENAEUS BECOMES BISHOP OF LYONS

Irenaeus (flourished 175–195), the bishop of Lyons, France, grew up in Asia Minor. He was a disciple of Polycarp (69–155) and therefore a spiritual grandson to the apostle John. He moved to Lyons where he became an elder (presbyter) in the church. When the bishop of Lyons died in the persecution of 177, Irenaeus succeeded him. His diocese included not only all of Gaul (modern-day France) but extended to Vienna as well. His major literary work, *Against Heresies*, refuted Gnosticism and Marcionism. Irenaeus followed Paul more closely than did the apostolic fathers after him. Theologically biblical rather than philosophical, he was the first theologian who wrote for the church. Above all he saw himself as a shepherd of God's flock.

164	220	238	300s
Oldest Mayan monuments erected	Chinese Han Dynasty ends	Goths begin invading Roman Empire	Villages appear in North America

190 ✝ CLEMENT OF ALEXANDRIA BECOMES HEAD OF CATECHETICAL SCHOOL

Clement (155–220), the first known Christian scholar, was an Athenian by birth. He traveled to the centers of learning in the eastern Roman Empire searching for a teacher to instruct him in the Christian faith. He found Pantaenus (d. 190), the founder of a school in Alexandria, Egypt. In about 190 Clement succeeded Pantaenus as head of the school, which became the official catechetical school of Alexandria. While in this post, Clement wrote three books that have survived. Clement adopted an allegorical method of interpreting the Bible, using Greek philosophy as a means of understanding Scripture. He taught Origen, who became the early theologian of the Eastern Church. Clement was forced to flee Alexandria in 202 during the persecution under Emperor Septimius Severus (145–211).

196 ✝ TERTULLIAN BEGINS TO WRITE

Tertullian (160–225), a lifelong resident of Carthage, North Africa, was educated in literature, rhetoric, and law. He was converted to Christ around age forty and soon became a leading teacher in the church of Carthage. Tertullian began to write soon after his conversion, and thirty-one of his writings have been preserved. He was one of the first to articulate the doctrine of the Trinity, stating that God is one substance and yet three persons. Tertullian's writings demonstrate his legal mind. He sought for perfect order and opposed all moral laxity in the church. Phrases such as "The blood of the martyrs is the seed of the church" and "What has Athens to do with Jerusalem?" come from his works. In about 206, Tertullian left the church to become a Montanist; yet, in his writings he continued to defend orthodox theology.

200 ✡ JUDAH THE PATRIARCH COMPILES THE MISHNAH

Following the defeat of Bar Kokhba (d. 135), an assembly of rabbis convened in Galilee and was named the "Sanhedrin" after the body by the same name that had ruled the Jews prior to the destruction of the Temple. The Sanhedrin's leader was called the patriarch. This council's goal was to make rabbinic Judaism the norm for succeeding ages. A major step in this process occurred in about 200 when Judah the Patriarch (135–220) compiled the Mishnah, a record

105	118–25	150	161–80
Paper invented in China	Pantheon built in Rome	Earliest Sanskrit inscribed in India	Emperor Marcus Aurelius reigns

of the rabbis' discussion regarding proper interpretation and application of the Mosaic law. The Mishnah is a collection of oral laws, traditions, and explanations of Scripture by Jewish teachers from as early as 300 BC. It was written in Hebrew and formed the core of the Talmud.

202 ✝ PERSECUTION BEGINS UNDER SEPTIMIUS SEVERUS

Septimius Severus (145–211), a man of African descent, was Roman emperor from 193–211. In 202, he enacted a law forbidding new conversions to Christianity. His motive was to unite all religions in worship of the sun. All gods could be accepted as long as their adherents acknowledged that the sun god was supreme. The law produced violent persecution, especially in Egypt and North Africa. As consequences of this law, Origen's father was beheaded in Alexandria and a young woman named Perpetua (d. 203), along with her fellow Christians, was killed by wild beasts at a public festival in Carthage. Many more unnamed believers also received their martyr's crown during this persecution.

205 ✝ ORIGEN BEGINS TO WRITE

Origen (185–254), considered the greatest scholar of his age, was born in a Christian family in Alexandria, Egypt. After her husband, Origen's father, was martyred in 202, Origen's mother hid her son's clothes to prevent him from turning himself in to the authorities to be martyred as well.

Origen was a prodigious scholar and lived an ascetic life, allowing himself only one coat but no shoes. A prolific writer, Origen authored more than two thousand works, including commentaries on almost every book of the Bible. His book *On First Principles* was the first systematic theology written. Origen was primarily responsible for making allegorical interpretation of the Bible the standard hermeneutic from his time through the Middle Ages. Because he included many concepts from Plato in his teaching, he is considered a father of both orthodoxy and heresy.

212 ✡ JEWS ARE GRANTED ROMAN CITIZENSHIP

Under the Sanhedrin's leadership, the Jews of Palestine were able to work out a way to be accepted by the Roman Empire. They were treated as other small

164	220	238	300s
Oldest Mayan monuments erected	Chinese Han Dynasty ends	Goths begin invading Roman Empire	Villages appear in North America

nations of the empire, except that Jews were excused from pagan observances. In 212, Emperor Carcalla (188–217) granted Roman citizenship to the Jews as well as to the other small nations of the empire. Yet in spite of peaceful relations with Rome, Palestine was impoverished, and the population declined as a result.

217 ✠ HIPPOLYTUS BECOMES FIRST ANTIPOPE

Hippolytus (160–236) was a presbyter and teacher in the church of Rome. Although he was that church's most important theologian in the third century, he was passed over for bishop in favor of a deacon named Callistus (d. 222), who served in that position from 217 to 222. Believing Callistus to be too lax on the issue of absolution for mortal sins, Hippolytus withdrew from the church with a few followers and claimed that he was the true bishop of Rome, thus becoming history's first antipope. He continued attacks on the succeeding bishops of Rome: Urban I (222–230) and Pontianus (230–235). Then as part of Christian persecution under Emperor Maximin (235–238), Hippolytus and Pontianus were exiled together to Sardinia where they came to agreement over their differences. Both resigned their positions, and their successor, Anterus (235–236), ended the schism.

219 ✡ RAV ARRIVES IN BABYLON

Through the second century the Jews of Babylon looked to the rabbis of Palestine for guidance, because the Sanhedrin patriarch in Palestine was considered to be the final authority in religious matters. Although many Palestinian rabbis had come to Babylon following the Bar Kokhba rebellion, Babylon did not become a center for Jewish scholarship until the arrival of Abba Arika (popularly called Rav) (d. 247) in 219. A Palestinian rabbi and disciple of Judah the Patriarch (135–220), Rav introduced Babylonian Jews to the Mishnah. Rav founded an academy at Sura, while Samuel Yarhinaa'ah (165–257), a wealthy Babylonian scholar, established one at Nehardea that relocated to Pumbeditha. These two schools became rivals to the declining Palestinian ones. They survived until the eleventh century as centers of Jewish scholarship.

220 ✠ CARTHAGE BECOMES NORTH AFRICAN CENTER FOR CHRISTIANITY

Carthage, on the northernmost coast of modern-day Algeria, became the Christian center for North Africa. In the West, Carthage's influence was second only to

Rome. Around 220, the first church council was held in Carthage and was composed of seventy African and Numidean bishops. By the time Cyprian became bishop in 248, the Carthage church was the largest in Africa. Church councils continued to be held in Carthage as late as 646.

232 ✝ EARLIEST KNOWN CHURCH IS BUILT

Early Christians worshiped in homes, some of which were eventually adapted to serve as church buildings. In Dura-Europos, Syria, such a house was excavated, dating from 232. A single entrance in the north wall opened into a vestibule and from there into a courtyard with a portico on the east side. In the northwest corner of the building a room with a cistern served as a baptistry. Two rooms on the house's south side had been combined into one with a small platform serving as an altar. A small room off of this larger room may have been used for the preparation of the Lord's Supper, and a room on the west side of the courtyard may have been used for instructing catechumens, believers being taught the basics of Christianity. Buildings such as this were the forerunners of every place of worship from one-room churches to cathedrals.

240 ✝ MANI PREACHES MANICHAEISM

Mani (216–276) grew up in southern Babylonia in an aristocratic Parthian family. Revelations he received at ages twelve and twenty-four led him in 240 to proclaim the truth he felt he had received. His teaching, called Manichaeism, presupposed a primal conflict between light and darkness. He taught that religious practice was to free particles of light, which Satan had stolen from the world of light and had imprisoned in the brain of man. Jesus, Buddha, the prophets, and Mani himself had been sent to aid in this process. Manichaeism spread throughout the Roman Empire and as far as China, becoming a major rival to Christianity in many regions. Mani himself was imprisoned in Persia by a competing religious group known as Zoroastrians, and in about 276 was skinned alive.

250 ✝ DECIUS PERSECUTES CHRISTIANS

Decius (190–251), a native of Pannonia (modern-day Hungary), was first proclaimed emperor by the Roman army. After the death of Emperor Philip in 249,

164	220	238	300s
Oldest Mayan monuments erected	Chinese Han Dynasty ends	Goths begin invading Roman Empire	Villages appear in North America

the Senate accepted him as the new emperor. Being a staunch defender of Roman traditions, Decius believed that the restoration of state cults was necessary to preserve the empire. Therefore, he issued an imperial order that all citizens make a sacrifice to the emperor. As a result, Fabian, the bishop of Rome, was executed in January 250 for not making a sacrifice. Thousands of other deaths followed. Fortunately for the church, Decius died in battle the following year. But following the persecution, a major crisis arose in the church over how to deal with Christians who sacrificed but later repented.

251 ✝ THE COUNCIL OF CARTHAGE MEETS

Between 249 and 251, during Emperor Decius's (201–251) persecution of the church, many professing Christians recanted their faith while under pressure from Roman authorities. However, the persecution abated when Decius was killed in battle. The church then was left with the problem of how to deal with the multitudes who had denied their faith but now desired readmittance to the church. In response to this, Cyprian (200–258), the bishop of the North African city of Carthage (in modern-day Tunisia), called a church council in 251. The Council of Carthage ruled that after a lengthy period of repentance and penance, the lapsed believers could be readmitted to the church. However, the stringent requirements of this decision were eased by later councils.

251 ✝ CYPRIAN WRITES ABOUT CHURCH UNITY

Born into a wealthy family in Carthage, North Africa, Cyprian (200–258) was converted to Christ in 246. Two years later he was installed as bishop of the church of Carthage, the largest in Africa. During a period of persecution under Emperor Decius (250–252), Cyprian continued his duties of bishop from hiding. During his absence, the church readmitted Christians who formerly had agreed to sacrifice to the Roman gods. From exile Cyprian insisted that they instead perform severe penance. After Cyprian's return, the threat of a new persecution united the church. Cyprian's most important treatise, *On the Unity of the Church,* argued for the equality of all bishops, an argument contrary to the bishop of Rome's claim of authority over other bishops. Cyprian is known for his statement, "There is no salvation outside the church."

105	118–25	150	161–80
Paper invented in China	Pantheon built in Rome	Earliest Sanskrit inscribed in India	Emperor Marcus Aurelius reigns

SACRIFICE TO THE ROMAN GODS

| January 3, 250 |

"Deliver us, Lord Jupiter!" shouted Trajanus Decius, emperor of Rome, as stones and arrows showered around him. "Deliver us, Lord Jupiter, for I have delivered all of Rome into your hands and the hands of our ancient gods!" cried the beleaguered monarch.

Decius's Roman troops gradually succumbed to the fatal blows of the barbarian Goths of King Kniva. Decius fell at last, one dark form among many, trampled underfoot by panic-stricken horses.

Decius had been emperor for just three years. Coming to power in a time when political turmoil threatened the Roman Empire, Decius sought to unite his subjects through forced submission to the ancient Roman gods. "Perhaps," he reasoned, "the gods will favor us once more, give us final victory over the pestilent Goths, and restore the glory of the Empire."

On January 3, 250, he published an imperial edict commanding all citizens of the empire to sacrifice to the Roman gods. Those who did so were given certificates as evidence of their compliance. Those who refused were imprisoned or executed.

Decius's edict initiated the first universal Roman persecution of the Christian church. Untold numbers of believers suffered the loss of family, freedom, and life itself. Among those martyred over the next two years were the bishops of Rome, Antioch, and Jerusalem.

When Decius died in battle against the Goths in June 251, the pogrom ended, but the lull revealed a spiritual war within the ranks of the Christian community itself.

Many believers had sacrificed to the gods to save their lives. Others had illegally obtained certificates without sacrificing. And now thousands of lapsed Christians begged to be received back into church fellowship.

A great controversy ensued. Some of those who had been imprisoned for their faith wrote letters of pardon to large numbers of those who had denied Christ. Some dishonest individuals produced amnesty papers in the name of dead martyrs.

Bishops were divided over how to treat the lapsed Christians. Some called for rigid excommunication. Some demanded a general amnesty. Eventually, they arrived at a consensus that those who had sacrificed to the gods should be readmitted to communion only when dying. Those who obtained a false Roman certificate but had not sacrificed to the gods could be readmitted upon repentance and penance. No forgiveness was to be offered to the unrepentant. However, bitter dissensions over the matter continued, with resulting schisms.

When another great persecution arose under Emperor Valerian in 257, a wider amnesty was offered to those who had defected during the days of Decius. This was not the sign of a weakened standard for Christian fidelity, but rather a gracious opportunity for the shunned to stand where once they had fallen. Many returned to the fold. Many, in turn, sacrificed their lives for Christ.

268–341 ✝ ANTIOCH COUNCILS MEET

Church councils meeting in Antioch, Syria, in 325, 330, and 341, played an important role in defining the nature of Christ. They influenced the decisions of the ecumenical church council of Chalcedon in 451. Facing accusations from the Alexandrian Church of Arianism—a heresy that denied the eternal existence of God the Son—the members of the Antioch councils took measures to distance themselves from Arius (d. 336) and his supporters. At the same time, they endeavored to highlight Christ's eternal equality with the Father. Later councils served to further distance the church from the Nestorian heresy, which split Jesus Christ into two distinct persons, one human and one divine; and the Monophysite heresy, which denied that Jesus had both divine and human natures.

270 ✝ ANTHONY LIVES AS A HERMIT

Regarded as the father of monasticism, Anthony (251–356) was born in Egypt, the son of wealthy parents. Shortly after his parents died, Anthony heard Matthew 19:21 read in church, "If you want to be perfect, go and sell all you have and give the money to the poor." In response, Anthony gave his property to the poor and initially placed himself under the supervision of an elderly Christian ascetic. Living on bread and water once a day and sleeping on bare ground in a tomb, he was besieged by demons. He eventually was the first Christian to withdraw to the desert, crossing the Nile to the East where he ultimately settled on a mountain near the Red Sea. Even there he was sought out by many would-be hermits. Anthony organized them into colonies, beginning the monastic movement.

303 ✝ MASS CONVERSION OF ARMENIA BEGINS

Armenia was a buffer nation between the Persian and Roman Empires. As a result, it had a turbulent history. The great missionary to Armenia was named Gregory the Illuminator (240–332). Gregory seems to have been of Armenian aristocracy and to have become a Christian while in exile in Cappadocia. Returning to Armenia, he converted his relative, King Tiridates III, to the Christian faith and baptized him on January 6, 303. When the nobles of Armenia followed their king in converting to the Christian faith, the general populace did as well. Many pagan priests were converted as well, with many of them entering

105	118–25	150	161–80
Paper invented in China	Pantheon built in Rome	Earliest Sanskrit inscribed in India	Emperor Marcus Aurelius reigns

THE GREAT PERSECUTION

February 23, 303

A reign that didn't end well.

When Diocletian became emperor of the Roman Empire in 284, Christians were encouraged because of rumors that his wife, Prisca, and daughter Valeria were believers. And, in fact, during the first nineteen years of his reign, Diocletian was relatively tolerant of the church. In civil affairs he had great organizational skills. To improve the management of the Roman Empire, he established his tetrarchy of two senior emperors called *augusti* (himself and Maximian) and two junior emperors called *caesares* (Galerius, his son-in-law, and Constantius Chlorus, the father of Constantine).

Gradually, life became more difficult for Christians. Deciding that religious unity would strengthen the empire, Diocletian published edicts in an attempt to guarantee the supremacy of the Roman state religion by eliminating Christianity.

On February 23, 303, the day of the Roman feast of Terminalia, Diocletian issued an edict that all copies of Scripture were to be burned, all churches destroyed and their property confiscated. Meetings for Christian worship were forbidden. The next day additional measures were announced: Christians who resisted no longer would have legal recourse and were to be deprived of all honors and public office. Thus the Great Persecution began, although it was not uniformly enforced by the four emperors. Many Christians first learned of the edicts as they watched their churches go up in smoke.

A third edict ordered the arrest of Christian clergy. This resulted in a state crisis, because the prisons filled and real criminals were crowded out. To deal with this problem, the next edict stated that Christian prisoners would be released if they made sacrifices to the Roman gods. The prison guards could compel them by any means possible to perform these sacrifices. In early 304, an edict was posted insisting that everyone in the Roman Empire—clergy and laity alike—sacrifice to the Roman gods. Every Christian was put in jeopardy.

In 305, Diocletian and Maximian abdicated in favor of Constantius and Galerius, effectively ending the persecution in the West since Constantius was not interested in enforcing the edicts. The persecution continued in the East until 311, when shortly before his death, Galerius relented and issued an edict of limited toleration, granting freedom of worship if Christians did not disturb the peace.

The years of the Great Persecution officially ended with a second edict of toleration, this time by Constantine in 313. The Edict of Milan was a great historical event for it granted religious liberty to Christians and pagans alike. Eusebius, the first church historian and a contemporary of these events, recorded the words of Constantine's edict: "We resolved . . . to grant both to the Christians and to all men freedom to follow the religion which they choose. . . . For by this means . . . the divine favor toward us which we have already experienced in many matters will continue sure through all time."

the Christian ministry. Gregory became bishop of the newly organized Armenian church. His son succeeded him as bishop and was present at the Council of Nicea in 325.

303 ✝ EMPEROR DIOCLETIAN PERSECUTES CHRISTIANS

Born in a humble family in Dalmatia (now part of Yugoslavia), Diocletian (245–313) was proclaimed emperor by the Roman Imperial Guard in 284 following the murder of Emperor Numerian. An able organizer, Diocletian established a new system of governance for the Roman Empire in which four rulers shared power. Believing that the old Roman religion would reinforce the unity of the empire, Diocletian issued four edicts in 303 which brought the most vicious of all persecutions upon the Christians of the empire. Diocletian ordered the army purged of all Christians, the destruction of church buildings, the prohibition of Christian worship, and the burning of Bibles. Bishops were arrested, imprisoned, tortured and in many cases killed. In addition, thousands of Christians were tortured and killed. The persecution continued even after the abdication of Diocletian in 305, until the Edict of Toleration in 311.

311 ✝ THE EDICT OF TOLERATION

The most vicious persecution of Christians in the Roman Empire began in 303 under Emperor Diocletian (245–313). When Diocletian abdicated his rule in the East, he was replaced by his son-in-law Galerius, who then intensified the effort to eradicate Christianity. On April 30, 311, while on his deathbed, Galerius—perhaps convinced that his fatal illness was God's judgment on him—issued the Edict of Toleration, which pardoned Christians and allowed them to resume practicing their faith. Soon the prisons were opened and thousands of Christians were released, bearing the scars of their torture. Galerius died five days after issuing his edict.

THE ERA OF THE CHRISTIAN ROMAN EMPIRE

312–590

The Emperor Constantine is one of the major figures of Christian history. After his conversion, Christianity moved swiftly throughout the empire, from the seclusion of the catacombs to the prestige of palaces. Christians were a minority at the beginning of the fourth century but by the century's end, the faith had grown to be the empire's established religion. Thus, the Christian church was joined to the power of the state and assumed a moral responsibility for society. To serve the state, it refined its doctrine and developed its structure. Monks arose to protest this secularization of the faith, but when barbarians shattered the government in the western half of the empire, even Benedictines enlisted as missionaries to the pagans.

BRUCE L. SHELLEY

✝

312 ✛ CONSTANTINE CONVERTS TO CHRISTIANITY

Constantine (285–337), the son of Constantius Chlorus, the western co-emperor of the Roman Empire, was proclaimed emperor by his troops at his father's death in 306. However, he had a rival for the throne in Maxentius. On October 26, 312, the night before the decisive battle between the two, Constantine saw a flaming cross in the sky with the words, "In this Sign Conquer." Later that night in a dream, Christ commanded Constantine to have his soldiers mark their shields with the letters *chi* and *rho,* the first two letters of the word *Christ* in Greek. Constantine did as instructed and was victorious in the ensuing battle, becoming the undisputed emperor of the West. In 313, Constantine issued the Edict of Milan, granting Christians freedom of worship. Because of Constantine, Christianity became the religion of the Roman Empire.

312 ✛ THE DONATIST SCHISM BEGINS

Donatists took their name from Donatus (d. 355) who was bishop of Carthage from 313 to 355. Beginning in 312, Donatus led a protest against the practices of the Catholic Church. In particular, he and his followers charged that certain Catholic bishops had handed over Bibles to the civil authorities to be burned during Emperor Diocletian's (245–313) persecution, an act they viewed as apostasy. Since these apostate bishops were ordaining Catholic pastors, the Donatists claimed themselves, not the Catholics, to be the true church. They also argued that the validity of the sacraments depended upon the morality of the pastor administering them. Donatists became a majority in many areas of North Africa but were vigorously opposed by Augustine (354–430), the bishop of Hippo.

313 ✛ THE EDICT OF MILAN BRINGS CHRISTIAN FREEDOM

In 312, Constantine (285–337) became the uncontested ruler of the Western Roman Empire when he defeated Maxentius at the Milvian Bridge. In January 313 in Milan, he met with Licinius, the emperor of the East. They determined to reverse the Roman government's previous policy toward the church. Their proclamation, known as the Edict of Milan, was that all persons, including Christians, were free to worship as they wished. Christians also were to receive compensation and the return of previously confiscated property. A new day had dawned for the Christians of the Roman Empire.

313	360	383	411
Oldest bridge built over the Rhine	Books begin to replace scrolls	Romans conquer Gaul and Spain	Augustine writes *City of God*

THE AMBIGUOUS EMPEROR

October 26, 312

Constantine was the first Christian emperor of the Roman Empire, but was he really a Christian?

Constantine was the son of Constantius Chlorus, the western emperor of the Roman Empire, and his concubine, Helena. When his father died in 306, Constantine was proclaimed emperor by his father's troops. Meanwhile, back in Rome the Praetorian Guard proclaimed Maxentius as Western emperor.

On October 26, 312, Constantine and his troops reached a point about five miles north of Rome, prepared to do battle with Maxentius the following day. That evening he saw a flaming cross in the sky with the Greek words "In this Sign Conquer." Then that night he had a dream in which Christ commanded him to have his soldiers mark their shields with the letters *chi* and *rho*, the first and second letters of the Greek word for Christ. The many Christians in his army were greatly encouraged the next morning when he ordered his troops to put the inscription on their shields.

In Rome, Maxentius spent the night before the battle performing sacrifices and divinations. The impending battle was shaping up to be between the army of Christ and the army of the Roman gods.

Maxentius decided to do battle directly in front of the Tiber River with the Milvian Bridge behind him, approximately a mile from the gates of Rome. According to Eusebius, a church historian who lived during the fourth century, the outnumbered forces of Constantine advanced "invoking the God of heaven and his son and word our Lord Jesus Christ, the saviour of all." Maxentius was thrown into the Tiber along with many of his troops, and Constantine entered Rome as the undisputed emperor of the western empire.

The following year Constantine met with Licinius, emperor of the eastern empire, and issued the Edict of Milan, granting Christians freedom of worship along with compensation and return of confiscated church property.

An uneasy peace existed between Constantine and Licinius until 323, when Constantine defeated Licinius in battle, becoming the sole emperor. He then founded the city of Constantinople (modern-day Istanbul) as capital of his empire.

Constantine is most remembered for his church policies. In addition to the Edict of Milan, he allowed bishops to settle civil lawsuits, he closed courts of law and workshops on Sundays, and he banned gladiatorial games. He also took an active roll in church affairs, summoning the Council of Nicea in 325.

But there was a darker side to Constantine. In 326, he had his wife, the sister of Maxentius, and one son executed under suspicious circumstances. He also never relinquished his position as chief priest of the pagan state religion, and his coins proclaimed his allegiance to the sun god. He delayed Christian baptism until shortly before his death. Yet whatever his personal spiritual state, it was because of Constantine that Christianity became the religion of the Roman Empire.

314 ✛ THE COUNCIL OF ARDES MEETS

The Donatists were unhappy with a 313 ruling against them by the Roman Council's eighteen bishops. Therefore, they appealed to Emperor Constantine (285–337) who in response called the Council of Ardes in Southern France in 314. This was the first time in history that Christians appealed a church decision to a secular ruler. The Council turned out to be the forerunner of the Council of Nicea (325). Present were thirty-three bishops from Gaul (modern-day France), Sicily, Italy, North Africa, and Britain, as well as thirteen presbyters and twenty-three deacons. The Council ruled against the Donatists, excommunicating Donatus (d. 355) their leader. In addition, the Council issued twenty-two decisions, including the directive that Easter be celebrated on the same day everywhere, and that participants in races or gladiatorial fights be excommunicated.

318 ✛ ARIAN CONTROVERSY BEGINS

Trained in Antioch, Arius (250–336) became a presbyter in Alexandria, Egypt. In about 318, he entered into a dispute with Alexander (d. 328), the bishop of Alexandria, over whether Jesus Christ was co-eternal with God. Alexander taught, "God is always, the Son is always" and that the Son is "the unbegotten begotten." Arius's view regarding the Son was, "There was when He was not." At a church council in Alexandria, Arius and his followers were deposed and excommunicated. However, Arius refused to accept this judgment and appealed directly to the citizens of Alexandria and to bishops who had been his fellow students in Antioch. The resulting public demonstrations and letter-writing campaign by the sympathetic bishops challenged the unity of the church. As a result, Emperor Constantine (285–337) intervened and called the Council of Nicea (325).

320 ✛ PACHOMIUS BEGINS FORMING MONASTIC COMMUNITIES

Pachomius (287–346), an Egyptian, became a Christian as a result of the kindnesses shown him by the Christians of Thebes while he served there as a soldier. After his discharge from the army in 313, he was baptized and for a few years lived as a solitary monk. Then, about 320, he settled in the abandoned village of Tabennisi to fulfill his vision of an ascetic community patterned after the early Christians in Jerusalem. As a result, Pachomius is considered the father of communal monasticism. By the time of his death in 346, Pachomius was abbot

313	360	383	411
Oldest bridge built over the Rhine	Books begin to replace scrolls	Romans conquer Gaul and Spain	Augustine writes *City of God*

general over thousands of monks. He established eleven monasteries, nine for men and two for women. He emphasized the need for complete obedience to superiors and the communal ownership of goods.

323 ✝ EUSEBIUS COMPLETES ECCLESIASTICAL HISTORY

The son of humble parents, Eusebius (260–340) was born and educated in Caesarea. In 314, he was elected bishop of Caesarea. Considered to be the father of church history, Eusebius's most well known work is his *Ecclesiastical History*, which he finished in 323. It is an invaluable history of the church, containing records of many events not found elsewhere in existing documents. When the Arian controversy erupted in 318, Eusebius criticized Bishop Alexander (d. 328) of Alexandria for being too quick to condemn Arius (250–336). In response, an Anti-Arian council was held in January 325 in Antioch, where Eusebius was provisionally excommunicated. Later that year he was exonerated at the Council of Nicea. However, Eusebius signed the Nicene Creed only under pressure from Emperor Constantine (285–337) as he was never fully sympathetic to it.

325 ✝ THE NICENE CREED IS WRITTEN

Arius (250–336) was a pastor from Alexandria, Egypt, who taught that God is unique and unknowable and cannot share his substance with anyone. He therefore proclaimed Jesus to be divine but not God. The bishop of Alexandria realized that for Jesus to be the Savior he had to be truly God. Soon the city erupted in riots over this theological issue. In 325, when Emperor Constantine (285–337) realized that the security of his empire and the unity of the church were in danger, he called the Council of Nicea in Asia Minor to resolve the issue. After debating, the bishops denounced Arianism and formulated a creed describing Jesus as "true God from true God, begotten not made, of one substance with the father." All but two of more than three hundred bishops signed the statement, and those two were exiled with Arius.

326 ✝ HELENA MAKES HER PILGRIMAGE TO JERUSALEM

Helena (248–327), Constantine's (285-337) mother, had lowly origins. The daughter of an innkeeper, she probably was the legal concubine of Constantius, who would become the joint emperor of the West from 293 to 306. In 292, Constantius put her away so he could marry the daughter of Emperor Maximian to improve his chances to become a Caesar himself. When Helena's son Constantine was proclaimed emperor by his troops in 306, she was restored to a place of honor. Following Constantine's conversion in 312, Helena also put her faith in Jesus Christ. In about 326, she made a pilgrimage to Jerusalem where her name is connected with many of the churches constructed on sites associated with the life of Christ. She personally supervised the building of a church at the site of Jesus' tomb.

328 ✝ FRUMENTIUS IS SHIPWRECKED ON THE ETHIOPIAN COAST

Early in the fourth century Frumentius (300–380) and his brother Aedesius, two Christians from Tyre, were shipwrecked on the coast of Ethiopia. They were taken as slaves to the court of the Ethiopian king in Axum. Gaining the king's favor, they were appointed to high offices and given the opportunity to preach the gospel freely. Many people converted to Christianity, and a fledgling church was formed. The brothers strengthened it by bringing additional Christians from Egypt. Aedesius eventually returned to Tyre. In about 341, Frumentius went to Alexandria to see Athanasius (296–373) the patriarch. (Patriarch was a term applied to the bishops of Rome, Jerusalem, Antioch, and Alexandria.) When Frumentius requested that he send priests to Ethiopia, Athanasius instead consecrated Frumentius as bishop of Axum. Frumentius returned to Ethiopia, serving as bishop until his death.

330 ✝ CONSTANTINE DEDICATES CONSTANTINOPLE

When Constantine (285–337) became the sole emperor of the Roman Empire, he realized that Rome was too far away from the eastern empire to deal with the problems there. At first he considered making the ancient city of Troy his capital, but decided instead on the site of Byzantium. Its location on the Bosporus Strait had military advantages since it had access to both the Rhine and the Danube, as well as to Persia. On May 11, 330, Constantine dedicated the new "Rome," calling it Constantinople, meaning "city of Constantine" (now Istanbul). Even though Constantinople was created under the Roman Empire,

313	360	383	411
Oldest bridge built over the Rhine	Books begin to replace scrolls	Romans conquer Gaul and Spain	Augustine writes *City of God*

A LIFE TRANSFORMED

November 13, 354

God is in the business of changing lives, and Augustine is a prime example.

Augustine was born on November 13, 354, in Numidia, North Africa (modern-day Algeria). His father was a minor noble who desired above all else that Augustine become cultured. His devout but domineering mother wanted above all else that her son become a Christian.

As a boy, Augustine was the exact opposite of what his mother desired. To her dismay, he became an accomplished thief and liar. As a student he added sexual promiscuity to his catalog of sins, eventually taking a mistress. In spite of his lifestyle, Augustine excelled academically and eventually became a professor.

Ambition brought Augustine to Milan, the imperial capital, in 384, as a teacher of rhetoric. There he met Ambrose, the bishop of Milan, who challenged him to consider Christianity.

Then came a day in 386 that changed Augustine forever. He was at his villa in Milan with his mother when Pontitian, an African Christian and an officer in the imperial household, stopped by for a visit. As they talked, Pontitian casually picked up a book lying on the table and was surprised to see that it was the epistles of Paul. That discovery prompted Pontitian to relate how he had come to put his faith in Christ. He also told how two friends of his had decided to join a monastery, their fiancées also becoming Christians and dedicating themselves to virginity. Hearing the story of the two young women committing themselves to chastity pierced Augustine to the core, and he realized his addiction to sex.

After Pontitian left, Augustine ran out of the house, overcome by his sin. In despair, he flung himself on the ground underneath a fig tree. There he babbled, "How long, how long? Tomorrow and tomorrow? Why not now? Why should there not be an end to my uncleanness now?"

Suddenly Augustine heard the plaintive voice of an unknown little girl singing a song with the simple words, "Take up and read." To Augustine these words came as the voice of God himself. Augustine jumped up and ran to get the book containing Paul's epistles. Opening its pages, his eyes fell on Romans 13:13-14: "We should be decent and true in everything we do, so that everyone can approve of our behavior. Don't participate in wild parties and getting drunk, or in adultery and immoral living, or in fighting and jealousy. But let the Lord Jesus Christ take control of you, and don't think of ways to indulge your evil desires."

Augustine later wrote, "Instantly as I reached the end of this sentence, it was as if the light of peace was poured into my heart, and all the shades of doubt faded away." He immediately went into the house and told his mother that her prayers had been answered.

A changed man, Augustine went on to become the bishop of Hippo in North Africa and the greatest theologian between the apostle Paul and John Calvin.

historians view its establishment as the beginning of the Byzantine Empire and a first step leading to the later division between the Roman Catholic Church and Eastern Orthodoxy.

341 ✛ ULPHILAS, TRANSLATOR OF GOTHIC BIBLE, BECOMES BISHOP

Ulphilas (311–381), a Goth from a Germanic tribe living in the Balkans, spent much of his early life in Constantinople. About 341, he was consecrated as a bishop by Eusebius of Nicomedia (d. 341), the bishop of Constantinople. He then returned to his native land as a missionary. He evangelized among the Goths living in Moesia (present-day Bulgaria). He translated the Bible into Gothic for the first time but omitted 1 and 2 Kings, believing that they would have a negative influence on the Goths who were already fond of war. Eusebius of Nicomedia led him into Arianism, denying that God the Son was eternal. Because of Ulphilas's influence, the Goths were Arians for centuries to come.

358 ✛ BASIL THE GREAT FOUNDS A MONASTERY

Born in Cappadocia (present-day eastern Turkey), Basil (329–379) was the oldest child of Christian parents. He, his brother Gregory of Nyssa (330–395), and Basil's close friend Gregory of Nazianzus (330–389) became known as the Cappadocian Fathers, theologians who had a profound impact on the development of Christian theology. After studying at the University of Athens, Basil returned to Cappadocia and in approximately 358 founded a monastery in Annesia. His *Rules* for the monastery became famous. It included monastic regulations and answers to practical questions. In 370, Basil became bishop of Caesarea in Cappadocia, devoting himself to making monasticism a core part of the church, performing works of charity, and above all, defending the orthodoxy of the Council of Nicea against Arianism.

363 ✛ JULIAN THE APOSTATE, THE LAST PAGAN EMPEROR, DIES

Roman Emperor Julian the Apostate (331–363) died on June 26, 363. The nephew of Constantine the Great (285–337)—the Roman Empire's first Christian emperor—Julian received his nickname, the Apostate, because he denounced the Christian faith in which he had been raised. Julian succeeded his

313	360	383	411
Oldest bridge built over the Rhine	Books begin to replace scrolls	Romans conquer Gaul and Spain	Augustine writes *City of God*

A DECEITFUL EMPEROR

June 27, 363

Born in 331, Julian was the nephew of Constantine the Great, the first Christian emperor of the Roman Empire, who had legalized Christianity. When Julian was six years old, Constantine died and the empire was divided among his three sons, Constantine II, Constans, and Constantius, all Julian's cousins. After wars between the sons, Constantius, also a Christian, emerged victorious as emperor.

Julian had received a Christian education but had secretly rejected it, seeing hypocrisy in the lives of his supposedly Christian teachers. He was baptized and even ordained to serve as a lector, one who read the Scriptures in worship services, but the austere Christianity that was forced on him made him a rebel. He studied in Athens, where he enthusiastically embraced the teachings of Homer, Plato, and Aristotle. While in Athens he became a convert to ancient Greek idolatry. He told his private confidants that he was in daily communication with Jupiter, Minerva, Apollo, and Hercules, who assured him of their personal special protection. However, he publicly concealed his politically incorrect commitment to the Greek gods.

In 356, Emperor Constantius made Julian the governor of Gaul (modern France), where Julian had distinguished himself in battle. Meanwhile, Constantius was in Constantinople (modern Istanbul) and was threatened by the Persians. He ordered some of Julian's troops to come to his aid. Not wanting to march the two thousand miles to Constantinople, Julian's troops mutinied against Constantius's orders and proclaimed Julian as emperor instead. This act of outright rebellion made civil war appear imminent, but Constantius died before it could occur, leaving Julian the undisputed emperor. It was not until just before Constantius died that Julian publicly revealed his allegiance to the Greek gods.

As emperor, Julian immediately set about restoring paganism, earning him the name of Julian the Apostate. In addition to levying heavy taxes on Christians, Julian also removed them from military and government offices and prohibited them from teaching school. He reopened the pagan temples and reinstituted the priesthood and the sacrifices.

In an effort to discredit the Christian holy places in Jerusalem, Julian decided to rebuild the Jewish Temple—not because he had any affection for the Jews, but he wanted to upstage the Christians. However, when the workers were laying the foundation, they struck underground deposits of gas that exploded and burned, ending the project.

After reigning for eight years, Julian went to war against the Persians. The Christians dreaded his return and were relieved to hear that he had died of battle wounds. On June 27, 363—the day after Julian's death—the army elected Jovian, a Christian general, as the new emperor. When news arrived that Julian had died and that his replacement was a Christian, great rejoicing filled the churches.

cousin Constantius as emperor and wasted no time reestablishing homage to the Greek gods. He removed Christians from government service, banned them from teaching in Roman schools or serving in the military, and taxed them heavily. In addition to hindering the lives of Christians, Julian renewed pagan rituals, reopened old temples, and supported pagan sacrifices. His changes were the final imperial effort to return the Roman Empire to pagan worship. All subsequent Roman emperors were at least nominal Christians.

366 ✝ DAMASUS I BECOMES POPE

Born in Rome of Spanish parents, Damasus (304–384) was made a deacon by Pope Liberius (d. 366). At the pope's death, a fierce controversy broke out over whether his supporters or those of his rival Ursinus would succeed him. Damasus was elected pope, but Emperor Valentinian had to suppress Ursinus's supporters who had set him up as a rival pope. Damasus played a vital role in restraining Arianism, the view that denied Christ's deity by asserting that Jesus was created by God the Father. He also commissioned his secretary, Jerome (345–419), to prepare a reliable Latin translation of the Bible. The result was Jerome's Vulgate, which became the authoritative Bible of the Roman Catholic Church.

367 ✝ ATHANASIUS DEFINES THE NEW TESTAMENT

Athanasius (295–373), bishop of Alexandria, Egypt, devoted his life to defending orthodoxy against Arianism. The church's struggle with heresy increased the urgency to distinguish between truly inspired writings and questionable ones. The canon (Greek for "standard") was generally identified as writings of apostolic origin and those writings used in the churches. By the end of the second century most churches recognized the four Gospels, Acts, and Paul's epistles. The disputed books were Hebrews, James, 2 Peter, 2 and 3 John, Jude, and Revelation. In his widely circulated Easter Letter of 367, Bishop Athanasius named the twenty-seven books that make up the New Testament as we know it, stating that those were the only books to be regarded as Christian Scripture. Although his proclamation was not immediately adopted universally, over time the church gradually came to accept the books on Athanasius's list.

313	360	383	411
Oldest bridge built over the Rhine	Books begin to replace scrolls	Romans conquer Gaul and Spain	Augustine writes *City of God*

372 ✝ MARTIN OF TOURS BECOMES BISHOP

Born in Pannonia (modern-day Hungary) of pagan parents, Martin (335–397) was enlisted by his father in the Roman army at the age of fifteen. When he was eighteen the plight of a naked beggar moved him to tear his own coat into two parts, giving half to the beggar. Subsequently, he had a vision of Christ wearing half of his cloak. Martin was baptized as a result of his vision. After obtaining a military discharge, he joined Hilary of Poitiers (315–368) in founding the first monastery in Gaul (modern-day France). Elected bishop of Tours in 372, he continued to practice and promote monastic life as well as rural evangelization. Due to his efforts, many churches were established throughout the countryside of Gaul.

378 ✝ GREGORY OF NANZIANZUS BECOMES BISHOP OF CONSTANTINOPLE

The son of the Catholic bishop of Nanzianzus, Cappadocia (now central Turkey), Gregory of Nanzianzus (330–389) was educated in Caesarea (in Cappadocia). While there he met Basil the Great (330–379), and the two men finished their education in Athens, Greece. Gregory followed Basil into the monastic life, studying the Bible in seclusion for most of two decades before being ordained in 362 as co-bishop of Nanzianzus alongside his father. In 374, Gregory returned to monastic life only to be called out again in 378 to be bishop of Constantinople. Second in influence only to Rome, Constantinople was the seat of Catholic orthodoxy in an age characterized by heresy. Among the Cappadocian Fathers, Gregory was christened "The Theologian" for his articulate defense against the prevailing Arian heresy that Jesus was inferior to God because he could not have existed before God "begat" him.

379 ✝ GREGORY OF NYSSA CHAMPIONS ORTHODOXY

Gregory of Nyssa (330–394) spent the first five decades of his life in the shadow of his older brother and teacher, Basil the Great (330–379). Like Basil, Gregory was born in Caesarea in Cappadocia (modern-day Turkey) and received a rigorous classical education. After practicing secular rhetoric and law, Gregory devoted himself to studying theology in a monastery. In 370, Basil, then bishop of Caesarea, made Gregory the bishop of Nyssa. As bishop, Gregory was distinguished for defending the orthodox Nicene faith against Arian heresies, but was removed for administrative failure. When Basil died in 379, Gregory took up his brother's mantle as the Catholic Church's champion of orthodoxy. After Gregory's death around 394, the depth and influence of his theological writings earned him the title "Father of the Cappadocian Fathers."

380 ✡ THE PALESTINIAN TALMUD IS COMPLETED

The Talmud is a collection of rabbinical laws, judicial decisions, and commentary on the law of Moses. The Talmud consists of two parts: the Mishnah, which is a collection of the oral laws of ancient Judaism, and the Gemara, which is a commentary on the Mishnah. Following the destruction of the Jewish Temple in 70, the Pharisees began putting their oral laws into writing. Rabbi Judah ha-Nasi (Judah the Prince) completed this process by 217. The Gemara, the additional comments added later, completed the Talmud. There are two versions of the Talmud: the Palestinian and the Babylonian. The Palestinian Talmud was completed about 380. It is about a third the length of the Babylonian, which was completed about 500 and has been the more accepted text for subsequent Judaism.

381 ✝ THE FIRST COUNCIL OF CONSTANTINOPLE MEETS

Theodosius I (346–395), an orthodox Christian, became emperor in 379. To restore church unity in the face of the Arian heresy, Theodosius called the First Council of Constantinople in 381. On the basis of the scholarship of the Cappadocian Fathers—Basil of Caesarea (329–379), his brother Gregory of Nyssa (330–395), and his friend Gregory of Nanzianzus (330–389)—the council accepted the Nicene Creed, which upheld the eternality of Jesus Christ and the doctrine that the Holy Spirit was of like substance to the other two persons of the Trinity. Thus, the First Council of Constantinople definitively defined the doctrine of the Trinity. Although it included only Eastern bishops, this council is considered to be the second ecumenical council.

385 ✝ BISHOP AMBROSE DEFIES THE EMPRESS

Ambrose (339–397), bishop of Milan, was a deeply spiritual man and one of the strongest leaders the church had known. Known for his intellect and ora-

313	360	383	411
Oldest bridge built over the Rhine	Books begin to replace scrolls	Romans conquer Gaul and Spain	Augustine writes *City of God*

tory, he was influential in the conversion of his young admirer Augustine (354–430). The mother of Emperor Valentinian, Empress Justina, was the true power behind the throne in the Western Roman Empire. She was an Arian, believing that God the Son was not eternal, while Bishop Ambrose held to the orthodox teachings of the Council of Nicea. In 385, Empress Justina demanded that Ambrose surrender his cathedral for the use of Arian congregations. When he refused, she ordered soldiers to surround the cathedral. Many expected a massacre. Inside the cathedral the congregation raised their voices in song, and the soldiers inexplicably dispersed. Imperial force had been met with impenetrable faith.

386 ✛ AUGUSTINE CONVERTS TO JESUS CHRIST

In Milan, Italy, in July 386, Aurelius Augustine (354–430) found faith in Jesus Christ and was freed of his enslavement to sexual immorality. That day, as a visitor testified of his conversion to Christianity, Augustine sensed the immense weight of his sin. After the visitor left, he flung himself on the ground in the garden. There he heard a child singing, "Take up and read." Thinking these words to be from God, Augustine took up a book of Paul's epistles. His eyes fell on Romans 13:13–14. The sentence "Let the Lord Jesus Christ take control of you, and don't think of ways to indulge your evil desires" pierced his soul and lit a flame of faith in Christ that never went out. His was one of the church's most celebrated conversions because he proved to be one of history's most prolific Christian thinkers.

398 ✛ CHRYSOSTOM BECOMES BISHOP OF CONSTANTINOPLE

John Chrysostom was born about 347 in Antioch into a Christian family of above average means. He first studied to be an attorney but then became interested in monasticism. After living as a hermit for ten years, he returned to Antioch where he was ordained as a deacon in 381 and a priest in 386. John Chrysostom was the great preacher of his day. His eloquence earned him the name *Chrysostom*, meaning "golden mouthed." In 398, he reluctantly was made bishop of Constantinople. In that position, his uncompromising zeal to reform the church raised the ire of the empress and many clergy. As a result, he was banished twice and died in 407 in transit to a place of exile.

443	455	542–94	593
Attila becomes Hun ruler	Vandals sack Rome	Plague kills half of Europe	Printing press invented in China

405 ✝ JEROME COMPLETES THE VULGATE

Eusebius Hieronymus Sophronius, known to us as Jerome (345–420), was born in northeastern Italy in about 345. He was a disciplined scholar and an ascetic Christian. For several years he lived in the Syrian Desert mastering Hebrew. By 383, he became secretary to Damasus (304–384), the bishop of Rome, and probably was the greatest Christian scholar in the world. His lasting achievement was translating the Old and New Testaments into Latin. Today we know his translation as the Vulgate. In 1546, the Council of Trent declared it to be the only authentic Latin text of the Bible. Although he included the books of the Apocrypha since they had been part of the Septuagint, which was the Jewish translation of the Old Testament, he did not consider them to be part of the inspired Word of God.

410 ✝ THE VISIGOTHS SACK ROME

The Goths were Germanic tribes that initially raided the northeastern frontiers of the Roman Empire during the third century. In the fourth century they split into two tribes, the Goths who lived in Dacia (now Romania and Hungary) and the Visigoths who lived north of the Black Sea. In 376, the Visigoths crossed the Danube and in 378 defeated the Roman army at Adrianople, killing the Emperor Valens. Under their king, Alaric (d. 410), the Visigoths attacked Rome in 408 and 409, in both cases accepting huge ransoms to lift their siege. On August 24, 410, Alaric captured Rome and looted everything except its churches. The sack of Rome was a great disillusionment to Christians and pagans alike, as both believed that personal piety guaranteed both political freedom and social security.

414 ✝ ✡ CHRISTIANS ORGANIZE THEIR FIRST
ATTACK ON JEWS IN ALEXANDRIA

Alexandria, Egypt, had been a cosmopolitan city since Alexander the Great founded it in 332 BC. From its beginning it had a sizable Jewish population. In the fourth century AD, relations between the Jews and Christians of Alexandria had become contentious. When Athanasius (295–373) was bishop of Alexandria, Jews joined the Arians, who denied Christ's deity, in rioting against him. Then in about 414, the Jews, threatened by Cyril the Patriarch (bishop) of Alexandria,

313	360	383	411
Oldest bridge built over the Rhine	Books begin to replace scrolls	Romans conquer Gaul and Spain	Augustine writes *City of God*

THE RESULTS OF A LONG-AGO DECISION

September 30, 420

Why do Roman Catholic Bibles have more books than Protestant Bibles?

The answer comes from the work of a man who died on September 30, 420. His name was Sophronius Eusebius Hieronymus, but history knows him as Jerome. Born of Christian parents in northeastern Italy, at the age of twelve he went to Rome to study. He was baptized there at nineteen.

Jerome became attracted to monasticism and lived as a monk near the ancient Syrian town of Chalcis. During this time he began mastering Hebrew and perfecting his Greek. He was ordained in Antioch and became a bishop without pastoral responsibilities. He next studied under Gregory of Nazianzus, one of the Cappadocian Fathers who had a profound influence on Christian theology.

In 386, Jerome moved to Bethlehem, where he spent the rest of his life. He served as the overseer of a monastery and the spiritual advisor to a local convent.

Jerome spent most of his time writing. His linguistic ability and scholarship were unsurpassed in the early church. His greatest contribution to the Christian world was his translation of the Bible. In 382, Pope Damasus commissioned Jerome, then no more than thirty-five years old, to produce a uniform text of the Latin Bible. He was to standardize the texts then in circulation.

Between 390 and 404, Jerome translated the Old Testament into Latin. In addition to the thirty-nine books of the Hebrew Old Testament, Jerome also translated fourteen Jewish religious books that the translators of the Septuagint had included. These fourteen books were never part of the Jewish Bible and were called the Apocrypha, which came to mean "spurious" or "not genuine." Even though Jerome included the Apocrypha with the Old Testament because the Septuagint had done so, in speaking of the thirty-nine books of the Old Testament, he wrote, "anything outside of these must be placed within the Apocrypha," the noncanonical books. In other words, Jerome saw a definite distinction between the thirty-nine inspired books and the Apocrypha.

Jerome's translation became known as the Vulgate. At the time of the Reformation, the Pope called the Council of Trent to attempt to stem the tide of Protestantism. There, in an attempt to differentiate the Roman Catholic Church from the Reformers, the council declared the Latin Vulgate, including the Apocrypha, to be the authoritative Bible, whereas the Reformers recognized only the original thirty-nine books of the Old Testament.

Although Jerome had included the Apocrypha in the Vulgate as uninspired books, the Council of Trent declared them to be inspired. Thus was born the difference between the Roman Catholic and the Protestant Bibles.

rioted and killed many Christians. The next day in response, with Cyril's encouragement, Christians attacked the synagogues and killed as many Jews as they were able to find. The surviving Jews fled Alexandria, ending the Jewish colony there.

423 ✝ SIMEON THE STYLITE LIVES ON A PILLAR

Perhaps the most well known of the early ascetics was Simeon the Stylite (390–459) who was born in Cilicia in modern southeastern Turkey. After being raised by his shepherd father, he moved to Antioch and became a hermit. For the next twenty years, he wandered through Northern Syria, living in several monasteries. In 423, Simeon ascended a pillar in Telanissus. He spent thirty-six years living a rigorously ascetic life on a small platform on the top of the pillar, which eventually reached sixty feet high after several additions. As Simeon's reputation spread through the surrounding areas, thousands came to see him and hear him preach. Simeon's followers multiplied, with Daniel the Stylite (409–493) being most famous among them. After Simeon died, a monastery was built on the site of his famous pillar.

428 ✝ NESTORIUS BECOMES BISHOP OF CONSTANTINOPLE

In 428 Theodosius (401–450), the eastern Roman emperor, promoted Nestorius (d. 451) to the position of bishop of Constantinople, modern-day Istanbul, Turkey. Nestorius had been a monk and an elder in Antioch, and was very well known for his preaching. At his post in Constantinople, Nestorius began teaching and was asked to declare whether *Theotokos* ("God-bearing") was an appropriate term for Mary, the mother of Jesus. His response was that the best title for Mary was *Christotokos* (Christ-bearing). In the ensuing debate, Nestorius was denounced as a heretic by Cyril (d. 444), the bishop of Alexandria. Then in 431, the Council of Ephesus removed Nestorius from his office. A Nestorian church continued on in the Middle East with some remnants still remaining today.

429 ✡ JEWISH PATRIARCHATE IS ABOLISHED

Shortly after the Romans destroyed Jerusalem in 70 AD, two central Jewish institutions known as the Patriarchate and the Sanhedrin came to the fore. The

Sanhedrin functioned as the Supreme Court of Judaism, while the Patriarchate took precedence in the eyes of the general public. Both Romans and Jews acknowledged the patriarch as the official representative of Judaism, even though he had no political power. He came to be recognized by the Roman government as the authority over the Jews. As the Roman Empire adopted Christianity, it simultaneously began removing Jews from public office. The patriarch lost his official prerogatives and the office was abolished in about 429 when Emperor Theodosius refused to appoint a successor to Gamaliel VI. This left the Sanhedrin as the only recognized central authority in Judaism.

431 ✛ THE COUNCIL OF EPHESUS MEETS

Concerned by the view of the Nestorians—who split Jesus Christ into two separate persons, one human and one divine—Emperor Theodosius II (401–450) called the Council of Ephesus to meet in 431. With sixty bishops present, the Council of Ephesus is considered to be the third General Council of the church. The council acted to excommunicate Nestorius (d. 451) and condemn his teaching. The Nestorians refused to accept the council's decision and proceeded to form a Nestorian church. The council also condemned Pelagianism, which had become popular in the West. This view taught that man has a free will and an innate ability to do good and rejected the concepts of original sin and predestination. Millennialism, the view that Christ will reign on earth for one thousand years, was condemned as well.

432 ✛ PATRICK EMBARKS ON HIS MISSION TO IRELAND

Born near Dumbarton, Scotland, Patrick (390–461) was the son of a deacon and Roman magistrate. At the age of sixteen he was captured by Irish pirates and sold into slavery in Ireland. Escaping to Gaul (modern-day France), he became a monk under Martin of Tours (335–400). After returning to his family in Britain, he had a vision in which he was called to preach to the heathen Irish. He was consecrated as a bishop and returned to Ireland with a missionary party in about 432. For the next thirty years Patrick ministered throughout Ireland and witnessed thousands converted to Christ. The churches he founded were independent of Rome. As a result of Patrick's labor, Ireland became a center of Christian influence for the rest of Western Europe.

443	455	542–94	593
Attila becomes Hun ruler	Vandals sack Rome	Plague kills half of Europe	Printing press invented in China

440 ✝ LEO I BECOMES BISHOP OF ROME

Born in Tuscany, Leo (400–461) became a prominent deacon and then an imperial diplomat. His wide-ranging abilities made him an obvious choice for bishop of Rome in 440. Leo was faced with heresies that threatened the integrity of the church. In response, he codified what he considered to be orthodox doctrine and made the papacy sovereign within the church. To adjust to the rapidly disintegrating Roman Empire, he attempted to achieve peace by negotiating with the enemies of the empire such as Attila the Hun (d. 453). Leo's efforts greatly stabilized the Western church in troubled times and set its course for future centuries. At the same time, his sermons revealed a genuine concern for the lives of individual believers. For his accomplishments, he is known as Leo the Great.

445 ✝ VALENTINIAN GIVES HIS EDICT

Valentinian III (419–455) became the emperor of the Western Roman Empire in 425, although for the first twenty-five of his thirty-year reign, he was co-regent with his mother. With the encouragement of Bishop Leo I of Rome (400–461), Valentinian issued an edict in 445 giving the bishop of Rome authority over all the provincial churches in the Western empire. This gave the Roman bishop important advantage in his struggle for power with the other patriarchs of the church.

451 ✝ THE COUNCIL OF CHALCEDON OPENS

The Council of Chalcedon was called by Emperor Marcian (396–457) to deal with the heresy of Eutyches (378–454), an elderly monk who blurred the distinction between Jesus' human and divine natures. More than five hundred bishops were present at the first session on October 8, 451. The council dealt not only with the heresy of Eutyches, but three others as well. The statement of faith issued by the council, called the Definition of Chalcedon, affirmed against Eutyches that the deity and humanity of Christ are distinct. Against Arius (250–336) they accepted the full deity of Christ, and against Apollinarius they maintained Christ's full humanity. Against Nestorius (d. 451) they declared that Christ is one person. Although the emperor intended the Definition to unite the empire, many churches in the Eastern Empire, especially those in Egypt and Ethiopia, rejected it.

313	360	383	411
Oldest bridge built over the Rhine	Books begin to replace scrolls	Romans conquer Gaul and Spain	Augustine writes *City of God*

452 ✝ ATTILA THE HUN INVADES ITALY

Known to Christian authors as the "Scourge of God," Attila was a powerful king who united the Huns, a Mongolian tribe that first invaded the Roman Empire in the 300s. In 440, Attila invaded the Balkans. He headed west in 450 when the sister of the Western emperor asked him to rescue her from a forced marriage. When he invaded France in 451, Attila finally was defeated by the armies of the Romans, Visigoths, and Franks. Attila next turned his attention to Italy, invading in 452. However, with famine and disease taking a high toll on his troops, he was persuaded to heed the pleas of Leo I, bishop of Rome, and returned to territory north of the Danube. One year later Attila died, leaving the Christian presence in central Europe severely eroded as a result of his invasions.

476 ✝ THE WESTERN ROMAN EMPIRE FALLS

The fifth century witnessed the decline of the Western Roman Empire. After the death of Emperor Valentinian III in 455, the Western Empire came under the influence of Germanic chiefs who held real power over puppet emperors. Finally in 476, the Germanic chief Odoacer (434–493) deposed the last Roman emperor, a youth named Romulus Augustulus, whose name recalled Rome's first king and first emperor. Odoacer proclaimed himself king according to the customs of the barbarians. Although the event was not regarded as of great importance at that time, in reality the center of world power had now shifted to Constantinople. In the West the power of the church was about to replace the power of the state.

496 ✝ CLOVIS, KING OF THE FRANKS, IS BAPTIZED

Clovis, king of the Franks from 481 to 511, first learned of Christianity when he married Clothilda of Burgundy who was a Christian. She continually attempted to convert Clovis, but he would have none of it until 496, when the prospect of losing a battle caused him to seek the aid of his wife's God. After winning the battle, he consented to be baptized on Christmas Day that year. Clovis then used his new religion as an excuse for expanding his territory, expelling the heretic Arian Visigoths out of southern France. However, his newly professed faith did not deter him from using brutality and treachery against his political opponents. With the support of the church he appointed clergy as envoys and governors in further successful attempts to extend his kingdom.

499 ✡ THE BABYLONIAN TALMUD IS COMPLETED

The Palestinian Talmud—a commentary on the Mishnah, the oral laws of Judaism added to those of Scripture—was completed about 380 in Tiberias. But the Babylonian Talmud was not finished until approximately 499. Just as there were academies for study of the Mishnah in Palestine, so there were similar academies in Babylonia (modern-day Iraq). The enrollments often numbered in the thousands. Students went from one academy to another, sometimes even between Palestine and Babylonia. It is likely that Rabina bar Huma who died in 499 was the final editor of the Babylonian Talmud. The Babylonian Talmud was regarded as authoritative in the Middle Ages.

500 ✝ DIONYSIUS THE PSEUDO-AREOPAGITE WRITES

Dionysius the Psuedo-Areopagite is the name given to an author who lived in the fourth or fifth century whose writings were initially attributed to Dionysius of Athens (Acts 17:34). The author was a mystical theologian whose works had a marked impact on the theology of the Middle Ages. His writings attempted a synthesis of theology and Neoplatonist philosophy. Central themes were the union between man and God and the progressive deification of man in which the soul is illuminated and ultimately given knowledge of God. He also taught that man is increasingly related to God by a series of graded levels corresponding to the hierarchy of the church. These hierarchies are designed to lead man to his deification.

520 ✝ IRISH MONASTERIES FLOURISH

Ireland was the center of vigorous missions-minded monasticism. Developing independently of Roman Catholicism, the Irish church was organized around monasteries, which were the centers of learning. The Bible was the primary subject of study, and Latin was the language of education. The Irish monasteries sent missionaries throughout their world—to the Orkney and Faroe Islands, to Scotland, Germany, Gaul (France), and even to Italy. They went individually

313	360	383	411
Oldest bridge built over the Rhine	Books begin to replace scrolls	Romans conquer Gaul and Spain	Augustine writes *City of God*

and in groups. Some were missionaries to pagans, others to nominal Christian populations. Their independence often made them an irritant to the Roman Catholic hierarchy. But they were so numerous that they remained a continuing influence in Western Europe until 950.

524 ✝ BOETHIUS WRITES THE CONSOLATION OF PHILOSOPHY

Anicius Manlius Torquatus Severinus Boethius was born about 480 to a noble Roman family and was educated in Athens and Alexandria. Boethius, a great intellectual, was an advisor to Theodoric the Ostrogoth king who began his rule in Italy in 493. In 523, Boethius was promoted to one of the most influential offices in the realm, but the next year he suddenly fell from favor and was sentenced to die for treason. The reason may have been that Theodoric was an Arian, believing Christ was a created being and not eternal, while Boethius and those arrested with him were orthodox Christians. While awaiting execution, Boethius wrote his most well known work, *The Consolation of Philosophy*, in which he described philosophy's role in leading a soul to God, without ever mentioning Christ or the Bible. This and other writings of Boethius strongly influenced the tone of intellectual life in the Middle Ages.

529 ✝ JUSTINIAN'S CODE IS PUBLISHED

The greatest of all the Byzantine Roman emperors, Justinian I, was born in 483 and succeeded his uncle Justin I as emperor in 527. Throughout his reign he was an energetic champion of Nicene orthodoxy, even though his wife, Theodora, was a Monophysite, emphasizing only Christ's divine nature. Upon becoming emperor, Justinian found the laws of the empire in disarray and appointed a panel of ten legal experts to consolidate Roman law. He declared the results of their successful effort in what has come to be known as the Justinian Code. This codification became the basic collection of Roman law, and it greatly influenced the development of canon law in the Western church.

529 ✝ THE SECOND COUNCIL OF ORANGE MEETS

There were two Councils of Orange in southern France. The first, held in 441, dealt primarily with disciplinary matters. The second, held in 529, addressed the

443	455	542–94	593
Attila becomes Hun ruler	Vandals sack Rome	Plague kills half of Europe	Printing press invented in China

heresy of Semi-Pelagianism. Pelagius had been a monk active in Rome (383–410) who had rejected the doctrines of original sin and predestination. Instead, he promoted the concepts of man's free will and natural capacity for good. Later followers of Pelagius, alarmed that Augustine's view of predestination seemed to undermine free will, developed a view known as Semi-Pelagianism in which the initial steps toward salvation were the result of the human will, with divine grace coming into play later. The Second Council of Orange ruled in favor of the view of Augustine, that every step toward salvation is the result of God's grace, not man's will.

540 ✝ BENEDICT WRITES HIS MONASTIC RULE

Born in approximately 480, Benedict of Nursia was educated in Rome. He found the immorality of the city so offensive that before he had finished his studies, he went to live as a hermit in a cave near Subiaco. Twice he became the abbot for a group of monks in the area. In about 520, Benedict established the monastery of Monte Casino where he spent the rest of his life. There, in about 540, he wrote the *Rule* for the monastery. The *Rule* became the constitution of the Benedictine order. Every monastery was to be self-supporting under the direction of an abbot. In the *Rule,* Benedict attempted to create an atmosphere where ordinary men could serve God and grow spiritually through a balanced life of work, reading, prayer, and worship. The *Rule* established a pattern for life in the monasteries of Europe.

544 ✝ DIONYSIUS EXIGUUS, INVENTOR OF DATING SYSTEM, DIES

Dionysius, a Scythian monk who called himself Exiguus (the less) out of humility, arrived in Rome shortly after 496. His summary of canon law was the first to gain wide usage and was used as late as the twelfth century. When called upon to create a new calendar for dating Easter in succeeding years, Dionysius abandoned the method of calculating it from the Jewish date of Passover, since with that method Easter didn't always fall on Sunday. He calculated the date from what he supposed to be the birth of Jesus. Although he was a few years off in his estimation of Jesus' birth, the date determined by Dionysius for the Incarnation is the basis of the Anno Domini system still used today.

313	360	383	411
Oldest bridge built over the Rhine	Books begin to replace scrolls	Romans conquer Gaul and Spain	Augustine writes *City of God*

553 ✝ THE SECOND COUNCIL OF CONSTANTINOPLE MEETS

The Council of Chalcedon in 451 had determined that Christ had two natures, human and divine. It proclaimed him true God and true man in one person. Opposition to this doctrine became known as "Monophysitism," the term coming from the Greek words *mono* meaning "only" and *fusis* meaning "nature." Monophysites downplayed the humanity of Jesus and emphasized the unity of his divine nature. Monophysitism was particularly popular in Egypt and the Middle East. Emperors Justin I and Justinian I appointed orthodox bishops in these areas, but they required police protection to stay in power. Then Emperor Justinian switched tactics—due in part to his Monophysite wife, Theodora—condemning three writings of orthodox theologians, called *The Three Chapters*. The Second Council of Constantinople in 553, the fifth ecumenical council, followed Justinian's lead and moved closer to the Monophysite position by condemning *The Three Chapters*. The council also affirmed the perpetual virginity of Mary.

563 ✝ COLUMBA EVANGELIZES SCOTLAND

Columba was born in Ireland in 521 to parents of royal lineage. After being educated in monastic schools and recognized as a scholar, he was ordained as a priest and spent nearly twenty years in Ireland as an evangelist, church planter, and founder of monasteries. In 563, Columba and twelve Irish monks moved to the small island of Iona off the coast of Scotland. There he founded a monastery whose purpose was to train evangelists to bring the gospel to Scotland. His monks played a central role in the evangelization of Scotland and England. He also encouraged the copying of the Scriptures and reportedly made three hundred copies of the Vulgate himself. Though born to royalty, Columba chose to serve a higher King.

THE CHRISTIAN MIDDLE AGES

590–1517

Most Christians saw the hand of God in the happy wedding of Christian church and Roman state. In the East the marriage continued for a millennium. A mystical piety flourished under the protection of Orthodox emperors until 1453, when invading Muslim Turks brought the Byzantine Empire to its final ruin. The fall of Constantinople, however, meant the rise of Moscow, the new capital of Eastern Orthodoxy.

It was a different story in the West. After the fifth century, when barbarian Germans and Huns shattered the Empire's defenses and swept into the eternal city of Rome itself, men turned to Augustine's *City of God* for explanations. They found a vision for a new age.

We call these centuries "medieval." People who lived in them considered them "Christian." Their reasons lay in the role of the pope, who stepped into the ruins of the fallen empire in the West and proceeded to build the medieval church upon Rome's bygone glory. As the only surviving link with the Roman past, the Church of Rome mobilized Benedictine monks and deployed them as missionary ambassadors to the German people. It took centuries, but the popes, aided by Christian princes, slowly pacified and baptized a continent and called it Christendom, or Christian Europe.

BRUCE L. SHELLEY

590 ✛ GREGORY THE GREAT IS ELECTED POPE

Born in Rome, Gregory (540–604) grew up in an educated Christian home. In 570, he became the prefect of Rome but gave that up to found seven monasteries, one of which he entered himself about 575. After being ordained as a deacon, he was elected pope in 590, becoming Gregory I. As pope, Gregory assumed many duties normally administered by civil authorities, thus taking an important step toward the forming of the Papal States. In church affairs Gregory maintained that God had entrusted the pope with caring for the entire church and therefore had universal jurisdiction over it. Gregory also had a major role in organizing and codifying Roman liturgy and music. The Gregorian Chant is named after him.

597 ✛ AUGUSTINE OF CANTERBURY EMBARKS ON A MISSION TO ENGLAND

Augustine (d. 604), having taken the name of the earlier bishop, was the prior of the St. Andrews monastery in Rome when Pope Gregory the Great (540–604) commissioned him in 596 to convert pagan England. Stopping along the way in Gaul (modern-day France), he arrived in England. He was welcomed by Athelbert (552–616), the king of Kent, whose wife was already a Christian. Within a short period of time, Athelbert and hundreds of his subjects were converted to Christ. In the same year, Augustine traveled to France to be consecrated as the first archbishop of Canterbury. Pope Gregory later made him metropolitan bishop of England. Augustine failed to win the allegiance of the Celtic church but was successful in spreading the gospel in Kent, eventually leading to the evangelization of all England.

601 ✛ KING ATHELBERT OF KENT IS BAPTIZED

Athelbert (552–616), son of the Saxon king of Kent, England, succeeded his father as king in about 580. In about 578, he married the Christian daughter of the king of the Franks. As part of a marriage agreement she was allowed to bring her chaplain, Liudhard, with her. Liudhard then was permitted to restore the old Roman church at Canterbury that had stood vacant for two hundred years. When Augustine arrived in England in 597, Athelbert met him under an oak venerated

594	1066	1200	1300
Buddhism becomes religion of Japan	Normans conquer Britain	Genghis Khan begins conquests	Renaissance begins in Italy

by the Saxons. Athelbert believed that the sacred tree would be able to cancel out any magic the Christians might use. He nevertheless allowed Augustine to establish a house in Canterbury and to use Liudhard's church. Within the year Athelbert was converted to Christ. Soon hundreds were baptized, and in 601 Athelbert himself was baptized, becoming the first Christian English king.

614 ✡ PERSIANS CONQUER JERUSALEM

The one period of respite for the Jews of Palestine from the domination of the Byzantine Empire came in 614 during the final war between Rome and Persia. In 603, King Chosroes II of Persia (r. 591–628) began attacking the eastern province of Rome, and in 614 he conquered Jerusalem with assistance from the Jews, who looked to Persia as their liberator. Chosroes killed and deported many Christians and turned control of the city over to the Jews. However, he soon realized that the Jews were not strong enough nor sufficiently numerous to defend Palestine by themselves. As a result, in 617 Chosroes returned Palestine to Christian allies. In 629, the Romans reconquered Jerusalem and restored Palestine to Byzantine control.

627 ✝ KING EDWIN OF NORTHUMBRIA, ENGLAND, IS BAPTIZED

Edwin (585–633), king of Northumbria, married Ethelburh, the daughter of King Ethelbert (552–616) of Kent in 625. A Christian like her father, Ethelburh was accompanied to Northumbria by her chaplain, Paulinus (d. 644). On the same day the following year, Edwin narrowly escaped an assassination attempt, and his wife gave birth to a daughter. Sobered by these experiences, he told Paulinus that he would become a Christian if Paulinus's God would give him victory over the West Saxons. Edwin won the battle and thereby became the most powerful king in England. Edwin was baptized in 627 and then sanctioned the conversion of the Northumbrians to Christianity.

634 ✝ SIGEBERT'S EFFORTS HELP CONVERT THE EAST ANGLES

One of the last pagan areas of England was the fiercely independent kingdom of East Anglia, including modern Norfolk and Suffolk on the southeastern coast. Redwald, who ruled East Anglia from about 599–625, was converted to Christianity at the court of King Athelbert (552–616) in Kent, but he reverted to paganism because of the influence of his wife. His son Eorpwald (r. 625–632) was converted to Christ by King Edwin (585–633) of Northumbria but soon was murdered because of his faith. Eorpwald's brother Sigebert, also a devout Christian, fled to France to avoid the wrath of his pagan stepfather, Redwald. After ten years Sigebert returned and successfully took the throne in about 634. As a result of Sigebert's efforts, the East Angles were converted to Christianity from paganism. After reigning until about 638, Sigebert retired to a monastery.

635 ✝ NESTORIAN MISSION TO CHINA

Nestorius (380–451) had been made Patriarch of Constantinople in 428 but was deposed three years later by the Council of Ephesus. He was probably orthodox but had not adequately stated his view of the relationship between Christ's human and divine natures. In 1623, a monument was discovered in China that chronicled the Nestorian missionary Alopen's arrival there in 635. Churches and monasteries were established, Christian literature was distributed, and the movement received the emperor's approval. Nestorian Christianity reached all the way to the border of Korea. Churches flourished until the tenth-century fall of the dynasty that had supported them. Traces of the Nestorian church remained until the thirteenth century, at which time it largely disappeared.

637 ☾ MUSLIM ARMIES CONQUER JERUSALEM

In 636, near where the Yarmuk River enters the Jordan, the armies of Islam engaged in what was to be the decisive battle against the armies of the Byzantine Empire for the control of Palestine. Though vastly outnumbered, the Muslims were victorious with few of the Byzantine army escaping. The following year the two principal Muslim armies converged in a siege on Jerusalem. The siege lasted four months as the Christians zealously defended their Holy City. When further defense appeared hopeless, Sophronius (560–638), the patriarch of Jerusalem, offered to surrender to Caliph Omar of Medina (581–644) if he would come to Jerusalem. The caliph came riding on a camel, accepted the surrender, and promised the Christians of Jerusalem freedom of worship and possession of the Church of the Holy Sepulcher. The Jews of Jerusalem also survived as a tolerated minority.

594	1066	1200	1300
Buddhism becomes religion of Japan	Normans conquer Britain	Genghis Khan begins conquests	Renaissance begins in Italy

A MAN NAMED MUHAMMAD

June 8, 632

He successfully invented a new religion.

Muhammad, the founder of Islam, the world's youngest major religion, was born in Mecca around 570. An orphan at a young age, he grew up in relative poverty, but at the age of twenty-five, Muhammad entered the service of a wealthy widow, fifteen years his senior, named Khadija. His marriage to her shortly thereafter provided him with instant wealth. Her affluence provided him with the luxury to indulge in a life of religious contemplation.

When he was about forty, Muhammad claimed that he received a prophetic call from Allah through the angel Gabriel. He began preaching monotheism, a final judgment, alms, prayer, and surrender to the will of Allah. In three years he attracted only twelve converts. Persecuted in his hometown of Mecca, he fled to Medina in 622. His flight to Medina is called the *Hegira* and is traditionally dated July 15, 622, which marks the beginning of the Muslim calendar.

During his time in Medina, Muhammad's revelations became more legalistic and secular. Islam, as his new religion was called, became both a community and a state with Muhammad as both its ruler and lawgiver.

Once he centralized his power in Medina, he was able to return to Mecca and conquer it in 630. By the time Muhammad died on June 8, 632, almost all of Arabia had embraced Islam. In the hundred years following his death, Islam spread like wildfire.

The successors of Muhammad encouraged *jihad*, or holy war, against non-Muslims and within a century built an empire stretching from northern Spain all the way across North Africa to India. Many of the areas conquered, such as Iraq, Syria, Palestine, and North Africa, were formerly Christian strongholds where the Christians chose conversion to Islam over death by the sword. Even western Europe was threatened until Charles Martel of France finally halted Islam's expansion, when he defeated the Muslims at the battle of Tours, France, in 732, exactly one hundred years after Muhammad's death.

Islam has continued to grow, and today more than one-fifth of the world's population is Muslim. In 1900, only 12 percent of the world's population embraced Islam; by 2000 the number had grown to 21 percent. Today, Islam is the fastest growing of the major religions. Most Muslims live in a belt stretching from West Africa to Southeast Asia. Islam is the majority religion in forty-two countries and territories, most of which prohibit Christian evangelism and exclude Christian missionaries.

In spite of the fact that Muhammad's followers have greatly increased their numbers and their political power, there is encouragement in that more Muslims came to Christ between 1980 and 2000 than in any earlier period of history.

664 ✠ THE SYNOD OF WHITBY MEETS

Seventh-century English Christianity was divided into the Roman Catholic Church and the Celtic church. One of the divisive issues was the date for Easter. This issue came to a head in 663 when King Oswy (611–670) of Northumbria, a Celt, realized that he would be celebrating Easter when his Roman Catholic wife was observing Lent. King Oswy called a synod at Whitby in Yorkshire in 664, with delegates from both movements. The Celts argued that their position could be traced through Columba (521–597) and Polycarp (69–155) to St. John, while the Romanists declared that their view went back to Peter and Paul. King Oswy decided in favor of the Roman position, stating that he would rather be on good terms with the keeper of heaven's gate than with Columba. This decision aligned the English Church with the Roman Catholic Church for the next 875 years.

676 ✠ CAEDMON CREATES CHRISTIAN POETRY IN ENGLISH

In about 676, an illiterate English herdsman named Caedmon (d. 680), following an evening of revelry, had a vision in which he was commanded to write poetry. In the vision he recited verses that he had never before heard. To his great surprise, the next day he could repeat the verses from his vision and create more. His employer introduced him to Hilda (614–680), the abbess of Whitby, who verified his gift by reading portions of Scripture to him and asking him to put them into poetry. He was able to do so by the next morning. Hilda then hired him for the abbey, and he spent the rest of his life turning Bible stories into verse. He is the earliest known Christian Anglo-Saxon poet.

680 ✠ THE THIRD COUNCIL OF CONSTANTINOPLE MEETS

In response to the rise of Islam in the mid-seventh century, Eastern Emperor Heraclius (575–641) sought to strengthen the church by unifying it. This meant trying to bring the Monophysites, who held that Christ had only one nature instead of two, back into the church. In 638, he proposed a compromise called Monothelitism that described Christ as having two natures, divine and human, but only one will. A few leaders in Egypt accepted the compromise, but most Eastern churches rejected it. The Third Council of Constantinople, the sixth ecumenical council, dealt with this issue. The council desired to achieve unity

594	1066	1200	1300
Buddhism becomes religion of Japan	Normans conquer Britain	Genghis Khan begins conquests	Renaissance begins in Italy

between the churches of Constantinople and Rome. It therefore rejected the compromise of Monothelitism and declared that Christ not only had two natures but also two wills. As a result of this council, the Nestorian and Monophysite churches separated themselves permanently from orthodoxy.

686 ✝ WILFRID COMPLETES THE EVANGELIZATION OF ENGLAND

The son of a Northumbrian noble, Wilfrid (634–709) studied Roman Catholicism at Canterbury. At the Synod of Whitby in 664, he was the leading spokesman for the Roman dating of Easter. Following the synod he was appointed bishop of York. In 678, the archbishop of Canterbury, concerned about Wilfrid's aspirations for power, divided the diocese of York into four sections, taking away three-quarters of Wilfrid's territory. Wilfrid appealed to Rome and won his case, but when he returned to England he was imprisoned by the king of Northumbria, whose new queen had an intense hatred for Wilfrid. In 686, after his release from prison, he went to Sussex, where he had success evangelizing the heathen Saxons of southernmost England, thereby completing the evangelization of England.

691 ☾ THE DOME OF THE ROCK IS COMPLETED

Less than seventy-five years after the founding of Islam, Caliph Abd al-Malik (646–705) completed the Dome of the Rock mosque on the Temple mount in Jerusalem. The building is the oldest surviving Muslim structure in the world. According to Muslim doctrine, during his Night Journey, the prophet Muhammad (570–632) traveled to Jerusalem, set foot on the giant rock on the Temple mount, and then ascended to heaven. The Dome was built directly over this rock, which is also the traditional site of Abraham's near-sacrifice of Isaac. After construction was completed, Abd al-Malik commemorated his accomplishment with an inscription that read, "This dome was built by the servant of God Abd al-Malik ibn Marwan, emir of the faithful, in the [Muslim] year seventy-two."

694 ✡ JUDAISM IS OUTLAWED IN SPAIN

The Jewish communities of Spain had flourished under the Roman Empire. By 415, a barbarian tribe called the Visigoths had taken control of Spain after conquering Rome in 410. The Visigoth king Recared (586–601) converted to Catholicism in 598, and the majority of the nobles followed suit. The church held successive councils in Toledo, the Visigoth capital of Spain, which increasingly instigated vicious anti-Semitism. This culminated in the Seventeenth Council of Toledo in 694, at which all Jews living in Visigoth Spain were declared slaves. Their possessions were confiscated, and Judaism was outlawed. All Jewish children over the age of seven were taken from their homes and raised as Christians.

711 ☪ MUSLIMS INVADE SPAIN

By 710, the Muslim armies had conquered most of North Africa. In that year a Muslim Berber chief named Tarif ibn Malluk led a raiding party across the Straits of Gibraltar into Spain, then known as Iberia. Cape Tarifa, the southernmost tip of Gibraltar, still carries his name. Encouraged by the success of this mission, Tarik ibn Aiyad (d. 720), another Berber, prepared a larger expedition, which in the spring of 711 landed an army of seven thousand Muslim horsemen on Gibraltar. From there the army marched north, defeating the Visigoths who controlled Spain and capturing Córdoba and Toledo. In 712, Musa ibn Nusayr (640–716), the governor of northwest Africa, arrived in Spain with a Muslim army of ten thousand and captured Seville and Merida. By 718, the Muslims controlled most of the Iberian Peninsula and had crossed the Pyrenees into southern France. The conquest of Spain was to be the most enduring Muslim achievement in Europe.

716 ✝ BONIFACE'S MISSIONARY CAREER BEGINS

Born in Devonshire, England, Boniface (675–754) was ordained at the age of thirty. Feeling called to evangelize Europe, he made his first missionary trip to the continent in 716. After laboring in Frisia, Holland, and Germany, he went to Rome in 723 and was consecrated as missionary bishop to Germany by Pope Gregory II (669–731). Boniface's missionary methods were vigorous and assertive. His most famous act was chopping down the sacred oak of the German thunder god. Throughout Germany, he preached, set up monasteries, organized bishoprics, trained clergy, and tore down pagan shrines. At the

594	1066	1200	1300
Buddhism becomes religion of Japan	Normans conquer Britain	Genghis Khan begins conquests	Renaissance begins in Italy

end of his career, he longed to return to still-pagan Frisia, where he had begun. He was martyred in Frisia in 754, ending his career as the most effective missionary of the Dark Ages (the fifth through eighth centuries).

726 ✝ EMPEROR LEO III DECLARES AN EDICT AGAINST WORSHIP OF IMAGES

Although pictures had been banned by church councils, they had become very popular from 400 on. It was suggested that the pictures of martyrs would help the illiterate to follow their positive examples. Then in 717, Leo III (680–741) took the empire's throne. Apparently believing that the veneration of images was an obstacle in evangelizing Jews and Muslims, in 726 Emperor Leo III issued an edict declaring all paintings, mosaics, and statues in churches to be idols and ordering them to be destroyed. In Rome, Pope Gregory II (669–731) rejected the decree, and his successor, Gregory III (731–741), called a council in 731 that affirmed this position. John of Damascus (675–749) wrote against iconoclasm, opposition to the use of images in worship, and advocacy of their destruction. This opposition, however, did not deter Leo or his successor, Constantine V (718–775). Their campaign against images went on unabated.

730 ✝ JOHN OF DAMASCUS WRITES FOUNT OF WISDOM

John (675–749) was born about 675 into a wealthy Christian home in Damascus. His father was the representative of Christians in the court of the caliph. John succeeded his father in the position; however, in about 716 he joined a monastery near Jerusalem. From 726 to 730 he wrote three treatises defending the use of images in worship, asserting that those opposed to them had a pessimistic view toward matter. John's most famous treatise was the *Fount of Wisdom*. In its first section he examined the philosophy of Aristotle, applying it to Christian theology in a manner that was followed by many theologians of the following centuries. In the second part, he answered heresies that had arisen in the church. John's lasting contribution was in systematizing the theology of Eastern Christianity. His approach is still authoritative in Eastern Orthodoxy.

1435	1475	1506–7	1517
First African slaves brought to Europe	First book printed in English	First maps of New World created	Ottomans conquer Egypt

731 ✝ BEDE COMPLETES ECCLESIASTICAL HISTORY OF THE ENGLISH PEOPLE

Born in Northumbria (now Durham, England), Bede (673–735) entered a monastery at the age of seven. The monastery soon moved to Jarrow where he lived for the rest of his life. In that isolated location he became one of the most educated men in Europe. After his ordination, he taught and wrote in the monastery. In 731, he completed his best-known work, *Ecclesiastical History of the English People*. It is a primary and, in many cases, sole source for much of early English history. Within a century of his death, he was ascribed the title, "The Venerable Bede." He was the father of English history.

732 ✝ ☪ THE BATTLE OF TOURS

Many consider the rise of Islam to be one of the most unique movements in history. In 622, the followers of Muhammad (570–632) were a persecuted band of religionists huddled in Mecca. Exactly one hundred years later they controlled much of the known world, from Spain on the west, to all of North Africa, Palestine, Syria, Persia, and even parts of India, until they were threatening Constantinople and France. Charles Martel (689–741) (*Martel* meaning "the hammer") was the military leader of the Franks, a German tribe that had invaded Gaul (modern-day France) and converted to Christianity. In 732, the Muslim army pushed northward into the territory of the Franks, and Charles Martel met them between Tours and Poitiers in Gaul. In a series of fierce battles, Martel and the Franks successfully pushed the Muslims back to Spain. Martel preserved Western civilization; if not for his victory at Tours, Western Europe today would be Muslim and speaking Arabic.

740 ✡ KHAZARS CONVERT TO JUDAISM

The persecution of the Byzantine Empire caused many Jews to flee to the little kingdom of Khazaria, located north of the Caspian and Black Seas with its capital, Atila, on the Volga River. In about 740, the king of Khazaria and the whole ruling class converted to Judaism. This event was a great encouragement to Jews throughout the world, for it meant that there was at least one place in the world where Jews were in authority. News of the mass conversion reached the Jews of Spain in the tenth century, and Hasdai Ibn Shaprut (915–970), the leader of the

594	1066	1200	1300
Buddhism becomes religion of Japan	Normans conquer Britain	Genghis Khan begins conquests	Renaissance begins in Italy

Spanish Jewish community, began corresponding with the Khazar king. In 965, Khazaria was severely oppressed by nearby Kiev. Greatly weakened and reduced in size, the kingdom disappeared from view after the twelfth century.

750 ✝ THE DONATION OF CONSTANTINE IS WRITTEN

In approximately 750, an unknown author fabricated a document entitled the *Donation of Constantine*. It claims to be written by Constantine (285–337) as a record of his conversion and faith and of the privileges that he conferred on Pope Sylvester I (d. 335) and his successors. These privileges included authority over all other churches, particularly those of Alexandria, Antioch, Constantinople, and Jerusalem. The pope also was given dominion over Rome, Italy, and all western regions. The pope was made the supreme judge of all clergy and was even offered the imperial crown, but he refused. These supposed grants were undoubtedly to support the universal claims of the popes and were frequently cited for that purpose. The document was not identified as a forgery until the fifteenth century.

753 ✝ THE SYNOD OF HIERIA ENDORSES ICONOCLASM

The controversy over the veneration of images or icons had begun with the edict of Emperor Leo III (680–741) in 726, outlawing their worship. In 741, Leo was succeeded by his son Constantine V (718–775), who continued the policy of his father. To gain ecclesiastical backing for his position, Constantine called the Synod of Hieria to deal with the issue. A total of 338 bishops met near Chalcedon, although the patriarchs of Alexandria, Antioch, and Jerusalem did not attend, nor did the pope. The synod ruled that by representing only the humanity of Christ, icon worshipers were either dividing his unity or confounding his two natures. The synod declared that all images of Mary or saints were idols and therefore to be destroyed. The decision of Hieria fueled the controversy, and many monks were martyred for the sake of their venerated icons.

756 ✝ PEPIN III DONATES LAND TO THE PAPACY

In 756, Pepin III (714–768), king of the Franks, granted the Lombard lands of central Italy to Pope Stephen II (d. 757). Known as the "Donation of Pepin," this act procured for the papacy political authority over much of central Italy. This newly explicit papal political power and the cooperation between pope and king were not without precedent, however, nor unexpected. Five years earlier, Pope Zacharias (d. 752) had supported Pepin's rise to kingship, and in 754 Stephen personally crowned Pepin as king. Pepin's donation, then, was the product of a growing collaboration between papacy and empire. It also reflected the increasing role of northern Europe in the religious and political medieval world. The Donation of Pepin set the stage for Pope Leo III (d. 816) to crown Pepin's son, Charlemagne (742–814), as Holy Roman Emperor in 800.

765 ✡ ANAN BEGINS KARAITE MOVEMENT

Around 765, Anan ben David established the Karaites, which means "the people of Scripture." The movement, located in Islamic-ruled Iraq, sought to reform Judaism by emphasizing study of the Jewish Bible. By the late eighth century the traditional writings of Jewish rabbis had come to be regarded as a higher authority than the Bible, and Anan and his followers believed this progression twisted the Jewish religion. Besides reestablishing Scripture as the key source for Jewish law and practice, Anan taught that all Jews should be allowed to interpret the Bible for themselves. Resulting from their own efforts to interpret Scripture, the Karaites were among the first to study Hebrew grammar, and they wrote a number of biblical commentaries.

768 ✝ CHARLEMAGNE CONQUERS WESTERN EUROPE

Charlemagne (742–814) became ruler of France in 768. He proceeded to conquer Germany and Italy, and then continued to fight throughout central Europe and northern Spain, setting up frontier areas that later were influential in the spread of Christianity throughout Europe. Because Charlemagne made profound religious, political, economic, and intellectual contributions that greatly influenced Western culture, he is often considered to be the founder of Europe.

768–814 ✝ CHARLEMAGNE'S REFORMS SPARK RENAISSANCE

With hopes of reestablishing the glory of the old Roman Empire, Emperor Charlemagne (742–814) pressed for many changes to the clergy. His goals were

594	1066	1200	1300
Buddhism becomes religion of Japan	Normans conquer Britain	Genghis Khan begins conquests	Renaissance begins in Italy

to produce a literate clergy and to preserve the classic ancient works, to create an enduring legacy of Christian scholarship and learning. As a result, illiteracy was attacked throughout the empire, new monasteries and schools were established in many regions, and there was a renewed focus on liberal arts as part of education. Charlemagne's reforms thus marked the beginning of a revival in learning and education for the whole population of the Holy Roman Empire in general, and for the church in particular.

781 ✛ ALCUIN OF YORK BECOMES AN ADVISOR TO CHARLEMAGNE

Alcuin of York (d. 804) was head of a cathedral school in York when Charlemagne (742–814) persuaded him to leave England to become a part of his court in France. Charlemagne was attempting to raise the level of education among the clergy in his kingdom and enlisted Alcuin as his royal advisor in this matter. Alcuin's chief duty was to teach Latin language, culture, and theology—subjects that had been neglected over the years. One of the results of Alcuin's work was the development of a style of handwriting called Caroline miniscule, which used both capital and lowercase letters and was easier to read than earlier styles. His writings on theological topics continue to be studied today. He is regarded as the most significant figure in the renaissance of classical and religious learning that began under Charlemagne.

787 ✛ SECOND COUNCIL OF NICEA SETTLES ICON CONTROVERSY

Although early Jewish and Christian practice forbad the worship of icons, by the early eighth century, the veneration of images had gained widespread acceptance in the church. Therefore, in 730, when Emperor Leo III (680–741) proclaimed this practice to be unlawful, there was a backlash against his decree. After several years of intense controversy that involved violent persecution on both sides, a council convened to decide the question. For more than a month in 787, the Second Council of Nicea (a city just east of modern-day Istanbul, Turkey) met to debate the issue. After eight sessions, attended by more than three hundred delegates, the council decided that icons could receive veneration but not adoration, which was reserved for God alone. Although this decision was not immediately accepted (Emperor Charlemagne [742–814] openly defied it), it eventually became the standard practice of the whole church.

1435	1475	1506–7	1517
First African slaves brought to Europe	First book printed in English	First maps of New World created	Ottomans conquer Egypt

800 ✛ CHARLEMAGNE IS CROWNED ROMAN EMPEROR

Leo III (d. 816) became pope in 795. The previous pope, Hadrian I (d. 795), and his followers were quick to accuse Leo of perjury and adultery and attempted to take his life. Charlemagne (742–814) rescued him from his accusers. In return on Christmas Day 800, Leo III crowned Charlemagne as Roman emperor. He was the first emperor of what later would be called the "Holy Roman Empire." Naming Charlemagne as emperor blurred the jurisdictions of church and state, in effect making Charlemagne, rather than Leo, the highest authority figure in the church. Although Leo III continued to voice theological pronouncements, many were, in fact, authored by the emperor, Charlemagne. The Roman Catholic Church canonized Leo III in 1673.

826 ✛ KING HARALD KLACK OF DENMARK IS CONVERTED

In approximately 822, Emperor Louis the Pious (778–840), son of Charlemagne (742–814), sent Archbishop Ebo (806–882) of Reims, France, to Denmark in an effort to expand the Christian religion into the north. The tide began to turn in 826 with the conversion of Harald Klack, an exiled Danish king, one of the many kings among whom Denmark was divided. Klack was baptized with four hundred of his followers in Mainz, Germany. Klack and his fellow Danes were the first fruits of what would become a rich spiritual harvest in Denmark.

827 ✛ ANSKAR EVANGELIZES DENMARK

When Harald Klack sought help from Emperor Louis the Pious (778–840) in regaining his throne in Denmark, Anskar (801–865), an educator at a French abbey, was recruited to accompany Harald back to Denmark. This trip marked the beginning of Anskar's relationship with Denmark. Anskar established a church at Hedeby, and a few important converts were made. Later, after being appointed archbishop of Hamburg, Anskar brought Danish boys to Germany to train them to return as evangelists to Denmark. It is unknown how influential the churches established under Anskar were, for paganism had a stronghold on the Scandinavian countries for more than a generation after Anskar's death. However, he played an important early role in what would later become the widespread conversion of Scandinavia.

594	1066	1200	1300
Buddhism becomes religion of Japan	Normans conquer Britain	Genghis Khan begins conquests	Renaissance begins in Italy

829 ✝ ANSKAR EVANGELIZES SWEDEN

In 829, the king of Sweden petitioned France to send Christian missionaries to his country. Anskar (801–865), who became known as the "apostle of the North," was sent, along with a fellow monk, because he had previously done evangelistic work in Denmark. Though the two men were robbed by Vikings on their journey to Sweden, once there the king supported them and they were able to make converts and to found several churches. In 831, Pope Gregory IV (r. 827–844) granted Anskar jurisdiction over future churches in Scandinavia. Even though widespread conversion did not take place for another century, Anskar laid a foundation for the future of Christianity in Scandinavia.

843 ✝ THE TREATY OF VERDUN DIVIDES THE CAROLINGIAN EMPIRE

After Charlemagne's (742–814) death, his only surviving son, Louis I (778–840), succeeded him as emperor of the Holy Roman Empire. Louis, known as Louis the Pious because he preferred doing missions work over conquering territories, divided the kingdom between his three sons after his death in 840. Louis' oldest son, Lothair I (795–855), immediately declared war on his two brothers. After three years of war, the brothers agreed to cease hostilities in the Treaty of Verdun. Lothair received the central and southern portions of the empire, extending into modern-day Italy. Louis II, the German (804–876), was given the eastern portion, which became Germany. Charles I the Bald (823–877) acquired the western portion, which is now France. These basic political divisions have remained intact until the present day and marked the end of the political unity of Christian Europe.

846 ✝ ☪ MUSLIMS ATTACK ROME

Approximately two hundred years after Muhammad's death (570–632), Muslims had conquered most of the Middle East, Asia Minor, and Northern Africa. By then, the once great city of Rome had become politically unstable and militarily weak. In 827, Muslim armies invaded the island of Sicily. After conquering the island, they invaded and conquered the Mediterranean islands of Corsica, Malta, Sardinia, and Pantellerva, before advancing on to the Italian mainland. By 846, Muslim pirates had reached Rome. They swept through the city, encountering little resistance. They plundered the cathedrals of St. Peter and St. Paul, then withdrew. Contemporaries interpreted the attack as God's judgment on Rome for its corruption.

858 ✛ NICHOLAS I BECOMES POPE

Also called Nicholas the Great, Nicholas I (820–867) was pope from 858 until his death. His tenure as pope was distinguished by controversies regarding the authority of the papacy. Nicholas I was able to work through the controversies, successfully gaining acceptance for papal rule over the church and firmly establishing Rome's primacy, both critical elements in the church's development over the following centuries. However, these controversies also served to lay the groundwork for the future split between the Eastern and Western churches.

861 ✛ EAST–WEST CONFLICT OVER PHOTIUS BEGINS

Photius (820–895), a prominent scholar of the Byzantine Renaissance, was chosen to be patriarch of Constantinople in 858. This event created great controversy in the Eastern church, because the followers of Ignatius (d. 877), his predecessor, did not recognize Photius as patriarch and attempted to excommunicate him. The leaders of the Eastern church supported him, but they were overruled by the pope, Nicholas I (820–867), who deposed Photius and reinstated Ignatius. Nicholas's claim of papal supremacy over all of Christendom widened an already existing breach between the Eastern and Western churches due to differences in doctrine, language, and worship. Considered to be the most distinguished scholar and politician to hold office as patriarch of Constantinople, Photius played an important role in history for the coming split between the Eastern and Western churches in 1054.

862 ✛ CYRIL AND METHODIUS BEGIN MISSION TO SLAVS

Cyril (826–869) was a scholar from Thessalonica, Greece, who had studied under the patriarch Photius (820–895) in Constantinople before being ordained and teaching philosophy in Constantinople. In 862, Prince Ratislav of Moravia, in the modern Czech Republic and Slovakia, was converted to Christianity and requested missionaries from Constantinople to combat the infiltration of Western culture and religion. Emperor Michael III (836–867) and patriarch Photius sent Cyril and his brother Methodius (815–885). The two brothers became known as the "apostles to the Slavs." Cyril's significant contributions include creating an alphabet that put the Slavonic language into writing for the first time, and then translating the Scriptures. After Cyril's death, Methodius continued his evangelism efforts throughout much of Eastern Europe. The "apostles to the Slavs" are credited with laying the foundations of the church in Slavic Europe, and their memories are still cherished by many Czechs, Croats, Serbs, and Bulgars.

864 + KING BORIS OF BULGARIA IS CONVERTED

King Boris (d. 907) of Bulgaria was converted and baptized about 864 by clergy sent to Bulgaria by patriarch Photius (820–895) of Constantinople. Boris encouraged the dissemination of Christianity throughout Bulgaria. However, he desired that the Bulgarian church be independent rather than fall under Byzantine rule. The patriarch rejected this idea, so Boris brought in Western missionaries from Rome, creating an East-West conflict within his own country. The Roman church also did not approve of the idea of an independent Bulgarian church. Eventually, the Byzantine orthodox clergy drove out the Western clergy but were forced to agree to a semiautonomous Bulgarian church. The next patriarch, Ignatius (d. 877), even named a Bulgarian as archbishop and gave him ten bishops to take back to Bulgaria. Boris also succeeded in substituting the Slavonic language for Greek for the liturgy of the Bulgarian church, another mark of independence.

869 + FOURTH COUNCIL OF CONSTANTINOPLE FAVORS IGNATIUS

Patriarch Ignatius (d. 877) of Constantinople was arrested and deposed in 858 for rebuking the immorality of Emperor Caesar Bardas (d. 866). Photius (820–895) was named patriarch in his place. However, Ignatius's supporters convinced Pope Nicholas I (820–867) to intervene and reinstate Ignatius in 863. Photius then managed to have the pope deposed, partly due to the support of the current emperor Michael III (842–867). However, Michael III's successor, Emperor Basil (812–886), restored Ignatius as patriarch during the Fourth Council of Constantinople in 869, which voted in favor of Ignatius over Photius. Later, after Ignatius's death, Photius convened his own Council of

Constantinople in 879, which annulled the decisions of the 869 council. Thus, the Fourth Council of Constantinople in 869 is not recognized by the Eastern church as the eighth ecumenical council, as it is by the Western church.

900 ✡ ☾ FIRST UNIVERSITY BEGINS IN CÓRDOBA, SPAIN

During the tenth century, Muslims ruled Córdoba, Spain. Islamic tolerance of both the Christian and Jewish religions cultivated an environment in which the three religious groups thrived alongside one another. The economic, cultural, and intellectual pursuits throughout the region combined to produce one of the most enlightened civilizations in history. In fact, scholarly interests were so great that the first university-like institution of learning was founded during this period of coexistence. Under Muslim tutors, Jews learned Arabic (the language of the Koran), becoming students of the Koran, as well as of their own Hebrew Bible. As a result, Moses ben Maimon, or Maimonides (1138–1204), a later native of Córdoba and one of the most revered Jewish sages, wrote in Arabic not Hebrew.

909 ✝ WILLIAM THE PIOUS ESTABLISHES MONASTERY AT CLUNY

In 909, a reform movement within the Roman Catholic Church led by William the Pious (d. 918), duke of Aquitaine, founded a new monastery at Cluny, France. The monastery strove for a return to strict adherence to the Benedictine *Rule* drawn up by Benedict of Nursia (480–547) and became the center of monastic reform for nearly two centuries. The order cultivated personal spiritual life and placed great emphasis on worship. During the eleventh and twelfth centuries, Cluny wielded great influence in the opposition of Pope Gregory VII (1023–1085) to clerical marriages and simony, the buying and selling of spiritual benefit. At the height of the reform, there were more than eleven hundred monasteries in Germany, France, England, Italy, and Spain associated with the Cluniac order.

930 ✡ THE AUTHORITATIVE TEXT OF THE HEBREW BIBLE IS ESTABLISHED

Due to the high regard in the ninth and tenth centuries for the emergent rabbinic tradition in Jewish culture, for many years the Hebrew Bible was seen as

594	1066	1200	1300
Buddhism becomes religion of Japan	Normans conquer Britain	Genghis Khan begins conquests	Renaissance begins in Italy

secondary in authority to the writings of the rabbis for law and practice. In fact, it was the tenth century before an authoritative version of the Hebrew Bible finally was determined for common use. By 930, the text was firmly in place, probably under the influence of the Karaites, "the people of Scripture," who flourished in the eighth century. This group of Jews, established by Anan ben David, sought to return the Jewish Bible to its original position as the primary authority for Judaism. With the establishment of an authoritative text, both personal interpretation and scholarly analysis were able to draw from the same source.

935 ✡ SAADIA BEN JOSEPH WRITES THE BOOK OF BELIEFS AND OPINIONS

Under the protection afforded Jews by the Islamic Empire, Jewish academies flourished in Iraq. The leaders of these institutions, known as *gaons,* were regarded as the final authority for Jewish practice. The most important gaon was Rabbi Saadia ben Joseph (882–942) of the academy in Sura. Saadia articulated Jewish law, a traditional topic for rabbinical writing, but also completed an Arabic translation of the Bible. He produced his greatest work, *The Book of Beliefs and Opinions,* in 935. It was the first systematic Jewish theological treatise ever written. Embracing the cultural changes that came with the spread of Islam, Saadia tried purposely to analyze Judaism against the backdrop of Islam and its intellectual life.

940 ✡ HASDAI IBN SHAPRUT BECOMES COURTIER TO THE MUSLIM RULER OF SPAIN

As the Islamic Empire strengthened in Spain, the caliph (the local ruler) used Córdoba—one of the great Islamic cities that attracted wealth, artists, and scholars—as his headquarters. In 940, Jewish Rabbi Hasdai Ibn Shaprut gained the caliph's favor and began serving as a courtier. His courtier-rabbi status, though unique at first, became a typical model for Jewish leaders in Spain during the tenth century. Many of these leaders wielded authority in the public life of the Islamic state and became involved in the intellectual life that flourished in the Muslim world. Hasdai not only was able to positively

1435	1475	1506–7	1517
First African slaves brought to Europe	First book printed in English	First maps of New World created	Ottomans conquer Egypt

affect the Jewish lifestyle, but his wealth afforded him influence in the literary development of Córdoba. He personally supported several poets, and with his assistance the golden age of Hebrew literature dawned in the Middle Ages.

955 ✝ OLGA OF RUSSIA IS CONVERTED

The first ruler in Russian lands known to convert to Christianity was Olga (d. 969), the grand duchess of Kiev from 945 to 964. In about 955, she accepted the Christian faith and traveled to Constantinople to be baptized. At that time Constantinople was the second most important religious center next to Rome. Olga returned to Kiev, the capital of the Russian realm, but unfortunately her faith had little influence upon her land. Kiev remained a pagan state under her son, Sviatoslav, who ruled from 964 to 978. However, Olga's grandson, Prince Vladimir (956–1015) of Kiev, who reigned from 978 to 1015, became the person responsible for bringing Orthodox Christianity to the people of Russia.

962 ✝ OTTO I REVIVES THE HOLY ROMAN EMPIRE

The Holy Roman Empire, originally founded in 800 by Charlemagne (742–814), was revived in 962 with the coronation of the German king, Otto I (912–973), as emperor. This was a revival of Charlemagne's alliance of church and state. Otto reasserted his right to appoint and control bishops. His policy was one of empowering the church in order to diminish the authority of secular rulers. Initially his empire included only Germany and part of Italy, but the Holy Roman Empire eventually spread over Western Europe and lasted from 962 until it was dissolved by Napoléon Bonaparte (1769–1821) in 1806.

988 ✝ RUSSIA IS CHRISTIANIZED

Tradition has it that, following a strong pagan revival, Prince Vladimir (956–1015) of Kiev—grandson of Olga (d. 969), the first Russian ruler to accept Christianity—sent out emissaries to study Judaism, Islam, Roman

THE HOLY ROMAN EMPIRE

February 2, 962

Pope John XII was one of the worst of a long line of reprobate Italian vicars. King Otto I was one of the best of a promising succession of German sovereigns. When Pope John crowned Otto as Roman Emperor on February 2, 962, he effectively signed his own political death warrant and the rebirth certificate of the Holy Roman Empire in one grand and ceremonious stroke.

The Holy Roman Empire was first born on Christmas Day 800. On that day, while Charlemagne, the conquering king of western Europe, was worshiping at St. Peter's Basilica, Pope Leo III stepped down from the altar and crowned him successor to the Caesars of Rome. But Charlemagne's heirs could not maintain his empire. Separate kingdoms once again arose with no central government to hold them together.

Near the end of the ninth century and through the first half of the tenth, the papacy fell into moral decadence. Immoral popes were seated and deposed at whim, the lives of many of them ending in murder or imprisonment. During this infamous period John XII became pope in 955.

Meanwhile in Germany, young Otto I was rising in power. Wielding Christianity as a unifying sword, King Otto formed wise and careful alliances with other German tribes. Appointing bishops at the same time as he anointed civil authorities, he gave generous land grants to the German church, building it into a national institution.

By sword point, Otto sought to bring a western Slavic tribe known as the Wends to the foot of the cross. Denmark, Poland, and Bohemia bowed to him as their feudal sovereign. And then, with his eye on the crown of the Holy Roman Empire, Otto led his army into Italy to rescue the widowed Adelaide, Italy's former queen who had been imprisoned by King Berengar II, her late husband's successor. Otto married Adelaide, reduced Berengar to a fief of the German crown, and returned to Germany.

Several years later, Otto came up against Berengar again when Pope John XII sent an appeal for his help against the king. This time Otto marched peaceably into Rome at the head of a massive army, and there, on February 2, 962, John XII crowned him emperor of the Holy Roman Empire.

Otto became greatly alarmed by the moral degradation of the papacy, and the next year he returned to Rome and brought Pope John to trial before an ecclesiastical court. Cardinals charged the pope with adultery, incest, and turning the papal palace into a brothel. They removed John from office, replacing him with Otto's choice, a capable but ecclesiastically unaccredited layman. The new pope, Leo VIII, and many successive popes would now answer to the Holy Roman emperor.

Thus began a "reformation" of the papacy that lasted nearly three centuries. From Otto the Great's time, the Holy Roman Empire would exist continuously until Napoléon I [Bonaparte] replaced it with his Confederation of the Rhine in 1806.

Christianity (Catholicism), and Greek Christianity (Orthodoxy). Vladimir married Anna, the sister of the Byzantine emperor and chose Orthodoxy. In 988, Vladimir proclaimed Christianity as the official Russian religion and ordered all his subjects to be baptized. The upper classes and city dwellers quickly adopted Christianity while the lower classes and rural areas remained pagan into the fourteenth and fifteenth centuries. The official religion of the state until 1917, the Russian Orthodox Church continues to have great political influence.

996 ☦ ☾ CALIPH EL HAKIM PERSECUTES COPTS IN EGYPT

Legend has it that Mark the Evangelist founded the church in Egypt, known as the Coptic Church. Throughout the ages, the Copts were persecuted by many of the conquerors and rulers of their homeland. In the early seventh century Persians exercised authority over the Copts until the Muslims conquered Persia. Since that time Muslim Arabs have had varying degrees of dominion in the area up to the present day. Among the most severe persecutions experienced by the Copts was one that took place during the devastating rule of Caliph el Hakim, who came into power in 996 and ruled until 1021. It is reported that el Hakim destroyed three thousand Egyptian churches and induced large numbers of Christians to abandon their beliefs under threat of death.

999 ☦ LEIF ERIKSSON CONVERTS

Despite his heritage as the son of pagan Norse leader Erik the Red (950–1003), who had settled in Iceland and founded Greenland, Leif Eriksson became a Christian in 999 through the influence of Norwegian King Olaf Tryggvason (969–1000). Leif then brought a priest to Greenland and, despite his father's objections, introduced Christianity to their small Norse settlement there. Though the population of the settlement was never much more than two thousand, the members succeeded in building churches and a cathedral. Eventually a bishop was established, becoming the civil and religious leader of the Norse community in Greenland. In 1000, Leif Eriksson was the first European to discover America by landing in what he called Vineland, which probably was Newfoundland.

594	1066	1200	1300
Buddhism becomes religion of Japan	Normans conquer Britain	Genghis Khan begins conquests	Renaissance begins in Italy

999 ✝ SYLVESTER II BECOMES POPE

After his education at a Benedictine monastery, Sylvester II (945–1003) studied in Spain and became a teacher at the cathedral school at Reims, France. Known for his abilities in mathematics, philosophy, and natural science, Sylvester is considered to be the one who introduced Arabic numerals to Western Europe and invented the pendulum clock. In 999, he became the first Frenchman elected pope, becoming head of the church at a time of great corruption. He stood against prevailing evils such as the secular control of church elections, nepotism, and simony. Sylvester also played a significant role in the spread of Christianity into Eastern Europe, establishing new bishoprics in Hungary and appointing the first archbishop of Poland.

1000 ✡ KALONYMUS FAMILY MOVES TO MAINZ

Prior to their exclusion from social and political activities in Europe, Jews spread to central Europe, as well as into France and England. While Jewish academies thrived under the Muslim Empire in Iraq during the tenth century, it was not until the beginning of the eleventh century that Jewish institutions were established in central European locations. Around 1000, a family of rabbis named Kalonymus journeyed from Lucca in Italy to Mainz, a prominent German city. Under their leadership rabbinic academies were established with a single-minded focus on the study of the Talmud and Jewish law. Thus began the tradition of Jewish scholarship in Western Europe.

1000 ✡ THE KHAZAR KINGDOM ENDS

Jewish persecution in the Byzantine Empire under a number of different rulers caused Jews to seek refuge in Khazaria. Established in the seventh century by the Khazars, a pagan people of Turkish heritage, Khazaria had developed into an assertive, albeit small kingdom. In the mid-eighth century Khazaria's ruler converted to Judaism, along with the entire upper class. To Jews throughout the world, the existence of the Khazar kingdom was evidence that, despite the loss of their homeland in the Middle East, God remembered them and had provided them a new home. Although rulers in the Byzantine Empire made some attempts to snuff out the Khazar kingdom, it was not until the attacks from the Russian force in Kiev in 965 that Khazaria buckled. The year 1000 saw the end of the Khazar kingdom.

1000 ✡ RABBENU GERSHOM'S SYNOD IN MAYENCE OUTLAWS POLYGAMY

Around the year 1000, Rabbenu ("Our Master") Gershom ben Judah (960–1040) brought together a Jewish synod in Mayence, France. Gershom's synod, much like the Christian councils of the day, discussed various issues affecting Jewish law and practice, and passed *takkanot* (ordinances or improvements). The synod outlawed the practice of polygamy, thereby adopting the standard of the Christian culture around them. In Christian Europe, where monogamy was the only form of marriage, the Jews were often judged as immoral because of their polygamy. Despite a deep respect for the forefathers in Scripture (who were polygamous), the Jews at the synod in Mayence upheld Gershom's call for monogamy. In addition, they required the wife's consent before a divorce could be granted.

1038 ✡ HAI, THE LAST INFLUENTIAL GAON, DIES

Judaism flourished in Iraq under Muslim rule, and the Jewish academies of Sara and Pumbeditha moved to Baghdad, where they attracted residents from throughout the Muslim world. The academy leaders were called *gaons*, and they were considered the supreme authority in Jewish law and religious practice. However, beginning in the eleventh century the Islamic Empire broke up into individual Islamic states and Iraq lost its leadership role, causing the gaons of Iraq to lose their role in the Jewish world. As a result, Jewish culture in Iraq became less important among the Jews elsewhere. Hai of Pumbeditha, who died in 1038, appears to have been the last gaon to possess international authority. The academy of Pumbeditha closed two years after his death.

1048 ✝ LEO IX BECOMES POPE

Born into a noble family in Alsace, Leo IX (1002–1054) performed military service before studying at Toul, in northeastern France. With the assistance of his relative Emperor Conrad II (990–1039), Leo later was appointed bishop of

Toul. Inspired by the religious work of the monastery at Cluny, Leo led reforms in a number of monasteries. In 1048, Leo became Leo IX when he was elected pope. With his assistant, Hildebrand (who would later become Pope Gregory VII), Leo IX traveled throughout Europe to promote a new view of church leadership. He convened numerous councils at Bari, Mainz, Reims, and Pavia to implement his reforms. The councils issued decrees focusing on abuses such as simony, which is the buying and selling of spiritual benefits, and marriage of the clergy. In later years Leo focused on defending Italy from the invading Normans. Leo IX was defeated by the Normans in 1053, the year before he died.

1049 ✛ HUGH RULES THE CLUNY MONASTERY AS ABBOT

Though he came from a noble family, Hugh (1024–1109) chose intellectual life over the life of a knight and, at the age of fourteen, joined the monastery at Cluny. Hugh became prior only four years later, and was named abbot of Cluny in 1049. Under Hugh's discipline, Cluny grew to the height of its prosperity, opening new houses of the order in France, Germany, England, Spain, and Italy, and building a beautiful abbey church. During his sixty-year rule at Cluny, Hugh saw the successful founding of the first Cluniac convent for nuns, participated in many church councils, and assisted in the arrangements for the first crusade.

1050 ✛ POPE LEO IX ESTABLISHES THE COLLEGE OF CARDINALS

In 1050, Pope Leo IX (1002–1054) altered the church office of cardinal by establishing the Sacred College of Cardinals in Rome. Until the eighth century, "cardinal" referred to priests in general and thereafter was used to refer to the priests and deacons advising Rome's bishop. Pope Leo's action in 1050 officially established the office of cardinal, whose members ranked as Roman princes during the Middle Ages. As a governing body of the church, the College of Cardinals became the pope's advisors and assumed administrative control of the Roman Catholic Church in his absence. Today, in addition to electing the pope, the primary work of the Sacred College is administrative. Cardinals are chosen by the pope. Since the Third Lateran Council (1179), the election of a pope is held at a secret conclave of the cardinals.

1054 ✦ THE EAST-WEST SCHISM SEPARATES ORTHODOX AND CATHOLIC CHURCHES

The Great Schism of 1054 signaled the separation of the Orthodox Church in the East from the Roman Church in the West. At the heart of their break was the Roman pope's claim to universal authority. The Orthodox Church, which had agreed to honor the pope, believed that church matters should be determined by a council of bishops, and would not grant the pope undisputed dominion. The two churches already had very distinct cultures and theologies. The Eastern church developed into the Eastern, Greek, and Russian Orthodox Churches while the Western Roman Church developed into the Roman Catholic Church. The East and West churches remained on friendly terms until Crusaders of the Fourth Crusade captured Constantinople in 1204.

1056 ✡ SAMUEL THE NAGID DIES

Samuel the Nagid (993–1055) was one of the most influential courtier-rabbis in the history of the Muslim Empire. Samuel gained his prominent position in the Muslim court of Granada, one of the small kingdoms of Islamic Spain, as a result of his uncanny ability to write in the difficult-to-master, elaborate style of Arabic required for diplomatic communications. In addition to earning him a role advising the prince of Granada, Samuel's character and political prowess made him, in effect, Granada's ruler. Samuel probably had military responsibilities as well. He also wrote many Jewish law and Hebrew grammar books and composed Hebrew poetry before his death around 1055. While many Muslims held him in high esteem, some were threatened by his authority. Jewish society revered Samuel for his knowledge, skill, elegant manner, and loyalty to his people.

1059 ✦ NICHOLAS DECREES THAT CARDINALS ELECT THE POPE

During the rule of Pope Nicholas II (1010–1061), significant steps were taken to establish procedures for electing future popes. In 1059, Nicholas decreed that the cardinals of the church were responsible for filling the office via election. The edict also made allowances for unusual situations. For example, the cardinals could meet outside of Rome if they so desired, and if an appropriate candi-

594	1066	1200	1300
Buddhism becomes religion of Japan	Normans conquer Britain	Genghis Khan begins conquests	Renaissance begins in Italy

date could not be found within the city of Rome they could look elsewhere. And finally, in the event that war or other events kept the pope outside of Rome, he would still exercise and carry full authority. By making the pope less identified with Rome alone, he became more connected to the entire Western church.

1065 ✡ RASHI RETURNS TO TROYES

Rabbi Solomon bar Isaac (1040–1105), known as Rashi, was born in Troyes in present-day France and was educated in the Talmudic academies of Worms and Mainz, Germany. Returning to Troyes in 1065, he opened his own Talmudic academy. During Rashi's lifetime, the Talmud—a collection of legal arguments, folklore, stories, and proverbs—became the main focus of study and meditation among Jews. Desiring to assist students in their study, Rashi and other leaders wrote commentaries on the Talmud. Rashi's commentaries on the Bible and the Talmud are distinguished by such clarity that they still remain authoritative today.

1066 ✡ JEWS ARE MASSACRED IN GRANADA

In 1066, the residents of Granada, a traditionally tolerant region in Muslim Spain, massacred the Jews living in their midst. Earlier, Rabbi Samuel the Nagid (993–1055) had become the primary advisor to the prince of Granada and had functioned as the de facto ruler of the small kingdom. He had successfully been able to deal with the jealousy many of the Muslims felt toward him. However, his son Yehosef, who succeeded him at his death, was one of those killed in the massacre. Although it was an isolated event in Muslim Spain, the massacre was a reminder that the Jews were regarded as aliens.

1066 ✝ WILLIAM THE CONQUEROR IS CROWNED KING OF ENGLAND

Victorious in battle during the Norman Conquest of England, William I of Normandy (1028–1087), known as William the Conqueror, was crowned king of England on December 25, 1066. Counted among the greatest and worst of men, William was respected for his pious conduct and reverent support of the church, and he was dreaded because of his sword and his will. Yet, because of his claims to the throne and able leadership, he obtained the loyalty of the pope, the

1435	1475	1506–7	1517
First African slaves brought to Europe	First book printed in English	First maps of New World created	Ottomans conquer Egypt

church, and much of the English nobility. William's rule, a unique mix of Saxon practices (already familiar in England) and bold new Norman ideas, created a lasting foundation for England's continued progress. In the end, William's endeavor to bring Norman and Christian ideals to England had enduring benefits, making him one of England's most significant reformers. William I reigned as king of the Norman dynasty until 1087.

1066 ✡ JEWS BEGIN SETTLING IN ENGLAND

As Jews traveled into central and Western Europe, eventually some moved to England. The first Jews most likely came to England from mainland Europe with William the Conqueror (1028–1087) in 1066. William's son, King Henry I (1068–1135), gave the Jews expanded business opportunities in London. By the time King Henry II (1133–1189) took the English throne, the Jewish population had grown in a number of cities throughout England, and many Jews were active participants in financing various endeavors, including royal projects.

1070 ✡ SOLOMON IBN GABIROL WRITES FONS VITAE

Around 1070, Solomon ibn Gabirol (1021–1070), a Jewish poet and philosopher from Malaga, Spain, completed *Fons Vitae*. Drawing heavily on the ideas of Plato (429–347 BC), *Fons Vitae* explores the universe as a cosmic battle between what Plato called "form" and "matter." The work had a great impact on a number of Catholic scholars and eventually became well read throughout Christian Europe, though most readers were unaware that the volume was authored by a Jew.

1071 ✝ ☾ SELJUK TURKS FROM ASIA CONQUER ASIA MINOR

Christian pilgrimages to the Holy Land were common during much of the medieval period. But in the eleventh century trouble in the Byzantine Empire made travel increasingly dangerous. Deaths of key rulers and leadership dissensions threatened the stability of the empire from within. Around this time Seljuk Turks, Islamic converts from Central Asia, were establishing an empire that spread from Mesopotamia to Syria to Palestine to Egypt. They were considered even more formidable than the Normans in the West, who simultaneously were conquering southern Italy. In 1071, the Seljuk Turks moved north and defeated Christian Byzantine forces at the Battle of Mazikert, near Lake Van in Armenia. The resulting request of Byzantine rulers to the pope for support in their fight against the Seljuk Turks contributed to the commencement of the Crusades.

1073 ✝ GREGORY VII BECOMES POPE

Gregory (1023–1085) began his life of church service as a Benedictine monk, taking the name Hildebrand, meaning "brilliant flame." In 1073, Hildebrand became Pope Gregory VII. Known for his spirit of reformation, Gregory made an attempt to unite the Eastern and Western churches but lacked support. He then focused on renewal of the Western church and on the development of church law. Gregory endeavored to enforce celibacy decrees for the clergy and opposed Holy Roman Emperor Henry IV (1050–1106) for choosing the church officials within his realm. Gregory's influence on the church's canon law shaped its policies for many years to come.

1077 ✝ EMPEROR HENRY IV SUBMITS TO THE POPE OVER INVESTITURE

When Pope Gregory VII (1023–1085) forbade the appointing of clergy by laymen, he thereby prevented the Holy Roman emperor, Henry IV (1050–1106) of Germany, from interfering in the selection of German church officials. However, Henry claimed the practice was an imperial divine right and sought Gregory's removal. In retaliation, the pope excommunicated Henry, whereupon imperial church officials, dreading their own exclusion, wavered in support of their king. Isolated and desiring reinstatement, Henry submitted himself before the pope at Canossa, in northern Italy, in 1077. Though Gregory heard Henry's plea and absolved him, scheming ensued and Henry deposed Gregory in 1084. Gregory's ban on lay investiture later was upheld by the Concordat of Worms in 1122.

1093 ✝ ANSELM BECOMES ARCHBISHOP OF CANTERBURY

Born in Aosta, Italy, Anselm (1033–1109) entered a monastery in France and eventually became its abbot. In 1093, at the request of King William II (1057–

1435	1475	1506–7	1517
First African slaves brought to Europe	First book printed in English	First maps of New World created	Ottomans conquer Egypt

1100) of England, Anselm left France to become archbishop of Canterbury. As archbishop, Anselm played a leading role in the academic reformation of the eleventh and twelfth centuries and worked to implement the reforms of Pope Gregory VII (1023–1085) in the English church. This, however, led to conflict with William II. Anselm refused to let the king choose church officials and was forced to leave England. King Henry I (1068–1135) asked him to return to Canterbury, but he too disagreed with Anselm, exiling him a second time. When Anselm finally compromised with the king and returned to England, he spent his remaining years enforcing clerical celibacy and other reforms of the pope. Anselm remained archbishop of Canterbury until his death in 1109.

1095 ✝ ☾ POPE URBAN II LAUNCHES FIRST CRUSADE

With the fall of Asia Minor to the Seljuk Turks, Alexius Comnenus (1048–1118), the Byzantine emperor, made an urgent request to the pope and Western rulers to send soldiers to help recover the lost territory. In addition, the Turks, in control of Jerusalem, were hindering Christian pilgrims from visiting the Holy Land. In answer to the emperor's appeal, Pope Urban II (1042–1099) announced the First Crusade in a sermon he delivered at Clermont, France, on November 27, 1095, at the Council of Clermont. In response, the crowd shouted, "God wills it!" This became the battle cry of the campaign. Mustering five thousand men, the First Crusade set out for Constantinople, eventually making its way to Jerusalem. The Crusaders captured Jerusalem in 1099.

1096 ✡ ☾ CRUSADERS MASSACRE JEWS IN RHINELAND

As enthusiasm mounted for the First Crusade, the motivation to conquer the unbelievers in control of Jerusalem spilled over toward the unbelievers closer to home: the Jews. The mobs sweeping across Europe on their way to the Holy Land found their first victims among the Jews of the Rhineland (in modern-day Germany). Massacres and forced baptisms resulted. Rather than be murdered, large numbers of Jews committed suicide, with the fathers first killing their families and then themselves. The ancient prosperous Jewish communities of the Rhineland were destroyed. This was just the beginning of the indignities wrought upon the Jews by the Crusaders.

594	1066	1200	1300
Buddhism becomes religion of Japan	Normans conquer Britain	Genghis Khan begins conquests	Renaissance begins in Italy

THE BEST SERMON EVER?

If you had just listened to a sermon on the will of God that was the greatest sermon you had ever heard, what would you do?

The place was Clermont, France, where Pope Urban II had called a church council. On November 27, 1095, the final day of the council, Urban II addressed the thousands assembled. Historians have deemed his sermon as possibly the most effective of all time.

The burning issue for Urban II was that in 1076, the Seljukian Turks had captured Jerusalem from the Arabs, making life intolerable for Christians living in Jerusalem or going there on pilgrimages.

The eloquent Urban II spoke in his native French to the assembled crowds:

Ye men of the Franks ... To you our words are spoken, and by you our message will be passed on ... God orders it.

From the borders of Jerusalem and the city of Constantinople evil tidings have come to my ears. ... An accursed race, estranged from God, has invaded the lands of the Christians in the East and has depopulated them by fire, steel and revenge. ... These Turks have led away many Christians as captives, to their own country; they have torn down the churches of Christ or used them for their own rites. In some they stable their horses. ...

Who will avenge these wrongs, unless it be you who have won glory in arms? ... If you would save your souls, then come forward to the defense of Christ. ... Labor for everlasting reward. ... You will earn the right to absolution from all your sins, and heaven is assured to any who may fall in this worthy undertaking. ... The wealth of your enemies will be yours; ye shall plunder their treasures and return home victorious. ... Take up your arms, valiant sons, and go—God guarding you. ...

The crowd rose as one, chanting, "God wills it! God wills it!"

The pope called back, "It is the will of God! ... You are soldiers of the cross. Wear on your breasts or shoulders the blood-red sign of the cross. Wear it as a token that his help will never fail you, as the pledge of a vow never to be recalled."

Thousands immediately took the vow and sewed a cross on their garments. The message raced throughout Europe by word of mouth. The next year the First Crusade left for Jerusalem with the rallying cry, "God wills it!"

The next two hundred years, the period of the Crusades, are the most embarrassing of all church history. Although the Crusaders were able to capture Jerusalem and hold it for a period of time, the Near East in general and the Muslims in particular have never forgotten the murder, rape, and pillage that characterized the Crusades. Probably never in history have so many calling themselves Christians been so misdirected in their cause. Their actions demonstrated that most of them knew nothing of the faith they claimed to represent.

And it all began with an eloquent sermon proclaiming the will of God.

1098 ✚ ANSELM WRITES <u>CUR DEUS HOMO</u>

Anselm (1033–1109), archbishop of Canterbury from 1093 until his death, was an important intellectual leader of his day. He was not as systematic as the medieval scholars who followed in his footsteps; most of his writings take the form of dialogues with his students. He wrote his most famous work, *Cur Deus Homo* (Why God Became Man), in 1098. In it, Anselm developed his understanding of the Atonement, man's reconciliation to God through Christ. Believing that the Atonement was essential to satisfy the majesty of God, Anselm's writing shifted away from the older view, held since the time of Origen (185–254), that the purpose of Christ's death was to pay a ransom to the devil.

1099 ✚ ☾ CRUSADERS CAPTURE JERUSALEM

Having set out to free the Holy Land from the grip of the Seljuk Turks, the First Crusade successfully captured Jerusalem on July 15, 1099. Their victory was bloody, with a horrendous massacre of Muslims within Jerusalem. Godfrey of Bouillon (1060–1100), who was selected to be defender of the Holy Sepulcher, did not live through the next year. His brother Baldwin (1058–1118) established the Kingdom of Jerusalem and was crowned king on Christmas Day 1100. The conquest of Jerusalem, along with Antioch and Tripoli, gave the Christians footholds of power in the region. These victories, however, would not be permanent.

1115 ✚ BERNARD FOUNDS A MONASTERY AT CLAIRVAUX

Bernard (1090–1153) grew up in a noble French family. Shortly after joining a Cistercian monastery, he moved to Clairvaux, France, in 1115 and established a new monastery there. Though devoted to the ascetic life at Clairvaux, Bernard became immersed in the political activities of his day. Bernard believed, as outlined in his *Twelve Steps to Humility,* that all Christians should focus on the soul, emptying it of worldly desires and achieving final union with God. He supported the Second Crusade but was also respected for his goodness, self-discipline, and personal charm. Considered by some to be the greatest medieval master of language, Bernard is honored by both Protestants and Catholics today. His beloved hymns include "Jesus, the Very Thought of Thee" and "O Sacred Head Now Wounded."

594	1066	1200	1300
Buddhism becomes religion of Japan	Normans conquer Britain	Genghis Khan begins conquests	Renaissance begins in Italy

1119 ✝ ✡ POPE CALLISTUS II WRITES BULL DEFENDING JEWS

In 1119, Pope Callistus II (1050–1124) issued a historic papal bull, *Sicut Judaeis*, defending the Jewish population throughout Europe. Callistus's defense came in response to the violence rained upon the Jews in the Rhineland during the First Crusade (1096). During his rule, Pope Gregory I (540–604) had made a similar attempt to protect the Jews. The terrible attack on Jews at the end of the eleventh century caused Callistus to reinforce the church's condemnation of violently attempting to convert Jews to Christianity. Throughout the next four centuries this papal decree was reissued more than twenty times. *Sicut Judaeis* granted the Jews "the shield of [the church's] protection" and declared "that no Christian shall use violence to force [Jews] into baptism."

1122 ✝ CONCORDAT OF WORMS ENDS INVESTITURE CONTROVERSY

Pope Nicholas II (1010–1061) in 1059 and Pope Gregory VII (1023–1085) in 1075 prohibited lay investiture, the practice of laymen appointing clerics to office. Gregory's ruling was repeated in 1076, 1078, and 1080, and was upheld by subsequent popes. The Concordat of Worms confirmed the decision in 1122. While the church won the battle of investiture, the emperor and other lay rulers still maintained a varying degree of control over church appointments.

1122 ✝ PETER ABELARD WRITES SIC AND NON

French philosopher, theologian, and teacher Peter Abelard (1079–1142) was an inventive thinker whose lectures attracted large crowds. His pupils included Peter Lombard (1095–1169), an Italian theologian, and many other great thinkers of the twelfth century. While teaching in Paris, Abelard roomed at the home of Fulbert, the canon of Notre Dame, and agreed to tutor Fulbert's niece, Héloise (1101–1164). Abelard and Héloise soon fell in love, and in 1116 Héloise gave birth to their son, Astrolabe. Abelard married Héloise secretly, but she joined a convent to protect Abelard's career. Fulbert was furious and had Abelard castrated. Abelard rose above the scandal and continued to be a popular lecturer. His most famous book was *Sic and Non*, in which he compared the contradictory statements between the Bible and the church fathers.

1435	1475	1506–7	1517
First African slaves brought to Europe	First book printed in English	First maps of New World created	Ottomans conquer Egypt

1123 ✝ LATERAN COUNCIL RATIFIES THE CONCORDAT OF WORMS

Held in the Church of St. John Lateran in Rome, the first of five Lateran Councils was summoned by Pope Callistus II (1050–1124) in 1123. The primary task of the council was to authenticate the Concordat of Worms, written in 1122, thereby signaling the end of the investiture controversy by condemning lay investiture, the practice that allowed rulers to make ecclesiastical appointments. In the spirit of Pope Gregory VII (Hildebrand) (1023–1085), many of the laws addressed reforms that affected ordinations and the appointing of church offices as well as making an attempt to curb the sale of indulgences.

1139 ✝ SECOND LATERAN COUNCIL RULES ON CHURCH REFORMS

Summoned by Pope Innocent II (d. 1143) in 1139, the Second Lateran Council held at the Church of St. John Lateran in Rome was concerned with church reform. The council prohibited the clergy from receiving payment for extreme unction and burial, from studying secular law or medicine, from marrying, and from using crossbows.

1141 ✝ BERNARD OF CLAIRVAUX DENOUNCES ABELARD AT THE COUNCIL OF SENS

The Council of Sens, held in 1141, was one of many councils held in Sens, France, to examine charges of heresy brought against Peter Abelard (1079–1142) by Bernard of Clairvaux (1090–1153). Abelard, a popular lecturer, was accused of having a deficient view of the Trinity. He, in return, accused Bernard of instituting unconventional practices at Clairvaux. Unable to persuade Abelard to retract, Bernard came to Sens determined to condemn Abelard for heresy. Abelard refused to defend himself and appealed his case to Pope Innocent II (d. 1143). The pope, however, declared Abelard to be a heretic and sentenced him to perpetual silence and banishment.

1141 ✝ HILDEGARD OF BINGEN BEGINS WRITING

German mystic, abbess, and author, Hildegard (1098–1179) reported her first vision from God when she was only three years old. Her parents sent her to a Benedictine convent for her education where, in 1141, Hildegard shared her revelations with her friends and superiors. Amazed by her gift, the women convinced Hildegard to record her visions. The resulting volume, *Scivias,* became a classic of medieval mystic literature. In her time Hildegard was regarded as a prophetess by the pope and other church authorities. One of her supporters, Bernard of Clairvaux, (1090–1153), had a lifelong correspondence with her, discussing many things including the need for reform within the church. Hildegard's writings cover topics ranging from science and medicine to hymnology and the lives of the saints.

1144 ✝ ✡ FIRST ACCUSATION OF BLOOD LIBEL OCCURS IN ENGLAND

Throughout the Middle Ages, the accusation of blood libel—the rumor that Jews murder Gentiles to use their blood for religious rituals—was used as a pretense for the persecution and murder of Jews. The first instance of this practice was in 1144 near Norwich, England. Several Jewish leaders were arrested and executed on the charge that they had kidnapped a local child. They were accused of crucifying the boy, stabbing his head to imitate Jesus' crown of thorns, and then using his blood as part of their Passover celebration. In 1247, the Roman Catholic Church officially declared the blood libel charges to be false; however, many continued to falsely accuse Jews of this gruesome practice. The Nazis revived blood libel rumors during their intense persecution of the Jews in the 1930s and 1940s.

1147 ✝ ✡ CRUSADERS MASSACRE JEWS IN RHINELAND FOR THE SECOND TIME

Just like the First Crusade of 1096, attacks on the Jews of the Rhineland characterized the early stages of the Second Crusade. Bernard of Clairvaux (1090–1153) prevented the carnage from being worse by preaching throughout Germany that the Jews were not to be persecuted. Yet in spite of his pleas, many Jews were murdered and others were forced to flee from their homes.

1147 ✝ ☾ THE SECOND CRUSADE ENDS IN DEFEAT

Although the West earned substantial victories in the Holy Land during the First Crusade, Muslim power continued to increase. Following a terrible massacre in December 1144, the Latin state of Edessa, established to the east of Antioch, fell to the Turks. The ruin of Edessa raised concerns about the permanence of the

1435	1475	1506–7	1517
First African slaves brought to Europe	First book printed in English	First maps of New World created	Ottomans conquer Egypt

Latin kingdom in Jerusalem. With the Holy Land under renewed threat, Louis VII (1120–1180) of France and Roman Emperor Conrad III (1093–1152) led forces to the Holy Land for the Second Crusade in 1147. To raise support, Pope Eugenius III (d. 1153) summoned Bernard of Clairvaux (1090–1153) to leave his monastery and rally support for the crusade. Bernard's enthusiastic and fervent message successfully inspired the participation of many soldiers. In spite of their objective to regain Edessa and conquer Damascus, the Second Crusade ended in utter defeat at Damascus.

1150 ✝ UNIVERSITIES OF PARIS AND OXFORD ARE FOUNDED

The University of Paris and the University of Oxford were both founded around 1150 and quickly became centers of learning in the Middle Ages. Receiving approval from political rulers and numerous popes, the University of Paris became famous primarily because of its schools for the arts and theology. The University of Oxford was a theological and philosophical school. Unlike the University of Paris and other schools in Europe, the University of Oxford emphasized undergraduate studies and developed a college system for the study of a variety of subjects. Oxford, which enjoyed a faithful alliance with the church, was less restricted by the power of the church than was Paris. Both universities were main centers for religious training.

1158 ✝ PETER LOMBARD COMPLETES FOUR BOOKS OF SENTENCES

Peter Lombard (1095–1169), an Italian theologian who taught in Notre Dame's cathedral school in Paris, wrote *Four Books of Sentences (Libri quatuor sententiarum)* in about 1158. A textbook of sorts, it articulated church doctrines and practices, supporting each with quotations from Scripture and writings of early church fathers as well as contemporary Christian thinkers such as Peter Abelard (1079–1142). It addressed the nature of God, man's sinful nature, man's redemption through Christ, and the sacraments. Lombard was one of the first to teach that there were seven sacraments, nearly three hundred years before that number was officially decreed. In addition, his ability to organize texts and to avoid extremes was noteworthy. Lombard's work became a standard text on Roman Catholic doctrine in the universities of Europe and influenced many into the 1600s. In England alone, 180 commentaries were written on it.

1159 ✡ ☾ MAIMONIDES LEAVES SPAIN

Maimonides (1135–1204), one of the most revered Jewish sages, was born in Córdoba, Spain, and was the son of a Jewish judge named Maimon. Maimonides' family was one of many that fled the Almohad persecution in approximately 1159, when Maimonides was still a young man. Persecution of Jews and Christians in Spain had begun around 1146 as a fanatical Moroccan Islamic group known as the Almohads gained control of Spain. The persecution was particularly trying for the Jewish population, because prior to the attack, the Jews had enjoyed a fruitful relationship with Muslims. The persecution brought about the end of the rich Jewish culture in Spain, and like others, Maimonides fled first to Morocco and then to Palestine. He finally settled in Egypt, where he became the most famous Jewish scholar of the Islamic age.

1162 ✝ THOMAS BECKET IS APPOINTED ARCHBISHOP OF CANTERBURY

Born to a merchant family in London, Thomas Becket (c.1118–1170) became chancellor to King Henry II (1133–1189) of England in 1154. Owing to their agreement on most issues, Becket and King Henry became good friends and drinking partners. In 1162, the archbishop of Canterbury died, and Henry, anxious to gain control of the church, nominated his loyal chancellor as the new archbishop. To Henry's great surprise, Becket immediately adopted the disciplines of his new religious role and began to live a pious and sober life. Becket's new devotion to the faith greatly affected Henry's ability to control the church from his secular throne. Despite King Henry's efforts to expand his authority, Becket would not allow it. Eventually murdered for his resistance to the king, Becket's loyalty to the church was a source of encouragement to many and became an example to later Christians struggling with problems of church and state.

1166 ✡ BENJAMIN OF TUDELA BEGINS TRAVELS IN DIASPORA

Benjamin (1127–1173) of Tudela (in modern-day northwestern Spain) was a Jew who spent at least five years, beginning in 1166, traveling among the various communities of the Jewish Diaspora during the twelfth century. The Diaspora was the dispersion of Jews outside the land of Israel beginning with the Babylonian captivity and continued by Alexander the Great (356–323 BC) and the

1435	1475	1506–7	1517
First African slaves brought to Europe	First book printed in English	First maps of New World created	Ottomans conquer Egypt

Romans after the fall of Jerusalem in AD 70. Benjamin was a fearless voyager and visited Jews in Damascus, Lebanon, Syria, Persia, Greece, India, and Iraq. He recorded details concerning their numbers, businesses, social conditions, factors in their environment, battles, and their city life. Each of Benjamin's voyages produced a wealth of information used by historians today to better understand the population and culture of various twelfth-century Jewish communities.

1171 ✝ ✡ JEWISH COMMUNITY OF BLOIS IS DESTROYED

The first blood libel, or ritual murder, accusation against the Jews in continental Europe occurred on May 26, 1171, in Blois, France. All fifty-one Jewish residents of the town were dragged to a wooden tower where they were given the option of Christian baptism or death. They all chose death and were burned alive. They chanted a Hebrew hymn as they died.

1173 ✝ PETER WALDO FOUNDS THE WALDENSES

In 1173, Peter Waldo (1150–1218), a wealthy merchant in Lyons, France, gave away his riches to the poor and began a life of voluntary poverty as a preacher. His disciples, who called themselves the Poor Men of Lyons, came to be known as the Waldenses. One of the unique marks of Waldo's preaching was his use of a French translation of the Bible, instead of the Latin Vulgate. The Waldenses, despite repeated confessions of orthodox faith, were eventually branded heretics. Though they would not renounce their vows of poverty, in the face of persecution many renewed their commitment to the church. Waldo and his followers were medieval forerunners of the Protestant Reformation. The Waldenses still exist today, primarily in Italy.

1176 ✝ THE BENEFIT OF THE CLERGY IS CREATED THEN ABOLISHED

In 1176, King Henry II (1133–1189) of England granted what became known as the Benefit of the Clergy. It stipulated that clergy and nuns would no longer be tried in secular courts but only in church courts, with their lesser punishments. These benefits were later expanded by King Edward III (1327–1377) to include literate laity on their first offense. As time passed and corruption increased, this

594	1066	1200	1300
Buddhism becomes religion of Japan	Normans conquer Britain	Genghis Khan begins conquests	Renaissance begins in Italy

benefit became more and more abused so that by the time of the sixteenth-century English Reformation, the Benefit of the Clergy was restricted. It was completely abolished in 1827.

1179 ✠ THIRD LATERAN COUNCIL CONVENES

In 1179, Pope Alexander III (1105–1181) convened the Third Lateran Council at the basilica church of St. John Lateran in Rome and renewed interest in the study of church law. At the Third Lateran Council he issued a decree that a two-thirds majority of cardinals was required to elect a pope, and a majority was necessary for decisions in religious communities. Another decree called for the founding of cathedral schools.

1182 ✠ MARONITES BECOME A UNIATE CHURCH

The churches of Eastern Christianity that are unified with the Roman Catholic Church are known as Uniate churches. These churches usually conduct mass in their own language and keep church law according to their own traditions. The Maronites of Syria took their name from Maron, a solitary monk who died in about 423. In 1182, they entered into an unstable relationship with the Roman Catholic Church, becoming a Uniate church. The only Roman Catholic Church in the East, Maronites use the Syriac language in their liturgy. Presently, the Maronites are the largest Christian church in Lebanon.

1187 ✠ ☾ SALADIN CAPTURES JERUSALEM

Appointed caliph in 1174, Saladin (1138–1193) controlled the region from Damascus, Syria, to the Nile. With his ability to unite his fellow Muslims, Saladin was determined to conquer Jerusalem. On July 5, 1187, the definitive battle was fought in the village of Hattin, on the hill where tradition sets the preaching of the Sermon on the Mount. The Muslim forces won a decisive victory over the Crusaders, killing some thirty thousand Christian soldiers. To his credit, Saladin's entry into the defeated Jerusalem on October 2, 1187, was not marked by the butchery that occurred during the Crusaders' conquering of Jerusalem ninety years earlier.

1435	1475	1506–7	1517
First African slaves brought to Europe	First book printed in English	First maps of New World created	Ottomans conquer Egypt

1189 ✝ ☾ THE THIRD CRUSADE IS THE CRUSADE OF KINGS

Following the capture of Jerusalem from the Crusaders by Saladin (1138–1193), the Third Crusade was organized in 1189. Led by Holy Roman Emperor Frederick I Barbarossa (1122–1190), Richard I (1157–1199) of England, and Philip II (1165–1223) of France, it became known as the Crusade of Kings. After Frederick was drowned along the way, Philip and Richard fell into contention and went on to the Holy Land separately. Philip started the battle for Acre, today's Akko, and then returned home, leaving Richard to lead the fight for the Holy Land alone. Under Richard, the Crusaders recaptured Acre, but were unsuccessful in reaching Jerusalem, having to settle for a three-year truce with Muslims that allowed Christian pilgrims safe passage to Jerusalem. Known as Richard the Lionhearted, Richard was an excellent warrior but an arrogant king, who made enemies wherever he went.

1190 ✝ ✡ JEWS ARE MASSACRED IN YORK

Beginning with the First Crusade, toward the end of the eleventh century, the formerly stable relations between Jews and Christians were significantly jeopardized. The violent and widespread massacres of Jews in the Rhineland during both the First and Second Crusades terrorized all of the Jews living outside the land of Israel. The earlier actions of the Crusaders led many of the Jews of York, England, to commit mass suicide in 1190, fearing an attack by soldiers similar to that of the Third Crusade. Those who survived were massacred by crusading warriors. To this day the terrible fate of the Jews in York is remembered each week in synagogues throughout Europe.

1192 ✝ JOACHIM OF FIORE ESTABLISHES THE ORDER OF SAN GIOVANNI

While on pilgrimage to the Holy Land, a young Cistercian monk named Joachim (1135–1202) received a vision that shaped his life, his beliefs, and his writings. He believed that there were three overlapping eras representing the Father (Adam to Christ), the Son (King Uzziah to the year 1260), and the Holy Spirit (St. Benedict to the end of the world). Joachim moved to Fiore, Italy, in 1192 and established the order of San Giovanni (St. John). During this period, he wrote *Concordance to the New and Old Testaments, Exposition of the Apocalypse,* and *Psaltery of Ten Strings.* Although the Fourth Lateran Council in 1215 and the

Synod of Arles in 1263 declared Joachim's theories heretical, his writings had noticeable influence on medieval reformers such as the Spiritual Franciscans.

1198 ✝ INNOCENT III BECOMES POPE

Having studied in Paris and at the University of Bologna, Giovanni Lotario de' Conti (1160–1216) was appointed as cardinal deacon at the age of thirty. During his tenure in that position, he wrote *On the Contempt of the World*, encouraging the practice of contemplation and asceticism. The book became popular throughout Europe, and in 1198, he was unanimously elected pope, becoming Pope Innocent III. A man of keen intellect, he successfully positioned the church to dominate all human relationships. His leadership in matters of church doctrine and practice were perhaps even more significant. The most powerful of the medieval popes, Innocent's crowning achievement was his convening of the Fourth Lateran Council in 1215, the decrees of which shaped church policy for centuries.

1200 ✝ SCHOLASTICISM IS POPULARIZED BY UNIVERSITIES

The founding of the major European universities (Paris, Oxford, Pisa, Bologna, and Salerno) propelled scholasticism to the forefront of Christian learning. The movement was essentially the application of Aristotle's philosophy to Christian thought. The Scholastics endeavored to unite faith and reason into one coherent system. Anselm of Canterbury (1033–1109), Peter Abelard (1079–1142), Peter Lombard (1095–1169), and Thomas Aquinas (1224–1274) were some of the most prominent Scholastics. Thomas taught that reason is sufficient to determine what God is not, and after eliminating what it is impossible for God to be, man is then able to know what God is. He declared that if Christian revelation and reason seem to conflict, revelation amends reason, not vice versa. In the following centuries humanism and the Reformation destroyed Scholasticism's idea of synthesis.

1202 ✝ POPE INNOCENT III CLAIMS POWER OVER SECULAR RULERS

Pope Innocent III (1160–1216), an effective statesman, began his reign by reorganizing the management of Rome. He was granted the right to choose the senator who ruled Rome and to receive an oath of allegiance from him. He desired to be the supreme authority in international affairs and the guardian of unity

1435	1475	1506–7	1517
First African slaves brought to Europe	First book printed in English	First maps of New World created	Ottomans conquer Egypt

throughout the Christian world. After Germany's rule over Italy collapsed with the death of the German emperor of the Holy Roman Empire, Henry IV (1050–1106), Innocent III was able to revive and expand the Papal States and to prevent the unification of Italy. In 1202, after his first choice for emperor attacked Italy, Innocent issued his famous letter, *Venerabilem,* which maintained the pope's right to accept or reject any recently elected emperor, thereby giving the pope ultimate control of the imperial throne.

1202 ✦ CONSTANTINOPLE SACKED DURING FOURTH CRUSADE

In 1202, Pope Innocent III (1160–1216) called for the Fourth Crusade to recapture Jerusalem. However, the few knights who responded to the call were unable to pay the passage fees demanded by the Venetians. A compromise was reached wherein the campaigners agreed to attack Constantinople, the capital of Eastern Christendom, in exchange for passage to Jerusalem. Unfortunately, after sacking the city, the Crusaders forgot about their original mission to the Holy Land and, instead, set up Latin rule in Constantinople. Though this achieved a temporary union between the Eastern and Western churches, the union was merely superficial and eventually led to Eastern Christians' resentment of Rome. In the end, conquering Constantinople served only to undermine the Eastern Empire's value as a defense against the continued attacks of Islam.

1209 ✦ FRANCIS OF ASSISI RENOUNCES WEALTH

Christened Giovanni but nicknamed Francesco by his father, a wealthy textile merchant, Francis of Assisi (1182–1226) experienced a comfortable childhood. As a young man he worked for his father and joined the military. During an illness, Francis began to reflect on his life. In 1205, he journeyed to Rome where he was so struck by the plight of a beggar that he gave the man his clothes. Traveling back to Assisi, Francis had a vision of God. However, upon arrival home in 1208, he was disowned by his father, who believed Francis was insane. During a morning mass the following year (1209), Francis was convicted by Jesus' command for the disciples to leave everything (Matthew 10:9-19). He took up a life of voluntary poverty and set out to preach the gospel. Though not by Francis's intent, his actions inspired many and the Franciscan order was born.

594	1066	1200	1300
Buddhism becomes religion of Japan	Normans conquer Britain	Genghis Khan begins conquests	Renaissance begins in Italy

1209 + A CRUSADE IS DECLARED AGAINST THE ALBIGENSIANS

The Albigensians believed in two gods: "Truth," the god of light, was derived from the New Testament, and "Error," the god of darkness, was derived from the Old Testament. The Albigensians did not believe in hell, thinking instead that unsaved souls would transmigrate into lower animals. When representatives of Count Raymond VI of Toulouse (1156-1222), a major advocate of the Albigensian cause, murdered an official emissary of Pope Innocent III (1160–1216), a crusade was launched against the Albigensians in the Provence region of France in 1209. The Albigensian Crusade crushed the heretics and Provence as well.

1212 + CHILDREN FORM CRUSADE ARMIES

In 1212, tens of thousands of children as young as six years old from western Europe set out to reclaim the Holy Land. Inspired by the preaching of a French boy named Stephen who said that Christ had appeared to him, the children formed groups and set out for Jerusalem. They believed that God would certainly return the city to innocent children. After reaching Genoa, Italy, and being refused passage to the Holy Land some returned to their homes. Others traveled on to Rome, where the pope told them to return home. Some went to Marseilles, France, where they were shipped to North Africa and sold as slaves.

1215 + KING JOHN ISSUES THE MAGNA CARTA

On June 15, 1215, at Runnymede, southwest of London, King John (1167–1216) of England issued the Magna Carta, meaning "Great Charter." The charter granted greater power to the *curia regis,* the feudal assembly that later became the British Parliament, and limited royal power. King John agreed to consult the assembly before instituting new taxes and to allow accused law-breakers to be tried by a group from their own social class. Also, the assembly was granted authority to depose the king if he violated the charter. However, the document limited these rights to the aristocracy. The Magna Carta became the foundation for present-day English law. It also became the foundation of most constitutional forms of government, including that of the

1435	1475	1506–7	1517
First African slaves brought to Europe	First book printed in English	First maps of New World created	Ottomans conquer Egypt

United States, creating stable governments under which the gospel could flourish.

1215 ✠ FOURTH LATERAN COUNCIL ISSUES DECREES

The Fourth Lateran Council, convened in 1215 by Innocent III (1160–1216), the powerful medieval pope, confirmed the election of Frederick II (1194–1250) as emperor of the Holy Roman Empire and denounced the Magna Carta. The council articulated the doctrine of transubstantiation, the belief that Christ is physically present in the bread and wine of the mass. It confirmed the Franciscan order but decreed that no new monastic orders were to be founded. It also decreed that Jews and Muslims were to wear distinctive dress, and it made provision for the upcoming Fifth Crusade. Covering the political, religious, and social arenas of thirteenth-century Europe, the council had profound and lasting effects on both church law and everyday life.

1220 ✠ DOMINIC ESTABLISHES ORDER OF PREACHERS

While serving as a prior, noble-born Dominic (1170–1221) witnessed the Albigensian heresy firsthand in southern France. Moved with compassion, Dominic initiated a preaching ministry to the Albigensians, a dualistic group that believed Truth was the god of the New Testament, and Error was the god of the Old Testament. Dominic lived a mendicant lifestyle, often preaching barefoot. A gifted organizer, he founded the Dominican Order to multiply his ministry of preaching the gospel.

1226 ✠ ☾ LOUIS IX BECOMES KING OF FRANCE

Louis IX (1214–1270) became king of France at the age of twelve. Deeply spiritual and ascetic, he avoided many of the luxuries enjoyed by other kings, choosing instead to build churches and hospitals. Louis also negotiated a treaty ceding land back to England, which he believed to have been unfairly acquired by previous French rulers. He used his political skills to limit the rights of nobles, increasing royal control. In 1248, he launched the Seventh Crusade, which was directed at Damietta, Egypt, where he was captured and later ransomed. Then in 1270, he led the Eighth (and final) Crusade. It was directed against Tunis in North Africa, where he died of a fever. Louis's piety, policies of fairness,

594	1066	1200	1300
Buddhism becomes religion of Japan	Normans conquer Britain	Genghis Khan begins conquests	Renaissance begins in Italy

and modest lifestyle led many Frenchmen to consider him the model Christian king. His reign is regarded as the apex of the French medieval monarchy, and the Roman Catholic Church canonized him in 1297.

1229 ✝ ☾ CRUSADERS NEGOTIATE THE RETURN OF JERUSALEM

In September 1228, eight years after becoming emperor of the Holy Roman Empire, Frederick II (1194–1250), king of Germany and Sicily, arrived in the Middle East to lead the Fifth Crusade. Finding the Muslim rulers of Egypt and Damascus in conflict, Frederick, known for his diplomacy with Christians and Muslims alike, negotiated a treaty with the Egyptian sultan Al-Kameel (r. 1218–1238). In 1219, Al-Kameel had offered William of Holland (1168–1222) the exchange of Jerusalem for territory at the mouth of the Nile River, but William was unsuccessful in completing the negotiations. Desiring peaceful relations, Frederick sought success where William had failed. Despite objections from the church, Frederick negotiated a ten-year treaty with Egypt that gave Christians dominion over Jerusalem (with the exception of the mosque of Omar), Bethlehem, Nazareth, and one pilgrimage route. On March 18, 1229, Frederick staged a coronation for himself in the Church of the Holy Sepulcher to celebrate the return of Jerusalem.

1232 ✝ ✡ BOOKS OF MAIMONIDES ARE BURNED IN MONTPELLIER

In the thirteenth century, efforts were made to undermine Judaism as a theological system. When Arabic-speaking Jews fled Almohad persecution in Spain beginning in about 1146, many went to Provence, France. They brought with them their broad philosophical training and what the traditional Provencal Jews saw as worldly manners. The philosophical works of Maimonides (1135–1204), written in Arabic, were controversial within the Jewish community. In 1232, members of the Dominican monastic order, who were in charge of eliminating Christian heresy, publicly burned the books of Maimonides in Montpellier, France.

1233 ✝ POPE GREGORY IX APPOINTS FIRST "INQUISITORS"

Despite earlier efforts by Pope Innocent III (1160–1216) to eliminate Albigensians, believers in a New Testament god of light and an Old Testament god of darkness, many followers remained in the mid-1220s. Following in the footsteps of his uncle Innocent III, Pope Gregory IX (1170–1241) asked Louis IX (1214–1270) to engage in another crusade against the sect. However, increased Albigensian presence in Spain and Italy particularly concerned Gregory, so he established an inquisition. A close friend of Francis of Assisi (1182–1226), Gregory appointed Franciscan and Dominican monks in 1233 to be the first "inquisitors." Hoping to obtain fair and principled judgment, Gregory became the first pope to contend with heresy through a formal church inquisition.

1242 ✝ ✡ KING JAMES I OF ARAGÓN FORCES JEWS TO CONVERT

Although Jews were allowed to live alongside Christians in Spain, in 1242, King James I (1208–1276) of the Spanish kingdom of Aragón signed a decree demanding that all Jews submit to the evangelistic preaching of the Dominican and Franciscan monks. Pope Innocent IV (1200–1254) followed James I's edict with similar commands to the monastic orders. James and Innocent commanded monks to preach in synagogues and civil officials to force Jews out of their homes to listen to the sermons. They both felt the use of force was appropriate to make the Jews comply. No longer hidden, the church's desire to be rid of Judaism was violently obvious.

1242 ✝ ✡ THE TALMUD IS BURNED IN PARIS

Catholic scholars found the Jewish Talmud offensive because of passages derogatory to Jesus and to Christianity. In 1236, a Jewish convert named Nicholas Donin testified before Pope Gregory IX (1170–1241) that the Talmud was heretical and blasphemous. As a result, Gregory condemned the Talmud, officially instructing the kings and church leaders of Europe to expose its secrets. King Louis IX of France (1214–1270) was the only monarch to respond to the pope's call. On June 25, 1240, a public debate commenced in Paris that was, in fact, a trial. Nicholas Donin, now a Franciscan, acted as prosecutor and a Jewish rabbi as defendant. As a result of the proceedings, the Talmud was declared heretical, and all the copies of it in Paris were collected and burned in 1242. The mountain of books was so high that it took a day and a half for them to burn.

1245 ✝ FIRST COUNCIL OF LYONS CONVENES

In 1245, Pope Innocent IV (1200–1254) convened the First Council of Lyons, or the thirteenth ecumenical council. Held in three sessions, the assembly looked to solve five problems afflicting Innocent: the misconduct of the clergy, the fall of Jerusalem, the control of the Byzantine Empire, the Mongol assaults in Europe, and the persecution of the church and of Innocent himself by the Holy Roman Emperor Frederick II (1194–1250). The conflict between Frederick and Innocent originated in the excommunication of Frederick by Pope Gregory IX (1170–1241), for his failure to lead a crusade as promised. Attempting to thwart the council, Frederick had blocked all routes to Lyons and prohibited his imperial clergy from attending. The Council voted to depose Frederick and recommended another crusade to claim Jerusalem, but no action was taken to carry out the decree.

1255 ✡ INNOCENT JEWS ARE CONVICTED OF BLOOD LIBEL

One of the most infamous incidents of Jewish slaughter as a result of accusations of blood libel occurred in Lincoln, England, in 1255. Blood libel was the superstition that Jews killed non-Jews, especially children, and used their victims' blood in religious rituals. In Lincoln about 1246, a poor woman named Beatrice gave birth to a son she named Hugh. In 1255, his body was found at the bottom of a well of a Jew named Copin. Copin and more than one hundred Jews were accused of scourging the boy, crowning him with thorns, and then crucifying him. Copin was sentenced to a cruel death and eighteen other Jews were hanged. Ninety more were imprisoned in London but were released upon payment of a large fine. In *The Canterbury Tales,* English poet Geoffrey Chaucer (1340–1400) memorialized the accusation of blood libel in Lincoln.

1263 ✝ ✡ NAHMANIDES LOSES DISPUTATION IN BARCELONA

As persecution of Jews increased in the thirteenth century, Jewish society, religion, and practices were scrutinized throughout Europe. Among the most well-known public debates during this period was the 1263 disputation in Barcelona. Under the influence of Dominican monks and Hebrew Christian

Pablo Christiani, the debate was held on July 20, 1263, and moderated by King James I (1208–1276) of Aragón, one of two Christian states in Spain. Defending the Jewish faith was Rabbi Moses ben Nahman, or Nahmanides (1194–1270) (also known as the Ramban), a leader at a Jewish academy in Aragón. Although Nahmanides lost the debate, the king was impressed with his argumentation and enabled him to escape to Palestine. The Jews left behind were forced to attend Dominican sermons.

1265 ✝ THOMAS AQUINAS BEGINS SUMMA THEOLOGIAE

Thomas Aquinas (1224–1274) was a Dominican monk who spent much of his life teaching in Paris. He wrote his principal work, *Summa Theologiae*, as a guide for instruction in undergraduate theological studies. Begun in 1265, *Summa Theologiae* is a systematic examination of the theological, philosophical, and moral issues of Aquinas's day. Its three major parts (focused on God, Man, and Christ) are organized according to the Scholastic method: Questions are posed and broken down into "articles," which then are individually addressed. Believing that reason and revelation supplement reading of Scripture, Aquinas used Christian thinkers and Aristotle in addition to the Bible to build his arguments. Unfortunately, due to illness in 1273, Aquinas was forced to discontinue his *Summa Theologiae*. Largely as a result of his *Summa,* Aquinas is known as the greatest philosopher and theologian of the medieval church.

1269 ✝ KUBLAI KHAN ASKS POPE TO SEND CHRISTIAN TEACHERS TO CHINA

In 1269, two Italian merchants, the Polo brothers, arrived in Acre on the coast of the Mediterranean with a letter from Kublai Khan (1214–1294), ruler of China's Mongol Empire. The letter requested that the pope send one hundred teachers to China so that the Chinese could study the science and religion of Europe. In 1271, the Polo brothers and one son, Marco (1254–1324), started back to China accompanied reluctantly by two Dominican monks. The perils of the journey, however, caused the monks to return to Europe. Less than ten years later when the rumor reached Europe that Kublai had been baptized, the pope dispatched five more monks, but they never got farther than Persia.

594	1066	1200	1300
Buddhism becomes religion of Japan	Normans conquer Britain	Genghis Khan begins conquests	Renaissance begins in Italy

1274 ✝ SECOND COUNCIL OF LYONS ASSEMBLES

The Second Council of Lyons—the fourteenth ecumenical council—assembled in 1274. The council, convened by Pope Gregory X (1210–1276), consisted of sixteen hundred clergy, including five hundred bishops and sixty abbots. Gregory hoped to organize another crusade to liberate Jerusalem, but because of his inability to establish peace in Europe, European kings refused to rally to his cause. The assembly did achieve a nominal reunion with the Orthodox Church and issued several new canons. Among them was the decision that, to avoid long intervals between popes, the cardinals could wait only ten days following the death of a pope before going into deliberation, and would forego salaries until a new pope was elected.

1280 ✡ MOSES DE LEON COMPOSES THE CORE OF THE KABBALAH

A form of Jewish mysticism known as the *kabbalah* arose in the twelfth and thirteenth centuries. Among those who contributed to the religious and intellectual style of kabbalah was Moses de Leon (1240–1305). De Leon composed the majority of the Zohar, a multivolume work that includes a commentary on the Torah. His writings develop the idea that the stories and laws found in Scripture create a map or pattern for God. De Leon believed that a holy life, marked by an accurate execution of rituals, allowed humanity to reinstate God's perfect order. By the sixteenth century, the Zohar was read far and wide and remains at the core of kabbalah practice.

1290 ✡ JEWS ARE EXPELLED FROM ENGLAND

Following official condemnation of the Talmud by Pope Gregory IX (1170–1241) in 1236, criticism of Jews increased and Jewish communities began to be displaced throughout Western Europe. King Edward I (1239–1307) of England issued a declaration in 1275, canceling all debts owed to Jews and forbidding Jews from making any further loans to non-Jews. Because money lending was a major business of the Jews, this decree significantly limited their ability to make a living. In addition, Edward arrested a number of Jewish leaders, demanding a ransom before releasing them. Finally, in 1290, King Edward expelled all Jews from England, confiscating all their assets for himself.

1435	1475	1506–7	1517
First African slaves brought to Europe	First book printed in English	First maps of New World created	Ottomans conquer Egypt

1291 ✚ ☾ CRUSADER PRESENCE IN PALESTINE ENDS

Between 1095 and 1270, eight major crusades attempted to drive Muslim forces out of the Holy Land and their strategic fortresses. Although the early crusades were successful, the later crusades were marked by failure, bickering, and tragedy. In 1291, al-Ashraf Khalil (r. 1290–1293), the Muslim sultan reigning in Cairo, Egypt, led an army to the last Christian stronghold in the Holy Land, the city of Acre on the Mediterranean coast. Although Pope Nicholas IV (1227–1292) had sent a mercenary army to protect the city, the Muslim armies drove the Christians out of Acre with little resistance. The fall of Acre marked the end of the Crusader era. Although some efforts were made to attempt another crusade, none were successful. As a result of the Crusades, European feudalism and papal power were weakened, but the Muslims were permanently imprinted with the brutal image of Christianity left by the Crusaders.

1294 ✚ JOHN OF MONTE CORVINO ARRIVES IN CHINA

In 1289, John of Monte Corvino (1247–1330), an Italian Franciscan monk experienced in missions, was dispatched to China by Pope Nicholas IV (1227–1292). He carried with him a letter for Kublai Khan (1214–1294), who had previously requested that the pope send missionaries. Traveling through Persia and India, John eventually made his way to the Mongolian capital of Khanbalik (Peking) in 1294, where the Mongolian ruler Khan Timor Olcheitu welcomed him. John successfully established a mission northwest of Khanbalik, in Tenduk. It was the first Franciscan mission in China. He later built three churches, translated Psalms and the New Testament into Chinese, and directed a native boys' choir that was popular with the Mongols. Through John's efforts, six thousand people converted to Roman Catholicism.

1302 ✚ UNAM SANCTAM PROCLAIMS PAPAL SUPREMACY

Pope Boniface VIII (1234–1303) issued the papal edict *Unam Sanctam* on November 18, 1302, in response to a dispute with Philip IV (1268–1314), king of France. The edict asserted that there was "neither salvation nor remission of sins" for those outside the church. Emphasizing the role of the pope as head of the church, the decree promised excommunication to anyone who rejected his supreme authority. It also articulated that the "temporal sword" (secular au-

594	1066	1200	1300
Buddhism becomes religion of Japan	Normans conquer Britain	Genghis Khan begins conquests	Renaissance begins in Italy

thority) was to submit to the "spiritual sword" (the clergy). The edict concluded with the message that submission to the Roman pope was necessary for salvation. *Unam Sanctam* marked the height of medieval papal power.

1306 ✡ PHILIP IV EXPELS JEWS FROM FRANCE

During the fourteenth century the Jews in France experienced three expulsions. The series of evictions began when King Philip IV (1268–1314) had borrowed all he could from the Jewish money lenders of France. In 1306, he arrested all of them, cancelled his debts to them, and then transferred all the debts owed to the moneylenders from others to himself. In addition, he confiscated all the remaining property of the Jews and expelled them from France. The Jews were allowed back in 1315, following Philip IV's death. Then once again, in 1320, Jewish communities were destroyed. A year later five thousand Jews were accused of poisoning wells and were executed, and the rest of the Jewish population in Paris was forced into exile. As a result, by 1322 there remained only a handful of Jews in France. While the Jews again were recalled in 1359, they all were finally expelled in 1394.

1309 ✝ PAPACY BEGINS "BABYLONIAN CAPTIVITY" IN AVIGNON

In 1309, at the encouragement of French King Philip IV (1268–1314), Pope Clement V (1264–1314) moved the papal office from Rome to Avignon, France. With this action, Pope Clement, recently elected by a Roman conclave where French emissaries were present, began what became known as the papacy's "Babylonian Captivity," a seventy-year period during which the popes—all Frenchmen—ruled from Avignon and were heavily influenced by the French kings. Clement, for example, appointed French cardinals to twenty-two of twenty-four posts. During this period, the papacy lost the respect of nations hostile to France. The Avignon years were distinguished by luxury in the papal court and an increase of papal taxation.

1311 ✝ POPE CLEMENT V SUMMONS THE COUNCIL OF VIENNE

Considered the fifteenth ecumenical council, the Council of Vienne was summoned by Pope Clement V (1264–1314) and remained in session from October

16, 1311 through May 6, 1312, deliberating primarily over questions about the Knights Templar, a wealthy crusading order. Philip IV, king of France (1268–1314), hoping to obtain the Templar wealth for himself, had ordered the arrests of Templars and tortured many of them in order to obtain confessions of heresy. Unfortunately, the recent relocation to Avignon placed the pope under Philip's influence, and the king successfully used these confessions to compel the pope and the assembly to abolish the Templar order. The council also made plans for another crusade, which Philip pledged to lead, though it never took place.

1312 ✛ KNIGHTS TEMPLAR ARE SUPPRESSED

When the Knights Templar, a militaristic religious order, lost their crusading objectives in the late thirteenth century, they became a secret organization, independent of secular control. The bankrupt king of France, Philip IV (1268–1314), set his eyes on their wealth and to that end pressured Pope Clement V (1264–1314) to dissolve their order. In 1312, Clement issued *Vox in excelso*, declaring the termination of the Knights Templar throughout Europe. One hundred twenty Templars were executed on charges of heresy and witchcraft, and Philip confiscated their wealth.

1320 ✛ SCOTTISH ASSERT THEIR NATIONALISM IN THE DECLARATION OF ARBOATH

After the Scots won their independence from England, Pope John XXII (1244–1334) excommunicated Robert the Bruce (1274–1329), Scotland's new king, for killing a rival in an argument, thereby denying Robert the right to the throne. In response, the Scottish noblemen drafted the Declaration of Arboath, a letter to the pope asserting that Robert was their king because of God's hand, the laws of their country, and the will of the people, and that they would not relent in their claim to independence. The declaration also asserted that the Scottish people were not seeking glory, but liberty for themselves and their posterity. Therefore, they requested that the pope recognize their sovereignty and order the king of England to do the same. It took the pope eight years to decide, but in 1328, he lifted his excommunication and acknowledged Robert's right to be king. The Declaration of Arboath was the most remarkable assertion of nationalism in Europe during the Middle Ages.

594	1066	1200	1300
Buddhism becomes religion of Japan	Normans conquer Britain	Genghis Khan begins conquests	Renaissance begins in Italy

1321 ✝ DANTE WRITES HIS <u>DIVINE COMEDY</u>

Dante Alighieri (1265–1321), an Italian poet, spent much of his life in exile due to political struggles in his native Florence. He is most well known for his epic poem *The Divine Comedy*. The poem consists of one hundred sections divided into three parts: *The Inferno, The Purgatory,* and *The Paradise.* They tell a story that begins at Easter, with the poet lost in a dark forest (representing Sin). Next, Virgil (Philosophy) volunteers to guide the poet through Hell to the Mount of Purgatory. Finally, Dante's idealized love, Beatrice (Theology or Religion), leads him to Paradise where he meditates on God's indescribable glory. Dante completed the work in 1321, shortly before his death.

1324 ✝ MARSIGLIO OF PADUA FINISHES <u>DEFENSOR PACIS</u>

Marsiglio of Padua (1275–1342) was born in Padua, Italy, and studied medicine and philosophy. He was rector of the University of Paris when he wrote *Defensor Pacis* (The Defender of the Peace) in 1324. The book develops both a philosophy of the state and a theology of the church, including a reproach of papal claims to secular power. He argues that the state, not the church, should bring peace and unity to society. Since Christ himself called for submission to temporal authority, Marsiglio declared the church's hierarchy was merely human and its only power was spiritual. Marsiglio's work was a precursor to the Reformation and was studied by the reformers.

1324 ✝ WILLIAM OF OCKHAM IS SUMMONED BEFORE THE POPE

William of Ockham (1280–1349), a Franciscan monk who studied and taught at Oxford, was an English philosopher and the most influential theologian of his day. He taught that the Scriptures were the only infallible source of authority and that the pope was not infallible. In Ockham's mind, church councils, not the pope, were the highest ruling authority in the church. He believed that God could be comprehended only by faith and not by reason. He was summoned before the pope in 1324 and eventually excommunicated. He is also remembered for his belief that "What can be done with fewer assumptions is done in vain with more" (known as Ockham's Razor), which had great influence on science by proposing that natural phenomena could be rationally examined.

1435	1475	1506–7	1517
First African slaves brought to Europe	First book printed in English	First maps of New World created	Ottomans conquer Egypt

1337 ✛ THE HUNDRED YEARS' WAR BEGINS

The Hundred Years' War was the defining event in the fourteenth and fifteenth centuries. Tensions between France and England had been high for nearly a hundred years. Edward III (1312–1377), who had recently become king of England, was the only direct male descendent of King Philip IV (1268–1314) of France, giving Edward a claim to the French throne. However, when King Charles IV (1294–1328) of France died without an heir, he was succeeded by his nephew Philip VI (1293–1350). Edward's claim to the throne against Philip IV started the Hundred Years' War in 1337, when the English attacked Flanders in northern France, gaining control of the English Channel. The war soon degenerated into a fight of attrition that lasted more than one hundred years. It was not until 1453 that the French, inspired by the devout Joan of Arc (1412–1431), drove the last of the British forces out of their country, thus ending the conflict.

1347 ✛ ✡ THE BLACK DEATH BEGINS

From 1347 to 1351, bubonic plague blazed across Europe. From its origins, apparently in central Asia, the plague moved through India to China and on into Italy. It spread through Switzerland, Germany, and Eastern Europe, eventually moving into France, Spain, and England. By the spring of 1349, the Black Death, as the plague became known, reached London. From there Scotland, Scandinavia, and the Baltic countries were afflicted. Up to 40 percent of those living in urban communities died. The effects of the Black Death included a renewed interest in piety and death, but it also led to the murder of Jews blamed for poisoning wells. In addition the ranks of the Dominicans, formerly respected scholars, were so decimated that they recruited the semiliterate to their order, resulting in much superstitious and heretical theology.

1350 ✛ BRETHREN OF THE COMMON LIFE FORMS

In the mid-fourteenth century a movement led by Gerhard Groote (1340–1385) sprang up in Germany and the Netherlands. Focused on the piety of the laity, the groups that surrounded Groote emphasized the inner life of the soul, seeking to imitate Christ by loving one's neighbor. They functioned outside of the bounds of the established church. Following Groote's death the leadership fell to Florentius Radewijns (1350–1400). This society, which began regularly meeting in Groote's hometown of Deventer, the Netherlands, became known as the Brethren of the Common Life. Their movement also labored to establish schools and encourage literacy. A number of influential people emerged from schools established by the Brethren of the Common Life, including Erasmus (1466–1536) and Thomas à Kempis (1380–1471).

1368 ✝ MONGOL DYNASTY DISAPPEARS FROM CHINA

In the fourteenth century, the Mongol Empire was the largest the world had ever seen. Its leaders conquered vast areas that included Korea, Central Asia, Persia, southern Russia, and China. Though not Christian themselves, the Mongol rulers were very tolerant of Roman Catholicism, and under their rule the number of Roman Catholics in China may have grown as high as one hundred thousand. But in 1368, Mongol rule fell to the Chinese Ming Dynasty. With the expulsion of the Mongols from China came a reaction against anything not Chinese. There is no record of any Christian churches in China from this time until the arrival of Jesuit missionaries in the late sixteenth century.

1373 ✝ JULIAN OF NORWICH RECEIVES HER REVELATIONS

Julian of Norwich (1342–1413) led a solitary life of prayer and meditation near St. Julian's Church in Norwich, England. Her famous book, *The Sixteen Revelations of Divine Love,* includes her account of May 8, 1373—a day when she claims to have received fifteen revelations of the suffering of Christ and of the Trinity, receiving one more on the following day. She meditated on the visions for twenty years before recording them in her book.

1378 ✝ THE GREAT PAPAL SCHISM BEGINS

Beginning in 1378, the loyalties of the churches of Western Europe were divided between two concurrent popes, with each attempting to excommunicate the other. Urban VI (1318–1389) was in Rome, backed by the German Empire, England, Hungary, Scandinavia, and most of Italy. In Avignon, France, Clement VII (1291–1352) was backed by France, Naples, Savoy, Scotland, Spain, and Sicily.

1435	1475	1506–7	1517
First African slaves brought to Europe	First book printed in English	First maps of New World created	Ottomans conquer Egypt

1378 ✝ CATHERINE OF SIENA TRIES TO HEAL GREAT SCHISM

By the age of sixteen, Catherine of Siena (1347–1380) knew she wanted to devote her life to a religious calling. Becoming a member of the Sisters of Penance, a Dominican lay order, she led a life of strict asceticism in her own home. Later in life, Catherine ventured out into public arenas, becoming particularly involved in political diplomacy and church reform. In 1378, after the death of Pope Gregory XI (1329–1378), whom she had earlier convinced to return to Rome from Avignon, France, Catherine actively worked to heal the Great Schism between two rival popes, endorsing the newly elected Urban VI (1318–1389).

1380 ✝ JOHN WYCLIFFE SUPERVISES BIBLE TRANSLATION

Known as the "Morning Star of the Reformation," John Wycliffe (1330–1384) was an Oxford theologian. He challenged papal control, church hierarchy and indulgences, and denied that Christ was literally present in the bread and wine of the Mass. Due to the support of Oxford University, Wycliffe was able to withstand the pope's accusations of heresy against him. Believing that people needed Scripture in their own language in order to have a relationship with God through Christ without church interference, Wycliffe and his Oxford companions completed the first English translation of the New Testament around 1380. They finished the Old Testament in 1382. Not knowing Hebrew or Greek, they translated from the Latin Vulgate. Wycliffe was condemned for heresy after his death. Consequently, his body was exhumed, burned, and his ashes scattered on the Swift River.

1382 ✝ LOLLARD REVIVAL IN ENGLAND
CONTINUES BIBLE TRANSLATION

The Lollards were English followers of John Wycliffe (1330–1384). The term *Lollard* was a derisive one, originally meaning "mumbler" or "mutterer." The initial Lollards were Wycliffe's fellow scholars at Oxford, but soon many laymen had been converted to Christ and joined the cause. In 1382, Wycliffe's followers, led by Nicholas of Hereford (d. 1420), finished the translation of the Latin Vulgate Bible into English. It was the first time in one thousand years that

594	1066	1200	1300
Buddhism becomes religion of Japan	Normans conquer Britain	Genghis Khan begins conquests	Renaissance begins in Italy

the Bible had been translated into a European language. The Lollard priests then took the English Bible into the villages of England. Wycliffe died two years later, but the revival based on his teachings continued. It is estimated that by the early fifteenth century half the English were Lollards.

1391 ✝ ✡ JEWS ARE FORCED TO CHOOSE MASS CONVERSION OR MASSACRE IN SPAIN

During the fourteenth century, the Black Death plague swept across Europe. The epidemic reached Spain in 1348, along with the accusation that Jews were responsible for the plague by poisoning wells. General hysteria was fanned by the anti-Jewish preaching of a Dominican monk, Vincente Ferrer (1350–1419), and the mood climaxed in a terrible persecution of Jews that began in Seville. On June 6, 1391, a mob attacked the Jewish quarter of Seville killing reportedly more than a thousand people, with thousands more converting to Christianity at swordpoint. The horror spread throughout Spain. Thousands of Jews were killed and thousands more were forced to be baptized. In 1391, while entire communities fled from the massacres, many Jews chose Christianity over death. Many of the forced converts, however, continued to practice Judaism secretly.

1395 ✝ LOLLARDS SUMMARIZE COMPLAINTS IN THE TWELVE CONCLUSIONS

The followers of John Wycliffe (1330–1384), called Lollards, were outspoken activists against the abuses of the church in fourteenth- and fifteenth-century England. The group originally began as a group of students and scholars at Oxford, but grew into a larger sect particularly among the middle class. Among their many complaints against the church were its hierarchy, the Eucharist, and its opposition to an English Bible. These complaints were summarized in the *Twelve Conclusions,* a document written in 1395 to define Lollard beliefs. Six years later, in 1401, Parliament responded with a statute called "On the Burning of a Heretic," which was aimed specifically at the Lollards. In spite of opposition, the Lollards played key roles in English revivals, and their ideas proved influential in England's move toward Protestantism under Henry VIII (1491–1547).

1435	1475	1506–7	1517
First African slaves brought to Europe	First book printed in English	First maps of New World created	Ottomans conquer Egypt

1409 ✝ COUNCIL OF PISA CONVENES

The Council of Pisa convened on March 25, 1409. It was the first of three Refor-
matory councils where the gathered dignitaries and leaders of the church, rather
than the pope, had the final authority. During the previous thirty-one years of
the Great Schism, the existence of two popes, one seated in Rome and the other
in Avignon, wreaked such havoc in Western Christendom that this council was
called to reconcile the division and bring reform. The council deposed Gregory
XII (1327–1417) (Rome) and Benedict XIII (1328–1423) (Avignon) and elected
Alexander V (1339–1410) as the new pope. However, the first two refused to re-
sign, resulting in three popes. Nevertheless, the Council of Pisa did lay the
groundwork for an eventual solution later at the Council of Constance.

1413 ✝ ✡ TORTOSA DISPUTATION BEGINS

Conversion to Christianity opened the door of opportunity for some Jews.
Joshua Lorca was a Spanish Jew who converted during the mass Christian conversion in the late fourteenth century. He became Geronimo de Santa Fe and
influenced Benedict XIII (1328–1423), a rival pope to the pope of Rome, to hold
a disputation between Christians and Jews in Tortosa, Spain. The public pro-
ceeding became more of a spectacle than a disputation. Beginning in 1413, it
continued until 1414 as more of a Christian harangue than a debate. One monk
after another lectured the Jewish rabbis that the Messiah had come in the person
of Jesus. The Jews were allowed only very limited responses. The result was that
many Jews simply converted.

1414 ✝ THE COUNCIL OF CONSTANCE CONVENES;
THE GREAT SCHISM ENDS

By 1414, the Great Schism with its three popes had become scandalous and intolerable. The German king, Sigismund (1361–1437), obliged the successor of Pope
Alexander V (1339–1410)—Pope John XXIII (1370–1419)—to convoke a council. The Council of Constance was held in the city of Constance in Southern Germany and was the best attended of all the ecumenical councils. It convened on
November 5, 1414, and ended on April 22, 1418. Germany, Spain, France, England, and Italy each had one vote. This council called for the resignation of Pope

594	1066	1200	1300
Buddhism becomes religion of Japan	Normans conquer Britain	Genghis Khan begins conquests	Renaissance begins in Italy

ited to the teaching of the Bible and rejected distinctions between priests and laity. They became a mass movement when forty thousand people assembled in July 1419 on a hill given the biblical name of Tabor. Led by military leader John Zizka (c.1358–1424), the Taborites were able to defeat the imperial army sent to destroy them. However, their success lasted only a short while, and in 1434, an army of the Catholic nobles defeated the Taborites, ending the movement.

1420 ✛ CRUSADE TARGETS THE HUSSITES

The death of Jan Hus (1373–1415) in 1415 made him a martyr and a national hero in Bohemia. His followers, known as Hussites, couldn't agree on the extent of reforms needed within the Catholic Church and consequently split into two groups. The moderates, called the Calixtines or Utraquists from the Latin word meaning "both," were willing to remain within the Catholic Church if Communion could be served to the laity. The more radical Taborites would make no concessions to Rome. In 1420, Pope Martin V (1368–1431) gathered 150,000 men from across Europe for a crusade against Bohemia. Five times in the following twelve years they advanced against the Hussites and five times were defeated. Ultimately the Utraquists reconciled with the church, and Hussism largely died out. Many Hussite teachings lived on in the Bohemian and Moravian Brethren groups.

1431 ✛ JOAN OF ARC IS MARTYRED

Joan of Arc was born a peasant around 1412 in Domrémy, France, during the Hundred Years' War when England sought to capture the French throne. From her early teens, Joan of Arc saw visions and heard voices telling her to liberate her country. She convinced young King Charles VII (1403–1461) of her special calling from heaven, insisting that France would prevail. With conviction and military genius, she led the French victoriously into battle at Orléans in 1429. Four other victories followed. Joan then led the king to Reims for his coronation. After that event, the voices and visions left her and she wished to return home. Returning to battle at the king's insistence, Joan was captured by England's allies and condemned as a heretic. Burned at the stake on May 30, 1431, the Maid of Orléans remains a national heroine of France.

1435	1475	1506–7	1517
First African slaves brought to Europe	First book printed in English	First maps of New World created	Ottomans conquer Egypt

1431 ✟ COUNCIL OF BASEL CONVENES

The Council of Basel, called by Pope Martin V (1368–1431), opened on July 23, 1431, and was characterized by the ongoing struggle for supremacy between the council and the pope. By 1433, the new pope, Eugene IV (1383–1447), recognized the authority of the council, which then turned its attention to the enactment of reforms, some of which limited the pope administratively and financially, and endeavored to bring reconciliation to the rebellion of the followers of the martyred Jan Hus (1373–1415) in Bohemia (modern-day Czech Republic). However, the Conciliar Movement was dealt a severe blow when Pope Eugene IV transferred the council to Ferrara, Italy, in 1438, and later to Florence and Rome. In defiance, the majority of the council refused to go to Ferrara and elected an antipope, Felix V (d. 1451), who served from 1439 to 1449. Felix V found little support outside Savoy and Switzerland.

1439 ✟ COUNCIL OF FLORENCE CONVENES

After the separation between the Greek church in the East and the Latin church in the West became permanent in 1054, the Latin church pressed for reunification. Finally, the Greek church agreed to a meeting, hoping thereby to secure assistance against the advancing Turks. Pope Eugene IV (1383–1447) transferred the Council of Basel being held in Basel, Switzerland, to Ferrara, Italy, deeming Ferrara more accessible to the Greek leaders. The first common session was held on October 8, 1438. When the city of Florence, Italy, agreed to fund the council, it was moved to Florence in 1439 and became known as the Council of Florence. Council members signed a superficial decree of unity between the Eastern and Western churches on July 5, 1439, which proved to be only temporarily successful.

1449 ✟ ✡ TOLEDO BANS JEWS FROM HOLDING OFFICE

In 1449, the city council of Toledo, Spain, issued a law prohibiting Christian converts who came from Jewish descent from holding any official office within the city. In response to the council's decree, Pope Nicholas V (1397–1455) signed a papal decree that attempted to counter the false notion that Jews could not be transformed by Christian conversion. Although Nicholas V excommunicated those who instituted the ban in Toledo, within two years the king of Castile officially made the ban law for all of Castile. The end result was that Jews in Spain were legally defined by their bloodlines, and "Jewish" people, formerly defined as a religious group that included all adherents to Judaism, became a racial group instead.

1450 ✛ MOVABLE-TYPE PRINTING IS INVENTED

Johannes Gutenberg (1397–1468), born in Mainz, Germany, is acknowledged as the inventor of printing with movable type. Gutenberg was looking for faster ways of producing books, which up until then were produced slowly by copyists using quills and reeds or by printing with hand stamps and woodcuts. The Renaissance produced a tremendous hunger for learning, and these methods could not keep up with the demand for books. Gutenberg developed an oil-based ink and a typecasting machine that used a tin alloy to cast movable metal type. Wine, cheese, or olive oil presses were modified so that the huge screw pressed the printing block against the paper. Using this method, a printer could make identical copies of a book quite quickly—about three hundred per day. The printing press soon was to be used by God to fuel the Reformation.

1450 ✛THE RENAISSANCE SPREADS THROUGH EUROPE

The Renaissance, or "rebirth," started in Italy during the fourteenth century and spread throughout Europe during the fifteenth and sixteenth centuries. It was typified by the spread of humanism, a return to classical values and the beginning of objective scientific inquiry. The invention of printing helped spread the new ideas. The presence of a wealthy leisured class made possible the patronage of artists and intellectuals. It became an age of transition between the Church-centered culture of the Middle Ages and modern civilization. For the church, the Renaissance can be dated from 1450, when Nicholas V (1397–1455) was pope. He was known for his patronage of the arts and for his efforts to restore Rome and build the Vatican library. Tired of monastic asceticism and church restrictions on intellectual inquiry, Western Europe replaced heavenly considerations with earthly interests. The resulting intellectual and religious climate helped prepare the way for the Reformation.

1435	1475	1506–7	1517
First African slaves brought to Europe	First book printed in English	First maps of New World created	Ottomans conquer Egypt

1453 ✛ THE BOHEMIAN BRETHREN ARE FORMED

The Bohemian Brethren, known later as the Moravian Brethren, were a group of Christians committed to fulfilling the law of Christ. The Brethren first formed under the preaching of Archbishop Rokycana (1390–1471) in Prague; they were later united with the followers of Peter Chelcicky (d. 1457). The Brethren society consisted of three groups: the beginners, the advanced, and the perfected (priests), who were held to a very high standard. The priests were to remain celibate, administer the seven sacraments, and maintain a high level of honesty and integrity. They eventually separated completely from the Catholic Church. The Brethren later expanded into synods and dioceses. During the mid-sixteenth century, persecution led to the dispersion of the Brethren into many isolated groups. Many of these groups were reunited later under the leadership of Count Zinzendorf (1700–1760) in Germany.

1453 ✛ ☪ CONSTANTINOPLE FALLS TO THE TURKS

By the late 1300s, the Ottoman Turks (Turkish Muslims) had started to build an empire that was destined to cover much of the Middle East, as well as parts of North Africa and southeastern Europe. With Constantinople threatened by Muslim invasion, the Greek Orthodox Church had agreed at the Council of Florence in 1439 to reunification with the Roman Church. Largely motivated by the hope of reinforcement against the Turks, the Greeks were to be disappointed in the little aid they received. Constantinople fell on May 29, 1453, to the Ottoman forces led by Mohammad II (1430–1481). The Byzantine Empire was no more; the reunification of the Eastern and Western churches was short-lived. Constantinople was renamed Istanbul, meaning "to the city." Istanbul remained the capital of Turkey from 1453 until 1923 when Ankara replaced it.

1456 ✛ GUTENBERG PRODUCES THE FIRST PRINTED BIBLE

Mass production of books was made possible with the invention of the printing press by Johannes Gutenberg (1397–1468). In Mainz, Germany, Gutenberg borrowed money from Johann Fust to finance his printing business. The first major book produced during the years 1453–1456 was the 42-line Gutenberg Bible, which was the Vulgate, Jerome's Latin translation of the Hebrew and

Greek texts. No two Bibles were alike since each had large capital letters and ornamentation added by hand after it came off the press. It is believed that about 160–180 copies were printed; large portions of 48 still exist. The Library of Congress, the British Library, and the Bibliothèque Nationale in Paris each has an excellent copy printed on vellum.

1460 ✠ HENRY THE NAVIGATOR DIES

The Portuguese prince, Henry the Navigator (1394–1460), sent out more than fifty expeditions to explore the northwest coast of Africa but never went on one himself. The purpose of these voyages was to establish Portuguese colonies, to break the Muslim hold on trade, and to spread Christianity. Unfortunately, almost from the first, Africans were brought back to Europe as slaves. By his death on November 13, 1460, Henry had substantially advanced the knowledge of navigation. He made possible the later explorations of Vasco da Gama (1469–1524) and Bartolomeu Dias (1450–1500).

1478 ✠ ✡ ☪ POPE SIXTUS IV AUTHORIZES THE SPANISH INQUISITION

Prodded by Queen Isabella (1451–1504), Pope Sixtus IV (1414–1484) authorized the Spanish Inquisition in 1478. Headed up by the Dominican order, the church hoped to identify and remove heresy among Christians. In 1483, Tomas de Torquemada (1420–1498) was appointed the Spanish Grand Inquisitor. He set up tribunals with such effectiveness that they lasted for three centuries. Persecution was leveled against Spanish Muslims called Moors, as well as Jews and Muslims who had been forced to convert to Christianity and who were suspected of duplicity. The grounds for arrest often were mere rumor, and all were presumed guilty until proven innocent. Torture was the primary means of extracting confessions, and burning was the principal means of execution. By Torquemada's death, two thousand had been executed as heretics under his authority.

1481 ✠ SAVONAROLA SPURS REVIVAL IN FLORENCE

Girolamo Savonarola (1452–1498) was a Dominican friar who brought revival to Florence, Italy, in 1481. Both an intellectual and a man of deep piety, he was

1435	1475	1506–7	1517
First African slaves brought to Europe	First book printed in English	First maps of New World created	Ottomans conquer Egypt

known for his asceticism, visions of ecstasy, and predictions of the future. Savonarola had been a preacher in Italy since 1845, steadily gaining influence and popularity. However, after having a vision of God's judgment on Florence, he took his message to the streets with increased passion. He moved large congregations to tears, had long lines outside of his church before services, and held huge bonfires to burn "sinful articles." Seemingly all of Florence got caught up in the popularity of his movement. Savonarola was influential even in setting up a new system of government after a French invasion. However, the revival and his popularity were short-lived. He was excommunicated for heresy and ultimately hanged in Florence.

1488 ✡ FIRST COMPLETE HEBREW OLD TESTAMENT IS PRINTED

For hundreds of years, the Hebrew Scriptures—the Old Testament of modern Bibles—were preserved through the painstaking and careful work of scribes who handwrote copies to pass on from generation to generation. The diligent and accurate preservation of the Old Testament text is due largely to groups such as the Masoretes, a group of scribes who arose at the end of the fifth century. However, with Johann Gutenberg's (1397–1468) invention of the printing press around 1450, the transmission of these ancient texts became much easier and more efficient. On February 23, 1488, the first complete Hebrew Bible was printed in Soncino, Italy. For the first time the Old Testament Scriptures were available in Hebrew in large numbers.

1492 ✝ ☾ THE LAST MUSLIM MOORS ARE REMOVED FROM SPAIN

The Moors were Islamic nomads from northwestern Africa. They joined the Arabs who came into Europe from North Africa in the seventh century, marching across the Pyrenees Mountains and advancing as far as Tours, France, before Charles Martel (689–741) defeated them in 732. They retreated to Spain, which then was divided into Islamic fiefdoms. Gradually, Christians took over power in the north and west of Spain. In the early thirteenth century, Christian kings joined to push the Moors out of central Spain, but they remained in the kingdom of Granada for three more centuries. Finally on January 2, 1492, the Moors in Granada surrendered to the army of King Ferdinand (1452–1516) and Queen Isabella (1451–1504). These were the years of the Spanish Inquisition,

594	1066	1200	1300
Buddhism becomes religion of Japan	Normans conquer Britain	Genghis Khan begins conquests	Renaissance begins in Italy

A KING WHO THREW HIS WEIGHT AROUND

June 28, 1491

Have you ever noticed how God sometimes uses unlikely characters to play important roles in executing his plan? A case in point is the four-hundred-pound founder of the Episcopal Church.

He was born on June 28, 1491, the second son of King Henry VII of England. Named after his father, young Henry was trained for a career in the church since, as second son, he was not born to be king. However, when his older brother, Arthur, died in 1502, young Henry became the heir apparent.

Henry was just seventeen when his father died and he began to reign as King Henry VIII. Honoring his father's dying request, he married his brother's widow, Catherine of Aragon, thus maintaining the alliance between England and Spain. Two weeks after their wedding in 1509, they were crowned king and queen of England. Henry turned over the management of his realm to his ministers, in particular to Thomas Wolsey, his chaplain. In 1515, Wolsey was made a cardinal by the pope and lord chancellor by Henry.

In the early years of his reign, Henry was concerned with two issues: the spreading Reformation and his inability to sire a male heir. In ecclesiastical matters, Henry VIII strongly supported the pope against the Reformation. In 1521, he coauthored a book, *Defense of the Seven Sacraments*, which became a best seller throughout Europe.

As Henry VIII grew older and larger, his preoccupation with his lack of a male heir grew. Catherine of Aragon bore him six children, but only one, Mary Tudor, survived infancy. To Henry, it was unthinkable that a girl would succeed him. When Catherine turned forty in 1526, it was obvious to Henry that she never would bear him a son.

By 1527, Henry was in love with twenty-year-old Anne Boleyn, the younger sister of an earlier mistress. Cardinal Wolsey tried to arrange a divorce from Catherine with the pope, but the issue dragged on for years. Finally, Henry defiantly took things into his own hands and made himself head of the Church of England. He felt it was the only way he could divorce Catherine. Henry named Thomas Cranmer, who had been influenced by Lutheranism, archbishop of Canterbury, and Cranmer reciprocated by granting Henry VIII's divorce from Catherine of Aragon. Before his divorce was final, Henry married Anne Boleyn, who was to be the second of his six wives.

More importantly for the future, Henry enacted a series of laws permanently separating the Church of England from the Roman Catholic Church. Today, the Church of England is known in the United States as the Episcopal Church and elsewhere as the Anglican Church.

Henry himself may never have subscribed to any Protestant doctrines and his motives may have been self-serving, yet God used him to begin the Reformation in England.

during which any Muslims who wished to remain in Spain were forced to convert to Christianity.

1492 ✡ FERDINAND AND ISABELLA ISSUE SPAIN'S EDICT OF EXPULSION

King Ferdinand (1452–1516) and Queen Isabella (1451–1504), desiring to create an entirely Catholic nation, sought to erase Judaism from Spain. In spite of pleas from their Jewish advisors, they issued the Edict of Expulsion on March 31, 1492, which decreed that every Jew who would not immediately be baptized had to leave Spain by August 2, 1492. Of the two hundred thousand Jews still living in Spain, many decided to be baptized, but one hundred thousand fled to Portugal and another fifty thousand went to North Africa or Turkey. Others went to the Netherlands, the only Christian country that would receive them. On the Jewish calendar, August 2 is the ninth day of the month of Ab, the same day on which the destruction of the Jewish temple occurred in 586 BC and again in AD 70.

1492 ✝ COLUMBUS DISCOVERS AMERICA

In a time when the meanings of names were taken seriously, Christopher Columbus (1451–1506), named after St. Christopher, the patron saint of travelers, believed that he was to take the name of Christ to foreign lands that did not know of him. Columbus became convinced that sailing west would be a much quicker route to the Far East. He eventually persuaded King Ferdinand (1452–1516) and Queen Isabella (1451–1504) of Spain to finance his journey to the Orient. On August 3, 1492, Columbus boarded the *Santa Maria* and set sail. On the morning of October 11, 1492, after three strenuous months at sea and with the crew on the brink of mutiny, a lookout spotted land. Setting foot on an island he named San Salvador, meaning "Holy Savior," Columbus's prayer was that "Thy holy name may be proclaimed in this second part of the earth."

1492 ✝ PAPAL CORRUPTION PEAKS WITH ALEXANDER VI

Through bribery and political intrigue, a Spaniard named Rodrigo Borgia was elected Pope Alexander VI (1431–1503) in 1492. Thirty-seven years

594	1066	1200	1300
Buddhism becomes religion of Japan	Normans conquer Britain	Genghis Khan begins conquests	Renaissance begins in Italy

THE OTHER DEPARTURE OF 1492

August 2, 1492

In 1492, Columbus sailed the ocean blue—but another departure from Spain also transpired in 1492, which for some was more momentous than the voyage of Christopher Columbus.

In 1469, Ferdinand, son of the king of Aragon, married his cousin Isabella, daughter of the king of Castile. Together they ruled a united Spain, and together they defeated the Muslim Moors, ending Islam's presence in Europe.

In 1479, Ferdinand and Isabella introduced the Inquisition in Spain, a tribunal to identify and remove heresy. The Jews of Spain were a particular target. Many Jews, while secretly adhering to Judaism, outwardly professed Christianity and were baptized to save their lives. The Spaniards derisively referred to them as *marranos*, from the word for "swine." The *marranos* had the legal rights of Catholic citizens, yet it was well known that privately many were still practicing Jews.

The Spanish Inquisition targeted all kinds of suspected enemies of the church, but the majority were Jews. In total, the Spanish Inquisition punished 341,000 people. Over 32,000 were burned to death. The final indignity forced on the Jews was the Edict of Expulsion signed by Ferdinand and Isabella. It decreed that every Jew who would not immediately be baptized had to leave Spain within three months of the deadline of August 2, 1492.

At this time there were still two hundred thousand Jews living in Spain. Many decided to be baptized, including the senior rabbi and a majority of the leading families. Approximately one hundred thousand fled to Portugal only to be expelled four years later. Another fifty thousand crossed the straits to North Africa or sailed to Turkey. Others went to the Netherlands, the only Christian country that would receive them.

Christopher Columbus set sail from Spain half an hour before sunrise on August 3, with his Jewish secretary Luis Torres, who had been baptized. Columbus always signed his name Colon, a common name among the *marranos* of Genoa, his home, evidence that Columbus may have been a Hebrew Christian himself.

August 2, 1492, was the ninth day of the month Ab on the Hebrew calendar. This was the same day as the destruction of the Jewish Temple in 586 BC, beginning the exile among the Babylonians and the same day as the destruction of the Temple by the Romans in AD 70, beginning the exile among the Gentiles. It was also the same day that the Jews were expelled from England in 1290.

The persecution and exile of the Jews from Spain was the most momentous event for Judaism between the middle of the second century AD and the Holocaust. The Spanish Jews have become known as the *Sephardi* Jews (a corruption of an old word for Spain). They remained dispersed until the creation of the state of Israel in 1948.

previously, his uncle Callistus III (1378–1458), pope from 1455 to 1458, named him archbishop of Valencia when Alexander was only twenty-five years old. Alexander VI was able, hardworking, handsome, and imposing, but he used his papacy to serve his own desires. He did much for the arts, and for the architecture and streets of Rome; however, he was preoccupied with furthering the marriages and careers of his numerous illegitimate children by several mistresses. His pontificate was directed almost solely by family and political aspirations, and he was responsible for the execution of Savonarola (1452–1498). This most corrupt papacy ended with his death in 1503.

1493 ✝ POPE ALEXANDER VI DIVIDES THE WORLD BETWEEN SPAIN AND PORTUGAL

Pope Alexander VI (1431–1503) had the reputation of being one of the most corrupt popes of his day. He did, however, clarify the land rights of Spain and Portugal, the two sea powers in the New World. As pope, he felt he had the authority to establish ownership of the lands in newly discovered America. After Columbus (1451–1506) returned from his first voyage in spring 1493, the pope decreed in two bulls to divide the New World between Spain and Portugal. The dividing line was negotiated a year later when representatives of the two countries met at Tordesillas, Spain. The Treaty of Tordesillas made the line of demarcation about 1,295 miles east of the Cape Verde Islands, which gave most of Brazil to Portugal and the rest of South America to Spain.

1493 ✝ POPE ALEXANDER VI AUTHORIZES MISSIONS TO NEW WORLD

New horizons for Christian missions opened up with the discovery of the New World by Christopher Columbus (1451–1506). From the time of Columbus on, expansion would carry a dual religious and political flavor. In 1493, Pope Alexander VI (1431–1503) issued a bull charging King Ferdinand with the responsibility "to bring the Christian faith to the peoples who inhabit these islands and the mainland, and to send to the said islands and to the mainland wise, God-fearing, and virtuous men who will be capable of instructing the indigenous people in good morals and in the Catholic faith." Immediately, missionary priests began accompanying the explorers to the New World.

594	1066	1200	1300
Buddhism becomes religion of Japan	Normans conquer Britain	Genghis Khan begins conquests	Renaissance begins in Italy

1497 ✛ SAVONAROLA IS EXCOMMUNICATED

Girolamo Savonarola (1452–1498), a prior at the Convent of San Marco in Florence, Italy, became the city's spiritual leader. He had become very popular among the people due to his attempts to reform church and state by boldly denouncing the abuses of the clergy and the evils of the ruling class. When Pope Alexander VI (1431–1503) ordered Savonarola to discontinue all preaching, he disobeyed. On May 13, 1497, Alexander VI excommunicated Savonarola from the church on the grounds that he had disobeyed his commands. The following year Savonarola was tried for sedition and heresy and was tortured. He was then hanged and his body publicly burned.

1497 ✛ ✡ PORTUGUESE JEWS ARE FORCED INTO MASS CONVERSION

Following their expulsion from Spain in 1492, approximately fifty thousand Jews crossed the border and sought refuge in Portugal. Unfortunately, Judaism remained legal in Portugal only four more years. In 1496, the king of Portugal outlawed Judaism, but when the Jews attempted to leave, he prevented them from doing so. On March 19, 1497, the king forced all of them to be baptized. Life for those baptized Jews was easier in Portugal than in Spain, allowing them to secretly preserve their Jewish heritage. This difference in level of persecution was aided also by Portugal's lax approach to the Inquisition.

1497 ✛ VASCO DA GAMA REACHES INDIA WITH MISSIONARIES

Because overland routes to India and the Far East in the fifteenth century were blocked by the Ottoman Turks, an all-water route was needed. To establish a route between Europe and India and to spread Christianity, Admiral Vasco da Gama (1469–1524) left Lisbon, Portugal, on July 8, 1497, and followed Bartolomeu Diaz's earlier route down the west coast of Africa to the Cape of Good Hope and then on into uncharted waters. He set out in four ships, accompanied by a number of missionary priests and with a staff mostly of convicts. Arriving in India he found—in addition to Muslims, Hindus, and Jews—Christians who claimed that their church had been founded by the apostle Thomas. Vasco da Gama made two other trips to India, dying at sea on December 24, 1524, during his third voyage.

1435	1475	1506–7	1517
First African slaves brought to Europe	First book printed in English	First maps of New World created	Ottomans conquer Egypt

TORTURE IN THE NAME OF CHRIST

September 16, 1498

What makes a religious person cruel?

Tomas de Torquemada had good religious genes. Born in Spain in 1420, he was the nephew of a prominent cardinal. After entering a Dominican monastery, Torquemada was made prior of another monastery. Subsequently, he was appointed confessor to King Ferdinand II and Queen Isabella, best known for sponsoring Christopher Columbus's voyage.

Back in 1163, Pope Alexander IV had encouraged princes and bishops to imprison heretics and confiscate their property. And beginning in 1231, Pope Gregory IX set up the Inquisition, a special church tribunal for combating heresy.

Prodded by Queen Isabella of Spain, Pope Sixtus IV authorized the Spanish Inquisition in 1478. No nation during this time period was more interested in keeping the Catholic faith pure than Spain. In 1483, Torquemada was appointed the Spanish grand inquisitor and became the most powerful person in Spain after the king and queen. In 1487, the persecution was leveled against the Spanish Muslims, called Moors, and Jewish and Muslim converts to Christianity who were suspected of duplicity. The conversion of the Muslims and the Jews to Christianity had been forced in almost all cases.

The Inquisition in Spain began by offering heretics the Edict of Grace, a period of thirty to forty days during which they could identify themselves and, on their confession, be assured of a pardon. The catch was that those who confessed their heresies, called *penitentes*, were forced to take a vow to reveal other heretics.

The grounds for a person's arrest were accusation by another, or even mere rumor. A person was assumed to be guilty until proven innocent. Torture was used regularly. Even when there was sufficient testimony from others to convict the accused, the victim was still tortured to extract a confession. Torture also was used to acquire names of additional heretics.

From the beginning, the primary means of execution was by fire. The tribunal established at Ciudad Real in 1483 burned 52 heretics in two years. When the Inquisition moved to Toledo in 1485, 750 penitentes were marched into the cathedral to be told that one-fifth of their property had been confiscated. Next the tribunal went to Avila, where 75 were burned at the stake and 26 corpses were exhumed and burned.

By the time of Torquemada's death, on September 16, 1498, two thousand heretics had been executed under his authority. The great irony is that Torquemada died hiding the fact that he himself had Jewish blood.

1498 ✛ LEONARDO DA VINCI PAINTS THE LAST SUPPER

Born in Florence, Italy, Leonardo da Vinci (1452–1519) was the illegitimate son of a notary and a peasant woman. In 1482, he entered the service of the Duke of Milan. In Milan from 1495 to 1498, he painted his masterpiece *The Last Supper* on the refectory wall of the Dominican convent of Santa Maria delle Grazie. The scene of the Last Supper is unusual in that it contrasts the calm peacefulness of the figure of Christ with the emotional turmoil seen in the disciples at the moment of betrayal by Judas Iscariot. Leonardo spent his last days near Amboise in France, where King Francis I (1494–1547) invited him to be a member of the court.

1501 ✛ PETRUCCI FIRST PRINTS MUSIC WITH MOVABLE TYPE

Soon after the invention of the printing press in 1453, simple musical compositions began to be printed. Ottaviano dei Petrucci of Venice was the first to publish more complex compositions with movable metal type. Petrucci (1466–1539) used a three-step process to print music. First the words were printed, then the staves, and finally the notes. Petrucci's work made musical compositions more accessible, enabling church music to progress from simple tunes and Gregorian chants to the more complex works of Haydn and Bach.

1506 ✛ WORK BEGINS ON ST. PETER'S BASILICA

In 1506, Pope Julius II (1443–1513) began construction on St. Peter's Basilica in Rome. The basilica was located on the traditional site of Peter's crucifixion, and his tomb is said to be under the central altar. Michelangelo (1475–1564), who was one of a number of artists to contribute to the basilica's construction, designed its dome. The church, which was completed in 1615 under Pope Paul V (1552–1621), is one of the largest in the world. Early in the project the pope commissioned Johann Tetzel (1465–1519) to raise money for construction by selling indulgences. The church claimed that the purchase of an indulgence allowed the merit of Christ and the saints to be transferred to a soul in purgatory, thus shortening its time there. Martin Luther (1483–1546) wrote his Ninety-Five Theses against this practice of selling indulgences.

1435	1475	1506–7	1517
First African slaves brought to Europe	First book printed in English	First maps of New World created	Ottomans conquer Egypt

1512 ✝ FIFTH LATERAN COUNCIL CONVENES

The Lateran Councils were ecumenical church councils that convened in the Church of St. John Lateran in Rome. In 1512, Pope Julius II (c.1443–1513) called for the Fifth Lateran Council. The pope summoned the church together as a response to the Council of Pisa (1511–1512), which had convened without papal authority and commissioning. Though needing to address clerical abuses, corruption, usury, and overall church reform, the council focused primarily on issues of protocol, authority, and the governing structure surrounding the gathering of councils. The failure of the pope and council to address the church's need for reform prepared the way for Martin Luther (1483–1546) to launch the Reformation.

1512 ✝ MICHELANGELO COMPLETES THE SISTINE CHAPEL

According to his own account, Michelangelo Buonarroti (1475–1564) initially was hesitant to undertake painting the frescoes of the Sistine Chapel. However, at the papal court's urging, Michelangelo began work on the ceiling in 1508. He planned and worked on the project for more than four years. Covering more than ten thousand square feet of surface, the work includes hundreds of characters, some as large as twelve feet high, and depicts a timeline of the biblical account from creation to the second coming of Christ. The finished product has come to be known as one of the single greatest artistic achievements of all time.

1513 ✝ LEO X BECOMES POPE

In a span of three days, Giovanni de' Medici (1475–1521) received holy orders, was consecrated as a bishop, and was crowned Pope Leo X of the Catholic Church on March 17, 1513. Chosen as a relief to the harsh policies and attitude of the previous pope, Julius II (c.1443–1513), Leo strove for peace within the church and the empire. A classic embodiment of the Renaissance, Leo delighted in the arts and humanist learning. His penchant for spending, however, led the church into more and more debt. As a result, Leo supported the sale of indulgences as a way to raise funds for the church. Martin Luther (1483–1546) would open the doors of reformation when he nailed his famous Ninety-Five Theses to the Cathedral door in Wittenberg, Germany, to attack the church's practice of indulgences.

594	1066	1200	1300
Buddhism becomes religion of Japan	Normans conquer Britain	Genghis Khan begins conquests	Renaissance begins in Italy

1513 ✝ RAPHAEL PAINTS SISTINE MADONNA

Raphael Sanzio (1483–1520), one of the greatest pupils of Leonardo da Vinci (1452–1519) and Michelangelo (1475–1564), is best known for his vivid and powerful paintings of the Madonna and the life of Christ. Commissioned by Pope Julius II (1443–1513) in about 1513, Raphael began working on an altarpiece that would be titled the *Sistine Madonna*. This work—first presented in Piacenza, a newly established city in the Papal States—depicts the Virgin Mary and the baby Jesus seemingly floating through the very frame of the picture, suggesting an infinite lightness and absence of mortality in these two holy figures. Raphael's artistic style and talent has become the benchmark for biblical art.

1514 ✝ BARTOLOME DE LAS CASAS CONVERTS

Bartolome de las Casas (1474–1566) was born in 1474 in Seville, Spain. In 1502, he went to the Caribbean island of Hispaniola, and he was ordained there as a priest in 1507. Several years after his profound conversion to Jesus Christ in 1514, he became a champion of the American Indians, seeking to end their slavery, to encourage their conversion, and to further their humane treatment. Even after returning to Spain in 1547, he worked tirelessly to improve the Indians' quality of life. He was a pioneer in the cause of human rights.

1516 ✡ THE FIRST ITALIAN GHETTO IS ESTABLISHED IN VENICE

In 1516, the city of Venice portioned off a neighborhood specifically for Jews. The Venetian ghetto, the first to be established in Italy, not only confined the Jewish population but became the model for such ghettos throughout Italy. In 1555, Pope Paul IV (1476–1559) commanded the separation of Jews from the rest of the Italian population, making ghettos a standard feature in Rome and papal territories. The typical Italian ghetto was surrounded by a gated wall, and the Jews were required to remain inside it at night. Starting with the first ghetto in Venice, Italy continued to require ghettos in major cities and small towns until 1732.

1516 ✡ ☾ OTTOMAN TURKS CONQUER PALESTINE

The Ottomans, a Turkish dynasty dating back to about 1300, conquered Constantinople in 1453. In 1516, the Turks defeated the Egyptian armies, giving

1435	1475	1506–7	1517
First African slaves brought to Europe	First book printed in English	First maps of New World created	Ottomans conquer Egypt

them control not only of Syria but of Palestine as well. The presence of the Ottoman Empire, an enemy of Europe, brought unity to the Middle East, and their influence often benefited the Jews in the area. The Ottoman sultan, Suleiman the Magnificent (1520–1566), used his power in the region to build the walls that still surround Jerusalem. The flag of the Ottoman Empire flew over Palestine for four centuries, until World War II.

1516 ✝ ERASMUS PUBLISHES THE GREEK NEW TESTAMENT

The Renaissance spurred a resurgence of interest in the classics. This interest extended to the study of original languages. Francisco Jiménez de Cisneros (1437–1517) began work in Spain to publish the first polyglot, or multi-translation, Bible including the Greek. By 1514, the New Testament was completed, but publishing delays prevented it from being released immediately. During this time, Desiderius Erasmus (1466–1536) of Rotterdam, the Netherlands, entered the race to publish the first Greek New Testament. Working with insufficient and incomplete manuscripts, Erasmus completed his Greek Testament in ten months, making it available for publication by 1516, beating the release of Jiménez's text. Though containing many errors, Erasmus's work challenged the Vulgate's supremacy and was the Greek text used by Martin Luther (1483–1546) and William Tyndale (1494–1536) to translate the New Testament into German and English.

THE REFORMATION ERA

1517–1648

Reform came with a fury. Martin Luther sounded the trumpet, and hosts of others rallied to the cause. The period we call the Reformation marks the mobilization of Protestantism: Lutheran, Reformed, Anglican, and Anabaptist. By the mid-sixteenth century the Reformation had shattered the traditional unity of Western Europe and had bequeathed to modern times religious pluralism. The Church of Rome resisted this attack on tradition and mustered new troops, especially the Society of Jesus. The church sent out fresh waves of missionaries to Asia, Africa, and Latin America, and waged war in France, the Netherlands, and Germany. But in the end, Christendom slipped into yesteryear. In its place arose the denominational concept of the church, which allowed modern nations to treat the churches as voluntary societies separated from the state.

BRUCE L. SHELLEY

1517 ✛ LUTHER'S NINETY-FIVE THESES LAUNCH THE REFORMATION

On October 31, 1517, Martin Luther (1483–1546) nailed his Ninety-Five Theses to the door of the Castle Church in Wittenberg, Germany. He had become convinced of justification by faith alone and therefore felt compelled to protest against the indulgence system of the church. In the Roman Catholic Church it was claimed that indulgences remitted the debt of temporal punishment owed to God after the guilt of the sin was forgiven. Indulgences were being sold in Germany by a Dominican friar named Johann Tetzel (1465–1519). Luther's theses were ninety-five arguments against the indulgences. His theses created an explosion of antichurch sentiment among the people and triggered many attempts by the church to silence him. However, Luther would not be silenced, claiming the supremacy of Scripture's authority over any ecclesiastical authority. Luther's Ninety-Five Theses marked the beginning of the Reformation.

1521 ✛ LUTHER DEFENDS HIMSELF AT THE DIET OF WORMS

After Martin Luther (1483–1546), a professor at the University of Wittenberg in Germany, nailed his Ninety-Five Theses to the door of the Castle Church in 1517, the church excommunicated him in January 1521, but agreed to hear his arguments that spring. On April 17, 1521, Luther came to the Diet of Worms to state his case; however, the assembly refused to hear him and demanded that he recant his writings. After a night of prayer, the next day Luther boldly refused to recant, stating, "I am bound by the Scriptures I have cited, for my conscience is captive to the Word of God. . . . I cannot do otherwise. Here I stand, may God help me. Amen." The fire of Reformation would continue to blaze.

1521 ✛ PHILIP MELANCHTHON'S <u>LOCI COMMUNES</u> IS PUBLISHED

Philip Melanchthon (1497–1560) was a professor of Greek at the University of Wittenberg when he embraced the cause of Martin Luther (1483–1546). Melanchthon was the son of George Scharzerd, but when he was young his great uncle gave him the Greek name Melanchthon, meaning "black earth." Melanchthon became the temporary leader of the Reformation when Luther was forced into hiding at Wartburg Castle after the Diet of Worms in 1521. That same year, Melanchthon released his first edition of *Loci Communes*, which was the first systematic exposition of Lutheran theology. It dealt primarily with

1519–21	1521	1531	1562
Ferdinand Magellan circumnavigates the earth	Hernando Cortés conquers Mexico's Aztec Empire	First stock exchange established in Antwerp	English enter slave trade

FROM HEAD TO HEART

December 27, 1518

Theological ideas alone cannot save, but they can be the seeds of spiritual transformation.

Ulrich Zwingli was not born an idealistic revolutionary. Although he was intelligent and well educated, it was his training not his spiritual passion that led him into the ministry. In short, the ideas of the Early Church Fathers made sense to Zwingli, but he lacked true spiritual devotion.

This rift between head and heart manifested itself when, amid his persuasive sermons and popular ministry in the Swiss town of Glarus, someone exposed Zwingli's wanton relationship with a mistress. His conscience was pricked but not yet transformed. At this time, Zwingli reluctantly accepted a post at Einsiedeln, a monastery and place of pilgrimage.

As he preached about God's grace, Zwingli began to find the rituals and trappings of the Roman Catholic Church lacking, and he publicly denounced the local seller of papal indulgences. Surmising that grace could not be bought and sold, Zwingli sought the Scriptures for an understanding of free grace.

Only God knows when Zwingli discovered this saving grace for himself, but at Einsiedeln, Zwingli publicly confessed his own sins and declared Christ's saving grace to be sufficient. Soon, officials from Zurich noticed his powerful oratory. They had reservations about his past reputation, but he appeared changed. They soon invited him to become priest at the Zurich Great Church. He arrived in Zurich on December 27, 1518.

Zwingli entered a city primed for the Reformation. His employers had little idea they were hiring a Reformer, and Zwingli himself might not have known how much he would change. Zurich's citizens, known for their fine army and penchant for political independence, were drawn to their new preacher.

Zwingli found himself preaching in the marketplace on Fridays so the crowds from surrounding villages might hear him. He proclaimed the sufficiency of faith in Christ, the deficiency of superstition and indulgences, the necessity of true repentance and godly living, and the importance of caring for the poor and needy, the widow and orphan.

And widows and orphans there would be. In the summer of 1519, the plague arrived in Zurich. Three out of ten people died. Zwingli diligently ministered throughout the ravaged city. While attending to the sick and dying, he also became ill and nearly died.

Zwingli eventually recovered and went on to become the leading figure in the Reformation in German-speaking Switzerland. But it was just a matter of time before war broke out between Protestants and the armies of the pope. A lifelong military chaplain, Zwingli died on the Kappel battlefield in 1531, defending a threatened freedom: the preaching of the gospel he had come to know and love.

justification by faith, the bondage of the will, and the relationship between the law and the gospel.

1522 ✟ LUTHER TRANSLATES THE NEW TESTAMENT INTO GERMAN

After posting his Ninety-Five Theses, Martin Luther (1483–1546) experienced great opposition from the Roman Catholic Church. In 1521, following the Diet of Worms, Luther went into hiding in Wartburg Castle, protected by the elector, Frederick the Wise (1463–1525). While in hiding, Luther took the opportunity to translate the New Testament from Greek into German. He completed the New Testament in the fall of 1522, and then translated the Old Testament from Hebrew, eventually finishing it in 1534. Luther's German Bible was as much a force in the German-speaking world as the King James Version later became in the English-speaking world.

1523 ✡ DAVID REUBENI APPEARS IN ITALY

In 1523, a young Jew from Ethiopia came to Venice proclaiming that he was a descendent of King David and a prince of the lost tribes of Reuben, Gad, and Manasseh, which he said were living in Ethiopia. As a result he became known as David Reubeni (d. 1538). He claimed he was sent by God to deliver the Holy Land from the Ottoman Empire. Next he traveled to Portugal where he attracted many followers among the Marranos, the Jews who had accepted Christian baptism. One of his followers, Solomon Molcho (d. 1532), was inspired to proclaim himself as the Messiah in Rome in 1530, and was burned alive two years later by the Inquisition. Reubeni was burned in Spain as a heretic in 1538.

1523 ✟ ZWINGLI LEADS THE SWISS REFORMATION

Ulrich Zwingli (1484–1531) was a scholar and priest who had served in the papal armies. In 1518, he became priest at the Great Church in Zurich. In this position Zwingli began a vast reform movement in 1523. The Zurich city council eventually broke with the diocese of Constance and adopted Zwingli's Sixty-Seven Articles, which radically changed church practices in terms of authority, worship, and sacraments. Zwingli's Swiss Reformation was more radical than the Lutheran reform movement, especially on the issues of public worship and

1519–21	1521	1531	1562
Ferdinand Magellan circumnavigates the earth	Hernando Cortés conquers Mexico's Aztec Empire	First stock exchange established in Antwerp	English enter slave trade

THE DIET OF WORMS

| April 17, 1521 |

It wasn't some kind of crazy fad diet.

Europe was in a state of flux during the early 1500s. The Renaissance celebrated humanism and undermined contemporary Christian culture. A threat to the church came from Martin Luther.

Luther, a professor at the University of Wittenberg in Germany, was forthright about his convictions regarding justification by faith, papal authority, and the sacraments. The Reformation had begun when Luther nailed his Ninety-Five Theses to the door of the Wittenberg Cathedral in 1517. The Theses consisted of ninety-five distinct propositions arguing against the supreme power of the pope, the greed within the church, and the abuse of indulgences. As a result, the Roman Catholic Church excommunicated Luther in January 1521. This move served to fuel rather than diminish public support for Luther.

Because of Luther's popularity, Emperor Charles V of the Holy Roman Empire, agreed to hear his arguments at a diet, a meeting of the empire's parliament, which was scheduled for the spring of 1521 in Worms, Germany. Representatives from the church wanted Luther arrested and condemned to death as a heretic without a trial. However, Luther was promised that he would be protected and given a fair trial at the diet.

At four o'clock in the afternoon on April 17, 1521, Luther arrived triumphantly in Worms. It was a dramatic contrast: Luther, a simple monk, standing before the powerful sovereign of the Holy Roman Empire. He was confronted immediately with a pile of his books and asked whether he acknowledged authorship of the writings. He quietly responded, "The books are all mine." They pressed him further, asking whether he would stand by them or recant anything in them. Luther was shocked, because he had been promised a hearing of his beliefs, not a demand for recantation. He replied, "This touches God and his Word. This affects the salvation of souls. Of this Christ said, 'He who denies me before men, him will I deny before my Father.' To say too little or too much would be dangerous. I beg you, give me time to think it over." After some deliberation and even though they felt he didn't deserve it, Luther was granted a one-day delay.

Luther spent the evening in prayer, carefully preparing his response. At six o'clock the following evening, he gave his famous answer: "Unless I am convinced by the testimony of Scripture or by clear reason (for I trust neither pope nor council alone, since it is well known that they have often erred and contradicted themselves), I am bound by the Scriptures I have cited, for my conscience is captive to the Word of God. I cannot and will not recant anything since to act against one's conscience is neither safe nor right. I cannot do otherwise. Here I stand, may God help me. Amen."

These famous words reverberated throughout the Reformation, inspiring many others to take their stand as well.

the sacraments. Zwingli was the founder of the Reformation in German-speaking Switzerland. He died in the battle of Kappel in 1531.

1524 ✦ THE PEASANTS' REVOLT ERUPTS

A revolutionary mass movement among German peasants began when the rulers laid taxes on them. Martin Luther's condemnation of the greedy clergy and princes helped ignite the uprising. The revolt lasted from June 1524 until May 1525. As many as three hundred thousand peasants participated in the uprising. Their agenda was to eliminate feudal dues and serfdom, reform the courts, modify tithes, and institute congregational election of pastors. Luther (1483–1546) strongly opposed the revolt, and this, combined with its poor direction and organization, led to the peasants' defeat. The Peasants' Revolt was detrimental to the Reformation. The Catholic Church portrayed the peasants' defeat as a divine judgment against Protestantism, turning the disillusioned peasants against Luther. As a result, the Reformation lost its appeal among the lower classes.

1525 ✦ THE ANABAPTIST MOVEMENT BEGINS

Often called the Swiss radicals or the left wing of the Reformation, the Anabaptists separated from Swiss Reformer Ulrich Zwingli (1484–1531) over the issue of infant baptism. They believed that only those who could understand and publicly confess their faith should be baptized. The movement, originally called the Swiss Brethren, originated and flourished in Zurich, Switzerland, under the leadership of Conrad Grebel (1498–1526) and Felix Manz (1498–1527). It then spread to Germany, Moravia, and the Netherlands. The Anabaptist movement began on January 21, 1525, when Grebel and Manz held their first adult "believer's baptism." Persecution quickly followed. Grebel died after being imprisoned in 1526, and the following year Manz was drowned in the Liemat River, the first Protestant martyred by other Protestants. The Anabaptists were predecessors of the Mennonite movement.

1525 ✦ THOMAS MÜNZER IS EXECUTED

Thomas Münzer (1490–1525) was a radical figure in the Reformation who became a leader in the Peasants' Revolt of 1524–1525. Initially he had been an associate of Martin Luther (1483–1546) and then received a call to preach at Zwickau, Germany, where he came in contact with a radical group called the Zwickau Prophets. However, he fell out of favor with them due to his violent anticlerical beliefs and his opposition to infant baptism. He then became a leader of the Peasants' Revolt. When the peasants were decisively defeated at Frankenhausen, Germany, in 1525, Münzer was captured and executed.

1525 ✝ TYNDALE'S NEW TESTAMENT IS PUBLISHED

While William Tyndale (1494–1536) was in school at Cambridge University in England, he embraced the doctrines of the Reformation. He also became convinced that in order for England to be evangelized, the people must have the Bible in English. Tyndale petitioned the bishop of London for permission to produce an English translation, but he was denied. Soon thereafter, Tyndale left England for Antwerp. There he translated the Scriptures into English while he was financed and protected by a group of English merchants. In 1525, he printed his first English New Testament. After being condemned for his actions in 1528, Tyndale was finally arrested in 1535 and executed the following year. However, Tyndale's legacy lives on, for his translation was the foundation for the King James Version, as well as the Revised Standard and the English Standard Versions that followed it.

1527 ✝ SATTLER IS MARTYRED FOR HIS SCHLEITHEIM CONFESSION OF FAITH

On February 24, 1527, the Anabaptists in Switzerland approved a confession of faith written by one of their leaders, Michael Sattler (d. 1527). The document, which was called the Brotherly Agreement of Some Children of God, was unanimously approved by those in attendance. The document contained seven major articles. The first was that baptism is reserved for those who make a trustworthy profession of repentance. The second article stated that any member who continues in sin after two warnings would be excluded from the fellowship. The third clause reserved the Lord's Table for baptized believers. The fourth called for separation from the world. The fifth article summarized the requirements for the pastorate. The sixth article banned church members from participating

1590	1607	1631	1647
Telescope invented	English colony established at Jamestown	Mount Vesuvius erupts, destroying towns	Bayonet invented in Bayonne, France

TWO OF A KIND

February 24, 1527

Michael and Margaretha Sattler's convictions consistently took them down the road less traveled and more dangerous.

Michael Sattler was a Catholic priest in southern Germany in the 1520s and Margaretha a member of a lay order in the Catholic Church. The two were of one mind regarding their faith in God and their love for each other. They boldly broke their vows of celibacy, married, and joined the fledgling religious movement known as the Anabaptists.

The Sattlers were attracted to the movement because it considered obedience to God to be of primary importance. They were also attracted to the movement because of its belief in believer's baptism and strict pacifism.

As Michael became an Anabaptist leader, he saw the need for structure within the movement, which needed written guidelines in order to preserve freedom, set boundaries, and protect themselves against fanatics. In Schleitheim, Germany, on February 24, 1527, Michael Sattler brought together a small group of Anabaptist leaders, who wrote and adopted seven articles of faith, which they called the "Brotherly Union." They now had an organized church.

Michael went to Rottenburg, where officials seized the "Brotherly Union" papers from him. Nineteen people, including Michael and Margaretha, were arrested and tried for violations of Catholic doctrine and practice such as baptism, the Eucharist, unction, and veneration of the saints. Michael was also charged with leaving his monastery, marrying, and promoting a pacifist attitude toward the Turks.

In court Michael refuted the charges except the last, for he did believe in a pacifist approach to the Turks. He insisted that the Anabaptists had done nothing against the Bible and requested a debate with the Catholic leaders. Sattler asserted that if he and the other Anabaptists could be proved in error, they would gladly accept their punishment. "But if we are not shown to be in error, I hope to God that you will accept teaching and be converted." The court did not take kindly to the suggestion of his "teaching" them and came back with the sentence: "Michael Sattler shall be committed to the hangman, who shall take him to the square and there first cut out his tongue, then chain him to a wagon, tear his body twice with hot tongs there and five times more before the gate, then burn his body to powder as an arch-heretic."

During his excruciating execution, Michael prayed with slurred speech, "Almighty, eternal God, Thou art the way and the truth; because I have not been shown to be in error, I will with Thy help on this day testify to the truth and seal it with my blood."

After Michael's death the authorities tried in vain to persuade Margaretha to recant, but she declared that she would forever remain true to her Lord and to her husband. Eight days after Michael's execution, Margaretha was drowned in the Neckar River that passes through Rottenburg.

in military service. The final section prohibits the taking of oaths. Soon after the confession was approved, Sattler, like many other Anabaptists, was martyred.

1529 + COLLOQUY OF MARBURG IS CALLED

The Colloquy of Marburg was called in 1529 by the Reformers in Marburg, Germany, to form a united front against Roman Catholicism. The main issue was the Lord's Supper. Ulrich Zwingli (1484–1531) argued that the bread and wine were symbols of Christ, and that Communion was a sign of the grace that already had been bestowed upon the believer. Luther (1483–1546) and his supporters took Christ's words literally rather than metaphorically, insisting on a real presence of Christ in the elements. The group came to a general agreement on many important doctrines and issued fifteen articles that stated their position. In spite of their agreements, the colloquy overall served to divide rather than unite Protestantism. Disagreements about the Lord's Supper set the pattern for denominational differences that continue today.

1529 + PROTESTANTS EMERGE AT THE DIET OF SPEYER

The term *Protestant* was first used in 1529 at the Diet of Speyer, the Holy Roman Empire's parliament meeting in Speyer along the Rhine River in Bavaria (present-day Germany). There, several German princes signed a formal protest to Emperor Charles V (1500–1558) challenging his demand that the rulers of Germany enforce the 1521 Edict of Worms that had declared Luther and his followers to be outlaws. The signatories became known as Protestants, and the name came to be applied to all who left the Catholic Church to join the Reformation.

1529 + ☪ TURKS BESIEGE VIENNA

After becoming Holy Roman Emperor in 1519, Charles V (1500–1558) began fighting vigorously to suppress the Lutheran movement and eliminate Protestantism throughout Europe. In 1529, just as Charles was preparing to take action against the Lutherans in his German territories, the Muslim Turks—led by Suleiman (1494–1566)—attacked Vienna, the capital of Charles's Austrian territories. The city of Vienna was vitally important to Germany, because if it were

1590	1607	1631	1647
Telescope invented	English colony established at Jamestown	Mount Vesuvius erupts, destroying towns	Bayonet invented in Bayonne, France

THE REEK OF PATRICK HAMILTON

February 29, 1528

He was Scotland's first.

Born around 1503, Patrick Hamilton was from a Scottish noble family. He was a distant relative of King James V and therefore, technically, royalty. During his short life, he passed a number of milestones in rapid succession. When a teenager, he was appointed the titular abbot of Ferne in Ross-shire, then entered the University of Paris and graduated in 1520.

In Paris, Hamilton was exposed to the teachings of Martin Luther that were spreading across Europe. He returned to Scotland in 1523, unhappy with the Roman Catholic Church, but as the second son, he was expected to pursue the study of theology. He entered St. Leonard's College at St. Andrews that same year, excited about Luther's teaching of justification by faith.

By 1525, books containing the heresies of Luther were forbidden by the Scottish Parliament. The next year, Patrick Hamilton let it be known publicly that he believed those doctrines. In response to an accusation of heresy in 1527, he went abroad to avoid further problems with the church.

However, this trip only served to strengthen his resolve as a follower of Luther. He went to Wittenberg, Germany, and personally met both Martin Luther and Philip Melanchthon. He also met William Tyndale, who was translating the Bible into English. While in Germany he wrote a short book entitled *Common Places*, which explained the principles and doctrines of the Reformation, emphasizing, in particular, justification by faith in Christ alone.

Soon he returned to Scotland, where he began preaching the doctrines of the Reformation. His preaching and family connections made him a considerable threat to the Roman Catholic Church, and in January 1528, Hamilton was called to meet with Archbishop Beaton and other Catholic theologians at St. Andrews. He was examined and sent home—perhaps in the hope that he would further incriminate himself or leave the country to save himself.

A month later, he again was summoned to appear before the archbishop and his council on thirteen charges of heresy. He was convicted and sentenced to be burned at the stake that same day, February 29, 1528. The execution was carried out in such haste that they did not have enough wood and gunpowder on hand to produce a huge blaze. As a result, Hamilton suffered a slow and horrible death. He was the first Protestant martyr in Scotland.

Hamilton's influence grew as word of his martyrdom spread, making him more popular in death than in life. Soon all of Scotland was discussing Reformed theology. One of his accusers, Alexander Alexius, was converted as a result of Hamilton's testimony and became a leader of the Reformation.

A witness of his burning later remarked, "The reek (stench of the smoke) of Patrick Hamilton has infected as many as it did blow upon."

to fall to the Turks, Germany itself would be left vulnerable to Turkish attack. Therefore, Emperor Charles set aside his religious differences with his German subjects, and German Protestant forces joined Charles in fighting the Turks. Because of this coalition, they were able to force Suleiman and the Turkish army to withdraw from Vienna.

1530 ✛ THE AUGSBURG CONFESSION IS READ PUBLICLY

Emperor Charles V (1500–1558) hoped that some conciliation between Catholics and Protestants would be possible during his reign, so he called the Diet of Augsburg. At this meeting on April 25, 1530, the Augsburg Confession was read aloud publicly in German, taking two hours. The Confession had been commissioned by John (1468–1532), elector of Saxony, and written by Martin Luther (1483–1546), Justus Jonas (1493–1555), Johann Bugenhagen (1485–1558), and Philip Melanchthon (1497–1560). The Confession was a summary of the evangelical faith from the perspective of these Reformers. The Catholic reply, called the Papalist Confutation, accepted parts of it but condemned others. Although the emperor demanded that the Reformers comply with the Confutation, Melanchthon wrote a reply that was added as an addendum to the Augsburg Confession. This document was the earliest formal creedal statement of Lutheranism and became the authoritative Confession of the Lutheran church.

1531 ✛ MEXICAN INDIAN REPORTS A VISION AT GUADALUPE

As the Spanish conquistadors moved through the Americas, Catholic missionaries usually followed close behind. This was the case as Franciscan missionaries arrived in Mexico City in 1524. The next year, an Indian convert named Quauhtlatoatzin (1474–1548) was baptized by a Franciscan priest, and his name was changed to Juan Diego. In 1531, Juan Diego reported having a vision of the Virgin Mary in Tepeyac, northwest of Mexico City. He claimed that she had appeared to him and charged him to tell the bishop to build a temple on that site. She then is said to have left an imprint of herself on Juan Diego's cactus-cloth garment. In the years since the reported vision, many miracles have been attributed to this imprinted garment, and millions have visited the shrine built on the site.

1590	1607	1631	1647
Telescope invented	English colony established at Jamestown	Mount Vesuvius erupts, destroying towns	Bayonet invented in Bayonne, France

1531 ✝ ✡ THE INQUISITION BEGINS IN PORTUGAL

Thousands of Spanish Jews fled to Portugal after their expulsion from Spain in 1492, but four years later they were forced to be baptized or leave Portugal. The Spanish Inquisition, which was authorized by Pope Sixtus IV (1414–1484) in 1478, did not spread to the neighboring kingdom of Portugal until 1531, when Pope Leo X (1475–1521) extended it to Portugal. An inquisition patterned after that in Spain was established with tribunals being set up in Lisbon and other major cities. The Jews who had not been baptized as Christians were the particular target. In all, approximately forty thousand Jews were brought to trial in Portugal and eighteen hundred were burned at the stake. The last burning in Portugal was on October 27, 1765.

1532 ✝ ✡ SOLOMON MOLCHO IS BURNED

In the early sixteenth century a Jew named David Reubeni (d. 1538) declared he was sent by God to free the Holy Land. Solomon Molcho (d. 1532) was among his followers. Reubeni and Molcho traveled to Rome and obtained an audience with Pope Clement VII (1479–1534). They attempted to gain the pope's approval for an army of Marranos—Jews who had undergone Christian baptism but were rumored to be secret Jews—to conquer the Holy Land. The pope, however, denied their request, threatening Molcho with execution. They next proceeded to entreat Holy Roman Emperor Charles V (1500–1558) to employ the Jews in the fight against the Turks. Their meeting was unfruitful again, and in 1532, Molcho was burned at the stake by the Inquisition in Mantua, Italy.

1534 ✝ HENRY VIII'S ACT OF SUPREMACY PASSES

King Henry VIII (1491–1547) of England was a devout Catholic who had received the title "Defender of the Faith" from Pope Leo X (1475–1521). However, in 1529, Henry began an assault upon papal control of England in order to divorce his wife Catherine of Aragon (1485–1536) and marry Anne Boleyn (1507–1537). In 1534, the English parliament passed the Act of Supremacy, declaring Henry to be "the only supreme head on earth of the Church of England," thus placing England outside the Roman Catholic Church's control. Appeals to Rome were forbidden, clergy were forced to submit to the throne, and church assets were appropriated. The Act of Supremacy laid the legal groundwork for the

1519–21	1521	1531	1562
Ferdinand Magellan circumnavigates the earth	Hernando Cortés conquers Mexico's Aztec Empire	First stock exchange established in Antwerp	English enter slave trade

THE FUGITIVE TRANSLATOR

Can you imagine William Tyndale on the Ten Most Wanted list?

Tyndale was born about 1494, and was educated first at Oxford, where he was ordained into the priesthood and then at Cambridge, where he joined the Reformation. After completing his education, he felt he needed to get away from the academic atmosphere of the university to be able to think, pray, and study the Greek New Testament on his own. His solution was to take a job as tutor for a wealthy family. During that time he became convinced that England would never be evangelized using Latin Bibles. He felt that "it was impossible to establish the lay people in any truth, except the Scripture were laid before their eyes in their mother tongue."

However, Tyndale's efforts to secure permission from the bishop of London to translate the Bible into English were unsuccessful, so he left England, never to return.

Tyndale settled in Antwerp, where sympathetic English merchants hid and protected him as he translated the New Testament from Greek into English and parts of the Old Testament from Hebrew. His first English New Testament was printed in Germany in 1525.

As Tyndale's English Bibles were smuggled into England, the archbishop of Canterbury and the bishop of London began attacking him fiercely. Finally on June 18, 1528, the English cardinal Thomas Wolsey ordered the ambassador to the Low Countries to demand that the Low Countries' regent arrest Tyndale and extradite him to England. It took his pursuers seven years to find him, but Tyndale was finally arrested near Brussels in 1535. He was held in a castle dungeon near Brussels for eighteen months before his trial.

A long list of charges was drawn up against him: He had maintained that faith alone justifies and that to believe in the forgiveness of sins and to embrace the mercy offered in the gospel was enough for salvation.

In his early forties, Tyndale was found guilty at his trial and condemned to death as a heretic. Referring to the king's opposition to his English Bible, Tyndale's final words were, "Lord, open the king of England's eyes." Then William Tyndale was strangled and his body burned.

The year that Tyndale died two English Bibles containing his translation of the New Testament were circulating England, awaiting the approval of King Henry VIII. When the first was presented to him, the king, not realizing it was Tyndale who had translated the New Testament, proclaimed, "In God's name let it go abroad among the people."

Two years later the king directed that every church in England display "one book of the whole Bible in English." Tyndale's dying prayer was answered.

Tyndale's Bible translations were his lasting legacy. They were so well done that they comprise 90 percent of the wordings of the King James Version published nearly one hundred years later and 75 percent of the wordings of the Revised Standard Version of 1952.

English Reformation. It is also the basis upon which English bishops today still are appointed by the sovereign.

1535 ✝ ANABAPTISTS EVENTUALLY LOSE IN THE MÜNSTER REBELLION

As the Reformation blossomed, it spread throughout Europe and in 1532, it reached the city of Münster in Westphalia, Germany, near the Netherlands. A group of Anabaptist settlers soon arrived, seeking to establish the kingdom of God in Münster. When the local bishop assembled an army to subdue this new group, they defended themselves and gained control of the city. In the summer of 1534, Jan of Leiden (d. 1535), who claimed to be receiving messages from God, assumed sole leadership of the city. In September, he took the title "King David," and instituted the practice of polygamy. He was able to hold off the bishop's army until the following summer, but then he was defeated and executed. For many years to come, most Europeans associated all Anabaptists with the Münster Rebellion.

1536 ✝ MENNO SIMONS IS BAPTIZED AS AN ANABAPTIST

Menno Simons (1496–1561), a Roman Catholic priest in the Dutch province of Friesland, was startled to hear that a man had been executed for being an "Anabaptist" (a rebaptizer). As Menno quietly studied the Scriptures he found no mention of infant baptism and became convinced of the doctrine of believer's baptism. However, he remained in the security of his parish until members of his own congregation, including his brother, staged a militant Anabaptist occupation of a nearby cloister and were executed. This event spurred Menno to repent of his apathy toward God's Word. In 1536, Menno renounced his priesthood and was baptized as a believer. He soon became the leader of the Anabaptists. His followers, who came to be called Mennonites, were heavily persecuted as they were neither Catholic nor identifiably Protestant.

1536 ✝ CALVIN PUBLISHES INSTITUTES OF THE CHRISTIAN RELIGION

John Calvin (1509–1564) was a French scholar who was converted to Christ and joined the Reformation. Because of the persecution of Protestants, he was forced to be continually on the move throughout France, Switzerland, and Italy. Despite the danger, he began writing his theology. In March 1536, he published the first

1519–21	1521	1531	1562
Ferdinand Magellan circumnavigates the earth	Hernando Cortés conquers Mexico's Aztec Empire	First stock exchange established in Antwerp	English enter slave trade

edition of his most influential work, *Institutes of the Christian Religion*. It was a small, seven-chapter volume, prefaced by a letter to King Francis I (1494–1547) of France defending the Protestants against their enemies. Calvin revised it five times, and by 1559, it had grown to seventy-nine chapters. The *Institutes* quickly became popular among Protestants as a cogent exposition and defense of their doctrines. It is the most influential Protestant systematic theology of all time.

1537 ✛ "MATTHEW'S BIBLE" IS PUBLISHED IN ENGLAND

Matthew's Bible, the first authorized English translation of the Bible, was published in England in 1537 by Thomas Matthew—which was actually a pen name that concealed the identity of the true editor, John Rogers (1500–1555). This version bore the words "Set forth with the king's most gracious license" on its title page. The Matthew's Bible included much of an earlier translation by William Tyndale (1494–1536). It was replaced in 1539 by the "Great Bible," which was basically a revision of the Matthew's Bible by Miles Coverdale (1488–1569) and published by royal authority.

1539 ✡ JURISDICTION OVER POLISH JEWS TRANSFERS FROM KING TO NOBILITY

Beginning with the Crusades and carrying through the fourteenth century, persecution in Western Europe drove Jews eastward. The expulsions from Spain, Portugal, and Italy in the fifteenth and sixteenth centuries greatly increased the migration. By contrast, Poland encouraged the immigration of Jews, who brought with them skills such as diplomacy, education, and business. In 1539, jurisdiction over Polish Jews was transferred from the Polish king to the land-owning nobility. This change in authority allowed Jews to rise as managers of great estates, and by 1600, Polish Jews were known for their craftsmanship and were involved in agriculture, tax collection, and trade. In Poland, Jews experienced a more normal life than they had previously in Europe.

1540 ✛ POPE PAUL III APPROVES JESUITS

Ignatius of Loyola (1491–1556) was a Spanish monk who became increasingly interested in mysticism and asceticism. After experiencing several visions, he wrote a manual called *Spiritual Exercises,* which dealt with personal spiritual warfare. In 1536, Loyola formed a brotherhood with six other like-minded men who were also interested in committing themselves to a life of poverty, chastity, and service to the pope. Their group, called the Society of Jesus, or the Jesuits, gained Pope Paul III's (1468–1549) formal approval in 1540. Loyola was chosen as general of the society. The Jesuits were known for their dedication and obedience to the pope, and for selfless missionary work, especially among the poor.

1542 ✡ ☪ SULEIMAN THE MAGNIFICENT COMPLETES THE WALLS OF JERUSALEM

After Selim the Grim (1467–1520), ruler of the Ottoman Empire, defeated the Mameluke sultan of Egypt and occupied Jerusalem in 1516–1517, the Christians and Jews of the Holy Land welcomed him. His early death in 1520 brought his son, Suleiman the Magnificent (1494–1566), to the throne of the empire in Constantinople (modern-day Istanbul). The Ottoman Empire reached its zenith during Suleiman's forty-six-year reign. In Jerusalem, Suleiman improved the status of Christians, and from approximately 1537 to 1542 he laid out the Temple area as it is today and rebuilt the walls and gates of Jerusalem, which had been without a wall since 1219. The Damascus Gate was the last to be finished in 1542. The walls still stand today.

1542 ✝ FRANCIS XAVIER BEGINS HIS MISSIONARY EFFORTS

Francis Xavier (1506–1552), the son of a Spanish high official, became a Jesuit priest after meeting Ignatius of Loyola (1491–1556). After working with Ignatius in the Society of Jesus, he sailed from Lisbon on April 7, 1541, to start his missionary career, reaching Goa on the west coast of India in 1542. He remained there for three years, preaching and ministering to the sick. He next found great success evangelizing pearl divers along the coast of southwestern India, baptizing thousands of them. By 1549, he had gone on to Japan. Pope Pius X named him the "Patron of Foreign Missions," and he was canonized in 1622.

1543 ✝ COPERNICUS WRITES ON REVOLUTIONS OF THE HEAVENLY SPHERES

Nicolas Copernicus (1473–1543) was a Polish astronomer, physician, and cleric. He was the first person to work out mathematically a heliocentric concept of the solar system, in which the earth and all planets revolve around the sun. Prior to Copernicus, the prevailing concept of the solar system was geocentric, with the planets, sun, and moon revolving around the earth. At the end of his life, in 1543, he published *On Revolutions of the Heavenly Spheres,* in which he described his new theory. He dedicated the book to Pope Paul III (1468–1549), but nonetheless both the Catholic Church and Martin Luther opposed the Copernican theory on theological grounds. *On Revolutions* was on the Catholic "Index of Forbidden Books" until 1758. The Copernican theory of the solar system became the foundation for modern astronomy.

1545 ✝ THE COUNCIL OF TRENT IS CALLED

To counter the success of the Protestant movement throughout Europe, Pope Paul III (1468-1549) called for a council of the church. The council's start was delayed for years due to conflict between Charles V (1500–1558), Francis I (1494–1547), and Pope Paul over its need and purpose. The council finally convened in Trent, Italy, in December 1545, with the purposes of settling the religious disputes with the Protestants, reforming ecclesiastical abuses, and beginning a crusade against Islam. The council met in three stages: 1545–47, 1551–52, and 1562–63. By the third meeting, all hope was gone for reconciliation with the Protestants. The decrees issued by the council provided the foundation for a revitalization of Catholicism and set the boundaries of the Catholic faith.

1548 ✡ FIRST JEWS SETTLE IN THE AMERICAS (BRAZIL)

Although the Inquisition began in Spain, it eventually spread to Portugal. As a result of the Portuguese Inquisition, many Jews were expelled from the country and forced to resettle in Brazil in 1548. This forced resettlement was the first permanent Jewish settlement in the New World. Although the Inquisition never was officially established in the Americas, the Jews in Brazil remained

1590	1607	1631	1647
Telescope invented	English colony established at Jamestown	Mount Vesuvius erupts, destroying towns	Bayonet invented in Bayonne, France

under constant threat of persecution. In 1580, when King Philip II of Spain (1527–1598) seized the throne of Portugal, putting Portugal under the auspices of the Spanish Empire, the Jews in Brazil were forced to go underground. They were later involved in the unsuccessful Dutch attempt to conquer Brazil.

1549 ✝ FRANCIS XAVIER OPENS JAPAN FOR ROMAN CATHOLIC MISSIONS

Regarded as the greatest Roman Catholic missionary, Francis Xavier (1506–1552) set out from India for Japan, arriving on August 15, 1549, with two other Jesuits and a Japanese interpreter. He spent two years in Japan teaching the Christian faith throughout the country. After his trip, many Jesuits followed him and subsequently many Franciscans as well. By 1581, there were more than two hundred churches and 150,000 Roman Catholics in Japan.

1549 ✝ CRANMER DRAFTS THE BOOK OF COMMON PRAYER

In 1547, Edward VI (1537–1553) inherited the throne of England. He commissioned a compellation of the existing English liturgy, with some additions, to direct the worship of the Anglican Church. Thomas Cranmer (1489–1556) drafted the *Book of Common Prayer,* Parliament approved it, and it was first used in 1549. The *Book of Common Prayer* replaced three Latin manuals. In 1552, some controversial portions of the book, such as prayer for the dead and certain ceremonial articles, were removed. After its abolition by Queen Mary (1516–1558) and restoration by Elizabeth I (1533–1603), the *Book of Common Prayer* was revised again in 1604. It was abolished again during the Protectorate under the Puritans. In 1662, the book was reestablished as the official service book of the Church of England as it still is today.

1551 ✡ ROYAL DECREE RECOGNIZES THE COUNCIL OF FOUR LANDS IN POLAND

The rallying point for the Jewish population of Poland was the Council of the Four Lands, which functioned as a parliament for the Polish Jewish community. The four lands were Great Poland with its capital Posen, Little Poland with

1519–21	1521	1531	1562
Ferdinand Magellan circumnavigates the earth	Hernando Cortés conquers Mexico's Aztec Empire	First stock exchange established in Antwerp	English enter slave trade

its capital Cracow, Polish Russia (Podolia and Galicia) with its capital Lemberg-Lwow, and Volhynia with its capital Ostrag. In 1551, a royal decree officially sanctioned its functions and powers. The council regulated the Jewish community's financial affairs, represented it at the royal court, directed religious observances, and supervised a hierarchy of Jewish courts. It met twice annually, and every Jewish community sent an official as its representative. The council functioned until 1764 when it was abolished by the Polish Parliament.

1553 ✠ THE FORTY-TWO ARTICLES ACT IS FORMULATED

During the reign of King Edward VI (1547–1553) the English Reformation took significant steps forward. One of these steps was the formulation of the Forty-Two Articles Act. Thomas Cranmer (1489–1556), the archbishop of Canterbury, drafted the Forty-Two Articles, which mirror the Augsburg Confession in their teaching on the Trinity and justification by faith. They followed Calvin in their outlook on predestination and the Lord's Supper. In 1553, they were adopted as the Anglican Church's first Protestant confession of faith. In 1562, the Convocation of Anglican Clergy modified and condensed the articles to thirty-nine.

1553 ✠ MARY TUDOR ASCENDS TO THE THRONE AND RESTORES CATHOLICISM

Queen Mary I (1516–1558) of England—daughter of Catherine of Aragon (1485–1536), the first wife of King Henry VIII (1491–1547)—was proclaimed queen of England on July 19, 1553, and quickly sought to return England to its Catholic roots. Initially she pledged to treat the Protestant minority with tolerance, but before long her patience with the Protestants grew thin. Fearing a revolt that would place her Protestant sister Elizabeth (1533–1603) on the throne, she issued an edict on March 4, 1554, outlawing Protestantism as a heresy. She earned the title "Bloody Mary" as she ruthlessly enforced the edict from 1555 until her death in 1558. In the end, her reign of terror claimed the lives of more than three hundred Protestants, including the archbishop of Canterbury, Thomas Cranmer (1489–1556), and deposed Bishops Hugh Latimer (1485–1555) and Nicolas Ridley (1500–1555).

1590	1607	1631	1647
Telescope invented	English colony established at Jamestown	Mount Vesuvius erupts, destroying towns	Bayonet invented in Bayonne, France

1553 ✝ ✡ COPIES OF THE TALMUD ARE BURNED IN ROME

Anti-Semitism was rampant in sixteenth-century Europe. One of the most flagrant examples took place on September 9, 1553. Cardinal Caraffa (1476–1559), who later became Pope Paul IV, organized the confiscation and public burning of copies of the Talmud in the streets of Rome. The cardinal, who organized the event with the support of Pope Julius III (1487–1555), chose September 9 because it was the Jewish holy day Rosh Hashanah, and he desired to make the event as painful as possible for the Jews. After the first burning in Rome, a wave of Talmud burning and Jewish persecution broke out through all of Italy. As a result, the Jews were forced to move their printing operations from Italy to Poland.

1555 ✝ HEAD OF ITALIAN INQUISITION BECOMES POPE PAUL IV

Giovanni Pietro Caraffa (1476–1559) descended from Italian nobility and worked his way up in the Roman Catholic Church from chamberlain to bishop to papal envoy. He then was appointed cardinal by Pope Paul III (1468–1549). A staunch supporter of the Counter-Reformation, he reorganized the Italian Inquisition. His election as Pope Paul IV in 1555 resolved the century-long conflict between the Inquisition and previous popes. He continued his fervent support of the Roman Inquisition, as well as anti-Spanish and anti-imperial policies. His extremism and his publication of the "Index of Forbidden Books" lessened his popularity.

1555 ✝ HUGUENOT REFUGE IS ESTABLISHED IN BRAZIL

The French Calvinists, called Huguenots, were greatly persecuted during the Reformation. During the reign of King Henry II (1519–1559) of France, the government instituted special courts whose function was to put the Huguenots on trial—and, in many cases, to execute them. However, as persecution of the Huguenots increased, so did the number of adherents to the Reformed faith in France. In 1555, King Henry's cousin, Admiral Gaspard de Coligny (1519–1572), who had become a Huguenot, sponsored an attempt to establish a colony in Brazil to which Huguenots could escape for refuge. The colony was established near the present site of Rio de Janeiro. However, the Portuguese would not allow the French to gain a foothold in their New World territory and destroyed the short-lived colony in 1557.

1519–21	1521	1531	1562
Ferdinand Magellan circumnavigates the earth	Hernando Cortés conquers Mexico's Aztec Empire	First stock exchange established in Antwerp	English enter slave trade

BLOODY MARY

March 4, 1554

Sometimes things get worse before they get better.

Born in 1516, Mary Tudor was the only surviving child of King Henry VIII and his first wife, Catherine of Aragon. She was raised a Roman Catholic. When she was fifteen her parents divorced, and mother and daughter went into separate exiles, never to see each other again. When she was seventeen, her parents' marriage was declared void after the birth of her half sister, Elizabeth, and Mary was declared a bastard, losing her right of succession to the throne. Later, when Parliament revoked the annulment of her parents' marriage and restored her legitimacy, Mary returned to prominence and became vocal about her Catholicism.

In 1544, Henry VIII wrote his will, designating the order of succession to the throne to be his only son Edward, Mary, and then Elizabeth, if either of the first two died without having produced an heir.

At the death of Henry VIII, his nine-year-old son, Edward, became King Edward VI. A godly boy, Edward moved England decisively toward Protestantism. Suffering from congenital syphilis contracted from his father, he died at the age of sixteen. A few weeks before his death, without authorization from Parliament, he amended his father's will by naming his cousin Lady Jane Grey, also an evangelical, as his successor instead of his sister Mary.

Jane Grey's reign lasted just nine days before she was replaced by Mary, who became Queen Mary I in 1553.

Upon becoming queen, Mary set about returning England to its Roman Catholic roots. At first Mary dealt tolerantly with the Protestants, hoping to convert them to Catholicism. But Mary quickly realized that her lenient approach with the Protestants was not working, and she feared a Protestant revolt would place her Protestant half sister, Elizabeth, on the throne. Therefore, on March 4, 1554, Mary issued an edict that reinstated Catholic worship and outlawed Protestantism.

She earned her title "Bloody Mary" in the enforcement of this edict, following the advice of her advisors to kill anyone who was a threat to her. Lady Jane Grey, her husband, and her father were executed, as well as a hundred lesser rebels who were part of a Protestant plot to take back the throne. Mary also held her half sister, Elizabeth, in the Tower of London for months, while investigating her role in the plot. Elizabeth survived, eventually succeeding Mary as queen.

In 1555, the reign of terror began with the execution of Protestant clergymen who refused to accept the reestablished Catholic creed. Each "heretic" was given a chance to recant and then was burned at the stake if they did not. Many Protestant ministers and leaders were executed, but most of the martyrs were laypeople who had converted to Christ as the Reformation spread through England.

In all, Bloody Mary's reign of terror claimed the lives of more than three hundred Protestants. It ended with her death in 1558.

1555 + PEACE OF AUGSBURG IS REACHED

After the Catholic emperor Charles V (1500–1558) was defeated by Protestant princes of Germany, he commissioned his brother Ferdinand to settle affairs with Germany at the Diet of Augsburg. The Peace of Augsburg was reached in 1555. The terms of the Peace of Augsburg gave each prince, whether Protestant or Catholic, absolute control over the religion in his domain, forcing all subjects to conform or emigrate. It gave Protestant rulers and cities protection equal to Catholic ones, but Calvinists and Anabaptists were excluded from this protection. By giving secular rulers control over religion in their domain, the agreement weakened true Christianity. It also signified the end of German political and religious unity. This agreement held until the Peace of Westphalia in 1648.

1555 + LATIMER AND RIDLEY ARE BURNED AT THE STAKE

Hugh Latimer (1485–1555) and then Nicolas Ridley (1500–1555) served as the English royal chaplain under King Henry VIII (1491–1547). However, when Henry's daughter Mary Tudor (1516–1558) ascended to the throne as Queen Mary I in 1553, Latimer and Ridley were removed from their leadership positions, tried as heretics, and condemned to death for their Protestant faith. On October 16, 1555, Latimer and Ridley were led out to be burned at the stake. As the fire was lit, Latimer said, "Be of good comfort, Master Ridley, and play the man. We shall this day light such a candle by God's grace in England as I trust shall never be put out." The candle lit by the faith of these men still blazes today.

1556 + THOMAS CRANMER IS BURNED AT THE STAKE

Thomas Cranmer (1489–1556) rose to prominence as the archbishop of Canterbury during the reign of King Henry VIII (1491–1547). However in 1553, Queen Mary I (1516–1558) ascended to the throne, and her horrific treatment of Protestants earned her the nickname "Bloody Mary" and soon engulfed Cranmer. He was sentenced to death as a heretic, but Mary and the Catholic bishops coaxed Cranmer into signing a recantation, secretly plotting to kill him anyway after his public confession of Catholicism. At the public ceremony, Cranmer instead denounced Catholicism and boldly affirmed

1519–21	1521	1531	1562
Ferdinand Magellan circumnavigates the earth	Hernando Cortés conquers Mexico's Aztec Empire	First stock exchange established in Antwerp	English enter slave trade

THE SURPRISE ENDING

October 16, 1555

Be thou faithful unto death.

In 1534, King Henry VIII separated the Church of England from the Roman Catholic Church. This action did not indicate a change in doctrine but merely meant that Henry VIII now controlled the English Church. However, Thomas Cranmer, the archbishop of Canterbury, was a committed Protestant believer. Cranmer appointed Hugh Latimer as royal chaplain. Latimer had experienced a dramatic conversion when another minister shared the gospel with him. Cranmer appointed Nicholas Ridley, who still espoused the Roman Catholic faith, as his own personal chaplain.

In 1547, Henry VIII died and was succeeded by his nine-year-old son, a sincere Christian, who became King Edward VI. During Edward's reign, Archbishop Cranmer had great influence, and the liturgy of English churches was changed from Latin to English. Ridley, now a convinced evangelical, became a bishop, and Latimer, no longer a bishop, was preaching every Sunday. Unfortunately, Edward died in 1553 and was succeeded by his half sister Mary Tudor, a Roman Catholic. She was crowned Queen Mary I and soon earned her nickname of "Bloody Mary." She replaced all bishops with Roman Catholics, and Cranmer, Latimer, and Ridley were imprisoned and condemned to death.

On October 16, 1555, Latimer and Ridley were led out of prison to be burned at the stake. As the fire was lit, Latimer said, "Be of good comfort, Master Ridley, and play the man. We shall this day light such a candle by God's grace in England as I trust shall never be put out."

Cranmer was then "degraded," a ceremony in which all symbols of his office of archbishop were removed from him. After much pressure Cranmer finally signed a recantation denouncing Luther and affirming the teachings of the Roman Catholic Church.

But Queen Mary and the Catholic bishops had no intention of sparing Cranmer. They planned to have him make a public statement of his conversion and *then* execute him.

On the appointed day, Cranmer was brought to the platform to speak to the assembled crowd. He confirmed his faith in God and in the Bible. Then to the horror of the church dignitaries, he said, "As for the Pope, I refuse him, as Christ's enemy and Antichrist, with all his false doctrine." Amidst an uproar Cranmer was pulled off the platform, but he broke away and ran straight to the stake and stood resolutely to be burned.

The flames soon consumed him, but his brave denunciation destroyed forever the power of Roman Catholicism in England, making it a Protestant nation. The deaths of Latimer, Ridley, and Cranmer indeed lit a candle that never has been put out.

his faith in God and the Bible. Then he broke away and ran straight to the stake and stood resolutely to be burned. The flames quickly consumed him, but Roman Catholicism in England never recovered from his denunciation.

1558 ✝ ELIZABETH I BECOMES QUEEN

When Henry VIII (1491–1547) died, his will stated that his son, Edward (1537–1553), was to succeed him, followed by his first daughter, Mary (1516–1558), and then his second daughter, Elizabeth (1533–1603). After Edward died, the country was torn apart by Mary's reign of terror, and Elizabeth inherited England's throne in 1558. By the time Elizabeth died forty-five years later, England had defeated the Spanish Armada, the country was thoroughly Protestant, the Union Jack flew over every ocean, and English culture was at its zenith. Elizabeth's keen intellect and ingenuity shaped her domestic and foreign policies. She sensed that the country was primarily Protestant and consequently reinstated Protestant policies and largely abolished religious persecution in England. Elizabeth died in 1603 and was succeeded by James I (1566–1625), the son of Mary Queen of Scots (1542–1587).

1559 ✝ "INDEX OF FORBIDDEN BOOKS" IS PUBLISHED

When Pope Paul IV (1476–1559) commissioned the Congregation of the Inquisition, one of their assignments was to produce a list of books that church members were not allowed to read. In 1559, this list was published under the title "Index of Forbidden Books." After the Council of Trent revised the list, Pope Pius IV (1499–1565) introduced a new index in 1564. This edition included ten principles for determining which books were to be included in future editions of the index. In the subsequent four centuries, several popes produced various editions. Vatican Council II (1962–1965) announced that no future revisions were to be produced. However, Catholics still are under obligation to avoid books that the church declares to be spiritually hazardous.

1559 ✝ JOHN KNOX RETURNS TO SCOTLAND

John Knox (1514–1572) was educated at St. Andrews University and ordained as a priest in the Roman Catholic Church. However, by 1542, he had

1519–21	1521	1531	1562
Ferdinand Magellan circumnavigates the earth	Hernando Cortés conquers Mexico's Aztec Empire	First stock exchange established in Antwerp	English enter slave trade

that was approved by the Synod of Heidelberg. The catechism was first published in Germany on January 19, 1563, and included a preface by Prince Frederick. Three other German editions were produced in 1563, followed by a Dutch edition in 1566. The Synod of Dort slightly revised the catechism between 1618 and 1619. Since then it has been translated into multiple languages and is one of the standard Reformed catechisms.

1563 ✝ FOXE'S BOOK OF MARTYRS IS PUBLISHED

John Foxe (1516–1587) was a Protestant educator in England with a keen interest in history. When Mary Tudor (r. 1553–1558) took the English throne and restored Roman Catholicism, Foxe and his wife fled England, taking refuge in Germany. Despite having to flee, Foxe continued to pursue his passion of writing about English church history, supporting his family with odd jobs and tutoring while he wrote. In Frankfurt, Foxe's interest turned to the martyrs of the Protestant Reformation after meeting Edmund Grindal (1519–1583), who was recording the stories of the martyrs. Foxe continued Grindal's work, and with the help of the printer John Day (1522–1584), published *Actes and Monumentes*, popularly known as *Foxe's Book of Martyrs*, in 1563. The four editions published during Foxe's lifetime profoundly influenced Elizabethan England.

1563 ✝ THE THIRTY-NINE ARTICLES ARE ISSUED

In response to the religious controversies of the sixteenth century, the 1563 Convocation of the Church of England revised the Forty-two Articles Act of 1553 into the Thirty-Nine Articles, which have remained nearly unchanged to this day. The intention was not to formulate a complete creedal system, but rather to define the position of the Anglican Church in relation to the issues of the day. The Thirty-Nine Articles cover the doctrines of Scripture, the Trinity, salvation, the sacraments, and the church's ministry. They still stand as the Church of England's official confession of faith.

1564 ✝ CALVIN DIES AND IS SUCCEEDED BY BEZA

Reformed Protestantism flourished under John Calvin (1509–1564) in Geneva, Switzerland. In 1558, Calvin asked Theodore Beza (1519–1605) to come to

been converted and had joined the Reformation. After being appointed preacher to a garrison of soldiers in 1547, Knox was captured and made a galley slave. Freed after nineteen months, he returned to England. During Edward VI's reign, Knox served as a chaplain to the king, but when Mary Queen of Scots (1542–1587) took the throne, Knox was forced to flee to the continent. Returning to Scotland in 1559, Knox became the leader of the Scottish Reformation and, after Mary was deposed, preached at the coronation of her son James VI (1566–1625). The relentless efforts of John Knox made Scotland the most Calvinistic country in the world and the birthplace of modern Presbyterianism.

1560 ✝ FIRST BOOK OF DISCIPLINE IS PUBLISHED

In an effort to delineate the parameters of congregational worship and governance in Scotland, a six-member panel of leaders was appointed by Parliament in 1560. Led chiefly by John Knox (1514–1572), this committee drafted the *First Book of Discipline*. Twenty-one years later, in 1581, the *Second Book of Discipline* was published. The *Books of Discipline* explained the relationship between church and state and defined the roles of church offices. Defining a church polity very similar to the structure in Geneva, the *Books of Discipline* served as the charter of Presbyterian government for the Church of Scotland.

1560 ✝ THE GENEVA BIBLE IS POPULARIZED

The Geneva Bible was an English translation made in 1560 by Protestant exiles in Geneva. Its translators likely included John Knox (1514–1572) and William Whittingham (1524–1579). The Old Testament was primarily a revision of the Great Bible, and the New Testament was primarily a revision of William Tyndale's work. The Geneva Bible's Calvinistic annotations bothered King James I (1566–1625) of England, but the increasingly Puritan populace embraced it wholeheartedly. It quickly became the household Bible of English-speaking Protestants and was used widely for two generations. It gradually was replaced by the 1611 Authorized Version. The last edition of the Geneva Bible was published in 1644.

1519–21	1521	1531	1562	1590	1607	1631	1647
Ferdinand Magellan circumnavigates the earth	Hernando Cortés conquers Mexico's Aztec Empire	First stock exchange established in Antwerp	English enter slave trade	Telescope invented	English colony established at Jamestown	Mount Vesuvius erupts, destroying towns	Bayonet invented in Bayonne, France

1561 ✦ THE COLLOQUY OF POISSY FAILS

In an attempt to produce a lasting peace between Roman Catholics and Protestants in France, Catherine de Médicis (1519–1589), the Queen Mother, called for a national council of the French Church. Catherine's desire was to obtain peace and harmony in France so that the nation could continue to develop and gain influence. However, since two church councils could not take place simultaneously, Pope Pius IV (1499–1565) reconvened the Council of Trent, which had adjourned in 1552, to prevent Catherine's council. However, Catherine went forward with her plan and titled the assembly a "colloquy" instead. The colloquy failed to meet any of Catherine's goals. She had underestimated the depth of theological differences between the Catholic and Protestant camps. Instead of resulting in peace, the assembly gave the appearance of royal approval of the Protestants, which increased the tension between the competing parties.

1562 ✦ WARS OF RELIGION IN FRANCE BEGIN

Following the death of King Henry II (1519–1559) of France in 1559, his successors struggled with the house of Guise. Catherine de Médicis (1519–1589) was the mother of Francis II (1544–1560), Charles IX (1550–1574), and Henry III (1541–1589), who all successively inherited the throne of France. When Francis II died unexpectedly a year after succeeding his father, Catherine became regent for Charles IX, her ten-year-old son. As the Guises were staunch Roman Catholics, Catherine sided with the French Protestants, called Huguenots. After the failure of the Colloquy of Poissy to settle the differences between Catholics and Protestants, in 1562, Catherine issued the Edict of St. Germain granting the Huguenots freedom of worship. In reprisal, two months later the Guises massacred Huguenots worshiping in the village of Vassy, thus beginning the Wars of Religion in France, which lasted on and off until 1570.

1562 ✦ GERMAN MINISTERS WRITE THE HEIDELBERG CATECHISM

In 1562, Zacharias Ursinus (1534–1583) and Kaspar Olevianus (1536–1587), two young German ministers, met in Heidelberg at the request of Elector Frederick III (1515–1576) to produce a catechism that could be used to teach children and provide doctrinal guidelines for pastors and teachers. With the help and advice of Heidelberg University faculty, the two men wrote the catechism

FROM APATHY TO COURAGE

January 31, 1561

A man of peace died in peace.

Born in 1496, Menno Simons grew up in the Dutch province of Friesland. At twenty-eight, he was ordained to the Roman Catholic priesthood and appointed to a parish near his home.

He settled into a routine of saying Mass, baptizing newborns, playing cards, and drinking with his fellow priests. Meanwhile, Simons was also reading Luther and began entertaining doubts concerning certain tenets of the Catholic faith.

His first doubts centered on whether bread and wine became the actual body and blood of Christ. An intense study of Scripture led him to the conclusion that he had been deceived by the teachings of the church. Yet he remained a Catholic priest. It was a comfortable living. It paid the bills.

Then troubling news reached his ears. A man in a nearby town had been executed for adhering to an unusual new doctrine: rebaptism! The death of this "Anabaptist" (rebaptizer) drove Simons to a renewed search of the Scriptures. He could find no mention of infant baptism, and he became more and more convinced that "believer's baptism" was instead the true Christian model. Still he remained a Catholic. It was safe. It was secure.

But then members of his own congregation, his brother Pieter among them, staged a militant Anabaptist occupation of a local cloister and were massacred by the authorities. Menno's soul was crushed. He realized that in his role as a spiritual leader he might have been able to prevent the tragedy. "The blood of these people, although misled, fell so hot upon my heart that I could not stand it, nor find rest in my soul," he wrote.

He repented of his sins, begging God for grace and a clean heart. He prayed for the courage to "preach His exalted adorable name and holy Word in purity, and make known His truth to His glory." Menno Simons was reborn.

As he began to preach the Bible, Menno's life became increasingly at risk. In 1536, he quietly renounced his priesthood, was rebaptized, and began an itinerant career of radical Biblical reform that lasted until his death.

As Menno Simons rose to a place of revered influence within the Anabaptist movement, his spirit of moderation helped unite various Anabaptist groups into one distinctive Christian body. Neither Catholic nor identifiably Protestant, Menno Simons's followers came to be called Mennonites and maintained a view of the church as a pure bride for Christ, untainted by earthly political allegiance. Believing that Jesus called Christians to forsake the sword for the Word of God, they refused to accept secular offices or join an army. As such, authorities everywhere, both civil and religious, viewed them as traitors. Many were martyred for their understanding of the example of Jesus Christ. But Menno Simons, a man of peace in a world of war, eluded capture to the end and died in his own bed on January 31, 1561.

Geneva to be a professor of Greek. Beza was a former Catholic lawyer who had been converted to Christ after a physical and spiritual crisis in 1548. Once in Geneva, Beza gained much influence in the movement, eventually becoming rector and teaching theology at the Genevan Academy. At Calvin's death in 1564, all of his responsibilities fell to Beza. This included heading the Genevan Academy, moderating the Company of Pastors of Geneva, working with the city magistrates, and being the leader and spokesperson for Reformed Protestantism.

1565 ✝ AUGUSTINIANS ARRIVE IN THE PHILIPPINES

After Magellan discovered the Philippine Islands for Spain in 1521, the first major missionary effort by the Roman Catholic Church came in 1565, with the arrival of Spaniard Miguel de Legaspi (1510–1572). The royal court of Mexico sent him to the Philippines accompanied by Augustinian priests. The Franciscans, the Dominicans, and the Jesuits closely followed the Augustinians. By 1620, approximately half of the population, now under Spanish rule, was nominally Roman Catholic. It was not until the United States took control of the Philippines from Spain in 1898 that Protestant missionaries were permitted. In 2000, the Philippines were 67 percent Roman Catholic and 17 percent evangelical.

1565 ✝ TERESA OF AVILA WRITES THE WAY OF PERFECTION

Teresa of Avila (1515–1582) became a nun and entered the Spanish Carmelite Convent of the Incarnation in 1533. There in the 1550s, she began to have heavenly visions and mystical experiences. Seeking to live a life of perfection, she founded a convent in Avila, Spain, under the original Carmelite Rule, and named it after St. Joseph. While there in 1565, she wrote *The Way of Perfection,* an instructional book for her nuns. This and her other written works teach a life of prayer, meditation, asceticism, and mysticism. From 1567, she worked to reform the Carmelite order throughout Spain, setting up several reformed convents obedient to the original Carmelite Rule. Teresa of Avila was a voice not only for mysticism but also for reform within the Catholic Church.

1566 ✡ JOSEPH NASI IS MADE DUKE OF NAXOS

Jews who were forced to convert to Christianity but secretly maintained their Jewish practices were called Marranos. In the sixteenth century, an influential

1590	1607	1631	1647
Telescope invented	English colony established at Jamestown	Mount Vesuvius erupts, destroying towns	Bayonet invented in Bayonne, France

Marrano named Doña Gracia Nasi (1510–1569) fled Portugal with her nephew, João (later Joseph) Nasi (1524–1579). After completing his studies, he worked for Nasi family enterprises in Antwerp, Belgium. João later joined his aunt in Istanbul, where he embraced Judaism and took the name Joseph Nasi. He obtained the Turkish sultan's permission to rebuild the ancient city of Tiberias as a city-state for Jews. Nasi rose to such power in the government of the sultan that he became the virtual ruler of the empire. In 1566, he was made Duke of Naxos and used his power and wealth to serve his Jewish people.

1566 ✝ THE SYNOD OF ANTWERP MEETS IN SECRET

As the Lowlands—known to us today as the Netherlands and Belgium—neared rebellion against Spanish rule, the underground Reformed church met in a secret synod at Antwerp to discuss their convictions and outline their beliefs. The assembly adopted the Belgic Confession, a Calvinistic creed written five years earlier in 1561, by Guido de Bres (1522–1567), who had been a fugitive preacher in the Lowlands. Drawing heavily from the writings of John Calvin (1509–1564), this confession was eagerly received by the Reformed churches of the Lowlands. The National Synod of the Netherlands adopted it following independence from Spain in 1619. The Belgic Confession is one of three standards of the Dutch Reformed Church, along with the Heidelberg Confession and the Canons of Dort.

1568 ✝ THE BISHOP'S BIBLE IS PUBLISHED

In 1560, the Geneva Bible was produced by English Protestant exiles in Geneva, Switzerland. This English translation of the Bible quickly became the household version of English-speaking Protestants, yet it contained Reformed notes that were not acceptable to the leaders of the English church and state. In response, they produced their own version, in 1568, and called it the Bishop's Bible. The church intended that the Bishop's Bible would replace their Great Bible, which had had royal approval—and, indeed, the Bishop's Bible was an improved translation. However, it was not as good of a translation as the Geneva Bible, and as a result, the Bishop's Bible never gained popular approval, nor was it recognized formally by Queen Elizabeth I (1533–1603).

1519–21	1521	1531	1562
Ferdinand Magellan circumnavigates the earth	Hernando Cortés conquers Mexico's Aztec Empire	First stock exchange established in Antwerp	English enter slave trade

1569 ✝ ✡ PAPAL STATES EXPEL THE JEWS

Pope Pius V (1504–1572) was determined to combat heresy wherever he found it. This included not only Protestantism but Judaism as well. For commercial reasons he permitted some Jews to live in ghettos in Rome and in Ancona, Italy; but in 1569, he issued his *Bull Hebraeorum Gens* in which he expelled all other Jews from the Papal States, some of whose families had lived there from antiquity.

1569–1572 ✡ ISAAC LURIA IS MAJOR INFLUENCE IN SAFED

A small town in the hills of Upper Galilee became a center for pious and mystical Jews. The town, Safed, hosted Jewish academies in the sixteenth century. Rabbi Isaac Luria (d. 1572), who lived in Safed and was known as the Ari, was a prophet of a new Jewish mysticism and became a major influence from 1569 to 1572. An immigrant from Cairo, Egypt, Luria explained Jewish sufferings as cosmic events related to the very nature of God. To Luria, Jewish rituals were a means for redeeming God himself and bringing in the messianic age. From Safed, his teaching spread throughout the Middle East, into Italy, and from there to the heart of Europe. Rituals and prayers devised by Luria are still found in Jewish prayer books today.

1572 ✝ QUEEN MOTHER ORDERS ST. BARTHOLOMEW'S DAY MASSACRE

While preparing for her daughter to marry the Protestant king of Navarre, Spain, Queen Mother Catherine de Médicis (1519–1589) of France also was plotting the assassination of Admiral Gaspard de Coligny (1519–1572), a French war hero and Huguenot leader. The wedding brought thousands of Protestants to Paris on August 18, 1572. On August 22, the assassination attempt failed. With the failed attempt threatening to embarrass the royal family, twenty-two-year-old King Charles IX (1550–1574) angrily shouted to his mother that she should just kill all the Huguenots in France. Catherine responded to this spontaneous demand with an order for all the Huguenot leaders in the city to be executed. The gates of the city were closed so that no one could escape, and on August 24, 1572—St. Bartholomew's Day—thousands of Huguenot men, women, and children were viciously executed, beginning with Admiral Coligny.

1590	1607	1631	1647
Telescope invented	English colony established at Jamestown	Mount Vesuvius erupts, destroying towns	Bayonet invented in Bayonne, France

ST. BARTHOLOMEW'S DAY

August 24, 1572

In Paris on August 18, 1572, hopes for peace existed between the warring Catholics and Protestants. On this day, a royal wedding between the Protestant King Henry of Navarre and the Catholic Margaret of Valois brought together the two hostile factions. Protestant and Catholic nobles who had fought each other for ten years turned out for the celebration. Thousands of Protestants came to Paris for the wedding, and the festivities lasted for days.

Calvinism had come to France in 1555. Soon there were two thousand French Reformed churches, and nearly half of the population had been won over to the Reformed faith. French Protestants became known as Huguenots.

While Catherine de Médicis, the Queen Mother, had been planning her daughter's wedding, she had also been plotting the assassination of Admiral Gaspard de Coligny, who was a leader of the Huguenots.

On August 22, the assassination attempt failed. This ignominious plot so soon after the royal wedding threatened to embarrass the royal family. Near midnight the following night, the twenty-two-year-old French king, brother of the bride, in a fit of rage shouted to his mother, "If you are going to kill Coligny, why don't you kill all the Huguenots in France, so that there will be no one left to hate me."

Following this impetuous directive, Catherine ordered the murder of all the Huguenot leaders currently in Paris, including those who had attended the wedding. The massacre began on August 24, 1572, St. Bartholomew's Day. Admiral Coligny was murdered first as he knelt in prayer.

Many of the Huguenot nobles who were guests at the royal wedding were lodged at the Louvre. They were called into the courtyard and shot one by one as they appeared.

During the night, the homes of Paris Huguenots each had been marked with white crosses. Before daybreak, messengers were sent throughout the city screaming, "Kill! Kill! The King commands it." A murdering frenzy fell on the whole city. Entire Huguenot families were taken into the streets and murdered. The dawn of St. Bartholomew's Day revealed thousands of martyred Huguenots.

The craze spread to the provinces in the following days and weeks, and the death toll was probably in the range of thirty to forty thousand. Admiral Coligny's head was embalmed and sent to Rome as a gift to Pope Gregory XIII. When news of the massacre reached Rome (along with Coligny's head), the pope and his cardinals attended a mass of thanksgiving.

But the savagery was not without cost to the king. Charles IX soon began having nightmares about the massacre. In less than two years, he was dying at the age of only twenty-four. His last days were plagued with visions of his victims. "What bloodshed, what murders!" he cried to his nurse. "What evil counsel have I followed? O my God, forgive me! . . . I am lost!"

1572–1573 ✛ PURITANS WRITE ADMONITIONS TO PARLIAMENT

During the reign of Queen Elizabeth I (1533–1603) in England, many Puritans found themselves becoming more and more estranged by the queen's religious policies. Unsatisfied with the episcopal government of the church and with various policies that appeared to be politically dictated, an anonymous tract titled "Admonition to Parliament" was printed in 1572. It was followed the next year by a second admonition. These complaints against church abuses and polity were written in hopes that Parliament would counter Elizabethan compromises by setting up a Presbyterian government in the church to be a better reflection of the continental Reformation. Controversy ensued, and Elizabeth effectively drove the movement underground. The admonitions, however, signaled a growing dissatisfaction in the rising Puritan movement, which would spread to the New World sixty years later.

1576 ✛ THE TORGAU ARTICLES ATTEMPT TO SETTLE THEOLOGICAL DIFFERENCES

After the Augsburg Confession was written, there were still a number of theological disagreements among Lutherans. In an attempt to settle these differences in a Christian manner, German Lutheran theologians adopted the Torgau Articles, which were accepted by most Lutheran theologians.

1577 ✛ FORMULA OF CONCORD ENDS LUTHERAN DOCTRINAL CONTROVERSIES

When the Torgau Articles were criticized as being too lengthy, six German Lutheran theologians led by Martin Chemnitz (1522–1586) and James Andreae (1528–1590) met in 1577 to revise them. The resulting Formula of Concord ended the doctrinal controversies of German Lutheranism that had arisen after the death of Martin Luther (1483–1546). It had two parts: the Epitome and Declaration. The Epitome described each doctrinal controversy and the arguments on each side. The Declaration was entitled "Thorough, Pure, Correct, and Final (Solid, Plain, and Clear) Repetition and Declaration of Some Articles of the Augsburg Confession."

1578 ✛ REFORMED AND ANABAPTIST LEADERS DEBATE PEACEABLY

Since the beginning of the Reformation, the debates between Anabaptists and their Reformed counterparts had been anything but peaceful. The Anabaptists renounced the close union between church and state that had been central to European governmental structures for more than a thousand years. They also rejected the practice of infant baptism. As a result, most Anabaptist leaders lived under threat of imprisonment or death from both Protestants and Catholics. However, in 1578, Anabaptist and Reformed leaders held a series of surprisingly peaceful debates. From February 27 until May 17, delegates from each side met in Emden, the Netherlands. The representatives debated topics such as the nature of the Trinity, the sin of mankind, sacramental theology, the resurrection, and the Christian's role in government and military service, thereby coming to a greater understanding of each other's positions.

1582 ✛ RICCI BEGINS MISSIONS IN CHINA

Matteo Ricci (1552–1610) was the founder of modern-times Roman Catholic missions to China. The Italian Jesuit arrived at the Portuguese trading settlement of Macao on the coast of China in 1582, and began avidly studying Chinese language and culture. He gained admittance to China the following year, but encountered significant popular resistance. He gained acceptance by embracing Chinese dress, culture, and language—and because his maps, books, and mechanical instruments were of interest to the educated Chinese. Ricci eventually settled in Peking among the Chinese literati and never left, dying there in 1610. In Peking he made several influential converts, including some among high court officials, and the Catholic Church began to grow. He opposed Buddhism and Taoism, but embraced classical Confucianism, making him a controversial missionary figure.

1587 ✛ MISSIONARIES ARE BANNED IN JAPAN

In 1549, the Jesuit missionary Francis Xavier (1506–1552) arrived in Japan. During his first years in Japan, many people simply thought that he was establishing a new Buddhist sect. However, it soon became apparent that he was teaching something different. Thirty years after Xavier's arrival, Jesuit missionaries could claim 130,000 converts. In 1587, Toyotomi Hideyoshi (1537–1598),

1519–21	1521	1531	1562
Ferdinand Magellan circumnavigates the earth	Hernando Cortés conquers Mexico's Aztec Empire	First stock exchange established in Antwerp	English enter slave trade

A POWER STRUGGLE OR A HOLY WAR?

July 29, 1588

Why is England largely Protestant and not Catholic?

In 1558, Elizabeth I, a Protestant, succeeded her Roman Catholic half sister, Mary Tudor, as Queen of England. Mary had done everything she could to make England Catholic. On the other hand, the pragmatic Elizabeth adamantly opposed allowing the pope to rule her country.

England's archrival at the time was Spain, which was Catholic. The Spanish king Philip II was Europe's most powerful monarch. The pope, Emperor Ferdinand I of the Holy Roman Empire, and the Catholic Mary Queen of Scots all encouraged Philip to invade England to restore Catholicism.

Queen Elizabeth cleverly toyed with King Philip, letting him think she might marry him or his son. Meanwhile, English pirates under the direction of Frances Drake plundered Spanish merchant ships with Elizabeth's tacit approval.

At this time the Netherlands were in revolt against Spain. Queen Elizabeth knew that as long as Philip was fighting in the Netherlands, he was less likely to invade England. Therefore Elizabeth secretly helped the Dutch rebels.

Then Queen Elizabeth received a financial windfall. Spanish ships carrying the payroll for their troops in the Netherlands were driven into England's ports by English pirates. Philip kept his temper, and Elizabeth kept the money.

But when Queen Elizabeth imprisoned the Catholic Mary Queen of Scots, Philip's patience ran out and he plotted to assassinate Elizabeth. When Elizabeth found out, she expelled the Spanish ambassador and began openly aiding the Netherlands. The lines were drawn. Both Elizabeth and Philip put all their resources into preparing for the war that would determine the mastery of the seas and the religion of England.

Queen Elizabeth assembled her fleet of thirty-four royal warships. In addition, she induced the owners of 170 merchant ships to equip their vessels with armaments to be available when needed. Meanwhile, Philip's Spanish Armada consisted of 130 ships, the most powerful navy the world had ever seen. On the morning the Armada sailed, every sailor took the Eucharist and all Spain prayed.

The battle's main action occurred off the coast of France. Shortly after midnight on July 28, Francis Drake set fire to several small boats and placed them in the wind to sail into the Spanish fleet. Panic seized the Spaniards as two ships caught fire and several of the largest became entangled with one another as they sought to escape the burning boats.

The coup de grâce for the Spanish came on the following day, July 29, 1588. The wind carried the broken Armada off into the North Sea, where heavy winds wrecked many of the remaining ships off the coast of Ireland.

Of the 130 ships that left Spain, just fifty-three returned, and they were so badly damaged that they were worthless. Of the twenty-seven thousand men who left, ten thousand returned, most of them wounded or sick.

England lost just sixty men and not one ship and would remain Protestant.

the Japanese Napoléon, issued a decree that banned missionaries from Japan. His decree, however, was neither obeyed nor enforced. In 1596, Hideyoshi began a more proactive persecution of the missionaries, and the next year twenty-six Christians were crucified in Nagasaki. In 1614, Christianity was officially outlawed in Japan, and the seventeenth century was marked by extreme persecution of Japanese Catholics.

1588 ✝ THE SPANISH ARMADA IS DEFEATED

In 1588, King Philip II (1527–1598) of Spain sent the 130-ship Spanish Armada to invade England and overthrow Elizabeth I (1533–1603), the Protestant queen of England. Possessing the most powerful navy in the world, Philip felt sure of victory. Hundreds of monks accompanied the Armada to reestablish Catholicism in England. To defend Protestant England, Elizabeth conscripted 170 merchant ships to accompany her thirty-four Royal Navy ships. Terrible storms forced the Armada into harbors in France. Early on the morning of July 28, 1588, English Admiral Francis Drake (1540–1596) lit a few small boats on fire and used the wind to carry them to the Spanish fleet. At noon that day, as the fire spread to the Spanish ships, the English defeated the Armada.

1589 ✝ MOSCOW BECOMES AN INDEPENDENT PATRIARCHATE

During feudal times, the Russian Orthodox Church had been a stabilizing force in the life of the Russian people. In the fourteenth century, as the divided feudal kingdoms began to unite around Moscow, Orthodox bishops acted as counselors to the princes of Moscow. In the fifteenth century, as the Byzantine Empire collapsed, the Russian Orthodox Church became autonomous from the Patriarchate of Constantinople. In 1589, Metropolitan Job (r. 1589–1605) was recognized as the first Russian patriarch, and the Moscow Patriarchate was established. The Eastern Orthodox bishops considered the Moscow Patriarchate to be the fifth-most-honored office in the Orthodox Church.

1590 ✡ JEWS BEGIN TO IMMIGRATE TO THE LOW COUNTRIES

In 1579, the Low Countries freed themselves from Spanish rule and instituted freedom of religion. The following year Spain annexed Portugal, and the Portu-

1519–21	1521	1531	1562
Ferdinand Magellan circumnavigates the earth	Hernando Cortés conquers Mexico's Aztec Empire	First stock exchange established in Antwerp	English enter slave trade

guese Inquisition that had been lax became much more aggressive in searching out crypto-Jews, those who had accepted Christian baptism but secretly still were practicing Judaism. As a result, by 1590, a steady stream of Jews immigrated to Amsterdam. Throughout the seventeenth century Amsterdam prospered, largely as a result of the skills the Jews brought with them. Trained in medicine, law, politics, business, and religion, the Jewish population made Amsterdam known as "The Dutch Jerusalem."

1598 ✛ EDICT OF NANTES SEEKS TO ENLARGE FRENCH PROTESTANT RIGHTS

Throughout sixteenth-century Europe, rulers proclaimed one religion for their region, and all subjects were expected to conform. The Edict of Nantes changed this practice in France. The edict was an agreement signed in 1598 between King Henry IV (1553–1610) of France and the French Protestant Huguenots after the formerly Protestant Henry converted to Catholicism in an effort to end the Wars of Religion. The Edict of Nantes enlarged the rights given to French Protestants to include civil equality, free exercise of religion, and fair administration of justice. This edict introduced the new concept of two religions tolerantly coexisting. King Louis XIV (1638–1715) revoked the Edict of Nantes in 1685.

1603 ✛ JACOBUS ARMINIUS ENUNCIATES ARMINIANISM

After a fifteen-year pastorate in the Dutch Reformed church, in 1603 Jacobus Arminius (1559–1609) became a professor of theology at the University of Leiden, where his lectures refined and disseminated the seeds of a theology later called Arminianism. The Reformed doctrine of predestination held that God predetermined whom he would save. Arminius believed that the Bible taught conditional election, with each person's free will determining his salvation. The controversy led to deep divisions in the church. The year after Arminius's death his followers wrote "The Remonstrance," which systematized Arminian theology. Arminianism holds that 1) God extends his offer of salvation to all who will believe, 2) Jesus Christ died for all people, 3) the Holy Spirit enables people to achieve a right relationship with God, 4) people can resist God's saving grace, and 5) Christians may lose their salvation.

1590	1607	1631	1647
Telescope invented	English colony established at Jamestown	Mount Vesuvius erupts, destroying towns	Bayonet invented in Bayonne, France

1605 ✛ THE GUNPOWDER PLOT FAILS

Alarmed at increasing religious persecution under England's Protestant King James I (1566–1625), thirteen Catholics devised a plot to blow up the Parliament building in 1605. The conspirators filled a cellar beneath the House of Lords with thirty-six barrels of gunpowder, intending to kill King James, his eldest son, and many Lords on the first day of Parliament. They hoped the plan would restore a Catholic monarch to the throne. However, the plot was exposed when a member of the House of Lords received an anonymous letter urging him not to attend Parliament. All thirteen conspirators died, either resisting arrest or by execution. Contrary to its intent, the scheme provoked increased hostility toward the Catholic faith in England. The failure of the Gunpowder Plot still is celebrated on Guy Fawkes Day, November 5, when the key conspirator of the plot is burned in effigy.

1606–1609 ✛ JOHANN ARNDT PUBLISHES FOUR BOOKS CONCERNING TRUE CHRISTIANITY

German Lutheran pastor Johann Arndt (1555–1621) was dismissed from his first pastorate for de-emphasizing the role religious pictures and ceremonies played in the German Lutheran church. At the heart of Arndt's dissent was his belief that orthodox traditions were meaningless without personal spiritual conversion. From 1606 to 1609, Arndt published his *Four Books Concerning True Christianity*. In them, Arndt advanced the mystical aspects of Martin Luther's (1483–1546) teaching, insisting that personal holiness could be obtained only through constant communication with and dependence upon God. The Thirty Years' War was only three years old when Arndt died in 1621. His books fueled the religious revival that swept Europe in the war's wake, influencing Pietism, Russian Orthodoxy, and even the Enlightenment.

1606 ✛ ROBERT DE NOBILI ARRIVES IN INDIA

The son of a wealthy Italian family, Robert de Nobili (1577–1656) joined the Jesuits despite his family's opposition. When de Nobili sailed to India as a missionary in 1605, the country was a Portuguese colony, and missionaries expected Indian converts to assume European cultural customs. Hoping to win

1519–21	1521	1531	1562
Ferdinand Magellan circumnavigates the earth	Hernando Cortés conquers Mexico's Aztec Empire	First stock exchange established in Antwerp	English enter slave trade

THEY WENT WITHOUT GOD

December 19, 1606

Everything that could possibly go wrong did.

Englishmen publicly claimed that the primary purpose in establishing the American colonies was to spread the gospel among the Indians. In truth, their motivation was greed. In 1606, the London Company was formed for colonial expansion and trade, obtaining a royal charter to found a colony in Virginia. Without taking time to prepare plans for the new colony, three ships carrying 105 colonists set out for Virginia on December 19, 1606.

The voyage took much longer than expected, forcing them to consume much of the rations en route that were to have sustained them through their first year. The leaders constantly fought with each other, and because they had no authority structure, conflicts went unresolved. In May the ships finally entered the Chesapeake Bay. The colonists named their colony Jamestown after their king, James I.

These men were unfit to build a colony. With few laborers or carpenters among them, the group consisted primarily of "Gentlemen," who came without realizing the hard work that would be necessary for the colony to succeed. The quarreling that began during their voyage continued on land. The Gentlemen refused to participate in any labor, instead setting off in search of gold and pearls. Only one minister had been sent with them—an indication of how interested England really was in evangelizing the Indians. Reverend Robert Hunt was a man of God whose passion to evangelize the Indians was not shared by anyone else.

They arrived too late to plant crops and were quickly running out of food. They lived in fear of Indian attacks and were sick from exposure, mosquitoes, and poor nutrition. The rift between the Gentlemen and the others continued to widen, and no one showed any interest in Reverend Hunt's continued pleas for reliance on God. By September 1607, half of the little colony had died.

Hunt's life was a vivid contrast. In addition to being a godly man of prayer, he labored energetically, taking charge of building the first mill for grinding corn and becoming the primary caregiver for the sick.

The colony at Jamestown became entirely dependent on the generosity of the Indians. Yet only Hunt thanked God for their assistance.

The sweltering heat in the summer of 1608 scorched the crops they planted. Starvation and disease claimed even more lives the second year than the first. Nine out of every ten people who embarked for Jamestown died, including Rev. Hunt. This pattern continued for years. In March 1621, there were only 843 settlers in Virginia. During the next year, 1,580 more people arrived but 1,183 died!

Even with this staggering death rate, the colonists refused to trust in God. Ship after ship arrived, with the investors always "forgetting" to send more ministers. In 1622, there were more than twelve hundred settlers on ten plantations scattered throughout Virginia, but just three ministers. So much for spreading the gospel among the Indians!

to Christ the Hindu priestly caste known as the Brahmins, and against the counsel of his superiors, de Nobili lived among them and adopted their cultural practices. De Nobili also urged the development of separate evangelistic missions for each caste or class of Indian people. De Nobili was one of the first missionaries to attempt to separate Christianity from its Western cultural bias. An estimated hundred thousand people became Roman Catholics through de Nobili's ministry and influence.

1608 ✝ ✡ JESUITS REJECT APPLICANTS WITH JEWISH BLOOD

The Jesuits, or the Society of Jesus, was a religious order of the Roman Catholic Church that first addressed the idea of blood purity at their Fifth General Congregation (1593–1594). This gathering ruled that no one with a Jewish parent would be admitted to the Jesuit order. In 1608, the Sixth General Congregation of the Society of Jesus ruled that no one could be admitted to the order with a Jewish ancestor in their lineage going back five generations. These rulings remained until 1946.

1609 ✝ JOHN SMYTH FOUNDS FIRST BAPTIST CHURCH IN AMSTERDAM

Minister John Smyth (1560–1612) was dismissed from the Church of England for his belief that those who called themselves Christians only for political reasons were not true members of the Christian church. Smyth and his followers fled to Holland where they found more religious tolerance. There Smyth was influenced by the Mennonite practice of baptizing believers. The common practice in the Protestant church at that time was infant baptism by sprinkling. In 1609, Smyth baptized himself and his followers upon their confession of faith, forming the first Baptist church in Amsterdam. Members of Smyth's congregation later migrated to America among the Pilgrims. Others founded the General Baptist movement in Great Britain.

1611 ✝ KING JAMES BIBLE IS FIRST PUBLISHED

In 1604, James I (1566–1625), newly crowned king and head of the Church of England, championed a new translation of the Bible. At that time, the Bishop's Bible was used in churches. Those who had Bibles at home read the Geneva Bi-

1519–21	1521	1531	1562
Ferdinand Magellan circumnavigates the earth	Hernando Cortés conquers Mexico's Aztec Empire	First stock exchange established in Antwerp	English enter slave trade

ble, which had Reformed notes in the margins, sparking theological controversy. Fifty-four scholars worked on the new translation, drawing on original texts as well as translations in several languages, and omitting marginal notes. The King James translation received wide acceptance, in part because its prose was well suited to being read aloud, significant in an era when many could not read. As a result, the new translation helped shape the development of spoken English. The King James Version remained the Bible of English-speaking Protestants for three hundred years.

1612 ✛ THOMAS HELWYS ESTABLISHES THE FIRST BAPTIST CHURCH IN ENGLAND

Thomas Helwys (1550–1616) and John Smyth (1560–1612) started a Baptist church in Amsterdam with Smyth as pastor. Helwys became pastor after Smyth's death. The church issued a Declaration of Faith, defining baptism as "the outward manifestation of dying with Christ and walking in newness of life; and therefore in nowise appertaineth to infants." In 1612, Helwys returned to England and established a church on Newgate Street that practiced believer's baptism with Mennonite-style pouring rather than immersion. It was the first known Baptist church in England.

1617 ✛ THE BOOK OF SPORTS CAUSES ESTRANGEMENT

By 1617, King James I of England (1566–1625) had made it clear that he intended to make no significant alterations to English church polity, which had been chiefly set up by Elizabeth I (1533–1603). Unsatisfied, the Puritans continued to oppose the English court. Therefore, James issued a decree authorizing the activities of the old English Sunday, including dancing, archery, and vaulting. This declaration, titled the Book of Sports, attacked the Puritan idea of the Sabbath by suggesting that the Puritans had a penchant for melancholy that repelled Roman Catholics, and that their Sabbatarian practices encouraged laziness and drunkenness. With pressure from Archbishop of Canterbury William Laud (1573–1645) and with greater force, Charles I (1600–1649) reissued this decree in 1633, causing further estrangement between Puritan revolutionaries and the king. The result was the English Civil War and the execution of Charles I in 1649.

1590	1607	1631	1647
Telescope invented	English colony established at Jamestown	Mount Vesuvius erupts, destroying towns	Bayonet invented in Bayonne, France

1617 ✝ JANSENISM BEGINS

Cornelius Otto Jansen (1585–1638) led a revival of Augustinian theology within the Catholic Church. From 1612 to 1617, he immersed himself in the writings of Augustine (354–430) and then in 1617 became director of a college in Louvain, France, where he found others open to his convictions. Jansen and his successors challenged the sacramentalism and hierarchical structure of the Counter-Reformation, the Catholic Church's response to the Reformation, and were devoted to reforming the church according to Augustinian standards. The Jansenists taught that grace is irresistible and that Christ died only for the elect. After Jansen's death in 1638, Antoine Arnauld (1612–1694) assumed leadership of the group, which included the French philosopher Blaise Pascal (1623–1662). Pope Innocent X (1574–1655) condemned Jansenism in 1653.

1618 ✝ THE SYNOD OF DORT BEGINS

After Jacobus Arminius's death in 1609, bitter controversy about the doctrine of unconditional predestination raged within the Dutch Reformed Church. Arminius's followers, by then called Remonstrants, wanted to modify the church's theology to recognize the role they believed human free will played in salvation. The Synod of Dort convened in 1618, with fifty-six delegates from the Netherlands, as well as advisors from Reformed churches in England, Scotland, and Germany. By this time political issues concerning state supervision of the church were also part of the controversy. The Remonstrant representatives refused to participate, denouncing the synod. The synod ruled the Remonstrants' Arminian teachings were not orthodox, and responded by producing the Cannons of Dort. This document reaffirmed the Reformed doctrines of grace as the standard for the Dutch Reformed Church. Remonstrant leaders were removed from their pulpits and exiled from the Netherlands.

1618 ✝ THE THIRTY YEARS' WAR BEGINS

By the early 1600s, the Peace of Augsburg (1555) was beginning to buckle under the ever-shifting weight of rulers choosing their country's religion. In 1608, Protestant princes formed the Evangelical Union, which the Catholic rulers soon countered with the Catholic League. Theological differences, however, were only part of the growing problem. Personal and national rivalries, eco-

1519–21	1521	1531	1562
Ferdinand Magellan circumnavigates the earth	Hernando Cortés conquers Mexico's Aztec Empire	First stock exchange established in Antwerp	English enter slave trade

A MOMENTOUS DOCUMENT

For the first time in recorded history, free men covenanted together to form a new civil government.

The date was November 11, 1620, and the place was the *Mayflower*, anchored off the coast of Cape Cod. One hundred two passengers including thirty-four children had crossed the ocean from England. Of the passengers, sixteen men, eleven women, and fourteen children were Pilgrims, having been associated with the Separatist church in Scrooby, England. Refusing to conform to the Church of England, they had first sought religious asylum in Leyden, Holland. After twelve years, they became concerned that their children no longer would identify themselves as English. Learning of the possibility of settling in America, they made arrangements with the Virginia Company to settle within the northernmost boundary of the Virginia Charter. However, fierce winds blew them off course to Cape Cod.

They decided to settle there but then realized that since they would not be under the Virginia Company, they would be on their own, for they had no agreement with the New England Company. On board the ship some of the non-Pilgrim bonded and contract servants greeted the new plan as an opportunity for rebellion. The Pilgrims saw that they must act quickly to prevent a mutiny.

The Pilgrim men then wrote up a compact, now known as the Mayflower Compact, and presented it to the rest. Forty-one of the sixty-five men signed it. Thirteen who didn't sign were sons of signers, covered by their fathers' commitments. The remaining men probably were too sick to sign. The compact read:

> Having undertaken, for the glory of God and the advancement of the Christian Faith and honor of our King and country, a voyage to plant the first colony in the northern parts of Virginia, do by these presents solemnly and mutually in the presence of God and one another, covenant and combine ourselves together into a civil body politic, for our better ordering and preservation and furtherance of the ends aforesaid, and by virtue hereof to enact, constitute and frame such just and equal laws, ordinances, acts, constitutions and offices from time to time, as shall be thought most meet and convenient for the general good of the colony. Unto which we promise all due submission and obedience. In witness whereof we have hereunder subscribed our names at Cape Cod, the 11th of November, in the year of the reign of our Sovereign King James of England . . . Anno Domini 1620.

Before leaving the Netherlands, the Pilgrims had knelt on the dock to ask God's blessing on their voyage, and now William Bradford recorded, "Being thus arrived in a good harbor and brought safe to land, they fell upon their knees and blessed the God of heaven."

During their first winter, forty-seven people died. These humble Christian men and women were to be the seeds of what would become the United States of America.

SQUANTO

March 22, 1621

In the year 1619, when many people were considering whether to go to the New World, one person had a unique reason—he was trying to go home.

An American Indian by the name of Squanto had come to England via the slave trade. In 1605, Squanto was captured by Captain George Weymouth and taken to England, where he learned English. He spent nine years there before returning home to his people, the Patuxets on Cape Cod in 1614, on a vessel captained by John Smith. He was not at home long before Captain Thomas Hunt, part of Smith's expedition, lured Squanto and twenty-six other unsuspecting Indians aboard his vessel, clamped them in irons, and took them to Spain, where he sold them into slavery. Squanto was delivered into the hands of local friars, who introduced him to the Christian faith.

Squanto did not remain long with the Spanish monks. Making his way to England, he managed to get passage on an American-bound ship in 1619. When Squanto arrived back on Cape Cod, to his great shock he learned that everyone in his tribe had died from smallpox.

A year after Squanto's return, in November 1620, the Pilgrims reached the shores of Cape Cod. The Pilgrims were members of the Separatist congregation of Scrooby, England, that had fled to Holland. Twelve years later, they set sail for America and settled in Plymouth.

The settlers discovered that Indians had cleared the land at Plymouth for planting, but it had not been farmed for some time. After a devastating winter, one day the following March, an English-speaking Indian walked into Plymouth. His name was Samoset. He had learned the language from English fishermen he had met along the Maine coast. The Pilgrims discovered from Samoset that they had settled on the homeland of the Patuxets, the tribe wiped out by disease four years earlier. God had led the Pilgrims to perhaps the one plot of uninhabited land on the East Coast, the very land where Squanto had grown up.

Samoset introduced the Pilgrims to Squanto on March 22, 1621. Squanto brought news that Massasoit, chief of the Wampanoag and leader of most of the surrounding tribes, was coming to visit the settlers that very day. When Massasoit arrived, Squanto helped the Pilgrims agree to a peace treaty with Massasoit that would last for decades.

When Squanto arrived in Plymouth, the Pilgrims were in desperate straits. Nearly half had died during the previous winter, lacking the skills for survival in their new land. Squanto showed the Pilgrims how to fertilize and protect the corn they planted, how to catch fish from the streams, and how to harvest the food the land provided. If God had not sent Squanto, the Pilgrims likely would not have survived. One of the Pilgrim leaders called him "a special instrument sent of God for our good, beyond our expectation."

nomic difficulties, and ambition to expand empires complicated religious tensions. In May 1618, Protestant nobles threw two Catholic Hapsburg rulers out of a high window in Prague, starting what would become known as the Thirty Years' War (1618–1648). Eventually involving all of central Europe, the war was characterized by religious–political allies temporarily winning ascendancy in their quest to gain territory and wipe out their enemy's religion, only to be driven back by the opposite faction.

1619 ✛ FIRST SLAVES ARRIVE IN VIRGINIA

When the first twenty African men arrived in Jamestown, Virginia, in 1619, the colony had no laws governing slavery. The men were put to work in the tobacco, rice, and cotton fields alongside Englishmen who had committed themselves to be servants in exchange for passage to the New World. Conditions were hard for both white and black men, most of whom survived their term of service and earned their freedom. Unlike the Englishmen, however, the Africans had not left their homes voluntarily. Therefore, they are recognized as having been slaves—the first of 399,000 Africans who were forced to migrate to the colonies that became the United States.

1620 ✛ MAYFLOWER COMPACT ESTABLISHES NEW GOVERNMENT

On November 11, 1620, forty-one men aboard the *Mayflower* signed the Mayflower Compact off the coast of Cape Cod. The authors, who were sixteen of the signers, were Pilgrims associated with the Separatist church in Scrooby, England. They had fled first to the Netherlands and then sought religious freedom in America. Because the ship had been blown off course and did not land in Virginia as intended, they no longer were under the jurisdiction of the Virginia Company, the sponsor of their voyage. This was the first time in recorded history that free men covenanted together to form a civil government with the authority to enact laws that the people promised to obey.

1621 ✛ SQUANTO SAVES THE PILGRIMS

When the Pilgrims arrived in Cape Cod in November 1620, they possessed very few survival skills for living in the New World. More than half of the group died

1590	1607	1631	1647
Telescope invented	English colony established at Jamestown	Mount Vesuvius erupts, destroying towns	Bayonet invented in Bayonne, France

from starvation and sickness the first winter. On March 22, 1621, an English-speaking Indian named Samoset introduced the Pilgrims to Squanto, another Indian. Squanto had been captured twice by slave traders, and he had learned to speak English while in Britain. Upon returning to America, Squanto discovered that smallpox had wiped out his tribe. The Pilgrims had settled on the land that had belonged to his eradicated tribe. That very day he assisted the newcomers in establishing a peace treaty with Massasoit, chief of the surrounding tribes. Squanto also taught the Pilgrims how to catch fish, fertilize corn, and harvest food in America. If God had not sent him, the Pilgrims might never have survived.

1622 ✛ POPE GREGORY XV CREATES THE SACRED CONGREGATION

Pope Gregory XV (1554–1623) created the Sacred Congregation for the Propagation of Catholic Faith on June 22, 1622. Originally lead by thirteen cardinals, this administrative department was commissioned to evangelize the Protestants in areas lost in the wake of the Reformation and to counter Protestant expansion in newly established colonies. The Sacred Congregation sponsored missionaries and established seminaries in foreign lands, published catechisms and other religious works in foreign languages, and poised the Catholic Church for expansion around the world.

1627 ✛ THE CODEX ALEXANDRINUS ARRIVES IN ENGLAND

The Codex Alexandrinus, a manuscript thought to have been written in the fifth century, is believed to have come from Alexandria, Egypt. It contains most of the text of the Bible in Greek uncial script (all capital letters). Although missing thirty-four New Testament chapters, it represents one of the most complete early copies of the Bible known at the time. The Eastern Orthodox bishop of Alexandria, Cyril Lucar (1572–1638), sent the Codex to King James I (1566–1625) of England, who had authorized the King James Bible. However, the Codex did not arrive in England until 1627, two years after James's death. In 1627, King Charles I (1600–1649) accepted the bishop's gift in place of his predecessor. The Codex Alexandrinus became a definitive text for subsequent scholarship as copies of it were disseminated from England.

1519–21	1521	1531	1562
Ferdinand Magellan circumnavigates the earth	Hernando Cortés conquers Mexico's Aztec Empire	First stock exchange established in Antwerp	English enter slave trade

AN INQUIRING MIND

June 19, 1623

Some children seem to be born with an "I'll do it myself" attitude.

Blaise Pascal, one of the greatest intellects of the Western world, had an unquench-able thirst to learn. He was born into an upper-class family in central France on June 19, 1623. His father, Etienne, was an attorney, magistrate, and tax collector who loved lan-guages and mathematics and was intensely interested in his children's education. Pascal's mother died when he was only three, and four years later, Etienne moved his family to Paris. There he homeschooled his three children, starting with the study of languages. He was of the opinion that it was best to withhold the study of geometry until they were proficient in languages, so they wouldn't be preoccupied with the fascination of mathematics.

However, when young Blaise was only twelve, his father discovered that his preco-cious son had taught himself geometry. At age sixteen, Pascal attracted the attention of mathematician and philosopher René Descartes by writing a book on the geometry of cones. Concerned by the long hours his father would spend adding up figures at night, Pascal put his problem-solving ability to work and invented the first mechanical calcu-lating machine when he was nineteen. Its principles have remained in use into modern times. Pascal also originated the theory of probability. In the field of physics he discov-ered a principle known as Pascal's Law, which is the foundation of modern hydraulics.

Pascal's remarkable mind was interested in things of the Spirit as well. Encouraged by his father to learn by observation and discovery, Pascal's inquiring mind devoured the Scriptures as well as scientific data. Just as he learned geometry on his own, so his spiritual journey to belief was a private one. On the night he put his faith in Christ he wrote:

> God of Abraham, God of Isaac, God of Jacob, not of the philosophers and scholars . . .
> He is to be found only by the ways taught in the Gospel. . . .
> "Righteous Father, the world has not known Thee, but I have known Thee." . . .
> Let me not be separated from Him eternally.
> "This is the eternal life, that they might know Thee, the only true God, and the one whom Thou has sent, Jesus Christ." . . .
> Let me never be separated from Him.
> We keep hold of Him only by the ways taught in the Gospel.

A few days after Pascal died, a servant of the house happened to notice a bulge in the lining of Pascal's coat. Carefully pulling the stitches, he discovered two small pieces of parchment in Pascal's handwriting—one a copy of the other. Dated Novem-ber 23, 1654, the document was a record of his intensely personal revelation on that night. It was apparently so important to Pascal that he made two copies and carefully sewed and unsewed the parchments into the coats he wore until his death eight years later.

1627 ✢ LA ROCHELLE IS BESIEGED

The religious policies of French Cardinal Armand de Richelieu (1585–1642), the most trusted advisor of France's young King Louis XIII (1601–1643), were based on advancing the power of France and himself, rather than on theological considerations. Richelieu wanted the Huguenots—the French Protestants—destroyed, not because they were Protestants but because the previous king, Henry IV (1553–1610), had given them several fortified cities and independent power within France in order to guarantee their security. Richelieu's efforts to eradicate the Huguenots led to armed conflict in the 1627 siege of La Rochelle, the main Huguenot stronghold. The Protestants successfully resisted the French army for one year, but eventually were forced to surrender. Only fifteen hundred of the city's twenty-five thousand inhabitants survived. Because Richelieu's concern was the Huguenots' political power rather than their religious beliefs, he ordered religious and civil tolerance of Protestants after their cities had been conquered.

1630 ✢ COMMUNION REVIVAL OCCURS AT SHOTTS

On June 21, 1630, several hundred Protestants crowded into Shotts, Scotland, to celebrate Communion. A relatively unknown preacher named John Livingstone (1603–1672) was scheduled to address the crowd. That morning, overwhelmed by a sense of his own unworthiness, Livingstone had fled from Shotts, only to be turned back by the conviction that his appointment to preach was of God. Soon after Livingstone began to speak, rain began to fall on the crowd that had been unable to squeeze inside the church. As the congregation scattered, he admonished them with the challenge that they should "flee only to Christ the City of Refuge." Before Livingstone could finish his sermon, the power of God fell in revival on the crowd. By nightfall, more than five hundred new believers came to faith in Scotland's best-known revival.

1630 ✢ PURITANS SETTLE IN MASSACHUSETTS

By 1629, the turmoil over whether the king or Parliament was the final authority in the land reached its peak in England. King Charles I (1600–1649) disbanded Parliament and ruled alone for the next eleven years. A group of Puritan businessmen, faced with increasing hostility toward their religious views and

1519–21	1521	1531	1562
Ferdinand Magellan circumnavigates the earth	Hernando Cortés conquers Mexico's Aztec Empire	First stock exchange established in Antwerp	English enter slave trade

A CITY UPON A HILL

Founding America was at times a depressing ordeal.

John Winthrop was a dedicated Puritan lawyer in England. Winthrop had been elected governor of the Massachusetts Bay Company prior to departing from England on the *Arabella* with some seven hundred colonists. Two years earlier sixty-six English settlers led by John Endicott had settled at Salem, Massachusetts, and the next year two hundred more had followed.

On June 12, 1630, John Winthrop stood at the rail of the *Arabella* as it entered Salem Harbor. He had been at sea for seventy-two days, and now he finally had arrived in New England. As the ship approached shore, the sight that greeted Winthrop perplexed him. Where was Salem? All that was visible was a collection of huts and canvas shelters. Stepping on shore, he realized to his great disappointment that this pathetic settlement was indeed Salem.

John Endicott, the acting governor, informed him that of the first two groups of settlers now only eighty-five remained. More than eighty had died, and the rest had returned to England. Many of those remaining planned to do the same.

As Winthrop surveyed the disheartening sight, he thought of the words he had written the day before to spell out his goals for the new colony, which he titled "A Model of Christian Charity":

> Thus stands the cause between God and us: we are entered into covenant with Him for this work. . . .
>
> Now the only way . . . to provide for posterity, is to follow the counsel of Micah, to do justly, to love mercy, to walk humbly with our God . . . for this end, we must be knit together in this work as one man. . . . We must hold a familiar commerce together in all meekness, gentleness, patience, and liberality. We must delight in each other, make one another's condition our own, rejoice together, mourn together, labor and suffer together, always having before our eyes our Commission and Community in his work, as members of the same body. So shall we keep the unity of the Spirit in the bond of peace. . . .
>
> We shall find that the God of Israel is among us, when ten of us shall be able to resist a thousand of our enemies, when he shall make us a praise and glory, that men of succeeding plantations shall say, "The Lord make it like that of New England." For we must consider that we shall be as a City upon a hill. . . .

Rekindled in his vision, John Winthrop went on to serve as governor of Massachusetts almost continually until his death in 1649. He was instrumental in shaping Massachusetts into a Christian commonwealth that went on to have a profound effect on the rest of the developing new nation.

DOES THE SUN CIRCLE THE EARTH?

| June 21, 1632 |

Five hundred years ago, being ahead of the curve in science could put you on a collision course with the church.

Galileo Galilei was born in Pisa, Italy, the day Michelangelo died (February 18, 1564) and the same year Shakespeare was born. He became the leading astronomer of his day and was given lifetime tenure as a professor at the University of Padua. In 1610, using his newly invented telescope that could magnify one thousand times, Galileo discovered four moons revolving around Jupiter. By analogy he reasoned that the planets revolved around the sun, agreeing with the view set forth by Copernicus a century earlier. The other professors at Padua refused to even look through his telescope. Galileo took this as his signal that he should leave Padua, going to Florence instead.

Galileo's conclusions brought to public attention the question of whether the earth circled the sun or the sun circled the earth. Soon Galileo was accused of contradicting the Bible. In 1615, a formal protest was lodged against Galileo before the Inquisition, a special tribunal set up in the medieval church to combat heresy. To answer his critics, Galileo went to Rome, hoping to convert the church leaders to his point of view. Galileo promoted his ideas so extensively in Rome that soon everyone in the city was discussing astronomy. However, the Inquisition directed Galileo to abandon his opinions and not discuss them further. In February 1616, the Inquisition published its edict: "The view that the sun stands motionless at the center of the universe is foolish, philosophically false, and utterly heretical." To avoid the threatened imprisonment, Galileo declared his submission to the decree.

Galileo was able to keep out of the public eye until 1632, when he published his major book on astronomy, which explained his understanding of the relationship between the earth and the sun. The book earned wide acclaim throughout the academic world, but the Inquisition immediately demanded that Galileo appear before it once again, accusing him of breaking his promise to obey the edict of 1616. Threatened with torture on June 21, 1632, Galileo agreed with the position of the church and declared the earth to be motionless with the sun moving around it. The next day, in spite of this denial of his convictions, the Inquisition found Galileo guilty of heresy and sentenced him to prison for an indefinite length of time. As penance, he was to recite seven penitential psalms daily for three years.

Fortunately for Galileo, after just three days in prison, the pope allowed him to be kept as prisoner in his own villa. There he was free to pursue his studies while his daughter, a nun, recited the penitential psalms for him.

dim financial prospects in England, broadened the charter of their Massachusetts Bay trading company to include colonization. The Great Migration from Britain to New England began in 1630. That year, almost one thousand settlers arrived in Salem and (present-day) Boston, Massachusetts. Only Puritans could hold public office in the new colony. This policy effectively created a theocracy in which religious principles guided civil government. For the first time, the authority for a colony's government resided in a colony, not in England.

1632 ✛ GUSTAVUS ADOLPHUS DIES SAVING GERMANY

During the Thirty Years' War (1618–1648), Protestants fought Catholics in Germany. By 1630, the Imperial Catholic forces had crushed all of the Protestant princes, and it seemed that the complete destruction of German Lutherans was imminent. At that point, King Gustavus Adolphus (1594–1632) of Sweden came to the rescue. With the assistance of troops provided by the marquis of Brandenburg and the duke of Saxony, Gustavus's skilled soldiers were victorious over the Catholic army. On November 16, 1632, Gustavus faced one final battle in southern Germany. After leading his troops in song and prayer, he charged with them into the Battle of Lützen. Although Gustavus was killed, his army was victorious, and German Protestantism was saved.

1632 ✛ COMENIUS WRITES THE GREAT DIDACTIC

Jan Amos Comenius (1592–1670) was born in Moravia, now the eastern Czech Republic. He studied theology and was ordained in the Brethren church. The advance of the Thirty Years' War compelled Comenius to move to Lissa, Poland, where he wrote *The Great Didactic*, his best-known work. In it, Comenius outlined a system of education that began with home-schooling then lead through public elementary and Latin middle schools to universities. He advocated equal education of girls and boys and rejected physical punishment in schools, both revolutionary ideas at the time. Central to Comenius's philosophy was his conviction that although traditional learning was important, the true goal of education should be ever-closer conformity to the image of Christ. Ultimately, Comenius believed moral transformation via education would result in peace for a war-torn world.

1590	1607	1631	1647
Telescope invented	English colony established at Jamestown	Mount Vesuvius erupts, destroying towns	Bayonet invented in Bayonne, France

1633 ✛ GALILEO IS FORCED TO RECANT

Italian physicist and mathematician Galileo Galilei (1564–1642) invented the telescope in 1610, making him the foremost astronomer of his day. One of the more significant things Galileo observed was that Jupiter's moons revolved around the planet. From this, Galileo reasoned that the sun, not Earth, was the center of the solar system, a theory Copernicus first proposed ninety years earlier. Although the idea gained widespread acceptance in Europe, in 1616, the Inquisition declared it heretical. Galileo received permission from the Roman Catholic Church to write an impartial book discussing the earth- and sun-centered models of the solar system and published *Dialogue Concerning the Two Chief Systems of the World* in 1632. In 1633, the Inquisition brought him to trial. Threatened with death if he did not renounce the Copernican theory, Galileo recanted and lived under house arrest until his death in 1642.

1633 ✛ VINCENT DE PAUL FOUNDS THE DAUGHTERS OF CHARITY

Born in southwestern France to peasant parents, Vincent de Paul (1581–1660) was ordained a priest in the Roman Catholic Church. While pursuing further theological studies in France, Vincent was captured by pirates and enslaved in Tunisia. Two years later, he escaped and made his way back to France. While there, he felt a strong calling to ministry among the poor. In 1625, Vincent founded the Congregation of Missions, also known as the Lazarists. Under that banner in 1633, he founded the Daughters of Charity, the first cloistered order of women dedicated to serving the sick and the poor. Through this and other efforts, he helped organize the ministries of the Catholic Church among the poor into the systems that continue to operate today.

1633 ✛ WILLIAM LAUD BECOMES ARCHBISHOP OF CANTERBURY

William Laud (1573–1645) was educated at Oxford University in England where he became convinced that the prevailing Calvinist thought had undermined the traditional order of worship in the Church of England and its episcopal organization. As chancellor of Oxford, Laud worked to restore pre-Reformation liturgy. Noting Laud's efforts, King Charles I (1600–1649), also interested in restoring the purity of the Anglican Church, appointed

1519–21	1521	1531	1562
Ferdinand Magellan circumnavigates the earth	Hernando Cortés conquers Mexico's Aztec Empire	First stock exchange established in Antwerp	English enter slave trade

Laud in 1633 to the church's highest position, archbishop of Canterbury. As archbishop, Laud enforced uniformity in Anglicanism without regard to objections of conscience. He systematically undermined the influences of both the Puritan and Roman Catholic churches in England. When England's political winds shifted back toward Puritanism, Parliament impeached and jailed Laud in 1641 for his zeal. Laud was executed for treason on January 10, 1645.

1636 ✛ HARVARD COLLEGE IS FOUNDED

In 1636, only six years after the founding of the Massachusetts Bay Colony, its Great and General Court voted to establish Harvard College. The first institution of higher learning in the United States, it was named after its benefactor, Puritan minister John Harvard of Charlestown. John Harvard died in 1638, leaving his library and half of his estate to the new school. Harvard began with one professor and nine students. Its classical academic offerings were based on the model of the university system in England. Harvard's early years reflected the Puritan philosophy of its founders, and many early graduates became ministers in the Puritan churches of New England.

1636 ✛ ROGER WILLIAMS FOUNDS PROVIDENCE, RHODE ISLAND

English Puritan Roger Williams (1603–1683) immigrated to Boston with his family in 1631. A Separatist, Williams believed that England had irreparably contaminated religious life by bringing the church under the government's control. In colonial New England, Williams spoke out against the Puritan church for not explicitly separating from the Church of England. Banished for his criticism, Williams and his followers fled to present-day Rhode Island in 1636, where Williams took the then-unusual step of purchasing from Native Americans the land on which he founded the city of Providence. In 1639, he founded America's first Baptist church in Providence. Returning to England in 1642, he secured a colonial charter for Rhode Island, which became a stronghold for religious liberty in New England. Williams died in 1683 without knowing that his ideals about the separation of church and state would become a cornerstone of American life.

1590	1607	1631	1647
Telescope invented	English colony established at Jamestown	Mount Vesuvius erupts, destroying towns	Bayonet invented in Bayonne, France

1637 ✛ ANNE HUTCHINSON IS TRIED FOR HERESY

Born in Lincolnshire, England, Anne Hutchinson (1591–1643) spent her formative years under the teaching of Puritan vicar John Cotton. In 1634, Anne and her husband, William, followed Cotton to Boston, Massachusetts, where Anne's nursing skills earned her great respect. She became known for her thorough Bible knowledge through midweek meetings she convened to discuss Cotton's sermons. Hutchinson emphasized the covenant of grace whereby God revealed himself to believers through the Holy Spirit. Initially, Cotton and others supported her position. But as Anne's following grew, some saw her as undermining the law-based foundation of male-dominated Puritan society. In 1637, Massachusetts Governor John Winthrop (1588–1649) tried Hutchinson for heresy, and the following year Hutchinson and her followers were banished from the state. They settled first in Rhode Island, then in present-day New York City where she and most of her family were killed by Native Americans in 1643.

1637 ✛ ANTI-CHRISTIAN EDICTS LEAD TO REBELLION IN JAPAN

Christianity was introduced into Japan by Catholic Jesuit Francis Xavier (1506–1552) in 1549. Although Japan was traditionally Buddhist, hundreds of thousands of Japanese joined the Catholic Church in the next half-century. In 1614, the emperor outlawed Christianity, attempting to consolidate his political power under Buddhism. Christians became the objects of persecution ranging from discrimination to crucifixion. However, missionaries continued to enter the country until 1637. That year in the wake of anti-Christian edicts, Christians joined a revolt against the emperor, who reacted by virtually closing off the nation to foreigners and forbidding Japanese nationals to leave. Christianity ceased to exist in any public sense. But thousands of Roman Catholics, posing nominally as Buddhists, took their faith underground, where it passed from generation to generation for more than two hundred years.

1638 ✛ COVENANTERS SIGN THE NATIONAL COVENANT

In 1638, a group of Scottish Presbyterians met and drafted what they called the National covenant, which was directed against King Charles I of England (1600–1649). Charles I had attempted to force the sacramental *Book of Com-*

1519–21	1521	1531	1562
Ferdinand Magellan circumnavigates the earth	Hernando Cortés conquers Mexico's Aztec Empire	First stock exchange established in Antwerp	English enter slave trade

AMERICA'S FIRST COLLEGE PRESIDENT

| August 27, 1640 |

He was a man of conviction, and it cost him his job.

"The Lord gave me an attentive ear and heart to understand preaching.... The Lord showed me my sins and reconciliation by Christ... and this word was more sweet to me than anything else in the world." So reads the testimony of Henry Dunster, born in 1609 in Bury, England. After receiving bachelor and master degrees at Cambridge University, he was ordained as a minister in the Church of England. As he served in his church, Dunster became increasingly disheartened by the corruption in the church and by its persecution of Christians who didn't conform to its doctrine. As a result, he fled to America in 1640.

Dunster's scholarly reputation preceded him to America. On August 27, 1640, shortly after arriving in Boston, Dunster was unanimously elected as the first president of America's first college, Harvard, in Cambridge, Massachusetts. The college had been struggling without a president for four years since its founding, but it flourished during the years of Dunster's administration. He strengthened the curriculum, erected buildings, attracted students, and taught full-time. He was a tireless fundraiser for Harvard, and although he himself was poor, he gave one hundred acres of his own land to the college.

The Baptist movement was making slow progress throughout New England at the time, and those who were leading the movement endured persecution in the Massachusetts Bay Colony. The more Dunster studied the more convinced he became of the Baptists' position. By 1653, he was so strongly opposed to infant baptism that he refused to have his fourth child baptized. This caused quite a stir within the Harvard community. Because of the controversy, he offered his resignation, but it was refused.

Dunster was such a beloved figure that had he been willing to keep silent regarding his view of baptism, he would have been able to keep his position at Harvard indefinitely. But he became so thoroughly convinced of the truth of believer's baptism that he preached a series of sermons against infant baptism. On one occasion he even disrupted a baptismal service in the church at Cambridge. For this latter incident he was indicted by the grand jury, found guilty of disturbing public worship, and sentenced to receive a public admonition.

Under these circumstances Harvard was too embarrassed to have Dunster remain as president, and so on October 24, 1654, the board accepted the resignation they previously had rejected. He had served Harvard as president for fourteen years.

Dunster spent the last five years of his life as pastor of the church at Scituate in the Plymouth Colony. The church's previous pastor, Charles Chauncy, succeeded him as president of Harvard.

Dunster held no animosities from this experience. At his death he bequeathed legacies to several of the people at Harvard who had called for his resignation.

mon Prayer on the Church of Scotland. The signers of the covenant, called Covenanters, committed themselves to maintain the freedom and autonomy of the Church of Scotland and to defend its Presbyterian government. Approximately three hundred thousand Scots signed the covenant.

1639–1640 ✠ BISHOP WARS ARE UNSUCCESSFUL

Charles I (1600–1649) of England was determined to impose Episcopal government upon the Church of Scotland. This led to the signing of the National covenant in Scotland in 1638, declaring Scotland to be Presbyterian. The growing hostilities between the king and the Scottish churches led to The Bishop Wars, two unsuccessful military campaigns by Charles I against the Scottish Presbyterians. This was a step leading to the English Civil War in 1642 and the eventual execution of Charles I in 1649.

1640 ✠ BAY PSALM BOOK IS PUBLISHED

As the Puritans settled Massachusetts beginning in 1628, they began to develop their own style of worship and church order. One of the earliest examples of this is the *Bay Psalm Book,* which was published in 1640. John Eliot (1604–1690), Richard Mather (1596–1669), and Thomas Welde (1595–1663) assembled the book, which was originally titled *The Whole Book of Psalmes Faithfully Translated into English Metre.* The book was the official hymnal of the Massachusetts Bay Colony until the 1750s. First printed by Stephen Daye in Cambridge, Massachusetts, it was the first English book known to have been printed in North America.

1640 ✠ CORNELIUS JANSEN'S AUGUSTINUS PUBLISHED

Although written eleven years before his death, Cornelius Jansen's most famous work, *Augustinus,* was not published until 1640. Jansen (1585–1638) was born in the Netherlands and studied Catholic theology in Belgium, France, and Spain. In Madrid, heavily influenced by the writings of Augustine (354–430), and alarmed at the expanding influence of Jesuit philosophy in the Catholic Church, Jansen wrote *Augustinus.* In it, he argued compellingly for irresistible grace and against man's ability to perfect himself. Three years after its publication, *Augustinus* was banned by the Catholic Church. But under the leadership

1519–21	1521	1531	1562
Ferdinand Magellan circumnavigates the earth	Hernando Cortés conquers Mexico's Aztec Empire	First stock exchange established in Antwerp	English enter slave trade

CIVIL WAR

July 2, 1644

When should Christians rebel?

In 1642, the Puritans of England thought the time had come. Charles I had been king of England since 1625. Charles, as head of the Church of England, supported the High Church Party within the church, with its tendencies toward Roman Catholicism, and sought to crush his Puritan opposition.

Earlier, in 1637, Charles set up his own downfall by ineptly handling the Scottish Church. Having declared himself the head of the Church of Scotland, Charles imposed a book of prayer on the Scottish Church that was more Roman Catholic than the one used by the Church of England. The Scots responded by signing the National covenant in 1638, which made the Scottish Church officially Presbyterian. The following year they revolted against Charles. Needing funds in 1640, Charles was forced to convene Parliament for the first time in eleven years to raise money to fight Scotland. Unfortunately for Charles, most of the members of the House of Commons were Puritans.

Charles's fatal blunder came in 1642, when he attempted to arrest five leaders of Parliament for treason. The result was civil war. Charles I had the support of the Anglican clergy and the nobility, while Parliament had the support of the Puritans and the merchant class.

The crucial battle of the civil war came in 1644. Oliver Cromwell, a godly Puritan, became the leading general of the Parliamentary army. In early summer he began a siege of the Royalist city of York. From his headquarters in Oxford, Charles I ordered his son Prince Rupert, with his army of twenty thousand, to go to York's relief. When Rupert arrived, the Parliamentary army retreated a few miles southwest to Marston Moor. On July 2, 1644, Prince Rupert, not content simply to relieve York, attacked the Parliamentary army as they were about to move south. Initially, the Royalists routed the right wing of the Parliamentary army. But on the left, Cromwell's cavalry defeated Rupert's cavalry and followed them in hot pursuit. When the rout was complete, they turned back to aid the Parliamentarian infantry. The result was a total victory for Cromwell with the Royal army in flight. The Battle of Marston Moor spelled doom for the Royalists. The king lost his army, and the queen escaped to France.

The Puritans' attitude in the civil war can be sensed in a letter that Cromwell wrote three days after the battle:

> Truly England and the Church of God hath had a great favor from the Lord, in this great victory given unto us, such as the like never was since this War began. It had all the evidences of an absolute victory obtained by the Lord's blessing upon the Godly Party principally. We never charged but we routed the enemy.... The particulars I cannot relate now; but I believe, of twenty thousand the Prince hath not four thousand left. Give glory, all glory, to God.

of Jean Du Vergier (1581–1643), Jansenism, as the philosophy came to be known, birthed a significant reform movement in the Roman Catholic Church.

1642 ✛ ENGLISH CIVIL WAR BEGINS

The English Civil War (1642–1648) pitted the monarchy under King Charles I (1600–1649) against Parliament in a struggle that culminated in the execution of the king in 1649 and the temporary establishment of a republican commonwealth in England. King Charles I, a staunch Anglican, believed that he had a divine right to sovereign rule. Parliament, composed largely of Puritans from society's gentry, merchant, and artisan classes, sought political, financial, and religious freedom from undue control by the Crown. In late 1641, some members of Parliament issued a Grand Remonstrance decrying Charles's reign. But this radical action drove many to the royalist side. In the months that followed, two opposing armies were raised in England. Puritans from the House of Commons gathered in southern England to challenge Charles and his group of lords in the north. On August 22, 1642, King Charles declared war on Parliament. Parliament was ultimately victorious, and Charles I was executed.

1643 ✛ SOLEMN LEAGUE AND COVENANT IS SIGNED

The English Civil War was well underway by 1643. That year the largely Puritan army of Parliament, in its conflict with the forces of King Charles I (1600–1649), sought help from the powerful army of Scotland. Signing the Solemn League and covenant was the price Parliament agreed to pay for Scotland's aid. Scotland was a stronghold of Presbyterianism, not of the Anglican Church. The Solemn League guaranteed the rights of the Presbyterian Church in Scotland and provided for the eventual reformation of English and Irish churches as well. In exchange, Scotland promised allegiance to both England's Parliament and to the Crown. King Charles II (1630–1685) signed the League and covenant in 1650 to enlist the support of the Scots to regain his throne.

1646 ✛ WESTMINSTER CONFESSION IS COMPLETED

In 1643, England was in its second year of civil war. The Puritans' desire to bring the Church of England into conformity with the Reformed churches abroad was a key issue. Scotland's staunch Calvinists, also under Anglican rule, wanted a voice in the reform as well. Parliament called an assembly to meet at Westminster to formulate a creed acceptable to English and Scottish churches. One hundred and twenty-one Puritan and Calvinist delegates met for three years. Doctrinal questions were resolved fairly quickly, following the tenets of orthodox Calvinism. Church and state issues took longer. The resulting Westminster Confession of Faith was finished in 1646. It prevailed in England for the next decade during the Commonwealth period and became the standard for the Presbyterian Church of Scotland. The Westminster Assembly was the greatest gathering of theologians of all time, and the Westminster Confession is still the most influential document of the Reformed faith.

1647 ✝ GEORGE FOX BEGINS TO PREACH

George Fox (1624–1691) had no formal education when he began preaching in England in 1647. A three-year quest for spiritual enlightenment resulted in Fox shunning church attendance, the sacraments, and ordained clergy. Instead, Fox believed that true spirituality came from God speaking directly to the human soul through the Holy Spirit. He stressed the priesthood of all believers (including women preachers), pacifism, and a simple lifestyle. Calling his followers "Friends of the Truth," Fox traveled extensively in Holland, Ireland, the West Indies, and North America, establishing local Friends congregations. Fox's teachings were often at odds with the Church of England, and he spent nearly six years in prison. On trial in 1650, Fox urged the judge to "tremble at the word of the Lord." The judge retorted by labeling Fox's Friends "Quakers," the name by which the sect has been known ever since.

THE AGE OF REASON AND REVIVAL

1648–1789

Novel schools of thought filled the seventeenth century. None was more powerful than Reason itself. It asked, "Who needs God? Man can make it on his own." Christians screamed their objections, but the idea spread until secularism filled the public life of Western societies. God remained, but only as a matter of personal choice.

Christians no longer could appeal to the arm of power to suppress such heresies. So, many of them turned instead to the way of the apostles: prayer and preaching. The result was a series of evangelical revivals, chiefly Pietism, Methodism, and the Great Awakening. Through preaching and personal conversions, evangelicals tried to restore God to public life.

BRUCE L. SHELLEY

1648 ✝ CAMBRIDGE PLATFORM HELPS LAY THE FOUNDATION FOR DEMOCRACY

In 1646, six years after the founding of the Massachusetts Bay Colony, the Colony's General Court authorized a synod of Puritan leaders to meet in Cambridge. The synod's goal was to develop statements on doctrine and polity that would distinguish Puritan life from that of other Protestant groups in New England. An epidemic delayed completion of the resulting document, known as the Cambridge Platform, until 1648. Most of its Reformed doctrinal statements were not unique to Puritanism, but the Platform's provisions for church governance through pastors, ruling elders, and deacons in autonomous congregations were a first for New England and laid the foundations for American democracy.

1648 ✝ ✡ CHMIELNICKI MASSACRES TARGET JEWS

In 1648, the Cossacks of the eastern Ukraine, along with Ukrainian peasants and Tatars from Crimea, were led by Bogdan Chmielnicki (1595–1657) in a revolt against their Polish rulers. Polish nobles, Catholic priests, and Jews were murdered in large numbers during the Chmielnicki Massacres. The Ukrainians, who were Orthodox Christians opposing the Catholic Church, targeted the Catholic priests; the peasants targeted the Jews, because the Jews collected taxes and often controlled the nobles' property where the peasants were enslaved. Some Jews made a public conversion to Christianity to save their lives, but others committed suicide. Thousands of Jews died in the massacres, which lasted until 1655.

1653 ✝ CROMWELL IS NAMED LORD PROTECTOR

Oliver Cromwell (1599–1658) began his political career in the House of Commons in 1628, at a time of great conflict in England. Cromwell distinguished himself as a military commander of the parliamentary army in the English Civil War opposing King Charles I (1600–1649), and later, Charles II (1630–1685). After forcing Charles II into exile, Cromwell, then commander in chief of the army, was named lord protector or titular head of state of England in 1653, in lieu of a king. After decades of conflict, England enjoyed relative

1649	1665	1675	1712
England becomes a Commonwealth	Isaac Newton develops theory of gravity	Speed of light calculated	Steam engine invented in England

peace under Cromwell's democratic parliamentary form of government, also known as the Commonwealth. Under Cromwell, England began diplomatic relations with other countries and rose to world-power status due to its supreme naval force. Cromwell, a Puritan, extended religious toleration to Quakers and Jews, and to a lesser extent, to Roman Catholics and Anglicans. He ruled as lord protector until his death in 1658.

1654 ✛ PASCAL IS CONVERTED

Blaise Pascal (1623–1662) was a French mathematician and physicist. He invented the first mechanical calculating machine, discovered the theory of probability, and articulated the principles of physics known as Pascal's Law, which is the foundation of modern hydraulics. Home-schooled by his father, Pascal learned languages, geometry, and physics at an early age. Because of his father's encouragement to learn as much as he could by observation and discovery, Pascal not only discovered truths in science and mathematics, but began to study the truth in Scripture as well. When he died, documents dated November 23, 1654, were found stitched inside his jacket. The handwriting was Pascal's, and it revealed his personal testimony of his conversion to Christ. After his death, *Pensées*—Pascal's defense of Christian faith—was published.

1654 ✡ FIRST PERMANENT JEWISH SETTLER ARRIVES IN WHAT IS NOW THE UNITED STATES

Jacob Barsimson was the first permanent Jewish settler in what became the United States. He came from Holland as part of a group sent by the Dutch West India Company to settle New Amsterdam, now New York City. He arrived on August 22, 1654, a month ahead of a group of Jews who emigrated from Brazil to America. Upon his arrival he was allotted a hut in the forest outside the settlement. Barsimson arrived a poor man, but over the years he prospered. He was the first Jewish citizen, a member of America's first Jewish congregation, and was laid to rest in America's first Jewish cemetery. By the time of the American Revolution (1775–1783) about two thousand Jews lived in the United States.

1757	1770s	1776–81	1789
British rule begins in India	Industrial Revolution begins in England	American Revolution	French Revolution begins

1654 ✡ FIRST GROUP OF JEWS ARRIVES IN NEW YORK

After the Dutch lost their settlement in Brazil to Portuguese forces, twenty-three Jews who had left Dutch Brazil in search of a safe haven arrived in New Amsterdam (present-day New York City) in 1654. As a result, when the later great migration of Jews from Eastern Europe to the United States occurred, a Jewish settlement awaited them. By 2000, there were more than 5.5 million Jews living in the United States.

1655 ✡ MENASSEH BEN ISRAEL GOES TO LONDON

Nearly four hundred years after their expulsion from England in 1290, Jews were allowed to return. The change was due in large measure to the efforts of Menasseh ben Israel (1604–1657), a rabbi in Amsterdam. After submitting a formal request to the English Parliament, he traveled to England in 1655 to argue in person the case for allowing Jews to return to England and to be able to maintain their religious practices. His presentation inspired Cromwell (1599–1658), the lord protector of England, to endorse unofficially the presence of Jews in England. As a result, a small Jewish community was established in London. Believing that England would benefit from the presence of Jews, King Charles II (1630–1685) officially approved of allowing Jews to live in Britain. By the close of the seventeenth century, Jews were accepted into English society.

1656 ✡ SPINOZA IS EXCOMMUNICATED

Born to Jewish parents in Amsterdam, the Netherlands, Benedict de Spinoza (1632–1677), an optical lens grinder by trade, became one of the foremost Rationalist philosophers of his day. Rationalists replaced faith in divine revelation with the belief that the reasoning power of the human mind was the only true source of knowledge and enlightenment. Spinoza reinterpreted God's creativity as purely natural activity. For example, Spinoza interpreted the Bible as being the product of its human authors' minds. Unorthodox views like this one won Spinoza censure from Protestants, Catholics, and his own synagogue, which excommunicated him in 1656. Spinoza's written work was significant in the popularization of Rationalism.

1649	1665	1675	1712
England becomes a Commonwealth	Isaac Newton develops theory of gravity	Speed of light calculated	Steam engine invented in England

1658 ✛ CONGREGATIONALISTS WRITE THE SAVOY DECLARATION

In 1658, about two hundred representatives from English Congregational and Independent churches met at the Savoy Palace in London to draw up the first English Congregational statement of doctrine and practice. In a relatively short time, the representatives came to a unanimous decision as to the contents. Very similar to the Westminster Confession except for the sections on church government, the declaration became the primary doctrinal statement for the Congregationalists of New England. The church polity section granted congregations complete autonomy under the headship of Jesus.

1660 ✛ JOHN OWEN IS EJECTED FROM CHRIST CHURCH

John Owen (1616–1683) studied classics and theology at Queen's College, Oxford. Although a Presbyterian, Owen was influenced by the writings of John Cotton and became convinced that the Congregational form of church government was more biblical. Serving from 1651 to 1660 as dean of Christ Church, Oxford, Owen significantly influenced the religious, political, and academic developments in England. Owen became the chief architect of the Cromwellian State Church, although he eventually opposed Cromwell (1599–1658) as lord protector. When the monarchy was reestablished in 1660, Owen was ejected from his post at Christ Church. For the next twenty-three years he was influential as a leader of Protestant nonconformity. He spent his time preaching and writing in England, declining offers to minister in Boston and to serve as the president of Harvard College.

1661 ✛ CLARENDON CODE ENFORCES THE CHURCH OF ENGLAND'S DOCTRINES

The Clarendon Code was a series of onerous statutes passed by the English Parliament beginning in 1661 to remove everyone not completely committed to the Church of England's doctrines from government or the ministry of the church. The Act of Uniformity (1662) required all ministers to receive Episcopal ordination if they had not been so ordained. The Five Mile Act (1665) forbade nonconforming ministers from coming within five miles of any town or borough. As a result of the Clarendon Code, two thousand pastors lost their churches.

1757	1770s	1776–81	1789
British rule begins in India	Industrial Revolution begins in England	American Revolution	French Revolution begins

1662 ✝ ACT OF UNIFORMITY SPAWNS DISSENTING ACADEMIES

The Dissenting Academies of England arose in response to the Act of Uniformity of 1662. They were established by English Nonconformist pastors to provide an alternative to the universities for young men who wished to be trained for the ministry. The first of these academies was probably established by Jarvis Bryan of Coventry sometime after 1663. The training that these academies offered in the new sciences often was superior to that of the traditional universities. The need for these academies ended in the nineteenth century as Nonconformists were allowed once again to attend the universities.

1662 ✝ HALF-WAY COVENANT EXPANDS CHURCH MEMBERSHIP IN MASSACHUSETTS

Because so many Puritan children in Massachusetts were reaching adulthood unconverted and therefore ineligible for church membership, the Massachusetts Synod of 1662 adopted the Half-way covenant. It allowed for baptized adults who professed faith and lived uprightly, but who had had no conversion experience, to be accepted as church members. Their children were recognized as "half-way" members and could not take Communion or participate in church elections. In practice, the Half-way covenant opened the doors of church membership to the whole community and was the catalyst for the spiritual decline of New England Congregationalism.

1665 ✡ SHABBETAI ZEVI PROCLAIMS HIMSELF MESSIAH

In 1665, Shabbetai Zevi (1626–1676), a Polish Jew who practiced a form of Jewish mysticism known as *kabbalah,* claimed to be the deliverer of the Jews. He became convinced he was the Chosen One after rumor had spread among Eastern European Jews that their Messiah would appear in 1648. Though denounced as a heretic for speaking God's name aloud (in Jewish tradition God's true name is considered unutterable), Zevi received homage from many Jews throughout Europe and the Middle East, including serious attention from rabbis and educated Jews. In a surprising turn, Zevi was imprisoned while attempting to overthrow a Turkish ruler, and when faced with execution or conversion, he became a Muslim. The shock hit Jewish communities with force, and many refused to believe he had rejected Judaism. To this day, the Turkish group

1649	1665	1675	1712
England becomes a Commonwealth	Isaac Newton develops theory of gravity	Speed of light calculated	Steam engine invented in England

Dönmeh secretly remains Jewish awaiting the return of Zevi, while publicly practicing Islam.

1667 ✝ MILTON WRITES PARADISE LOST

John Milton (1608–1674) felt a call to serve God from the time he entered school in England at age seven. He spent the next fifteen years acquiring a remarkable education in England and Italy. By the time he graduated, Milton could speak or read seven languages. He sided with the Parliamentarians in England's Civil War, earning him a post in Cromwell's Commonwealth government. By 1655, Milton was totally blind. Three years later, Cromwell (1599–1658) died. When Charles II (1630–1685) returned in 1660 to reestablish the monarchy, Milton went into hiding for fear of his life. Working from memory and aided by people who read and took dictation for him, Milton devoted his final years to writing poetry. *Paradise Lost,* an epic poem on the creation and fall of man, was published in 1667 and became Milton's defining work.

1669 ✝ REMBRANDT COMPLETES THE RETURN OF THE PRODIGAL SON

Rembrandt van Rijn (1606–1669) produced more than twenty-three hundred known works of art. Born into a prosperous family in Leyden, the Netherlands, Rembrandt began studying art at age fourteen and first attained success as a portrait painter. Rembrandt's personal life was tumultuous, with bankruptcy, the death of his only son, and marriages resulting in censure from the strongly Calvinistic society in Amsterdam. The vast majority of his religious paintings, intimate in detail and size, were intended for private contemplation rather than for public display. By contrast, Rembrandt's last painting, *The Return of the Prodigal Son,* was almost nine by seven feet. In it, a repentant son kneels at the feet of his father, who leans over him with outstretched arms. It was finished in 1669, and many scholars consider it Rembrandt's last testimony. He died the same year.

1675 ✝ SPENER'S PIA DESIDERIA CHALLENGES BELIEVERS

Philipp Jakob Spener (1635–1705) was born in Germany at the height of the Thirty Years' War. He grew up in the Lutheran Church, which by this time had become dry and formal. As a student in Geneva, Switzerland, Spener was exposed

1757	1770s	1776–81	1789
British rule begins in India	Industrial Revolution begins in England	American Revolution	French Revolution begins

to Reformed theology. The Reformed doctrines of repentance and regeneration revitalized Lutheranism for Spener, who emerged as a leader of the Pietist movement in Germany. His best-known work, *Pia Desideria,* or "Pious Desires," was published in 1675. In it Spener challenged believers to seek an active faith rooted in personal study of the Bible and manifested in acts of love. As a result, Spener became a controversial figure in the church. But it was his emphasis on practical spirituality that eventually revitalized the German Lutheran Church.

1678 ✦ JOHN BUNYAN PUBLISHES THE PILGRIM'S PROGRESS

With the restoration of England's King Charles II (r. 1660–1685) to the throne in 1660, a decade of religious toleration in England came to an end. Puritans who conscientiously objected to the rites of the Church of England faced persecution and imprisonment. Among them was a Bedford tinker turned preacher named John Bunyan (1628–1688). Bunyan was born into a modest country home and received little formal education. Following his conversion, Bunyan continued to support his family by mending pots and pans while preaching occasionally in his home church in Bedford, England. He was arrested in 1660 for preaching and spent most of the next twelve years in jail. During his imprisonment, Bunyan wrote *The Pilgrim's Progress*. First published in 1678, Bunyan's allegory of the Christian life has remained in print for more than three centuries and has been translated into more than two hundred languages.

1680 ✦ JOACHIM NEANDER DIES

A student of literature and music, Joachim Neander (1650–1680) was born in Bremen, Germany, and led a wild and careless life. After a miraculous escape from death, Neander became a Christian and joined the Lutheran Church. At age twenty-four he became the headmaster of a Reformed grammar school in Düsseldorf. A few years later, Neander was suspended. Rather than protest the circumstances, he returned to Bremen. That summer, Neander lived in a cave overlooking the Rhine River, where he began writing poetry and hymns. He died, probably of the plague, three years later at the age of thirty. Sixty of Neander's hymns were published in 1680, the year of his death. Among them was "Praise to the Lord, the Almighty, the King of Creation." Neander is considered the first great poet of the German Reformation.

1649	1665	1675	1712
England becomes a Commonwealth	Isaac Newton develops theory of gravity	Speed of light calculated	Steam engine invented in England

A TINKER'S PILGRIMAGE

February 18, 1678

For a century after it was first published, one book's popularity was exceeded only by that of the Bible. Yet its author was a tinker—a mender of pots and pans.

John Bunyan seems an unlikely candidate to have written *any* book. Born in Bedford, England, in about 1628, he received little formal education. But he was skilled with his hands and served as an apprentice to his father, a tinker. Bunyan owned no books until he was married, but his wife's dowry consisted of two Puritan classics. She was a Christian, but Bunyan still was an unbeliever.

While working as a tinker, Bunyan often overheard a group of women discussing the Bible. He later wrote, "I thought they spoke as if joy did make them speak.... They were to me as if they had found a new world." Irresistibly drawn by their conversations, one day he marveled "at a very great softness and tenderness of heart, which caused me to fall under the conviction of what by Scripture they asserted." Shortly thereafter he experienced their joy when he put his trust in the Lord Jesus as his Savior.

Bunyan's path after his conversion, however, was neither smooth nor straight. He struggled with his daughter's blindness, poverty, his wife's death, and his desire to preach the gospel when it was forbidden by law. In 1660, remarried and the father of six, John Bunyan was imprisoned for preaching without a license. He was denied a license because he had little education and disagreed with the Church of England.

Intermittently in and out of prison for twelve years, he made shoelaces in his cell to support his family and spent many hours writing. His manuscript began, "As I was walking in the wilderness of this world . . . I dreamed, and behold I saw a man clothed with rags, a book in his hand, and a great burden upon his back. I looked, and saw him open the book and read therein, and as he read, he wept and trembled . . . and broke out with a lamentable cry saying, 'What shall I do to be saved?'" The manuscript, titled *The Pilgrim's Progress*, told the story of Pilgrim's quest to answer that question.

First licensed for print on February 18, 1678, *The Pilgrim's Progress* is the best known of Bunyan's fifty-eight books. It remains in print three hundred years later and has been translated into more than two hundred languages.

Bunyan died ten years later. In the words of *The Pilgrim's Progress*, "Now at the end of this valley was another, called the Valley of the Shadow of Death, and Christian must needs go through it, because the way to the Celestial City lay in the midst of it."

1680 ✝ RICHARD CAMERON DELIVERS THE SANQUHAR DECLARATION

King Charles II (1630–1685) of England's oath in 1650 to establish Presbyterianism throughout his realm won him the Scottish crown. But he later revealed his insincerity when he reestablished the Anglican Church in Scotland in 1662. Opposition quietly simmered beneath the surface until 1680, when covenanter Richard Cameron (1648–1680) rode into the Scottish city of Sanquhar and delivered what became known as the Sanquhar Declaration. The declaration rejected Charles II as king and declared war on him as a tyrant and as the chief persecutor of the covenanters. It also rejected his brother, the Duke of York, as heir apparent because he was Roman Catholic. Although initially regarded as a futile protest by a small minority, within nine years the declaration became Britain's position.

1682 ✝ PENN FOUNDS PENNSYLVANIA

William Penn (1644–1718) was born in London and was the son of an admiral in the Royal Navy who had captured Jamaica for England. After a godless youth, Penn became a member of the Society of Friends, or Quakers, in 1666. Two years later, Penn was imprisoned for speaking out against the Church of England. After his release he grew increasingly discouraged with England's persecution of those who dissented from the views of the state church. King Charles II (1630–1685) owed Penn's father a debt, and in 1681, Penn persuaded the king to cancel it in exchange for a huge land grant west of the colonies in New England. In 1682, Penn laid out the city of Philadelphia on his newly gained land and published the "Frame of Government" for Pennsylvania, which allowed unprecedented religious freedom for anyone who believed in God. Pennsylvania was the first seat of true religious toleration in America.

1685 ✝ EDICT OF NANTES IS REVOKED

After nearly forty years of war in France between the Catholics and Protestants (called Huguenots), King Henry IV (1553–1610) of France brought peace by issuing the Edict of Nantes in 1598. Legally recognizing Protestants' rights, the edict granted the Huguenots relative religious freedom. However, the Catholic majority continued to fight the Huguenots in many French towns. In 1685,

1649	1665	1675	1712
England becomes a Commonwealth	Isaac Newton develops theory of gravity	Speed of light calculated	Steam engine invented in England

THE EXTINGUISHING OF PROTESTANTISM IN FRANCE

October 18, 1685

Why is France today considered a mission field?

The Wars of Religion began in France in 1562, between the Roman Catholics and the French Protestants called Huguenots. The Huguenots were led by the family of Henry of Navarre, a minor kingdom including a small portion of southern France and the present Spanish province of Navarre. Henry inherited the throne of Navarre from his staunchly Calvinistic mother. When his cousin King Henry III of France died in 1589, he became heir to France's throne. His Calvinism made him an unacceptable candidate in Catholic France until he embraced Catholicism in 1593. He was then crowned King Henry IV.

Once king, however, he did not forget his Huguenot roots, and in 1598, he issued the Edict of Nantes. This agreement gave the Huguenots freedom of religion in certain areas of the country. It provided the Huguenots with a state subsidy for their troops and pastors and allowed them to retain control of approximately two hundred towns. The Edict of Nantes was historically unique in that it was the first time freedom was granted to two religions to exist in a nation side by side.

By the late 1600s, Henry IV's grandson Louis XIV was king of France. But Louis XIV shared none of his grandfather's empathy for the Huguenots, and on October 18, 1685, he revoked the Edict of Nantes. All Huguenot worship and education were forbidden, and all Huguenot churches were either destroyed or turned into Catholic churches. Huguenot clergy were given fourteen days to leave France, but the remaining Huguenots were forbidden to emigrate. All children within France were to be baptized by a Catholic priest and raised as Catholics, and Huguenots were allowed to remain in only a few specified towns.

Mounted soldiers were housed in the homes of Huguenots. The troops were given license to do anything they pleased short of murder. Obstinate Huguenot men were imprisoned. The women sometimes fared better as they were sent to convents where they often received unexpectedly sympathetic treatment from the nuns.

Of the 1.5 million Huguenots living in France in 1660, over the next decades four hundred thousand risked their lives by escaping across the guarded borders. Geneva, a city of sixteen thousand, welcomed four thousand Huguenots. An entire quarter of London was soon populated with French workers. The elector of Brandenburg gave such a friendly reception to Huguenots that over a fifth of Berlin was French by 1697. Holland welcomed thousands and gave them citizenship. Many Huguenots fled to South Carolina and to the other colonies as well.

At the height of the Reformation nearly half of France's population was Huguenot. But as a result of the revocation of the Edict of Nantes and the intense persecution that followed, today less than one percent of the French share the faith of the Huguenots, making France a mission field for the gospel.

EVEN THE WIND AND WAVES OBEY HIM

> November 5, 1688

The God who controls the winds controls the nations.

The 1660s through the 1680s were tough times for God's people in England and Scotland. After the ascendancy of the Puritans to political power during the English civil wars of the 1640s and the execution of King Charles I, Oliver Cromwell, a Puritan Independent, set up a commonwealth with himself as its head. Following his death in 1658, his son Richard succeeded him for one year and then resigned. During the Cromwells' rule, the Puritans experienced their peak of political power and enjoyed religious freedom.

The Presbyterians controlling Parliament were no fans of the Cromwells. Therefore, in 1660, Parliament invited Charles II, the second son of Charles I, to the throne. They were influenced by the fact that ten years earlier Charles II had become a Presbyterian in order to gain Scottish support for his recovery of the throne. But Charles II turned out to be no friend of God's people. Under the Act of Uniformity of 1662, all ministers were given a deadline by which they were required to receive Episcopal ordination. This resulted in the "Great Ejection," in which about two thousand Presbyterian, Independent, and Baptist pastors were forced from their churches. The Five Mile Act of 1665 forbade them from coming within five miles of any British town.

On his deathbed in 1685, Charles II publicly acknowledged his conversion to Roman Catholicism, which he had kept secret for years. This explained his animosity toward the Presbyterians who had brought him to the throne.

Charles II was succeeded by James II, another Roman Catholic. James II intensified the persecution of the Scottish covenanters who resisted the Episcopal government being forced upon the Church of Scotland. Many lost their lives. Since James II had pushed for a Catholic succession, the birth of his son brought the issue to a crisis. His daughter Mary had married William of Orange, who was raised as a follower of John Calvin and had become head of state of the Netherlands. William also had strong claims to the throne of England. The thought of James's Catholic son as heir to the throne was too much for the Protestant nobles of England and they invited William and Mary to take the throne.

On November 1, 1688, William set out with his navy across the English Channel to invade England. The wind was so strong that it kept many of the English ships imprisoned in the Thames River, unable to attack William. The sight of William's fleet sailing along the English coast was a stirring spectacle to the beleaguered Protestants of England. On November 5, 1688, William's fleet landed and William of Orange and his troops began what became known as the Glorious Revolution.

James II fled to France. The next month, as the Protestants of England celebrated their first Christmas in years worshiping as they wished, James was attending Mass in France.

God used the wind to keep England a Protestant nation.

eighty-seven years later, King Louis XIV (1638–1715) revoked the edict under pressure from the Catholic Church. Renewed persecution forced many Huguenots to flee to Germany, England, and the Netherlands.

1687 ✛ NEWTON PUBLISHES PRINCIPIA MATHEMATICA

Sir Isaac Newton (1642–1727) was educated at Trinity College in Cambridge, England, and became a professor of mathematics and physics at Cambridge University. Newton, an Anglican, was an ardent Bible student and was active in Bible distribution, but he hid the fact that he did not believe in the deity of Christ. In 1687, Newton published his discoveries about the mechanics of earth and space in his *Philosophiae Naturalis Principia Mathematica*, or "Mathematical Principles of Natural Philosophy." The *Principia* is considered a landmark in the history of science. In it, Newton postulated the theory of universal gravitation, demonstrating how it explained both the behavior of falling bodies on the earth, and the motions of planets and other bodies in space.

1688 ✛ ENGLAND'S GLORIOUS REVOLUTION BEGINS

James II (1633–1701), a Roman Catholic, reigned as king of England from 1685 to 1688. In June 1688, when his wife gave birth to a son who would be heir to the throne, the nobles of England, Ireland, and Scotland determined that they could not tolerate another Catholic king. Instead they pledged their support to William of Orange (1650–1702). William, a Protestant who followed the teachings of John Calvin (1509–1564), left his kingdom in the Netherlands on November 1, 1688. Crossing the English Channel with his navy, William was assisted by strong winds that kept the English army from setting sail to attack his fleet. Arriving in England on November 5, 1688, William of Orange and his army were victorious in what we now know as the Glorious Revolution. James II fled to France.

1689 ✛ THE BILL OF RIGHTS AND THE TOLERATION ACT ARE CODIFIED IN ENGLAND

In 1689, as one of his first acts as king of England, William of Orange (1650-1702) codified in twin acts many of the triumphs won by Puritans and other Protestants in the previous decades of revolution: the Bill of Rights and the

1757	1770s	1776–81	1789
British rule begins in India	Industrial Revolution begins in England	American Revolution	French Revolution begins

Toleration Act. Nonconformists, as those who disagreed with the Church of England were known, were granted relative religious freedom in England. They were allowed to have their own places of worship and to choose their own pastors and teachers.

1692 ✝ WITCH EXECUTIONS END IN SALEM

In 1692, Samuel Parris (1653–1720), the pastor in Salem, Massachusetts, warned his congregation that witches could be anywhere, even in their church. Parris's concern stemmed from the recent experiences of his daughter and several of her teenage friends, who had experienced convulsions, trances, and hallucinations. The witch hunt began at a meeting at the Parris home, and eventually about one hundred and fifty people were accused of witchcraft and arrested. Nineteen were convicted as witches and hanged. The final executions in Salem took place on September 22, 1692, when one man and seven women were hanged on Witches Hill. The following year Parris repented of the part he played in the witch hunts and publicly denounced his behavior in a sermon.

1692 ✝ CHINA LIFTS THE BAN ON CHRISTIANITY

In 1692, Manchu Emperor K'ang Hsi (1654–1722) issued an edict granting toleration to Christians. The edict's effect was to open most of China to Jesuit missionaries, who were soon joined by Dominicans and Franciscans. The first Protestant missionary, Robert Morrison (1782–1834), did not arrive in China until 1807.

1698 ✝ FRANCKE OPENS THE FIRST ORPHANAGE IN HALLE

While teaching Hebrew at the University of Leipzig, Germany, August Hermann Francke (1663–1727) heard Pietist Philipp Jakob Spener (1635–1705) preach. In 1687, Francke was converted and began holding Bible studies for students at the university. These lead to a revival at the school, but Francke was forced to leave because of his evangelical views. In 1692, Francke accepted a professorship at the University of Halle as well as a pastorate at a nearby church. There, led by his deeply held belief that genuine spirituality expresses itself in acts of love, Francke initiated a ministry to the poor. In 1698, he opened the first

1649	1665	1675	1712
England becomes a Commonwealth	Isaac Newton develops theory of gravity	Speed of light calculated	Steam engine invented in England

THE SHAME OF SALEM

September 22, 1692

It became a literal witch hunt.

It all began in 1692, when the young daughter of Samuel Parris, pastor of the church in Salem, Massachusetts, exhibited strange, psychotic symptoms, including violent convulsions and trancelike states. The hysteria soon spread to several other teenage girls within her social sphere.

Parris was at first ashamed and then alarmed by these manifestations in his daughter and her friends. When pressed, the girls blamed witches for their torment. In a sermon, Parris told his parishioners that witches were everywhere, including in their church.

The ensuing witch hunt was organized in a meeting held at the Parris home. Eventually, approximately 150 suspected witches were imprisoned and nineteen were hanged. Most of the victims were either social outcasts or members of families who had opposed the ministry of Samuel Parris. Many were middle-aged women with no male relatives to defend them.

The final executions occurred on the morning of September 22, 1692, on Witches Hill in Salem. Eight New Englanders, including seven women and one man, were hanged.

Gathered at the foot of the scaffold were people representing every age group. Eighty-nine-year-old Simon Bradstreet, recent governor of Massachusetts Bay Colony, as well as the other original Puritans still alive, had left England over a half century earlier to create a Christian commonwealth in the New World. They viewed their own children as unfaithful to their Puritan upbringing and felt their utopia was being judged because of their wayward progeny.

Also present at the gallows was sixty-one-year-old William Stoughton, the judge at the witch trials. His generation watched the execution with resignation. The witches as well as the magistrates who condemned them were all of their age.

Representative of the younger generation was twenty-nine-year-old Cotton Mather, a brilliant young clergyman. Mather himself had been one of those who had examined the witches. He was to become a leading theologian of his day.

Present also at the gallows were the young girls who had been the accusers of the witches. Their shrieking and twitching reminded everyone what the witches had done.

From the last of the original Puritans who had helped create Massachusetts as God's "City on a Hill" to the youngest children who would someday be citizens of the future United States of America, this crowd at the final witch hanging represented a unique moment in American history.

After the executions, the neighboring ministers took action to end the witch trials. A year later Samuel Parris, by then realizing his own responsibility for these shameful events, described his remorse for the executions in a sermon. He acknowledged that the wounds of their victims "accuseth us as the vile actors."

modern orphanage in Halle. But rather than segregate these children from society, Francke established associated schools and job-training programs of such caliber that middle-class and aristocratic children were educated side by side with the poor. As a result, Halle became a center for Pietism in Germany.

1700 ✚ THE ENLIGHTENMENT IS BORN

The Enlightenment was a philosophical movement based on faith in human ability that sought to formulate and defend truth on the basis of reason alone. Eighteenth-century Germany was the birthplace of the Enlightenment, and also where it had its greatest impact. This philosophy led to the widespread rejection of both supernatural revelation and the belief that man is sinful. The movement perceived God as having placed within man a natural theology that led to both morality and immortality.

1700 ✚ PETER THE GREAT PROMOTES MISSIONS IN SIBERIA

Russia began commercial expansion into northern Asia in approximately 1500. But two hundred years passed before the area now known as Siberia came under the political control of Russia. Russian Czar Peter the Great (1672–1725) sought to extend the reach of the Russian Orthodox Church for reasons more political than religious. Yet because of Peter's sponsorship, by 1750, priests and monks carried Orthodox Christianity as far east as the Bering Sea. Church affiliation among many ethnic Russians in Siberia proved to be nominal, but among indigenous people groups, Russian Orthodoxy took root and flourished for centuries.

1701 ✚ YALE COLLEGE IS FOUNDED

In 1701, at the urging of Congregational pastors in the colony, the Connecticut General Assembly adopted "An Act of Liberty to Erect a Collegiate School, wherein Youth may be instructed in the Arts & Sciences who through the Blessing of Almighty God may be fitted for Publick Employment both in Church and Civil State." The Collegiate School opened its doors that same year in the Killingworth, Connecticut home of its first rector, Congregational pastor Abraham Pierson (1645–1707). In 1716, the school was relocated to New Haven, Connecticut, and was renamed Yale to honor Elihu Yale (1649–1721), who had

1649	1665	1675	1712
England becomes a Commonwealth	Isaac Newton develops theory of gravity	Speed of light calculated	Steam engine invented in England

donated 417 books to the school's library. Among early notable students were theologian Jonathan Edwards (1703–1758) and missionary David Brainerd (1718–1747). The college expanded to include graduate programs and became Yale University in 1887.

1704 ✛ POPE CONDEMNS CHINESE RITES

Jesuit monk Matteo Ricci (1552–1610) set the standard for Jesuit relations with China by articulating Christianity to the Chinese in their own terms. Ricci believed that the Chinese worshiped the true God in their own way; consequently, Jesuit missionaries usually tolerated indigenous rites in honor of ancestors and Confucius. The Dominican and Franciscan orders eventually joined the Jesuits in China, and by the late sixteenth century the Jesuits' lenient practices sparked heated debate. Though Jesuit skill with astronomy and mathematics had won the favor of Chinese scholars and officials, the Dominicans argued that their policy of allowing traditional Chinese rites permitted superstition to enter the church. In 1704, Pope Clement XI (1649–1721) issued a decree condemning the Chinese rites. Despite the pope's condemnation, the Jesuit method of accommodation survived as a missionary strategy.

1706 ✛ DANISH-HALLE MISSION IS FOUNDED

In 1706, King Frederick IV (1671–1730) of Denmark founded a mission to the Danish colonies in India. Two of August Francke's (1663–1727) former students in Halle, Germany were the first missionaries, and it became known as the Danish-Halle Mission. The various business endeavors Francke started raised funds for the missionaries and published their letters from India. The Danish-Halle Mission operated for more than 250 years.

1707 ✛ ISAAC WATTS WRITES <u>HYMNS AND SPIRITUAL SONGS</u>

Isaac Watts (1674–1748), born in Southampton, England, served as a pastor in London for most of his life and wrote such well-known hymns as "Joy to the World," "When I Survey the Wondrous Cross," "O God Our Help in Ages Past," and "Jesus Shall Reign." Most of these hymns were first published in 1707 in *Hymns and Spiritual Songs,* a collection unlike any other before it. These

1757	1770s	1776–81	1789
British rule begins in India	Industrial Revolution begins in England	American Revolution	French Revolution begins

hymns broke the English taboo against singing anything other than Psalms in public worship.

1708 ✝ ALEXANDER MACK FOUNDS THE CHURCH OF THE BRETHREN

Alexander Mack (1679–1735) of Schriesheim, Germany, was born to Reformed parents but was drawn to the more radical Pietist movement led by E. C. Hochmann von Hochenau (1670–1721). Persecution of Pietists caused Mack to move to Wittgenstein, Germany, where in 1708, he and seven others started a fellowship that became the Church of the Brethren. Many of their rituals, such as foot washing and the holy kiss following Communion, came directly from Scripture. They also emphasized believer's baptism and practiced triple immersion. Due to continued persecution, the Brethren eventually set out for America. The first group arrived in Pennsylvania in 1719, and the second group, led by Mack, followed in 1729. Mack guided the Brethren until his death.

1708 ✝ THE SAYBROOK PLATFORM IS FORMED

By the start of the eighteenth century the churches of New England were faced with a congregational polity that seemed ineffective for solving disputes and promoting piety within the church. In an effort to curb this decline, the Congregational Church of Connecticut met in Saybrook and formed the Saybrook Platform. Building upon the ideas of Puritan preachers such as Cotton Mather (1663–1728), the Saybrook Platform declared that a board made up of lay and clerical representatives would be responsible for making authoritative judgments for the church, as well as for resolving disputes. This marked an important break with the congregational polity set up by the churches of Massachusetts Bay, moving toward a more Presbyterian model of church governance. The Saybrook Platform became the most important confessional document for the churches of New England.

1717 ✝ ANTI-CHRISTIAN EDICTS ARE FORMED IN CHINA

In the sixteenth and seventeenth centuries, Jesuit missionaries experienced great success in China, with early Manchu emperors graciously welcoming

1649	1665	1675	1712
England becomes a Commonwealth	Isaac Newton develops theory of gravity	Speed of light calculated	Steam engine invented in England

Christianity and allowing missions to be founded throughout the Chinese provinces. Dominican and Franciscan missionaries joined the Jesuits, and by the early 1700s there were at least 250,000 Chinese Roman Catholics. Unfortunately, the disagreement between Jesuits and Dominicans over the role of Chinese rites was very damaging to relations with China. Pope Clement XI (1649–1721) issued a decree in 1704 to end the Chinese rites, but this declaration only served to irritate K'ang Hsi (1654–1722), China's emperor. As a result, Emperor K'ang Hsi banished all missionaries in 1717. Persecution of Christians followed and continues today.

1721 ✝ PETER THE GREAT PUTS THE CHURCH UNDER HIS CONTROL

In 1721, Russian czar Peter the Great (1672–1725) issued a "Spiritual Regulation" and established his own Holy Synod as a means to bring the Russian Orthodox Church under his control. Composed of twelve members nominated by the czar, the synod officially replaced the patriarch, the head of the Russian Orthodox Church in Moscow. The Holy Synod, which became the dominant authority over the church, turned Christian ministers into a police force of sorts, strengthening the state's control of clergy and church members alike. The Russian government controlled the church for nearly two hundred years. Following the Communist Revolution of 1917, the synod was finally abolished and the patriarch temporarily restored.

1722 ✝ ZINZENDORF FOUNDS HERRNHUT

Count Nikolaus Ludwig von Zinzendorf (1700–1760), the founder of the Moravian Church, was born to an Austrian noble family. As a young man he was interested in foreign missions, but was pressured by his family into a government job. In 1722, he invited a group of Moravian Protestant refugees to live on an estate he purchased at Berthelsdorf, outside of Dresden, Germany. Zinzendorf called the newly formed Christian community "Herrnhut." He retired from his Saxon civil service job in 1727 to devote himself full time to the religious colony. Zinzendorf's "heart religion" emphasized a deep mystical, spiritual, and experiential faith that manifested itself in community and worldwide evangelism. The community at Herrnhut was the beginning of the Moravian Church.

1757	1770s	1776–81	1789
British rule begins in India	Industrial Revolution begins in England	American Revolution	French Revolution begins

1726 ✝ REVIVAL COMES TO THE CHURCH OF THEODORUS FRELINGHUYSEN

By the beginning of the eighteenth century in America, the evangelistic fervor that had first been present in New England had passed with the deaths of its founders. Many church members were theologically knowledgeable but remained unconverted. Immigrants were increasingly unchurched. Through the influence of Rationalism, the role of the Word of God was rapidly being displaced by human reason. It was in this setting that revival began through New Jersey pastor Theodorus J. Frelinghuysen (1691–1774). Born in the Netherlands, Frelinghuysen grew up in Dutch Calvinistic pietism. In his late twenties, he felt called to preach among the Dutch Reformed congregations in America and immigrated to New Jersey in 1720. Frelinghuysen was an eloquent preacher who emphasized the need for personal spiritual regeneration. Around 1726, God lit the first sparks of a revival in Frelinghuysen's church that would become known as the Great Awakening.

1726–1760 ✝ THE GREAT AWAKENING REVIVES THE COLONIES

The Great Awakening is the name given to the revivals occurring in the American colonies from 1726 to 1760. The movement was led by the preaching of Jonathan Edwards (1703–1758) and George Whitefield (1714–1770) and reached its peak in 1740. Jonathan Edwards was a pastor first in Northhampton, Massachusetts, and then in Stockbridge, Massachusetts, briefly becoming president of the College of New Jersey (later Princeton University). Whitefield toured the colonies, calling all to repent and believe in Christ. By 1740, evangelical Christianity was firmly established on American soil. The revival birthed numerous universities, including Princeton University, the University of Pennsylvania, Rutgers, Brown, and Dartmouth.

1726 ✝ LOG COLLEGE IS FORERUNNER OF PRINCETON UNIVERSITY

In 1726, William Tennent (1673–1746), a Presbyterian minister in Neshaminy, Pennsylvania, began training his sons and other young men for the ministry. In 1735, the teaching became formalized and Tennent erected a modest structure that was referred to as the "log college." The name stuck, and the men who attended were referred to as the "New Side" Presbyterians, the "Old Side" being

1649	1665	1675	1712
England becomes a Commonwealth	Isaac Newton develops theory of gravity	Speed of light calculated	Steam engine invented in England

THE ANTIDOTE TO DISUNITY

August 13, 1727

It's a familiar story—people couldn't get along.

In 1700, Count Nikolaus Ludwig von Zinzendorf was born in Dresden, Germany, in a Pietist noble family. The Pietists were Lutherans who sought to know Jesus personally and to live a godly life. At the age of six, Zinzendorf committed his life to Jesus. In child-like simplicity he wrote love letters to his Savior and threw them out the windows of the castle. At ten, he was sent to school in Halle, the center of German Pietism.

In 1721, he purchased his grandmother's estate containing the village of Berthelsdorf. Soon thereafter a leader of the Moravians, the spiritual descendants of Jan Hus, came and asked him if oppressed Moravians could take refuge on his estate. Zinzendorf agreed, and in December 1722, the first ten Moravians arrived. They were given a plot of land that was named *Herrnhut*, meaning "The Lord's Watch."

Soon ninety Moravians lived on Herrnhut. Because the Pietist pastor of the Lutheran church in Berthelsdorf shared the Moravians' vision in his preaching, Lutheran Pietists soon became part of Herrnhut, as did Reformed and Anabaptists. By 1727, the population had reached three hundred, but divisions were arising.

Language barriers and squabbles over the church liturgy sprang up between the Moravians and the Lutherans. Zinzendorf, determined not to let Herrnhut destroy itself, moved there himself, going house to house to encourage unity in the community. He organized the people into prayer bands of two or three.

Then on Sunday, August 13, 1727, the Lutheran church pastor gave an early morning address at Herrnhut to prepare them for the Lord's Supper. The people walked to the church in Berthelsdorf feeling united as never before and expectantly awaited the service, which began with the singing of a hymn. The congregation became gripped with such emotion that the sound of weeping nearly drowned out the singing. Zinzendorf led the congregation in a prayer of confession for their earlier broken fellowship. Then they partook of the Lord's Supper together. After the service people who had previously been fighting embraced one another, pledging to love each other from that time on.

The residents of Herrnhut saw that day as their Pentecost. Soon an around-the-clock prayer ministry began at Herrnhut and continued for one hundred years.

The Moravians became the first missionary-sending Protestant church. When Zinzendorf died thirty-three years later, 226 missionaries had been sent out from Herrnhut. One of every sixty of the early Moravians had become a missionary.

The day before he died, Zinzendorf asked a Moravian friend, "Did you ever suppose in the beginning that the Savior would do as we now really see in the various Moravian settlements . . . amongst the heathen? . . . What a formidable caravan from our church already stands around the Lamb."

those who rejected the validity of the Great Awakening. The Log College closed with the death of William Tennent in 1746, but his vision lived on. Later that year, alumni and supporters of the Log College founded the College of New Jersey, which eventually became Princeton University.

1727 ✛ HERRNHUT WITNESSES REVIVAL

In 1727, five years after the founding of the Moravian religious community on the estate of Count Nikolaus Ludwig von Zinzendorf (1700–1760), discord developed between the residents of Herrnhut and the Lutheran Pietists with whom they worshiped. During the summer of 1727, Zinzendorf organized the people into prayer groups to build unity. On Sunday, August 13, as they were singing the first hymn of worship at the Lutheran church, the spirit of revival swept through the service, resulting in weeping, prayers of confession, and heartfelt reconciliation among the worshipers. The residents of Herrnhut saw that day as their Pentecost. The Moravians, as they came to be known, were the first missionary-sending Protestant church.

1728 ✛ ✡ ☾ FIRST TRAINING INSTITUTE FOR EVANGELIZING JEWS AND MUSLIMS

It was not until the Reformation that the church began to take any interest in evangelizing Jews and Muslims. This interest did not become serious until the Moravians and the Pietists emerged. The first Protestant effort to evangelize Jews began through the efforts of three men: Ezra Edzard (1629–1708), J. H. Callenberg (1694–1760), and A. H. Francke (1663–1723). They established the *Institutum Judaicum et Muhammedicum* at Halle in Germany to train missionaries to evangelize Jews and Muslims.

1728 ✛ THE HOLY CLUB BEGINS

The Holy Club was started in 1728, when Oxford University student Charles Wesley (1707–1788) began a small Christian group with two friends. The name of the group came from other students, who teased Wesley and his friends, calling them the "Holy Club" or "Methodists." Later, Charles's brother John (1703–1791) took over leadership of the group, and by 1733,

1649	1665	1675	1712
England becomes a Commonwealth	Isaac Newton develops theory of gravity	Speed of light calculated	Steam engine invented in England

when George Whitefield (1714–1770) joined, there were eight or nine members. The club focused on self-discipline and encouraged its members to maintain pious lives characterized by good works. Unfortunately, their efforts lacked faith in Jesus Christ for salvation, and their religious routines served only to highlight how far they were from perfection. Of the members of the Holy Club, only Whitefield was converted to Christ while still at Oxford.

1729 ✛ BACH WRITES ST. MATTHEW PASSION

Johann Sebastian Bach (1685–1750) was born in Eisenach, Germany. He was a committed orthodox Lutheran his entire life. Bach was a regular church musician by age fifteen, and at twenty-three he became the court organist for the Duke of Weimar. During his lifetime, Bach was better known as an organist than as a composer. Only nine or ten of his compositions were published while he was alive. However, in the mid-nineteenth century, a rediscovery of Bach's work began. Felix Mendelssohn's discovery of Bach's *St. Matthew Passion,* his greatest work, composed in 1729, made Bach known as a composer. Since that time, many have regarded him as the greatest sacred composer in church history. He often wrote on his compositions *I.N.J.,* the Latin initials for "In the name of Jesus."

1732 ✛ FIRST MORAVIAN MISSIONARIES SAIL FOR WEST INDIES

Leonhard Dober (1706–1766) and David Nitschmann (1696–1772) were the first Moravian missionaries to set out from Herrnhut, their headquarters in Saxony, Germany, where Christians from Moravia had taken refuge in the early eighteenth century. After walking to Copenhagen, Dober and Nitschmann set sail for the West Indies on October 8, 1732. Paying their own way, they had no formal support system. Over a fifty-year period, the Moravians preached the gospel throughout the West Indies, and by the time missionaries from other Christian denominations arrived, they had baptized approximately thirteen thousand converts. By the mid-eighteenth century, more than two hundred additional Moravian missions were established around the world in Australia, North and South America, Tibet, Russia, and parts of Africa.

1757	1770s	1776–81	1789
British rule begins in India	Industrial Revolution begins in England	American Revolution	French Revolution begins

1735 ✡ ISRAEL BEN ELIEZER FOUNDS HASIDISM

Largely in reaction to the Jews' primarily intellectual study of the Talmud, Israel ben Eliezer (1700–1760)—known as Israel Baal Shem Tov ("Master of the Good Name")—began teaching a mystical form of Judaism in about 1735 that came to be known as Hasidism. He articulated a spiritual life in which ordinary Jews, not just intellectuals, could participate. Making use of the *kabbalah*, or Jewish mysticism, Hasidism first swept through the Jewish community of the Ukraine, then through Hungary and northern Rumania, attracting as much as half of the Jewish population of these areas. Hasidism included ecstatic worship and was led by charismatic rabbis known as *zaddikim*. Many Jews made pilgrimages to the zaddikim seeking inspiration or a blessing.

1735 ✝ JONATHAN EDWARDS PREACHES DURING THE GREAT AWAKENING

Revival came to the Massachusetts town of Northampton in 1735, through the preaching of Jonathan Edwards (1703–1758). Throughout the fall Edwards preached with passion, attempting to convert the lost members of his church. At the end of December, "the spirit of God began extraordinarily to set in and wonderfully to work amongst us," he later wrote. In a matter of a few days several church members were converted. Eventually people were converted in every home in Northhampton. Jonathan Edwards went on to become one of America's greatest theologians.

1735 ✝ GEORGE WHITEFIELD IS CONVERTED

Educated at Oxford's Pembroke College and a member of the Holy Club along with the Wesley brothers, George Whitefield (1714–1770) became convinced of the necessity of conversion in 1735, and subsequently experienced spiritual rebirth himself. A year later, he was ordained in the Church of England. Traveling to the New World seven times, Whitefield is considered to be the founder of American revivalism and was the leader of the Great Awakening in America. During his six-week tour of New England in 1740, he preached more than 175 times to tens of thousands. In addition to his American tours, he made fourteen visits to Scotland. In his thirty-four-year career, Whitefield delivered more than

1649	1665	1675	1712
England becomes a Commonwealth	Isaac Newton develops theory of gravity	Speed of light calculated	Steam engine invented in England

THE HOLY CLUB

May 5, 1735

It was a religious club that produced mostly poor results.

Charles Wesley and two friends began a Christian small group at Oxford University in 1728. John Wesley, who already had graduated from Oxford, returned the following year as a tutor and assumed its leadership. Oxford students made fun of the group, referring to it as the "Holy Club" or "Methodists." By the time George Whitefield joined the group in 1733, the group included eight or nine dedicated members.

The focus of the Holy Club was on religious self-discipline. They woke up early for lengthy devotions, took Communion each Sunday, fasted every Wednesday and Friday, and observed Saturday as the Sabbath in preparation for the Lord's Day. They were motivated by the belief that they were working for the salvation of their souls. Yet their self-discipline brought them neither happiness nor salvation.

The lifestyle of the Holy Club had a catastrophic effect on the life of William Morgan, one of the founders. He lost his mind and eventually his life in his struggle to achieve self-disciplined perfection.

Whitefield was the first Holy Club member to question their practices. He read a book through which, in his words, "God showed me that I must be born again, or be damned!"

His solution, however, was to try to be born again through further extremes of self-denial. During Lent of 1735, he ate only a little coarse bread with tea. By Holy Week he was so weak he could not study or even walk up a flight of stairs. His grades began to suffer and his tutor wondered if he was going mad. His physician put him in bed where he remained for seven weeks.

Having hit bottom in his efforts to earn his salvation, Whitefield described what happened next:

> God was pleased to remove the heavy load, to enable me to lay hold of his dear Son by a living faith, and by giving me the Spirit of adoption, to seal me, even to the day of everlasting redemption.
>
> O! With what joy—joy unspeakable—even joy that was full of and big with glory, was my soul filled when the weight of sin went off and an abiding sense of the love of God broke in upon my disconsolate soul! Surely it was a day to be had in everlasting remembrance. My joys were like a spring tide and overflowed the banks.

Later he declared, "I knew the place: it may be superstitious, perhaps, but whenever I go to Oxford I cannot help running to the place where Jesus Christ first revealed himself to me, and gave me the new birth."

On May 5, 1735, Whitefield sent a letter to John Wesley, attempting to share what had happened to him. He wrote, "Into his all gracious arms, I blindly throw myself."

It would be three more years before the Wesleys found Jesus' gracious arms.

fifteen thousand sermons to millions of people, and his unrehearsed style of preaching irreversibly affected American evangelistic preaching.

1735 ✦ THE WESLEYS GO TO GEORGIA

Charles (1707–1788) and John Wesley (1703–1791) were born in Epworth, Lincolnshire, England. While studying at Oxford they were involved in the Holy Club, a group started by Charles to promote the practice of Christian duties. John was invited by the Society for the Propagation of the Gospel to be a missionary to the Indians and colonists of Georgia. He went in 1735, accompanied by his brother Charles. However, the mission was unsuccessful, and upon returning to England Wesley wrote, "I went to Georgia to convert Indians; but, oh, who shall convert me?" Though the mission was a failure, it succeeded in introducing the brothers to Moravian Christians whose teachings eventually lead to their conversions.

1738 ✦ JOHN AND CHARLES WESLEY ARE CONVERTED

Despite having been sent as missionaries from England to Georgia, it was not until later that brothers Charles (1707–1788) and John Wesley (1703–1791) were converted to Christ. In 1738, Charles read Martin Luther's (1483–1546) commentary on Galatians for the first time, and as he later wrote, found himself "at peace with God and rejoiced in hope of loving Christ." Charles went on to write 7,270 hymns, becoming known as the "sweet singer of Methodism." On May 24, 1738, three days after Charles's conversion, John's heart too was "strangely warmed" while listening to the reading of Luther's preface to the book of Romans. Of that day he wrote, "Then it pleased God to kindle a fire which I trust shall never be extinguished." This experience made a powerful evangelist out of John, who later became known as the "founder of Methodism."

1739 ✦ REVIVAL BEGINS AT FETTER LANE WATCH NIGHT SERVICE

The Moravian congregation at the Fetter Lane Chapel in London, England, met on New Year's Eve, 1738, for their annual Watch Night service. Following Moravian custom, they held a prayer service and "love feast" as a prelude to the Lord's Supper. About sixty people were in attendance, including George Whitefield (1714–1770), John (1703–1791) and Charles (1707–1788) Wesley, and other former members of the "Holy Club" at Oxford University. Much to the surprise of those

1649	1665	1675	1712
England becomes a Commonwealth	Isaac Newton develops theory of gravity	Speed of light calculated	Steam engine invented in England

A HEART STRANGELY WARMED

May 20, 1738

They were missionaries while still themselves a mission field.

John and Charles Wesley were born in 1703 and 1707 respectively, the fifteenth and eighteenth children of Samuel and Susanna Wesley.

At Oxford they met frequently with George Whitefield and others for Bible study and reflection. John was the leader of their group that was mockingly called the "Holy Club."

In 1735, the Wesleys sailed to America to become missionaries in the colony of Georgia. During the long journey the ship was buffeted by a violent storm, and John was left cowering in fear of death. He was amazed at the sense of peace that he observed among the Moravian Christians aboard the same ship. He was shaken, realizing that they had something he didn't have.

On January 24, 1738, he wrote in his journal, "I went to America to convert the Indians; but O! who shall convert me?"

After a short and unsuccessful time in America, the brothers returned to England where they came under the influence of Peter Boehler, another Moravian. Boehler's teachings on justification by faith, not works, were convincing. The Wesleys began eagerly reading Martin Luther's writings on Galatians and Romans, coming to the realization that their theology had been resting on works, not faith. This doctrine was now clear in their minds, but they had not yet experienced it in their hearts.

On May 20, 1738, the brothers and some friends stayed up all night praying for Charles, who was quite ill. They also were praying that God would open their hearts so they could truly believe and have assurance of salvation. The next day, Charles believed and gave his life to Christ for the first time. "I now found myself at peace with God, and rejoiced in hope of loving Christ."

For three days John wrestled with what happened to his brother. He wanted to believe, but couldn't and became very depressed. Then on May 24, 1738, he wrote in his journal:

In the evening I went very unwillingly to a society in Aldersgate Street, where one was reading Luther's preface to the Epistle to the Romans. About a quarter before nine, while he was describing the change which God works in the heart through faith in Christ, I felt my heart strangely warmed. I felt I did trust in Christ, Christ alone for salvation; and an assurance was given to me that he had taken away my sins, even mine, and saved me from the law of sin and death.

When John went to Charles to tell him the good news, he found Charles up late writing a hymn to celebrate his own conversion. They sang the hymn together.

John and Charles Wesley went on to lead the great Methodist revival that changed English society. Charles wrote almost eight thousand hymns by the time he died in 1788. John preached nonstop until his death in 1791.

in attendance, at about three in the morning they were greatly moved by the Holy Spirit and experienced what Whitefield called "a Pentecostal season indeed." What took place at this small Moravian service began what came to be known in England as the Evangelical Revival. Through Whitefield and the Wesleys, all of England was affected by the Fetter Lane Watch Night Revival.

1739 ✝ WHITEFIELD PREACHES IN THE OPEN AIR

George Whitefield (1714–1770) first preached in the open air at Bristol, England. In 1739, while he took a break from his time in America to raise money for an orphanage, Whitefield's preaching at open-air meetings began to have an astounding impact throughout England. Returning to the American colonies, Whitefield became the leader of the Great Awakening that had begun in 1735 under the preaching of Jonathan Edwards (1703–1758). Whitefield continued the practice of open-air preaching until the end of his life, usually delivering at least twenty sermons a week, traveling great distances to carry his message to millions of people.

1739 ✝ JOHN WESLEY BEGINS ITINERANT PREACHING

Believing his God-given mission was to evangelize Great Britain, in April 1739, John Wesley (1703–1791) set out to preach the gospel. At his friend George Whitefield's (1714–1770) prompting, Wesley preached in the open air for the first time at Kingswood in Bristol, England. As Wesley's evangelical preaching caused many churches to close their doors to him, he realized that open-air preaching was the most effective way for him to reach the masses. Seeing the need to follow up with recent converts, he formed fellowships, which led to the formation of Methodism. In his lifetime, he rode 250,000 miles on horseback, preached 42,000 sermons, and published 233 books. Wesley remained a member of the Church of England until his death.

1741 ✝ JONATHAN EDWARDS PREACHES
"SINNERS IN THE HANDS OF AN ANGRY GOD"

In 1735, the Great Awakening began in New England in the village of Northampton, Massachusetts, under the leadership of Jonathan Edwards.

1649	1665	1675	1712
England becomes a Commonwealth	Isaac Newton develops theory of gravity	Speed of light calculated	Steam engine invented in England

SINNERS IN THE HANDS OF AN ANGRY GOD

July 8, 1741

It was the most famous sermon ever preached in America.

The preacher was Jonathan Edwards, pastor of the Congregational Church in Northampton, Massachusetts, and a future president of Princeton College. The date was Saturday, July 8, 1741, and the place was Enfield, Connecticut, where Edwards had been invited to speak.

Enfield was not a religious place. The Great Awakening had touched surrounding towns, but not Enfield. With curiosity and nonchalance, the crowd entered the meetinghouse to hear Edwards speak.

Then Edwards began. He did not sound like the evangelists of today. He wrote out his sermons word for word and then usually read them. Listening to Edwards was like listening to a lecturer who made his case in an even-tempered, intellectually demanding style in which he tried to develop each step of his argument logically.

The title of Edwards's sermon was "Sinners in the Hands of an Angry God," and his text was Deuteronomy 32:35: "Their foot shall slide in due time" (KJV).

Edwards explained his text:

As he that walks in slippery places is every moment liable to fall, he cannot foresee one moment whether he shall stand or fall the next; and when he does fall, he falls at once without warning: which is also expressed in Psalm 73:18-19. "Surely thou didst set them in slippery places: thou castedst them down into destruction: How are they brought into desolation as in a moment!" . . .

The bow of God's wrath is bent, and the arrow made ready on the string, and justice bends the arrow at your heart, and strains the bow, and it is nothing but the mere pleasure of God, and that of an angry God, without any promise or obligation at all, that keeps the arrow one moment from being made drunk with your blood. Thus all you that have never passed under a great change of heart, by the mighty power of the Spirit of God upon your souls; all you that were never born again, and made new creatures, and raised from being dead in sin, to a state of new, and before altogether unexperienced light and life, are in the hands of an angry God.

As Edwards preached, members of the audience cried out, "What shall I do to be saved? O, I am going to hell!" Some crowded toward the pulpit begging him to stop. The noise was so loud at one point during the sermon that Edwards asked everyone to be quiet so that he could be heard.

He ended the sermon by saying: "Let everyone that is out of Christ now awake and fly from the wrath to come. The wrath of Almighty God is now undoubtedly hanging over a great part of this congregation. Let everyone fly out of Sodom: 'Haste and escape for your lives, look not behind you, escape to the mountain, lest you be consumed.'"

The little town of Enfield was never the same.

When Edwards was invited to speak in Enfield, Connecticut, on July 8, 1741, he faced an indifferent audience as the Awakening had made little impact on the town. The title of his sermon that evening was "Sinners in the Hands of an Angry God." As Edwards preached in his even-tempered, logical style about God's wrath and human sinfulness, the attitude of his audience moved from indifference to fear for their souls. Some began to weep, crying out, "What shall I do to be saved?" Edwards ended his sermon with a call to come to Christ, and the town of Enfield was never the same.

1741 ✟ HANDEL WRITES MESSIAH

George Frideric Handel (1685–1759) was of Lutheran heritage and possessed uncommon musical talent. Handel did not come from a musical family, and his father wanted him to study law. Despite his father's wishes, Handel mastered harpsichord, organ, violin, and oboe by the age of seventeen. He began composing in Hamburg, where German opera was flourishing. Moving to England, Handel wrote approximately forty operas, which were popular among English aristocrats. Eventually he began composing oratorios. His *Messiah,* composed in only three weeks during 1741, tells the story of Christ from prophecy to fulfillment and has been performed more than any other choral work in history. Handel, master of the English oratorio, inspired later composers like Haydn (1732–1809), Beethoven (1770–1827), and Mendelssohn (1809–1847).

1742 ✟ DAVID BRAINERD IS APPOINTED MISSIONARY TO THE INDIANS

Born in Haddam, Connecticut, David Brainerd (1718–1747) experienced a profound conversion at the age of twenty-one. Desiring to go into the ministry, he studied at Yale and was first in his class, but he was expelled for an offhand remark he made that reflected his involvement in the Great Awakening. In November 1742, Brainerd was commissioned as a missionary to the Indians. Serving in Massachusetts, New Jersey, and Pennsylvania, Brainerd saw more than 130 Indians put their faith in Christ within four years. Becoming terminally ill with tuberculosis, Brainerd spent a short while studying at the College of New Jersey and then accepted the invitation to spend his last days at the home of his friend Jonathan Edwards (1703–1758). Following Brainerd's death in October

1649	1665	1675	1712
England becomes a Commonwealth	Isaac Newton develops theory of gravity	Speed of light calculated	Steam engine invented in England

MESSIAH

September 14, 1741

He wrote the world's most beautiful music in an amazingly short period of time.

George Frideric Handel was born in1685. Handel's father was the town surgeon of Giebichenstein, a suburb of Halle, Germany. George was the second child and was baptized as a Lutheran the day after he was born.

When Handel began showing an interest in music, his father, determined that his son be a lawyer, forbade him to have anything to do with music. A sympathetic relative, however, secretly gave young Handel access to a clavichord and Handel taught himself to play.

When Handel was six years old he accompanied his father to the court of a duke to whom his father had been appointed surgeon. While there, Handel went up and played the organ after a Sunday worship service. Hearing the lad play, the duke was so impressed that he urged the father to give his son a formal music education. As a result, Handel was allowed to study under the organist of the Liebfrauenkirche in Halle. By the time he was twelve, Handel had written his first composition and was proficient enough at the organ to serve as his teacher's substitute.

At the age of twenty-seven Handel moved to England, where he spent the rest of his life. But life as a composer and musician was not easy. Finally in 1741, his health began to fail, and he was facing debtor's prison.

Then two events occurred that turned Handel's life around. A friend gave him a libretto for an oratorio on the life of Christ, with the words taken from the Bible. Then three Dublin charities commissioned him to compose a work for a fund-raising benefit.

On August 22, 1741, Handel sat down to begin composing. He became so absorbed in his work that he hardly took time to eat. On September 14, 1741, he finished his composition and named it simply *Messiah*. In just twenty-four days he had written 260 pages of music. Considering the short time involved, it was the greatest feat in the history of musical composition. Later, in describing his experience he alluded to the apostle Paul and said, "Whether I was in the body or out of my body when I wrote it, I know not."

Dublin hosted the premier performance of *Messiah* on April 13, 1742. The king was in attendance at the London premier a year later. As the choir began to sing the "Halleluiah Chorus" the king rose to his feet and the whole audience followed his lead, beginning a tradition that continues to this day.

Messiah was Handel's last public performance, on April 6, 1759. At the end of the concert he fainted by the organ and died just eight days later. He was buried in Westminster Abbey, where his statue shows him holding the manuscript from *Messiah*, opened to "I know That My Redeemer Liveth."

THE TIMES AND SEASONS ARE GOD'S

| November 3, 1745 |

What a difference a year can make.

David Brainerd, a twenty-seven-year-old missionary to the Indians of Crossweeksung, New Jersey, baptized fourteen converts one Sunday in 1745. This was part of what he called "a remarkable work of grace" with which God had blessed his labors among the Native Americans of New Jersey and Pennsylvania.

David Brainerd was born in 1718 in Haddam, Connecticut, and orphaned at the age of fourteen. His plans to farm the land he had inherited changed when he experienced a profound conversion in 1739. That same year he entered Yale at the age of twenty-one, aspiring to the Congregational ministry.

At Yale, he became a leader in the Great Awakening, a revival then sweeping through New England. He was expelled from the university in his third year when he was overheard questioning the salvation of a faculty member. After his expulsion, he continued his studies for the ministry, living with a local minister. Subsequently, he was licensed to preach and ordained as a Presbyterian minister before becoming a missionary to the American Indians of New Jersey and Pennsylvania.

On Sunday, November 3, 1745, Brainerd joyously baptized six adults and eight children, bringing the total to forty-seven baptized believers. One was an eighty-year-old woman. Two were fifty-year-old men who were notorious drunkards before putting their trust in the Lord Jesus. One of the men was a murderer as well. Because of the terrible lives these men had led, Brainerd delayed baptizing them until he saw a radical change in their lives. But changed they were, and Brainerd finally felt at peace about baptizing them. Brainerd wrote in his journal, "Through rich grace, none of them have been left to disgrace their profession of Christianity by any scandalous or unbecoming behavior."

A year later this remarkable work of God among the Indians continued, but David Brainerd's work was coming to a close. Brainerd was dying of tuberculosis at the age of just twenty-eight. He sadly realized that he must return to New England where friends and family could care for him during his last days.

Desperately weak in body on November 3, 1746, Brainerd spent the day bidding farewell to his beloved Indian flock. He visited every family in their home and exhorted each person from God's Word. The tears flowed freely as he left each house. His farewells took most of the day and in the evening he rode off, his mission completed.

A year later, David Brainerd died, at the age of twenty-nine.

1747, Edwards published Brainerd's diary, which became a devotional classic and a source of great inspiration for the cause of cross-cultural missions.

1746 ✝ PRINCETON UNIVERSITY IS FOUNDED

Disappointed with the liberalism of Yale University, the Presbyterian synods of New Jersey and New York decided to found their own college to prepare men for the ministry, building on the foundation of the Log College founded by William Tennent (1673–1746). Specifically, pastors Jonathan Dickenson (1688–1747) and Aaron Burr Sr. (1716–1757) were concerned with Yale's expulsion of David Brainerd (1718–1747) due to his involvement in the Great Awakening. The College of New Jersey, which later became Princeton University, received its charter from the governor of New Jersey in 1746. Classes began in May 1747, with Brainerd as the first official student and Dickinson as the first president. Initially, the college was located in Dickinson's home in Elizabethtown, New Jersey, but he died the same year. Aaron Burr Sr. succeeded Dickinson as president, and under his leadership the students moved to Burr's parsonage in Newark, New Jersey, and then finally to Princeton. Burr was succeeded as president by his father-in-law, Jonathan Edwards (1703–1758).

1748 ✝ JOHN NEWTON IS CONVERTED

Son of a merchant sea captain, John Newton (1725–1807) was forced into the British Royal Navy at age nineteen. Following a failed attempt at escape, Newton was humiliated and flogged. He found work with a slave trader shipping slaves from Africa. On March 21, 1748, a great storm at sea nearly sank his ship in the North Atlantic, and Newton turned to God in faith. He left the sea in 1755, and became curate of Olney in Buckinghamshire, England. Newton is best known for his hymn "Amazing Grace."

1750 ✝ JONATHAN EDWARDS IS DISMISSED FROM HIS CHURCH

On June 22, 1750, the church in Northampton, Massachusetts, voted to dismiss Jonathan Edwards (1703–1758), their pastor of twenty-three years. In spite of great successes during the Great Awakening, Edwards had fallen out of favor with the people over his stand against the open Communion practiced by his

1757	1770s	1776–81	1789
British rule begins in India	Industrial Revolution begins in England	American Revolution	French Revolution begins

grandfather Solomon Stoddard (1643–1729). However, the next summer Edwards was called as pastor to the church in the small frontier village of Stockbridge, Massachusetts. There he was able to devote much of his time to writing. During the next seven years Edwards wrote some of his most influential works, such as *Freedom of the Will, The End for Which God Created the World, The Nature of True Virtue,* and *Original Sin.* God used Edwards's dismissal to enrich his people forever through these books.

1750 ✛ NEW ENGLAND THEOLOGY EVOLVES

Jonathan Edwards (1703–1758) wrote his treatise titled *Freedom of the Will* in defense of the Great Awakening. In order to explain man's accountability for his actions and God's sovereignty over man's will, Edwards argued that God must incline the human will to understand and accept the gift of salvation. The successors of Edwards, who included Jonathan Edwards Jr. (1745–1801), Timothy Dwight (1752–1817), Samuel Hopkins (1721–1803), and Nathaniel Taylor (1786–1858), built on his theology. Later successors sometimes softened Edwards's view of God's sovereignty, and in their thinking, the primary work in salvation shifted from God to man. This subtle dilution of Edwards's theology became known as New England Theology. It controlled Congregational schools from 1750 until the influx of German higher-critical theology in the late nineteenth century.

1750 ✛ INDUSTRIAL REVOLUTION BEGINS

Since the Middle Ages, the Western world had primarily been an agrarian society. However, in the middle part of the eighteenth century, much of the Western world began to manufacture goods primarily through steam power that was fueled by coal instead of by water or wind power. The steam engine invented by James Watt (1736–1819) allowed tasks, once dependent upon man or animal power, to be accomplished much more quickly and efficiently. Soon the steam engine locomotive and steam-powered ship were transporting people farther and more quickly than ever before. Another outcome of the Industrial Revolution was the invention and proliferation of factories. These factories, in spite of often dangerous working conditions, created the necessary means for the development

1649	1665	1675	1712
England becomes a Commonwealth	Isaac Newton develops theory of gravity	Speed of light calculated	Steam engine invented in England

AMAZING GRACE

March 21, 1748

Born in London in 1725, John Newton, a sea captain's son, lost his mother when he was six. However, before she died she prayed that he would become a minister. Newton went to sea with his father at age eleven. After an unsuccessful stint in the Royal Navy, he went to work for a slave trader.

In March 1848, Newton was in a violent storm that changed him forever. He went to bed that night and was awakened by the storm. Within a few minutes the ship was a virtual wreck, filling with water. Working frantically, the crew finally was able to plug the leaks. Exhausted, Newton heard himself say to the captain, "If this will not do, the Lord have mercy upon us." Newton was instantly taken aback by his own words that reflected the first time he had desired God's mercy in years. Then the thought went through his mind, *What mercy can there be for me?*

As the storm continued the next day, March 21, 1748, Newton sadly concluded that there had never been a sinner as wicked as he and that his sins were too great and too many to be forgiven. His journal records the deliverance from that storm and his spiritual deliverance as well: "[This] is a day much to be remembered by me, and I have never suffered it to pass wholly unnoticed since the year 1748. On that day, the Lord sent from on high and delivered me out of the deep waters. . . ."

Later he wrote: "I stood in need of an Almighty Saviour, and such a one I found described in the New Testament. . . . I was no longer an infidel; I heartily renounced my former profaneness, and I had taken up some right notions; was seriously disposed, and sincerely touched with a sense of the undeserved mercy I had received, in being brought safe through so many dangers."

Although he continued sailing and working in the slave trade for a time, Newton studied the Bible, prayed, read Christian books, and finally left the sea behind. In 1764, at age thirty-nine, John Newton began a new life as a minister in the Church of England, later writing his autobiographical hymn, "Amazing Grace."

Throughout his life, he stopped to thank God on his "anniversary." The last entry in his journal was written on March 21, 1805, an anniversary of his deliverance. He wrote simply, "Not well able to write; but I endeavor to observe the return of this day with humiliation, prayer, and praise."

AN INFLUENTIAL LIFE

September 24, 1757

The impact of a life matters more than its length.

Aaron Burr Sr. was born in Connecticut and graduated first in his class at Yale in 1735. He then became pastor of the Presbyterian Church of Newark, New Jersey.

When a student named David Brainerd was expelled from Yale because of his involvement in the Great Awakening, Aaron Burr along with Jonathan Dickinson, pastor of the Presbyterian Church in Elizabethtown, New Jersey, took an active interest in his case. The two pastors were particularly upset when their alma mater refused to readmit Brainerd after his apology for the offhand comments that had caused his expulsion. This action by Yale confirmed the conviction of the Presbyterian Synods of New Jersey and New York that they should found their own college to prepare men for ministry.

The College of New Jersey, which was to become Princeton University, received its charter from the governor of the state in 1746. Aaron Burr was the youngest of the organizing seven trustees.

The college began in May 1747, in Jonathan Dickinson's home in Elizabethtown, New Jersey, with David Brainerd as its first official student. The original students studied in Dickinson's library, attended classes in the parlor, and ate meals in the dining room with the family. Just four and a half months later they would accompany the family to Dickinson's funeral.

Aaron Burr was persuaded then to take charge of the college. The students bid farewell to the grieving Dickinson family and moved six miles to Newark, where they boarded in the town and held their classes at the Burr parsonage. Burr did the teaching with the assistance of one tutor. A year later, Aaron Burr was formally elected the college's second president.

Burr was still a bachelor when he accepted the position. Some years earlier he had met fifteen-year-old Esther Edwards, daughter of Jonathan Edwards. Unable to forget about fair Esther, Burr made a courting visit to the Edwards's home. Esther accepted his declaration of love, and they were married at Burr's church in Newark.

In 1755, Burr resigned the pastorate to devote himself full-time to the college. He supervised the erection of the college's first building in Princeton, New Jersey. In 1756, Burr and the now seventy students and two tutors moved to Princeton into glorious Nassau Hall, the largest stone building in the colonies.

The governor died the following year, and Burr traveled to Elizabethtown to deliver the funeral sermon. Returning to Princeton seriously ill himself, Aaron Burr died on September 24, 1757, at the age of only forty-one.

Burr's father-in-law, Jonathan Edwards, was chosen five days later to follow his son-in-law as the college's next president.

Esther survived her husband by less than a year, succumbing to smallpox at the age of twenty-six. She left two children, four-year-old Sarah and two-year-old Aaron Jr. Sarah later married Connecticut Chief Justice Tapping Reeve, and Aaron Jr. became the third vice president of the United States.

of the middle class. The industrial revolution changed the structure of society in the Western world, providing Christians with both effective tools and challenges.

1759 ✝ VOLTAIRE WRITES <u>CANDIDE</u>

The French philosopher Voltaire (1694–1778) was one of the most articulate spokesmen for the Age of Enlightenment, advocating the use of reason to reevaluate traditional ideas and institutions. Educated by French Jesuits, Voltaire developed a distaste for what he considered to be the superstition and intolerance in the Catholic Church. He then was influenced by the English Deists. Voltaire's most well-known writing, *Candide,* was published in 1759. It is a satirical critique of the common ideas about good and evil. Thirty-nine of his works eventually were banned by the Roman Catholic Church. Voltaire, who worked to ordain tolerance as the distinguishing characteristic of society, epitomized the self-sufficient humanist. His beliefs were widely held among the educated in the 1700s and 1800s.

1759 ✝ EUROPEAN NATIONS BEGIN TO OUTLAW JESUITS

The Society of Jesus, better known as the Jesuits, was founded in Italy in 1540 by Ignatius of Loyola (1491–1556). The brotherhood grew rapidly and spearheaded the Roman Catholic attack on the Reformation. However, they were not popular with absolute monarchs. In 1758, an assassination attempt on the king of Portugal was blamed on the Jesuits, and as a result they were expelled from Portugal in 1759. In 1764, they were suppressed in France and three years later in Spain.

1769 ✝ JUNÍPERO SERRA FOUNDS FIRST OF NINE MISSIONS IN CALIFORNIA

Junípero Serra (1713–1784), a Franciscan missionary to the Indians of Mexico and the California coast, came from the island of Majorca in the Mediterranean. Serra earned a doctorate in theology, but turned away from a more privileged life at the university to establish missions in America. In 1769, Serra entered California with a Spanish army of conquest, but he was the first to defend the lives of the native Indians. Serra's work titled *Representación* describes his expectations for conduct in the missions he established. He spent his life in ministry, traveling be-

1757	1770s	1776–81	1789
British rule begins in India	Industrial Revolution begins in England	American Revolution	French Revolution begins

tween the missions he established, baptizing six thousand and confirming five thousand in his lifetime. San Diego, San Gabriel, San Francisco, San Juan Capistrano, and Santa Clara are among the cities that developed around the missions founded by Serra.

1767 ✡ MOSES MENDELSSOHN BECOMES A DEFENDER OF JUDAISM

The Jewish Enlightenment movement started in Germany with Jewish philosopher Moses Mendelssohn (1729–1786). Committed to the Enlightenment philosophies of the eighteenth century, Mendelssohn was interested in showing that Jewish beliefs constituted an acceptable intellectual view of the world. Among his achievements was a German translation of the Hebrew Bible, which he encouraged all Jews to study. Mendelssohn believed Jews could practice their faith while becoming involved in the cultural and civic duties of the nations where they happened to reside. In 1769, at the height of his career, Mendelssohn held a public debate with a Christian apologist and from that time on became a defender of Judaism in print. He was the grandfather of composer Felix Mendelssohn (1809–1847).

1771 ✝ FRANCIS ASBURY IS SENT TO AMERICA

Francis Asbury (1745–1816) was converted at fourteen in England and began preaching at sixteen. His parents were some of the early followers of John Wesley (1703–1791). In 1771, Asbury was among four men who left England to answer Wesley's call for volunteers to sail to America as missionaries. Once in America he traveled to preach the gospel wherever he could, a commitment that set the standard for the early American Methodist itinerant preachers. When the Revolutionary War broke out, Asbury was the only Methodist missionary to remain in America. Later he was appointed joint superintendent of the Methodists in the United States. By the end of his life, Asbury had ordained more than four thousand preachers, and there were more than 214,000 Methodists in the United States. He is known as the father of American Methodism.

1772 ✡ VILNA RABBIS EXCOMMUNICATE THE HASIDIM

Hasidim, who first appeared in Eastern Europe in the 1730s under the leadership of Israel ben Eliezer (1700–1760), practiced a mystical form of Judaism in

1649	1665	1675	1712
England becomes a Commonwealth	Isaac Newton develops theory of gravity	Speed of light calculated	Steam engine invented in England

THE COWPER BROTHERS

March 10, 1770

They are in heaven together.

John and Ann Cowper had seven children, but only two survived infancy: William, born in 1731, and John, born in 1737. John Sr. was rector of Berkhamsted, Hertfordshire, England, and the family was strongly evangelical. The one weakness Rev. Dr. Cowper passed on to his son William was chronic depression. Today he would be diagnosed as having a bipolar disorder.

In 1764, during one of his hospitalizations, William was converted through the evangelistic efforts of his doctor. Despite his mental illness, he became one of England's greatest poets, writing the lyrics to hymns such as "O for a Closer Walk with Thee" and "There Is a Fountain Filled with Blood." His brother John, however, remained unconverted.

In September 1769, John became so ill that his friends insisted William come to visit him. After ten days John was much improved, and William returned home, mystified as to why his brother refused to trust in Jesus even when he was facing death.

The following February, William was again summoned because of John's failing health. John continued in great suffering until March 10, 1770, when William heard him quoting the words, "Behold, I create new heavens and a new earth" to which he added, "Ay, and he is able to do it too."

The following day William wrote to a Christian friend about what had happened:

I am in haste to make you a partaker of my joy. . . . Yesterday, in the afternoon, my Brother suddenly burst into tears, and said with a loud cry, "Oh! forsake me not!" I went to his bed-side, and . . . found that he was in prayer. Then, turning to me, he said, . . . "I have felt that which I never felt before; and I am sure that God has visited me with this sickness, in order to teach me what I was too proud to learn in health. I never had satisfaction till now. The doctrines I had been used to referred me to myself for the foundation of my hope, and there I could find nothing to rest upon. The sheer anchor of the soul was wanting. I thought you wrong, yet wanted to believe as you did. I found myself unable to believe, yet always thought that I should one day be brought to do so. You suffered more than I have done, before you believed these truths, but our sufferings, though different in their kind and measure, were directed to the same end. . . . These things were foolishness to me once, I could not understand them, but now I have a solid foundation and am satisfied.". . . The good I enjoy, comes to me as the overflowing of his bounty. But the crown of all his mercies is this, that he has given me a Saviour, and not only the Saviour of mankind, but my Saviour."

John Cowper died ten days later.

contrast to the intellectualism of traditional Talmud study. As a result of their teachings, the Hasidim were considered a threat to the authority of the rabbis who led the *yeshivas*, the Jewish institutes where students studied the Talmud. Led by Elijah ben Solomon Zalman (1720–1797)—the *gaon*, or leader of the yeshiva of Vilna, Lithuania—the leaders of the Eastern European yeshivas excommunicated the Hasidim in 1772 and burned their books. Despite the opposition, Hasidism continued to spread.

1773 ✝ POPE CLEMENT XIV SUPPRESSES THE JESUITS

In 1773, pressure from Portugal, Spain, France, and various Italian states caused Pope Clement XIV (1705–1774) to issue the papal bull *Dominus ac Redemptor noster*, officially dissolving the Jesuit order. However, this did not mean the order was extinguished. Jesuits continued to teach throughout Germany and Austria, where they were protected by both Frederick II (1712-1786) of Prussia and Empress Catherine the Great (1729–1796) of Russia. The Jesuits also continued their activities and maintained their possessions in England, where Roman Catholic bishops were discouraged from implementing the pope's ruling. This was also true in the United States, where the Jesuits continued their work almost uninterrupted.

1775 ✝ AMERICAN REVOLUTION BEGINS

On the morning of April 19, 1775, in Lexington and Concord, Massachusetts, the first shots of the American Revolution were fired. Dissatisfaction with British rule among the colonial Americans had been increasing for several years. However, after the Intolerable Acts were passed in 1774, war was inevitable. On May 10, 1775, Benedict Arnold (1741–1801) and Ethan Allen (1738–1789) led a group of American troops to Fort Ticonderoga, where they defeated the surprised British forces, beginning the war in earnest. That summer, the Continental Congress appointed George Washington (1732–1799) commander of the Colonial army. The next year, the new nation formally declared independence from British rule. After six years of war, the British surrendered to the American forces at Yorktown, and the United States of America emerged. No country in the world would be so strongly influenced by biblical Christianity.

1649	1665	1675	1712
England becomes a Commonwealth	Isaac Newton develops theory of gravity	Speed of light calculated	Steam engine invented in England

THE METHODIST PARSON

August 7, 1771

His life was an example of what God can do with one man.

Francis Asbury was born in 1745 to a poor family near Birmingham, England. His parents had been among the early converts of John Wesley, the founder of Methodism.

When Asbury was a boy, his mother surrounded him with prayer, Scripture, and hymns. She invited everyone she met who seemed "religious" to stay at her house. Young Asbury didn't get into much trouble, but his peers jeeringly called him "Methodist Parson," a cutting insult because Methodism at that time was seen as a crazy new religion.

At the age of thirteen, Asbury began asking his mother questions about the Methodists. She arranged for a friend of hers to take him to the town of Wednesbury so that he could see for himself.

He was particularly impressed with the spontaneity of a Methodist service he attended. Soon thereafter, when Asbury and a Christian friend prayed together in his father's barn loft, he trusted the Savior he had heard about for so long.

His great excitement about his salvation led him to become a local traveling preacher at the age of seventeen, while also continuing his work as a blacksmith's apprentice. By the age of twenty, he was ministering full-time in various Methodist preaching circuits throughout England.

On August 7, 1771, at the age of twenty-one, Asbury answered John Wesley's call for Methodist preachers to go to America. When Wesley announced, "Our brethren in America call aloud for help," Asbury answered, "Here am I, send me."

Once in America, Asbury was chosen to be one of the first two Methodist superintendents in the Methodist Episcopal Church, a new denomination that was born from his leadership. He subsequently changed his title to "bishop."

Asbury defined the role of an itinerant minister. His motto was, "Go into every kitchen and shop; address all, aged and young, on the salvation of their souls." He urged all Methodist ministers to do the same. He became a circuit rider, visiting camp meetings, revivals, and conventions on horseback.

Asbury traveled constantly for forty-five years, covering about three hundred thousand miles, mostly on horseback, and crossing the Appalachians more than sixty times. He literally had no home of his own in America but found shelter wherever he could.

When Asbury came to America in 1771, the country was home to approximately three hundred Methodists and four ministers, all on the Atlantic seaboard. When Asbury died in 1816, the denomination had spread into every state and over 214,000 people in America called themselves Methodists. Asbury himself had ordained more than four thousand Methodist ministers and had preached more than sixteen thousand sermons.

"DON'T FIRE UNTIL YOU SEE THE WHITES OF THEIR EYES"

June 16, 1775

In times of battle, men's thoughts often turn to prayer—and for good reason!

On June 16, 1775, a significant prayer meeting took place in Boston. The day before, the Patriots had learned of English General Gage's plan to occupy the southern projection of Bunker Hill on the Charleston peninsula, across the Charles River from Boston. In the twilight of June 16, twelve hundred Patriot troops gathered on the Cambridge Common. There Samuel Langdon, the gray-haired president of Harvard College, led them in prayer concerning the awesome task before them. He prayed, "O may our camp be free from every accursed thing! May our land be purged from all its sins! May we truly be a holy people and all our towns cities of righteousness!"

After the prayer, the patriot commander William Prescott led the troops to a rise near Bunker Hill overlooking the British army that occupied Boston. All through the night they worked preparing fortifications to withstand the British soldiers the next day.

General Gage committed twenty-two hundred British soldiers, a third of all his troops to the operation. At two in the afternoon the cannon fire from the British ships in Boston Harbor intensified against the patriot position as the British troops crossed the Charles River in small boats and then formed themselves into long lines. As the church bells tolled three o'clock, Gage's field commander, General William Howe, began leading his troops up the long hill. Behind him two rows of British soldiers, stretching the complete width of the peninsula, advanced up the open slope toward the patriot position.

The British troops were puzzled that the patriots did not fire a single shot at them as they advanced, even though they were well in range. Prescott, the patriot commander, had commanded his men with the now famous words, "Don't fire until you see the whites of their eyes." The young soldiers bravely did as they were told and were victorious. Seeing the countless red-coated British soldiers lying all around them, they knew that God had given them the victory.

Corporal Amos Farnsworth of the Massachusetts militia wrote in his diary that night, "O, the goodness of God in preserving my life, although they fell on my right hand and on my left! O may this act of deliverance of thine, O God, lead me never to distrust thee; but may I ever trust in thee and put confidence in no arm of the flesh!" Another soldier, Peter Jennings, wrote to his mother, "God, in His mercy to us, fought our battle for us, and although we were but few . . . we were preserved in a most wonderful way, far beyond expectation."

God answered the prayers of the previous night's prayer meeting.

1775 ✛ HENRY ALLINE CONVERTS

Known for bringing the Great Awakening to Nova Scotia, Henry Alline (1748–1784) was born to Congregational parents in Rhode Island. He moved to Nova Scotia, and in 1775, having experienced a dramatic conversion, Alline felt called to preach the gospel. A second experience, which gave him the sense that he needed only Christ, not a theological education, to qualify for the ministry, empowered Alline to begin a lifetime of preaching. His message centered on the need for a new birth. God used him to start a revival known as the New Light movement in the maritime colonies of Canada. The movement resulted in many Congregationalists becoming Baptists in Nova Scotia, and as a result, many evangelical churches were established in the province.

1775 ✛ FIRST INDEPENDENT BLACK BAPTIST CHURCH IS FOUNDED IN AMERICA

The first independent black church likely was one founded in 1775 in Silver Bluff, South Carolina. The successful establishment of this church led to the formation of other black congregations in Savannah, Boston, New York, Philadelphia, and other cities throughout the United States.

1779 ✛ COWPER AND NEWTON PUBLISH OLNEY HYMNS

William Cowper (1731–1800), a descendant of the English poet John Donne (1573–1631), became chronically depressed following an attempted suicide in his youth. But then he started reading the Bible and was converted to Christ. In 1767, he moved to Olney in Buckinghamshire, England, and was befriended by John Newton (1725–1807), a pastor who had been a slave trader before his conversion. Newton and Cowper wrote and published *Olney Hymns* in 1779. Cowper composed sixty-eight of the 348 hymns, including the well known, "O for a Closer Walk with God!" and "There is a Fountain Filled with Blood." The collection also included hymns by Newton, his most familiar being, "Amazing Grace" and "Glorious Things of Thee Are Spoken."

1780 ✚ ROBERT RAIKES BEGINS SUNDAY SCHOOL

Robert Raikes (1735–1811) followed his father as publisher of the *Gloucester Journal* in Gloucester, England, a position which afforded him the opportunity of helping those in need. In 1780, after consulting the pastor of a nearby church, Raikes set up a Sunday school for the city's growing number of neglected children. During the week and on Sunday, the teachers at the school taught Bible, reading, and other basics. The undertaking was quickly duplicated at other parishes, but concern that educating the poor would lead to revolution brought much opposition as well. Raikes, however, used his newspaper to promote his Sunday school idea, and within six years two hundred thousand children were being educated in English Sunday schools. The idea soon spread to Scotland, Ireland, Wales, and the Americas.

1781 ✚ CORNWALL'S CHRISTMAS REVIVAL FOCUSES ON PRAYER

Cornwall's Christmas Revival was unique in that it was largely a prayer movement without the involvement of any significant preachers. Most gatherings were prayer meetings rather than evangelistic meetings. It started in 1781, when a Christmas morning service in Cornwall, England, turned into six hours of prayer. After a brief break with their families, many gathered again at the church that evening to continue praying. This prayer revival continued daily, with prayer meetings held most evenings until midnight through March. The revival was also unique in that it was interdenominational, with Baptists, Methodists, and Anglicans gathering together to pray for the revival of England. Many unbelievers were drawn to these large meetings and were converted. Cornwall's Christmas Revival was one of the first events in the Second Great Awakening, which spread throughout England, America, and many other nations.

1781 ✚ KANT PUBLISHES HIS <u>CRITIQUE OF PURE REASON</u>

Immanuel Kant (1724–1804), was the most influential philosopher of modern times. A professor of logic and metaphysics in Königsberg, Prussia, he published *Critique of Pure Reason* in 1781. At the heart of *Critique* was Kant's case for human freedom and his explanation of knowledge and morality. By demonstrating that rational knowledge is derived only from logic, mathematics, and

1649	1665	1675	1712
England becomes a Commonwealth	Isaac Newton develops theory of gravity	Speed of light calculated	Steam engine invented in England

physics, Kant argued that neither reason nor experience can provide metaphysical or abstract knowledge. Kant's belief that knowledge of God is unattainable made a significant impact on Protestantism, providing a foundation for later liberal theology. Though he eventually articulated moral arguments for God, immorality, and freedom, Kant maintained that these premises were produced only by reason and therefore were not scientifically demonstrable conclusions.

1782 ✡ HOLY ROMAN EMPEROR JOSEPH II ISSUES EDICT OF TOLERANCE

Joseph II (1741–1790), king of Austria and the Holy Roman emperor, issued the Edict of Tolerance in 1782, which abolished the Jews' special poll tax, the yellow badge they had been forced to wear, the ban on Jews from attending universities, and the ban on Jews leaving their homes on Sundays and Christian holidays. On the other hand, it prohibited the use of Hebrew or Yiddish in any business documents or public records and introduced military service for Jewish males. In spite of the Edict of Tolerance, the Jews soon discovered that their newly gained rights were often denied by bureaucrats.

1784 ✝ METHODIST CONFERENCE FORMS IN CHURCH OF ENGLAND

In 1739, John Wesley's (1703–1791) successful preaching led him to establish Methodist societies to support recent converts. The name came from the Wesley's earlier Holy Club at Oxford University whose members were derisively called "Methodists." When Wesley filed a Deed of Declaration in the Court of Chancery in 1784, the societies became an official "Yearly Conference of People Called Methodists" that listed one hundred preachers. The authority to appoint ministers to its "Preaching Houses" was included in the deed. In addition, the deed called for preachers to be ordained in the Church of England, though few followed the provision. Following Wesley's death, the one-hundred-person limit was extended to include all English Methodist preachers.

1784 ✝ JOHN WESLEY WRITES THE ARTICLES OF RELIGION

In 1784, John Wesley (1703–1791) wrote the Articles of Religion as the official doctrinal standard for American Methodists. His Twenty-Four Articles of Religion were a revision of the Thirty-Nine Articles of the Church of England. Wesley removed everything from the Thirty-Nine Articles having to do with ritual or Calvinism. He did not add anything uniquely Methodist as this was already available in his sermons and in his "Notes on the New Testament." The American Methodists added one article affirming their loyalty to the American government. The resulting Twenty-Five Articles were officially adopted by the Baltimore Conference later that year.

1784 ✝ THOMAS COKE COMES TO AMERICA

Born in Brecon, Wales, England, Thomas Coke (1747–1814) earned his doctorate in civil law at Oxford University and was ordained in the Church of England. While serving as the curate in South Pertherton, however, Coke was removed from his office because of his Methodist beliefs. Coke, a good preacher with a sharp legal mind, earned the respect of John Wesley (1703–1791) and served as superintendent of the Methodist circuit in London. In 1784, Coke sailed to America after John Wesley appointed him to assist Francis Asbury (1745–1816) as joint superintendent for America. Next to John Wesley, Thomas Coke was the most significant figure in early Methodism.

1784 ✝ THE METHODIST EPISCOPAL CHURCH IS FOUNDED IN AMERICA

Thomas Coke (1747–1814), the devoted English Methodist, came to America with instructions from John Wesley (1703–1791) for Francis Asbury (1745–1816), the leading Methodist preacher in the United States. In 1784, the two men organized what became known as the Christmas Convention, chaired by Coke. The meeting was held in Baltimore and led to the official formation of a new American denomination called the Methodist Episcopal Church. In accordance with Wesley's recommendation, the conference adopted the Articles of Religion and established a rule of discipline. Coke, who had been ordained superintendent by Wesley, ordained Asbury as a fellow superintendent. At its founding, the denomination included eight thousand members, and more than one hundred itinerant preachers, with eight hundred regular preaching locations and sixty chapels.

1649	1665	1675	1712
England becomes a Commonwealth	Isaac Newton develops theory of gravity	Speed of light calculated	Steam engine invented in England

1784 ✛ CHRISTIANITY COMES TO KOREA

In 1783, Lee Seung-hoon, a Korean Confucian scholar accompanying an envoy to Peking, China, read Jesuit literature there and was baptized a Christian. He then returned to Korea and baptized two of his friends in 1784. From Seung-hoon's testimony, Catholicism spread throughout Korea. For nearly one hundred years and despite terrible persecutions by Confucian rulers in 1791, 1801, 1839, 1846, and 1864, the hidden Catholic Church in Korea grew to more than 17,500 members. Protestantism was introduced by Suh Sang-yum who was converted by Scottish missionaries in Manchuria in 1878. Although it was against the law to do so, Sang-yum returned with parts of Scripture translated into Korean and quietly converted the first Korean Protestant Christians. The first Presbyterian and Methodist missionaries arrived in 1884. By 2000, there were more than 7 million evangelical Christians in South Korea and approximately 355,000 in North Korea.

1786 ✛ THOMAS COKE LEADS THE FIRST
METHODIST MISSION TO WEST INDIES

In addition to serving as joint superintendent of Methodism in the newly formed United States of America, Thomas Coke (1747–1814) rightly bears the title of "father of Methodist Missions." In 1786, he wrote the first Methodist tract on missions and that same year set out to establish a mission in Nova Scotia. However, a severe storm forced his ship to land in Antigua, West Indies, where he was thrilled to find an open door for missionaries. Missions in the British West Indies and the other British colonies became his passion for the remainder of his life.

1787 ✛ THE ABOLITION MOVEMENT BEGINS

The Abolition Society, formed in Britain in 1787 by Thomas Clarkson (1760–1846) and William Wilberforce (1759–1833), was the first organized group that sought to abolish slavery. In 1807, the society successfully lobbied Parliament to outlaw the slave trade within the British Empire. Slavery itself continued, but in 1823, the Anti-Slavery Society was formed in Britain under the direction of a member of Parliament named Thomas Forwell Buxton (1786–1845). Finally in

1757	1770s	1776–81	1789
British rule begins in India	Industrial Revolution begins in England	American Revolution	French Revolution begins

1833, the British Parliament passed legislation that abolished all slavery throughout the empire. The anti-slavery movement gained strength and subsequently spread to North America.

1787 ✛ SECOND GREAT AWAKENING BEGINS AT HAMPDEN-SYDNEY COLLEGE

The second national revival in the United States is known as the Second Great Awakening. The era energized the spiritual life of Americans following the Revolutionary War and confronted two major challenges. First, Deism was popular among educated society and centered on thinking of God on the basis of reason not faith. Secondly, the challenges and dangers of life on the Western frontier resulted in churches being few and far between. The much-needed revival came first to colleges in the East, where in 1787, Hampden-Sydney College experienced a spiritual awakening. From Hampden-Sydney, revival spread to Washington College, Yale, Williams, Dartmouth, and Amherst. Carried along by students and preachers alike, the Second Great Awakening lasted from 1787 to 1825, sweeping the land from East to West.

1649	1665	1675	1712
England becomes a Commonwealth	Isaac Newton develops theory of gravity	Speed of light calculated	Steam engine invented in England

THE AGE OF PROGRESS

1789–1914

The Age of Progress saw Christians of all sorts wage a valiant struggle against the advance of secularism. Out of the evangelical awakenings came new efforts to carry the gospel of Christ to distant lands, and to begin a host of social service ministries in industrialized Europe and North America. From the ramparts of Rome, a defensive papacy fired a barrage of missiles aimed at the modern enemies of the Catholic faith. In spite of Christians' best efforts, however, Christianity was slowly driven from public life in the Western world. Believers were left with the problem we recognize in our own time: How can Christians exert moral influence in pluralistic and totalitarian societies where Christian assumptions about reality no longer prevail?

BRUCE L. SHELLEY

1789 ✛ REVOLUTION RADICALIZES FRANCE

In eighteenth-century France, excesses by the monarchy, the nobility, and the clergy led to intense political and social upheaval. The middle classes demanded political power, refusing to submit to the nobility and the clergy. The peasants demanded redistribution of land and an end to feudalism. An intense distrust of the Catholic Church had developed, due primarily to the church's increased wealth and power. The Enlightenment had bred ideas of Deism and naturalism that compounded the newly found aversion toward organized religion. The fighting began with the storming of the Bastille on July 14, 1789, and the revolution continued for ten years. The revolution overthrew the monarchy and abolished the old feudal system, but it also attempted to abolish the church in France by removing all vestiges of Christianity from French culture. Although the Catholic Church regained some privileges later under Napoléon Bonaparte (1769–1821), it never regained its former place in French society.

1791 ✡ CATHERINE THE GREAT ESTABLISHES THE PALE OF SETTLEMENT

In the 1770s, Poland was divided three times between Prussia, Austria, and Russia, and the majority of Polish Jews came under Russian authority. Russia, which had been closed to Jews, suddenly had one million Jewish inhabitants. Desiring to keep Jews separate from the rest of her subjects, in 1791 Empress Catherine the Great (1729–1796) of Russia restricted Jews to an area known as the Pale of Settlement. That region included the areas they already inhabited and territories taken from the Ottoman Empire along the Black Sea that the empress wished to colonize. In one form or another, the Pale of Settlement was enforced until the Russian Revolution in 1917.

1791 ✛ THE FIRST AMENDMENT TO THE U.S. CONSTITUTION IS RATIFIED

In order to ratify the American Constitution, several states demanded that certain rights be added to the document. This Bill of Rights constitutes the basic freedoms of American citizens. The first amendment declares that "Congress shall make no law respecting an establishment of religion, or prohibiting the free exer-

1791	1793-4	1808	1846
U.S. Bill of Rights written	Reign of Terror in France	Napoleon controls almost all Europe	One million Irish starve in Potato Famine

cise thereof; or abridging the freedom of speech, or of the press; of the right of the people peaceably to assemble and to petition the government of a redress of grievances." The Supreme Court has ruled that the freedom of religion does not apply when it results in antisocial or self-harming behavior. In 1947, the *Everson v. Board of Education* verdict stated that there was a "wall of separation between church and state." This decision has resulted in the removal of prayer, Bible reading, and most religious-related activities from American public schools.

1791 ✡ FRANCE GRANTS CIVIL RIGHTS TO JEWS

When the French Revolution occurred in 1789, it had positive results for the Jews of France. During the Revolution, in the first debate in the French National Assembly on the status of the Jews, many radicals fought bitterly against granting equal rights to Jews. Nevertheless, on September 27, 1791, the National Assembly granted Jews their full civil rights, becoming the first European nation to do so. The rationale was simply that all Frenchmen were equal.

1791 ✝ SCHLEIERMACHER PUBLISHES ON RELIGION

Frederick Ernst Daniel Schleiermacher (1768–1834) was born to a Pietistic German family and studied at Halle, the center of Pietism, under Moravian teachers. As a university student, Schleiermacher rejected much of Pietism and became fascinated by debates concerning the teaching of Immanuel Kant (1724–1804). In 1799, Schleiermacher published his first major work, *On Religion: Speeches to Its Cultured Despisers*. The book, which gives theological voice to Romanticism, describes religion as a "sense and taste for the infinite" and argues that life becomes dreadful without religion. Schleiermacher rejected the orthodox doctrine of Christ, seeing him merely as a person, thus paving the way for future liberal views of Christ as merely a man inspired by God.

1792 ✝ THE CLAPHAM SECT IS FORMED

Around 1792, a small group of influential Christians living near Clapham, a village south of London, joined forces to promote Christian action, particularly the abolition of slavery. Working tirelessly to influence public opinion and to exert pressure on the government, they accomplished the abolition of the slave

1856	1903	1905	1914
Transatlantic cable developed	Wright brothers make first flight	Albert Einstein develops Theory of Relativity	Panama Canal completed

trade in 1807, and the emancipation of all slaves throughout the British territory in 1833. Members of the close-knit group included William Wilberforce (1759–1833) and Zachary Macaulay (1768–1838) (members of Parliament), John Venn (1759–1813) (rector of Clapham), Henry Thornton (1760–1815) (banker whose home was the meeting place), Hannah More (1745–1835) (writer and educator), and Lord Teignmouth (1751–1834) (governor-general of India). In addition to facilitating the end of slavery in the British Empire, they worked for reform in England's schools and prisons. God used a small group of committed believers to change their world.

1792 ✝ HANNAH MORE PUBLISHES CHEAP REPOSITORY TRACTS

Growing up in England, Hannah More (1745–1833) mastered French, Latin, Italian, and Spanish at an early age, and was gifted in mathematics and poetry. She administered a school with her three sisters and became an important social and literary figure in London. After the death of two literary friends, More lost interest in the London social scene and decided to devote her abilities to serving God. John Newton (1725–1807), author of "Amazing Grace," became her spiritual advisor. She wrote many books and essays on the importance of education and Christianity in establishing moral laws. In 1792, she published a series called *Cheap Repository Tracts,* which explained religious truth and responsibility. The series was sponsored by William Wilberforce (1759–1833) and Henry Thornton (1760–1815) of the Clapham Sect and sold 2 million copies in the first year. Hannah More wrote throughout her life, becoming the first evangelical to use novels for religious or moral purposes.

1793 ✝ FESTIVAL OF REASON DEGRADES CHRISTIAN INFLUENCE IN FRANCE

With the triumph of the French Revolution, its leaders tried to abolish the church in France. Festivals such as the Festival of Reason in 1793 were part of a concerted effort to erase any vestige of a Christian culture from the nation. To that end, Notre Dame Cathedral—formerly a Christian center for intellectual and spiritual reform—became the Temple of Reason. Catholic priests were forced to take an oath to the newly created Civil Constitution. The Catholic Church denounced the Civil Constitution and, as a result, Catholic clergy endured cruel mistreatment.

1791	1793-4	1808	1846
U.S. Bill of Rights written	Reign of Terror in France	Napoleon controls almost all Europe	One million Irish starve in Potato Famine

"EXPECT GREAT THINGS"

May 31, 1792

Fellow ministers called him "the harebrained enthusiast," but we know him as the father of modern missions.

William Carey was born in 1761 to a poor Anglican family in rural England. At the age of fourteen he began training as a shoemaker's apprentice. Providentially, fellow apprentice John Warr was a Christian.

Carey was uncomfortable with the evangelical arguments Warr presented to him, and over time Carey began to feel a "growing uneasiness and stings of conscience gradually increasing" in regard to Warr's beliefs. Over the next two years, he came to "depend on a crucified Saviour for pardon and salvation."

Although he did not attend high school, Carey possessed a keen intellect. He taught himself five languages, and by the end of his life he knew dozens of languages and dialects.

Carey became a Calvinistic Baptist preacher, who was burdened for overseas missions. He published a pamphlet called *An Enquiry into the Obligations of Christians to use Means for the Conversion of the Heathens*.

For years Carey tried to convince fellow Baptist ministers of the need to form a missionary society in order to spread the gospel across the world. Although the leaders of the denomination kept putting him off, he persisted.

On the evening of May 30, 1792, Carey preached at the annual Baptist association meeting. His text was Isaiah 54:2-3, and his theme was "Expect great things from God; attempt great things for God." He urged his fellow pastors to commit to venture forth among the nations with the gospel, having confidence that God would bless the message and extend his kingdom. Carey's address made a profound impression on the ministers in attendance.

The nest day, May 31, 1792, they agreed to form the "Baptist Society for Propagating the Gospel among the Heathen." Later it was renamed the Baptist Missionary Society.

In 1793, Carey and two other missionaries sailed for India where Carey worked until his death in 1834. His comprehensive approach to missions included evangelization, church planting, and Bible translation. He also established schools, hospitals, and a savings bank; founded the Agricultural and Horticultural Society of India; started a Bengali newspaper; and supervised the start of India's first printing press, paper mill, and steam engine. He also taught languages at a local college, wrote a Bengali-English dictionary, and founded the first Christian college in Asia. In all, Carey translated the complete Bible into six languages and portions of it into twenty-nine others.

He expected great things from God, attempted great things for God, and God brought them to pass.

1793 ✛ WILLIAM CAREY SAILS FOR INDIA

William Carey's (1761–1834) vision for evangelizing the entire world was unlike that of his predecessors, which had focused on territories of the missionary's homeland. Converted at eighteen and ordained in 1787, Carey mastered Latin, Greek, Hebrew, Italian, and Dutch. Following the establishment of the Particular Baptist Society for Propagating the Gospel among the Heathens (now the Baptist Missionary Society), Carey sailed for India in 1793. Carey and his fellow missionaries established twenty-six churches and more than 125 schools. He translated Scripture into at least thirty-five languages, including Bengali and Sanskrit. India's first medical mission, bank, girls' school, printing operation, paper mill, steam engine, and Bengali newspaper are among his other accomplishments. The father of Modern Missions, Carey baptized eighteen hundred converts, and his work prompted the creation of numerous other missionary societies.

1795 ✛ ROBERT AND JAMES HALDANE ARE CONVERTED

Brothers Robert (1764–1842) and James Haldene (1768–1851) were raised by uncles after losing their parents when very young. They were educated in Dundee and Edinburgh, Scotland, after which they joined the navy. Both had left the navy before they were converted in 1795. James then became an influential itinerant preacher, and Robert attempted to set up agencies for financing foreign missions. However, the Church of Scotland opposed foreign missionary work, so Robert redirected his efforts and finances to establishing preaching tabernacles and theological seminaries throughout Scotland. In 1797, James founded the Society for Propagating the Gospel at Home and, in 1799, became the first Congregational pastor in Scotland. By 1801, he was pastor of the huge Tabernacle in Edinburgh, where he ministered for almost fifty years.

1795 ✛ LONDON MISSIONARY SOCIETY IS FORMED

One of the first societies of its kind, the Missionary Society (renamed London Missionary Society in 1818) was founded in 1795 by a group of Anglicans, Congregationalists, Presbyterians, and Methodists who met at Baker's Coffee House in London to pray for and plan for foreign missions. With the formation of the

1791	1793-4	1808	1846
U.S. Bill of Rights written	Reign of Terror in France	Napoleon controls almost all Europe	One million Irish starve in Potato Famine

society they pooled their efforts to promote Christian missions. One of the society's unique founding principles was that no particular denomination should be promoted by the missionaries, and that church government should instead be set up by those converted. The first mission was made up of twenty-nine missionaries who ventured to Tahiti in 1796. The London Missionary Society eventually became the Council for World Missions (CWM). In subsequent years, the CWM initiated large-scale mission efforts in China, India, South East Asia, and East Africa.

1796 ✝ HANS NIELSEN HAUGE IS CONVERTED

Hans Nielsen Hauge (1771–1824) was raised in the pious Lutheran home of a Norwegian farmer. In 1796, he experienced a dramatic conversion, after which he devoted himself to full-time evangelism as a lay preacher. He traveled throughout Norway, usually on foot, exhorting Norwegians to repent. He was quite successful, quickly gathering many followers. At this time itinerant preaching was illegal in Norway, and Hauge was sent to prison from 1804 to 1811. After a long trial he was ordered to pay a fine for unlawful preaching and criticizing the clergy. His followers, who came to be called "Haugeans," helped him buy a farm near Oslo where he wrote many widely circulated books. Toward the end of Hauge's life, his relations with the authorities became much friendlier. Hauge is regarded as the founder of the Christian laymen's movement in Norway.

1797 ✝ METHODISTS BEGIN TO SEPARATE FROM CHURCH OF ENGLAND

In 1787, the "Preaching Houses" established by John Wesley (1703–1791) were registered as dissenting churches under the Toleration Act of 1559. The Methodist's *Plan of Pacification* in 1795 furthered their detachment from the Church of England, because it permitted Communion and baptism, as well as marriage and funeral services, to be carried out in Methodist chapels. The *Plan* also allowed preachers with full connection to the Methodist Conference to be considered ordained ministers. In 1797, six years after Wesley's death, Alexander Kilham (1762–1798) formed the Methodist New Connection, the first Methodist group to break officially from the Church of England. The principles of the New Connection eventually were taken over by the main Methodist bodies.

1856	1903	1905	1914
Transatlantic cable developed	Wright brothers make first flight	Albert Einstein develops Theory of Relativity	Panama Canal completed

1797 ✝ SECOND GREAT AWAKENING SPREADS WESTWARD IN THE UNITED STATES

Excitement and emotion characterized the Second Great Awakening in America when it spread westward. In 1797, the revival started in three Presbyterian churches led by James McGready (1769–1817) in Logan County, Kentucky. His fiery preaching, with its vivid descriptions of heaven and hell, shook the apathy from his congregation. When one of his churches invited the other Presbyterian and Methodist churches of the area to its annual Communion service in 1800, the revival spread to the visiting churches.

1799 ✡ NAPOLÉON BREAKS DOWN GHETTO WALLS

After Napoléon Bonaparte (1769–1821) seized power in France in 1799, he conquered much of Europe. In an effort to promote the legal equality of all men, Napoléon's armies broke down the walls of Jewish ghettos whenever he encountered them. Napoléon's destruction of the Roman Ghetto, established by Pope Paul IV (1476–1559) in the sixteenth century, also sent a message to the Catholic Church, whose authority Napoléon refused to recognize. Though some of the ghettos eventually would be rebuilt, and though Napoléon himself placed some limits on Jewish settlement, he was considered a liberator by many Jews in the eighteenth century.

1801 ✝ CONCORDAT IS RATIFIED BETWEEN NAPOLÉON AND PIUS VII

Following the French Revolution of 1789 and the de-Christianization of France in the 1790s, Pope Pius VII (1740–1823) at long last reached an agreement with Napoléon Bonaparte (1769–1821), then first consul of France. The concordat was ratified on June 16, 1801, and "restored the altars" of Christianity. It also declared that sixteen pre-revolution bishops would be reinstated and thirty-two new bishops would be installed. Although this restoration of the church recognized that the majority of French citizens were Roman Catholics, the favorable terms were hindered significantly only a year later by the publication of Napoléon's *Organic Articles,* in which he assumed complete control of the French church. The *Organic Articles* remained law until 1905.

1791	1793-4	1808	1846
U.S. Bill of Rights written	Reign of Terror in France	Napoleon controls almost all Europe	One million Irish starve in Potato Famine

THE CANE RIDGE REVIVAL

| August 6, 1801 |

Some called it America's Pentecost.

The state of the American frontier in the late 1700s was one of growing religious indifference. Christianity was on the decline as the settlers began to experience economic success.

Settlers went to the frontier to get land, not religion. Referring to Lexington, Kentucky, in 1795, Methodist James Smith feared that "the Universalists, joining with the Deists, had given Christianity a deadly stab hereabouts."

James McGready arrived in Kentucky in 1798 to pastor three small frontier Presbyterian churches. His fiery preaching and vivid depictions of heaven and hell snatched the apathy from his congregations. When the Red River church started to plan their annual Communion gathering in 1800, they decided to invite other local Presbyterian and Methodist churches to participate. The typically reverent, quiet Communion service of Presbyterianism turned surprisingly emotional and ecstatic. The ministers and parishioners alike were amazed at how God had worked in their midst. Although somewhat wary of emotionalism, the ministers began to plan a larger Communion service weekend for the following summer at Cane Ridge.

Word of the upcoming camp meeting had spread throughout the frontier. On August 6, 1801, the Cane Ridge Revival began. For seven days, thousands of people descended on the Cane Ridge meetinghouse in Bourbon County, Kentucky, about twenty miles west of Lexington. They gathered together to worship, fellowship, and celebrate the Lord's Supper.

Friday and Saturday were solemnly observed, devoted to fasting and praying in preparation for Sunday's Communion. But as thousands more than expected arrived, the crowds grew restless and sabotaged the traditional Presbyterian routine. One after the other, preachers began to take the stage, with the large crowd occasionally growing into a frenzy. Some ministers encouraged ecstasy and emotionalism, while others fought to maintain control of their audience and to return the focus to the solemnity of the Lord's Supper.

The Cane Ridge meeting was both a beginning and an end. It was the end of the long-preserved Scotch-Irish Presbyterian tradition of lengthy, highly ritualized large-group Communion services. The emotional events of Cane Ridge forced the end of that tradition. The meeting was also the beginning of a new institution: organized camp meetings and revivals that turned the American frontier from apathy back to Christianity.

Estimates of attendance at Cane Ridge vary widely from ten to twenty thousand. There were one to three thousand reported conversions. The banner year for camp meetings was 1811, when as many as one-third of all Americans attended at least one such meeting.

1801 ✝ CANE RIDGE REVIVAL ESTABLISHES CAMP MEETINGS

Camp meetings were a significant part of the Second Great Awakening, the revival that swept the United States from 1787 to 1825. The Cane Ridge Revival in Bourbon County, Kentucky, from August 6 to 13, 1801, was the first large camp meeting. It lasted for six days and drew a crowd of between ten and twenty thousand people from many different denominations. As many as three thousand conversions were reported. The success of the revival at Cane Ridge established the camp meeting as an integral part of frontier religious life during the early 1800s. Ten years later in 1811, it was estimated that one-third of all Americans had attended a camp meeting.

1802 ✝ YALE COLLEGE WITNESSES REVIVAL

When the Second Great Awakening in America reached Yale College in 1802, one-third of Yale's students converted, largely due to the preaching of Timothy Dwight (1752–1817), the president of Yale. Dwight was the grandson of Jonathan Edwards (1703–1758), the great theologian and preacher of the First Great Awakening. From Yale, the revival spread to other colleges and into the American West.

1804 ✝ THE BRITISH AND FOREIGN BIBLE SOCIETY IS FORMED

The formation of the British and Foreign Bible Society (BFBS) in 1804 ushered in the aggressive modern movement of distributing Bibles. The goal of the BFBS was "to encourage the wider circulation of the Holy Scriptures, without note or comment" to the colonies of Europe and England, in addition to all English churches. Founded by a predominantly Anglican group of evangelicals, the BFBS started its work in India around 1811 and inspired the establishment of similar societies in America (1816) and Russia (1819).

1806 ✝ HOLY ROMAN EMPIRE IS DISSOLVED

On August 6, 1806, due to persistent pressure from Napoléon Bonaparte (1769–1821), Emperor Francis II (1786–1835) resigned and the Holy Roman Empire was dissolved. By the mid-seventeenth century, lack of imperial re-

1791	1793-4	1808	1846
U.S. Bill of Rights written	Reign of Terror in France	Napoleon controls almost all Europe	One million Irish starve in Potato Famine

form and the stress of the Protestant Reformation had weakened the empire's relationship with the church, making it vulnerable to Napoléon's assault. It was replaced by Napoléon's Confederation of the Rhine.

1806 ✡ JEWISH NOTABLES AND SANHEDRIN ASSEMBLE IN FRANCE

In 1806, Napoléon Bonaparte (1769–1821), who had crowned himself emperor of the French, called together an assembly of Jewish notables, composed of delegates who were elected by the Jews of his empire. Napoléon then assembled a group of rabbis he called the Sanhedrin, to give religious sanction to the assembly's decisions. The meeting resulted in a number of resolutions, including an affirmation that French Jews did indeed love their fellow non-Jewish Frenchmen, and a decree giving French courts authority over Jewish courts. It was the Sanhedrin that attracted most of the public attention. Since it met secretly, it fueled conspiratorial speculation and contributed to anti-Semitism in France.

1806 ✝ SAMUEL MILLS LEADS PRAYER MEETING IN HAYSTACK

Samuel Mills (1783–1819) was converted in his youth during the revivals that swept through New England. The son of a Congregational minister, Mills attended Williams College in Williamstown, Massachusetts. There he set up the Society of the Brethren, whose purpose was to spread the gospel to the world. One day in 1806, the group found themselves caught in a rainstorm while they met for prayer. Mills led the young men to the shelter of a haystack where the prayer meeting could continue. There at the haystack, four of the five committed themselves to being foreign missionaries. This was the beginning of the foreign missionary movement among students in America and led to the formation of the American Board of Commissioners for Foreign Missions, which sent the first American missionaries to India in 1812.

1807 ✝ ENGLISH PARLIAMENT VOTES TO ABOLISH THE SLAVE TRADE

In 1807, British Parliament voted to abolish the slave trade—the first victory in the campaign to emancipate slaves in the British Empire. The abolitionist

1856	1903	1905	1914
Transatlantic cable developed	Wright brothers make first flight	Albert Einstein develops Theory of Relativity	Panama Canal completed

movement, begun in the late eighteenth century, was led by William Wilberforce (1759–1833) and the Clapham Sect (est. 1792). He was joined by friends John Newton (1725–1807), author of the hymn "Amazing Grace," and Thomas Clarkson (1760–1846), who spent his fortune on the battle. Campaigning throughout England and in the House of Commons, the group used the increasingly popular values of liberty and happiness to undermine the main arguments for slavery, which were namely, economics and national policy. Due to their convincing arguments and ability to influence public opinion, the abolitionists were able to achieve victory in Parliament. The abolition of slavery itself was adopted in 1833.

1807 ✝ ROBERT MORRISON ARRIVES IN CHINA

Robert Morrison (1782–1834), the youngest son of Scottish Presbyterian parents, felt called to missions in his early twenties. While attending a Congregationalist seminary near London, Morrison heard the London Missionary Society call for missionaries to China. Morrison responded, and after two more years training in medicine and Mandarin Chinese and a sea voyage of nine months, landed in Macao on September 4, 1807. Locating in Canton, Morrison immersed himself in language and culture study, becoming fluent in Cantonese, Mandarin, and written Chinese. In 1810, Morrison completed translating the book of Acts, and in 1819, the entire Bible. With the Bible translation as a text, Morrison helped found an English-Chinese College that trained Chinese in evangelism. Morrison, the father of Protestant missions in China, died in Canton in 1834.

1808 ✝ ANDOVER THEOLOGICAL SEMINARY IS FORMED

In 1808, Andover Theological Seminary was formed on the campus of Andover Academy in Andover, Massachusetts. It was the first theological seminary in the United States. The seminary began as a reaction against the appointment of a Unitarian, Henry Ware (1764–1845), as professor of divinity at Harvard. The new seminary initially required all faculty to subscribe to the Andover Creed, grounded in the theology of John Calvin (1509–1564) and Jonathan Edwards (1703–1578). In 1931, the seminary merged with Newton Theological Institute to become Andover Newton Theological School.

1791	1793-4	1808	1846
U.S. Bill of Rights written	Reign of Terror in France	Napoleon controls almost all Europe	One million Irish starve in Potato Famine

1810 ✝ AMERICAN BOARD OF COMMISSIONERS FOR FOREIGN MISSIONS IS ESTABLISHED

The American Board of Commissioners for Foreign Missions (ABCFM) was the first foreign missionary society organized in America. It was established in Massachusetts as a Congregational Church ministry in 1810, following the petition of several Andover Seminary students—including Samuel Mills (1783–1819) and Adoniram Judson (1788–1850)—to go to the mission field. In 1812, Adoniram Judson and fellow missionaries set out for India. This voyage was followed by missions to the Near East in 1818 and to Hawaii in 1819. The primary tasks of ABCFM missionaries were evangelism and church planting. These activities were supplemented and aided by translating Scripture, while social concerns were of secondary importance. Within fifty years the ABCFM established missions in Asia, China, Japan, and Africa, as well as among American Indians and African Americans.

1810 ✡ REFORM JUDAISM BEGINS

In the early nineteenth century, several Jewish rabbis in Germany started reforming Jewish traditions. In 1810, Rabbi Israel Jacobson (1768–1818) in Seesen, Germany, began to use the German language instead of Hebrew for liturgy and sermons, and to incorporate organ music. In addition to the service changes, he called the synagogue a temple. Jacobson later moved to Berlin and began a temple in his home. By 1818, a reform temple had also been built in Hamburg. Berlin and Hamburg, having many wealthy and educated Jews, became centers of Reform Judaism. The reformers' general desire was to reestablish Judaism as a religious system, de-emphasizing the identification of Jews as a nation. In Reform Judaism, rituals contributing to the formation of a Jewish-nationalist identity were removed or pronounced insignificant.

1811 ✝ CAMPBELLS FOUND THE DISCIPLES OF CHRIST

Following futile attempts to unify churches that had separated from the Church of Scotland, Scots-Irish minister Thomas Campbell (1763–1854) immigrated to America in the early nineteenth century. Hoping to establish unity among Christians, Campbell and his son Alexander (1788–1866) toured Pennsylvania, Ken-

1856	1903	1905	1914
Transatlantic cable developed	Wright brothers make first flight	Albert Einstein develops Theory of Relativity	Panama Canal completed

UNDER A HAYSTACK

June 29, 1810

Foreign mission organizations are common in America today, but in the 1800s there was not a single foreign missions board in the United States. God was to begin the American foreign missions movement in a very unlikely place—a haystack!

Williams College in Williamstown, Massachusetts, was just twelve years old in 1805, when the Second Great Awakening visited the school. In the spring of 1806, Samuel Mills, the son of a Congregational minister, joined the freshman class with a passion to spread the gospel around the world. He began leading a prayer group of four other students who had been touched by the revival. They met three afternoons a week in the maple grove of nearby Sloan's Meadow.

One sultry day in August 1806, a violent thunderstorm interrupted their prayer time and they took refuge on the sheltered side of a large haystack. There in the sanctuary of the haystack, Mills directed their prayers to their personal missionary obligations. God spoke to them as they prayed, and four of the five committed themselves to serving God overseas if he so led. The Haystack Prayer Meeting was not only the beginning of the first American student mission society, but was also the beginning of the foreign missions movement itself in America. In two years their prayer group took the name The Society of the Brethren, with the motto "We can do it if we will."

Two years later many of the group enrolled at Andover Seminary in Andover, Massachusetts, where they were joined by Adoniram Judson and others interested in world missions. There they continued to believe that God was calling them to the mission field, but there was no foreign missions board in America to send them.

The students took their problem to the seminary faculty and to pastors in the area. In response, the teachers and pastors met at the home of Moses Stuart, a member of the Andover faculty. Their advice was that the students submit their case to the General Association, a body made up of the Congregational Churches of Massachusetts, which was to begin meetings the following day in Bradford, Massachusetts.

Acting on this advice, the students wrote a letter explaining their plight and soliciting the association's help. Adoniram Judson, Samuel Mills, and two others signed the letter. Originally Luther Rice and James Richards also signed but removed their names so there wouldn't be too many, lest the number of potential missionary candidates needing support would scare the Association.

Two days later, on June 29, 1810, the Association responded to their request by forming the American Board of Commissioners for Foreign Missions, the first foreign missions board in America. A year later the board sent out Adoniram Judson and three other men with their families as their first missionaries.

From that humble beginning, the foreign missions force of the United States has grown to more than sixty thousand missionaries sent out by hundreds of missions boards.

tucky, West Virginia, Tennessee, Ohio, and Indiana. The message they preached was that there were only two basic requirements for Christian unity, confessing Jesus as Lord and baptism by immersion. In 1811, Alexander Campbell organized the Disciples of Christ. In 1832, they united with the Christian Church of Barton Stone (1772–1844). From this union, the Churches of Christ later emerged.

1812 ┼ ADONIRAM JUDSON SAILS FOR INDIA

While attending Andover Seminary, Adoniram Judson (1788–1850) played a significant role in establishing the American Board of Commissioners for Foreign Missions (ABCFM). The inaugural mission to India in 1812 included Judson and his wife, Ann (1789–1826), who became missionaries to Burma. Judson was convinced that to be effective, he needed to master the local language and religion, which was Theravada Buddhism. In addition to devoting his time to preaching and training pastors and evangelists, Judson created a Burman dictionary and translated Scripture into their native language. Returning to America only once, Judson spent most of his life in Burma. In 2000, there were 2 million Christian believers in Myanmar (formerly Burma), and 40 percent of the Karen people, the tribe to whom Judson directed his ministry, were Christians.

1812 ┼ CHURCH MISSIONARY SOCIETY IS ESTABLISHED

Formed in the late eighteenth century, the Society for Missions in Africa and the East, was one of the first major evangelical Anglican mission groups. Its first mission to Sierra Leone in 1804, however, was carried out by German Lutherans because no English ministers were able to go. Following this mission, the society sent English laymen to New Zealand in 1809, and men from both Germany and England sailed to southern India a few years later. In 1812, the society was established officially and renamed the Church Missionary Society. Among the first to send single women into the field, the organization took the name Church Mission Society in 1995 and has remained an Anglican organization.

1812 ┼ PRINCETON SEMINARY IS FOUNDED

Archibald Alexander (1772–1851) had a conversion experience at the age of seventeen, causing him to leave his position as a private tutor and enroll at Liberty

1856	1903	1905	1914
Transatlantic cable developed	Wright brothers make first flight	Albert Einstein develops Theory of Relativity	Panama Canal completed

Hall (now Washington and Lee University) to study theology. He then entered the Presbyterian ministry, first as an itinerant minister on the Ohio-Virginia frontier, and later as pastor of the Third Presbyterian Church of Philadelphia and moderator of the Presbyterian General Assembly. In his final address as moderator in 1808, he suggested the formation of a Presbyterian seminary in America. As a result of his leadership, Princeton Theological Seminary was founded in 1812 in Alexander's home of Princeton, New Jersey. Alexander was its sole faculty member for the first year, and he continued teaching there until his death in 1851.

1813 ✠ J. A. NEANDER IS APPOINTED PROFESSOR OF CHURCH HISTORY

Johann August Wilhelm Neander (1789–1850) was born David Mendel in a Jewish family in Germany. At age seventeen, he was converted to Christ and changed his name. He was initially interested in theology, but church history began to captivate his mind. In 1813, he was appointed professor of church history in Berlin. Many students enjoyed Neander for his excellent scholarship, his sacred devotion, and his ability to highlight unique details in history. Neander believed that church history was an essential part of the church's mission and ministry, rather than a mere academic pursuit. His most detailed works, *History of the Planting and Training of the Christian Church* and *A General History of the Christian Religion and Church,* were translated in the 1880s, extending Neander's influence to the English-speaking world.

1813 ✠ INDIA IS OPENED TO MISSIONS

Prior to 1813, mission work in India was discouraged because the East India Company feared missionary activity could give Indians a negative impression of Europeans. Although some missionaries, like William Carey (1761–1834), managed to obtain entrance into the country, it was not until the East India Company Charter was renewed in 1813 that the official missionary restrictions were lifted. This new freedom to pursue missions made it possible for groups from Sweden, Norway, Germany, Switzerland, and Denmark to become more active, and by the late twentieth century British missionaries were outnumbered by Americans. The British government endorsed missionary schools will-

1791	1793-4	1808	1846
U.S. Bill of Rights written	Reign of Terror in France	Napoleon controls almost all Europe	One million Irish starve in Potato Famine

ing to consent to secular control but, aside from abolishing certain Hindu practices, maintained religious neutrality in India.

1814 ✝ JESUITS ARE REESTABLISHED

Though Pope Clement XIII (1693–1769) suppressed the Jesuits (Society of Jesus) in 1773, the society continued on in the United States, England, Germany, and Austria. With support and protection from many in these countries, the order grew and was able to regain much of its former strength. The Jesuits were finally restored in 1814, when Pope Pius VII (1742–1823) brought the order into full communion with the church. Today, the Jesuit order is a major resource for the Roman Catholic Church throughout the world.

1815 ✝ ✡ POPE PIUS VII REESTABLISHES THE GHETTO OF ROME

The conquering armies of Napoléon Bonaparte (1769–1821) broke down the Jewish ghettos wherever they encountered them, including the ghetto in Rome, which was nearly two hundred years old. Like other European ghettos, the Roman Ghetto separated the Jews from the rest of the population and forced desolation and poverty on the Jewish population. The Roman Ghetto, as well as those in other papal territories, was perhaps unique in that it was established by the church under the decree of Pope Paul IV (1476–1559). In 1815, after Napoléon's defeat, Pope Pius VII (1742–1823) reestablished the ghetto of Rome, forcing Jews to live within its confines. While many ghettos were reestablished in the nineteenth century, the Roman Ghetto was among the few where the walls Napoléon destroyed were actually rebuilt.

1816 ✝ THE AMERICAN BIBLE SOCIETY IS FOUNDED

Modeled after the successful British and Foreign Bible Society (BFBS), the American Bible Society (ABS) was founded in 1816 in New York City by representatives of regional Bible societies throughout the country. Within a year, forty-one local and regional societies became auxiliary members of the ABS. John Quincy Adams (1767–1848) and Francis Scott Key (1779–1843) were among the ABS's first officials. As Bibles became plentiful in America, the ABS

1856	1903	1905	1914
Transatlantic cable developed	Wright brothers make first flight	Albert Einstein develops Theory of Relativity	Panama Canal completed

expanded their efforts to the translation and international distribution of Bibles in other languages.

1816 ✝ AMERICAN COLONIZATION SOCIETY IS FORMED

The American Colonization Society originally was founded in 1816, by Robert Finley (1772–1817) with the help of the United States government. The society's purpose was to return freed slaves to Africa, and it established the nation of Liberia to that end. The society also raised money to buy slaves and give them freedom. The founders hoped that the return of Christian freed men to Africa would be a means that God would use to evangelize the African continent. The society itself experienced many setbacks in seeing its vision come to fruition. The first group of 114 that returned to Africa was almost completely wiped out by disease. When the society's authority to govern Liberia was denied by the British, an independent government was set up in 1847 that was both sponsored by and modeled after the United States. By 1867, approximately ten thousand freed slaves had been transported to Liberia.

1816 ✝ NETTLETON LEADS THE BRIDGEWATER REVIVAL

As America's Second Great Awakening waned, Asahel Nettleton (1783–1844) tapered off his traveling evangelistic ministry and became pastor of the Congregational church in Bridgewater, Connecticut. The Bridgewater church was struggling with issues of pride and disharmony, and Nettleton's sermons addressing the need for love and unity seemed to have little effect. He decided that if his preaching was ineffectual, maybe God would use his silence. So, one Sunday in 1816, Nettleton did not show up for church, leaving a room full of waiting people. This unique rebuke by their pastor stirred the congregation into organizing a day of prayer and confession to deal with the problems in their church. By the time Nettleton returned to the Bridgewater pulpit, the church was experiencing an exciting revival that soon spread to other towns.

1816 ✝ HALDANE BEGINS GENEVA'S SECOND REFORMATION

Robert Haldane (1764–1842) left Scotland in 1816 in order to begin a new ministry on the European continent. He first went to France but then settled in

1791	1793-4	1808	1846
U.S. Bill of Rights written	Reign of Terror in France	Napoleon controls almost all Europe	One million Irish starve in Potato Famine

Geneva, Switzerland. A revival began quietly among divinity students at a local Geneva college. Groups of twenty to thirty young men gathered daily at Haldane's apartment after their seminary classes to hear him discuss theology. These young men reported learning more from Haldane during those afternoons than during their entire course of study at the seminary. They in turn became the carriers of revival throughout Switzerland and the French-speaking world, extending as far as Quebec, Canada, in what soon became known as Geneva's Second Reformation.

1816 ✝ RICHARD ALLEN IS APPOINTED BISHOP OF AFRICAN METHODIST EPISCOPAL CHURCH

Richard Allen (1760–1831) was born a slave in the United States. At seventeen, he was converted to Christ through the Methodists and started preaching the gospel. After teaching himself to read and write, Allen purchased his freedom. Continuing to preach, he worked several trades and headed for Philadelphia. There Allen worshiped regularly at St. George's Methodist Church. However, upon learning that the church had decided black parishioners could sit only in the balcony, Allen and his black friend Absalom Jones (1746–1818) walked out of the church, followed by other black parishioners. Allen and Jones then founded the Free African Society, the first American organization founded by African Americans for African Americans. A few years later, Allen founded Bethel Church in Philadelphia for black Methodists. Due to the uneasiness of white Methodists toward them, Allen's congregation joined other black churches to form the African Methodist Episcopal Church. Allen was appointed its first bishop in 1816.

1816 ✝ ROBERT MOFFAT GOES TO AFRICA

While apprenticing as a gardener at High Leigh, Cheshire, England, Robert Moffat (1795–1883) was converted through the Methodists and, while attending a missionary meeting, he decided to devote his life to foreign missions. With little education and the somewhat hesitant support of the London Missionary Society, Moffat set sail for South Africa in 1816. He served for more than fifty years, mostly in Great Namaqualand (West Namibia) and in Kuruman,

1856	1903	1905	1914
Transatlantic cable developed	Wright brothers make first flight	Albert Einstein develops Theory of Relativity	Panama Canal completed

Bechuanaland (Botswana). He was a proficient translator of Bechuana, completing translations of the Bible, various hymns, *The Pilgrim's Progress,* and textbooks in their native language. In addition, his evangelistic efforts along with those of his son-in-law, David Livingstone (1813–1873), saw the establishment of many churches with trained African pastors. Known as the father of South African missions, Moffat was awarded an honorary doctorate by Edinburgh University in 1872.

1817 ✝ ELIZABETH FRY ORGANIZES RELIEF IN NEWGATE PRISON

Born to English Quakers, Elizabeth Gurney Fry (1780–1845) underwent an awakening while listening to the preaching of an American Quaker. She married an affluent London merchant in 1800, who supported her ministry to the needy. While raising eleven children, Elizabeth donated clothes and medicine, rallied for school enrollment, encouraged Bible reading, started more than five hundred libraries in British coastguard stations, and founded the "Nursing Sisters of Devonshire Square" for nurses in training. Elizabeth's greatest passion, however, was reforming prisons. After having spent years teaching female prisoners in Newgate Prison to read and sew, she founded the Association for the Improvement of the Female Prisoners in Newgate in 1817. She campaigned for female wardens, education, and privacy for female prisoners. Elizabeth published notes from her prison tours in England and Scotland and testified in the House of Commons. She later traveled to France and northern Europe, inspiring prison reform there as well.

1818 ✡ HAMBURG TEMPLE IS OPENED

Reform Judaism began in Germany in the early nineteenth century with reformers trying to remove any practice or ritual that identified Jews as foreigners. Among the changes they initiated, Reform Jews began referring to their synagogues as temples and started using German, the national language, in their services instead of Hebrew. The Hamburg Temple, which opened its doors in 1818, was the first Jewish place of worship built by Reform Jews. A revised prayer book, which included prayers in German, was used at the Hamburg Temple. From Germany, Reform Judaism spread to the United States.

1791	1793-4	1808	1846
U.S. Bill of Rights written	Reign of Terror in France	Napoleon controls almost all Europe	One million Irish starve in Potato Famine

THE PATIENT LABORER

June 6, 1819

The seeds of evangelism bear fruit in God's time, not man's.

Pioneer missionary Adoniram Judson graduated from Brown University as valedictorian at the age of nineteen and then graduated in 1810 in the first class of Andover Theological Seminary. He and his wife journeyed from America to Burma (now Myanmar), arriving in 1813. Shortly thereafter they were joined by two other missionaries. However, after six years of labor not one Burmese person had trusted in Christ.

Then on June 6, 1819, Judson received a letter from Moung Nau, a Burmese man who had shown great interest in the gospel but up to that point had not acted on it. The letter read as follows:

I, Moung Nau, the constant recipient of your excellent favor, approach your feet. Whereas my Lord's three [i.e. three missionaries] come to the country of Burma—not for the purposes of trade, but to preach the religion of Jesus Christ, the Son of the eternal God—I, having heard and understood, am, with a joyful mind, filled with love.

I believe that the divine Son, Jesus Christ, suffered death, in the place of men, to atone for their sins. Like a heavy-laden man, I feel my sins are very many. The punishment of my sins I deserve to suffer. Since it is so, do you, sirs, consider that I, taking refuge in the merits of the Lord Jesus Christ, and receiving baptism, in order to become his disciple, shall dwell one with yourselves, a band of brothers, in the happiness of heaven, and therefore grant me the ordinance of baptism.

Moreover, as it is only since I have met with you, sirs, that I have known about the eternal God, I venture to pray that you will still unfold to me the religion of God, that my old disposition may be destroyed, and my new disposition improved.

Three weeks later Moung Nau was baptized and the barrier of unbelief was broken.

What enabled Adoniram Judson to faithfully labor so many years before seeing any fruit? His motivation is evident in the following lines, which he penciled on the inner cover of a book used in his translation of the Bible into Burmese:

In joy or in pain,
Our course be onward still;
We sow on Burma's barren plain;
We reap on Zion's hill.

Today there are more than 1.5 million believers in Myanmar, and 40 percent of the Karen people to whom Adoniram Judson directed his ministry are now Christians.

1819 ✝ CHANNING EMBRACES UNITARIAN CHRISTIANITY

Born in Newport, Rhode Island, William Ellery Channing (1780–1842) earned his B.A. from Harvard where he had a conversion experience. In 1803, he became the pastor of Federal Street Congregational Church in Boston where he spent the rest of his life. In 1819, he delivered a sermon at an ordination in which he embraced the basic ideas of Unitarianism by denying the Trinity, the deity of Christ, total depravity, and Christ's atoning sacrifice. While Channing upheld the Resurrection, New Testament miracles, and the moral purity of Christ, he confessed that though the Bible contained inspiration, it was not itself an inspired book. In 1820, he coordinated the meeting of liberal ministers at the Berry Street Conference, which soon after became the American Unitarian Association.

1819 ✡ HEP! HEP! RIOTS BEGIN

The early nineteenth century witnessed the fall of the empire established by Napoléon Bonaparte (1769–1821). To reestablish the monarchies and their territories, representatives of the European powers that had been conquered by Napoléon's armies gathered at the Council of Vienna. Although the council granted these various rulers their right to rule, the gathering refused to uphold the rights that Napoléon had given to the Jews. Echoing the sentiment of Vienna, anti-Semitic riots broke out in Germany in 1819 and 1820. For reasons that are unclear, the rallying cry was "Hep! Hep!" The riots spread throughout Germany, reaching as far as Denmark and Poland. The response of many German Jews was to assimilate as much as possible into secular society, believing that if they became fully German they would be treated as such.

1821 ✝ LOTT CAREY BECOMES THE FIRST BLACK MISSIONARY TO AFRICA

Lott Carey (c.1780–1829) was born into slavery in Virginia. Although raised by his devout Baptist grandmother, as a young man Carey shunned Christianity. In 1807, Carey was converted and taught himself to read in order to study the Bible. He became a Baptist laypastor while continuing to work to earn his family's freedom. Burdened for the evangelism of Africa, Carey founded the Rich-

1791	1793-4	1808	1846
U.S. Bill of Rights written	Reign of Terror in France	Napoleon controls almost all Europe	One million Irish starve in Potato Famine

LOTT CAREY

January 23, 1821

His life spanned two continents.

Lott Carey didn't know the exact year of his birth because records of slave births weren't kept, but he estimated it to be around 1780 on a plantation near Richmond, Virginia. His grandmother, a devout Baptist, cared for him while his parents worked. She taught him the suffering of slaves in America and the need of those remaining in Africa to hear about Jesus.

As a young man working as a slave laborer, Carey showed no signs of espousing his grandmother's faith. Then in 1807, Carey was in the gallery of the First Baptist Church in Richmond and heard a sermon about Jesus telling Nicodemus that he must be born again. Carey was profoundly moved and put his trust in Jesus Christ. After he was baptized, he determined to learn to read the Bible for himself. After he taught himself to read and write, he continued his education in a night school started by a white Baptist named William Crane.

Carey earned repeated promotions at the Shockoe tobacco warehouse where he worked. Around the age of thirty-three he purchased freedom for himself and his two children for $850—much more than his annual salary. His first wife had died, and he later remarried.

Carey began preaching to gatherings of African Americans, eventually forming and becoming the pastor of a black church. Meanwhile, through his night classes with William Crane, he became very interested in African missions.

His church grew to over eight hundred members, while he remained respected and secure in his position at the tobacco warehouse. Yet his burden for missions to Africa increased, and finally he decided to go there himself.

In his final sermon to his congregation, Carey said, "I am about to leave you and expect to see your faces no more. I long to preach to the poor Africans the way of life and salvation. I don't know what may befall me, whether I may find a grave in the ocean, or among the savage men, or more savage wild beasts on the coast of Africa; nor am I anxious what may become of me. I feel it my duty to go."

On January 23, 1821, Carey sailed with his family as the first black missionary to Africa. In Liberia he founded and served as pastor of Providence Baptist Church. He helped to establish schools and was the first president of the Monrovia Baptist Missionary Society. When the white governor of the colony was forced to leave because of illness, he appointed Carey as provisional governor.

In 1829, as Carey was preparing to rescue some of his men who had been imprisoned while negotiating with a native tribe, he and seven coworkers died in an explosion of gunpowder apparently set off by an overturned candle. It had been eight years since Carey had set sail for Africa and forty-nine since he had been born a slave in America.

mond (Virginia) African Missionary Society. On January 23, 1821, Carey sailed with his family to become the first black missionary to Africa. He settled in Liberia, then a newly established haven for freed slaves. Carey helped set up a mission and schools and was serving as Liberia's interim governor at the time of his death in 1829.

1821 ✛ SCHLEIERMACHER PUBLISHES THE CHRISTIAN FAITH

Friedrich Schleiermacher (1768–1834) was among the most prominent German theologians of the nineteenth century. In 1821, while a professor at the newly established university in Berlin, Schleiermacher published his magnum opus, *The Christian Faith*. In it, he rejected both historic orthodoxy and strict natural theology. Instead, he posited a religion loosely based on Christian orthodoxy but ultimately defined in terms of human experience. For Schleiermacher, the basis of religion was the human self-consciousness. A right self-understanding would result in a feeling of divine dependence. This self-understanding was the basis for all religion. He also rejected the divine nature of Christ, claiming that Jesus was a man whose intense dependence on God resulted in his full experience of God's existence. Schleiermacher's work helped shape the developing theological liberalism of the early twentieth century.

1822 ✛ THE SOCIETY FOR THE PROPAGATION OF THE FAITH

In 1815, the Catholic bishop Louis-Guillaume-Valentin Dubourg (1766–1833) of New Orleans traveled to Lyons, France, to collect money for his diocese. While there he shared with Mrs. Petit, a woman from the United States, his idea of founding a missionary society to evangelize the Louisiana Territory. Her brother wrote a letter to Pauline Marie Jaricot (1782–1862) of Lyons, who then conceived a plan in which parishioners would contribute one penny per week to propagate missionary efforts. In 1822, Bishop Dubourg sent his vicar-general from New Orleans to Lyons to discuss a possible American counterpart to the missionary effort. However, after meeting in Lyons, they decided that American and European societies would be united as the Society for the Propagation of the Faith. The society was formally established on May 3, 1822, and became the primary institution for funding Catholic missions in the nineteenth century.

1791	1793-4	1808	1846
U.S. Bill of Rights written	Reign of Terror in France	Napoleon controls almost all Europe	One million Irish starve in Potato Famine

AN ATTORNEY WHO SWITCHED CLIENTS

October 10, 1821

In 1818, a twenty-six-year-old man named Charles Finney began a law apprenticeship in Adams, New York. Although having had a limited formal education, within just three years he became a junior partner in the law firm.

As Finney studied law, the authors he read often quoted the Bible. Realizing his own ignorance of the Scriptures, he began to study them for himself.

When a new minister came to the local Presbyterian church, Finney began to attend. In the summer of 1821, the pastor took a trip and told his replacement just to read sermons from a book. Surprisingly, the Holy Spirit began to move among the church members, and Finney started to spend a lot of time wondering about his own salvation.

He later recounted what happened on October 10, 1821:

Just before I arrived at the office, something seemed to confront me with questions like these: . . . "Did you not promise to give your heart to God? And what are you trying to do? Are you endeavoring to work out a righteousness of your own?"

Just at that point the whole question of God's salvation opened to my mind. . . . I saw that his work was a finished work; that instead of having, or needing, any righteousness of my own to recommend me to God, I had to submit myself to the righteousness of God through Christ. It was full and complete, and all that was necessary on my part was to . . . give up my sins and accept Christ. Salvation, it seemed to me, instead of being a thing to be wrought out by one's own works, was a thing to be found entirely in the Lord Jesus Christ.

Instead of going to his office, Finney went into a nearby woods and spent the morning wrestling with God in prayer until he reported, "I found that my mind had become most wonderfully quiet and peaceful."

The next day, a client who was a deacon from his church came into his office and reminded him, "Mr. Finney, do you recollect that my case is to be tried at ten this morning?"

Finney replied, "Deacon, I have a retainer from the Lord Jesus Christ to plead His cause, and I cannot plead yours."

Charles Finney went on to become the leading revivalist of the nineteenth century with approximately a half million people coming to Christ through the influence of his ministry. Beginning in upstate New York, his revivals swept through New York City, Philadelphia, Boston, and Rochester. In 1835, he became professor of theology at the newly formed Oberlin Collegiate Institute, now Oberlin College. He served as the college's president from 1851 to 1866. Theologically, Finney was his own man. His point of departure was Calvinism, but he placed great emphasis on man's ability to repent and made perfectionism the trademark of Oberlin theology.

It all started on that fateful day in 1821, when Charles Finney switched from the practice of law to pleading the cause of Christ.

1824 ✝ FINNEY ORDAINED AND BEGINS REVIVALS

Charles Finney (1792–1874) was born in Connecticut and raised in Oneida County, New York. While working as an attorney, Finney started attending church with a friend but was skeptical at first. After studying Scripture for himself, Finney put his faith in Christ. He soon began preaching and was ordained a Presbyterian minister in 1824. That year, the Female Missionary Society of the Western District commissioned Finney to evangelize settlers in New York. Finney held evangelistic meetings, often lasting for days, and his preaching led to many revivals. Over the next eight years, Finney held revivals throughout the eastern United States, in cities such as New York, Boston, Philadelphia, and Rochester. His teaching emphasized mankind's ability to repent and to achieve sinless perfection.

1824 ✝ THE AMERICAN SUNDAY SCHOOL UNION IS FOUNDED

The American Sunday School Union was founded in 1824 as an outgrowth of the Sunday and Adult School Union in Philadelphia. Its purpose was to develop Sunday schools "wherever there is a population." Run mainly by the laity, the society established thousands of schools, especially on the frontier along the Mississippi River. Following the Civil War, however, an increasing number of denominations began assuming responsibility for their own Christian education. In 1970, the American Sunday School Union changed its name to the American Missionary Society, redirecting its focus to assisting multicultural communities.

1824 ✡ REFORM CONGREGATION IS FOUNDED
IN CHARLESTON, SOUTH CAROLINA

Although Reform Judaism took root in Germany in the early nineteenth century, the majority of synagogues built in the United States were Orthodox. However, Reform Judaism spread to the United States within fifteen years of its 1810 beginning in Europe. The first Reform congregation was established in Charleston, South Carolina, in 1824. Shortly thereafter, a Reform synagogue named the Emanu-El Temple was founded in New York City. The changes peculiar to American Reform Judaism included the use of the organ, mixing of the

1791	1793-4	1808	1846
U.S. Bill of Rights written	Reign of Terror in France	Napoleon controls almost all Europe	One million Irish starve in Potato Famine

AN APE OF A COLD GOD

August 26, 1824

Baptism didn't do him any good.

Karl Marx was born on May 5, 1818, in Truer, Prussia, descending from a distinguished line of Jewish scholars. His father was an attorney, who became a Lutheran when an 1816 Prussian decree prohibited Jews from holding prestigious law positions. Karl and his siblings were baptized on August 26, 1824.

Karl was confirmed at fifteen and for a while appeared to be a committed Christian. However, as he continued his education, all appearances of Christianity faded away. He received a doctorate in philosophy from Jena University and settled in London in 1849, where he remained for the rest of his life.

Marx was a poet, whose early writing revolved around two themes: his love for Jenny von Westphalen, whom he married in 1841, and the destruction of the world. In one poem he wrote, "We are the apes of a cold God." One of his favorite phrases was from Faust: "Everything that exists deserves to perish." The theme of a coming apocalyptic conflagration occupied his thinking throughout his life. This vision of doomsday was an artistic notion in Marx's mind, not a scientific conclusion. It was a theory from which he as a political scientist worked backwards.

Many of his favorite phrases showed his disdain for religion: "Religion is the opiate of the people"; "Religion is only the illusionary sun around which man revolves, until he begins to revolve around himself."

What kind of fruit would attitudes like these produce in a man's life? Marx had a very unhealthy lifestyle. He smoked and drank heavily. He seldom bathed or washed. He was totally incompetent at handling money. He never seriously tried to get a job but, instead, lived off loans from family and friends that he never repaid.

Marx was saved financially by substantial inheritances that provided an annual income equal to three times the earnings of a skilled workman at that time. Even with this generous inheritance, all Marx and his wife knew how to do was spend and borrow. The family's silver service was often at the pawnbrokers, as were their clothes.

In spite of writing about the struggle of the working class, Marx personally knew only one member of that class, a woman named Lenchen Demuth, who was the Marx family's servant from 1845 until her death in 1890. Although Marx collected reports of many low-paid workers, he never found evidence of a worker who was paid no wages at all. Yet one such person lived in his own house. Lenchen never received a cent from Marx for her labors, only room and board. Marx fathered a son, Freddy, by her but convinced his protégé Friedrich Engels to claim paternity in his stead. Freddy was allowed to visit Lenchen only by coming to the back door. Marx met his son once, at the back door, but Freddy never realized that the radical philosopher was his father.

Marx's life serves as an example of the wasted potential of a human heart without God.

sexes during worship, and the introduction of English to the service. Like the reformers in Europe, Reform Jews in the United States hoped to promote the identity of Jews as assimilated American citizens rather than foreigners.

1825 ✛ AMERICAN TRACT SOCIETY BEGINS ITS PUBLICATIONS

In 1825, the New York and Massachusetts Tract Societies merged to form the American Tract Society. The society pioneered many innovative printing techniques and by 1830 had printed more than 5 million tracts, in addition to books and other periodicals. Although intentionally nondenominational, the society represented mainline Calvinism during its early years. In spite of its unwillingness to oppose slavery, the society continued to flourish during the 1850s and 1860s. After the Civil War, the society was heavily involved in the evangelism of freed slaves. As support waned in the early twentieth century, the society ceased publication of other materials and began to focus exclusively on the publication of small tracts and pamphlets. The American Tract Society continues to publish more than 30 million tracts annually.

1825 ✛ LA REVEIL REVIVAL SPREADS THROUGH EUROPE

As the Second Great Awakening was sweeping through the United States, the first signs of reawakening in Europe were seen in Geneva in 1810, spreading to French-speaking Swiss churches in 1825. *La Reveil* (literally "the Awakening") was a spiritual reaction against the Rationalism and materialism that had increasingly characterized the churches on the Continent since the Enlightenment. The newly revived pastors preached the supremacy of God in human affairs, the Bible as the standard for truth, and personal spiritual awakening as the evidence of saving faith. *La Reveil* spread from Switzerland to France and the Netherlands by 1825, touching a thousand congregations with renewal and drawing several thousand new believers to saving faith in Christ.

1826 ✛ THOLUCK BEGINS TEACHING AT HALLE

Friedrich August Gottreu Tholuck (1799–1877) was a German Protestant theologian whose undergraduate studies at Breslau and Berlin focused on Eastern languages. After he was converted to Christ, however, he redirected his study to

1791	1793-4	1808	1846
U.S. Bill of Rights written	Reign of Terror in France	Napoleon controls almost all Europe	One million Irish starve in Potato Famine

theology. In 1826, after a short term teaching theology at Berlin, Tholuck was appointed professor of theology at the University of Halle, where he stayed for forty-nine years. An opponent of rationalism, he wrote commentaries on John, Romans, Hebrews, Psalms, and the Sermon on the Mount. Involved in the revival movements of his day and acclaimed for his ministry to students, Tholuck did much to further the cause of evangelical scholarship during his lifetime.

1827 ✡ CZAR NICHOLAS I ISSUES THE CANTONIST DECREES IN RUSSIA

Russian rulers were threatened by the significant presence of the Jewish population since the division of Poland in the 1770s. In 1827, Czar Nicholas I (1796–1855) devised a scheme to absorb Jews into Russian culture. Nicholas issued the Cantonist Decrees (a canton being a military recruiting district), which forced Jewish community leaders to provide a certain number of Jewish recruits between the ages of twelve and twenty-five who were then required to complete twenty-five years of military service. Twelve-year-olds had to spend an additional six years in training before their twenty-five-year commitment began. The czar created Cantonist battalions, which forced the Jewish boys into Russian Orthodox Christianity. In addition to creating a captive audience for religious conversion, the czar's Cantonist Decrees caused much dissension among Jews, as leaders tended to protect their own families, sending the poor instead.

1829 ✝ MENDELSSOHN CONDUCTS BACH'S ST. MATTHEW PASSION

Jakob Ludwig Felix Mendelssohn-Bartholdy (1809–1847) was born in Hamburg, Germany, and was raised in Berlin by Jewish converts to the Lutheran church. Mendelssohn was a gifted pianist and a precocious composer who had written twelve symphonies by the age of twelve. His musical mentors introduced him to the compositions of Johann Sebastian Bach (1685–1750), whose work at the time was largely ignored by all but a small circle of musical connoisseurs. Mendelssohn loved Bach's music. At age twenty, Mendelssohn conducted Bach's *St. Matthew Passion* oratorio, which had not been performed since before Bach's death in 1750. The concert marked the beginning of a revival of Bach's music that continues today. Mendelssohn went on to write his own oratorios, including *Elijah* (1846), considered to be the premier choral work of the nineteenth century.

1856	1903	1905	1914
Transatlantic cable developed	Wright brothers make first flight	Albert Einstein develops Theory of Relativity	Panama Canal completed

1830 ✝ JOSEPH SMITH JR. FOUNDS THE MORMON CHURCH

On April 6, 1830, Joseph Smith Jr. (1805–1841) and five others met in Fayette, New York, to found a new religious society called the Church of Christ. Eventually renamed the Church of Jesus Christ of Latter-day Saints, it is popularly known as the Mormon Church. Smith claimed to have found their Scripture, *The Book of Mormon*, on "golden plates" he unearthed from a hill near Palmyra, New York, then translated from "reformed Egyptian hieroglyphics." No one but Smith ever saw the golden tablets. Today, the Mormons claim more than eleven million members, more than half of whom live outside the United States.

1830 ✝ JOHN NELSON DARBY BEGINS DEVELOPING DISPENSATIONALISM

In 1825, a group of men led by John Nelson Darby (1800–1882) began meeting in Dublin because of their dissatisfaction with the Protestant churches of the area. The group was particularly interested in eschatology. In 1830, Darby visited Margaret MacDonald in Port Glasgow, Scotland, and heard how earlier in the year she had received a revelation that a select group of Christians would be raptured before the time of the Antichrist. Darby began popularizing the doctrine of the pretribulation rapture of the church in prophecy conferences. In succeeding years he developed his theology of dispensationalism from his premise of the pretribulation rapture.

1831 ✝ EVANGELICAL SOCIETY OF GENEVA IS FORMED

Orthodox Christianity in Geneva, Switzerland, had sunk to a low point since the days of John Calvin (1509–1564). In this climate in 1816, Louis Gaussen (1790–1863) became pastor of the village parish of Satigny near Geneva after being converted to Christ through the ministry of Robert Haldane (1764–1842). Gaussen republished the Helvetic Confession in French. In 1831, Gaussen and two colleagues formed the Evangelical Society of Geneva for the distribution of Bibles and tracts. As a result, he was suspended by the local consistory. Undaunted, the Evangelical Society also founded a new theological school where Louis Gaussen became professor of dogmatics.

1791	1793-4	1808	1846
U.S. Bill of Rights written	Reign of Terror in France	Napoleon controls almost all Europe	One million Irish starve in Potato Famine

LATTER-DAY SAINTS?

April 6, 1830

It's amazing what can result from unsubstantiated claims.

In 1820, a fourteen-year-old boy named Joseph Smith Jr. claimed to have received a vision in which God the Father and God the Son appeared to him and told him they had chosen him to launch a restoration of true Christianity. He apparently was not overly moved by this revelation because he went back to digging for Captain Kidd's treasure with his father and his brother.

When he was seventeen, he claimed to have been visited by an angel named Moroni who supposedly told him that he would receive the "golden plates" of *The Book of Mormon* to translate. In 1827, Smith alleged that he unearthed the plates in the hill Cumorah, near Palmyra, New York. Smith claimed he translated the "reformed Egyptian hieroglyphics" with the help of miraculous glasses he supposedly received from Moroni. Oliver Cowdery, a schoolteacher and a convert of Smith's, assisted in his translation, although no one but Smith ever saw the golden tablets. In 1829, during the translation, the "Prophet," as Smith liked to be called, alleged that John the Baptist was sent by Peter, James, and John to bestow the "Aaronic Priesthood" on himself and Oliver. They completed their translation in early 1830, and *The Book of Mormon* was published and copyrighted.

On April 6, 1830, Joseph Smith Jr., his two brothers Hyrum and Samuel, Oliver Cowdery, and David and Peter Whitmer Jr. met in Fayette, New York, to found a new religious society they called the Church of Christ. Eventually known as the Church of Jesus Christ of Latter-day Saints, the Mormon Church was begun.

Soon after their founding, the Mormons moved to Kirtland, Ohio, where in six years they grew to more than sixteen thousand members. Accusations that Smith's religion was a hoax caused the new church to move several times. From Ohio they moved to Jackson County, Missouri, and then on to Nauvoo, Illinois. Despite the moves, their problems followed them to each new location. The trouble heightened in Nauvoo when their practice of polygamy became known. Although the exact number of Smith's wives is unknown, it has been estimated to be as high as fifty. When Smith called for destruction of an outspokenly anti-Mormon newspaper, the state of Illinois stepped in and jailed Joseph Smith and his brother Hyrum. On June 27, 1844, an angry mob stormed the jail and murdered both men.

After the death of Joseph Smith, Brigham Young became the leader of the Mormons. Young led the group across the Great Plains and over the Rocky Mountains to the Salt Lake Valley in 1846. Under his leadership the Mormons were granted recognition as a legitimate religion. Brigham Young had twenty-seven wives and fifty-six children.

Today the Mormons claim more than eleven million members, over half residing outside the United States.

1831 ✛ PLYMOUTH BRETHREN BEGIN

The Plymouth Brethren formed under the leadership of John Nelson Darby (1800–1882) as a protest to both the formalism of worship and the spiritual deadness of the Church of England. They desired to remove the barriers that divided Christians and return to the simplicity and authenticity of worship in apostolic days. In 1831, the group formalized their first congregation in Plymouth, England. Their numbers grew rapidly, despite significant church divisions. In 1848, there was a split between the mainstream of the movement (Open Brethren) and the Darbyist group (Exclusive Brethren). Today the Brethren continue to be an influential denomination in many parts of the world.

1831 ✛ TONGUES ARE SPOKEN IN EDWARD IRVING'S CHURCH

Edward Irving (1792–1834), ordained by the Church of Scotland in 1815, played an important role in preparing for later charismatic and millenarian movements. In July 1822, when he was thirty, Irving was called to the Caledonian Chapel in London, where his forceful preaching style attracted great crowds. Under Irving's leadership, the church quickly became the largest in London. His teaching emphasized the supernatural and the imminence of Christ's return. In the fall of 1831, members of Irving's church began to speak in tongues, practice faith healing, and have prophetic visions, although Irving himself did not possess these gifts. After his death, some of Irving's followers formed the Catholic Apostolic Church.

1833 ✛ SLAVERY IS ABOLISHED IN THE BRITISH EMPIRE

William Wilberforce (1759–1833) decided that he could best serve God through a career in politics. Elected to the English Parliament in 1780, he devoted his life to the fight against slavery. Largely as a result of his efforts, the slave trade within the British Empire was abolished in 1807. Just before his death on July 29, 1833, Wilberforce was gratified to learn that a bill abolishing slavery itself in all British territories finally was assured of passage.

1791	1793-4	1808	1846
U.S. Bill of Rights written	Reign of Terror in France	Napoleon controls almost all Europe	One million Irish starve in Potato Famine

DEDICATION TO A CAUSE

July 26, 1833

He never gave up.

William Wilberforce was born to affluence in Hull, England, in 1759. His schooling began at Hull Grammar School, where he came under the influence of two brothers, headmaster Joseph Milner and teacher Isaac Milner.

Wilberforce developed a social conscience at a young age. When he was only fourteen he wrote a letter to the local newspaper on the evils of the slave trade. He completed his education at St. John's College, Cambridge, where he largely wasted his time. However, in 1780 he was elected to Parliament where he became a supporter and confidant of British Prime Minister William Pitt, the Younger. Pitt persuaded Wilberforce to focus his efforts on the abolition of slavery.

In 1785, Wilberforce was looking for a traveling companion for a European tour when he ran into Isaac Milner, his old grade-school teacher who then was a tutor at Cambridge. On an impulse he invited Milner on the trip, expenses paid, and Milner accepted. Had Wilberforce known that Milner was a committed Christian, he would not have extended the invitation.

As Wilberforce and Milner traveled together, they began arguing about religion. By the end of their trip, Wilberforce had given intellectual assent to many of the teachings of the Bible, but once back home he returned to politics and put religion on a back burner.

The next year Wilberforce took Isaac Miner on another tour of Europe. This time they studied the Greek New Testament together. Wilberforce later said, "I now fully believed the gospel and was persuaded that if I died at anytime I should perish everlastingly."

By October 1785, Wilberforce was miserable, realizing that he must choose between Christ and the world. Deciding that he needed to talk about it with someone, Wilberforce went to see his boyhood hero John Newton, the author of "Amazing Grace." On December 7, 1785, he left John Newton's home with the decision settled. He had chosen Christ and committed himself to being God's man in politics.

Wilberforce became the leader of a group of wealthy Anglican evangelicals who lived mainly in the hamlet of Clapham, three miles from London. They became known as the Clapham Sect, although they were in no sense a sect. They were more like a close family, determined to change the world for Jesus. They determined which wrongs needed to be righted and then delegated to each person the work he could best perform for their mutual goals.

Wilberforce and his friends' first great achievement was the abolition of the slave trade in 1807. But abolition itself proved a tougher goal to achieve.

On July 26, 1833, Wilberforce was on his deathbed at the age of seventy-three. Late that evening he received word that the Emancipation Act freeing the slaves of the British Empire was assured of passing. His final political goal had been reached. Three days later he died.

1833 ✛ AMERICAN ANTI-SLAVERY SOCIETY SEEKS IMMEDIATE ABOLITION

The American Anti-Slavery Society was founded in Philadelphia in 1833, by members of local and state abolitionist organizations, many of them followers of the revivalist Charles Finney (1792–1875). The abolition of slavery in the British Empire, also in 1833, served as the catalyst for the organization's founding. The main goal of the society was the immediate abolition of slavery, but many realized that the process would be a gradual one. The organization, however, lacked unity and was considered extreme by many supporters of abolition. The disunity in the society caused it to become ineffective by 1840.

1833 ✛ MASSACHUSETTS DISESTABLISHES THE CONGREGATIONAL CHURCH

In 1631, the Massachusetts General Court declared that only church members could vote, making Congregationalism the state religion of Massachusetts. The First Amendment of the Constitution took effect in 1791, prohibiting an officially established national church. However, throughout most of New England both political meetings and church services took place in the same building. In 1824, the Congregational meetinghouse in Deerfield was the first to be used solely for worship. Finally, in 1833, the state of Massachusetts disestablished the Congregational Church.

1833 ✛ JOHN KEBLE'S SERMON LAUNCHES THE OXFORD MOVEMENT

On July 14, 1833, John Keble (1792–1866)—professor of poetry at Oxford University from 1831 to 1841—preached his famous sermon entitled "National Apostasy," from which arose the Oxford, or Tractarian, Movement. The movement began as a reaction against liberalism in the Anglican Church and ended as a movement toward Roman Catholicism. Several of its leaders ultimately left the Church of England and became Roman Catholics.

1835 ✛ FINNEY WRITES LECTURES ON REVIVALS

Charles Finney (1792–1875) came to be known as the "father of Modern Revivalism." He was dramatically converted while working as a legal apprentice in upstate

1791	1793-4	1808	1846
U.S. Bill of Rights written	Reign of Terror in France	Napoleon controls almost all Europe	One million Irish starve in Potato Famine

New York. Without delay, Finney began preaching in the area's villages, and then in the large East Coast cities, working out his technique and theology as he went. Confrontational, energetic, and possessing a penetrating gaze, Charles Finney brought the enthusiasm of camp meetings into the churches. In 1835, Finney wrote *Lectures on Revivals of Religion* based on his experiences. His "New Measures" included prayers for people by name in public, women praying in public, a designated "anxious bench" for convicted sinners, and long, protracted meetings.

1836 ✝ GEORGE MÜLLER OPENS ORPHANAGES

George Müller (1805–1898) was born in Prussia, but became a naturalized British citizen after finishing his theological studies. In 1836, he started his first orphanage in Bristol, soon adding other houses and then moving into the suburbs. He followed the principle of making his financial needs known only to God through prayer, rather than asking other people for financial help. His autobiography, *Narrative of the Lord's Dealings with George Müller,* acquainted people all over the world with his work and faith. Beginning in 1875, he and his second wife toured forty-two countries over a seventeen-year period, generating additional awareness of his work with orphans.

1836 ✝ HAWAIIAN REVIVAL BRINGS THOUSANDS TO CHRIST

Titus Coan (1801–1882) was a missionary in Hawaii who supervised a teacher training college and led a small church of about twenty-three members in Hilo. He longed for revival in Hawaii, and in November 1836, he embarked on a ministry tour of the island. He preached several times a day in each village he entered, drawing large crowds and often preaching through the night. Many were converted, including the high priest and priestess of the volcano, the most influential pagan leaders. Word of the revival had spread by the time he returned to Hilo a month later, and his small church began growing. Whole villages moved to Hilo to attend Coan's church. The revival soon spread to other Hawaiian islands as well, and as a result, thousands were converted to Christ.

1836 ☿ ☾ POSITION OF CHIEF RABBI IS CREATED FOR OTTOMAN EMPIRE

By the end of the eighteenth century, the declining strength of the Ottoman Empire—the Muslim empire that ruled modern-day Turkey and much of the

1856	1903	1905	1914
Transatlantic cable developed	Wright brothers make first flight	Albert Einstein develops Theory of Relativity	Panama Canal completed

Middle East—was apparent to the powers in Europe who had investments to protect within the empire. Influenced by the opinions of these European rulers, the Ottoman sultans issued a variety of laws designed to centralize their control of the empire. Among the decrees affecting Jewish life was the creation of the position of chief rabbi, also referred to as the grand rabbi or *hakham bashi*, who was required to make regular reports to the Ottoman government. While the Ottoman authorities intended the reports of the chief rabbis to strengthen their control over their Jewish subjects, the new rabbinical office actually afforded a greater autonomy to Jewish communities.

1836 ✡ GERMAN JEWS BEGIN IMMIGRATION TO THE UNITED STATES

A large number of German Jews began immigrating to the United States in 1836, drawn by the developing cities and inexpensive land in America. In California, they put their business skills to use by becoming gold prospectors. In cities such as New York, they tended to gather in neighborhoods with other German-speaking Jews, putting their retail and trade abilities to use in everything from pushcarts to storefronts. Despite the existence of Reform Judaism in Germany, the majority of German Jews arriving in America were more traditional and orthodox in their beliefs and practice than were Jews arriving from other nations.

1837 ✝ AUBURN DECLARATION REAFFIRMS NEW SCHOOL COMMITMENT TO CALVINISM

At the 1837 General Assembly of the Presbyterian Church in the USA, the Old School Presbyterians who controlled the church accused the New School Presbyterians of heresy by placing too much emphasis on man's initiative in salvation. As a result, the assembly forced three presbyteries controlled by the New School out of the church. In response, the New School Presbyterians issued the Auburn Declaration in August 1837, which reaffirmed their commitment to Calvinism. However, the 1838 General Assembly refused to reconsider their decisions of the previous year. Consequently, the New School and Old School Presbyterians functioned as separate denominations until 1869, when the two factions reunited based on the language of the Auburn Declaration.

1791	1793-4	1808	1846
U.S. Bill of Rights written	Reign of Terror in France	Napoleon controls almost all Europe	One million Irish starve in Potato Famine

A THEOLOGIAN BECOMES PRIME MINISTER

October 29, 1837

How would you like to have a godly theologian lead your nation? It happened.

On October 29, 1837, a son was born to the pastor of the Reformed state church in Maasslius, the Netherlands. His name was Abraham Kuyper. Growing up in a pastor's home, young Kuyper was disenchanted by the church. In spite of his alienation, he enrolled in the pre-theology curriculum at the University of Leiden.

At this time Modernism, the belief system that exalts human reason over divine revelation, was taking over the theological faculties of Dutch universities. Kuyper did not escape this influence. He entered the university a person of orthodox faith but within a year and a half had become a religious liberal.

The next major event in Kuyper's religious pilgrimage was reading an English novel his fiancée had given to him. *The Heir of Redclyffe* by the Christian author Charlotte Mary Yonge proved to be life changing. Kuyper so identified with the story's proud hero that when the hero knelt and wept before God with a broken and contrite heart, Kuyper did the same. Only later would he truly understand what had occurred in his heart. From that moment on he found himself despising what he once admired and seeking what he once despised.

The final step in his pilgrimage came in his first pastorate. There was a group of individuals of low social status in his church who knew more about the Bible than he did. They had a Calvinistic worldview that he envied, even though he now had a doctorate in theology. The debates Kuyper had with these folk proved to be short lived as he agreed with them more and more that the Bible taught God's sovereign grace. He later wrote, "Their unremitting perseverance has become the blessing of my heart, the rise of the morning star for my life." The wisdom and faith of these simple people taught him to find rest for his soul "in the worship of a God who works all things, both the willing and the working, according to his good pleasure."

Now fully embracing orthodox Calvinism, Kuyper held major pulpits in Utrecht and Amsterdam. Taking up the cause for private schools, he joined the Anti-Revolutionary Party, which opposed godless revolution and made orthodox Calvinism a political force. Eventually he became the head of the party, and beginning in 1874, served repeatedly in the legislature of the Netherlands, as a member of one or the other house. He edited his party's daily newspaper and wrote 16,800 editorials for it. In 1880, Kuyper and others founded the Free University of Amsterdam, which was dedicated to Reformed theology. Kuyper became the professor of systematic theology.

In 1901, Abraham Kuyper became prime minister of the Netherlands, holding the position for four years. Through that role, God used him to shape a nation.

WHEN GOD WENT TO HAWAII

Some go to Hawaii for more than the scenery.

Titus Coan was converted at a Charles Finney revival in western New York State. Graduating from seminary in 1834, Coan went as a missionary to Hilo, Hawaii, then known as the Sandwich Islands. Having a burning desire to bring revival to Hawaii, he applied himself vigorously to learning the native languages of Kau and Puna, and by 1836 was fluent enough to preach in both.

Coan's official responsibility was to train teachers and oversee about two dozen schools. But Coan's vision went far beyond teacher training. His prayer was that Hawaiians would come to Christ, and he determined to take the gospel directly to the people himself. In November 1836, he gave his students a long Christmas vacation and went on a walking tour of the island. He preached each time he came to a village. As he had hoped, crowds of people gathered to hear him. He was able to preach in three to five villages a day.

When Coan reached the Puna region, large crowds gathered to hear him. In the largest city he preached ten times in two days. Many wept as they came to understand that Christ had paid the penalty for their sins on the cross.

A particularly stunning conversion in Puna was that of the high priest of the volcano. Idolatry, drunkenness, adultery, and even murder marked his priesthood. Yet upon his conversion, he became a man filled with zeal for God. His sister, the high priestess of the volcano, was initially hostile to the gospel but put her faith in Christ after seeing the change in her brother.

When Coan returned home to Hilo a month later, he found a heightened interest in the way of salvation. People, in some cases entire villages, who had heard him preach in their villages in Kau and Puna now came to Hilo to hear more. Hilo's population grew to ten thousand as people moved there just to hear Coan preach. On Sundays the two-hundred-by-eighty-five-foot building would be packed, with hundreds more listening outside. The Hawaiians decided they needed a bigger church and in three weeks built a building large enough to hold two thousand people.

In spite of thousands of conversions in 1836 and 1837, the church's membership didn't grow until 1838 and 1839. The slow growth reflected a flaw in Coan's missionary methodology, not disinterest on the part of the new converts. Coan would record the date of each person's conversion and then would wait months before recontacting the people to find out if their conversion was real. Only then would they be invited to join the church. It wasn't until July 1, 1838, that the first converts were finally baptized and received into the church. On that stirring day 1,705 were baptized. By 1853, fifty-six thousand of the seventy-one thousand native Hawaiians were professing Christians.

1837 ✡ MOSES MONTEFIORE IS KNIGHTED

Moses Montefiore (1784–1885), a wealthy English stockbroker, was also the president of the Board of Deputies that represented British Jews. In 1824, he retired from business to devote his life to the oppressed Jews of the world. He was the last of the *shtadtlanim*, prominent Jews whose social standing enabled them to intervene on behalf of persecuted Jews in foreign governments. He was a friend of Queen Victoria (1819–1901), who knighted him in 1837. In 1840, he not only secured the release of Jews accused of blood libel in Damascus, but also persuaded the sultan of Turkey to forbid any further arrests on that charge.

1839 ✝ WILLIAM C. BURNS PREACHES AT THE KILSYTH ANNIVERSARY REVIVAL

In 1839, William Hamilton Burns (1779–1859) wanted to stir the hearts of his congregation and bring revival once again to Kilsyth, Scotland. He decided to celebrate the hundred-year anniversary of the revival the town had experienced under James Robe (1688–1753) by holding services at Robe's grave. He invited his son, William Chalmers Burns (1815–1868), to preach at some of the services. What was planned to be a brief visit turned into many weeks as the people of Kilsyth responded in droves to the young Burns's preaching. Although pleased with the revival he was witnessing, young Burns's true longing was to bring the gospel to unreached people. Therefore, at the peak of his ministry in Scotland, young Burns departed to join Hudson Taylor (1832–1905) in bringing the gospel to inland China.

1840 ✝ LIVINGSTONE SAILS FOR AFRICA

In 1840, David Livingstone (1813–1873) received his medical degree from the University of Glasgow and sailed for Africa the same year. There he married Mary, the daughter of missionary pioneer Robert Moffat (1795–1883). He fixed his goals on taking Christianity to Africa and exploring the land, as well as fighting to end the slave trade. Due in large measure to Livingstone's reports on the scourge of slavery, it soon was outlawed in the civilized world. When Livingstone had not been heard from in quite some time, a *New York Herald* correspondent named Henry Stanley (1841–1904) traveled to the heart of Africa to

1856	1903	1905	1914
Transatlantic cable developed	Wright brothers make first flight	Albert Einstein develops Theory of Relativity	Panama Canal completed

LIVING BY FAITH

| November 21, 1839 |

What would it be like to live by faith, telling your needs to no one but God?

God leads different people in different ways, but he led George Müller to trust him for everything in life and to let his needs be known to God alone.

Müller was born in Prussia in 1805, and though he trained for the Lutheran ministry, led a degenerate life of petty thievery. When he was twenty, a friend invited him to a private home one Saturday evening for a group time of prayer and the reading of a printed sermon (it was illegal in Prussia for laymen to explain the Scriptures). He was intrigued just hearing about such a gathering. Once he arrived, the meeting both puzzled and thrilled Müller, and he realized that his advanced education had not given him the power to pray as eloquently as these simple tradesmen. That night Müller went home feeling that he had found what he had been seeking. God had begun a work of grace in his heart, and he went to sleep peaceful and happy in Jesus.

God continued to work in his life, and in 1829 Müller went to London to train as a missionary to the Jews. Müller soon became convinced of the teachings of the Plymouth Brethren, a group of Christians who functioned without a paid clergy. Over the next years he ministered at several Plymouth Brethren chapels in England.

Earlier in his life, while a student in Halle, Germany, Müller had observed the orphanages that August Francke, German Pietist, had begun in 1696. Through the years he thought about founding an orphanage, and on November 21, 1835, after reading a book about Francke's life, he felt God definitely lead him to start an orphanage in Bristol, England. He immediately asked God for a building, funds to support it, and godly people to operate it. His orphanage was operational within five months and remained the major project of his life.

George Müller continually trusted God for the daily operations of the orphanage. November 21, 1839, four years after his decision to start the orphanage, is a case in point. On that day some small contributions were received, enough for the next day's breakfast for the children but not enough for dinner. Müller described that day's staff meeting in his journal: "Our comfort . . . is 'The morrow shall take thought for the things of itself. Sufficient unto the day is the evil thereof.' Matthew 6:34. We separated very happy in God, though very poor, and our faith much tried."

Two and a half hours before dinner the next day, a large box arrived at the orphanage with a generous contribution plus some valuable items that could be sold. The joy of George Müller and his fellow workers was indescribable, as God once more had provided for his orphans.

search for him. When he finally found him, Stanley uttered the now-famous words, "Dr. Livingstone, I presume."

1840 ✛ ✡ ☾ MONTEFIORE INTERCEDES IN DAMASCUS BLOOD LIBEL AFFAIR

As the Ottoman Empire attempted to centralize its control, conflicts between Muslims, Christians, and Jews continued in Syria. In the Syrian capital of Damascus in 1840, a Jewish barber was accused of murdering a Christian monk and using his blood to celebrate the Jewish Passover. The accusation of "blood libel"—the belief that Jews murdered non-Jews and used their blood in secret rituals—while common in medieval Europe, was unknown in the Middle East. What became known as the Damascus Affair resulted in the imprisonment of nine Jewish religious leaders and children. Confessions obtained through torture precipitated violent attacks on Jews by Christians and Muslims. Eventually, England sent British Jew Sir Moses Montefiore (1784–1885) to intercede on behalf of his terrorized people. Montefiore's diplomacy, with the efforts of others, obtained the release of the nine prisoners.

1842 ✛ TREATY OF NANKING OPENS CHINA

In the early part of the nineteenth century, British merchants were heavily involved in the Chinese opium trade. In 1839, however, the Chinese government declared the opium trade illegal and began to impound opium from the public markets. They also demanded that British merchants and mariners agree not to import opium into China. The British refused to comply with the demands and war soon broke out. Within three years, the British had defeated the Chinese on land and sea, and the Treaty of Nanking was signed on August 29, 1842. In addition to granting the British the colony of Hong Kong, the treaty opened several Chinese towns to British trade and settlements, which in turn effectively opened China to Christian missionaries.

1843 ✡ B'NAI B'RITH IS ESTABLISHED

As Jews immigrated to America and many Jewish businessmen achieved financial success, a desire grew among the wealthy to coordinate their philanthropic efforts. In 1843, B'nai B'rith, Hebrew for "Children of the covenant," became

1856	1903	1905	1914
Transatlantic cable developed	Wright brothers make first flight	Albert Einstein develops Theory of Relativity	Panama Canal completed

the first nonreligious Jewish organization founded in the United States. Similar to other fraternal orders, B'nai B'rith established lodges and focused its work on general Jewish service to the community. Sponsoring the Anti-Defamation League of B'nai B'rith as well as the B'nai B'rith Hillel Foundations on college campuses, B'nai B'rith remains the largest Jewish fraternal order.

1843 ✛ KIERKEGAARD PUBLISHES PHILOSOPHICAL FRAGMENTS

Søren Kierkegaard (1813–1855), a leading Danish philosopher and writer, is considered to be one of the founders of existentialism. Using the pseudonym Johannes Climacus, he published *Philosophical Fragments* in 1844. The nature of faith preoccupied him, and he frequently used words such as *irrational, leap of faith, paradox,* and acceptance of the "absurd." Until the twentieth century, little was known of Kierkegaard outside of Denmark. From that time his writings have become a major influence in philosophy, psychology, and theology.

1843 ✛ PHOEBE PALMER WRITES THE WAY TO HOLINESS

Few women mounted a public platform in the 1840s and 1850s, but Phoebe Worrall Palmer (1807–1874) had something to share. Phoebe Palmer, the wife of a New York physician, had suffered the loss of three young children. Earnestly desiring a deeper faith, Phoebe experienced it on July 26, 1837. She began to share her story of the Holy Spirit's indwelling power at a weekly gathering in New York City known as the "Tuesday Meeting for the Promotion of Holiness." In 1843, a collection of her essays was published as *The Way to Holiness*. Enormously successful, by the time of the Civil War it had appeared in thirty-six editions. Her preaching and publishing were influential in promoting holiness as well as the role of women in religious leadership.

1844 ✛ "THE GREAT DISAPPOINTMENT" LEADS TO FORMATION OF THE SEVENTH-DAY ADVENTIST CHURCH

William Miller (1782–1849)—farmer, army captain in the War of 1812, and licensed Baptist minister—calculated that Christ's return would be within a year of March 21, 1843. When Christ failed to return during that period, Miller

1791	1793-4	1808	1846
U.S. Bill of Rights written	Reign of Terror in France	Napoleon controls almost all Europe	One million Irish starve in Potato Famine

LITTLE WOMAN, LONG SHADOW

December 12, 1840

She stood just four feet three inches tall.

On December 12, 1840, a tiny baby girl was born into an aristocratic family in Albemarle County, Virginia. Her name was Charlotte Diggs Moon, but everyone called her "Lottie." Her stature was small, yet her intellect and strength of character were enormous. In a day when embroidery and dancing distinguished most young ladies, Lottie spoke six languages fluently and earned a master's degree in education from the Albemarle Female Institution in 1861.

Lottie came from a family of dedicated Southern Baptists and attended church most of her life. But at seventeen, she was a staunch skeptic. Faith seemed antithetical to intellect, and Lottie had no need for it.

In December 1858, Dr. John Broadus—who eventually would be one of the first four professors at Southern Baptist Theological Seminary—was holding evangelistic meetings at his Charlottesville Baptist Church. Lottie went to one of the services, intending to scoff.

That night a barking dog kept Lottie awake. As she was in the habit of using otherwise wasted hours to consider various intellectual propositions, she decided to ponder the merits of Christianity. As she laid in the dark, Lottie mentally reviewed Dr. Broadus's sermon, adding to it the Bible texts and arguments she'd heard throughout her life. By the time she got to the evangelist's altar call, the Spirit of God prompted her to respond, and Lottie Moon, the brilliant skeptic, believed. When she finished her prayer of commitment to Jesus, she realized that the dog had stopped barking.

While working as a teacher at age thirty-three, Lottie heard a call to missions "as clear as a bell." In July 1873, the foreign mission board of the Southern Baptist Convention appointed her its first unmarried woman missionary to China.

Lottie arrived in Shantung (now Shandong) Province that year and settled in the city of Tengchow (now Qingdao), where she opened a school for girls. Over time, the focus of her ministry became personal evangelism among the poor.

In 1888, she persuaded the women of the Southern Baptist Convention to take an annual missions offering for China's poor. By 1912, thousands of people were dying of starvation every day in famine-ravaged Shantung Province. Lottie's cupboard was always open to the poor, even when she herself had to go without food.

Christmas Eve 1988 arrived, and as Southern Baptist women collected their special missions offering many were looking forward to meeting the woman who inspired their gifts. At seventy-two, Lottie Moon was coming home. But that same night, she died of complications from starvation, while aboard a ship in a Japanese harbor.

Lottie Moon helped pioneer the role of unmarried women missionaries in evangelism and planted more than thirty Chinese churches. The Lottie Moon Christmas Offering continued after her death, and by 1995 it had raised over 1.5 billion dollars for missions.

recalculated the date to be October 22, 1844. When that date came and went without the Second Coming, Miller's followers referred to the experience as "The Great Disappointment." Many left the group, but those who remained formed the foundation for what became the Seventh-Day Adventist Church.

1844 + THE YMCA IS FOUNDED

In 1844, George Williams (1821–1905) met with twelve young men in his London home in what was to be the first meeting of the Young Men's Christian Association (YMCA). The purpose of the YMCA was to win young men to Jesus Christ. Williams's Bible studies grew, and the movement spread to the United States, France, Holland, and throughout the British Empire. Gradually, recreation and relief work were added to its programs, and eventually the movement was secularized.

1844 + METHODISTS AND BAPTISTS SPLIT OVER SLAVERY

Twenty years before the American Civil War, several denominations and individual churches split over the issue of slavery. In 1834, a Methodist anti-slavery association was founded, and in 1844, the Southern Methodists withdrew from the denomination. The Southern and Northern Methodist churches did not reunite until 1939. Baptists formed the American Baptist Anti-Slavery Society in 1840, and in 1845, the southern Baptists split from the north and formed the Southern Baptist Convention. Just as the churches divided over the issue of slavery, the nation itself was about to divide.

1845 + JOHN HENRY NEWMAN BECOMES A ROMAN CATHOLIC

The Oxford Movement, also called the Tractarian Movement, was an Anglo-Catholic revival within the Church of England. The leader of the movement was John Henry Newman (1801–1890), who began disseminating his views in 1833, by publishing *Tracts for the Times*. Of the ninety tracts distributed by the Tractarians, Newman authored twenty-three. The Anglo-Catholic movement was very successful, attracting hundreds among the clergy. Finally, on October 9, 1845, John Newman joined the Roman Catholic Church and was named a cardinal in 1875.

1791	1793-4	1808	1846
U.S. Bill of Rights written	Reign of Terror in France	Napoleon controls almost all Europe	One million Irish starve in Potato Famine

1846 ✛ EVANGELICAL ALLIANCE IS FORMED

The Evangelical Alliance was formed in 1846 to further the cause of reconciliation and cooperation among Christian groups and across national boundaries. At the initial London conference, some nine hundred clergymen and laymen met to confess the unity of the Christian church. An American branch was formed in 1867, and it also drew support in Europe. In 1951, the Evangelical Alliance was one of the founders of the World Evangelical Fellowship.

1848 ✛ ILLINOIS INSTITUTE IS FOUNDED, LATER TO BECOME WHEATON COLLEGE

In 1848, a group of Wesleyans founded the Illinois Institute in Wheaton, Illinois. On January 9, 1860, the school was rechartered as Wheaton College, with Jonathan Blanchard (1811–1892) as president over the twenty-nine students. Warren Wheaton, a founder of the city of Wheaton, donated the land for the school. The college became one of the top academic colleges in the nation and an influential leader in evangelical Christian higher education.

1848 ✛ KARL MARX PUBLISHES COMMUNIST MANIFESTO

On the eve of the German revolution of 1848, Karl Marx (1818–1883) and his friend Friedrich Engels (1820–1895) wrote the *Communist Manifesto*, a pamphlet that presented the authors' political ideology. It was a systematic statement of Marxism: History is a series of class conflicts; the proletariat will overthrow the bourgeoisie; a classless society will be the result; and means of production will be publicly owned. Marx and his followers believed that "man shall live by bread alone," that religion is the "opiate of the people," and that "only labor creates value." The writings of Karl Marx laid the foundation for socialism and communism, which would be primary challenges to the gospel for the next century and a half.

1851 ✛ HARRIET BEECHER STOWE PUBLISHES UNCLE TOM'S CABIN

An abolitionist and writer, Harriet Beecher Stowe (1811–1896) was born in Litchfield, Connecticut, in 1811. While teaching and then writing for magazines in Connecticut, Ohio, Maine, and Massachusetts, Beecher Stowe became increasingly concerned with the elimination of slavery. She and her seminary

1856	1903	1905	1914
Transatlantic cable developed	Wright brothers make first flight	Albert Einstein develops Theory of Relativity	Panama Canal completed

GO FOR ME TO CHINA

December 2, 1849

Hudson Taylor was the child of devout parents and no stranger to the Bible, but at the age of seventeen, he was still a stranger to a personal walk with God.

The summer of 1849 broke warm with promise in Taylor's heart, when at last he had accepted the joyful realization God granted him of Christ's sufficiency for his sins. Many years later Taylor recalled:

> Well do I remember that occasion, how in the gladness of my heart I poured out my soul before God, and again and again confessing my grateful love to Him who had done everything for me — who had saved me when I had given up all hope and even desire of salvation — I besought Him to give me some work for Him . . . that I might do for Him who had done so much for me. . . . For what service I was accepted, I knew not. But a deep consciousness that I was not my own took possession of me, which has never since been effaced.

Taylor's inner change was outwardly visible that summer. He loved spending time in the Bible and in prayer. He was so filled with the joy and wonder of salvation that he used his free time to share his faith with others.

But as fall and then winter set in, a coldness crept over Taylor's spirit. He doggedly continued to do the things he felt a Christian should do. But Bible study and prayer lost their sweetness. He went to church only out of duty, and his soul grew weary in its struggles with sin.

On Sunday, December 2, 1849, Hudson Taylor awakened feeling as sick in his physical body as he had been feeling in his spirit. As the rest of his family went to church, he stayed behind in the quiet house and began a letter to his sister: "Pray for me, dear Amelia. Thank God I feel very happy in His love, but I am so unworthy of all His blessings. I so often give way to temptation. . . . Oh that the Lord would take away my heart of stone and give me a heart of flesh!"

Tormented by his thoughts, Taylor laid down his pen, and then, like Jacob of long ago, he decided that he would "lay hold of God and not let go except Thou bless me." What God did over the next few hours was so precious that Taylor never spoke of it in detail. But he did add this postscript to the letter to his sister: "Glory to God, my dear Amelia. Christ has said 'Seek and ye shall find,' and praise His name, He has revealed himself to me in an overflowing manner. . . . He has given me a new heart."

What filled Hudson Taylor with such praise? Six words from God that day: "Then go for me to China."

Hudson Taylor did go to China and founded the China Inland Mission, which became the largest missionary organization in the world.

professor husband, Calvin Stowe (1802–1886), harbored fugitive slaves in their home while in Cincinnati. Beecher Stowe's most influential work was *Uncle Tom's Cabin, or Life among the Lowly,* which was released in 1851–52 in the magazine *National Era.* It was published as a book in 1852. *Uncle Tom's Cabin* played a key role in popularizing the anti-slavery movement.

1854 ✛ CHARLES SPURGEON BEGINS HIS PASTORATE IN LONDON

Charles Haddon Spurgeon (1834–1892) was converted in 1850, after taking refuge from a snowstorm in a Methodist chapel. After a brief Baptist pastorate near Cambridge, England, he became pastor of the New Park Baptist Chapel in Southwark, London, in 1854 at age nineteen. He remained there the rest of his life. His preaching attracted such large crowds that the congregation built Metropolitan Tabernacle with seating for sixty-five hundred. Spurgeon preached there from 1861 until just before his death in 1892. The Tabernacle served not only as a preaching place, but as an educational and social center for the city. Spurgeon's tremendous gift for preaching is evidenced by the fact that his sermons are still popular and readable today, more than a century later.

1854 ✛ HUDSON TAYLOR ARRIVES IN CHINA

From the age of five, James Hudson Taylor (1832–1905) desired to be a missionary to China. Although chronic health problems almost derailed his dream, he fulfilled his goal when he arrived in Shanghai in 1854. Taylor soon began making evangelistic excursions into inland China in spite of the danger resulting from political unrest and mistrust of foreigners. Much of his success was due to his adoption of native dress and his facility with the language. When the interior of China was opened to Westerners in 1865, Taylor founded the China Inland Mission.

1854 ✛ MARY'S "IMMACULATE CONCEPTION" IS DECLARED

As early as the seventh century, there was debate within the church about the Catholic doctrine of the sinlessness of Mary and whether or not she had original sin. By 1476, the doctrine, along with the Feast of the Conception of Mary, was adopted and celebrated by the Roman Church. In 1854, "Immaculate" was added

1856	1903	1905	1914
Transatlantic cable developed	Wright brothers make first flight	Albert Einstein develops Theory of Relativity	Panama Canal completed

to the title when Pope Pius IX (1792–1878) issued a papal bull stating that, "From the first moment of her conception, the Blessed Virgin Mary was, by the singular grace and privilege of Almighty God, and in view of the merits of Jesus Christ, Saviour of Mankind, kept free from all stain of Original Sin." Protestants rejected the dogma.

1855 ✛ CONFESSIONAL LUTHERANISM WINS OVER REVIVALISTS

Lutheranism in America changed significantly from the mid-1700s, when the Lutheran Church was first organized in America, to the mid-1800s. European Lutheran theology quickly took on many characteristics of American Protestantism as the immigrants assimilated. Great debate ensued among Lutherans regarding the extent of the theological Americanization, with Samuel Simon Schmucker (1799–1873) leading the Revivalist, or American, side. In 1855, Schmucker attempted to have Lutherans adopt his Definite Synodical Platform, a revision of the Augsburg Confession along Revivalist lines. This precipitated a great clash of interests that resulted in the European Lutherans, or Confessional Lutherans, mobilizing themselves and defeating the Definite Synodical Platform. The Confessional Lutheran position was strengthened by the great numbers of Lutherans who emigrated from Germany and Scandinavia during the time of this Lutheran theological debate.

1856 ✛ MOODY COMES TO CHICAGO

Shortly after his conversion in Boston at age eighteen, Dwight L. Moody (1837–1899) moved to Chicago in 1856. He found success as a salesman, but it wasn't long before he turned more and more toward Christian work. By 1860, he was working full-time with the YMCA, ministering to young men and establishing Sunday school programs for poor children. By the early 1870s, he was a well-known evangelical leader in Chicago and by 1875, was known throughout the world after a very successful evangelistic tour of Great Britain with his song leader Ira Sankey (1840–1908). Returning to America, Moody focused his efforts on revival meetings in large cities. He also invested himself in education, founding Moody Bible Institute in Chicago, and boys' and girls' schools in his hometown of Northfield, Massachusetts. From 1875 until 1899, D. L. Moody was the chief spokesman for American evangelicals.

1791	1793-4	1808	1846
U.S. Bill of Rights written	Reign of Terror in France	Napoleon controls almost all Europe	One million Irish starve in Potato Famine

A SMALL BEGINNING

October 22, 1851

Imagine a theological seminary with a faculty of one.

Archibald Alexander was born in 1772, to a Presbyterian family near Lexington, Virginia. At the age of seventeen he became the tutor for the family of a general in the army of the new nation. Mrs. Tyler, an elderly woman in the general's home, took young Archibald under her wing. She was a Baptist who viewed Presbyterians as sound in doctrine but often not having the experience of spiritual rebirth.

The general hired a millwright, who also was a Baptist, for his plantation. One day the millwright asked Archibald whether he believed that to enter the kingdom of heaven one must be born again. Uncertain how to answer, Archibald said yes. The millwright then asked him whether he had experienced the new birth. Archibald answered, "Not that I know of."

"Ah," said the millwright, "if you had ever experienced this change, you would know something about it!"

The conversation got Alexander thinking. Surely the new birth was in the Bible, but he had never heard any Presbyterians talk about it.

Old Mrs. Tyler had poor eyesight and would frequently ask Alexander to read to her. On Sunday evenings Alexander was asked to read to the whole family. One particular Sunday night he read the family a sermon on Revelation 3:20, where Jesus says, "Behold I stand at the door and knock. . . ." As Alexander read the sermon, every word seemed to apply to him. By the time he finished, his voice was quivering with emotion. He laid down the book and ran to his room. Shutting the door, he fell to his knees and poured out his soul in prayer, inviting Jesus into his life. He had not prayed long when he was overwhelmed by a joy that he had never experienced. The joy was accompanied by a full assurance that, if he were to die, he would go to heaven.

Giving up tutoring, Alexander went to study theology at Liberty Hall (now Washington and Lee University) and entered the Presbyterian ministry. After serving as an itinerant minister on the Ohio-Virginia frontier, he became president of Hampden-Sydney College in 1796 at the age of twenty-four.

In 1807, Alexander became pastor of the Third Presbyterian Church of Philadelphia and moderator of the Presbyterian General Assembly. In his final address as moderator in 1808, he suggested the formation of a Presbyterian seminary in America. As a result of his leadership, Princeton Theological Seminary was founded in 1812, with Alexander as its sole faculty member for the first year. The first fall he had three students, who were joined by six more in the spring and five more during the summer. Alexander's modest home served as library, chapel, and classroom. He continued teaching at Princeton Seminary until his death on October 22, 1851.

1857 ✝ PRAYER MEETING REVIVAL BEGINS IN NEW YORK

In the summer of 1857, the North Dutch (Reformed) Church on Fulton Street in New York City decided to hire lay evangelist Jeremiah Lanphier (1809–c.1890) to minister to the immigrants living in poverty around their church. When Lanphier had difficulty reaching the church's neighbors, he decided to start a daily noon-hour prayer meeting for businessmen to gather and pray for revival. The first day—September 23, 1857—he knelt alone. As he prayed, men slowly trickled in, with six in attendance by one o'clock. Each day, the group grew and within a month averaged more than one hundred. Soon many other local churches and even the police and fire stations were housing noontime prayer meetings. Within two years, approximately one million converts were added to the churches of America.

1857 ✝ HAMILTON'S WESLEYAN METHODIST REVIVAL FUELS PRAYER REVIVAL

The Methodist lay preachers Walter and Phoebe Palmer (1807–1874) led very successful camp revival meetings during the summer of 1857 throughout Ontario, Canada. By October, the crowds reached five thousand during the week and twenty thousand on the weekends. During their return trip home by train to New York, the Palmers became separated from their luggage and ended up spending the night in Hamilton, Ontario, while waiting for their bags to arrive. A local Methodist pastor heard of their presence and requested that they preach at an impromptu Friday night service. One night turned into several weeks as the crowds grew and several hundred souls came to Christ, including the mayor of Hamilton. The Hamilton revival was reported widely in Christian newspapers and journals, which helped fuel the laymen's prayer revival that soon swept the United States.

1858 ✝ PATON SAILS FOR NEW HEBRIDES

John Gibson Paton (1824–1907), son of a devout Christian man, left home to devote his life to mission work. Having applied for a post as a tract distributor, Paton began training at the Free Church Normal Seminary in Glasgow, Scotland. While preparing for foreign mission work, he continued his studies in medicine and theology, and worked for the Glasgow City Mission for ten years.

1791	1793-4	1808	1846
U.S. Bill of Rights written	Reign of Terror in France	Napoleon controls almost all Europe	One million Irish starve in Potato Famine

THE FULTON STREET PRAYER MEETING

September 23, 1857

What do you do if you announce a prayer meeting but no one comes?

The summer of 1857 was a frustrating time to be a Christian in New York City. In the commercial district wealthy bankers and businessmen thanked God for their profitable deals. Yet in the vast slums poverty was inescapable.

Jeremiah Lanphier was a man who wanted to make a difference. Born south of Albany, he had come to New York City to enter the mercantile business. Then at the age of thirty-three he unexpectedly discovered that Jesus Christ was real and that he had paid the penalty for Jeremiah's sins. Lanphier gave his life to Jesus and joined Brick Presbyterian Church, spending much of his spare time as a street evangelist. In the summer of 1857 the North Dutch (Reformed) Church on Fulton Street decided to hire a full-time lay evangelist to reach the immigrants living in the surrounding neighborhoods. They chose Jeremiah Lanphier.

Lanphier began praying, *Lord, what do you want me to do?* The answer he received was that God wanted people to pray. He decided to have a prayer meeting for businessmen from noon to one o'clock in the afternoon when they could come for a few minutes or for the whole hour.

Lanphier printed up a handbill inviting the public to a weekly prayer meeting at noon on Wednesdays in the third-floor meeting room of North Dutch Church on Fulton Street. The first prayer meeting would be held September 23, 1857.

The appointed day arrived, and at noon Lanphier went to the room and knelt to pray. Twenty minutes passed and still he was alone. Finally at 12:30 one man entered the room and without saying a word knelt down next to Lanphier. Then another man came, followed by another until by one o'clock there were six.

The following week there were twenty. By the first week of October the meetings were held daily and the number increased to forty. The fourth week they averaged over one hundred with many under conviction and inquiring how they might be saved.

New York City was to see a great need for God when on October 18, a financial panic seized the city, collapsing the economy into a brief but steep recession. "The Fulton Street Meetings," as they became known, soon filled the rooms at North Dutch Church and spilled over into the nearby John Street Methodist Church. Before long many other churches welcomed people to pray both at noon and before work in the morning. Even police stations and firehouses opened their doors to meet the need for places to pray. Within six months, ten thousand businessmen were gathering for prayer daily.

Although the revival was the most spectacular in New York City, businessmen's prayer meetings sprang up in many cities around the country. Within the next two years approximately one million converts were added to America's churches.

On April 16, 1858, following his ordination as a Reformed Presbyterian minister, Paton sailed with his wife to New Hebrides (present-day Vanuatu). Following the deaths of his wife and infant son, Paten left the islands to regroup. In 1866, he returned to the island of Aniwa, and over the next fifteen years he saw the majority of the native people put their faith in Jesus Christ.

1858 ✛ BERNADETTE SOUBRIOUS CLAIMS A MIRACLE AT LOURDES

On February 11, 1858, fourteen-year-old Bernadette Soubrious (1844–1879) was gathering firewood on the banks of the Gave de Pau River in Lourdes, France, when she reported seeing a bright light in a grotto. The light formed the figure of a beautiful lady whom Bernadette recognized as the Virgin Mary. Bernadette reported that the Virgin asked her to deliver a message of repentance and prayer to the world. Crowds began following Bernadette to the grotto, hoping to witness another miracle. She had seventeen additional visions through July 16, 1858, seen only by her, causing many to dismiss them as the product of superstitious hysteria. A decade later, the Catholic Church officially recognized Bernadette's experience as miraculous, largely because visitors to the spring inside the grotto claimed miraculous healing. She was canonized in 1933.

1858 ✛ ✡ FIRST JEW IS SEATED IN ENGLISH HOUSE OF COMMONS

Prior to 1828, only Anglicans could be elected to the English House of Commons because members had to swear allegiance to the Thirty-Nine Articles of the Church of England. In 1828, all Protestants were allowed to be elected, and the following year Roman Catholics were as well. In 1847, a Jew named Baron Lionel de Rothschild (1808–1879) was elected but was not allowed to be seated because of the required oath "on the true faith of a Christian." He repeatedly was elected but was not seated because the House of Lords refused to eliminate the oath. Finally, in 1858, Rothschild was seated in the House of Commons, and in 1885, his son became the first practicing Jew to join the House of Lords.

1859 ✛ JAPAN REOPENS TO FOREIGN MISSIONARIES

In the mid-nineteenth century, for the first time in more than 250 years, missionaries made their way back into Japan. Following a treaty between France

1791	1793-4	1808	1846
U.S. Bill of Rights written	Reign of Terror in France	Napoleon controls almost all Europe	One million Irish starve in Potato Famine

THE PRECOCIOUS YOUNG PASTOR

| August 16, 1859 |

Would your church call a nineteen-year-old pastor? Here's one that did.

On a Saturday afternoon in December 1853, a nineteen-year-old lad made his first trip to London from Cambridge on the Eastern Counties Railway. No one observing him would have guessed that this young fellow was about to begin a ministry to the city of London that would last thirty-eight years.

His name was Charles Haddon Spurgeon. His father and grandfather were Congregational pastors. His grandfather had been the pastor of the Independent Church in Essex for fifty-four years, and his father pastored a number of independent churches throughout England. The family had descended from Huguenots who had fled France and settled in Essex.

When Spurgeon was just ten years old he met a pastor friend of his grandfather's, while vacationing at his grandfather's home. The friend was extremely impressed at how well Spurgeon read from the Bible in the Sunday service. Before leaving the next day, the pastor told the family he had a conviction that someday Spurgeon would preach the gospel to thousands.

After being converted at a Primitive Methodist chapel at the age of sixteen, Spurgeon began to study the issue of baptism. He became convinced that the New Testament taught baptism was to be for believers and by immersion. In spite of their belief in infant baptism, his parents encouraged him to follow his own convictions, and so he was baptized. Shortly thereafter, Spurgeon joined a Baptist church in Cambridge.

He soon discovered his gift of preaching, and in spite of his young age he was in much demand. After accepting a brief pastorate near Cambridge, eighteen-year-old Spurgeon was called the following year to the pastorate of the New Park Street Baptist Chapel in London. It was a small church, but within a few weeks of his arrival he was attracting great crowds. The chapel soon proved to be too small, so the church decided to enlarge the building. During construction the church moved to a large hall, but once again the crowds wanting to hear Spurgeon preach surpassed what the hall could accommodate. The decision was finally made to build a tabernacle sufficiently large to seat the crowds coming to hear the twenty-five-year-old preacher. On August 16, 1859, the cornerstone of the Metropolitan Tabernacle was laid. The church was built to hold sixty-five hundred worshipers. Metropolitan Tabernacle opened debt free in May 1861. Spurgeon preached there until shortly before his death in 1892.

The Metropolitan Tabernacle was more than just a preaching station. It was an educational and social center. Spurgeon founded a pastor's college and an orphanage, both of which continue to minister to this day. He also began a literature ministry and provided many services to the nearby slums. Spurgeon's Metropolitan Tabernacle was one of the great churches of all time.

and the Japanese government, Japan opened its borders for trade, and in May 1859, the first Protestant missionaries arrived. Despite more than two centuries of severe persecution of Christians in Japan, both Protestant and Roman Catholic missionaries found secret groups of Christians who had maintained the faith for generations, without the aid of formal education or clergy.

1859 ✛ DARWIN PUBLISHES THE ORIGIN OF SPECIES

In 1831, Charles Darwin (1809–1882) graduated from Christ College in Cambridge, England, intending to become a clergyman. However, he continually vacillated between faith and agnosticism, a tension that brought him psychosomatic pain as well. He became a "naturalist" and began formulating his theory of evolution during a five-year voyage around South America from 1831 to 1836. Upon his return he started studying the transmutation of species. In 1857, a debate at Oxford between T. H. Huxley (1825–1895), Darwin's representative, and Bishop Samuel Wilberforce (1805–1873) resulted in firmly pitting evolution and religion against each other. Darwin had hesitated in publishing his theories, apparently due to his own inner conflict. However, after A. R. Wallace (1823–1913) published a theory similar to evolution, Darwin finally published *On the Origin of Species by Means of Natural Selection, or the Preservation of Favoured Races in the Struggle for Life* in 1859.

1860 ✛ THE SEVENTH-DAY ADVENTIST CHURCH IS FOUNDED

Ellen Gould White (1827–1915) was a teenager when William Miller (1782–1849) predicted the second coming of Christ in 1843 and again in 1844, resulting in "The Great Disappointment." As one of those who remained committed to the movement, White became the most prominent leader of the Seventh-Day Adventist Church, formally organized in Battle Creek, Michigan, in 1860. Over her lifetime, White claimed to have experienced some two thousand visions, one of which was a vision confirming worship on Saturday rather than on Sunday.

1860 ✛ JAMAICA EXPERIENCES REVIVAL

As word of the amazing laymen's prayer revival in the United States spread to Jamaica, believers there fervently prayed that revival would also come to them.

1791	1793-4	1808	1846
U.S. Bill of Rights written	Reign of Terror in France	Napoleon controls almost all Europe	One million Irish starve in Potato Famine

A PEEP OF DAY MEETING

It all began with people praying.

In 1860, Christians in Jamaica had heard about the prayer revival sweeping the world. Wanting to become part of it, they held "peep of day" (dawn) prayer meetings throughout the island. Most were held in plantations so that people could meet for prayer before they went out to work the fields.

Their prayers for revival were first answered in a Moravian chapel. The Moravians were the spiritual descendants of Jan Hus, the Czech reformer martyred in 1415. They had settled at Herrnhut, Germany, and had become a major missionary-sending movement. Theodor Sonderman, a Moravian missionary from Germany, regularly visited the town of Clifton, Jamaica, as part of his ministry.

On September 28, 1860, Sonderman began what he expected to be a typical Moravian service. A hymn was sung, followed by an opening prayer. Then someone else prayed, and another and another. Even children led in prayer. As one boy poured out his soul to God, Sonderman saw tears streaming down everyone's cheeks as they cried to God for mercy. Even notorious sinners groaned to God in prayer. When a young girl prayed, men started to tremble on their knees. So many people were weeping that Sonderman became concerned for maintaining order. The meeting finally broke up after three hours so that Sonderman could deal with those who were in greatest distress.

After four weeks Theodor Sonderman was dealing with over three hundred inquirers, and the revival was still continuing. It spilled over into other denominations, including the Anglicans, Baptists, Congregationalists, Methodists, and Presbyterians.

At the Mount Carey Chapel the local justice of the peace presided over the Sunday morning service because there was no pastor. Even so, twelve hundred crowded into the chapel. In three smaller communities, three thousand were awakened to faith in Christ with no pastor preaching.

Among the Methodists of Montego Bay, the chapel of eight hundred members witnessed 547 people come to Christ. The eighty Baptist churches of Jamaica reported twelve thousand conversions during the revival. The Congregational churches grew so much that the missionary board called in its missionaries, leaving the church in able local hands, while the Presbyterian churches of Jamaica saw over three thousand conversions in 1860 and another seventeen hundred the following year.

A Congregational minister summarized the results of the revival: "It closed the rum shop and the gambling houses, reconciled long-separated husbands and wives, restored prodigal children, produced scores of bans to be read for marriage, crowded every place of worship, quickened the zeal of ministers, purified the churches, and brought many sinners to repentance. It also excited the rage of those ungodly people whom it had not humbled."

And it all began with prayer.

In September 1860, the much-anticipated revival began in a Moravian chapel in the town of Clifton and quickly spread throughout the island, crossing denominational boundaries to the Anglicans, Presbyterians, Methodists, Congregationalists, and Baptists. Individuals of all ages and classes gathered together on plantations and in churches for prayer meetings and services in all parts of the island. Many meetings numbered more than a thousand people. During the last few months of 1860, several thousand Jamaicans professed faith in Christ, drastically changing the culture of this nation of recently liberated slaves.

1860 ✝ WOMEN'S UNION MISSIONARY SOCIETY IS ESTABLISHED

The eighteenth century saw a significant increase in foreign missions, including an increase in single women choosing to be missionaries. Among the faith missions established to support missionaries during the last half of the nineteenth century, a variety of influential societies were founded, supported, and managed by women. Established in 1860, the Women's Union Missionary Society was the first missionary society of this kind in the United States. Other societies founded by and for women included the Female Education Society and the Church of England Zenana Missionary Society in Britain. Like other faith missions, the Women's Union Missionary Society developed a comprehensive ministry of evangelism, education, and medical care, attempting to meet the needs of the whole person. Today the society has merged with the Bible and Medical Missionary Fellowship.

1860 ✡ ALLIANCE ISRAÉLITE UNIVERSELLE IS FOUNDED IN PARIS

In 1860, the Alliance Israélite Universelle was established in Paris, focusing on assisting Jews in the Middle East, where France had numerous settlements. In addition to working for the freedom and well-being of Jews in French territories, the alliance sought to improve the status of Jews around the world. Its most significant achievement was the creation of a network of educational institutions through which religious and general education was available to Jews throughout the Middle East and North Africa. The school system, which taught classes in both French and Hebrew, included an agricultural program in Palestine. The alliance, with its Western bias, provided Jewish students an understanding of Western culture and society.

1791	1793-4	1808	1846
U.S. Bill of Rights written	Reign of Terror in France	Napoleon controls almost all Europe	One million Irish starve in Potato Famine

1861 ✝ UNITED STATES CIVIL WAR BEGINS

On April 12, 1861, the newly seceded Confederate States of America opened fire on the United States at Fort Sumter off the coast of Charleston, South Carolina. After thirty-six hours, the fort fell to the Confederacy. The opening shots in the American Civil War had been decades in the making as the Southern states increasingly longed for freedom from the Northern conceptions of union and liberty. Slavery, which eventually became the war's defining issue, was simply one manifestation of the deep philosophical differences between North and South. Christians on both sides defended their positions from the Bible and prayed for an end to America's bloodiest war. Their prayers were answered on April 9, 1865, when the Confederacy surrendered to the sovereignty of the United States of America.

1861–1865 ✝ REVIVALS ARE COMMON DURING THE AMERICAN CIVIL WAR

During the American Civil War, preaching and praying in both the North and South tended to emphasize God's blessing for their side. In the battlefields and among the soldiers, however, preachers usually emphasized the need for personal repentance and faith. Revivals were common among the ranks of both the Confederate and Union armies with thousands of soldiers being converted. Some have suggested that the Confederate troops in particular were the most evangelical army of all time.

1862 ✡ MOSES HESS PUBLISHES ROME AND JERUSALEM

When Moses Hess (1812–1875) published his work *Rome and Jerusalem* in Germany in 1862, it became the first Jewish book to present the idea of establishing a Jewish homeland. Hess was not alone in his beliefs, and the following decades saw a growing number who planned to settle in Palestine in hopes of building a nation in the land of Israel.

1863 ✝ GENERAL STONEWALL JACKSON'S CAREER CUT SHORT

General Thomas "Stonewall" Jackson (1824-1863) was one of the greatest tactical geniuses of military history. He was converted to Jesus Christ in 1848 while fighting in the Mexican War. Jackson did not support the secession of the southern

1856	1903	1905	1914
Transatlantic cable developed	Wright brothers make first flight	Albert Einstein develops Theory of Relativity	Panama Canal completed

REVIVAL IN THE ARMY

August 21, 1863

Reverend J. W. Jones was a Chaplain in the army of Northern Virginia during the Civil War. In his book, *Christ in the Camp,* he related how God worked among the Confederate Army troops. Jones attributed thousands of conversions directly and indirectly to a day of prayer and fasting that Jefferson Davis, president of the Confederacy, called for on August 21, 1863.

Robert E. Lee issued the following message in response to President Davis's request:

> Soldiers! We have sinned against Almighty God. We have forgotten His signal mercies, and have cultivated a revengeful, haughty, and boastful spirit. We have not remembered that the defenders of a just cause should be pure in His eyes; that "our times are in His hands;" and we have relied too much on our own arms for the achievement of our independence. God is our only refuge and our strength. Let us humble ourselves before Him. R.E. Lee, General

A revival of sorts had begun and the soldiers were receptive to a day dedicated to prayer and fasting. The services were well attended, and many miraculous events resulted from the day's observance. The following excerpts are from letters during that period.

Reverend Haley wrote, "There are religious revivals all over the army. Many are turning to God."

Chaplain Tomkies of the Seventh Florida Regiment wrote, "On last evening fifteen were buried with Christ in Baptism. . . . Each evening scores of soldiers are inquiring, 'What shall we do to be saved?'"

The chaplain of the Tenth Alabama Regiment wrote, "I believe that 100 anxious souls presented themselves for prayer last night after the sermon."

The *Richmond Christian Advocate* reported:

> Not for years has such a revival prevailed in the Confederate States. . . . The Pentecostal fire lights the camp, and the hosts of armed men sleep beneath the wings of angels rejoicing over the many sinners that have repented. The people at home are beginning to feel the kindling of the same grace in their hearts. It is inspiring to read the correspondence, now, between converts in the camp and friends at home, and to hear parents praise God for tidings from their absent sons who have lately given their hearts to the Lord. "Father is converted," says a bright-faced child of twelve years; "Mamma got a letter to-day, and father says that there is a great revival in his regiment." What glorious news from the army is this!

The revival spread at home in Virginia as well.

states, yet his loyalty as a Virginian caused him to accept a commission in the Army of Northern Virginia in 1861. He earned the nickname "Stonewall" in the first battle of Bull Run when his brigade stood firm against attack—like a stone wall. From 1861 to 1863, Jackson demonstrated his tactical genius in multiple campaigns. He prayed passionately before making every decision. During the battle of Chancellorsville in 1863, Jackson was wounded by errant fire from his own troops. On May 10, 1863, the great Christian general passed into the peace of God.

1864 ✝ SAMUEL CROWTHER IS NAMED BISHOP IN WEST AFRICA

Samuel Ajayi Crowther (1806–1891) was born in Yorubaland (present-day Nigeria). Captured by slave traders at fifteen and then freed by the British navy, he was taken to Sierra Leone. There, he put his faith in Christ and took his English name, Samuel. Excelling in school, he became a teacher for the Church Missionary Society and traveled to London in 1843, for ordination as an Anglican priest. Convinced that Africa's greatest need was native African missionaries, he returned home to preach the gospel. Among his first converts were his long-lost mother and sister. In 1864, Crowther became the first African Anglican bishop when he was made bishop of Western Africa. With an all-African staff energized by his unflagging vision, Crowther strengthened the Anglican Church and evangelized the tribes of the Niger territories.

1864 ✝ POPE PIUS IX WRITES THE SYLLABUS OF ERRORS

Beginning in 1849, a call sounded within the Catholic Church to condemn formally the errors brought by modern liberalism. Bishops began working on the list of errors in 1852, completing it in 1864. On December 8, 1864, Pope Pius IX (1792–1878) issued the *Syllabus of Errors*, a list of eighty errors and refutations under ten subheadings: 1) Pantheism, Naturalism, and Absolute Rationalism; 2) Moderate Rationalism; 3) Indifferentism and False Tolerance in Religious Matters; 4) Socialism, Communism, Secret Societies, Bible Societies, and Liberal Clerical Associations; 5) the Church and Its Rights; 6) the State and Its Relation to the Church; 7) Natural and Christian Ethics; 8) Christian Marriage; 9) Temporal Power of the Pope; and 10) Modern Liberalism. This document was immediately controversial throughout Europe because it was seen as a formal rejection of modern culture.

1856	1903	1905	1914
Transatlantic cable developed	Wright brothers make first flight	Albert Einstein develops Theory of Relativity	Panama Canal completed

1865 ✛ AFRICAN AMERICAN CHURCHES BREAK FROM WHITE CONTROL

During the aftermath of the Civil War, freed slaves began to leave white churches to form their own denominations and churches. In the South, African Americans founded the Colored Methodist Episcopal Church and the Colored Cumberland Presbyterian Church. Black Baptists, although slow to organize, eventually formed the National Baptist Convention. Already established Northern denominations, such as the African Methodist Episcopal Church, increased their influence in the South. In addition to the denominational expansion, many communities of freed slaves formed independent churches. As these groups continued to prosper, the denominations formed colleges and began publishing periodicals. In later years, many African American Baptist churches were instrumental in the expansion of the Holiness movement. These developments produced the black church movement in America, which has had a primary influence on African American culture.

1865 ✛ HUDSON TAYLOR FOUNDS THE CHINA INLAND MISSION

In 1854, James Hudson Taylor (1832–1905) became the first foreign missionary to enter inland China. He originally was backed by the Chinese Evangelization Society, but quickly severed his ties with them because of his displeasure with their fund-raising methods. Instead, he worked on his own, depending solely on God for support. When Taylor had to return to England because of illness, his burden for inland China grew stronger, and he tried in vain to find a mission to back his return. Therefore, in 1865, Taylor founded the interdenominational China Inland Mission, which in 1866, fulfilled his dream of sending missionaries to all twelve unreached provinces of inland China. The CIM missionaries, known for wearing Chinese dress and depending on God alone for support, numbered 641 by 1895. By 1914, the China Inland Mission was the largest missionary organization in the world, reaching its peak in 1934 with 1,368 missionaries.

1867 ✛ SCRIPTURE UNION IS FOUNDED IN ENGLAND

Founded in 1867, as the "Children's Special Service Mission" in England, the Scripture Union became an international, interdenominational, evangelical youth organization promoting Bible reading. Its main thrust is youth work and child evangelism, especially through groups in schools. The union publishes books, Sunday school materials, and training literature for all ages. A distinction of the organization is that it is controlled largely by laypeople.

1870 ✝ FIRST VATICAN COUNCIL DECLARES PAPAL INFALLIBILITY

The First Vatican Council was convened by Pope Pius IX (1792–1878) and met from December 8, 1869, to July 18, 1870. The pope had come to the papal throne in 1846, and had a very strong influence over this council. He and his supporters felt that the time had come to officially endorse papal absolutism, which had been a controversial issue within the church but had gained ground under powerful popes during the previous centuries. The council consisted of 276 Italian bishops and 265 from the rest of Europe. After months of intense debate, the council endorsed papal primacy and infallibility.

1870 ✝ ✡ THE GHETTO OF ROME IS ABOLISHED

The ghetto in Rome first established in 1555 by Pope Paul IV (1476–1559) was destroyed by Napoléon Bonaparte's (1769–1821) armies and then was reestablished by Pope Pius VII (1742–1823) in 1815. While the official purpose of the ghetto was to separate Jews from non-Jews, the state of life inside its walls was so deplorable that it served to destroy both the wealth and morale of the Jews. The Roman Ghetto was finally abolished in 1870, when the Roman Catholic Church lost much of its secular authority to the Italian nationalists. The new government of the Italian nationalists came to power on October 13, 1870, bringing freedom to the Jewish community.

1871 ✝ BISMARCK BEGINS HIS CAMPAIGN AGAINST THE CATHOLIC CHURCH

When Prussia defeated France in 1870, Chancellor Otto von Bismarck (1815–1898), son of Prussian aristocrats, seized his opportunity to establish a German empire. Fragmented since the dissolution of the Holy Roman Empire in the early nineteenth century, a united Germany would be much stronger than the sum of its parts. In 1871, Bismarck arranged for William I (1797–1888) to be

1856	1903	1905	1914
Transatlantic cable developed	Wright brothers make first flight	Albert Einstein develops Theory of Relativity	Panama Canal completed

crowned emperor of Germany and established an elected governing body. His actions fully united more than two dozen kingdoms, states, and cities into the new Germany. Knowing two-thirds of his German empire was Protestant, Bismarck thought making the Roman Catholic Church the enemy would further unite Germany. He closed Catholic schools, prohibited priests from preaching against the state, and opposed the Vatican at every opportunity. In the end, however, it was Bismarck who was forced to relent, and Germany and the Vatican resumed diplomatic relations in 1882.

1872 ✛ BETHEL INSTITUTIONS MEET PRACTICAL NEEDS

Friedrich Bodelschwingh (1831–1910), a pietistic Lutheran pastor and social reformer, was born in Westphalia, Germany. In 1872, he was appointed the head of a home for epileptic children in Bielefield, Germany. He named the institution "Bethel," or House of God. As a fruit of the revival in Europe and as part of the German Protestant Innere Mission movement, Bethel embraced the philosophy that the love of Christ is demonstrated by meeting practical human needs. The work rapidly expanded to include the education of lay ministers, seminarians, and secondary students who were involved in ministry to institutionalized people, refugees, paroled convicts, and in missions work in East Africa. Today, under the German Evangelical Church, Bethel Institutions house more than ten thousand individuals, making them one of the most significant social outreach ministries in Europe.

1873 ✡ UNION OF AMERICAN HEBREW CONGREGATIONS IS FOUNDED

In the United States, the Reform Judaism movement blossomed in the late nineteenth century, particularly from the efforts of Rabbi Isaac Mayer Wise (1819–1900). Wise, who served as a rabbi in Albany, New York, before taking a position with a synagogue in Cincinnati, Ohio, devoted his life to unifying Reform Jews throughout the United States. In 1873, Wise established the Union of American Hebrew Congregations and two years later, a Reformed Jewish seminary he called Hebrew Union College. The foundation of these American Jewish institutions was part of Wise's effort to assist Jews in achieving a normal life in the United States. Wise's actions and the movement's ideology were specifically outlined in the Pittsburgh Platform of 1885, which denounced any

BAPTISM OF FIRE

October 6, 1871

You have to be careful what you pray for.

In 1871, Dwight L. Moody was a well-known evangelical leader in Chicago. Seven years before, he had founded the Illinois Street Church, which today is Moody Memorial Church. In the late 1860s, he was president of the Chicago YMCA and built 3,000-seat Farwell Hall, the first YMCA building in America. He preached there on Sunday nights because congregational attendance had outgrown the Illinois Street Church.

At the time Moody was struggling with what God wanted him to do. He knew that he had to decide between being a social-religious organizer through the YMCA and being an evangelist. His inner conflict began to diminish the power of his preaching. This became especially clear to two women in his church, Sarah Anne Cook and a Mrs. Hawxhurst. They became convinced that Moody needed the baptism of the Holy Ghost and of fire. The women shared their concern with Moody and eventually set up a weekly Friday prayer time with him. Moody's spiritual frustration was so great that as they prayed on October 6, 1871, he rolled on the floor asking God to baptize him with the Holy Spirit and fire.

The next Sunday night Farwell Hall was full as Moody preached on "What then shall I do with Jesus which is called Christ?" He closed by saying, "I wish you would take this text home with you and turn it over in your minds during the week, and next Sabbath we will come to Calvary and the cross, and we will decide what to do with Jesus of Nazareth." Then his song leader, Ira Sankey, sang:

Today the Saviour calls,
For refuge fly
The storm of Justice falls,
And death is nigh.

Suddenly Ira's voice was drowned out by the sound of fire engines rushing past the hall. It was the Great Chicago Fire and it lasted until Wednesday. Everything that held Moody to Chicago was in ashes. The only chain still binding him there was his own will. Weeks later that last chain snapped, and he surrendered his will to God. Moody went on to become the leading evangelist in the English-speaking world at the end of the nineteenth century. He traveled over one million miles and presented the gospel by voice and written word to over one hundred million people.

On the twenty-second anniversary of the Great Chicago Fire, Moody spoke reflectively: "I have never seen that congregation since, and I never will meet those people again until I meet them in another world. But I want to tell you of one lesson I learned that night, which I have never forgotten, and that is, when I preach, to press Christ upon the people then and there, and try to bring them to a decision on the spot. . . . I have asked God many times to forgive me for telling people that night to take a week to think it over."

effort to establish a national homeland for Jews and dismissed the majority of traditional Jewish rituals.

1873 ✛ LOTTIE MOON ARRIVES IN CHINA

After earning a master's degree in classics from Albemarle Female Institution, Charlotte "Lottie" Diggs Moon (1840–1912) began teaching in Georgia. Feeling called as a missionary, Moon joined the Southern Baptist Convention, and in 1873, she arrived in Tengzhou, China. After working for twelve years at a girls' school, Moon relocated to P'ing-tu, becoming the first single woman to independently open a Chinese missionary post. Moon employed friendship as the basis of her evangelism. Her church-planting efforts in P'ing-tu led to the establishment of thirty churches. Known for her extreme generosity, Moon died of starvation on Christmas Eve 1912. The Southern Baptist Convention still collects the annual Christmas Offering for Foreign Missions established by Moon and renamed the Lottie Moon Christmas Offering after her death.

1873 ✛ MOODY'S BRITISH CAMPAIGN WITNESSES ANSWERS TO PRAYER

Dwight L. Moody (1837–1899), the American evangelist, traveled to England in 1873 to hold evangelistic meetings. He agreed to preach once for an old friend pastoring a London church. The congregation was cold and unresponsive to his morning sermon, and Moody regretted having committed to the evening service as well. Unknown to him, a bedridden woman from the church had been praying for months for Moody to come and bring revival. When she heard of his unannounced visit, she fasted and prayed all afternoon for the evening service. Much to Moody's surprise, that evening almost the entire congregation answered his altar call. As a result, the church received four hundred new converts. This answer to one woman's prayer opened the door for Moody to preach to 2.5 million people throughout England during the next two years.

1875 ✛ REVIVAL IS SPARKED AT THE FIRST KESWICK CONVENTION

In 1875, at the end of American evangelist Dwight L. Moody's (1837–1899) two-year evangelistic tour of England, the vicar of Keswick, a town in England's Lake District, invited him to speak there. God used Moody to spark a revival in

1791	1793-4	1808	1846
U.S. Bill of Rights written	Reign of Terror in France	Napoleon controls almost all Europe	One million Irish starve in Potato Famine

AN UNEXPECTED ARRIVAL

June 17, 1873

In the late nineteenth century, Anglo-American communications were difficult for everyone. Yet God was in charge then, too.

On June 17, 1873, Dwight L. Moody and his new and inexperienced song leader, Ira Sankey, along with their wives and the Moody children, arrived in Liverpool, England, to hold evangelistic meetings. They had come at the invitation of three Christian men who had promised to pay their travel expenses even though the men had never actually met Moody. Having exhausted all his own funds for the steamship tickets, Moody arrived in England only to learn that two of the men had died and the third had forgotten his promise. No arrangements had been made for any meetings, there was no sponsoring committee and no funds. They were stranded with no money three thousand miles from home.

Moody said to Sankey, "God seems to have closed the doors. We'll not open any ourselves. If He opens the door, we'll go in. If He doesn't, we'll return to America."

At their hotel that night Moody remembered that the one specific invitation he had received from England was from George Bennett, a young chemist in York who was the founder/secretary of the local YMCA. Moody had only vaguely replied to Bennett's invitation when he had first received it. Telling Sankey, "This door is only ajar," Moody had the secretary of the Liverpool YMCA send Bennett a telegram: "Moody here—are you ready for him."

Since he had received no firm reply to his invitation, Bennett had not pursued the idea any further and had told only one person that he had sent the invitation. Thus he was justifiably shocked when he received Moody's telegram. Bennett replied with a telegram to Moody: "Please fix date when you can come to York." Moody replied immediately, "I will be in York tonight ten o'clock—Make no arrangements till I come."

Bennett appeared dazed as he met Moody at the train station that evening. Over supper Moody suggested a course of action. "I propose we make arrangements tomorrow, Saturday, to commence meetings Sunday." As they ate, they came up with a plan to have posters printed and posted on Saturday as soon as Bennett could find a place for him to preach.

Starting that Sunday, Moody began holding services in local churches including one pastored by F. B. Meyer. Initially the meetings were only moderately successful, but the experience of having Moody preach in his church was life changing for Meyer. In the church's small vestry room, Moody and Meyer prayed many hours for England, kneeling together at the leather-covered table in the center of the room. Moody later referred to that little room as "the foundation from which the river of blessing for all England had sprung," for during the next two years, two and a half million people heard Moody preach throughout England. It was the greatest British revival since John Wesley's day.

Keswick that birthed the annual summer Keswick Convention, a nondenominational gathering of evangelicals that continues there today. The hallmarks of Keswick are prayer, Bible study, and dependence on the Holy Spirit. Thousands have been called into ministry and missions at the Keswick Convention.

1875 ✛ MARY BAKER EDDY WRITES SCIENCE AND HEALTH

In 1875, Mary Baker Eddy (1821–1910), the founder of the Christian Science Church, published *Science and Health, With a Key to Scripture.* She claimed that God had dictated it to her, although she hired a pastor to correct its bad grammar. Eddy proposed that all sickness was a result of mental error and that the way to cure sickness was not with medicine, but by the practice of a spiritual science that she had rediscovered from Jesus. She banned preaching in her churches, replacing it with readings from selected Bible texts and from her book. Mary Baker Eddy claimed that her teachings guaranteed health; however, she suffered considerably at the end of her life, requiring large doses of morphine to cope with her pain.

1876 ✛ CALVIN COLLEGE IS FOUNDED

On March 15, 1876, G. E. Boer (1832–1904) founded a school to train ministers for the Christian Reformed Church, a denomination composed of immigrants from Holland. During its first session, the school in Grand Rapids, Michigan, had only seven students. In 1894, the school began to admit students who did not plan to study for the ministry. The curriculum was expanded in 1900, and the name was changed to John Calvin Junior College. Twenty years later, the college began offering baccalaureate programs and was known simply as Calvin College. The college and seminary, now offering multiple undergraduate and graduate degrees, remain the center of the intellectual and spiritual life of the Christian Reformed Church.

1876 ✛ BIBLE CONFERENCE MOVEMENT BEGINS

In July 1876, a small group of Christian men met in Swampscott, Massachusetts, for fellowship and Bible study. They called their group "Believers' Meeting for Bible Study." This meeting marked the birth of the Bible Conference movement.

1791	1793-4	1808	1846
U.S. Bill of Rights written	Reign of Terror in France	Napoleon controls almost all Europe	One million Irish starve in Potato Famine

The "Believers" meeting became an annual and growing event. From 1883 to 1897, the group met annually in Niagara-on-the-Lake, Ontario, hence becoming known as the Niagara Bible Conferences. The conferences typically began with a Wednesday-night prayer meeting, and then a week followed with two morning, two afternoon, and one evening Bible lesson. The meetings were strongly influenced by the Plymouth Brethren and the teachings of J. N. Darby (1800–1882).

1876 ✝ JEHOVAH'S WITNESSES PUBLISH THE WATCHTOWER

The Watchtower Bible and Tract Society of New York, more commonly known as the Jehovah's Witnesses, grew out of a Bible study group started by Charles Taze Russell (1852–1916) in 1870. After years of independent Bible study, Russell began to teach his small group of followers an extreme form of Adventism. In 1876, Russell published the first edition of his magazine, *Zion's Watchtower.* The magazine, now known simply as *The Watchtower,* is currently published in 106 languages with a claimed circulation of 64 million. After Russell's death in 1916, his followers took the name Millennial Dawnists, but today they are known as Jehovah's Witnesses. In 2004, they claimed their membership to be 6 million in 230 countries.

1876 ✡ ☾ JEWS ARE GRANTED CITIZENSHIP IN THE OTTOMAN EMPIRE

Because of the weakness of the Ottoman Empire, which extended from Bulgaria to North Africa, and the fear that its collapse would upset the balance of power in Europe, the European nations began to exert pressure on the empire to institute reform. In particular, they pressured its leaders to assure the rights of their subject peoples. The changes had long-term effects on the Jews of the empire. In 1839, the empire granted civil equality to non-Muslims. Then finally in 1876, citizenship was granted to all Ottoman subjects, including the Jews.

1876 ✝ MARY SLESSOR SAILS FOR AFRICA

Mary Slessor (1848–1915) was converted to Christ as a teenager in Scotland. While helping young people in Dundee, Scotland, she became interested in the United Presbyterian Church's mission to Nigeria. In 1876, Slessor set sail for

1856	1903	1905	1914
Transatlantic cable developed	Wright brothers make first flight	Albert Einstein develops Theory of Relativity	Panama Canal completed

Nigeria where she worked among the Ibo tribe. She personally cared for multiple babies in the fight against twin killing. Slessor, affectionately known as "the White Queen," established fifty locally run churches and schools, and when British rule was established in Nigeria she became the first female magistrate in 1892. In addition to encouraging trade between inland regions and the coast, Slessor established the Hope Waddell Institute, where Africans were instructed in medicine and other trades. As a result of her work, the Ibo tribe became one of the most Christian peoples of Africa.

1877 ✝ THE PACIFIC GARDEN MISSION IS FOUNDED

On September 15, 1877, in the midst of Chicago's skid row, George Roger Clarke (d. 1892) and his wife, Sarah, opened the doors to Clarke's Mission. The mission outgrew its one-room facility within three years, and the Clarkes procured a new building called the Pacific Beer Garden. At the prompting of Dwight L. Moody (1837–1899), they renamed their mission the Pacific Garden Mission. Among the mission's more famous converts were Billy Sunday (1862–1935), a baseball player for the Chicago White Stockings who went on to become a famous evangelist, and Mel Trotter (1870–1940), a derelict who later founded a similar mission in Grand Rapids, Michigan. The ongoing success and influence of the Pacific Garden Mission makes it a leader among urban rescue ministries.

1878 ✝ BOOTHS FOUND THE SALVATION ARMY

William Booth (1829–1912) and his wife, Catherine (1829–1890), had been ministering among the unchurched slum dwellers of London for over a decade when, in 1878, they founded the Salvation Army with Booth as its first general. Claiming that "we can't get at the masses in a chapel," the Booths and their army preached in taverns, jails, theaters, factories, and poorhouses, and held open-air meetings with live bands playing loud music. Food centers, night shelters, and employment exchanges were opened. Souls were saved, lives transformed. When Booth died at age eighty-three, he left behind him a committed body of sixteen thousand officers to lead his army of socially conscious and spiritually vibrant believers. The Salvation Army was one of the nineteenth century's most successful revival movements, and the Booths' vision continues to inspire selfless and compassionate social work among the urban needy of the world.

1791	1793-4	1808	1846
U.S. Bill of Rights written	Reign of Terror in France	Napoleon controls almost all Europe	One million Irish starve in Potato Famine

1879 ✛ FRANCES WILLARD BECOMES PRESIDENT OF THE NATIONAL WOMAN'S CHRISTIAN TEMPERANCE UNION

Frances Willard (1839–1898) was an accomplished educator and diligent activist for suffrage and women's rights. Converted to Christ while attending Northwestern Female College in Evanston, Illinois, she became a Methodist. Willard devoted sixteen years to educational administration before becoming involved in the temperance movement. In 1879, she became the president of the National Woman's Christian Temperance Union, retaining the office until her death. Prominent in national reform political circles, she helped organize the Prohibition Party in 1882. Willard's unique role lay in combining conservative ideals with a commitment to radical social reform.

1880 ✛ ABRAHAM KUYPER FOUNDS THE FREE UNIVERSITY OF AMSTERDAM

Abraham Kuyper (1837–1920) was brought up in a strict Dutch Reformed home where the value of books and learning was emphasized. After earning a doctorate from the University of Leyden in the Netherlands in 1867, Kuyper became pastor in Beesd. He was then called to a church in Amsterdam in 1870, and his involvement in politics increased. In 1872, Kuyper became the editor of *De Standard,* a local Christian newspaper. Two years later, Kuyper was elected to the national parliament. During his time in the pastorate and parliament, Kuyper had become increasingly burdened about the need for a university where Christian leaders could receive a specifically Christian education. While in the parliament, he enabled legislation to be enacted that allowed for equal treatment of private religious universities. This laid the foundation for Kuyper to help establish the Free University of Amsterdam in 1880, where he became professor of systematic theology.

1880 ✛ MOODY LEADS NORTHFIELD CONFERENCES

In the summer of 1880, Dwight L. Moody (1837–1899) launched the first of his annual Northfield Conferences in his hometown of Northfield, Massachusetts. Moody's goal for the conferences was to offer laypeople in-depth

1856	1903	1905	1914
Transatlantic cable developed	Wright brothers make first flight	Albert Einstein develops Theory of Relativity	Panama Canal completed

Bible training and a time of spiritual renewal. As was the case with most other Bible conferences of the day, the Northfield Conferences promoted dispensational premillennialism. Also, Moody's association with the Keswick movement in England resulted in an emphasis on the Holy Spirit's power in sanctification. The meetings were held in 1880 and 1881, and then were suspended while Moody spent several years in England. When Moody returned in 1885, the conferences were reinstated and held annually until after his death.

1881 ✝ CLARK FOUNDS THE CHRISTIAN ENDEAVOR SOCIETY

In February 1881, Pastor Francis E. Clark (1851–1927) of Williston Church in Portland, Maine, founded the Christian Endeavor Society. His goal in founding the youth organization was to sustain and build on the results of a week of prayer at his church the previous month. The weekly meetings and monthly consecration meeting were organized and led exclusively by youth. The aim was to evangelize young people and to train them to serve. As the societies multiplied around the country, Clark later became the full-time president of the organization. The organization was the first of many similar nondenominational youth societies that sprung up in the late nineteenth and twentieth centuries.

1881 ✡ ELIEZER BEN YEHUDA ARRIVES IN PALESTINE

The articulation of the desire to establish a Jewish nation, which began with Moses Hess's work *Rome and Jerusalem* (1862), found a new voice in Eliezer Ben Yehuda's (1858–1922) publications. Ben Yehuda spent his life on efforts to restore what he considered the lost aspects of Judaism, specifically the use of Hebrew as a living language and the settlement of their ancient homeland in Israel. In 1881, he and his wife relocated to Palestine, where Ben Yehuda told her he would talk to her only in Hebrew, the proper language of the Jews. In addition to publishing newspapers in Hebrew, he compiled a seventeen-volume historical dictionary of Hebrew that is still the most comprehensive resource available on the language. When Israel became a nation, Hebrew was declared the official Jewish national language.

1791	1793-4	1808	1846
U.S. Bill of Rights written	Reign of Terror in France	Napoleon controls almost all Europe	One million Irish starve in Potato Famine

1881 ✡ MASS MIGRATION OF JEWS FROM EASTERN EUROPE TO THE UNITED STATES BEGINS

While the Russian persecution of Jews in 1881 coincided with the beginning of mass migration to the United States from Eastern Europe, violence was not the primary reason for the emigration. In fact, a large number of Eastern European Jews fled from areas where they had been relatively safe. Instead, the main force driving them to seek refuge in America was to flee poverty. The New World offered agricultural and business opportunities in addition to religious freedom. Unfortunately, many of the Jewish immigrants ended up in the slums of American cities. Many Russian Jews found work in New York City in the garment industry, where their skill excelled. The mass immigration, one of the most pronounced movements in Jewish history, forever altered the fabric of Jewish life in the United States.

1882 ✡ LEON PINSKER PUBLISHES <u>AUTOEMANCIPATION</u>

Although the book *Rome and Jerusalem* by Moses Hess (1812–1875), published in 1862, advocated the establishment of a Jewish state, relatively little action was taken to achieve this goal. In 1882, Russian Jew Leon Pinsker (1821–1891) wrote *Autoemancipation,* carrying the message to a new generation of Jews. Pinsker's articulation of the hope for a Jewish nation was particularly meaningful, and a movement began among his fellow Eastern European Jews following the terrible Russian persecutions of 1881. Feeling that all hope of normal relations with Gentiles was gone, the Jews of Russia were the first to press for the formation of a Jewish state.

1882 ✡ FIRST ALIYAH BEGINS TO PALESTINE

In 1882, a year after Eastern European Jews started their mass migration to the United States, Jews began a slow immigration to Palestine, their ancient homeland. The immigration to Palestine, which was ruled by the Turks at the time, is typically divided into six waves. The term used for these migrations was *aliyah,* the Hebrew word for "going up." The first aliyah lasted for just over twenty years and consisted of approximately twenty-five thousand Jews moving to Palestine. In contrast, during the same period more than a million

1856	1903	1905	1914
Transatlantic cable developed	Wright brothers make first flight	Albert Einstein develops Theory of Relativity	Panama Canal completed

Jews immigrated to the United States. The first aliyah would be the smallest wave in terms of numbers.

1882 ✡ BILU MOVEMENT IS ORGANIZED

Toward the end of the nineteenth century a number of Jewish organizations, generally identified as the *Hibbat Zion* (Love of Zion) movement, arose in eastern Europe. The common desire of these groups was to establish a Jewish nation. The first to immigrate to Palestine was the Bilu movement organized in 1882, whose name is an acronym for "House of Jacob, go, let us go!" In Palestine, the Bilu settled among Jews who had been living there since the Ottoman conquest in the fifteenth century. They attempted to set up agricultural colonies. While they did not possess the skills required for farming, they survived with the financial assistance of Baron Edmond de Rothschild, a wealthy French Jewish philanthropist.

1883 ✝ BOYS' BRIGADE IS ESTABLISHED

In 1883, Sir William A. Smith (1854–1914) established the first chapter of the Boys' Brigade in Scotland. The brigade's aim was "the advancement of Christ's Kingdom among boys and the promotion of habits of obedience, reverence, discipline, self-respect and all that tends toward a true Christian manliness." The organization became a model for subsequent uniformed groups for boys and girls, such as the Boy Scouts. In 1971, the organization's executive committee ruled that it was necessary for each chapter to remain church based so that the boys would acquire genuine Christian faith. With more than 140,000 boys aged eight to nineteen in the United Kingdom and eighty thousand boys in other countries enrolled, the brigade remains one of the largest organizations of its type.

1884 ✝ PROTESTANT MISSIONARIES ARE INTRODUCED TO KOREA

In the 1880s, Western nations established treaties with Korea that called for freedom of religion. As a result, beginning in 1884, Protestant missionaries—primarily Presbyterians and Methodists—from the United States, entered Korea for the first time. Protestant Christianity had been introduced a year

1791	1793-4	1808	1846
U.S. Bill of Rights written	Reign of Terror in France	Napoleon controls almost all Europe	One million Irish starve in Potato Famine

earlier by Korean native Suh Sang-yum (1849–1926), who was converted to Christ in Manchuria. Through Sang-yum's witness and the work of missionaries, it is estimated that by 1910, there were 167,000 Protestants in Korea. A number of medical and educational institutions were established as well. By 2000, the evangelical churches of Korea had grown to more than 7 million members. Ten of the world's eleven largest churches are in Seoul, Korea.

1886–1893 ✛ ANDOVER CONTROVERSY ENDS IN SMYTH'S REMOVAL

Between 1886 and 1893, a theological debate took place among the faculty members of Andover Theological Seminary in Andover, Massachusetts, involving "future probation." The seminary originally was founded by New England Congregationalists in response to the Unitarian theology that Harvard began to embrace. The issue of "future probation" was brought to the forefront as the faculty developed a theology of missions. Egbert C. Smyth (1829–1904) and other faculty members argued in the *Andover Review* for future probation, stating that those who die without hearing the gospel will have an opportunity in their future life to accept or reject the gospel before experiencing final judgment. Smyth eventually was removed from his position at Andover Seminary, but in 1891, the Supreme Court of Massachusetts overturned his removal.

1886 ✛ THE STUDENT VOLUNTEER MOVEMENT BEGINS

In 1882, Robert Wilder (1863–1938), the son of a former missionary to India, enrolled at Princeton University. During his time at Princeton, Wilder helped start the Princeton Foreign Mission Society. During his senior year, Wilder and his friends began boldly praying for one thousand missionaries to be sent out from American colleges. In the summer of 1886, Dwight L. Moody (1837–1899) allowed Robert Wilder and nine other students to speak at a Northfield Bible conference. During the conference, one hundred students pledged themselves as foreign missionaries. In 1891, these missionary candidates met for the first Student Volunteer Conference. During the next seventy-six years, the Student Volunteer Movement met every four years. By 1948, more than twenty thousand foreign missionaries had been sent out as a direct result of the movement.

1856	1903	1905	1914
Transatlantic cable developed	Wright brothers make first flight	Albert Einstein develops Theory of Relativity	Panama Canal completed

1887 ✝ B. B. WARFIELD BECOMES PROFESSOR AT PRINCETON SEMINARY

Benjamin Breckinridge Warfield (1851–1921) was the greatest theologian of his time. After graduating from Princeton University he went to Europe to pursue graduate studies in math and science. However, he decided in 1872 to enter the ministry instead. Warfield returned to the United States and entered Princeton Theological Seminary, graduating in 1876. He was professor of New Testament at Western Theological Seminary from 1879 to 1887. In 1887, he became professor of theology at Princeton Seminary, where he taught until his death in 1921, just hours after teaching his last class. While at Princeton, Warfield became his generation's leading exponent of Calvinistic theology in general and the authority of Scripture in particular. He was an outspoken critic of the liberal scholarship of his day and a prolific author. His collected works fill ten volumes.

1889 ✝ MOODY BIBLE INSTITUTE IS FOUNDED

The Chicago Evangelization Society of Dwight L. Moody (1837–1899) founded the Bible Institute for Home and Foreign Missions in 1889. The school, which was renamed Moody Bible Institute in 1900 after Moody's death, was established to counter the growing influence of the liberal theology being taught in seminaries at the time. Support for the school came from financially successful Chicago businessmen who were evangelical Christians. Moody Bible Institute was a groundbreaking institution in the early twentieth century, and its curriculum became a model for many other Bible institutes. The institute went on to become the world's greatest missionary training school.

1891 ✡ JEWS ARE EXPELLED FROM MOSCOW AND ST. PETERSBURG

After the assassination of Czar Alexander II (1818–1881) of Russia in 1881, his son, Czar Alexander III (1845–1894), launched pograms against the Jews that included mass murder, rape, and looting. The anti-Semitic "May Laws" of 1882 also had a terribly negative impact on the Jewish businessmen living in Moscow and St. Petersburg. Despite the limits of the Pale of Settlement—a region Catherine the Great (1729–1796) established to keep Jews in a contained area—Jewish professionals, such as doctors, lawyers, and entrepreneurs, had

1791	1793-4	1808	1846
U.S. Bill of Rights written	Reign of Terror in France	Napoleon controls almost all Europe	One million Irish starve in Potato Famine

been given permission to live in Russia's largest cities. In 1891, all the Jews of Moscow and St. Petersburg were ejected and forced to move back to the Pale, in most cases losing all of their assets.

1891 ✡ BARON MAURICE DE HIRSCH ESTABLISHES THE JEWISH COLONIZATION ASSOCIATION

Baron Maurice de Hirsch (1831–1896) was a wealthy Jewish financier and philanthropist living in England. In 1891, he founded the Jewish Colonization Association to coordinate agricultural settlements in the New World. During the association's first year, Hirsch purchased land in Argentina to support the settlement efforts of fifty Jewish families who had emigrated from Russia to South America. Not only did Hirsch proceed to purchase more than 1.5 million additional acres in Argentina through the association, but he also assisted groups of Jewish settlers to establish villages. By the turn of the twentieth century, there were twenty Jewish villages on land provided by Hirsch, and at its height, the Jewish population of the region was about thirty thousand.

1893 ✝ SUDAN INTERIOR MISSION BEGINS

In 1893, two Canadians named Roland Bingham (1872–1942) and Walter Gowans (1868–1894), and an American named Thomas Kent, arrived in Sudan (present-day Nigeria) to spread the gospel. Bingham, the only one of the three to survive the first year, set up the first missionary station on the Niger River, thus establishing the Sudan Interior Mission. In the 1980s, the Sudan Interior Mission united with the Ceylon and India General Mission, the Puna India Village Mission, and the Bolivia Indian Mission and changed their name to simply SIM. In 2001, the mission had 1,693 missionaries from twenty-six countries on fifty-four mission fields.

1894 ✡ THE DREYFUS AFFAIR BEGINS

On October 15, 1894, Captain Alfred Dreyfus (1859–1935) of the French army was arrested on charges of treason. The accusations were based on forged documents that purported to prove that Dreyfus, a Jew, was a spy for the German government. Because of the strong anti-Jewish feelings of many French leaders, when the documents were discovered to be in error, the army attempted to cover up the entire affair. After spending five years on Devil's Island, an island for criminals, Dreyfus was released, though he was not acquitted until 1906.

1894 ✝ ✡ COHN'S ORGANIZATION IS THE FORERUNNER OF CHOSEN PEOPLE MINISTRIES

Leopold Cohn (d. 1937), a Jew from Hungary, immigrated to the United States in 1892. Not long after his arrival in New York City, Cohn became a Christian. In 1894, he founded the Williamsburg Mission and began printing a newsletter called "Chosen People." In 1924, the organization's name was changed to the American Board of Missions to the Jews, and at Cohn's death in 1937, his son Joseph assumed the leadership of the mission. In 1986, the nearly one-hundred-year-old organization, headquartered in Charlotte, North Carolina, changed its name to Chosen People Ministries.

1895 ✝ BILLY SUNDAY BEGINS HIS EVANGELISTIC MINISTRY

William "Billy" Sunday (1862–1935), was a professional baseball player with the Chicago White Stockings. In 1886, he was converted to Christ at Chicago's Pacific Garden Mission. Five years later he ended his baseball career to work for the YMCA. After two years he became an advance man for evangelist J. Wilbur Chapman (1859–1918). In 1895, when Chapman ended his evangelistic ministry, he invited Billy Sunday to take his place. Over the next ten years, Sunday acquired his own informal preaching style, which appealed to the masses. He preached to more than 100 million people during his lifetime, and it is estimated that as many as one million people were converted to Christ in his evangelistic meetings.

1895 ✝ THE AFRICA INLAND MISSION IS FOUNDED

Peter Cameron Scott (1876–1896) established the Africa Inland Mission (AIM) in 1895. A Scottish missionary to Kenya, Scott greatly desired to impede the spread of Islam into southern Africa. Although he died only a year after found-

1791	1793-4	1808	1846
U.S. Bill of Rights written	Reign of Terror in France	Napoleon controls almost all Europe	One million Irish starve in Potato Famine

ing AIM, his vision was carried on by the missionary board. By 2000, the society had more than eight hundred missionaries in fourteen African countries.

1895 ✛ ✡ FREUD PUBLISHES HIS FIRST WORK ON PSYCHOANALYSIS

In 1895, the Jewish-Austrian psychiatrist Sigmund Freud (1856–1939) published his first extended work on psychoanalysis, which he titled *Studies on Hysteria*. Psychoanalytic theory was a significant step in the evolution of Rationalism, in which man's reason replaced God as the source of determination and truth. In Freudian theory, man's unconscious governed his reasoning, and therefore his behavior. Psychotherapy had two goals: to raise unconscious thought to conscious levels through techniques such as hypnosis and free association, and through analysis, to lessen its effects on behavior. Freud believed the unconscious consisted of suppressed emotional energy. Therapists who disagreed with Freud's emphasis on repressed sexuality founded variant schools of psychoanalysis. These schools, with Freudian theory at their root, have profoundly influenced the disciplines of psychiatry and psychology, including many forms of Christian counseling.

1895 ✛ ☾ TURKS MASSACRE 300,000 ARMENIAN CHRISTIANS

Beginning in 1895, Turkish forces commenced a terrible massacre of the Armenian Christians living in Turkey, killing at least three hundred thousand. The genocide, which lasted until 1897, was the first of two large Armenian massacres to take place in Turkey within a twenty-year period, the second occurring in 1915. Both campaigns sought to annihilate the Armenians, a people with Christian roots since ancient times.

1895 ✛ WORLD STUDENT CHRISTIAN FEDERATION IS FOUNDED

The World Student Christian Federation was founded in Sweden in 1895, combining forty autonomous Christian student groups from around the world. Led by John R. Mott (1865–1955), then student secretary of the International Committee of the YMCA, this group actively pursued the cause of Christ in world missions. Unfortunately the organization gradually moved away from its evangelical beginnings, shifting its emphasis from missions to the ecumenical movement.

1856	1903	1905	1914
Transatlantic cable developed	Wright brothers make first flight	Albert Einstein develops Theory of Relativity	Panama Canal completed

1896 ✡ HERZL PUBLISHES <u>THE JEWISH STATE</u>

After reporting on the Dreyfus Affair (1893), Theodor Herzl (1860–1904), a Hungarian reporter who covered Paris news, was overwhelmed at the hatred for Jews that the French leadership displayed. The racism he witnessed caused Herzl to spend the rest of his life seeking a solution to anti-Semitism. A Western European of Jewish descent, Herzl initially knew very little about his faith. When he published *The Jewish State* in 1896, Herzl argued for the establishment of a Jewish state. Although he found little support from the Jews of Western Europe, the Jews of Eastern Europe hailed him as a hero.

1897 ✡ HERZL COORDINATES THE FIRST ZIONIST CONGRESS

Following the publication of his work *The Jewish State* in 1896, Theodor Herzl (1860–1904) coordinated the First Zionist Congress in 1897. Held in Basel, Switzerland, the gathering defined the purpose of Zionism as a movement aimed at obtaining "a national home for the Jewish people in Palestine, guaranteed by public law." After the Congress adjourned, Herzl began negotiating with England, hoping to start a Jewish settlement in Uganda. But Palestine remained the focus of most Zionists, and when England showed little interest in Herzl's Ugandan proposal, he turned his attention back to creating a Jewish nation in Palestine.

1897 ✝ CHRISTIAN AND MISSIONARY ALLIANCE IS FOUNDED

In 1897, two missionary societies that had been formed by A. B. Simpson (1843–1919), a former Presbyterian minister, combined their resources and efforts to form the Christian and Missionary Alliance (CMA) denomination. The new denomination continued to carry Simpson's focus on mission work that the Christian Alliance, founded for home missions, and the International Missionary Alliance, established for foreign missions, had begun a decade earlier. In addition to missions, one of the central beliefs of Simpson and the CMA is called the Fourfold Gospel, which describes Jesus as Savior, Sanctifier, Healer, and Coming King. By the twenty-first century, the denomination included more than fifteen hundred churches. Continuing their original missionary focus, the CMA has more than twelve hundred missionaries in more than fifty nations worldwide.

1791	1793-4	1808	1846
U.S. Bill of Rights written	Reign of Terror in France	Napoleon controls almost all Europe	One million Irish starve in Potato Famine

DETOUR TO LIFE

January 19, 1897

He had walked in their shoes—until the night he sold them.

The son of a saloonkeeper, Mel Trotter learned bartending from his father. But as a young man, Trotter resolved to escape the saloon and left home to take up barbering. He was such a successful barber that, unfortunately, he had enough income to gamble and drink.

Trying to escape big-city temptations, Mel Trotter moved to Iowa around 1890 and managed to stay sober long enough to marry. But his wife soon discovered that she was married to an alcoholic. He repeatedly vowed to stop drinking, once staying sober for eleven months. But even the birth of a beloved son could not keep him from drinking. After one ten-day binge, Trotter returned home to find his wife weeping over the dead body of their two-year-old son.

Trotter left his son's funeral for a saloon. Then he hopped a train to Chicago, running from the certainty that he couldn't conquer his addiction. He knew his life was running out, so he resolved to end it in anonymity.

On the night of January 19, 1897, homeless, hatless, and coatless, Mel Trotter sold his shoes for one last drink before committing suicide. The alcohol barely warmed him as he trudged barefoot through a Chicago blizzard, trying to find Lake Michigan so he could drown his sorrows forever. Passing the darkened businesses on Van Buren Street, Trotter stumbled. A young man stepped out of the doorway of the only lit building, helped Trotter up, and invited him inside. Trotter followed, too numb to read the sign over the door: Pacific Garden Mission.

The man sat Trotter down in a warm room full of derelict men. The mission's superintendent, Harry Monroe, was in the middle of his evening message but stopped when he saw Trotter. Monroe felt compelled to pray aloud, "Oh, God, save that poor, poor boy." Monroe then shared the story of his own troubled life before he met Christ. "Jesus loves you," he concluded, "and so do I. He wants to save you tonight. Put up your hand for prayer. Let God know you want to make room in your heart for Him." Barely understanding what he was doing, Trotter raised his hand. Something inside him rose up and accepted the invitation in simple faith. And in that moment, the shackles of alcoholism and despair fell away.

Trotter spent the next forty-three years ministering to men and women he met on the streets, as lost and hopeless as he had been. His message was simple: "God loves you in the midst of the deepest failure and despair, and his love has the power to change even the most ruined life." For forty years he served as the supervisor of a rescue mission in Grand Rapids, Michigan. Alumni of his mission founded sixty-eight other rescue missions across the United States.

Mel Trotter's life didn't end that dark night in Chicago—it began!

THE BOXERS

August 3, 1900

This was not a boxing match; it was a struggle of life and death.

In the latter half of the nineteenth century China had opened itself to foreign missions because of Western pressure. The results, however, were not all positive. Disease accompanied the missionaries, and life expectancy dropped to forty years. Rebellions were frequent.

By 1898, the young emperor of China, Kuang-hsu, determined that the only hope for his nation was Christian moral and social reforms. He invited an influential Baptist missionary to the palace to help him draw up his reforms. The very day the missionary arrived at the palace the emperor was overthrown by a secret Chinese society that feared he would sell out to foreigners.

The secret society called itself Righteous and Harmonious Fists, but Westerners nicknamed them the "Boxers." The Boxers were desperate to hold on to the old pagan Chinese religions and had formed secret cells across China. They performed black-magic rituals that even included human sacrifices to temple idols.

Following the coup, the Boxers installed the emperor's mentally ill aunt as empress. At their urging, the new empress sent a secret decree to officials in the provinces calling on them to kill all foreigners and to exterminate Christianity. The messengers to southern China altered one Chinese character in the decree to make it read "protect" instead of "kill" foreigners. So the bloodletting was confined to the north. When the disobedience of the messengers was discovered, their bodies were cut in half.

Most local Chinese officials sought to protect the missionaries. The magistrate at Fenchow in north Shandi province was particularly friendly to them, so a missionary couple living there invited five missionaries from other areas to stay with them in July when the mob violence was at its peak. However, no sooner had the missionaries arrived than the vindictive provincial governor appointed a new magistrate for Fenchow. The new official ordered the missionaries out of Fenchow and gave them armed guards supposedly for their protection.

The missionaries apparently could read the handwriting on the wall. On August 3, 1900, Lizzie Atwater, an American missionary wife and mother wrote to her family:

Dear ones, I long for a sight of your dear faces, but I fear we shall not meet on earth. They beheaded thirty-three of us last week in Taiwan. I am preparing for the end very quietly and calmly. The Lord is wonderfully near, and He will not fail me. I was being restless and excited while there seemed to be a chance of life, but God has taken away that feeling, and now I just pray for grace to meet the terrible end bravely. The pain will soon be over, and oh the sweetness of the welcome above!

Twelve days later the guards assigned to them by the magistrate murdered the seven missionaries and their children.

1899 ✛ BUSINESSMEN FOUND THE GIDEONS

In 1898, two businessmen named Samuel E. Hill (1867–1936) and John H. Nicholson (1859–1946) met in the Central Hotel of Boscobel, Wisconsin, and discovered they both were Christians. They met again on July 1, 1899, along with William J. Knights (1853–1940), and formed the Gideons, now known as Gideons International. Currently, with 263,000 members in 179 countries, the Gideons aim is to win people to a saving knowledge of Jesus Christ through service, personal testimony, and the distribution of free Bibles "in the traffic lanes of everyday life." In 1908, the Gideons began placing Bibles in hotels, hospitals, prisons, rescue missions, schools, and through police and military chaplains. The organization is the oldest Christian business and professional men's association in the United States. In 2002, the Gideons distributed nearly 60 million free copies of Scripture.

1900 ✛ BOXER REBELLION BEGINS IN CHINA

As the twentieth century approached, Western powers were anxious to gain access to China's resources. Meanwhile, a secret Chinese society that called itself the Righteous and Harmonious Fists was determined to drive out foreigners and retain the old Chinese religions. The Boxers, as they were nicknamed by Westerners, overthrew the emperor in 1900, replacing him with Empress Tsu Hsi (1834-1908), whom the Boxers could control. The Boxers began a violent assault on Christian missionaries and their converts. In Beijing, foreign diplomats and their families took cover in a makeshift fort for more than a month until an international force arrived and crushed the Boxer forces. A total of 188 missionaries and their children died in the rebellion, along with more than thirty thousand Chinese Christians. In the aftermath of the rebellion, the empress's Ch'ing dynasty was destroyed, and foreign access to China continued unabated until World War II.

1901 ✛ OZMAN SPEAKS IN TONGUES AT PARHAM'S BETHEL BIBLE COLLEGE

On January 1, 1901, Agnes N. Ozman (1870–1937), a student at Bethel Bible College in Topeka, Kansas, became the first of the modern Pentecostals to speak

1856	1903	1905	1914
Transatlantic cable developed	Wright brothers make first flight	Albert Einstein develops Theory of Relativity	Panama Canal completed

in tongues. The leader of the school, a former Methodist pastor named Charles F. Parham (1873–1929), explained the event as the baptism of the Holy Spirit and began to teach all over the country about the gift of tongues. One supporter described Ozman's experience as the "touch felt round the world." The Pentecostal revival spread to Missouri, Texas, and eventually Los Angeles. From Los Angeles, it blossomed into a worldwide movement. The Pentecostal revivals, Charismatic renewals, and "third-wave" theologies of the twentieth century all trace their roots to Ozman's experience in 1901.

1901 ✛ AMY CARMICHAEL FOUNDS DOHNAVUR

Amy Wilson Carmichael (1867–1951), one of India's best-known missionaries, was born in Northern Ireland into a committed Presbyterian family. Carmichael became the first missionary supported by the Keswick Convention's Missions Committee. She arrived in India in 1895. Her efforts to rescue little girls who otherwise would have become temple prostitutes led, on March 7, 1901, to the establishment of the Dohnavur Fellowship—a home providing physical and spiritual refuge for abandoned children. Carmichael lived Dohnavur's motto: "To preach Jesus Christ as Lord and ourselves servants for Jesus' sake," serving for fifty-six years without furlough until her death in 1951. Thousands of abandoned children have passed through Dohnavur's doors into fellowship with Christ. Dohnavur Fellowship continues today as a native-led ministry to the needy among all ages and castes in India.

1901 ✛ ABRAHAM KUYPER BECOMES PRIME MINISTER OF THE NETHERLANDS

Abraham Kuyper (1837–1920), born in the Netherlands in a Reformed family, became a religious liberal as he prepared for the ministry. Later, as a pastor, he returned to his orthodox Calvinist roots. Kuyper was drawn into politics and in 1867, became head of the Anti-Revolutionist Party, which opposed the Godless cultural revolution then taking root in the Netherlands. Championing state support of private schools and suffrage for the middle class, Kuyper was elected to the Legislature in 1874. In 1880, he founded the Free University of Amsterdam to expand the influence of Calvinism. Six years later, Kuyper led a mass exodus of one hundred thousand orthodox Christians from the Reformed Church to

1791	1793-4	1808	1846
U.S. Bill of Rights written	Reign of Terror in France	Napoleon controls almost all Europe	One million Irish starve in Potato Famine

form a new denomination called the Gereformeerde Kerk, now the second largest Protestant church in Holland. At the age of sixty-five in 1901, Kuyper was elected Prime Minister of the Netherlands, where he served until 1905.

1902 ✛ REUBEN TORREY BEGINS WORLDWIDE EVANGELISM

Born in Hoboken, New Jersey, Reuben Torrey (1856–1928) was educated at Yale Divinity School and was ordained a Congregationalist minister. He served pastorates in Garettsville, Ohio, and Minneapolis, Minnesota, before accepting Dwight L. Moody's invitation to become superintendent of his Chicago Training Institute, later called Moody Bible Institute. In 1902, Torrey decided to devote his time to mass evangelism, his greatest passion. For four years he conducted a number of preaching tours overseas, including trips to Australia, India, China, New Zealand, Great Britain, and Canada. Torrey later became dean of the Bible Institute of Los Angeles (BIOLA). He was a transitional figure between the revivalism and millenarianism of the later 1800s and the fundamentalism of the 1900s.

1904 ✛ WELSH REVIVAL SPREADS AROUND THE WORLD

Beginning in 1904, the greatest evangelical awakening of all time occurred throughout the world. The revival started in January 1904 in a church in New Quay, Cardiganshire, and spread from there throughout Wales and continued for two years with thousands coming to Christ. Church leaders came from around the world to witness the revival for themselves, then returned home, spreading the revival everywhere from Asia, Africa, and North and South America. It is estimated that more than 5 million people were converted to Christ by 1906.

1904 ✛ AZUSA STREET REVIVAL COMMENCES

The Azusa Street Revival began in 1906 when William J. Seymour (1870–1922), an African American preacher who had recently moved from Houston to California, began holding small meetings with his followers in a rundown industrial building at 312 Azusa Street in downtown Los Angeles. Quickly gaining a reputation as a place for spiritual revival, the Azusa Street location attracted visitors

1856	1903	1905	1914
Transatlantic cable developed	Wright brothers make first flight	Albert Einstein develops Theory of Relativity	Panama Canal completed

from around the world who attended the services that were held three times a day. In addition to witnessing miraculous healings at the gatherings, participants began speaking in tongues. The fellowship also shared a strong belief that Jesus would return at any moment. Though the Azusa Street Revival dwindled by 1909, it was a major contributor to the founding of the Pentecostal movement.

1904 ✡ THE SECOND ALIYAH BEGINS

The second wave of Jewish immigration to Palestine, or *aliyah*, which began in 1904 and lasted until 1914, brought about forty thousand Jews to the region. A major cause of the immigration was the persecution of Jews in Russia during 1903. Many of the Jews from the second aliyah banded together to form *kibbutzim,* collective farms owned by the members where families raised their children communally. Eventually there would be two hundred kibutzim in Palestine. The young men of the second aliyah who had been part of Jewish self-protection groups in Russia formed Hashomer, the Association of Jewish Watchmen in 1909, to protect the Jewish settlements in Palestine. They eventually became responsible for the defense of all Jewish villages.

1905 ✡ <u>PROTOCOLS OF THE ELDERS OF ZION</u> APPEARS IN RUSSIA

Anti-Semitism flourished during the reign of Russian Czar Nicholas II (r. 1894–1917). In December 1905, the *Protocols of the Elders of Zion* was published after circulating in manuscript form in the royal court in Russia. The document was a forgery claiming to be the records of a worldwide Zionist meeting of leaders plotting to take over the world. Though proven false, the spurious document continues to circulate among right-wing extremists and anti-Israel Arab groups today.

1906 ✝ REVIVAL OVERFLOWS AMONG THE MIZO PEOPLE

The Mizo Christians in Lushai, India, heard news of the great Welsh Revival and a subsequent indigenous Indian revival in nearby Khasi Hills. They prayed for similar revival in their primarily pagan community, and their prayers were answered. One evening in 1906, a group of Mizo Christians felt the outpouring of the Holy Spirit as they sang "God Be with You Till We Meet Again" in farewell to three friends. They continued in prayer and praise throughout the night as many others

1791	1793-4	1808	1846
U.S. Bill of Rights written	Reign of Terror in France	Napoleon controls almost all Europe	One million Irish starve in Potato Famine

NAVIGATOR

March 25, 1906

Dawson Trotman was born in Arizona on March 25, 1906. The family moved to California and his parents eventually divorced.

In high school Trotman was both president and valedictorian of his class, and he also led the Christian Endeavor Society at Lomita Presbyterian Church. But he was living a double life. After graduating from high school, he turned his back on his spiritual charade and immersed himself in the Roaring Twenties.

When the police picked up Trotman for drunkenness, his mother asked a Christian neighbor to pray for her wayward son. The next day the neighbor called her back saying, "We spent the night praying, and the Lord showed me a vision of Trotman holding a Bible, speaking to a large group of people. And the burden has lifted. Don't worry about Trotman any more."

Two nights later, Trotman went back to visit his old Christian Endeavor group at church. Their Scripture-memorization contest captivated his interest, and over the next two weeks he memorized twenty verses. As he walked to work one day, one of those verses flashed into his mind: "But as many as received him, to them gave he power to become the sons of God, even to them that believe on his name" (John 1:12, KJV). He prayed a simple prayer, "O God, whatever it means to receive Jesus, I want to do it now."

After committing his life to Christ, Trotman joined a group dedicated to personal evangelism. He discovered that the words of God that he had memorized were a powerful witness to others. Bible memory became a discipline that would shape his future life and ministry.

He started a discipling group he called the "Minute Men." Then one day he met a sailor, and that meeting crystallized Trotman's vision. Thousands of young men were spending months each year aboard ships at sea, and Trotman saw the potential of training sailors to disciple their comrades. In 1933, the Minute Men became the Navigators. By 1945, Bible-memorizing Navigators had a presence on more than eight hundred navy ships, stations, and army bases. When World War II ended, thousands of former sailors went to college on the GI Bill, and the Navigators followed them onto campuses across the United States.

In 1950, Billy Graham asked Trotman to develop a follow-up program for crusade converts. The Navigators' philosophy significantly influenced other ministries as well, including Wycliffe Bible Translators, Operation Mobilization, Mission Aviation Fellowship, and Campus Crusade for Christ.

In 1956, at the Navigators annual summer conference at Schroon Lake in the Adirondacks of New York, Trotman saw a girl fall out of a speedboat and dove into the lake to rescue her. He held her above water long enough for others to pull her out, but then sank himself. Before anyone could reach him, Dawson Trotman drowned.

The caption under his obituary photo in *Time* magazine said simply, "Always holding someone up."

joined them. Several set out to bring the revival to nearby villages, often finding that the Holy Spirit was already moving there. This revival was followed by a period of persecution of Christians. However, in 1913, revival returned again to the Mizo people, and today Mizoram is India's most Christian province.

1906 + SCHWEITZER WRITES IN QUEST OF THE HISTORICAL JESUS

Albert Schweitzer (1875–1965), theologian, philosopher, musician, and medical missionary, won the Nobel Peace Prize in 1952, after forty years of ministering to the needs of the people of the Congo. As a theologian, Schweitzer was a strange combination of liberal and literalist. His popular 1906 work, *In Quest of the Historical Jesus,* presented a Jesus more driven by first-century Jewish messianic expectations than by his divine calling as the "Lamb of God who taketh away the sins of the world." Two additional books, *On the Edge of the Primeval Forest* (1921) and *The Jungle Hospital* (1948), chronicled his experiences in the Congo and set forth his philosophy of "reverence for life."

1907 + THE KOREAN PENTECOST BEGINS

Although Korea was one of the last Far Eastern nations to hear the gospel, the Korean church flourished at the turn of the century, transforming the country's culture and becoming a powerful force for God in Asia. Starting in 1903, revivals began within the Korean church that strengthened its members and added many new converts. These revivals set the stage for the "Pentecost" of 1907. This outpouring occurred at a New Year's Day Bible conference for Korean church leaders. During a concert of prayer, where everyone prayed aloud at the same time, fifteen hundred men became simultaneously convicted of their sins and began crying to God for mercy. These leaders became the carriers of revival back to their own congregations throughout the country. Approximately fifty thousand Koreans were converted during the 1907 Korean Pentecost.

1908 + GOFORTH LEADS THE MANCHURIAN REVIVAL

Jonathan Goforth (1859–1936) was a missionary to China at the turn of the century, during the deadly Boxer Rebellion. Longing to bring revival to the Chinese church, he traveled to Korea in 1907, after hearing the news of the great revival

1791	1793-4	1808	1846
U.S. Bill of Rights written	Reign of Terror in France	Napoleon controls almost all Europe	One million Irish starve in Potato Famine

there. He began praying that the Holy Spirit would move in a similar way in China. In February 1908, Goforth was asked to conduct meetings in Mukden, China. On the fourth day of meetings, several church elders were convicted of their sins and began publicly confessing them, starting a torrent of confession and reconciliation among the church leadership and missionaries, which then spread to the people. Hundreds of people who had drifted from the church in Mukden returned. Mukden was the first of thirty-six revival campaigns Goforth conducted in six provinces of China, helping to establish the indigenous Chinese church.

1908 ✝ THE FEDERAL COUNCIL OF CHURCHES IS FORMED

By the turn of the twentieth century, the social gospel, the belief that Christians are called to work to correct the flawed social order, had become the major agenda of many Christian denominations. The founding convention of the Federal Council of Churches was held in Philadelphia from December 2 to 3, 1908. Formed largely in answer to the growing emphasis on the needs of society, initial membership included more than thirty American denominations. In 1950, the Federal Council merged with thirteen other liberal interdenominational organizations to form the National Council of Churches.

1909 ✝ POPULAR REFERENCE BIBLE IS NAMED FOR EDITOR C. I. SCOFIELD

Cyrus Ingerson (C. I.) Scofield (1843–1921) first came into the public eye in 1873, as the U. S. Attorney for the district of Kansas, but the church knows him as the editor of the perennially popular Scofield Reference Bible. Converted to Christ in 1879, Scofield turned from law to theology, becoming pastor of a Congregational church in Dallas, now Scofield Bible Church. During his pastorate he began work on an annotated Bible with a focus on biblical prophecy. In 1909, the *Scofield Reference Bible* was published. It popularized dispensationalism, a theology that divides history into seven distinct eras or dispensations.

1909 ✡ TEL AVIV IS FOUNDED

In 1909, a group of Jewish settlers moved a short distance north of the seaport of Jaffa (ancient Joppa) to found Tel Aviv, the first all-Jewish community on the

1856	1903	1905	1914
Transatlantic cable developed	Wright brothers make first flight	Albert Einstein develops Theory of Relativity	Panama Canal completed

coast of the Mediterranean Sea in Palestine. Thirty-nine years later, on May 14, 1948, independence of the state of Israel would be declared from Tel Aviv.

1910 ✛ EDINBURGH MISSIONARY CONFERENCE IS PIVOTAL FOR FOREIGN MISSIONS

The 1910 World Missionary Conference held in Edinburgh, Scotland, was a pivotal event in the history of foreign missions for mainline denominations. Present for the ten-day conference were 1,355 delegates from missionary societies representing major Protestant denominations. At this conference the International Missionary Council was born as well as the movement that culminated in the formation of the World Council of Churches in 1948.

1910 ✛ PUBLISHING OF THE FUNDAMENTALS BEGINS

The Fundamentals, a series of short books conceived by wealthy California oilman Lyman Stewart (1840–1923), were published between 1910 and 1915. Each volume contained essays defending what Stewart considered to be essential Christian truths. Sixty-four respected American and British writers contributed, including E. Y. Mullins (1860–1928) of Southern Baptist Seminary and B. B. Warfield (1851–1921) of Princeton Seminary. R. A. Torrey (1856–1928), an evangelist and educational leader, assisted Stewart in editing the series. Of about ninety articles, one-third were written to affirm God's inspiration of Scripture, others were written to support the virgin birth of Christ, miracles, Jesus' resurrection, and the historicity of the Genesis Creation story. As an attempt to counteract the liberal theology of the day, 3 million free copies were distributed to every known Christian worker and theological student in America.

1913 ✛ WILLIAM WADE HARRIS MAKES HIS FIRST MISSIONARY JOURNEY

William Wade Harris (1865–1929), the most successful missionary in West Africa's history, was born in the Grebo tribe of Liberia that freed American slaves had colonized in 1847. Raised in the Methodist church, Harris joined the Episcopal Church in 1888. While jailed for political activism in 1910, he experienced a vision in which the angel Gabriel anointed him a prophet. On July 27, 1913,

1791	1793-4	1808	1846
U.S. Bill of Rights written	Reign of Terror in France	Napoleon controls almost all Europe	One million Irish starve in Potato Famine

Harris began his first missionary journey from Liberia, traveling east to Ivory Coast, which was a Catholic mission field at that time. Harris denounced the traditional religions, preached Christ, and baptized one hundred thousand or more new Christians in the following eighteen months. Harris ministered in adjoining West African countries until he was deported back to Liberia in 1914, where he died in 1929. Today there are more than two hundred thousand members of Harrist churches in Ivory Coast alone.

1913 ✡ ANTI-DEFAMATION LEAGUE OF B'NAI B'RITH IS FORMED

Seventy years after its founding, the first non-religious Jewish fraternal order, the B'nai B'rith, formed the Anti-Defamation League of B'nai B'rith in 1913. The league was founded to oppose anti-Semitism and to guarantee justice for all Jewish Americans.

THE AGE OF IDEOLOGIES

1914–2000

In the Age of Ideologies, new gods arose to claim the loyalties of secular people. Nazism exalted the state, Communism worshiped the party, and American democracy revered the individual's rights. Supposedly enlightened, modern nations waged two global wars in an attempt to establish the supremacy of these new deities. When no single ideology prevailed, a cold war of coexistence settled upon the once-Christian nations. Through these troubled times the denominations struggled over orthodox and liberal theologies, sought fresh ways to recover a lost unity, and reflected a new hunger for apostolic experiences.

After World War II, vigorous new Christian leadership emerged in the Third World, offering fresh hope for a new day for the old faith. Had missionaries from the neopagan nations of Europe and North America succeeded in giving Christianity a stake in the future, by carrying the gospel to Africa and Latin America?

Only time will tell. But Christians can hope, because faith always reaches beyond earthly circumstances. . . . Church history provides a quiet testimony that Jesus Christ will not disappear from the scene. . . . His truth endures for all generations.

BRUCE L. SHELLEY

1914 ✝ WORLD WAR I BEGINS

World War I erupted on June 28, 1914, with the assassination of the Austro-Hungarian crown prince in Serbia. Ambassadors and peace advocates worked desperately to overcome the tensions in Europe, but armies marched to war, many expecting to be home by Christmas. Most armies, however, were unable to break through enemy lines, and World War I—the first war fought on land, sea, and in the air—quickly reached an impasse. Industrial advances allowed for a steady provision of weapons to the combat zone, and for three years the devastating conflict took the lives of more than 12 million people. The cost to the church and foreign missions was extensive as well, with funding and travel greatly inhibited. The aftermath of the war created enormous needs for relief for those left destitute.

1914 ✝ THE ASSEMBLIES OF GOD ARE ORGANIZED

The Pentecostal movement began in the early twentieth century, emphasizing a "baptism of the Holy Spirit" evidenced by speaking in tongues. The largest denomination to develop from the movement was the Assemblies of God (AOG). In April 1914, American Pentecostal leaders met in Hot Springs, Arkansas, to discuss basic beliefs, church order, missions, pastors, and education. Desiring to change existing churches rather than organize new ones, they formed the Assemblies of God as a casual fellowship of churches. Like other Protestant denominations, the AOG believe in the orthodox doctrines of the faith, but unlike other denominations, the AOG emphasize baptism of the Holy Spirit as a second blessing for believers. In 2000, there were more than 16 million AOG members throughout the world.

1915 ✝ ☾ ARMENIANS ARE MASSACRED DURING WORLD WAR I

During World War I, the world stood by while the Turks slaughtered the Armenians, who had been a Christian nationality since ancient times. While conflict between Turks and Armenians was not new (a previous massacre of Armenians occurred in 1895–1897), this genocide was exacerbated by the fact that Armenians lived, almost equally divided, between Russia and Turkey, two countries on opposing sides in World War I. In 1915, Turkish forces brutalized their Armenian population, killing approximately one million people via mass

1914–18	1915	1918–20	1929
World War I	Mohandas Gandhi leads Indian Nationalist movement	Influenza kills 20 million	U.S. stock market crashes

murder, riots, and death marches. Though other nations spoke out against the horrors in Turkey, no one took action to stop the genocide.

1917 ✛ WILSON LEADS AMERICA INTO WWI ON CHRISTIAN PRINCIPLES

In 1913, Woodrow Wilson (1856–1924), a devout Christian and the son of a Presbyterian minister, was inaugurated as the twenty-eighth president of the United States. In 1914, shortly after Wilson's inauguration, Archduke Francis Ferdinand (1863–1914) was assassinated and World War I began. The United States, however, stayed out of the conflict until Wilson's second term. In 1917, when the Germans sank five American vessels in the Atlantic Ocean, Wilson asked Congress for a declaration of war. Soon American troops were sent to Europe, Germany surrendered, and President Wilson was influential in peace negotiations. His perspective on the war and its aftermath was shaped by his Christian principles. His intent was to spread American democratic Christianity throughout the world. Unfortunately he had a debilitating stroke in 1919, without having accomplished his goals.

1917 ✡ BALFOUR DECLARATION PROMISES ENGLAND'S SUPPORT OF ISRAEL

The Balfour Declaration was the single most important document in the establishment of the state of Israel. David Lloyd George (1863–1945), prime minister of England, and Arthur Balfour (1848–1930), his foreign secretary, issued the Balfour Declaration on November 2, 1917. It promised that England would support and help facilitate the establishment of a national home for the Jewish people in Palestine. Chaim Weizmann (1874–1952), an influential Jewish chemistry professor and Zionist, had greatly influenced Lloyd George and Balfour, winning them over to the Zionist cause. In 1949, Weizmann became Israel's first president.

1917 ✡ BRITISH CAPTURE JERUSALEM

Turkey, which controlled Palestine, joined Germany in declaring war on the Allies during World War I. Concerned that Jews or Arabs would create a disturbance in Palestine during the course of the war, the Turkish government arrested

AN UNLIKELY THREESOME

November 2, 1917

What do a lapsed Baptist, a member of the English landed gentry, and the inventor of synthetic acetate have in common? Would you believe God used them to return the Jews to their land?

It all began in 1874, in the hamlet of Motol in what is today Belarus. Chaim Weizmann was born the third of fifteen children to Ezer Weizmann, a lumberman. In spite of the family's meager resources, the children were able to attend the Jewish school in their village and then go on to advanced training.

In 1900, Chaim received a Ph.D. in chemistry from the University of Fribourg and four years later became a professor of chemistry at the University of Manchester in England.

From childhood on, Weizmann had a passion for Zionism, the movement for reestablishing a Jewish national state in Palestine. As a leading academic in England he was able to use his position to share his passion with the influential politicians of his day.

Two of Weizmann's converts, Arthur Balfour and David Lloyd George, were leaders of Parliament. Balfour was the last representative of England's traditional landed class to lead England. Weizmann had a decisive discussion with Balfour in 1914 that brought Balfour to tears and made him a committed supporter of Zionism.

David Lloyd George, a Welshman, was the grandson of a Baptist pastor. His father died when he was just one year old, leaving the family in dire poverty. His mother and her children were taken in and provided for by her brother, also a Baptist minister. David, however, lost his faith as a boy. As an adult and a leader of Parliament, he was infamous for his marital infidelity.

During World War I, Lloyd George, already a Zionist thanks to his contact with Weizmann, was put in charge of the entire War Office. By 1916, England was facing a huge military logistic problem. The country was running out of natural acetate, a crucial ingredient in the manufacture of munitions. Chaim Weizmann saved the day by quickly inventing a new process for extracting acetate from corn. The British would not run out of bullets!

Gratitude for Weizmann's discovery served the cause of Zionism well when, also in 1916, Lloyd George became prime minister and Balfour his foreign secretary. When the British army fought the Ottoman Empire for control of Palestine, the British government issued the Balfour Declaration on November 2, 1917, to rally Jewish support for its effort. The key paragraph read, "His Majesty's Government views with favour the establishment in Palestine of a national home for the Jewish people . . . and will use their best endeavors to facilitate the achievement of this object."

The Balfour Declaration became the single most important document in the establishment of the state of Israel. In 1949, Chaim Weizmann became Israel's first president.

God used Lloyd George, Balfour, and Weizmann to return the Jews to their land.

many settlers and expelled many more. Turkey's fears were enhanced when Jews were discovered engaging in espionage for England. This discovery increased the persecution of the Jews. As a result, when the British army captured Jerusalem in 1917, the Jews welcomed British General Edmund Allenby (1861–1936) as a liberator. The British capture of Jerusalem proved to be a major step toward Israel becoming a nation.

1917 ✝ RUSSIAN REVOLUTION NEGATIVELY AFFECTS THE CHURCH

The Russian Revolution of 1917, in which the Communists came to power, had a terrible effect on the church, which found itself persecuted on all sides. In 1918, Vladimir Lenin (1870–1924), the first Communist dictator, banned churches from owning property, making public worship more difficult, though not illegal. The same decree outlawed teaching any religion to those under eighteen. Communism, with its atheistic ideology, proved to be a formidable enemy of the gospel for the rest of the century.

1917 ✝ INTERDENOMINATIONAL FOREIGN MISSION ASSOCIATION IS FOUNDED

In March 1917, leaders of the South Africa General Mission invited leaders of three other mission agencies to meet together for prayer and discussion about how to increase the overall ministerial efficiency of evangelical mission agencies. As a result of this meeting, the Interdenominational Foreign Mission Association (IFMA) was formed with seven organizations as charter members. Holding its members to strict standards of financial accountability and fidelity to conservative Biblical theology, the IFMA currently has more than one hundred member agencies representing more than ten thousand American missionaries and five thousand foreign missionaries.

1919 ✡ THIRD ALIYAH BEGINS

At the end of World War I, Britain received a mandate to establish a Jewish state while maintaining the borders of other peoples in Palestine. The Jewish Agency, which was established to assist in administering the mandate, promoted Jewish immigration and settlement in Palestine. Thus, in 1919, the third *aliyah*—or wave of immigration—began. The majority of Jews who came to the region were

1939–45	1945	1989	1999
World War II	United Nations founded	Berlin Wall falls	Europe adopts Eurocurrency

FROM CONSCIENTIOUS OBJECTOR
TO WAR HERO

Life on the farm in 1887 was tough in Fentress County, Tennessee, where a boy named Alvin York was born. His father, William, needed to farm, hunt, and blacksmith to support a family that eventually included eleven children.

York worked on the farm, and he especially enjoyed hunting with his father and even became a crack shot at an early age. But in 1911, York's father died from a kick by a mule, leaving York as chief provider for the family.

Floundering under the responsibility of caring for this large family, York began drinking the local moonshine. Once when York lurched home at midnight from a night of drinking and fighting, his mother plaintively asked him, "When are you going to be a man like your father and grandfather?"

She had nagged him for years about his drunkenness but had never before compared him to his father and grandfather. Both were legendary for their fairness and honesty.

His mother's words made York suddenly realize that his life was hopeless and that all he deserved was God's wrath. Of that moment he later said, "God just took ahold of my life. My little old mother had been praying for me for so long, and I guess the Lord finally decided to answer her." In the wee hours of New Year's Day, 1915, a new era dawned for Alvin York.

At the next revival at a nearby church, York walked down the aisle and to his neighbors' amazement publicly dedicated his life to God. He soon became a song leader and an elder in the church.

Things were going well for York until 1917, when the United States declared war on Germany. Joining the army was the last thing York wanted to do because his church opposed war as a violation of the commandment "Thou shalt not kill." Then he received a notice requiring him to register with his draft board, the head of which was his pastor. He was in a quandary, as was his pastor. He applied to be a conscientious objector but was turned down. He had no choice but to go to war.

On September 26, 1918, the battle for the Argonne Forest began. The great achievement of the battle—in fact the greatest single military achievement of the war—was performed by a corporal from Tennessee by the name of Alvin York. As a member of a patrol sent to silence a group of German machine-gun nests, York single-handedly killed more than twenty Germans and took 132 prisoners. He forced a German major to order all his soldiers to surrender. Everything took place within three hours and fifteen minutes.

For his heroism Corporal York, soon to be Sergeant York, received the Congressional Medal of Honor. General Pershing called him "The greatest civilian soldier of the war."

Zionists from Poland who favored the development of a Jewish nation in Israel. Known as Labor Zionist *halutsim* (pioneers), the immigrants from the third aliyah involved themselves in farming and manual labor. This period of immigration, which lasted until 1923, also saw the increased use of Hebrew among Jewish immigrants. More than thirty-five thousand Jews immigrated to Palestine during the four years of the third aliyah.

1919 ✚ FIRST ANNUAL INTERVARSITY CONFERENCE MEETS IN ENGLAND

The first annual InterVarsity conference was held in 1919 in England. The intent of the gathering was to plan and coordinate evangelistic and missions events at British colleges and universities. Conference attendees included representatives of Christian organizations already operating on English college campuses. These conferences led to the official formation of InterVarsity Christian Fellowship in 1927. The InterVarsity movement spread to Canada in 1928, and to the United States in 1941. Today, InterVarsity Christian Fellowship continues to flourish.

1919 ✚ KARL BARTH WRITES <u>COMMENTARY ON ROMANS</u>

The spiritual and social dynamics of two world wars shaped the faith of theologian Karl Barth (1886–1968). Pastoring on the Swiss border during the dark days of World War I, Barth witnessed the political compromise of the German church and the spiritual powerlessness of Christian liberalism. Driven to the Bible to find answers for a world at war, Barth published his *Commentary on Romans* in 1919. A revised edition in 1922 shook the foundations of liberalism and introduced a "neoorthodoxy" to European theology. Although his theology was a reaction against liberalism, he refused to see the Bible as God's inspired Word. He argued instead that the Bible becomes the Word of God as the Holy Spirit speaks to the reader through it. Barth was the most influential European theologian of the twentieth century.

1920 ✡ ☾ ARAB RIOTS BEGIN IN PALESTINE

In anticipation of the British Mandate over Palestine that was to begin July 1, 1920, the first Arab riots took place in March 1920, during Passover in Jerusalem.

In April, several Jews were killed defending Tel Hai, a settlement in Upper Galilee. In May, there was an outbreak of hostility in Jaffa, leading to larger revolts in many other cities, with forty-seven Jews killed and seventy-three wounded. These violent revolts were a chilling foreshadow of the years to come and demonstrated Arab capability and willingness to launch numerous militant and strategic attacks all across Palestine.

1920 ☪ ✡ BRITISH MANDATE OVER PALESTINE BEGINS

Following World War I, one of the many results of the Treaty of Versailles was the establishment of the mandate system as a way to distribute and organize the lands formerly controlled by Germany and the Ottoman Empire. Consequently, England was given the mandate over Palestine, effective July 1, 1920. This declaration set up British oversight of the land until a self-sustaining Jewish government could be formed. The mandate was accepted by the League of Nations in 1922, resulting in years of bloody conflict between Jews and Arabs. The mandate ended with the establishment of the state of Israel in 1948.

1921 ✝ FIRST CHRISTIAN RADIO BROADCAST IS AIRED

KDKA in Pittsburgh, Pennsylvania, was the first radio station in the United States. Owned by the Westinghouse Company, the first KDKA broadcast announced the 1920 election results to people listening on homemade radio devices. The audience quickly grew as people began buying radio sets, creating an immediate need for new programs. A choir member at Calvary Episcopal Church in Pittsburgh, working as an engineer for Westinghouse, suggested broadcasting a live church service. On January 2, 1921, the first Sunday of the New Year, the first Christian radio broadcast was aired. Due to the popularity of the broadcast, the Calvary church service became a regular feature on KDKA. By 1928, there were sixty religious radio stations in the United States.

1921 ✝ SIMON KIMBANGU EXPERIENCES HIS FIRST HEALING

Simon Kimbangu (1889–1951), a Baptist lay pastor in Central Africa (modern-day Democratic Republic of Congo), experienced visions that changed the course of his life. Just before Kimbangu turned thirty, Christ called him to evan-

1914–18	1915	1918–20	1929
World War I	Mohandas Gandhi leads Indian Nationalist movement	Influenza kills 20 million	U.S. stock market crashes

gelize his fellow Africans and to establish indigenous evangelical churches on the continent. Kimbangu performed his first healing on April 6, 1921. Thousands flocked to N'Kamba, Congo, to hear Kimbangu preach and to witness the Holy Spirit's power. Within months the Belgian authorities arrested him for endangering public security, and he spent the rest of his life in prison. One hundred thousand of Kimbangu's followers were deported; another 150,000 were martyred. Today, the more than 7-million-member Church of Jesus Christ on Earth through the Prophet Simon Kimbangu (EJCSK), is the largest independent church on the African continent and the first indigenous African church to join the World Council of Churches.

1921 ✡ EINSTEIN WINS THE NOBEL PRIZE
Albert Einstein (1879–1955) was one of many German Jewish intellectuals to immigrate to the United States to escape Nazism. Coming to America in 1934, Einstein was a theoretical physicist whose theory of relativity revolutionized modern scientific thought and forever altered conceptions about space and time. His work also formed a theoretical base for the study of atomic energy. In 1921, Einstein was awarded the Noble Prize.

1923 ✝ MACHEN CHAMPIONS ORTHODOX REFORMED THEOLOGY
Passionately engaged in the battle against modernism that was dividing many American denominations, J. Gresham Machen (1881–1937) became the champion of Orthodox Reformed theology. *Christianity and Liberalism,* published in 1923, was his strong and influential apologetic for orthodoxy. As professor of New Testament at Princeton Theological Seminary, Machen fought for his seminary's long-standing Reformed position. In 1929, when he lost the battle for keeping Princeton Seminary theologically conservative, he founded Westminster Theological Seminary.

1923 ✝ AUBURN AFFIRMATION SUPPORTS THEOLOGICAL DIVERSITY
In 1923, a group of liberal Presbyterian ministers met in Auburn, New York, to "safeguard the unity and liberty" of the Presbyterian Church. In fact, they were meeting because they were opposed to an action of the denomination's general

1939–45	1945	1989	1999
World War II	United Nations founded	Berlin Wall falls	Europe adopts Eurocurrency

assembly that required candidates to the ministry to subscribe to five fundamental doctrines prior to ordination. In response, the Auburn group published in January 1924 what became known as the Auburn Affirmation, which was a plea for theological diversity within the church. It was signed by 1,274 pastors. By 1926, the General Assembly of the Presbyterian Church USA had adopted the affirmation's position, an action that became a defining moment in the Presbyterian Church USA's move away from orthodoxy toward liberal theology.

1924 ✝ DALLAS THEOLOGICAL SEMINARY IS FOUNDED

In 1924, Evangelical Theological College was established by Lewis Sperry Chafer (1871–1952). Chafer studied at Oberlin College and was a traveling evangelist, eventually becoming the pastor of First Congregational Church in Dallas, Texas. It was during his tenure at First Congregational that Chafer founded the three-year graduate school. After two successful years it moved to its present campus and in 1936 was renamed Dallas Theological Seminary and Graduate School of Theology, a name that was shortened in 1969 to Dallas Theological Seminary. The seminary, which has always been nondenominational, has been a champion of dispensational theology.

1924 ✡ FOURTH ALIYAH BEGINS

In 1924, the fourth *aliyah,* or wave of immigration to Palestine, began with many Jews emigrating from Poland, as in the third aliyah. The immigrants of the third aliyah were Zionists who set up farms and communes and were more philosophically interested in developing a distinctly Hebrew culture. Most of the Jews of the fourth aliyah, which lasted until 1931, were more interested in fleeing the growing anti-Jewish sentiment in Poland than in agricultural purposes. During this seven-year period, a variety of Jewish organizations like the Haganah, a Jewish defense organization, the Hebrew University, and the Histadrut, the General Federation of Hebrew Workers, were founded in Palestine. The developing presence of an organized Jewish community also led to increased tension with the native Arabs. More than eighty thousand Jews immigrated to Palestine during the fourth aliyah.

1914–18	1915	1918–20	1929
World War I	Mohandas Gandhi leads Indian Nationalist movement	Influenza kills 20 million	U.S. stock market crashes

1924 ✡ THE JOHNSON ACT SHAPES UNITED STATES IMMIGRATION

From the turn of the twentieth century until the post–World War I years, the American public became increasingly distrustful of immigrants. In response to this, Congress passed a series of laws that severely restricted immigration. The Immigration Act of 1924 was the culmination of these laws. Introduced by Congressman Albert Johnson (1869–1957) of Washington, the Johnson Act shaped U.S. immigration policy until the 1960s. Under its provisions, only 165,000 immigrants could enter the country annually. Based on the census of 1890, a certain number from each foreign nationality were allowed to enter the U.S. every year. This equation intentionally excluded immigrants from Southern and Eastern European countries, such as Italy and Russia. In particular, the Johnson Act ended the mass immigration of Jews to America, so that in the 1930s and early 1940s, America was closed to Jews seeking to flee Hitler and the Holocaust.

1925 ✡ HITLER PUBLISHES MEIN KAMPF

After a failed military coup to overthrow the government of Bavaria, Adolf Hitler (1889–1945) was imprisoned in Landsberg, Germany, for nine months. During this time he wrote his autobiography and political manifesto, *Mein Kampf* ("My Struggle"). It clearly revealed Hitler's violent anti-Semitism and was followed the next year by a second volume entitled, *Die Nationalsozialistische Bewegung* ("The National Socialistic Movement"). Initially, *Mein Kampf* was not widely distributed and made little impact in Germany or elsewhere. However, when Hitler rose to power, the book's sales multiplied rapidly. The book ominously foreshadowed the future Holocaust.

1925 ✡ HEBREW UNIVERSITY IS OPENED

Early proponents of the Zionist movement began discussing the establishment of a Jewish university in Jerusalem. In 1914, a plot of land was purchased on Mount Scopus in Jerusalem. The building and construction began in 1918, with the school's cornerstone being laid by Chaim Weizmann (1874–1952). On April 1, 1925, Lord Arthur J. Balfour (1848–1930)—the British statesman responsible for the Balfour Declaration—opened the Hebrew University. The war of independence in 1948 cut off the university from Israeli West Jerusalem, necessitating construction of a new campus in the heart of the Israeli section of Jerusalem.

1939–45	1945	1989	1999
World War II	United Nations founded	Berlin Wall falls	Europe adopts Eurocurrency

With the reunification of Jerusalem after the Six Day War, the original campus was restored and expanded, and in 1981, Mount Scopus once again became the university's main home.

1925 ✛ SCOPE'S MONKEY TRIAL ENDS WITH A GUILTY VERDICT

William Jennings Bryan (1860–1925) was a newspaper editor, lawyer, congressman, secretary of state, fundamentalist Christian apologist, and three-time Democratic presidential candidate, but he is best remembered by the distorted media depiction of his opposition to evolution in the Scopes Monkey Trial of 1925. At the trial of John T. Scopes (1900–1970), who was accused of teaching evolution in a public school, Bryan argued on behalf of biblical authority and the Genesis account of creation. Though Bryan was reasonable in his defense of the Bible, the national press portrayed him as uncultured, anti-intellectual, and the one real "monkey" in this debate on mankind's origins. Instead of a significant cultural dialogue, the trial became an antifundamentalist media campaign, increasing respect for the evolutionary position. Scopes was found guilty on July 21, 1925, and Bryan died the following Sunday.

1929 ✛ WESTMINSTER SEMINARY IS FOUNDED

In 1929, liberals within the Presbyterian Church gained control of the board of directors of Princeton Theological Seminary in Princeton, New Jersey, which had been the bastion of conservative theology since its founding in 1812. As a result of the doctrinal shift, J. Gresham Machen (1881–1937), professor at Princeton Seminary and the leading conservative scholar of his day, resigned and founded Westminster Theological Seminary in Philadelphia. On September 25, 1929, Westminster opened, and it eventually became the leading Reformed seminary in America.

1929 ✛ THE STOCK MARKET CRASHES

On October 24, 1929, the New York Stock Market crashed and continued to fall until the mid-1930s, triggering the Great Depression that lasted until World War II. A quarter of America's labor force became unemployed. An entire generation—one that had never known want and had been assured by the popular

1914–18	1915	1918–20	1929
World War I	Mohandas Gandhi leads Indian Nationalist movement	Influenza kills 20 million	U.S. stock market crashes

THE MONKEY TRIAL

July 21, 1925

At the Scopes "Monkey" Trial, was Scopes found guilty or innocent?

The issue of evolution had become more and more divisive ever since Charles Darwin published his *Origin of Species by Means of Natural Selection* in 1859. Following World War I, many prominent members of the emerging Fundamentalist movement went aggressively on the attack against evolution, believing that it undermined the authority of the Scriptures. One of the leading critics of evolution was William Jennings Bryan, a three-time Democratic nominee for president.

In 1915, Bryan threw himself into leadership of the Christian movement in America. As he saw the country's moral standards crumbling around him, he became convinced that a prime cause was Darwin's view of the origin of man.

Due in large measure to Bryan's efforts, the opposition to evolution became a national force in the 1920s. A number of Southern states passed laws outlawing the teaching of evolution in the public schools. The law passed in Tennessee was one of the strongest.

Within two weeks after the governor of Tennessee signed the bill into law, the American Civil Liberties Union (ACLU) announced that they would test the law and would provide counsel to any teacher in Tennessee willing to be the defendant in the case. Some prominent citizens of Dayton, Tennessee, persuaded John Scopes, a young science teacher, to break the law and allow himself to be arrested. The ACLU provided him with a star-studded defense team headed by Clarence Darrow, a religious skeptic and the nation's most famous trial attorney. The attorneys for the prosecution asked William Jennings Bryan to lead their team.

The resulting "Monkey Trial," as the Scopes trial came to be known, proved to be one of the first great media events in history, with reporters packing the little town of Dayton and wiring their stories around the world. There was even a nationwide radio hookup.

Bryan gave an impassioned speech for the prosecution, and then the drama of the trial reached its crescendo when Darrow called Bryan as an expert witness on the Bible for the defense. Bryan's difficulty in answering many of Darrow's questions brought him ridicule from the press. A tired old man at this point, Bryan's testimony consisted of more fervor than fact. The following day, the judge struck all of Bryan's testimony as a defense witness from the record.

It took only a few minutes on July 21, 1925, for the jury to find Scopes guilty. He was fined one hundred dollars, but the Tennessee Supreme Court later threw out the conviction on a technicality. The big story nationally, however, was that the most famous trial lawyer of the day had humiliated the nation's greatest orator. The Bible had won in Dayton, but in the eyes of the nation's press, evolution had won.

William Jennings Bryan died in his sleep the following Sunday.

liberalism of the day that things always inevitably improve—saw its dreams shattered. Theological liberalism that had won the day in the 1920s with its assurances of an optimistic future was dealt a severe blow by the depression and a fatal blow by World War II. Less optimistic theologies like those of Karl Barth (1886–1968), Reinhold (1892–1970), and H. Richard Niebuhr (1894–1962) were deemed more realistic by the major denominations. The Depression, on the other hand, caused evangelical and fundamentalist Christianity to become more separatist and ingrown as it endeavored to survive.

1929 ✡ ☾ RIOTS RAGE IN JERUSALEM; MASSACRES OCCUR IN HEBRON AND SAFED

Following a short period of relative stability, an outbreak of Arab hostility toward the Jews in Palestine erupted in 1929, sparked by disputes over Jewish rights to pray at the Wailing Wall, the western wall of the Temple Court. On August 23, a mob of Arabs attacked the Jews of Jerusalem, and the violence quickly spread. On August 24, Arabs of Hebron massacred seventy Jewish men and women, including infants and the elderly. Another slaughter occurred a few days later in Safed, with eighteen Jews killed and numerous others wounded. In the span of a few days, cities all across Palestine had been destroyed, with many Jews killed or wounded. British authorities eventually regained order, but the Palestinian riots refocused international attention on Palestine and the tension between Arabs and Jews.

1929 ✡ RAS SHAMARA TABLETS ARE DISCOVERED

The first tablets of a remarkable ancient library were discovered in 1929, at the tell of Ras Shamara in Northern Syria. Scholars immediately began working to translate and to publish the texts. Ras Shamara was the site of Ugarit, a major Canaanite city in the ancient Middle East that was destroyed by invaders in the early twelfth century BC. The clay tablets were written in cuneiform, wedge-shaped characters pushed into wet clay with a reed stylus. The writing is still legible and relates the history and mythology of the ancient civilization in two languages: Ugaritic and Akkadian. The former language was unknown before the tablets were discovered. Both languages are related to and shed light on ancient Hebrew.

1914–18	1915	1918–20	1929
World War I	Mohandas Gandhi leads Indian Nationalist movement	Influenza kills 20 million	U.S. stock market crashes

1929 ✝ LATERAN TREATY IS FORMED BETWEEN MUSSOLINI AND POPE

In 1929, the Lateran Treaty was signed between the Vatican and the Italian Kingdom. In bringing the pope to the table, anticlerical Italian dictator Benito Mussolini (1883–1945) settled an old dispute from 1870, when Italy wrested the city of Rome from the hands of the church. In the Lateran Treaty, Pope Pius XI (1857–1939) officially recognized Italy as a kingdom and Rome as its capital. In return, Mussolini recognized the Vatican City as an independent, sovereign state, with the Pope as its ruler. Catholicism was declared Italy's "sole religion," and the Vatican was compensated for the 1870 seizure of Rome. By signing the treaty, the church forfeited its right to political involvement, and Mussolini won the right to approve any new Italian bishop.

1931 ✝ C. S. LEWIS IS CONVERTED

Born in Belfast, Ireland, Clive Staples (C. S.) Lewis (1898–1963) was raised in the Church of England, but was what he called "a happy atheist" by the time he was fourteen. His conversion in 1931 was after a prolonged intellectual struggle, from which he concluded that the Christian faith was the only reasonable way to comprehend humanity and the universe. To his surprise he found himself sincerely believing in Jesus Christ. Not long after his conversion, Lewis, who taught at both Oxford and Cambridge Universities in England, wrote an autobiographical novel titled *The Pilgrim's Regress* (1933). A prolific writer, Lewis wrote fiction, apologetics, theology, children's books, poetry, and literary criticism. Much of his work seeks to articulate the truth of Christianity to the unbelieving age of the mid-twentieth century. Lewis believed reason comprehended truth, and imagination led to understanding. Among his most well-known works are *The Screwtape Letters, Mere Christianity,* and The Chronicles of Narnia.

1931 ✝ DONALD FULLERTON BEGINS THE PRINCETON EVANGELICAL FELLOWSHIP

In 1931, the mother of a Princeton University student asked Donald B. Fullerton (1892–1985), a former missionary to India and Afghanistan living in a nearby town, to disciple her son. Fullerton, a 1913 Princeton graduate, agreed and met initially with five students. The group eventually became known as the Princeton Evangelical Fellowship (PEF). Fullerton taught two Bible classes a week and after

1939–45	1945	1989	1999
World War II	United Nations founded	Berlin Wall falls	Europe adopts Eurocurrency

moving to Princeton in 1953 led personal Bible studies with interested students. He continued until his retirement in 1976. Alumni of the PEF include prominent seminary professors, scientists, denominational leaders, influential authors, as well as missionaries in more than twenty-five countries. As an independent group from a single university, the PEF has contributed more leaders to the Christian world than probably any other Christian college group. Today, the organization continues Fullerton's vision with an expanded full-time staff supported by alumni.

1931 ✛ HCJB IS THE FIRST MISSIONARY RADIO STATION

On Christmas Day 1931, *The Voice of the Andes* radio program began broadcasting from Ecuador on HCJB Radio. The establishment of HCJB, the first missionary radio station, was soon followed by the founding of the Far East Broadcasting Company (FEBC), Trans World Radio (TWR), Radio ELWA, and others. In 2004, with an estimated 1.2 billion radio sets in use around the world, shortwave radio stations broadcast in multiple languages, reaching billions of listeners, including more than a billion people who cannot read.

1932 ✡ FIFTH ALIYAH BEGINS

In 1932, just before the Nazi party came into power in Germany, the fifth wave of immigration, or *aliyah*, to Palestine began. As persecution of the Jews in Germany and other parts of Europe increased, the number of Jews coming to Palestine grew as well. The fifth aliyah continued until 1939, when the British, who coordinated the administration in Palestine, issued laws known as the White Papers, which limited Jewish immigration to the area. The laws were part of an effort to appease the Arabs in Palestine, who opposed any further development of Jewish communities on Palestinian territory. Despite the Arab and British opposition, during this period nearly a quarter of a million Jews migrated to Palestine, making it the largest immigration wave prior to Israel's becoming a nation in 1948.

1933 ✛ NAVIGATORS IS FOUNDED

During the 1920s, Dawson Trotman (1906–1956) was living a reckless life of drinking and gambling. While visiting his old Christian Endeavor group from

HE LIVED TO TRANSLATE

August 10, 1933

God can be trusted to work out the details.

William Cameron Townsend was born in California in 1896. He came to a personal faith in Jesus Christ as Lord and Savior at an early age and at the age of twelve joined the Presbyterian Church in which he was raised.

In 1917, Townsend went to Guatemala to sell Spanish Bibles to the rural Cakchiquel Indians. He soon realized that the Indians had no use for Spanish Bibles, but the Scriptures had not been translated into their own native language. One day an Indian asked him, "Why, if your God is so smart, hasn't he learned our language?"

Townsend then determined that he would translate the New Testament into Cakchiquel. Upon its completion in 1929, the Cakchiquels exclaimed, "Now God speaks our language!" This motivated Townsend to translate the Bible into yet another language.

A missionary friend, L. L. Legters, urged Townsend to come to Mexico, where at least fifty Indian tribes had no Bible in their language. Then news from Mexico came that a new Socialist president had confiscated all religious property and had ordered all foreign missionaries to leave the country.

Legters traveled to America's East Coast, to Keswick, a Bible conference ground in New Jersey where on August 10, 1933, the assembled group held a day of prayer for Mexico and Townsend's vision for translating the Bible into the country's tribal languages. When Keswick's director, Addison Raws, announced that the leaders would be fasting for the day, no one went to the dining hall.

After the day of prayer, those at Keswick were so sure God would answer their prayers that they encouraged Townsend and Legters to go immediately to Mexico and ask permission to do their translation work. Townsend and Legters followed those promptings, and through an amazing series of contacts, Townsend met Mexican's director of rural education. The director gave Townsend permission to study Mexico's rural education system for six weeks and was very pleased with the analysis Townsend wrote.

Confident that Mexico would be open to them, Townsend and Legters organized a three-month translation school in an Arkansas barn. They called it Camp Wycliffe, after John Wycliffe, the first translator of the Bible into English. The three students and four faculty members sat on nail kegs in the barn.

Townsend went to Mexico in 1935 with the students and began to translate the Bible into tribal languages. Wycliffe Bible Translators grew to become the largest independent Protestant mission agency in the world. At the time of Townsend's death in 1982, half of the world's five thousand languages still did not have any portion of Scripture, but half did—because of Cameron Townsend.

church, Trotman became captivated by their Scripture memorization contest. He began memorizing Scripture verses, which led to his conversion a few weeks later. Trotman started a discipling group called the Minute Men. Meeting a sailor crystallized Trotman's vision to train Christian sailors to disciple their comrades. In 1933, the organization became known as the Navigators. The motto was "To Know Christ and to Make Him Known." Scripture memorization was a key part of their training program. By 1945, Bible-memorizing Navigators were active on more than eight hundred navy ships, stations, and army bases. The Navigators' philosophy significantly impacted other ministries such as Wycliffe Bible Translators, Operation Mobilization, Mission Aviation Fellowship, and Campus Crusade for Christ.

1933 ✡ BOYCOTT AGAINST JEWS BEGINS IN GERMANY

On April 1, 1933, less than a month after the election of Adolf Hitler (1889–1945), the new German government organized a boycott of businesses owned by Jews. The nationwide boycott served the Nazi government's initial plan to make life so difficult for the Jews that they would leave the country. Within a week, Jews were removed from all civil service positions, and within ten days the definition of "non-Aryan," a person with even one Jewish grandparent, became a legal racial status in Germany. As the restrictions on the Jews grew, hatred of them increased as well, and signs saying Jews Not Wanted were posted in businesses, restaurants, and hotels throughout the country.

1934 ✝ BARMEN DECLARATION CHALLENGES HITLER

When Adolf Hitler (1889–1945), leader of the Nazi Party, became chancellor of Germany in 1933, he already had plans to stamp out the church. As Nazis increasingly challenged the church's authority, a group of Protestant leaders formed an alliance called the Confessing Church. Its spiritual constitution was spelled out in the *Barmen Declaration* of 1934, calling for a return to the doctrines of the Reformation and to the gospel of Jesus Christ. Largely written by theologian Karl Barth (1886–1968), the *Barmen Declaration* affirms Christ's lordship and provided a biblical challenge to Hitler's totalitarian aims. The Confessing Church did not, however, speak against Hitler openly; thus the

1914–18	1915	1918–20	1929
World War I	Mohandas Gandhi leads Indian Nationalist movement	Influenza kills 20 million	U.S. stock market crashes

movement failed to be the prophetic moral voice that Germany so desperately needed in its darkest hour.

1934 ✝ CAMERON TOWNSEND FOUNDS CAMP WYCLIFFE FOR BIBLE TRANSLATION

American missionary Cameron Townsend (1896–1982) became a Bible translator in 1926, in order to give a Mayan tribe in Guatemala the Bible in their native tongue. Townsend believed that the most effective way to evangelize native tribes was to provide them with Bibles in their own language. In 1934, he founded Camp Wycliffe, named for John Wycliffe (1330–1384), who translated the Bible into English. The camp became the Summer Institute of Linguistics (SIL) in 1942. SIL equips people to analyze and reduce unwritten languages into written form. The work of missionaries serving under SIL's sister organization— Wycliffe Bible Translators—has made Wycliffe a pioneer in the missionary movement to reach unreached peoples. Wycliffe has translated portions of the Bible into more than twenty-five hundred languages, and currently supports more than five thousand missionaries in seventy countries around the world.

1935 ✡ NUREMBURG LAWS INTENSIFY JEWISH PERSECUTION

On September 15, 1935, the German Reichstag adopted the Nuremberg Laws on Race and Citizenship. The laws became the official justification of racial discrimination in Germany. The legislation stated that only those of German blood (or closely related) were eligible for citizenship in the Reich. Also, only citizens were granted "full political rights." The Nuremberg Laws removed Jews from any positions of leadership in the army and prevented them from being citizens of the Reich. It also prohibited Germans from marrying or having any sexual contact with Jews. In the following years, these sentiments were intensified, and the full-scale persecution of Jews began in Germany.

1936 ✝ NGARUAWAHIA EASTER WEEK PROMPTS REVIVAL

Each Easter, many Christians in New Zealand gathered in Ngaruawahia for a week of worship. In 1936, many prayed that this might be the year they would experience revival. The revival historian J. Edwin Orr (1912–1987) was to be the

1939–45	1945	1989	1999
World War II	United Nations founded	Berlin Wall falls	Europe adopts Eurocurrency

PLAY BALL!

October 27, 1935

Name a professional baseball player who spoke to larger crowds than he played for.

His name was Billy Sunday, and he was born near Ames, Iowa, in 1862. His father, a Union soldier, died before he ever saw his son. Unable to provide for all her children, his mother was forced to send Sunday and a brother to an orphanage.

After high school, Sunday moved to Marshalltown, Iowa, where he played on the local state-champion baseball team. His amazing speed attracted the attention of the Chicago White Stockings, and he signed with Chicago in 1883.

One Sunday afternoon in Chicago in 1886, Sunday and some of his teammates went to a saloon, and after drinking their fill, went outside and sat down on the curb. Across the street a Christian band was playing gospel songs that Sunday remembered his mother singing years before in their log cabin. Sunday began to sob. One of the band members walked over to him and said, "We are going down to the Pacific Garden Mission. Won't you come?"

Sunday hesitated for a moment before jumping to his feet. He told his teammates on the curb, "I am going to Jesus Christ. We've come to a parting of the ways." Most of them laughed, but one friend encouraged him to go.

Billy Sunday walked to the mission, where he fell to his knees and into the arms of the Savior. Dreading his return to the ballpark the next day, he was pleasantly surprised to find his teammates supportive of what he had done.

Sunday joined a Presbyterian church and regularly went to Bible studies at the YMCA. In 1888, he married Helen Thompson, the sister of the White Stockings' batboy.

In 1891, Sunday ended his baseball career in order to work full time for the YMCA, for a fraction of his earnings as a baseball player. Two years later, he went to work as an advance man for evangelist J. Wilbur Chapman. When Chapman suddenly stopped traveling in 1895, he invited Sunday to hold evangelistic services for him in Garner, Iowa. Sunday did so and from then on was never without invitations to preach.

Sunday held evangelistic crusades in small midwestern towns and gradually went to the larger cities of the Midwest and the East. The climax of each service came after the sermon when he invited members of the audience to "walk the sawdust trail" to the front, indicating their decision to commit their life to Christ. His most successful crusade was in New York City where 98,264 people "hit the sawdust trail."

Billy Sunday preached his last sermon on October 27, 1935. No one else did more in the early days of the twentieth century in America to keep the Christian faith vital and growing. During his lifetime he preached to more than one hundred million, and hundreds of thousands put their faith in the Lord Jesus through his ministry.

speaker, further fueling the hopes and prayers for revival. Despite the expectations, most of the week-long meetings came and went uneventfully. After the meeting on Friday night, Orr met with a group of twelve young men who were disappointed about the lack of revival in their midst. Orr encouraged them to confess their sins. They were convicted, and as they began sincerely confessing and asking forgiveness of each other, the long-awaited revival began and spread quickly, in spite of its late start. On Saturday evening, one thousand people returned to the main tent to praise God for igniting revival among them, which they then carried back to their home churches.

1936 ✡ ARAB RIOTS RESULT IN THE FORMATION OF THE PEEL COMMISSION

As Palestine became a haven for Jews fleeing persecution in Europe during the 1930s, Arabs of Palestine increasingly resented the growing Jewish presence. In 1936, the Arab Higher Committee was formed with support from Germany and Italy, the Axis powers in World War II. The committee spread propaganda about the Jews that led to a number of Arab attacks on Jewish communities in Palestine. The violence, which lasted for three years, was ignored by England and its armed forces in Palestine until attacks were made on British stations. One of the results of the campaign was England's formation of the Peel Commission, which determined that the Jewish and Arab communities had irreconcilable differences and that Palestine should be divided.

1937 ✝ POPE PIUS XI CRITICIZES NAZISM AND COMMUNISM

In their early years, Italian Fascists supported the Catholic Church. So when Pius XI (1857–1939) became pope in 1922, he was content to work with them. However, he remained concerned with the atheism of Communism. In 1929, the Vatican signed the Lateran Treaty with Italian premier Benito Mussolini (1883–1945), in which the Italian government recognized the sovereignty of the Vatican City, and Pius recognized Italy as a sovereign state with Rome as its capital. In 1933, Pius signed a concordat with German chancellor Adolf Hitler (1899–1945) that many interpreted as his qualified approval of the Nazis. However, by 1937, Pius realized the dangers of both the Nazis and the Communists and issued two encyclicals—one condemning Nazism and the other condemning Communism.

1939–45	1945	1989	1999
World War II	United Nations founded	Berlin Wall falls	Europe adopts Eurocurrency

1937 ✛ CHILD EVANGELISM FELLOWSHIP IS FOUNDED

Child Evangelism Fellowship (CEF) is an international organization founded in 1937 by Jesse Irvin Overholtzer (1877–1955). Told as a boy that he was too young to understand religion, Overholtzer did not put his faith and trust in Christ until he was in college. He became a pastor, and after reading a sermon by Charles Spurgeon (1834–1892) on children's ability to understand and truly believe the gospel, was inspired to start Child Evangelism Fellowship. The heart of the organization's efforts revolve around preaching the gospel to children and providing them a foundation to grow up in a local church fellowship. The ministry became the world's largest organization evangelizing children. With more than twelve hundred workers and approximately forty thousand volunteers, CEF is active in every state in the U.S. and in more than one hundred fifty countries.

1938 ✡ KRISTALLNACHT ACCELERATES PERSECUTION OF GERMAN JEWS

When the Nazi party came to power in Germany in 1933, a variety of laws and boycotts heightened the persecution of German Jews. It was not until 1938, however, that the first widespread violence was directed against the Jewish community. During the night of November 9, Jews were attacked and Jewish establishments were destroyed throughout Germany. The night became known as Kristallnacht, or the "Night of Broken Glass," because of all the broken storefront windows. Despite claims that the violence was an outbreak sparked by the murder of a German official in Paris, Kristallnacht was in fact the result of an organized effort on the part of Nazi government agencies. The Jews were forced to pay for the damage, faced more regulations, saw their children removed from German schools, and were sent to concentration camps.

1938 ✛ DAVID MARTYN LLOYD-JONES JOINS THE STAFF OF WESTMINSTER CHAPEL

As a young man, David Martyn Lloyd-Jones (1899–1981) was trained in Wales as a physician. However, early in his practice he came to see his

1914–18	1915	1918–20	1929
World War I	Mohandas Gandhi leads Indian Nationalist movement	Influenza kills 20 million	U.S. stock market crashes

THE FIGHT AGAINST LIBERALISM

| January 1, 1937 |

Friend and foe alike considered him to be the leading conservative Christian apologist of his time.

Born in 1881, J. Gresham Machen grew up in a Presbyterian family in Baltimore. He majored in classics at Johns Hopkins University and graduated first in his class in 1901. He then entered their graduate program, but after one year transferred to Princeton Seminary. Following his graduation in 1905, he studied for a year in Germany then returned to Princeton as a professor of New Testament.

Machen was known for his scholarly writing on New Testament topics and for his defense of conservative theology. He became nationally recognized after publishing *Christianity and Liberalism* in 1923. He maintained that liberalism was not a variety of Christianity, but was instead an entirely different religion. He wrote, "Liberalism appeals to man's will, while Christianity announces, first, a gracious act of God."

Machen's convictions caused him to become a controversial figure both at Princeton Seminary and within his denomination, the Presbyterian Church U.S.A., as these institutions were beginning to shift toward a more liberal theological stance. Princeton's drift into liberalism was heartbreaking for Machen, who fought to keep the seminary committed to the creeds of the Presbyterian Church. He pleaded with the seminary faculty to make a stand for "the full truthfulness of the Bible as the Word of God and for the vigorous defense and propagation of the Reformed or Calvinistic system of doctrine."

It was a losing battle. Princeton officially reorganized in 1929, to ensure a more inclusive theological curriculum. This left Machen and other Reformed professors worried about the lack of evangelical training for future Presbyterian ministers. In response, Machen and other Reformed faculty members left Princeton and founded Westminster Theological Seminary in Philadelphia. They envisioned Westminster Seminary as an institution that would train Presbyterian ministers with a focus on academic excellence and theological orthodoxy. Gresham Machen was a professor of New Testament there until his death.

At Westminster, Machen continued to fight liberalism within the Presbyterian Church. In 1933, he helped form the conservative Independent Board for Presbyterian Foreign Missions in order to counteract the liberalism infiltrating Presbyterian missions. The Presbyterian General Assembly rejected this new mission board, and in 1935, Machen was suspended from the ministry of the Presbyterian Church for refusing to break his ties to the Independent Board.

Machen then played a central role in founding a new denomination, the Presbyterian Church of America (later the Orthodox Presbyterian Church), which continued to uphold theological orthodoxy.

In December 1936, while on a speaking tour in Bismarck, North Dakota, Machen came down with pneumonia, but he continued his preaching until finally he was hospitalized. When a friend visited him on New Year's Eve, Machen told him about a vision of heaven he had had: "Sam, it was glorious, it was glorious." He added later, "Sam, isn't the Reformed Faith grand?" He died the next day, on January 1, 1937.

patients' illnesses as deeper issues than physical or psychological diagnoses. He put his faith in Christ and studied theologians like John Owen (1616–1683) and Jonathan Edwards (1703–1758). In 1927, Lloyd-Jones was ordained to the ministry. He spent eleven years as an evangelist and preacher in south Wales before becoming co-pastor with G. Campbell Morgan (1863–1945) at London's Westminster Chapel in 1938. He spent another thirty years at Westminster Chapel powerfully preaching from the Scriptures. In 1943, Campbell Morgan retired, leaving Lloyd-Jones as the sole preacher of the church. Thousands found Christ and grew in their faith under Lloyd-George's preaching.

1939 ✝ BACK TO THE BIBLE BROADCAST BEGINS

On May 1, 1939, a young preacher by the name of Theodore Epp (1907–1985) went to Nebraska with the vision of starting a radio broadcast that would encourage Christians in their faith and spread the gospel. He called it *Back to the Bible*. Epp also had a strong burden for foreign missions. He used his broadcast to raise awareness and support for missions and also expanded radio broadcasts overseas. In 1954, *Back to the Bible* opened its first international office in Canada; offices in England, Sri Lanka, France, the Philippines, Australia, South Africa, India, Ecuador, and Jamaica soon followed. Through the years, the ministry continued to expand worldwide. Since Epp's retirement in 1984, his vision has continued under able leadership.

1939 ✝ ✡ WORLD WAR II BEGINS

In the 1930s, Fascist power in Europe grew rapidly under dictators Adolf Hitler (1889–1945) in Germany and Benito Mussolini (1883–1945) in Italy. In August 1939, Italy and Germany created an alliance known as the Axis, to which Japan was later added. On September 1, 1939, German armies invaded Poland, drawing Europe into World War II. In all, fifty-seven nations declared war, leading eventually to the loss of tens of millions of lives. World War II dealt a death blow to religious liberalism, which had taught that "every day and in every way we are getting better and better." Germany, with its intellectual and spiritual leadership as well as newly developed technology, had delivered to the world destruction instead of progress.

1914–18	1915	1918–20	1929
World War I	Mohandas Gandhi leads Indian Nationalist movement	Influenza kills 20 million	U.S. stock market crashes

1939 ✡ POGROMS SWEEP VIOLENTLY THROUGH POLAND

At the time of the German invasion in 1939, Poland had the greatest number of Jews of any country in the world. The Nazis brought their anti-Semitic laws with them into Poland, the Jewish religious and cultural center in Europe. In Polish territory, the Germans took their anti-Semitic sentiment even further than they had in Germany. As in Germany, regulations severely restricted Jewish life, but in addition, Jews were tortured and shot at random. The organized persecutions, or pogroms, were so violent and prevalent that more than 250,000 Jews were killed before the end of the year.

1940 ✡ GHETTOS ARE ESTABLISHED IN POLAND

Following their occupation of Poland in 1939, the Germans established Jewish ghettos in 1940. Ghettos were set up in Warsaw, Cracow, and other Polish cities that possessed railway connections. The entire Jewish population from each city was packed into the walled neighborhoods. Jews living in hundreds of Polish towns and villages were sent into these city ghettos. Any Jew found outside of a ghetto was executed. From the beginning, the Jews were used as slave labor for activities related to the war, and life in the ghettos became increasingly difficult as the war progressed. Within two years, the Germans liquidated the ghettos, sending the majority of Jews to concentration camps and death camps.

1940 ✡ SIXTH ALIYAH BEGINS

In 1940, the sixth *aliyah,* or immigration of Jews to Palestine, began. The first five were the major waves that started before the Nazi persecution of the Jews began in Germany in 1933. The sixth migration to Palestine took place during the war and at the height of the Holocaust in Europe. Immigration was hindered during this period by the British who ruled Palestine. It was common for boats carrying immigrants to be turned away. Nevertheless, the sixth aliyah lasted for about four years, until Britain made immigration to Palestine completely illegal. Approximately twelve thousand Jews successfully made their way to Israel during the sixth aliyah. Despite the British limitations, Germany's defeat opened the door for the largest migration to Palestine, which came with Israel's declaration of independence.

1939–45	1945	1989	1999
World War II	United Nations founded	Berlin Wall falls	Europe adopts Eurocurrency

1940 ✡ ORTHODOX JUDAISM REVIVES IN AMERICA WITH THE ARRIVAL OF JOSEPH ISAAC SCHNEERSOHN

Hasidim—the adherents of an ultra-orthodox form of Judaism, founded in Eastern Europe by Israel Baal Shem Tov in the 1700s—immigrated to America from 1880 to 1925. However, the movement never took hold until 1940, with the arrival of Rabbi Joseph Isaac Schneersohn (1880–1950), a Lubavitcher grand rabbi, called a *rebbe*. Schneersohn and his successor and son-in-law, Rabbi Menachem Mendel Schneersohn (1902–1994), began a program for the Lubavitch Hasidim to evangelize American Jews to return to Orthodoxy. They established Jewish day schools, summer camps, and youth groups. When his father-in-law died in 1950, Menachem Mendel Schneersohn led the movement for the next forty-four years from its headquarters in the Crown Heights section of Brooklyn, New York. By the 1990s, there were 150,000 Jews living in Hasidic communities in New York and New Jersey.

1940 ✝ FIRST CHRISTIAN TELEVISION BROADCAST IS AIRED

On March 24, 1940, Dr. Samuel McCrea Cavert of the Federal Council of Churches in America officiated at an Easter service in New York City. The service was televised on the NBC station W2XBS in New York City. It was the first Christian television broadcast. No one watching that initial broadcast could have anticipated the degree to which television would be used to spread the gospel in the years to come.

1941 ✡ JEWS ARE PROHIBITED FROM EMIGRATING FROM GERMANY

In the 1930s, Jews living in Germany became increasingly threatened and restricted by the anti-Jewish laws, boycotts, and riots. Beginning in 1938, the German government decided to assist Jews who wanted to leave the country. Hoping to raise anti-Jewish sentiment in neighboring countries by flooding them with Jews, the Germans set up emigration offices in Vienna, Berlin, and Prague. Besides promoting Jewish emigration, the offices also served to speed up the process of confiscating the property of those Jews who left Germany. Despite Germany's support of Jewish emigration, the majority of countries in Europe were unwilling to accept many Jewish refugees. In 1941, however, the

1914–18	1915	1918–20	1929
World War I	Mohandas Gandhi leads Indian Nationalist movement	Influenza kills 20 million	U.S. stock market crashes

government changed their policy, and rather than promoting emigration the Germans prohibited emigration and began killing Jews instead.

1941 ✧ EICHMANN INITIATES HIS FINAL SOLUTION

In 1941, the German government decided to initiate what they called the "final solution to the Jewish problem." The Nazis' goal was to totally exterminate the Jewish population throughout Europe. Coordinated by Adolf Eichmann (1906–1962), the Final Solution was centered in Poland, where the largest population of Jews resided. Organized as if it were just another military operation, the plan was to kill approximately 11 million Jews by collecting them throughout Europe, transporting them to central camps, and forwarding them to death camps. The death camps, like the one established at Auschwitz, were equipped with gas chambers hidden as showers. The terrifying Final Solution of Nazi Germany resulted in the deaths of more than 6 million Jews before the end of World War II.

1941 ✧ FIRST DEATH CAMP IS ESTABLISHED IN CHELMNO

In the 1930s, along with imposing restrictions on Jews in Germany, the German government began building concentration camps. The camp in Dachau, built in 1933, was one of the first erected. Originally the camps held a variety of people the Germans considered dangerous, not just Jews. By 1936, the German secret police, known as the Gestapo, was placed in charge of running these camps. Within a year, Jews were being sent to camps simply because of their heritage. With the implementation of the Final Solution—the coordinated operation designed to exterminate the Jewish population in Europe—some of the camps were converted to "death camps" to carry out the Nazi plan. The first death camp, where Jews were murdered with carbon monoxide or prussic acid gasses, was established in Chelmno in western Poland in 1941.

1941 ✧ GERMANY INVADES SOVIET UNION
AND ESTABLISHES EINSATZGRUPPEN

In June 1941, the German army invaded the Soviet Union. As part of their war effort, the Germans formulated killing squads in the Soviet provinces. Known

1939–45	1945	1989	1999
World War II	United Nations founded	Berlin Wall falls	Europe adopts Eurocurrency

as *Einsatzgruppen,* or "action groups," the squads were used to murder Jews, communists, gypsies, and anyone else who was perceived as a threat. The Einsatzgruppen possessed authority similar to that of the Gestapo, the secret police of Nazi Germany, and worked their way through Germany's acquired territory gathering Jews for execution. Large groups of Jews were killed by drowning, shooting, and asphyxiation. In one mass murder in September 1941, an Einsatzgruppen composed of Germans and Ukrainians killed at least thirty-three thousand Jews.

1941 ✛ NIEBUHR WRITES THE NATURE AND DESTINY OF MAN

Reinhold Niebuhr (1892–1971) was an American theologian who began his career as a religious liberal and political pacifist. But the day-to-day dynamics of his urban-industrial Detroit pastorate, coupled with the onset of World War II, turned him into a champion of social activism and a new heresy called neo-orthodoxy. In 1941, he helped found the journal *Christianity and Crisis,* challenging the nation's Christians to reject neutralism in the war. The same year, Niebuhr's influential theological work *The Nature and Destiny of Man* defined the neo-orthodox view of man and criticized both the liberal and Marxist views of human nature.

1941 ✛ BULTMANN CALLS FOR DEMYTHOLOGIZATION OF THE NEW TESTAMENT

In 1941, Rudolf Bultmann (1884–1976), the influential German theologian and professor of New Testament at the University of Marburg, wrote an essay titled "Neues Testament und Mythologie" (New Testament and Mythology). In his essay, Bultmann argued that both conservatives and liberals were misinterpreting the gospels. He suggested that the conservatives were wrong to accept the history of the gospels and that the liberals were wrong to reject the *kerygma,* what the early church preached about Jesus. Instead, the historical narratives of the gospels should be "demythologized," with the central kerygma to be reinterpreted and expressed in existential terms. A call for life-changing decision could then be made from this "demythologized kerygma." Bultmann's demythologization theory has remained an influential teaching among liberal theologians during the post–World War II era.

1914–18	1915	1918–20	1929
World War I	Mohandas Gandhi leads Indian Nationalist movement	Influenza kills 20 million	U.S. stock market crashes

1941 ✝ YOUNG LIFE BEGINS

Seeking to advance his evangelistic work among high-school students, James Rayburn Jr. (1909–1970), a student at Dallas Theological Seminary, initiated after-school Bible studies in Gainesville, Texas, in 1938. As he developed his strategy for reaching more students with the gospel, Rayburn targeted leaders in the school and built personal relationships with the students while continuing meetings in homes. Rayburn asked other seminary students to join the effort. In response to their positive results, a Chicago businessman provided financial support, which made it possible for Rayburn to expand the ministry. The ministry was officially incorporated on October 16, 1941, as Young Life. Young Life leaders seek to model the Christian life for students on a personal level, in order to share Jesus Christ with them.

1941 ✝ THE UNITED STATES ENTERS WORLD WAR II

On December 7, 1941 the Japanese air force attacked the American naval base at Pearl Harbor in Hawaii, sinking 17 ships and destroying 170 airplanes. The following day, the United States entered World War II. Four years later, in 1945, the Allies were finally able to defeat Germany, Italy, and Japan. The United States suffered casualties of more than 405,000 dead and 670,000 wounded. Many of the returning servicemen had become Christians during the war. They had seen the world in its spiritual poverty and desired to help. After attending school on the G.I. Bill, many returned as missionaries to the lands where they had earlier fought.

1942 ✡ MASS TRANSPORTS TO AUSCHWITZ BEGIN

As part of their "final solution" initiative designed to annihilate all European Jews, the Nazis designated certain concentration camps to collect Jews from the ghettos. The Jews were then transported in boxcars to Polish concentration camps. Death camps were constructed, where Jews were gassed in groups of seven hundred or more. One of the main concentration camps converted to a death camp was Auschwitz. Like other death camps, Auschwitz was equipped with a set of gas chambers, which appeared to be large shower rooms. The mass transportation of Jews to Auschwitz began in 1942. In all, approximately two and a half million Jews were murdered at Auschwitz.

1939–45	1945	1989	1999
World War II	United Nations founded	Berlin Wall falls	Europe adopts Eurocurrency

1942 ✝ NATIONAL ASSOCIATION OF EVANGELICALS IS FOUNDED

The National Association of Evangelicals (NAE) was founded during a meeting of evangelical leaders at the Hotel Coronado in St. Louis, Missouri, from April 7 to 9, 1942. The NAE was intended to be an evangelical substitute for the liberal-leaning Federal Council of Churches. The NAE's statement of faith is a clear declaration of the Bible's inspiration, infallibility, and authority as the Word of God. Throughout the latter half of the twentieth century, the NAE established a number of subsidiary operations such as missions, politics, relief organizations, and Christian schools.

1943 ✡ GERMANY IS DECLARED FREE OF JEWS

Less than two years after implementing the Final Solution, the Nazi plot to kill all European Jews, Germany declared that there were no more Jews living within its borders. Unlike other countries such as Italy, where Germany's plan was in place but not rigorously enforced, the Germans were extremely efficient at expediting the roundup and extermination of entire Jewish communities. By the end of World War II, despite its utter military defeat at the hands of the Allies, Germany had achieved its goal of devastating the Jewish population throughout Europe. There were essentially no Jews left in Germany, and Jews of Eastern Europe, once a center for Jewish culture, were either scattered or dead.

1943 ✡ WARSAW GHETTO UPRISING BEGINS

In 1942, after the first mass deportation of Jews from the Warsaw Ghetto, the Jewish Fighting Organization formed in the ghetto. Able to smuggle some weapons into the ghetto, the group participated in street fighting in January 1943. Sparked by a second wave of deportations to death camps, the fighting continued for four days and killed twenty German soldiers. As a result, a twenty-four-hour curfew was imposed on Jews. The Gentile Polish resistance movement supplied additional weapons, giving Jews in the ghetto renewed hope. On April 19, 1943, the Germans returned to Warsaw to wipe out the ghetto. Upon arrival they faced a Jewish attack so ferocious that their only strategy was to burn the ghetto. Fighting continued until May 8, when the headquarters of the Jewish Fighting Organization was destroyed.

1914–18	1915	1918–20	1929
World War I	Mohandas Gandhi leads Indian Nationalist movement	Influenza kills 20 million	U.S. stock market crashes

1943 ✝ NATIONAL RELIGIOUS BROADCASTERS IS FOUNDED

In 1943, the National Association of Evangelicals (NAE) founded the National Religious Broadcasters (NRB), with the purpose of protecting the Christian broadcaster's right to communicate the gospel. In 2001, the NRB left the NAE and became an independent organization. Now with more than seventeen hundred member organizations broadcasting to more than one million viewers and listeners, the NRB continues to grow. Its headquarters are located in Washington, D.C.

1944 ✡ JEWISH BRIGADE IS FORMED

During World War II, the Jews of Palestine were perplexed by the lack of sympathy shown by the British government officials ruling Palestine. Britain, hoping to win the Arabs to the side of the Allies, severely restricted Jewish immigration, frustrating the thousands attempting to escape persecution in Europe. Hoping that the British would favor the Jewish position in the Middle East following the war, Palestinian Jews participated in Britain's war effort. They also wanted to contribute to Germany's defeat and the end of the Holocaust. Thus, a multitude of Jews fought for Great Britain during World War II, and in September 1944, the Jewish Brigade of twenty-five thousand Palestinian Jews was formed within the British army. They carried a flag that included a yellow Star of David.

1944 ✝ YOUTH FOR CHRIST IS FOUNDED

Youth for Christ was founded in 1944, in Winona Lake, Indiana, as an interdenominational youth organization seeking to share the gospel with teenagers and young adults. The organization featured Saturday night youth rallies, with Billy Graham and Chuck Templeton as evangelists. Over the years, YFC's emphasis changed to promoting high-school Bible clubs. In the 1960s, these clubs became known as Campus Life. Youth for Christ International was launched in 1968 to reach teens in other countries.

1945 ✝ DIETRICH BONHOEFFER IS EXECUTED

In the mid-1930s, some German Christians looked to Hitler (1889–1945) as the savior of their nation. But Lutheran pastor Dietrich Bonhoeffer (1906–1945) recognized Hitler's Nazism as the dehumanizing, anti-Christian movement that it was. Prior to and during World War II, Bonhoeffer wrote prolifically about the Christian life and trained ministers in an underground seminary until he was forbidden to publish or preach. Joining a conspiracy against Hitler, Bonhoeffer worked in the military intelligence service as a double agent on behalf of the conspirators. Arrested in 1943, for smuggling Jews into Switzerland, he pastored his fellow prisoners until he was executed for treason on April 9, 1945. His writings have inspired many to be faithful to Jesus' teachings.

1945 ✡ LIBERATION OF CONCENTRATION CAMPS IS COMPLETE

In 1945, with the defeat of Germany fast approaching, the Nazis evacuated the concentration camps of Poland. As the armies of the Soviet Union gained ground in Eastern Europe, the prisoners were put on "death marches" heading westward to Germany. It is estimated that at least a quarter of a million Jews died in these marches, only months before the end of World War II. American and Soviet troops liberated the remaining concentration camps. Almost all the victims of the camps who lived to see the liberation were starving, having worked as slave labor for the German war effort. The slave laborers literally were being worked to death; their average lifespan while in the camps was only nine months. The last death camp to be liberated, at Gross-Rosen, Germany, was freed by the Russian army on May 8, 1945.

1945 ✡ JEWS STRUGGLE AGAINST BRITAIN'S IMMIGRATION RESTRICTIONS

In 1945, Britain, appointed by the League of Nations to rule Palestine, outlawed the immigration of Jews into the region. Since 1939, the British had been very strict about immigration, turning boats loaded with refugees back to sea. A group of Jews known as the Revisionists declared war on the British, and their campaign to undermine the British government led to the sweeping arrest of Jews and the establishment of confinement camps in Cyprus. Those who immigrated illegally were detained at the camps. As tensions intensified between Britain and the Palestinian Jews, the struggle was approaching full-blown war. In 1947, Britain ceased efforts to reconcile Arabs and Jews in Palestine, deferring to the General Assembly of the United Nations.

1914–18	1915	1918–20	1929
World War I	Mohandas Gandhi leads Indian Nationalist movement	Influenza kills 20 million	U.S. stock market crashes

1945 ✛ ATOMIC BOMB FALLS ON HIROSHIMA

After careful deliberations, the United States government chose not to launch a ground invasion of Japan in 1945. Instead, they decided the most effective way to end World War II would be to unveil a secret weapon that American scientists had only recently perfected. On August 6, 1945, at approximately 8:15 a.m. local time, the American bomber *Enola Gay* dropped the first atomic bomb, "Little Boy," on the Japanese city of Hiroshima. The force of the bomb was so great that every building in a 1.5-mile radius was leveled with ninety-two thousand people killed and a similar number injured. A second atomic bomb, "Fat Man," was dropped three days later on the city of Nagasaki. It destroyed one and one half square miles and killed forty thousand. On August 15, the Japanese army unconditionally surrendered to the Allies, and World War II was over.

1945 ✛ EVANGELICAL FOREIGN MISSIONS ASSOCIATION IS FORMED

In 1945, the Evangelical Foreign Missions Association was established. Initially formed in Chicago, today the association has sixty-four members that serve nearly seven thousand missionaries in approximately 120 regions. Still striving to fulfill its original purpose of providing "a medium for voluntary united action among the evangelical foreign missionary agencies," the group's Washington, D.C. office represents missionaries and their purposes to foreign governments.

1945 ✛ MISSION AVIATION FELLOWSHIP IS FOUNDED

Mission Aviation Fellowship (MAF) was founded on May 20, 1945, to assist in transporting missionaries in particularly remote areas. Originally named the Christian Airmen's Missionary Fellowship, the group started in California. Led by Christian military airmen from World War II, by the 1950s, MAF was seen as fulfilling an essential role in international missions. Over the next forty years, MAF established twelve strategically located bases around the globe. The organization, which serves multiple missionary groups, flies more than one hundred planes in more than twenty countries. Each year MAF pilots collectively fly more than 30 million miles.

1939–45	1945	1989	1999
World War II	United Nations founded	Berlin Wall falls	Europe adopts Eurocurrency

1945 ✝ JOHN STOTT BEGINS HIS MINISTRY AT ALL SOULS CHURCH

John R. W. Stott (1921–) was ordained in the Church of England and became curate (1945–1950) and then rector (1950–1975) of All Souls Church, Langham Place, London. At a strategic location on the doorstep of London University and the British Broadcasting Company, Stott's ministry at All Souls launched him into a place of leadership in the evangelical movement around the globe. His numerous books also have served to give him worldwide influence. Stott was a major contributor in the writing of the Lausanne covenant, presented at the International Congress on World Evangelization in 1974.

1946 ✝ INTERVARSITY CHRISTIAN FELLOWSHIP HOLDS ITS FIRST URBANA MISSIONARY CONFERENCE

In May 1941, the British college organization of InterVarsity Christian Fellowship was incorporated in the United States. In 1946, the organization held its first mission convention in Toronto, Canada, with 575 students in attendance from 151 colleges and universities. A number of those college students, fresh from the battlefields of World War II, were burdened to return to those lands with the gospel of Jesus Christ. Two years later, the mission convention relocated to the campus of the University of Illinois in Urbana, Illinois. That year 1,331 students from 254 schools attended the convention, and the Urbana tradition was born. Since then the convention has been held every three years, and the attendance has grown to twenty thousand.

1946 ✡ REVISIONISTS BLOW UP THE KING DAVID HOTEL

During the fourth *aliyah,* or wave of immigration, to Palestine in 1924–31, the Revisionists, a group of politically conservative Jews, grew in number. The Revisionists opposed the Labor Zionist party, whose members were more involved in Jewish culture. As disagreements between the parties increased during the 1930s, the Revisionists separated themselves from the Jewish Defense Organization known as the Haganah and formed their own military group, known as the Irgun. Toward the end of World War II, as the British opposed Jewish immigration, the Irgun fought against the British army. In June 1946, their campaign to undermine the government led to the

1914–18	1915	1918–20	1929
World War I	Mohandas Gandhi leads Indian Nationalist movement	Influenza kills 20 million	U.S. stock market crashes

SCROLLS FOR SALE

November 29, 1947

Some important stories don't make the news.

On November 29, 1947, headlines around the world proclaimed that the United Nations had voted to establish two separate states in Palestine, one Jewish and one Arab.

However, another event happened that day that was to influence biblical studies forever. The story begins about a year earlier, when three Bedouin teenagers— Muhammed Ahmed el-Hamed, Jum'a Muhammed Khalib, and Khalil Musa—found three scrolls covered with strange writing, while exploring a cave near the Dead Sea.

In April 1947, an uncle of one of the boys took the scrolls to Bethlehem and showed them to a Muslim sheikh, who sent them to a Bethlehem shoemaker and part-time antiquities dealer, known as "Kando."

Meanwhile, Khalil Musa and some other Bedouins brought George Isaiah, a Syrian Orthodox merchant from Jerusalem, to see the cave. They found four more scrolls. Isaiah told the Syrian Orthodox Metropolitan in Jerusalem about the scrolls, and he offered to buy them. In July, when Jum'a, Musa, and Isaiah tried to bring the four scrolls to the Syrian Orthodox Metropolitan, they were mistakenly turned away. Instead they sold the four scrolls to Kando, the Bethlehem merchant, who in turn sold them to the Metropolitan for $97.20. One of the experts the Metropolitan consulted regarding his purchase was Eleazar Sukenik, a noted professor at the Hebrew University in Jerusalem.

When Sukenik learned that an antiquities dealer was offering ancient scrolls for sale, he made a secret trip to Bethlehem. He purchased two of the scrolls on November 29, 1947, the day the United Nations voted to create a Jewish state. A month later he purchased a third.

In 1954, the Syrian Orthodox Metropolitan placed an ad in the *Wall Street Journal,* offering his four scrolls for sale. Sukenik's son, Yigael Yadin, an Israeli general and leading archaeologist, was in the United States when the ad appeared. Yadin was able to purchase the scrolls for $250,000. Those four together with the three purchased by his father now reside in an exhibit in the Israel Museum called The Shrine of the Book.

The Dead Sea Scrolls, dating from 250 BC to AD 68, are considered by many to be the most important archaeological discovery of all time. They apparently were the library of the Essenes, a Jewish sect that had lived at nearby Qumran. When the invading Roman armies reached southern Judea in AD 68, the Essenes hid their library in caves.

The scrolls range in length from the complete book of Isaiah to thousands of small fragments. At least one fragment from every Old Testament book except Esther has been found. Evidence shows that originally about three hundred books were hidden, a third of them portions of the Old Testament.

The greatest value of the Dead Sea Scrolls is that they demonstrate the accuracy of our current text of the Hebrew Old Testament, showing it to be virtually the same as that in 250 BC.

arrests of thousands of Jews. In response to the mass arrests, the Irgun blew up a wing of the King David Hotel in Jerusalem and all of the government offices housed there. Ninety-one were killed in the explosion.

1947 ✡ ☾ UNITED NATIONS VOTES TO PARTITION PALESTINE

Since receiving a mandate from the League of Nations in 1920, England had attempted to solve the Arab-Jewish conflict in Palestine. The influx of Jewish immigrants at the end of World War II increased these tensions, and England eventually deferred to the General Assembly at the United Nations. On November 29, 1947, the U.N. voted to partition Palestine into two states. The Negev Desert (in southern Palestine), and the coastal region and eastern Galilee (in northern Palestine) were set aside for Jews, while Arabs were given the Gaza Strip (the southern coast) and the remaining areas of Palestine. Jerusalem was designated as an international city. The motion, which the United States and the Soviet Union supported, was denounced by the League of Arab States, which supported the cause of the Palestinian Arabs.

1947 ✝ ✡ DEAD SEA SCROLLS ARE DISCOVERED

In 1947, in caves on the northwestern side of the Dead Sea in Israel, ancient scrolls were discovered dating back to the period between 250 BC and AD 68. The scrolls are believed to be the library of the Essenes, a Jewish priestly sect living at Qumran in the Dead Sea region. They vary in length, from the complete book of Isaiah to thousands of small fragments. Many consider the Dead Sea Scrolls to be the most important archaeological discovery of all time.

1947 ✝ FULLER THEOLOGICAL SEMINARY IS FOUNDED

Fuller Theological Seminary was founded in 1947 as a "Christ-centered, Spirit-directed training school" in Pasadena, California. The school received its name, inspiration, and early funding from Charles E. Fuller (1887–1968), the preacher on the nationally distributed radio program, *The Old-Fashioned Revival Hour*. Fuller Seminary became controversial as it changed its position on biblical inerrancy and introduced "New Evangelicalism" to the theological

1914–18	1915	1918–20	1929
World War I	Mohandas Gandhi leads Indian Nationalist movement	Influenza kills 20 million	U.S. stock market crashes

BIRTH OF A NATION

May 15, 1948

They came from all over the world.

In 63 BC, the Roman armies invaded the land of Israel and made it part of the Roman Empire. Then Jesus came, and in response to the Jews' rejection of him as their Messiah he predicted just before his death in AD 33 that the Jewish Temple would be completely destroyed (Luke 21:6). In addition, he foretold that a foreign army would conquer Jerusalem and that the Jewish people would be forcibly dispersed throughout the world (Luke 21:20-24). This prediction was fulfilled in AD 70 when, in response to an earlier Jewish revolt, the Roman armies destroyed the city of Jerusalem and its Temple, killing hundreds of thousands of Jews and taking captive most of the survivors.

Since their dispersion by the Romans, Jews have been scattered throughout the world. Then in the late 1800s a Jewish movement called Zionism arose. Its goal was to create an independent Jewish state in Palestine. In a 1917 attempt to win Jewish support for World War I, England issued the Balfour Declaration, declaring England's support for "the establishment in Palestine of a national home for the Jewish people." Following World War I, the League of Nations placed Palestine under England's control.

As Nazi persecution of Jews increased during the 1930s, large numbers of refugees fled to Palestine. In response, the Palestinian Arabs revolted against the British from 1936 to 1939. In 1939, Britain decided to limit Jewish immigration, arousing militant Jewish resistance.

Following World War II, during which six million Jews were murdered by the Nazis in the Holocaust, the British continued to limit Jewish immigration to Palestine. In response, large-scale Jewish resistance movements rose up among the Jews already in Palestine. Finally England decided to turn the problem of Palestine over to the United Nations.

When the matter came to a vote in the UN on November 29, 1947, due largely to U.S. President Harry Truman's strong support, the General Assembly endorsed a plan to create separate Jewish and Arab states, with Jerusalem as an international zone.

The British Mandate was scheduled to end on May 15, 1948, at which time their troops would begin leaving. The day before, a historic meeting was held in the exhibition hall of the art museum in Tel Aviv. At exactly 4:00 p.m. David Ben Gurion called the meeting to order. The audience rose and sang "Hatikvah," the Jewish national anthem, accompanied by the Palestine Symphony Orchestra. Then David Ben Gurion read in Hebrew, Israel's Declaration of Independence. It ended with the words, "We . . . hereby proclaim the establishment of the Jewish State in Palestine, to be called Israel." Everyone in the audience stood to their feet and applauded, many with tears streaming down their faces.

An independent Jewish state of Israel existed for the first time in over two thousand years.

scene. As a result, several prominent professors left the faculty and went to more conservative theological institutions.

1948 ✡ ISRAEL DECLARES INDEPENDENCE

On November 29, 1947, the General Assembly of the United Nations endorsed a plan to create separate Jewish and Arab states in Palestine. The British mandate over Palestine was scheduled to end on May 15, 1948, at which time the English troops would be leaving. In anticipation of the end of the British presence in Palestine, David Ben Gurion (1886–1973) called to order a historic meeting on May 14, 1948. After the assembled body sang the "Hatikvah," the Jewish national anthem, Ben Gurion read Israel's Declaration of Independence. For the first time in more than two thousand years, there was an independent Jewish state of Israel.

1948 ✡ ☾ ISRAEL'S WAR OF INDEPENDENCE BEGINS

On May 15, 1948, the day after Israel declared its independence, it was attacked by five Arab nations: Egypt, Iraq, Lebanon, Syria, and Jordan. Though greatly outnumbered and poorly armed, the Israelis were able to repulse the invading nations. By the end of 1948, they had defeated the Arab nations and in so doing had conquered half of the territory the United Nations had planned for the new Arab nation. The other half was divided between Jordan and Egypt. Israel controlled the western half of Jerusalem and Jordan the eastern half, including the Old City and the Temple mount.

1948 ✝ FAR EAST BROADCASTING AIRS ITS FIRST BROADCAST

On December 20, 1945, the Far East Broadcasting Company (FEBC) was incorporated, with John Broger (1913–) as president and Robert Bowman (1915–) as vice president. In April 1946, Broger arrived in Shanghai and began to talk with missionaries about starting a Christian radio station. In August, he traveled to Manila, the Philippines, for the purpose of establishing a FEBC base there. The first signal from KZAS—the station based in the Philippines—went on the air on June 4, 1948. The singing of "All Hail the Power of Jesus' Name" was the first sound transmitted. Today the FEBC broadcasts in Asia, Eastern Europe, Latin America, and Australia.

1914–18	1915	1918–20	1929
World War I	Mohandas Gandhi leads Indian Nationalist movement	Influenza kills 20 million	U.S. stock market crashes

1948 ✝ WORLD COUNCIL OF CHURCHES IS FORMED

At the end of World War II, all that most of the world wanted was to find ways to live in peace. To promote international cooperation, fifty-one nations signed the charter of the United Nations at a 1945 conference in San Francisco. Since early in the century, the church too had been moving toward an international, ecumenical league. On August 23, 1948, delegates from 147 mainline denominations from forty-four nations gathered in Amsterdam to form the World Council of Churches. It is the largest agency of cooperation among liberal Christian churches. Originally claiming to be a "fellowship of churches which confess the Lord Jesus Christ as God the Saviour according to the Scriptures," the Council's focus became increasingly social and more radically political as the decades passed.

1949 ✝ EVANGELICAL THEOLOGICAL SOCIETY FORMS

Early in 1949, the faculty of Gordon Divinity School suggested a regular meeting of evangelical scholars to discuss theological issues. The result of this suggestion was the first meeting of the Evangelical Theological Society (ETS) on December 27–28, 1949, when sixty evangelical theologians met in Cincinnati, Ohio, to found the organization. The doctrinal basis for entrance into the society was simply an affirmation of the inerrancy of Scripture. Affirmation of the orthodox conception of the Trinity was later added as a prerequisite for membership. Both national and regional meetings are held annually in the United States.

1949 ✝ BILLY GRAHAM HOSTS HIS FIRST CRUSADE IN LOS ANGELES

In 1949, while serving as president of the Northwestern Schools in Minneapolis, Minnesota, William ("Billy") Franklin Graham Jr. (1918–) held evangelistic meetings in an enormous canvas tent in Los Angeles, California, where several celebrities were converted to Christ. William Randolph Hearst (1863–1951) took note of both the meeting and Graham and instructed his newspapers to "puff Graham." Almost immediately, Graham, an ordained Southern Baptist minister and Wheaton College graduate, became known throughout the United States. Within a few short years he was hosting evangelistic crusades at stadiums in the country's largest cities. In his lifetime, Graham has preached the

1939–45	1945	1989	1999
World War II	United Nations founded	Berlin Wall falls	Europe adopts Eurocurrency

gospel to more than 110 million people in eighty different countries, more than any person in history.

1949 ✝ AWAKENING OCCURS IN NEW HEBRIDES

After World War II, not a single church in the Hebrides Islands off the coast of Scotland had any youth in attendance. Then in 1949, an eighty-four-year-old blind woman named Peggy Smith had a vision of churches filled with young people. As a result, her pastor, James Murray MacKay, began regular prayer meetings for revival. After several months of prayer, the revival began one night when a young deacon prayed, "O God are my hands clean? Is my heart pure?" MacKay invited the Scottish revivalist Duncan Campbell (1898–1972) to preach at a series of meetings. After the second night's service, the congregation remained outside the church and others left their homes to join them. Soon six hundred people streamed back into the church, spending the night in repentance and prayer. The revival spread throughout the islands, so that on Sundays the roads were crowded with people walking to church.

1949 ✡ ISRAEL IS ADMITTED TO THE UNITED NATIONS

After declaring its independence in 1948, the nation of Israel was attacked by her Arab neighbors. Among her supporters, however, were the Soviet Union and the United States. In addition, the General Assembly of the United Nations had helped to establish the state of Israel by voting, on November 29, 1947, to divide Palestine between the Jews and Arabs. In 1949, while in the midst of waging a war of independence, Israel held national elections, was recognized as a sovereign state by the United Nations, and was admitted as a member of the General Assembly.

1950 ✝ BILLY GRAHAM ASSOCIATION IS FOUNDED

As he rose to fame after his 1949 Los Angeles Crusade, Billy Graham (1918–) began to be accused of using his ministry success to enrich himself. During his 1950 Portland, Oregon, crusade, Graham's closest advisors persuaded him that the establishment of a nonprofit organization would be necessary to prevent false accusations, as well as for the management of the financial affairs of his crusades.

1914–18	1915	1918–20	1929
World War I	Mohandas Gandhi leads Indian Nationalist movement	Influenza kills 20 million	U.S. stock market crashes

On September 17, 1950, the Billy Graham Evangelistic Association (BGEA) was incorporated in Minneapolis, Minnesota. Although Graham was the president, day-to-day operations were the responsibility of the secretary-treasurer, George Wilson (1914–1999). Wilson was initially the business manager at Northwestern Schools, where Graham then served as president. The headquarters of the BGEA today are in Charlotte, North Carolina, where it oversees the Billy Graham Training Center, Blue Ridge Broadcasting, and the Samaritan's Purse relief organization, in addition to other international ministries.

1950 ✛ CHRISTIAN BOOKSELLERS ASSOCIATION IS FOUNDED

Officially organized on November 17, 1950, the Christian Booksellers Association (CBA) is the trade association for the Christian bookstore industry. Its purpose is the "development and retail distribution of Christ-honoring product." At its annual international convention, more than three thousand vendors gather to present their products for the Christian market. In addition to books, the CBA convention showcases Christian music and gift items.

1950 ✛ WORLD VISION IS FOUNDED

Founded in 1950 by Robert Willard Pierce (1914–1976), World Vision International became the most well-known evangelical relief organization in the world. Pierce, an evangelist who originally served with Youth for Christ, had also been a filmmaker and a war correspondent. His experience with orphans while covering the Korean War inspired him to found the child sponsorship program for which World Vision is best known. In addition to assisting children, the organization provides disaster relief, coordinates community development projects, distributes Bibles, conducts mission research, and helps establish churches. World Vision operates nearly five thousand programs in more than one hundred countries.

1950 ✛ MISSIONARIES ARE FORCED TO LEAVE CHINA

Following World War II (1939–1945), as many as three thousand missionaries returned to China. However, their missions were cut short in 1949, when Chinese communist leader Chairman Mao Zedong (1893–1976) established the

1939–45	1945	1989	1999
World War II	United Nations founded	Berlin Wall falls	Europe adopts Eurocurrency

A LIFE-CHANGING PRAYER

January 18, 1951

You never know how God will answer.

Amy Carmichael was born in 1867, in Millisle, County Down, Northern Ireland, a town dominated by the Carmichael flour mills. At the age of twelve, she was sent to a Wesleyan Methodist boarding school in Yorkshire, England. At a service for children when she was fifteen, Carmichael heard the song lyrics "Jesus loves me this I know, for the Bible tells me so." In the quiet moments following the song, Carmichael realized that, in spite of her mother's teaching that Jesus loved her, she had never opened the door of her heart to invite him in. "In His great mercy the Good Shepherd answered the prayers of my mother and my father and many other loving ones, and drew me, even me, into His fold."

After the death of her father she went to England to live in the home of Robert Wilson, a cofounder and chairman of the Keswick Convention, a summer gathering of English evangelicals. Under Wilson's influence, Carmichael became interested in missions and sailed for Japan in 1893, as the first Keswick missionary with the Church Missionary Society. After spending less than two years in Japan and Ceylon, poor health forced her to return to England.

In November 1895, she again left England to work with the Church of England Zenana Missionary Society in southern India. Traveling on evangelistic trips throughout India she became aware that many young Indian girls were offered by parents or guardians as temple prostitutes, a practice that was later outlawed. Touched by their plight, Carmichael began rescuing young girls from this fate.

By 1901, she, along with the Indian colleagues and converts from her many trips, settled in Dohnavur. In 1926, she founded the Dohnavur Fellowship, a home and school for rescued children. Here the Indian children were educated and trained to serve God as Christian nurses, teachers, and evangelists. These children and workers became her family. Amy Carmichael was known at Dohnavur Fellowship as "Amma" or Mother. So committed was Amy Carmichael to India that from the time she arrived there in 1895, she never returned to England.

In 1931, Carmichael visited a Dohnavur dispensary and was concerned about the Fellowship's financial support. Seeking God's guidance regarding money, she prayed, "Do anything, Lord, that will fit me to serve thee and to help my beloveds."

Later that day she visited a house she had rented for another dispensary. There in the darkness she fell into a newly dug pit, breaking her leg and twisting her spine. As a result of her fall, she was bedridden for the last twenty years of her life. Yet, from her bed she remained in charge of Dohnavur and developed a ministry of writing prose and poetry, through which the work of Dohnavur became known around the world.

In 1938, Carmichael believed that God gave her a promise that she would die in her sleep. This she did on January 18, 1951.

People's Republic of China. As a result, missionaries were forced to leave the country in 1950. At the time, there were approximately one million Chinese believers. Yet by the year 2000, the number of Christians in China had grown to approximately 75 million. God chose to have the missionaries removed before the great harvest, that he alone might receive the glory.

1950 ✝ THE ASSUMPTION OF MARY DRIVES WEDGE BETWEEN CATHOLICS AND PROTESTANTS

For years, the Roman Catholic Church had held a tradition that when the Virgin Mary died, she was bodily raised and glorified as a prefiguration of the resurrection awaiting all Christians. On November 1, 1950, Pope Pius XII (1876–1958) declared the Assumption of Mary to be an article of faith in the Roman Catholic Church, thus driving another wedge between Roman Catholicism and Protestantism.

1950 ✡ FIRST WOMAN SUCCEEDS HER HUSBAND AS RABBI

With the exception of a nineteen-year period from 1899 to 1919, when a woman acted as the spiritual leader of a Reform Jewish synagogue in England, no woman had ever served as a rabbi until 1950. That year Mrs. Paul Ackerman, the widow of Rabbi William Ackerman of Temple Beth Israel in Meridian, Mississippi, succeeded her husband as rabbi. Although she hadn't had rabbinical training, a ruling from Reform Judaism granted her full powers of rabbi, and the state of Mississippi gave her authority to perform marriages. In 1972, the Central Conference of Reform Rabbis formally voted to accept women into the rabbinate.

1953 ✝ BILL BRIGHT FOUNDS CAMPUS CRUSADE FOR CHRIST

In 1951, William R. Bright (1921–2003), a successful California entrepreneur, had a vision of fulfilling the Great Commission by evangelizing college campuses. Campus Crusade for Christ was officially incorporated on August 28, 1953. Bright's goal was to reach college and university campuses throughout America by spreading the gospel and equipping new believers to share Christ with others. Campus Crusade's outreach includes more than forty ministries.

1939–45	1945	1989	1999
World War II	United Nations founded	Berlin Wall falls	Europe adopts Eurocurrency

Today, Campus Crusade for Christ International is located in Orlando, Florida. In 2004, the nondenominational group had more than thirteen thousand staff members and one hundred thousand volunteers working in 167 countries.

1954 ✛ FELLOWSHIP OF CHRISTIAN ATHLETES IS FOUNDED

The Fellowship of Christian Athletes (FCA) was founded on November 12, 1954, by Don McClanen (1925–), a basketball coach in Norman, Oklahoma. The organization's mission is to "see the world impacted for Jesus Christ through the influence of athletes and coaches." With its headquarters in Kansas City, Missouri, FCA ministers to hundreds of thousands of men, women, boys, and girls through summer camps as well as school chapters known as FCA huddles. With the support of many famous athletes, FCA encourages student athletes to have personal relationships with Jesus.

1955 ✛ KENNETH TAYLOR BEGINS WORK ON LIVING LETTERS

In 1955, Kenneth Taylor (1917–) began paraphrasing the King James Version of the Bible into modern English while commuting to his downtown Chicago job. He wanted to provide his ten children with a more readable version of the Bible than the language of the King James Version. However, when Taylor was unable to find a publisher willing to market his paraphrase, he and his wife, Margaret, formed Tyndale House Publishers to publish *Living Letters,* a paraphrase of the New Testament Epistles. The Billy Graham Evangelistic Association soon offered *Living Letters* as a premium, and it became a best seller. Taylor eventually completed a paraphrased version of the entire Bible, which was published in 1971 as *The Living Bible* and subsequently sold more than 40 million copies.

1955 ✛ L'ABRI FELLOWSHIP IS FOUNDED

Francis Schaeffer (1912–1984), a graduate of Faith Theological Seminary, was ordained by the Bible Presbyterian Church. He served as a pastor in Pennsylvania and Missouri before moving to Switzerland as a missionary of the Independent Board of Presbyterian Foreign Missions. While in the Swiss Alps in 1955, Schaeffer and his wife, Edith, founded L'Abri Fellowship to combat the

PLANTING GOSPEL SEED

July 20, 1953

One plants, another waters, but God gives the increase.

In early 1832, James Taylor, a pharmacist in Yorkshire, England, knelt in the back of his shop beside his pregnant wife, Amelia, and prayed, "Dear God, if you should give us a son, grant that he may work for you in China."

God gave them a son a few months later, and they named him James Hudson Taylor. By the time Hudson was seventeen, he was a typical rebellious teenager and had no interest in being a missionary. But that summer when his mother was visiting her sister, she felt led to lock herself in a room to pray for Hudson's salvation and not come out until she had the assurance that her prayer had been answered. Back home that afternoon, Hudson picked up a gospel tract on Christ's death on the cross for sinners and accepted the Savior.

Within months after Hudson experienced his new birth, his call to China was confirmed during a night of prayer, which he described as being filled "with unspeakable awe and unspeakable joy."

With a sense of urgency, Hudson finished school and sailed for China at the age of twenty-one. At that time there were 350 baptized Chinese believers. During his first term he married and made several evangelistic trips into the closed interior of China but was forced to return to England because of illness.

In England he regained his health and felt an increasing burden for the millions in China's interior. When the interior of China was opened to Westerners and Hudson could find no mission willing to back him, he founded the China Inland Mission (CIM) in 1865.

Initially Hudson prayed for twenty-four workers, two for each unreached province. The first fifteen sailed in May 1866 and by 1882, the China Inland Mission had workers in every province. By 1895, it had 641 missionaries, and by 1914, the China Inland Mission was the largest missionary organization in the world, reaching its peak in 1934 with 1,368 missionaries ministering to five hundred thousand baptized believers. But then civil war broke out between the Chinese Nationalists and the Communists. The two enemies joined forces to fight Japan; but after the war they went back to fighting each other. By September 1949, the Chinese Communists had won, and the Nationalists retreated to the island of Taiwan. The last CIM workers left China on July 20, 1953, leaving behind about one million believers.

The first two decades under Communism were ones of intense persecution. Yet by 1980, there were two million believers.

Since the early 1980s, the growth of the church in China has no parallels in history. In 2000 there were approximately seventy-five million Christians in China.

The sacrificial seed sown by the missionaries of CIM and other missions bore fruit a thousandfold, yet God chose to have the missionaries removed before the harvest that he alone might receive the glory.

FULFILLING THE VISION

August 28, 1953

His mother's prayers had far-reaching effects!

In Coweta, Oklahoma, in 1921, a mother prayed over her yet-unborn son, dedicating him to the Lord's service. When the baby was born, his parents named him William Bright. As a child he showed little interest in spiritual things, but his mother continued to pray.

Bill Bright graduated from college in 1943 and went west to Los Angeles to seek his fortune in business. There he quickly achieved his dream of financial success.

After receiving repeated invitations, Bright began attending meetings for college students and young professionals led by Dr. Henrietta Mears at Hollywood Presbyterian Church. There, after a particularly challenging teaching on finding happiness at the "center of God's will," Bill went home yearning for this inner happiness. He later recalled,

> As I returned to my apartment that night I realized that I was ready to give my life to God. . . . I knelt down beside my bed that night and asked the questions which Dr. Mears had challenged us to pray, "Who art Thou, Lord? What wilt Thou have me to do?"
>
> In a sense this was my prayer for salvation. It wasn't very profound theologically, but God knew my heart and He interpreted what was going on inside of me. Through my study I now believed Jesus Christ was the Son of God, that He died for my sin, and that, as Dr. Mears had shared with us, if I invited Him into my life as Savior and Lord, He would come in.

Bright enrolled at Fuller Theological Seminary in Pasadena. In 1948, he married his wife, Vonette, whom Henrietta Mears had also led to Christ.

Late one night in 1951, while studying for an exam, he had a powerful vision of helping to fulfill the Great Commission by evangelizing college campuses. He shared it the next morning with Dr. Wilbur Smith, his professor and mentor. Smith responded with, "This is of God! This is of God!" The next day Smith told him, "I believe God has given me the name for your vision—Campus Crusade for Christ."

After much prayer, Bill and Vonette decided that he should leave seminary to pursue his vision. Bright sold his business and rented a house one block from the UCLA campus. He formed Campus Crusade for Christ, and within a few months 250 students had given their lives to Jesus.

Campus Crusade quickly spread to other campuses throughout the country, and Bright officially incorporated it on August 28, 1953.

Bill Bright's vision and ministry shaped Campus Crusade into one of the largest interdenominational mission agencies in the world, with approximately twenty-two thousand full-time workers in 156 countries by 2001. Its most substantial mark on world missions is the *Jesus* film, which has been viewed by more than 4 billion people in more than 650 languages, with 121 million reported conversions since 1979!

development of moral and intellectual relativism in the twentieth century. *L'Abri*, French for "shelter," consisted of a number of chalets. It became a place for people to come to study both Scripture and the arts, and to receive guidance from the Schaeffers. An English branch of L'Abri was established in 1958.

1956 ✝ AMERICAN MISSIONARIES ARE MARTYRED IN ECUADOR

American missionaries Nate Saint (1923–1956), Jim Elliot (1927–1956), Peter Fleming (1928–1956), Ed McCully (1927–1956), and Roger Youderian (1924–1956) had spent three months preparing for a face-to-face meeting with the primitive Auca Indians of Ecuador. It was to be the first step in establishing relationships that the men and their families hoped would eventually lead the Aucas to Christ. Instead, on January 6, 1956, after the men reported landing and meeting with a few Aucas, they were ambushed and killed. Nevertheless, within two years, Elisabeth Elliot (1926–), Jim Elliot's widow, and Rachel Saint (1914–1994), Nate Saint's sister, were living among the Aucas. Over time, many of the Aucas repented, turned to Christ, and became ministers to their own people. The martyrs' story became a touchstone for the modern Protestant missionary movement.

1956 ✝ FIRST ISSUE OF <u>CHRISTIANITY TODAY</u> IS PUBLISHED

The Christian periodical *Christianity Today* was founded as a result of Billy Graham's (1918–) desire for a magazine to provide ministers and laypeople with theological depth. The first issue was dated October 1956. To counterbalance mainline Protestantism's widely circulated *Christian Century*, the new magazine sought to encourage a biblically conservative worldview. Now exceeding the circulation of *Christian Century*, *Christianity Today* is quoted in the secular press more than any other religious periodical. Headquartered in Carol Stream, Illinois, the magazine continues to maintain a conservative theological and political stand.

1956 ✡ ☪ ISRAEL EVACUATES THE SINAI

Unwilling to accept the formation of Israel, Jordan and Egypt developed guerrilla operations known as *fedayeen*, from the Arabic word for "one who sacrifices himself for his country." In addition to *fedayeen* attacks in Israel, Arab states boycotted Israel and all who did business with her. In the 1950s, Egypt, backed by the Soviet Union, increased raids and conquered the Suez Canal. On October 29, 1956, Israel responded by seizing the Sinai Peninsula, annihilating many of the Egyptian forces in less than a week. The action, though planned with France and England, was not tolerated internationally. In exchange for a secure Israeli-Egyptian border and removal of the Egyptian blockade, Israel evacuated the Sinai.

1958 ✝ PAUL YONGGI CHO'S CHURCH BEGINS

After graduating from the Full Gospel Bible Institute in Korea, Paul Yonggi Cho (1936–) founded the Yoido Full Gospel Church in Seoul, Korea. The first service was held on May 15, 1958, with six people in attendance. In its beginning stages, the church met in a simple shelter of army tents that were pieced together. In 1960, Cho was ordained by the Korean Assemblies of God, and the Yoido church joined the Assemblies of God denomination in 1962. A vigorous strategy of multiplying home cell groups led to the explosive growth of the membership. By 2003, the church claimed a membership of 780,000. Because of the church's prominence, Cho became a world leader in the Pentecostal movement.

1958 ✝ BILL BRIGHT FINALIZES THE FOUR SPIRITUAL LAWS

Bill Bright (1921–2003), founder of Campus Crusade for Christ, worked for years on the evangelistic tool he called "God's Plan," later renamed the "Four Spiritual Laws." In 1958, he completed the project by adding the first law, deciding to emphasize God's love first, instead of starting with man's sinfulness as he had in prior versions. The Four Spiritual Laws are 1) God loves you and offers a wonderful plan for your life; 2) Man is sinful and separated from God; thus he cannot know and experience God's love and plan for his life; 3) Jesus Christ is God's only provision for man's sin. Through him you can know and experience God's love and plan for your life; and 4) We must individually receive Jesus Christ as Savior and Lord; then we can know and experience God's love and plan for our lives.

1914–18	1915	1918–20	1929
World War I	Mohandas Gandhi leads Indian Nationalist movement	Influenza kills 20 million	U.S. stock market crashes

THE GATES OF PEARLY SPLENDOR

January 9, 1956

On New Year's Day 1956, five missionaries packed for their attempt to contact the fierce Auca Indians of Ecuador. Nate Saint, the pilot, was going to fly them to Palm Beach, where they had previously exchanged gifts with the Aucas from the air. Jim Elliot, Pete Fleming, Ed McCully, and Roger Youderian collected what they would need for their mission. As Elisabeth Elliot helped her husband, she wondered, *Will this be the last time I'll help him pack?*

On January 3, their departure date, after breakfast and prayer the five men sang one of their favorite hymns:

We rest on thee, our Shield and our Defender,
Thine is the battle, thine will be the praise.
When passing through the gates of pearly splendor
Victors, we rest with thee through endless days.

Once on the beach they waited for contact with the Aucas. On Friday, January 6, the missionaries were encouraged by a visit from three Aucas.

No Aucas appeared on Saturday, but on Sunday morning Nate spotted some tribesmen walking toward their beach. At twelve thirty Nate made his prearranged radio call to his wife, Marj: "This is the day! Will contact you at 4:30."

When 4:30 came, the missionary wives switched on their radios. Silence. Sundown came, and still no word. The wives slept little that night.

On Monday morning, January 9, 1956, Johnny Keenan, another missionary pilot, flew to the beach. As Elisabeth Elliot awaited his report, a verse ran through her mind: "When thou passest through the waters, I will be with thee; and through the rivers, they shall not overflow thee" (Isaiah 43:2, KJV).

At 9:30 a.m., the pilot's report came in. Marj Saint shared it with the other wives. "Johnny has found the plane on the beach. All the fabric is stripped off. There is no sign of the fellows."

Radio station HCJB in Ecuador flashed the news to the rest of the world: "Five men missing in Auca territory." By noon a ground party was organized to go to the site. The search party located four of the five bodies, but Ed McCully's had been swept away by the river. The other four were buried on Palm Beach.

What happened to the Aucas? By the end of 1958, Elisabeth Elliot and Rachel Saint, Nate's sister, were living among them, and one by one the Aucas put their faith in Jesus Christ.

The five men who murdered the missionaries each, not only became Christians, but also spiritual leaders. After they believed, they shared how, after murdering the missionaries, they heard singing from above the trees. Looking up they saw what appeared to be a canopy of bright lights. God was welcoming his children home.

1959 ✛ MCGAVRAN ESTABLISHES THE INSTITUTE OF CHURCH GROWTH

In 1959, the Institute of Church Growth was established in Eugene, Oregon, by former missionary to India, Donald A. McGavran (1897–1991). The institute examined the forces behind the success of large churches and determined that the most successful congregations contained "a section of society in which all members have some characteristics in common." McGavran's practical philosophy of church growth, which was adopted by a number of evangelical pastors, targeted specific communities of individuals. From 1964 to 1980, McGavran published his ideas in the *Church Growth Bulletin*; and his theories, especially about allowing Christians to maintain cultural barriers, were particularly influential in white, middle-class suburbs. In 1965, the Institute of Church Growth joined Fuller Theological Seminary, as part of the School of World Mission.

1960 ✛ THE CHARISMATIC MOVEMENT BEGINS

In November 1959, while meeting with a group of ten Episcopalians from a neighboring church, pastor Dennis Bennett (1917–1991) of St. Mark's Episcopal Church in Van Nuys, California, reported experiencing the "baptism of the Holy Spirit." Others at the meeting also claimed to have had the experience. On April 3, 1960, Bennett shared his experience with his parishioners at each of the church's three services. After the second service, an associate pastor resigned in protest, and at the third service Bennett himself resigned. Jean Stone (1924–), a member of the church, contacted *Newsweek* and *Time* magazines, both of which picked up the story. As the story went public, the charismatic movement was born and soon spread throughout the world.

1960 ✛ YOUTH WITH A MISSION IS FOUNDED

In December 1960, Loren Cunningham (1935–) founded Youth with a Mission (YWAM). Cunningham's vision focused on engaging energetic young people in mission activities. Although his intention was to align YWAM with the Assemblies of God, the denomination in which he was raised, the denomination declined. After a successful eight-week mission trip to the Bahamas in 1964, Cunningham decided to make YWAM an interdenominational organization. In addition to operating the Pacific and Asia Christian University in Kailua-Kona, Hawaii, YWAM sends more than fifty thousand young missionaries on

1914–18	1915	1918–20	1929
World War I	Mohandas Gandhi leads Indian Nationalist movement	Influenza kills 20 million	U.S. stock market crashes

short-term mission trips to countries around the world each summer. YWAM's mission efforts usually include distributing Bibles, performing drama or music, and holding evangelistic assemblies.

1960 ✡ EICHMANN IS BROUGHT TO ISRAEL

In 1960, Adolf Eichmann (1906–1962), the Nazi official primarily responsible for coordinating the near extermination of Jews during World War II, was captured by Israel's security service in Argentina. The trial of Adolf Eichmann took place in Jerusalem and revealed that in 1941, Eichmann was authorized to implement a systematic annihilation of the entire Jewish population in Europe, as the "final solution of the Jewish problem." The Polish work camp at Auschwitz became a major death camp under Eichmann's direction, and by 1942, gas chambers disguised as showers, able to kill seven to eight hundred Jews at one time, were in place. In 1962, Eichmann was hanged for committing crimes against humanity, the only crime in Israeli law that carries the death penalty.

1960 ✛ SEVENTEEN AFRICAN NATIONS ACHIEVE INDEPENDENCE

For centuries, the continent of Africa was dominated by colonial powers. However, 1960 was the great year of independence for African nations, when seventeen were set free from colonial domination. The seventeen were Benin, Cameroon, Central African Republic, Chad, Gabon, Ivory Coast, Madagascar, Mali, Mauritania, Niger, Nigeria, Republic of Congo, Senegal, Somalia, Togo, Upper Volta, and Zaire. By 1994, every nation in Africa had achieved independence. Independence brought increased religious freedom to much of Africa, but the persecution of Christians by Muslims also escalated in Sudan and northern Nigeria. At the same time, many African nations have been led by corrupt rulers, who have enriched themselves and their own ethnic groups. Ethnic cleansing has brought death and refugee status to millions in Rwanda, Burundi, Congo, Liberia, Sierra Leone, Sudan, and Uganda.

1962 ✛ THEOLOGICAL EDUCATION BY EXTENSION BEGINS

By the mid-twentieth century, the church was rapidly expanding in Latin America. The rate at which pastors were needed exceeded the rate at which the few seminaries could train them. In addition, many pastors were men who had full-time jobs to support their families, limiting their options to leave to attend a seminary. In 1962, with almost sixty thousand pastors lacking adequate training in Scripture and theology, the Evangelical Presbyterian Seminary of Guatemala started Theological Education by Extension (TEE), to help pastors obtain knowledge of Scripture and training in ministry. The programmed textbook, which allowed for personalized study, became the foundation for the new style of seminary education. Counseling, supervision, and testing took place during regular student meetings with a seminary professor at a central location. From Guatemala, the TEE movement moved throughout Latin America, as well as to Africa and Asia.

1962 ✝ VATICAN COUNCIL II BEGINS

In 1958, Archbishop Angelo Roncalli became Pope John XXIII (1881–1963) and brought to the office his goal of *aggiornamento*, "bringing the Church up to date." On October 11, 1962, at St. Peter's Basilica in Rome, the pope opened the Second Vatican Council, which consisted of two thousand clergy from around the world. Unlike previous popes, John allowed the council free discussion, and the resulting decrees of Vatican II were far reaching. The council redefined the church, changed its relationship with Protestants, accepted religious liberty, encouraged Bible study, and permitted worship in local languages, rather than in Latin. The response was mixed. By 1976, thousands of priests and nuns had joined the laity, church attendance was down by one-third, and confessions by over half; but, at the same time, many Catholic laypersons had begun reading their Bibles.

1965 ✝ THE JESUS REVOLUTION IS BIRTHED

In 1965, Chuck Smith (1927–), a Pentecostal pastor in Southern California, had a burden to reach counterculture young people for Christ. Smith and his wife began by leading a few hippie youths to Christ and starting a commune dedicated to Bible study and evangelism. His church grew rapidly, with more than two hundred coming to Christ each week. More than nine hundred were baptized in the Pacific Ocean each month, in front of thousands of spectators. Full-page photographs of the "Jesus People" revival appeared in many secular magazines. Eventually Smith's California congregation, called Calvary Chapel, grew to become one of the twenty largest churches in the world. The revolution moved

1914–18	1915	1918–20	1929
World War I	Mohandas Gandhi leads Indian Nationalist movement	Influenza kills 20 million	U.S. stock market crashes

A DATE WE REMEMBER

November 22, 1963

Who died on November 22, 1963? Many will correctly answer, "President John F. Kennedy."

But another person, who was mightier than President Kennedy in God's kingdom, died that day. His name was C. S. Lewis.

"C. S." stood for Clive Staples, but to his friends he was "Jack." Born near Belfast, Ireland in 1898, Lewis was raised as an Anglican. But when he was ten, his mother died of cancer, and Lewis wanted nothing to do with a God so cruel as to take his mother. Before long he had become an atheist.

After graduating from Oxford, he spent the first thirty years of his academic career as a fellow of Magdalen College. From there he became chair of Medieval and Renaissance English at Cambridge University.

Lewis's spiritual pilgrimage began in 1926, with a conversation with another fellow of Magdalen College. Lewis was surprised to learn that his cynical friend believed in the Trinity. This revelation challenged Lewis's atheistic presuppositions.

His next step was a memorable spring day in 1929. While riding on a bus, Lewis pondered the various philosophers he had read. Taking Hegel's idea of the absolute and combining it with Berkeley's concept of Spirit, he conceived of a being he could call "God." He didn't know anything about this God, but when he got off the bus, he knew he believed something he hadn't before—that an absolute Spirit or God existed.

Some months later he began to formulate a mental vision of Absolute Spirit, conceiving of it as someone who said, "I am the Lord." Lewis finally admitted that God was God, and for the first time in years he prayed.

But the real turning point came two years later, in 1931. On this particular afternoon, Lewis and his brother rode a motorcycle forty miles to visit the Whipsnade Zoo. Following them by car were three friends and their dog. Lewis stayed behind with the dog, which wasn't allowed in the zoo.

As Lewis relaxed in the park, he came to the realization that sometime during the previous few hours he had come to an important conclusion. He knew that when he had left for Whipsnade he did not believe Jesus Christ was the Son of God, but somehow when he arrived, he believed! Without consciously thinking about it, he had passed from merely believing in God to trusting in Christ as his Savior.

In 1941, Lewis burst onto the literary scene as author of *The Screwtape Letters*. Books then began to flow from his pen at an amazing rate, one or more a year. Titles such as *Mere Christianity*, *Surprised by Joy*, *A Grief Observed*, and The Chronicles of Narnia have been used by God to change lives of people of all ages around the world.

C. S. Lewis is considered the most influential Christian author of the twentieth century—quite a leap from the atheism of his youth.

WHATEVER HAPPENED TO THAT
DANCING INSTRUCTOR?

February 20, 1967

Listening to the radio changed his life.

D. James Kennedy grew up in the 1930s in Chicago and attended the University of Tampa on a music scholarship. Jim became an Arthur Murray dance instructor, and before long was a nationally competitive dancer.

When nineteen-year-old Anne Lewis entered the Tampa Arthur Murray studio for a lesson one evening, Jim told a friend, "That's the girl I'm going to marry." Three and a half years later, his prediction came true!

During their courtship, Anne, who was a Christian, challenged Jim about what he believed. He believed in God and assumed he was a Christian, but Anne's questions threw him.

One Sunday in 1955, Jim woke up with a hangover. The radio was on and tuned to a message by Dr. Donald Grey Barnhouse from Tenth Presbyterian Church in Philadelphia. Dr. Barnhouse asked, "Suppose that you were to die today and stand before God and He were to ask you, 'What right do you have to enter into My Heaven?'—what would you say?" Jim listened to Barnhouse's explanation of salvation and redemption. Realizing he had no right to enter heaven at that point, he gave his life to Christ.

He made an overnight, 180 degree turn away from his former lifestyle. Shortly thereafter, he drove to see Anne with an engagement ring in his pocket. He said, "I have quit my job at the studio, which means I'm almost flat broke. I am going into the ministry, and I know you always said you wouldn't want to be a preacher's wife. Will you marry me?" Anne was taken aback but said yes.

After graduating from seminary, he went to Fort Lauderdale in 1959 to start a church. After ten months, attendance at Coral Ridge Presbyterian Church was down to seventeen! Jim and Anne were discouraged but didn't give up. Jim went to Atlanta to conduct an evangelism conference with a seminary friend, and there he discovered what he felt were the tools for successful one-on-one evangelism. He went home to teach these tools to his little flock. In one month, his church grew from 17 to 66, and then to 122 the next year. By 1974, Coral Ridge had over three thousand members.

Pastors from all over wanted to know how he did it. In answer, Jim held his first Evangelism Explosion (EE) clinic on February 20, 1967, to train pastors in his unique method of lay evangelism. Thirty-six pastors attended his first clinic. Since 1967, EE clinics have trained thousands of pastors, and in 1996, EE International reached its goal of planting EE teams in all 211 of the world's nations.

D. James Kennedy, the former dancer from Tampa, continues to evangelize the world through Evangelism Explosion and his radio and television ministries from Coral Ridge Presbyterian Church in Fort Lauderdale.

throughout the country, recruiting new Jesus People from among the countercultural ranks. There are currently more than six hundred Calvary Chapels, each pastored by a convert of the movement.

1965 ✝ EAST TIMOR, INDONESIA, EXPERIENCES REVIVAL

During the 1960s, the majority of professing Christians in the Timor Evangelical Church in Indonesia were also involved in magic, sorcery, promiscuity, and drunkenness. In response to this challenge, the church at Soe, East Timor, Indonesia, began conducting evangelistic meetings early in 1965. A revival began and quickly spread from Soe to Kupang, on to Niki-Niki, and then beyond Timor. From 1965 to 1972, one hundred thousand people in East Timor were converted to Christ from animism, in addition to large numbers of nominal Christians who experienced a new awakening.

1966 ✝ CHINESE CHURCH EXPERIENCES GROWTH THROUGH PERSECUTION

In 1966, perhaps fearing he was losing his grip on China, Communist Chairman Mao Zedong (1893–1976) began a brutal campaign known as the Cultural Revolution. By creating distrust of all foreign influences, a hatred for the Christian faith developed. Due to the Cultural Revolution's terrible persecution of Christians, the Chinese church of about one million was forced underground. When the oppression diminished and Christian churches were allowed to reopen after more than a decade, they resurfaced stronger than ever. Meeting as small groups in private homes had strengthened the Christians in China, similar to the way persecution had strengthened Christians in the early fourth century. As horrible as the Cultural Revolution was, it removed the trappings of Western culture from Christianity in China, allowing the Chinese to embrace true faith. The church grew so explosively that there were approximately 75 million Christians in China by 2000.

1967 ✝ FIRST EVANGELISM EXPLOSION SEMINAR IS HELD

In 1959, D. James Kennedy (1930–) started Coral Ridge Presbyterian Church in Fort Lauderdale, Florida. Forty-five people attended the first service, but in less

1939–45	1945	1989	1999
World War II	United Nations founded	Berlin Wall falls	Europe adopts Eurocurrency

than a year the congregation dwindled to only seventeen. While conducting a conference on evangelism with a seminary friend, Kennedy realized he needed to provide his congregation with the tools for one-on-one evangelism. Within one month of receiving Kennedy's evangelism instruction, Coral Ridge had sixty-six members, and a year later there were one hundred and twenty-two. Because other pastors inquired about Kennedy's technique of lay evangelism, he held the first Evangelism Explosion (EE) clinic on February 20, 1967. By 1974, Coral Ridge had more than three thousand members, and by 1996, EE International had teams in all 211 of the world's countries.

1967 ✡ ☾ SIX DAY WAR

In 1967, Egypt and Syria, falsely claiming that Israel was preparing war, sent troops to the Sinai Peninsula and forced the United Nations Emergency Forces based there to leave. On June 5, 1967, Israel responded with a preemptive strike, demolishing the Egyptian air force in just three hours. Israeli forces captured the Gaza Strip and the Sinai, then conquered the Old City of Jerusalem, the West Bank, and the Golan Heights. The conquest took six days. Israelis celebrated their rescue of the holy sites in Jerusalem, planning to exchange the captured Arab territories for recognition of the state of Israel and a peace treaty with their Arab neighbors. The Arab nations, however, continued to reject Israel's existence, and as a result the captured territories were not relinquished.

1968 ✝ MARTIN LUTHER KING, JR. IS ASSASSINATED

On April 4, 1968, Dr. Martin Luther King Jr. (1929–1968), a leading voice for civil rights, was assassinated in Memphis, Tennessee. King had served as president of the Southern Christian Leadership Conference and as pastor for two Baptist churches, in Montgomery, Alabama, and Atlanta, Georgia. As a leader of the civil rights movement, his message was one of nonviolence. Known for his "I Have a Dream" speech, King also led the "Walk for Freedom" in Montgomery, which ended the segregation of public buses in the city. While many, including some white Christians, resisted his demand for equal rights, King was *Time* magazine's Man of the Year in 1963, and won the Nobel Peace Prize in 1964.

1914–18	1915	1918–20	1929
World War I	Mohandas Gandhi leads Indian Nationalist movement	Influenza kills 20 million	U.S. stock market crashes

THE OLD CITY UNDER JEWISH CONTROL

| June 7, 1967 |

On June 7, 1967, the army of Israel captured the Old City of Jerusalem. The previous month the Egyptians had decided to attempt once more to conquer Israel. They poured one hundred thousand troops into the Sinai Peninsula, ordered the UN peacekeepers out, and made a military alliance with neighboring Jordan. Israel felt its only hope was to launch a preemptive strike, which it did on June 5. Jordan and Syria immediately entered the war. Two days later, the Israelis captured the Old City, which had been part of Jordan. As a result of this military victory in what is known as the Six Day War, Israel once again possessed her ancient capital. It had been 1,897 years since Jews last had controlled Jerusalem in AD 70.

During Jesus' ministry he had predicted that Jerusalem and its Temple would be destroyed.

> He said, "The time is coming when all these things will be so completely demolished that not one stone will be left on top of another." (Luke 21:6)
> When his disciples asked him, "When will all this take place? And will there be any sign ahead of time?" Jesus answered, "When you see Jerusalem surrounded by armies, then you will know that the time of its destruction has arrived. . . . There will be great distress in the land and wrath upon this people. They will be brutally killed by the sword or sent away as captives to all the nations of the world." (Luke 21:7, 20, 23-24)

From the beginning of Jesus' ministry he warned the Jews of God's coming wrath unless they repented (Matthew 3:7). In response to the Jews crucifying their Messiah, God sent the Roman armies to conquer Galilee and Samaria and then to surround and destroy Jerusalem (cf. Matthew 21:37–22:7). It happened in AD 66, when the last Roman prefect stole from the Temple treasury, triggering a Jewish rebellion. To quell the rebellion the Romans sent four legions, which arrived the following year. After a siege, Jerusalem fell in AD 70. The Roman general Titus completely destroyed the city and Temple.

Jesus had also prophesied that following its defeat "Jerusalem will be . . . trampled down by the Gentiles until the age of the Gentiles comes to an end" (Luke 21:20, 24). Does this mean that "the age of the Gentiles," or as other translations put it, "the times of the Gentiles," ended on June 7, 1967, when the Jews gained control of Jerusalem?

Revelation 11:2 seems to answer no. It states that the Gentiles "will trample the holy city for forty-two months," apparently the three and a half years prior to the second coming of Christ, implying that the Jews will not be in control of Jerusalem at that time. If this explanation is correct, the times of the Gentiles did not end on June 7, 1967. They will end at the Second Coming.

1968 ✝ THE FOURTH ASSEMBLY OF THE WORLD COUNCIL OF CHURCHES SPURS LIBERATION THEOLOGY

The World Council of Churches was founded in Amsterdam in 1948. Throughout the twentieth century it became increasingly involved in political activities, especially within developing nations. In 1968, the World Council's fourth assembly, in Uppsala, Sweden, defined *mission* in a horizontal way, as "humanization." By its action and decisions, the World Council made the purpose of the church more about saving the oppressed from the oppressor, and less a matter of bringing saving faith to the world. This emphasis on salvation as liberation grew in popularity, while evangelicals argued that liberation theology meant supporting man-centered goals, as opposed to proclaiming a uniquely Christian message.

1969 ✝ REVIVAL SWEEPS THROUGH INDEPENDENT BAPTIST CHURCHES

In 1969, revival occurred throughout the Independent Baptist Churches of America, regardless of location. The revival was fueled by weekly evangelistic services, as well as by large Sunday school and Saturday morning programs that relied on extensive busing ministries. Independent Baptists became role models for other American churches on how to grow by reaching the lost. Of the one hundred largest churches in America, more than sixty are Independent Baptist, including six of the ten largest churches.

1970 ✝ ASBURY COLLEGE EXPERIENCES REVIVAL

In 1970, Asbury College in Wilmore, Kentucky, experienced its greatest revival. Similar revivals had taken place in 1905 and in the 1940s, laying the groundwork for what happened in 1970. Although many on campus had been praying for revival all fall, it unexpectedly arrived during a routine chapel meeting one morning in February. The college dean, Custer Reynolds, decided not to speak on the scheduled topic, but instead offered a testimony and encouraged the students to share what God was doing in their lives. The routine fifty-five-minute chapel service ended up lasting 185 hours, having a profound impact on the students, faculty, and the larger community. Students experienced the presence of God as they recommitted their lives to him. As Christian magazines and major American newspapers carried the stories of what was happening at Asbury, similar revival spread to an estimated 130 other colleges.

1914–18	1915	1918–20	1929
World War I	Mohandas Gandhi leads Indian Nationalist movement	Influenza kills 20 million	U.S. stock market crashes

1971 ✛ SASKATOON EXPERIENCES REVIVAL

Saskatoon, Saskatchewan, located in the heart of Canada's "Bible Belt," had more churches per capita than any other Canadian city. However, the area's pastors believed the community was in need of revival. Several pastors from different denominations met weekly for more than a year to pray for revival. On October 13, 1971, the Saskatoon revival began at Ebenezer Baptist Church, where twin evangelists Ralph and Lou Sutera (1932–)were holding meetings. Their emphasis on forgiveness and reconciliation spoke powerfully to the members of the church, and the revival quickly spread to other local churches. Daily meetings with thousands in attendance lasted for eight weeks, profoundly affecting not only local Christians, but the entire community. The Canadian Revival Fellowship was formed as a result of the Saskatoon Revival, and it helped bring revival to many other communities across Canada, the U.S., and Europe.

1972 ✡ ☾ ISRAELI ATHLETES ARE KILLED AT THE MUNICH OLYMPICS

At 4:30 a.m. on September 5, 1972, eight Arab terrorists stormed into the Olympic village and raided the apartment building that housed the Israeli athletes. Two Israeli athletes were killed in the assault and nine more were taken hostage. The terrorists demanded the release of two hundred Arab prisoners held in Israeli prisons. After day-long negotiations proved unsuccessful, the terrorists headed for the military airport in Munich to fly back to the Middle East. German sharpshooters killed three of the Palestinians as they were boarding helicopters, and in the ensuing gun battle the terrorists killed all nine hostages. Two more terrorists were also killed.

1973 ✛ THE U.S. SUPREME COURT SUPPORTS ABORTION

On January 22, 1973, the United States Supreme Court issued its controversial *Roe v. Wade* decision. The majority decision of the Court was that states could not restrict the right of a woman to have an abortion in the first two trimesters of a pregnancy, and they could allow an abortion in the third trimester, if the circumstances warranted it. In so doing, the Court essentially opened the door for abortion on demand. Between 1973 and 2004, since *Roe v. Wade*, approximately 40 million legal abortions were performed in the United States. Every

1939–45	1945	1989	1999
World War II	United Nations founded	Berlin Wall falls	Europe adopts Eurocurrency

January 22, on state capital grounds all over the country, pro-life advocates gather to protest the devastating effects that abortion has had on millions of mothers and children. The abortion issue is a constant source of controversy, as Americans continue to debate its ethical basis.

1973 ✝ PRESBYTERIAN CHURCH IN AMERICA IS FORMED

What is today the Presbyterian Church in America was organized in December 1973, as the National Presbyterian Church, with approximately 260 churches and forty thousand communicant members. At its second general assembly in 1974, the denomination changed its name to the Presbyterian Church in America (PCA). In 1982, the Reformed Presbyterian Church Evangelical Synod joined the denomination, bringing with it covenant College in Lookout Mountain, Georgia, and covenant Theological Seminary in St. Louis, Missouri. The PCA Church adheres to the Westminster Confession of Faith, and the Longer and Shorter Westminster Catechisms. The PCA is one of America's fastest-growing denominations, with approximately thirteen hundred congregations in 2004 and more than three hundred thousand members.

1973 ✝ ✡ JEWS FOR JESUS IS FOUNDED

Jews for Jesus was founded on September 17, 1973, in the San Francisco Bay Area, by Moishe Rosen (1932–), a long-time missionary to the Jewish people. During his twenty-three years as executive director of the organization, Rosen formulated evangelistic methods and materials to communicate the gospel to Jews. As the group gained momentum, many Jewish leaders began to oppose its ministry. Jews for Jesus is now an international ministry, with offices in Israel, Brazil, and Germany.

1973 ✡ ☪ WAR BEGINS IN ISRAEL ON YOM KIPPUR

Following the Six Day War in 1967, Israel experienced economic growth and renewed hope. Israel's lack of focus on defense during this period led to Egyptian and Syrian attempts to regain the Suez Canal and the Golan Heights, sites lost in the Six Day War. On October 6, 1973, supported by the Soviet Union, Syria attacked Israel from the north, and Egypt attacked in the Sinai region.

1914–18	1915	1918–20	1929
World War I	Mohandas Gandhi leads Indian Nationalist movement	Influenza kills 20 million	U.S. stock market crashes

THE PRESIDENT'S HATCHET MAN

August 12, 1973

God's dealings with us may be a painful process.

Charles Colson was a senior partner in a prestigious Washington D.C. law firm when in 1969, he received a phone call from President Richard Nixon. The president needed him. A *Wall Street Journal* headline summed up his role as special counsel to the president: "Nixon Hatchet Man. Call It What You Will, Chuck Colson Handles President's Dirty Work." Then came the Watergate scandal, and Colson resigned his position to form his own law firm.

In March 1973, he went to visit Tom Phillips, a previous client and president of the Raytheon Company. When Colson mentioned that he had heard Phillips had become involved in some religious activities, Phillips replied, "Yes, that's true, Chuck. I have accepted Jesus Christ. I have committed my life to him, and it has been the most marvelous experience of my whole life."

That summer, while on vacation with his wife in the Boston area to get away from the Watergate hearings, Colson found himself calling Tom Phillips, who invited him to his home the evening of August 12, 1973. That evening Phillips straightforwardly told Colson about Jesus and read to him from C. S. Lewis's book *Mere Christianity*. Lewis's description of pride as a cancer hit Colson like a torpedo. Phillips gave Colson a copy of the book.

Back in his car, Colson began crying uncontrollably and tearfully prayed to God, "Take me! Take me!"

A short time later, words that he initially hadn't understood now fell naturally from his lips: "Lord Jesus, I believe you. I accept you. Please come into my life. I commit it to you."

Colson soon became part of a small prayer group that included Congressman Al Quie of Minnesota. Supported by these new brothers in Christ, Colson decided to plead guilty to a Watergate crime of which he had not been charged—passing derogatory information to the press about antiwar activist Daniel Ellsberg. He was sentenced to a prison term of one to three years. After Colson had been in prison for nearly seven months, his family began falling apart. His wife was near the breaking point, and his son was in jail for narcotics possession.

At this point Al Quie called and said, "There's an old statute someone told me about. I'm going to ask the president if I can serve the rest of your term for you." Overwhelmed, that night Chuck Colson completely surrendered himself to God. Two days later, the judge at his trial released him from prison because of his family problems. As he left prison a Christian federal marshal told him that he had felt God would set Chuck free that day. Colson replied, "Thank you, brother, but he did it two nights ago."

In 1976, Chuck Colson founded Prison Fellowship, which ministers in six hundred prisons in eighty-eight countries with fifty thousand volunteers.

The incursions began on Yom Kippur, a religious holiday observed even by nonreligious Jews, catching the nation by surprise. However, Israel, backed by the United States, quickly recovered and had penetrated twenty-five miles into Egypt by the time a cease-fire was called. Although Israel's military once again demonstrated its superior skill, the initial trauma of the surprise attack had a devastating effect on Israel's sense of security.

1974 + LAUSANNE CONGRESS ON WORLD EVANGELIZATION IS HELD IN SWITZERLAND

The Lausanne Congress on World Evangelization was held July 16–25, 1974, in Lausanne, Switzerland. Assembled by 142 evangelical leaders from around the globe, the council consisted of nearly four thousand participants from 150 nations and was chaired by Billy Graham (1918–). The conference theme was "Let the Earth Hear His Voice." The congress maintained that Western missionaries should continue work in Third World developing countries, countering suggestions that Third World missions should be suspended. The congress adopted the Lausanne covenant, drafted by John R. W. Stott (1921–), which is a document that emphasizes the authority of the Bible and its call to missions.

1974 + FIRST VINEYARD CHURCH IS ESTABLISHED

The first Vineyard congregation was established in July 1974, by Kenn Gullickson, who had been ordained by Calvary Chapel in Southern California. It all began with a meeting of five people at a friend's house. At each gathering, Gullickson sat on a stool, playing his guitar to lead worship, and then taught from the Bible. Weekly attendance quickly grew to more than a thousand. Another strand of the Vineyards began in October 1976, in a home fellowship led by Carol Wimber, wife of John Wimber (1934–1997), then pastor of the Calvary Chapel of Yorba Linda, California. In 1982, with his ministry emphasizing "signs and wonders," John Wimber left Calvary Chapel to join the Vineyard movement, soon becoming its leader. In 1985, the Association of Vineyard Churches was founded. By 1997, there were more than four hundred Vineyard congregations in the United States and nearly two hundred overseas.

1914–18	1915	1918–20	1929
World War I	Mohandas Gandhi leads Indian Nationalist movement	Influenza kills 20 million	U.S. stock market crashes

1974 ✛ CAMPUS CRUSADE "EXPLO" IS HELD IN KOREA

In June 1972, more than 180,000 people gathered in Dallas, Texas, for Explo '72, a Campus Crusade for Christ–hosted event intended to motivate Christians to fulfill the Great Commission. On the heels of Explo '72, Bill Bright (1921–2003) and the leaders of Campus Crusade began planning a larger evangelistic training event in Seoul, South Korea. Explo '74, which opened in August 1974, far surpassed everyone's expectations. Delegates from every province in South Korea and seventy-eight other countries attended the event. Official police estimates numbered the crowd at more than 1.3 million during two of the evening rallies, making the convention the largest Christian gathering in history. In the four years following Explo '74, the South Korean church grew from 3 to 7 million members.

1975 ✛ NORTH VIETNAM CONQUERS SOUTH VIETNAM

In 1945, North Vietnam declared itself a Communist republic. Continual warfare plagued Vietnam from 1941 to 1985, first under the Japanese, then against the French, the Americans, and their neighboring countries. In 1975, North Vietnam defeated South Vietnam and its American allies. It also ruled Cambodia from 1978 to 1985. As a result of the Communist victory, there is no religious freedom in the country. Persecution of Christians is as severe as almost anywhere in the world. The Vietnam War also was a major event in the history of the United States, as many young Americans rejected not only their nation's participation in the war but traditional American values as well.

1975 ✛ WILLOW CREEK COMMUNITY CHURCH IS FOUNDED

Market research revealed to Bill Hybels (1951–) that suburbanites found church hard to relate to, as well as dull, and they liked to remain anonymous. Desiring to minister to people in Chicago's suburbs, Hybels began Willow Creek Community Church at a movie theater in Palatine, Illinois, on October 12, 1975. Within the year, one thousand people were attending, and by the year 2004, Willow Creek's five weekly services regularly attracted seventeen thousand people to the church's enormous mall-like building in South Barrington, Illinois. Church services, held in a seven-thousand-seat auditorium, require minimal participation and include entertaining music, drama, and a sermon. Willow Creek focuses on five "core values" (grace, groups, growth, gifts, and

1939–45	1945	1989	1999
World War II	United Nations founded	Berlin Wall falls	Europe adopts Eurocurrency

good stewardship), and coordinates three thousand small groups. Today, ten thousand churches follow Hybels's example and participate in the Willow Creek Association, established in 1992.

1976 + CHARLES COLSON FOUNDS PRISON FELLOWSHIP

After the Watergate scandal leading to the resignation of President Richard Nixon (1913–1994), Charles Colson (1931–) resigned from the White House staff and started his own law firm. In 1973, one of Colson's clients shared his Christian testimony with him, and shortly thereafter, Colson put his own faith in Jesus Christ. Supported by a group of Christian friends, Colson decided to plead guilty to a Watergate crime, even though he had not been charged. He was sentenced to a prison term of one to three years. During his incarceration and after his release, Colson developed a burden for the spiritual welfare of other prisoners, and in 1976, he founded Prison Fellowship, a Christian ministry active in six hundred prisons throughout the world.

1977 + FOCUS ON THE FAMILY BEGINS BROADCASTING

In 1977, after working for fourteen years in the University of Southern California's School of Medicine, licensed psychologist Dr. James C. Dobson (1936–) began broadcasting a radio program called *Focus on the Family,* from a two-room office suite in Pomona, California. Dobson was distressed by the disintegration of the American family that he had observed during his years as a psychologist, and he felt that God was calling him to address the problem. On his radio program, Dobson presents biblical solutions to family problems. By 2004, the daily program was syndicated on more than six thousand radio stations worldwide. The Focus on the Family organization, now headquartered in Colorado Springs, Colorado, has become a leading evangelical organization and an active proponent of family values, lobbying against pornography, gay marriage, and other family-related issues.

1977 + THE ALPHA COURSE IS FIRST OFFERED

In 1977, Charles Marnham, a clergyman at Holy Trinity Brompton, an Anglican parish in London, England, devised a simple plan to present the basics of the Christian faith to new believers in a casual setting. His relaxed and informal pro-

1914–18	1915	1918–20	1929
World War I	Mohandas Gandhi leads Indian Nationalist movement	Influenza kills 20 million	U.S. stock market crashes

gram was called the Alpha Course. Alpha represents an acronym: A—anyone interested in learning more about Christianity; L—learning and laughter; P—pasta (eating together to build community); H—helping one another; A—ask anything. Each session of the program begins with a meal at which people can get acquainted. After this, the larger group is divided into small groups for discussion. In 1990, Nicky Gumbel began leading the Alpha Course, reshaping it into a ten-week course to reach the unchurched, and placing emphasis on evangelism. Through the year 2004, more than 2 million people will have taken the Alpha Course.

1978 ✝ ASSOCIATION OF CHRISTIAN SCHOOLS INTERNATIONAL IS FOUNDED

On July 10, 1978, three Christian school associations merged to form the Association of Christian Schools International (ACSI) in LaHabra, California. In 1994, ACSI moved to Colorado Springs, Colorado, as it continued to grow and expand. Currently the ACSI has eighteen regional offices in North America and includes in its membership more than five thousand Christian schools in more than one hundred countries.

1978 ✡ ☾ CAMP DAVID ACCORDS LEAD TO AGREEMENT

Following a diplomatic visit to Israel by Egyptian president Anwar Sadat (1918–1981) in November 1977, the two long-time enemies began peace talks in 1978, at Camp David, in the Catoctin Mountains of Maryland—largely as a result of the persistent urging of U.S. president Jimmy Carter (1924–). Organized by Carter, the conference between Sadat and Israeli prime minister Menachem Begin (1913–1992) led to an agreement in which Israel surrendered the Sinai region to Egypt, in exchange for Egypt's political recognition of Israel and a more stable alliance between the two nations. For their efforts, Sadat and Begin received the 1978 Nobel Peace Prize. Unfortunately, Sadat was assassinated in 1981 as a result of his stand.

1979 ✝ JESUS FILM IS INTRODUCED

Campus Crusade for Christ, International, founded in 1953, is known for its innovative evangelistic efforts. In 1979, Campus Crusade purchased the rights to a feature-length production depicting the life of Jesus, based on the Gospel of

Luke. The project was made possible by a substantial donation from billionaire Nelson Bunker Hunt. Following the success of the film's release in the United States, efforts were turned abroad. By January 1, 2004, more than five billion people worldwide had viewed the JESUS film since 1979, the audio having been translated into 857 languages. Nearly 200 million people have made professions of faith as a result of seeing the film.

1979 ✛ EVANGELICAL COUNCIL FOR FINANCIAL ACCOUNTABILITY IS FOUNDED

In 1977, Congress threatened to pass legislation to regulate the financial activity of evangelical organizations unless they policed themselves, and the Evangelical Council for Financial Accountability (ECFA) was founded on May 9, 1979, in response. In an effort to regulate and promote the trustworthiness of evangelical nonprofit organizations, the ECFA requires that members have an independent board of directors and adhere to a code of financial ethics and accountability. The ECFA gained prominence in the wake of the televangelist scandals in the mid-1980s, when the Christian public wanted to ensure that the money they were contributing was not being misused. Membership in the ECFA is voluntary, and each organization submits itself to an annual financial review.

1979 ✛ JERRY FALWELL FOUNDS THE MORAL MAJORITY

Jerry Falwell (1933–) was converted to Christ in 1952, and ordained by the Baptist Bible Fellowship in 1956, after graduating from Baptist Bible College in Springfield, Missouri. That same year he founded the Thomas Road Baptist Church in his hometown of Lynchburg, Virginia. Falwell initially avoided political involvement, but beginning in the 1970s, his articulation of conservative positions became more public, especially in regard to abortion and prayer in public schools. His increasingly political concerns led Falwell to found the Moral Majority in 1979. The Moral Majority registered millions of voters who helped elect Ronald Reagan (1911–2004) as president of the United States in 1980 and 1984. Falwell, who disbanded the Moral Majority in 1989, remains active in politics, speaking out on such issues as abortion, homosexuality, and pornography.

1914–18	1915	1918–20	1929
World War I	Mohandas Gandhi leads Indian Nationalist movement	Influenza kills 20 million	U.S. stock market crashes

1979 ✝ SOUTHERN BAPTIST TAKEOVER

After many years of control by more liberal leadership, the conservative membership of the Southern Baptist Convention (SBC)—a denomination consisting of more than forty thousand congregations in the southern part of the United States—decided in 1979 to campaign for the election of one of their own. They succeeded in electing Adrian Rogers (1931–) as SBC president. As president, Rogers had the authority to select leaders for committees, including missionary boards, Sunday school, and even the trustees of SBC seminaries. Following this success, conservatives have been successful in electing their SBC presidential candidate every year since. By the late 1980s, all SBC seminaries and mission boards were run by conservatives. In the 1990s, moderates formed the Cooperative Baptist Fellowship, which remains in the SBC but supports its own seminary, missionaries, and publishing efforts.

1980 ✝ JOHN PIPER ENTERS THE PASTORATE

Born in Tennessee and raised in South Carolina, John Piper (1946–), the son of a Southern evangelist, is a graduate of Wheaton College and Fuller Seminary. He received a doctorate in theology from the University of Munich in 1974. Piper spent the next six years teaching Bible at Bethel College in St. Paul, Minnesota. Feeling God's call to the pastorate, he preached his first sermon as pastor of Bethlehem Baptist Church in Minneapolis, Minnesota, on July 6, 1980. Deeply influenced by the writings of theologian Jonathan Edwards, Piper began to articulate the doctrine of Christian hedonism, that God is most glorified in us when we are most satisfied in him. In 1986, his publication of *Desiring God* launched a global speaking and writing ministry that catapulted him into leadership of the growing movement toward Reformed theology.

1982 ☿ ☾ ISRAEL LAUNCHES WAR IN LEBANON

In 1982, Israeli Prime Minister Menachem Begin (1913–1992) commenced Israel's first offensive military initiative where the existence of Israel was not directly threatened. The mission was to destroy the bases of the Palestine

1939–45	1945	1989	1999
World War II	United Nations founded	Berlin Wall falls	Europe adopts Eurocurrency

PHYSICIAN OF SOULS

February 26, 1981

His was an unusual path to the pulpit.

David Martyn Lloyd-Jones was born in Wales in 1899, and at twenty-two earned a medical degree under the most renowned physician in England. But Lloyd-Jones believed there was a soul sickness that ran far deeper than any physical ailment. He determined that what people needed most is life from God. As he studied and pondered these truths and came to understand that through Christ's death on the cross people could have eternal life, Lloyd-Jones himself was born again. This experience changed his life—and its direction from medicine to the pastorate. His theological education came from books of great theologians like John Owens and Jonathan Edwards. "I devoured these volumes and just read them and read them," Lloyd-Jones wrote. "It is certainly true that they helped me better than anything else." In 1927, he was ordained in George Whitefield's Tabernacle in London as a Calvinistic Methodist.

In 1938, after an eleven-year evangelistic and preaching ministry in South Wales, Lloyd-Jones was invited by the aging G. Campbell Morgan to become copastor with him of Westminster Chapel in London. His formal induction service in September 1939 was canceled, for fear of a Nazi bombing raid.

Lloyd-Jones spent the next thirty years preaching at the church, seeing it through the difficult war years. He became the sole pastor when Morgan retired in 1943. Under his leadership, Westminster Chapel became recognized as the leading evangelical pulpit of England. His ministry there was characterized by his careful exposition of the Bible and his uncompromising Reformed theology. At the same time, he was known for his genuine piety, his family life, his sense of humor, his skill as a counselor, and his deep desire for renewal in the evangelical church. Thousands found Christ and grew in their faith under Lloyd-Jones's preaching. He deserves to be included among the great preachers of all time.

In 1968, illness forced him to end his ministry at Westminster. But Lloyd-Jones was later convinced that God removed his preaching ministry so that he could write. He began editing his sermon transcripts for publication and wrote many books that still remain in print.

Lloyd-Jones was a student of church history, and among the quotes he treasured most was a statement by John Wesley, who said of the early Methodists, "Our people die well." Lloyd-Jones knew the power behind those words. Physical death did, indeed, lose its sting for those who were confident of their life in eternity.

His turn to die came in the waning days of winter in 1981. On Thursday evening, February 26, 1981, in a trembling hand Lloyd-Jones wrote a note to his dear wife and children: "Do not pray for healing. Do not hold me back from glory." His request was honored. The next Sunday, Dr. David Martyn Lloyd-Jones entered glory to meet face-to-face the God he so cherished.

Liberation Organization (PLO) in southern Lebanon, from which attacks were being launched against northern Israel. After Israel invaded Lebanon and destroyed the PLO camps, General Ariel Sharon (1928–) marched his troops to Beirut, Lebanon's capital city. General Sharon incurred much criticism by allowing Lebanese Christians into the Palestinian refugee camps of Sobra and Shatila, where they massacred the Palestinian refugees under Israel's care. While the Lebanon War achieved its objective by inhibiting the PLO, the campaign spawned significant unrest within Israel and cost Israel much international sympathy. The Israeli army withdrew from Lebanon in 1985.

1985 ✛ GORBACHEV BECOMES GENERAL SECRETARY OF SOVIET COMMUNIST PARTY

In March 1985, Mikhail Gorbachev (1931–) became general secretary of the Communist Party of the Soviet Union. In an effort to salvage the failing Communist system, Gorbachev initiated a program designed to make the Union of Soviet Socialist Republics (USSR) a more open society. Gorbachev then became president of the USSR in 1989. His regime was noted for *glasnost* (openness) and *perestroika* (reform), and in 1990, he was awarded the Nobel Peace Prize. His administration saw the disintegration of the USSR, and in 1991, he resigned as president of a USSR that no longer existed. The breakup of the Soviet Union under Gorbachev's policies opened up the entire region for the gospel.

1987 ✡ ☾ INTIFADA BEGINS ON WEST BANK

On December 6, 1987, an Israeli shopper was stabbed to death in the Gaza Strip. The next day, four Palestinians from the Jabalya refugee camp in the Gaza Strip were killed in an unrelated traffic accident. Some Palestinians, however, surmised that the crash was not accidental but an act of vengeance. This accusation led to mass rioting in Jabalya, and a seventeen-year-old Palestinian was killed by Israeli police during the riots. The riots spread throughout the West Bank and continued to intensify. Although the riots of this period, which has come to be known as *Intifada* or "shaking off," were at first disorganized, Palestinian leaders soon organized the violence into a guerrilla war against the Israelis. The violence and rioting continued until 1993.

1939–45	1945	1989	1999
World War II	United Nations founded	Berlin Wall falls	Europe adopts Eurocurrency

1987 ✝ TELEVANGELISM SCANDALS ARE REVEALED

In the 1970s, evangelicals combined evangelism and entertainment in several popular and profitable television programs. However, scandals unmasked several high-profile televangelists. On March 19, 1987, Jim Bakker (1940–) resigned from his ministry because of sexual improprieties and was sentenced to prison for financial misconduct. Jimmy Swaggart (1935–), who sought to debunk Bakker, confessed during his broadcast on February 21, 1988, to voyeuristic liaisons with a prostitute. Oral Roberts (1918–), on one of his television broadcasts, declared that God would "call me home" if viewers did not donate millions to save his financially troubled empire. As a result of these scandals, the ratings for the programs plummeted, and financial support for Christian television programs fell drastically.

1989 ✝ BERLIN WALL COMES DOWN

On November 9, 1989, the Berlin Wall was dismantled, after standing for nearly thirty years as an international symbol of division. The wall, erected in August 1961 by Nikita Khrushchev (1894–1971), the leader of the Soviet Union, had divided East Berlin (under the control of the Russians) from West Berlin (under the control of the Allies). The Berlin Wall was demolished by a joyful crowd of young men, celebrating the reunion of Berlin and East and West Germany. The tearing down of the wall was a direct answer to the prayers of Germany's Christians. The subsequent reunification of Germany marked the end of the persecution of Christians in East Germany.

1990 ✡ JEWISH EMIGRATION FROM SOVIET UNION PEAKS

The Soviet Union and its succeeding nations have been the greatest source of Jewish immigrants. Until 1971, the Communist government allowed only a trickle of Jews to leave the country. In 1959, only three were permitted to emigrate. In 1971, because of the pressure from worldwide Jewry, Jewish emigration was allowed to increase. With the onset of *glasnost* (openness) and *perestroika* (reform) under Mikhail Gorbachev (1931–), emigration peaked in 1990, when 213,437 Jews were able to leave the Soviet Union. Most immigrated to either Israel or the United States.

1914–18	1915	1918–20	1929
World War I	Mohandas Gandhi leads Indian Nationalist movement	Influenza kills 20 million	U.S. stock market crashes

1990 ✝ PROMISE KEEPERS IS CONCEIVED

On March 20, 1990, Bill McCartney (1940–), head football coach of the University of Colorado, had a conversation with a friend on the way to a Fellowship of Christian Athletes meeting. They discussed a vision to fill the university's football stadium with men worshiping God. Their first event brought more than four thousand men to the stadium, and by 1993, they were attracting crowds of fifty thousand. Promise Keepers had become a full-fledged evangelical movement and organization, aimed at discipling men to be leaders at both home and church. Holding rallies in sports stadiums throughout the nation, Promise Keepers enjoyed much success throughout America. However, by 1998, they had fallen on financial hard times and were forced to cut back on their rallies.

1993 ✡ ☾ OSLO ACCORDS ARE SIGNED

In the summer of 1993, the Israeli government and leaders from the Palestine Liberation Organization (PLO) met secretly in Oslo, Norway, and negotiated a peace treaty. On August 20, Israeli Prime Minister Yitzhak Rabin (1922–1995) and PLO Chairman Yasser Arafat (1929–2004) announced the agreement in Oslo, with a formal signing ceremony on September 13, 1993, in Washington, D.C. The heart of the agreement was mutual recognition of the PLO and Israel, with the goal of Palestinian autonomy. The Israeli government agreed to withdraw their troops from the Gaza Strip and West Bank and allowed for Palestinian self-government in those areas for five years, during which a permanent agreement would be negotiated. In the ensuing years, however, agreement was not reached, and when the two parties met in 2000, the negotiations ended in failure. Since 2000, violence has escalated, with frequent Palestinian suicide bombings followed by Israeli retaliation.

1994 ✡ ☾ ISRAEL SIGNS A PEACE TREATY WITH JORDAN

On July 25, 1994, King Hussein I (1935–1999) of Jordan and Israeli Prime Minister Yitzhak Rabin (1922–1995) met in Washington, D.C. and signed the Washington Declaration, which affirmed five principles for reaching a lasting peace between the two nations. Then on October 26, 1994, at Wadi Araba on the border between Israel and Jordan, King Hussein and Rabin signed a peace treaty

1939–45	1945	1989	1999
World War II	United Nations founded	Berlin Wall falls	Europe adopts Eurocurrency

which established a solid framework for future relations. Jordan thus became only the second Arab nation to make peace with Israel, following the example of Egypt's treaty in 1978.

1995 ✡ RABIN IS ASSASSINATED

The signing of the Oslo Accords in 1993 by Israeli Prime Minister Yitzhak Rabin (1922-1995) infuriated many Orthodox Jews. They were upset at the prospect of losing control of certain holy sites, and many Israelis, religious or not, refused to trust the Palestine Liberation Organization. In reaction, a Jewish fanatic assassinated Rabin on November 4, 1995, following a peace demonstration in Tel Aviv, Israel. Rabin's death postponed indefinitely any hope of peace with the Palestinians, because Rabin's successor, Shimon Peres (1923–), was unable to garner public support amid continued terrorist attacks.

2000 ✡ ☪ ARIEL SHARON VISITS THE TEMPLE MOUNT

On September 28, 2000, Ariel Sharon (1928–), leader of the conservative Likud Party of Israel, visited the Temple Mount in Jerusalem, accompanied by hundreds of Israeli soldiers sent to protect him. Shortly before the visit, Palestinian leader Yasser Arafat (1929–2004) proclaimed that Jews have no right to visit the site, which is considered holy by Christians, Jews, and Muslims alike. Sharon claimed that his visit was a gesture of peace; however, the Palestinians claimed that Sharon had desecrated their holy place, and they responded by intensifying the violence against the Israelis. Within hours of Sharon's visit, Palestinian youths in the West Bank city of Ramallah hurled rocks at Israeli police. In the Palestinian *intifada* (uprising) that followed, suicide bombers increasingly attacked Israeli public places, intensifying the long-standing Israeli-Palestinian conflict.

2000 ✝ MISSIONARY MOVEMENT SEEKS TO FULFILL THE GREAT COMMISSION

The AD 2000 and Beyond Movement, begun in 1989, was the most global and focused missionary movement of all time. Its goal was "the gospel for every person and a church for every people" by the year 2000. Missiologists have identi-

1914–18	1915	1918–20	1929
World War I	Mohandas Gandhi leads Indian Nationalist movement	Influenza kills 20 million	U.S. stock market crashes

fied approximately twelve thousand different people groups in the world, and the goal was to establish a self-propagating church in each of them. The goals were not reached by 2000, but great strides were made. The movement focused on the sixteen hundred people groups with a population of more than ten thousand but with less than 2 percent professing evangelical Christians. By the end of 2000, church-planting teams existed in 1,084 people-groups, and 487 of these had a congregation of more than one hundred. In 2000, Christian radio reached 99 percent of the world's population in their own language, and only 6.3 percent of the world's population lived in a culture without a witnessing church.

2000 ✝ BGEA ORGANIZES AMSTERDAM CONFERENCE

From July 29 to August 6, 2000, approximately ten thousand evangelists from 209 nations and territories of the world gathered in Amsterdam for a time of encouragement, training, and networking to maximize the thrust of the gospel in the next millennium. Organized by the Billy Graham Evangelistic Association (BGEA), the meeting was the largest ever of its kind. Unfortunately, eighty-one-year-old Billy Graham was not able to attend, because he was undergoing medical treatment. The conference issued the Amsterdam Declaration: A Charter for Evangelism in the Twenty-first Century.

1939–45	1945	1989	1999
World War II	United Nations founded	Berlin Wall falls	Europe adopts Eurocurrency

INDEX

A

Aaron 8, 12–13, 59, 75
Abba Arika (also known as Rav) 108
Abd al-Malik (caliph) 145
Abelard, Peter 171–172, 174, 179
Abijam (king of Judah) 23
Abimelech (of Shechem) 17
Abraham/Abram 2–4, 6, 12, 21, 145
Ackerman, Mrs. Paul (rabbi) 455
Ackerman, William (rabbi) 455
Acre 178, 186, 188
Act of Uniformity 279–280, 286
Adams, John Quincy 339
Aedesius 120
Africa Inland Mission 398
African American Churches 382
African Methodist Episcopal
    Church 341, 382
Agag (king of Amalek) 50
Ahab (king of Israel) 24–27, 31
Ahaz (king of Judah) 32, 34
Ahaziah (king of Israel) 25–27
Albigensians 181–183
Alcuin of York 151
Alexander (bishop of Alexandria) 118–119
Alexander II (Russian czar) 396
Alexander III (pope) 177
Alexander III (Russian czar) 396
Alexander IV (pope) 210
Alexander Janneus (high priest and king
    of Judea) 64
Alexander the Great 54–57, 59, 128, 175
Alexander V (pope) 196
Alexander VI (pope) 206, 208–209
Alexander, Archibald 337, 371
Alexandria 55–57, 102, 106–107, 118–
    120, 124, 128, 130, 135, 149, 260
Aliyah (immigration of Jews to
    Israel) 393, 406, 417, 422, 428, 437

Al-Kameel (Egyptian sultan) 183
Allen, Ethan 314
Allen, Richard (bishop of African
    Methodist Church) 341
Allenby, Edmund (British WWI
    general) 417
Alliance Israélite Universelle 378
Alline, Henry 317
Alopen (Nestorian missionary) 142
Amaziah (king of Judah) 28–29
Ambrose (bishop of Milan) 121, 126
American Civil War 379
American Sunday School Union 348
American Tract Society 350
Amon (king of Judah) 36
Amos (prophet) 29–30
Anabaptists 220–222, 228, 236, 248
Anan ben David 150, 157
Ananias (of Damascus) 80
Andover Theological Seminary 334,
    343, 395
Andreae, James 247
Anglican Church 205, 232–233, 242,
    266, 272, 284, 356, 381
Anselm (archbishop of
    Canterbury) 167, 170, 179
Anskar 152–153
Antiochus III (Seleucid king) 58–59
Antiochus IV Epiphanes (Seleucid
    king) 58–59, 60–62
Antwerp, Synod of 244
Arab riots 419, 426, 433
Arafat, Yasser 483–484
Archbishop of Canterbury 140, 145,
    167, 170, 175, 205, 233, 236–237, 255,
    266
Ardes, Council of 118
Arianism 112, 119, 122, 124
Aristobulus I (high priest and ruler of
    Judea) 63–64

Aristobulus II 64–66
Arius 112, 118–119, 132
Arles, Synod of 179
Armenian massacres 399, 414
Arminius, Jacobus 251, 256
Arnauld, Antoine 256
Arndt, Johann 252
Arnold, Benedict 314
Asa (king of Judah) 23, 25
Asbury College Revival 470
Asbury, Francis 312, 315, 320
Asia Minor 55, 65, 84, 86, 88, 94, 98–99,
    102–103, 105, 119, 153, 166, 168
Assemblies of God 414, 460, 462
Assumption of Mary 455
Assyrian Eponym lists 31
Athaliah (daughter of Ahab) 25–27
Athanasius (bishop of Alexandria) 120,
    124, 128
Athelbert (king of Kent) 140, 142
Attila the Hun 132–133
Auburn Declaration 358
Augsburg Confession 225, 233, 247, 370
Augsburg, Peace of 236, 256
Augustine (bishop of Hippo) 116, 121,
    127, 136, 139–140, 256, 270
Augustine of Canterbury 140
Augustinians 243
Auschwitz 439, 441, 463
Avignon 189–190, 193–194, 196
Avila 210, 243
Azusa Street Revival 405

B
B'nai B'rith 363, 411
Baasha (king of Israel) 23–24
Bach, Johann Sebastian 297
Bakker, Jim (American
    televangelist) 482
Baldwin (king of Jerusalem) 170
Balfour Declaration 415, 449
Balfour, Arthur (British foreign
    secretary) 415–416
Balkans 122, 133
Bar Kokhba 103, 106, 108
Barnabas 80, 82–84, 90

Barth, Karl 419, 426, 430
Basel, Council of 200
Basil (bishop of Caesarea) 122,
    125–126
Basil (emperor) 155
battle of Bunker Hill 316
Battle of Lützen 265
Battle of Marston Moor 271
Battle of Mazikert 167
battle of Qarqar 31
Becket, Thomas 175
Bede 148
Begin, Menachem (Israeli prime
    minister) 477, 479
Belgic Confession 244
Belshazzar (son of Nebuchadnezzar)
    44–46
ben Eliezer, Israel 298, 312
Ben Gurion, David 449–450
ben Israel, Menasseh 278
ben Judah, Gershom. See Gershom ben
    Judah
Ben Yehuda, Eliezer 392
Benedict of Nursia 136, 156
Benedict XIII (pope in Avignon) 196,
    198
Benefit of the Clergy 176
Benjamin of Tudela 175
Bennett, Dennis (pastor) 462
Bernard of Clairvaux 172–174
Bernice (sister and wife of Agrippa) 84
Bethlehem 19, 30, 66–67, 69–72, 129,
    183, 447
Beza, Theodore (successor to John
    Calvin) 242
Billy Graham Evangelistic
    Association 452–453, 456, 485
Bingham, Roland (founder of SIM) 397
Bishop Wars 270
Bishop's Bible 244
Bismarck, Otto von (chancellor) 383
Black Death 192, 195
Black Obelisk 31
Blanchard, Jonathan (president of
    Wheaton College) 367
Blois, France 176

Blood libel   173, 176, 185, 361, 363
Boer, G. E. (founder of Calvin
   College)   388
Boethius   135
Bohemia   198–200
Boleyn, Anne   205, 226
Bonhoeffer, Dietrich   443
Boniface   146
Boniface VIII (pope)   188
Booth Catherine (wife of William
   Booth)   390
Booth, William (founder of the Salvation
   Army)   390
Boris (king of Bulgaria)   155
Boxer Rebellion   402–403, 408
Boys' Brigade   394
Brainerd, David   291, 304, 306–307, 310
Bright, Bill   455, 458, 460, 475
British and Foreign Bible Society   332,
   339
British Mandate over Palestine   419–420
Bryan, Jarvis   280
Bryan, William Jennings   424–425
Bugenhagen, Johann   225
Bultmann, Rudolf   440
Bunker Hill, battle of   316
Bunyan, John (author of The Pilgrim's
   Progress)   282–283
Burma   337, 343
Burns, William Chalmers   361
Burns, William Hamilton   361
Burr, Aaron, Sr.   307, 310
Buxton, Thomas Forwell   321
Byzantine Empire   122, 139, 141–142,
   148, 161, 166, 185, 202, 250
Byzantium   120

C
Caedmon   144
Caesar Augustus   30, 65–66
Caesar Bardas (emperor)   155
Caleb   13–15
Callenberg, J. H.   296
Callistus   108
Callistus II (pope)   171–172, 208
Callistus III (pope)   208

Calvin College   388
Calvin, John   121, 228, 242, 244, 286–
   287, 334
Cambridge Platform   276
Cambridge University   221, 287, 465
Cameron, Richard   284
Camp David Accords   477
Campbell, Alexander   337
Campbell, Duncan (Scottish
   revivalist)   452
Campbell, Thomas   335
Campus Crusade for Christ   407, 430,
   455, 458, 460, 477
Canaan   2, 5, 7, 12–14, 16
Cane Ridge Revival   331–332
Cappadocian Fathers   122, 125–126, 129
Carcalla (emperor)   108
Carey, Lott (first black missionary to
   Africa)   344–345
Carey, William (missionary to
   India)   327–328, 338
Carmichael, Amy   404, 454
Carter, Jimmy   477
Carthage, North Africa   106, 110
Catherine de Médicis (queen of Henry II
   of France)   240, 245–246
Catherine of Aragon (first wife of Henry
   VIII)   205, 226, 233, 235
Catherine of Siena   194
Catherine the Great (Russian
   empress)   314, 324, 396
Cavert, Samuel McCrea   438
Chafer, Lewis Sperry (founder of Dallas
   Theological Seminary)   422
Chalcedon, Council of   132, 137
Channing, William Ellery   344
Chapman, J. Wilbur (American
   evangelist)   398, 432
Charlemagne (Holy Roman
   emperor)   150–153, 158–159
Charles I (Charles the Bald, Carolingian
   emperor)   153
Charles I (king of England)   255, 260,
   262, 266, 268, 270–272, 276, 286
Charles II (king of England)   272, 276,
   278, 281–282, 284, 286

Charles IV (king of France)   192
Charles IX (king of France)   240,
   245–246
Charles Martel   143, 148, 204
Charles V (emperor)   219, 223, 225–226,
   231, 236
Charles VII (king of France)   199
Chaucer, Geoffrey   185
Chelcicky, Peter   202
Chemnitz, Martin (German Lutheran
   theologian)   247
Child Evangelism Fellowship   434
China   109, 142, 186, 188, 192–193, 248,
   288, 291–292, 334, 361, 363, 365, 368–
   369, 382, 386, 402–403, 408, 453, 457,
   467
China Inland Mission   368–369, 382, 457
Chmielnicki, Bogdan   276
Cho, Paul Yonggi   460
Chosroes II (king of Persia)   141
Christian and Missionary Alliance   400
Christian Booksellers Association   453
Christian Endeavor Society   392
Christian Reformed Church   388
Christian Science Church   388
Christianity Today magazine   459
Christmas Revival   318
Church of England   205, 226, 232, 237,
   242, 254, 266–267, 271–273, 279, 282,
   284, 288, 319–320, 329, 354, 356, 366,
   374, 446
Church of Scotland   239, 270–271, 273,
   286, 328, 335
Church of the Brethren   292
Churches of Christ   337
Clarendon Code   279
Clark, Francis E. (founder of Christian
   Endeavor Society)   392
Clarke, George Roger   390
Clarkson, Thomas   321, 334
Claudius (emperor)   84, 86
Clement (bishop)   95
Clement V (pope)   189–190
Clement (Christian scholar)   106
Clement VII (pope in Avignon)   193,
   226

Clement XI (pope)   291, 293
Clement XIII (pope)   339
Clement XIV (pope)   314
Clermont, Council of   168
Clothilda of Burgundy (wife of
   Clovis)   133
Clovis (king of the Franks)   133–134
Cluny (monastery)   156, 163
Coan, Titus (missionary to Hawaii)
   357, 360
Cohn, Leopold   398
Coke, Thomas   320–321
Coligny, Gaspard de, (leader of the
   Huguenots)   234, 245–246
Colossae   92
Colson, Charles   473, 476
Columba (evangelist to Ireland and
   Scotland)   137, 144
Columbus, Christopher   206–208, 210
Comenius, Jan Amos   265
Communism   417, 433, 457
Comnenus, Alexius (Byzantine
   emperor)   168
Concentration camps   439, 441, 444
Confessional Lutherans   370
Congregational Church   292, 335, 344,
   356
Conrad II (emperor)   162
Conrad III (emperor)   174
Constance, Council of   196
Constantine the Great   117, 122–123
Constantine V   147, 149
Constantinople   117, 120, 122–123, 125–
   127, 130, 133, 139, 142, 145, 148–149,
   154–155, 158, 164, 168–169, 180, 202,
   213, 230
Constantinople, Fourth Council of   155
Constantinople, Second Council of   137
Constantinople, Third Council of   144
Constantius Chlorus (father of
   Constantine)   113, 116–117
Copernicus, Nicolas   231
Corinth   85–88
Cornelius   80
Cotton, John (Puritan vicar)   268, 279
Council of the Four Lands   232

Covenanters 268, 284, 286
Coverdale, Miles 229
Cowper, John 313
Cowper, William 313, 317
Cranmer, Thomas 205, 232–233, 236–237
Cromwell, Oliver 271, 276–277, 286
Crowther, Samuel (bishop) 381
Crusades, the 167–170, 173, 177–178, 180–183, 188, 229
Cunningham, Loren (founder of YWAM) 462–463
Cyprian (bishop of Carthage) 109–110
Cyril (bishop of Alexandria) 128, 130
Cyril (evangelist to the Slavs) 154–155
Cyrus II (Cyrus the Great) 45–46

D
da Gama, Vasco 203, 209
Dallas Theological Seminary 422, 441
Damasus I (pope) 124
Daniel, the prophet 39, 41, 44–47, 59–60, 73, 130
Dante (Alighieri) 191
Darby, John Nelson 352, 354
Darius (king of Persia) 46, 48, 54, 56
Darwin, Charles 376, 425
David (king of Israel) 19–23, 53, 72
Day, John 242
de Bres, Guido 244
de Cisneros, Francisco Jiménez 214
de las Casas, Bartolome 213
de Legaspi, Miguel 243
de Nobili, Robert 252
de Paul, Vincent 266
de Richelieu, Armand (cardinal) 262
de Santa Fe, Geronimo 196
Dead Sea Scrolls 447–448
Deborah (judge of Israel) 16
Decius (emperor) 109–111
Definite Synodical Platform 370
Delilah (wife of Samson) 18
Demetrius I Soter (ruler of Syria) 61
Dias, Bartolomeu 203
Diego, Juan (Quauhtlatoatzin) 225
Diocletian (emperor) 113–114, 116

Dionysius Exiguus 136
Dionysius the Pseudo-Areopagite 134
Disciples of Christ 335
Dobson, Dr. James C. (founder of Focus on the Family) 476
Dominic (founder of Dominican Order) 182
Domitian (Caesar) 98–99
Donation of Pepin 149–150
Donatus (bishop) 116, 118
Donin, Nicholas 184
Donne, John 317
Dort, Canons of 244
Dort, Synod of 242, 256
Drake, Francis 249–250
Dreyfus, Alfred (Jewish French army captain) 397
Dubourg, Louis-Guillaume-Valentin 346
Dunster, Henry (first president of Harvard College) 269
Dwight, Timothy (successor to Jonathan Edwards) 308, 332

E
Ebo (archbishop) 152
Eddy, Mary Baker (founder of Christian Science Church) 388
Edict of Nantes 251, 284–285
Edward I (king of England) 187
Edward III (king of England) 176, 192
Edward VI (king of England) 232–233, 235, 237, 239
Edwards, Jonathan 291, 294, 298, 302–304, 307–308, 310, 332, 334, 436, 479–480
Edwin (king of Northumbria, England) 141–142
Edzard, Ezra 296
Ehud (judge in Israel) 15–16
Einstein, Albert 421
El Hakim (caliph) 160
Elah (king of Israel) 24
Eliot, John 270
Elizabeth I (queen of England) 232, 238, 244, 247, 249–250, 255

Elliot, Elisabeth (wife of Jim Elliot) 459, 461
Elliot, Jim (missionary martyr) 459, 461
Engels, Friedrich 349, 367
English Civil War 255, 270, 272, 276
Enlightenment, the 252, 290, 312, 350
Eorpwald 142
Ephesus 85–87, 94, 99, 102, 131
Ephesus, Council of 130–131, 142
Episcopal Church 205
Epp, Theodore 436
Erasmus 193, 214
Erik the Red 160
Eriksson, Leif 160
Esau (son of Isaac) 4–5
Esther (Jewish queen of Persia) 49–51
Eugene IV (pope) 200
Eugenius III (pope) 174
Eusebius Hieronymus Sophronius. See Jerome
Eusebius of Nicomedia 122
Eutyches (monk) 132
Evangelical Council for Financial Accountability 478
Evangelical Foreign Missions Association 445
Evangelical Revival 302
Evangelical Theological Society 451
Evangelism Explosion 467
Everson v. Board of Education (Supreme Court decision regarding church and state) 325
Ezekiel, the prophet 40, 42–43
Ezra, the prophet 46–49, 51–53

F

Fabian (bishop of Rome) 110
Falwell, Jerry 478
Faroe Islands 134
Felix (Roman governor) 91
Felix V (antipope) 200
Fellowship of Christian Athletes 456
Ferdinand (king of Spain) 204, 206–208, 210
Ferdinand I (Holy Roman emperor) 249

Ferdinand, Francis (archduke) 415
Ferrer, Vincente (Dominican monk) 195
Festus, Porcius 84
Final Solution, the 439, 441–442, 463
Finley, Robert 340
Finney, Charles 347–348, 356, 360
First Vatican Council 383
Five Mile Act 279, 286
Fleming, Peter 459
Florence, Council of 200, 202
Focus on the Family 476
Four Spiritual Laws 460
Fox, George 273
Foxe, John 242
Foxe's Book of Martyrs 242
Francis I (king of France) 211, 229, 231
Francis II (emperor) 240, 332
Francis of Assisi 180, 184
Francke, August Hermann 288
Frederick I Barbarossa 178
Frederick II (Holy Roman emperor) 182–183, 185
Frederick II of Prussia 314
Frederick III (German elector) 240
Frederick the Wise 218
Free University of Amsterdam 359, 391, 404
Frelinghuysen, Theodorus J. 294
French Revolution 325–326, 330
Freud, Sigmund 399
Frumentius (bishop of Axum) 120
Fry, Elizabeth Gurney 342
Fulbert (canon of Notre Dame) 171
Fuller Theological Seminary 448, 458, 462
Fuller, Charles E. (founder of Fuller Theological Seminary) 448
Fust, Johann 202

G

Galerius (emperor) 113–114
Galilee 58, 66, 74, 97, 106
Galileo (Galilei) 264, 266
Gamaliel VI 131
Garden of Gethsemane 78, 81

Gaussen, Louis   352
Geneva Bible   239, 244, 255
Gershom ben Judah   162
Ghetto of Rome   245, 339, 383
Gideon   16–17
Gideons International   403
Godfrey of Bouillon   170
Goforth, Jonathan   408–409
Golgotha   77–78
Gorbachev, Mikhail   481–482
Gowans, Walter (missionary to the
   Sudan)   397
Graham, Billy   407, 443, 451–452, 459,
   474, 485
Great Awakening   294, 296, 298, 302–
   304, 306–308, 310, 317
Great Awakening, Second   318, 322, 330,
   332, 336, 340, 350
Great Schism   164, 194, 196
Grebel, Conrad (Anabaptist leader)   220
Gregory I (pope)   140, 171
Gregory II (pope)   146–147
Gregory IV (pope)   153
Gregory IX (pope)   183–185, 187, 210
Gregory of Nazianzus (bishop of
   Constantinople)   122, 129
Gregory of Nyssa (bishop of Nyssa)   122,
   125–126
Gregory the Illuminator (bishop of
   Armenia)   112, 114
Gregory VII (pope)   156, 163, 167–168,
   171–172
Gregory X (pope)   187
Gregory XI (pope)   194
Gregory XII (pope)   196, 198
Gregory XIII (pope)   246
Gregory XV (pope)   260
Grindal, Edmund   242
Groote, Gerhard   192
Gullickson, Kenn   474
Gumbel, Nicky (leader of the Alpha
   Course)   477
Gundaphorus (king in India)   83
Gustavus Adolphus (king of
   Sweden)   265
Gutenberg, Johannes   201–203

H

Habakkuk, the prophet   38
Hadrian (emperor)   103
Hadrian I (pope)   152
Hagar (concubine of Abram)   3
Haggai, the prophet   47–49
Hai of Pumbeditha   162
Haldane, James   328
Haldane, Robert   328, 340–341, 352
Haman (Persian prime minister)   49–50
Hamburg Temple   342
Hamilton, Patrick (first Protestant martyr
   in Scotland)   224
Handel, George Frideric   304–305
Hanukkah   61
Harald Klack (king of Denmark)   152
Harris, William Wade   410
Harvard, John   267
Hasdai Ibn Shaprut   157
Hasidim   312, 438
Hasidism   298
Hauge, Hans Nielsen   329
Hebrew Bible   34, 53, 156, 204, 312
Hebrew University   422–423, 447
Heidelberg Catechism   240
Heidelberg Confession   244
Helena (mother of Constantine)   117,
   119
Helwys, Thomas   255
Henry I (king of England)   166, 168
Henry II (king of England)   166, 175–176
Henry II (king of France)   234, 240
Henry III (king of France)   240, 285
Henry IV (German emperor)   167, 180
Henry IV of France (Henry III of
   Navarre)   246, 251, 262, 284–285
Henry the Navigator   203
Henry VIII (king of England)   195, 205,
   226–227, 233, 235–238
Heraclius (Eastern emperor)   144
Herod (governor of Judea)   49, 66–67
Herod Agrippa I   81, 84
Herod Agrippa II   84
Herod the Great   72
Herrnhut (Moravian Christian
   community)   293, 295–297, 377

Herzl, Theodor (Zionist and author of The Jewish State)   400

Hess, Moses (author of Rome and Jerusalem)   379, 392–393

Hezekiah (king of Judah)   34–35

Hideyoshi, Toyotomi   248

Hilda (abbess of Whitby)   144

Hildebrand (Pope Gregory VII)   163, 167, 172

Hildegard of Bingen   172

Hill, Samuel E. (cofounder of the Gideons)   403

Hippolytus (Roman antipope)   108

Hirsch, Baron Maurice de (founder of Jewish Colonization Association)   397

Hitler, Adolf   423, 430, 433, 436

Hochmann von Hochenau, E. C. (Pietist leader)   292

Holy Club   296, 298–301

Holy Roman Empire   151–153, 158–159, 180, 182–183, 219, 223, 249, 332, 383

Hopkins, Samuel (successor to Jonathan Edwards)   308

Hosea, the prophet   34

Hoshea (king of Israel)   33

Hugh (abbott of Cluny)   163

Huguenots   234, 240, 245–246, 251, 262, 284–285, 375

Hundred Years' War   192, 199

Hunt, Nelson Bunker   478

Hus, Jan (reformer)   197–200

Hutchinson, Anne   268

Huxley, T. H.   376

Hybels, Bill (pastor of Willow Creek Community Church)   475–476

Hyrcanus II (ruler of Palestine under Rome)   64–66

I

Ignatius (bishop of Antioch)   102

Ignatius (patriarch of Constantinople)   154–155

Ignatius of Loyola   229–230, 311

"Immaculate Conception"   369

Independent Baptist Revival   470

Indonesian Revival   467

Innocent II (pope)   172

Innocent III (pope)   179–183

Innocent IV (pope)   184–185

Innocent X (pope)   256

Interdenominational Foreign Mission Association   417

InterVarsity Christian Fellowship   419, 446

Irenaeus (bishop of Lyons)   105

Irving, Edward   354

Isaac (son of Abraham)   3–4, 12, 21, 145

Isabella (queen of Spain)   203–204, 206–207, 210

Isaiah, the prophet   5, 32–35, 46, 72

Ishmael (son of Abraham)   2–3

Israel Baal Shem Tov   298, 438

J

Jackson, Thomas "Stonewall" (American Confederate general)   379

Jacob (son of Isaac)   4–5, 7, 12, 71, 368

Jamaica Revival   376–377

James (brother of Jesus)   81, 83, 93, 100

James I (king of Aragón)   184, 186

James I (king of England, also James VI of Scotland)   238–239, 252–255, 260

James II (king of England)   286–287

James, the apostle (son of Zebedee)   353

Jan of Leiden   228

Jansen, Cornelius   256, 270

Jaricot, Pauline Marie   346

Jason (Jewish high priest)   59

Jehoahaz (king of Israel)   28, 37–38

Jehoash (king of Israel)   28–29

Jehoiachin (king of Judah)   37, 40–41

Jehoiakim (king of Judah)   37–41

Jehoram (king of Israel)   25–27

Jehoshaphat (king of Judah)   25–26

Jehovah's Witnesses   389

Jehu (king of Israel)   26–28, 31

Jephthah (king of Israel)   18

Jeremiah, the prophet   37, 39–41, 43, 46

Jeroboam I   22–24, 29

Jeroboam II   29–30, 34

Jerome (translator of the Vulgate)   124,
    128–129, 198, 202
Jerome of Prague   198
Jesus Christ   44, 54, 71, 73, 75, 77, 79, 86,
    89, 94, 102, 112, 118, 120–121, 126–
    127, 131, 213
JESUS Film   477–478
Jews for Jesus   472
Jezebel (wife of Ahab)   24, 26–27
Joachim of Fiore   178
Joan of Arc   192, 199
Joash (king of Judah)   27–28
John (king of England)   181
John Chrysostom   127
John Hyrcanus (son of Simon
    Maccabeus)   63
John Mark   82, 84
John of Damascus   147
John of Monte Corvino (monk)   188
John the Baptist   72, 74, 353
John XII (pope)   159
John XXII (pope)   190
John XXIII (antipope)   196, 198
John XXIII (pope)   464
John, elector of Saxony   225
John, the apostle (son of Zebedee)   75,
    81, 98–100, 104–105, 144, 353
Johnson Act   423
Johnson, Albert (congressman)   423
Jonah, the prophet   33, 37
Jonas, Justus   225
Jonathan (son of Saul)   20, 62–63
Jones, Absalom   341
Joram (king of Israel)   26
Joseph (son of Jacob)   5–7
Joshua (leader of Israel)   2, 13–14, 17
Josiah (king of Judah)   36–38
Jotham (king of Israel)   29, 32
Judah ha-Nasi (rabbi)   126
Judah the Patriarch   106, 108
Judas Iscariot   75, 211
Judas Maccabeus   60, 62
Judas Maccabeus (son of Mattathias and
    leader of the Maccabees)   61
Judson, Adoniram (missionary to
    Burma)   335–337, 343

Julian of Norwich   193
Julian the Apostate (emperor)   122–123
Julius Caesar   65, 67
Julius II (pope)   211–213
Julius III (pope)   234
Justin I (emperor)   135, 137
Justina (empress)   127
Justinian I (emperor)   135, 137

K
Kabbalah   187
Kalonymus (rabbinical family)   161
Kant, Immanuel   318, 325
Keble, John   356
Kennedy, D. James   466–467
Kent, Thomas (missionary to the
    Sudan)   397
Keswick Convention   386
Key, Francis Scott   339
Khan Timor Olcheitu   188
Khanbalik (Mongolian capital)   188
Khazaria, kingdom of   148, 161
Khrushchev, Nikita   482
Kierkegaard, Søren   364
Kilham, Alexander   329
Kilsyth Anniversary Revival   361
Kimbangu, Simon   420
King, Martin Luther, Jr.   468
Knights, William J. (cofounder of the
    Gideons)   403
Knox, John   238–239
Korea   142, 193, 321, 394, 408, 460, 475
Kristallnacht   434
Kublai Khan   186, 188
Kuyper, Abraham   359, 391, 404

L
La Reveil Revival   350
La Rochelle (Huguenot stronghold)   262
Lanphier, Jeremiah   372–373
Lateran Councils   172, 212
Lateran Treaty   427, 433
Latimer, Hugh (English bishop)   233,
    236–237
Laud, William (archbishop of
    Canterbury)   266

Lausanne Congress on World
  Evangelization   *474*
League of Corinth   *55*
League of Nations   *420, 444, 448–449*
Leah (wife of Jacob)   *5*
Lenin, Vladimir   *417*
Leo I (bishop of Rome)   *132–133*
Leo III (emperor)   *147, 149–152, 159*
Leo IX (pope)   *162–163*
Leo X (pope)   *212, 226*
Leonardo da Vinci   *211, 213*
Lewis, C. S.   *427, 465, 473*
Liberation Theology   *470*
Liberius (pope)   *124*
Licinius (emperor)   *116–117*
Liudhard (Frankish chaplain)   *140*
Livingstone, David   *342, 361*
Livingstone, John (pastor)   *262*
Lloyd George, David (British prime
  minister)   *415–416*
Lloyd-Jones, David Martyn (physician
  and pastor)   *434, 436, 480*
Log College   *294, 307*
Lollards   *194–195*
Lombard, Peter (Italian
  theologian)   *171, 174, 179*
Lorca, Joshua   *196*
Lot (nephew of Abraham)   *2*
Lothair I (Carolingian emperor)   *153*
Louis I (Louis the Pious, Holy Roman
  emperor)   *152–153*
Louis II (German emperor)   *153*
Louis IX (king of France)   *182, 184*
Louis VII (emperor of France)   *174*
Louis XIII (king of France)   *262*
Louis XIV (king of France)   *251, 285,
  287*
Luke (Gospel writer)   *84, 90, 93*
Luria, Isaac (rabbi, also known as
  Ari)   *245*
Luther, Martin (leader of the
  Reformation)   *211–212, 214–216,
  218–221, 224–225, 231, 247, 252, 300*
Lutheran Church   *281–282, 370*
Lützen, battle of   *265*
Lyons, Councils of   *185, 187*

M
Macaulay, Zachary (English abolitionist
  and member of Parliament)   *326*
Maccabean Revolt   *61*
Maccabees, the   *61*
Machen, J. Gresham (Princeton
  theologian)   *421, 424, 435*
Mack, Alexander (founder of Church
  of the Brethren)   *292*
MacKay, James Murray (Scottish
  pastor)   *452*
Magi (Persian astrologers and
  astronomers)   *71*
Magna Carta   *181–182*
Maimonides (also known as Moses ben
  Maimon)   *156, 175, 183*
Malachi, the prophet   *54*
Malaga, Spain   *166*
Manasseh (king of Judah)   *15, 35–36, 40*
Mani (founder of Manichaeism)   *109*
Manichaeism   *109*
Manz, Felix (Anabaptist leader)   *220*
Mao Zedong (Communist dictator in
  China)   *453, 467*
Marcian (emperor)   *132*
Marcion (heretic, founder of
  Marcionism)   *103–104*
Marcus Aurelius (Roman emperor)
  105
Margaret of Valois (queen of France, wife
  of Henry of Navarre)   *246*
Mark (Gospel writer)   *90, 95*
Mark Antony   *66–67*
Marnham, Charles (Anglican clergyman
  and founder of the Alpha Course)
  476
Maronites   *177*
Marranos (Jews accepting Christian
  baptism)   *207, 218, 226, 243*
Marsiglio of Padua (rector at the
  University of Paris)   *191*
Marston Moor, battle of   *271*
Martel, Charles. *See* Charles Martel
Martin of Tours (bishop of Tours)   *125,
  131*
Martin V (pope)   *198–200*

Marx, Karl   349, 367
Mary (mother of Jesus)   67, 71–72, 130,
   137, 149, 213, 225, 369, 374, 455
Mary I (Mary Tudor, Bloody Mary,
   queen of England)   205, 232–233,
   235–238, 242, 249
Mary Magdalene   78
Mary Queen of Scots   238–239, 249
Masada   97
Massachusetts Bay Colony   267,
   269–270, 276, 289
Massasoit (American Indian chief)   258,
   260
Mather, Cotton (Puritan preacher)   289,
   292
Mather, Richard (Puritan)   270
Mattathias (progenitor of the
   Maccabees)   60–61
Matthew (Gospel writer)   90
Matthew, Thomas (pen name for Bible
   editor John Rogers)   229
Maxentius (rival of Constantine)
   116–117
Maximian (emperor)   113, 120
Maximin (emperor)   108
Mayflower Compact   257, 259
Mazikert, battle of   167
McCartney, Bill (founder of Promise
   Keepers)   483
McClanen, Don (founder of Fellowship
   of Christian Athletes)   456
McGavran, Donald A. (founder of the
   Institute of Church Growth)   462
McGready, James (Presbyterian revival
   leader)   330–331
Melanchthon, Philip (Reformation
   leader)   216, 224–225
Melito (bishop of Sardis)   105
Menahem (king of Israel)   30
Mendelssohn, Felix (composer)   297,
   312
Mendelssohn, Moses (Jewish
   philosopher)   312
Mendelssohn-Bartholdy, Jakob Ludwig
   Felix (composer)   351
Menelaus (Jewish high priest)   59

Menno Simons (Anabaptist)   228, 241
Methodism   300, 302, 312, 315,
   320–321
Methodist Church   341
Methodist Episcopal Church   315, 320
Methodius (evangelist to the Slavs)
   154
Metropolitan Job (Russian
   patriarch)   250
Micah, the prophet   35
Michael III (emperor)   154–155
Michelangelo   211–213, 264
Milan, Edict of   30, 113, 116–117
Miller, William (Baptist minister)   364,
   376
Mills, Samuel (founder of the Society of
   the Brethren)   333, 335–336
Milton, John (poet)   281
Mishnah, the (collection of oral laws and
   traditions by Jewish leaders)   106,
   108, 126, 134
Mission Aviation Fellowship   407, 430,
   445
Moffat, Robert (Methodist missionary)
   341–342, 361
Mohammad II (leader of the Ottoman
   forces)   202
Molcho, Solomon   218, 226
Mongol Empire   186, 193
Montanus (pagan priest)   104
Monte Casino (monastery)   136
Montefiore, Moses (English Jewish
   leader)   361, 363
Moody Bible Institute   370, 396, 405
Moody, Dwight L.   370, 385–387,
   390–391, 395–396
Moon, Lottie (missionary to
   China)   365, 386
Moral Majority   478
Moravian Brethren   199, 202
Moravian Church   293
Mordecai   49–51
More, Hannah (English
   abolitionist)   326
Morrison, Robert (Protestant
   missionary)   288, 334

Moses (Hebrew leader and prophet) *7–8,
10, 12–14, 25, 75, 79–80, 83, 94, 126*
Moses ben Nahman (rabbi, also known
as the Ramban or Nahmanides) *186*
Moses de Leon (composed the
kabbalah) *187*
Mott, John R. (leader of World Christian
Fellowship) *399*
Mount of Olives *73, 76, 78*
Muhammad (founder of Islam) *143,
145, 148, 153*
Müller, George (founder of orphanages
in Bristol, England) *357, 362*
Mullins, E. Y. (contributor to The
Fundamentals) *410*
Münzer, Thomas (Reformation
leader) *220*
Musa ibn Nusayr (governor of northwest
Africa) *146*
Mussolini, Benito (Italian premier)
427, 433, 436

N

Nabonidus (son-in-law of
Nebuchadnezzar) *45*
Nadab (king of Israel) *24*
Nahum, the prophet *37*
Nantes, Edict of *251, 284–285*
Napoléon I (emperor of France, also
known as Napoléon Bonaparte)
*158–159, 324, 330, 332–333, 339,
344, 383*
Nasi, Doña Gracia (influential
Marrano) *244*
Nasi, Joseph (Duke of Naxos) *243*
National Association of
Evangelicals *442–443*
National Religious Broadcasters *443*
Nazis *173, 428, 430, 434, 437, 439–440,
442–443, 449, 463*
Neander, Joachim (writer of
hymns) *282*
Neander, Johann August Wilhelm
(German church historian) *338*
Nebuchadnezzar (king of Babylon)
38–45, 47, 49, 52

Nehemiah, the prophet *42, 52–53*
Neo-Orthodoxy *440*
Nero (Roman Caesar) *87, 95–97, 99*
Nestorius (bishop of
Constantiople) *130–132, 142*
Nettleton, Asahel *340*
Newman, John Henry *366*
Newton, Isaac *287*
Newton, John (author of the hymn
"Amazing Grace") *307, 309, 317,
326, 334, 355*
Nicanor (Seleucid general) *60–62*
Nicea, Council of *104, 114, 117–119,
122, 127*
Nicea, Second Council of *151*
Nicholas I (Russian czar) *351*
Nicholas II (pope) *164*
Nicholas II (Russian czar) *171, 406*
Nicholas IV (pope) *188*
Nicholas of Hereford *194*
Nicholson, John H. (cofounder of the
Gideons) *403*
Niebuhr, H. Richard (theologian) *426*
Niebuhr, Reinhold (theologian) *440*
Ninty-Five Theses *211–212, 216, 218*
Nixon, Richard *473*
Noah *2*
Northfield Conferences *391*
Numerian (emperor) *114*
Nuremburg Laws *431*

O

Octavian (Caesar) *65–67*
Odoacer (Germanic chief) *133*
Olaf Tryggvason (Norwegian king)
160
Olevianus, Kaspar (German
minister) *240*
Olga (grand duchess of Kiev) *158*
Omar (caliph of Medina) *142, 183*
Omri (king of Israel) *24*
Onesimus (slave) *92*
Onias III (Jewish high priest) *59*
Operation Mobilization *407, 430*
Orange, Councils of *135*
Origen (theologian) *106–107, 170*

Orr, J. Edwin (historian) *431*
Orthodox Church *58, 164, 202*
Oslo Accords *483–484*
Oswy (king of Northumbria) *144*
Othniel (judge in ancient Israel) *15*
Otto I (German emperor of the Holy Roman Empire) *158–159*
Ottoman Empire *214, 218, 230, 324, 357, 363, 389, 416, 420*
Ottoman Turks *202, 209, 213*
Overholtzer, Jesse Irvin (founder of Child Evangelism Fellowship) *434*
Owen, John (theologian) *279, 436, 480*
Oxford University *194, 266, 296, 299–300, 356*
Ozman, Agnes N. *403*

P

Pablo Christiani (Jewish Christian) *186*
Pachomius (father of communal monasticism) *118*
Pacific Garden Mission *390, 398, 401, 432*
Pale of Settlement *324, 396*
Palmer, Phoebe Worrall (author of *The Way to Holiness*) *364*
Pantaenus (founder of a school in Alexandria, Egypt) *106*
Papal States *140, 180, 213, 245*
Parham, Charles F. (leader of Pentecostalism) *404*
Parris, Samuel (pastor in Salem, Massachusetts) *288–289*
Pascal, Blaise *256, 261, 277*
Passover *8, 34, 65, 72–78, 103, 136, 173, 363*
Patmos (island) *98–99*
Paton, John Gibson *372*
Patriarchate (Jewish institution) *130*
Patrick (missionary to Ireland) *131*
Paul III (pope) *229, 231, 234*
Paul IV (pope) *213, 234, 238, 330, 339, 383*
Paul V (pope) *211*
Paul, the apostle *3, 80, 82–85, 87–93, 95–97, 121, 144*

Paulinus (chaplain of Kent) *141*
Pekah (king of Israel) *32–33*
Penn, William *284*
Pentecost *79, 295*
Pepin III *149*
Perpetua (Christian martyr) *107*
Peter the Great (Russian czar) *290, 293*
Peter, the apostle *75–76, 78–81, 83, 87, 94–95, 144, 353*
Petrucci, Ottaviano dei *211*
Pharaoh *6–8, 10, 38, 40, 42*
Philip (emperor) *109*
Philip II (king of France) *178*
Philip II (king of Spain) *232, 249–250*
Philip IV (king of France) *188–190, 192*
Philippines, the *243*
Photius (patriarch of Constantinople) *154–155*
Pierce, Robert (founder of World Vision) *453*
Pierson, Abraham (pastor) *290*
Pilgrim's Progress, The *282–283, 342*
Pilgrims *254, 257–259*
Pinsker, Leon (author of *Autoemancipation*) *393*
Piper, John (author of *Desiring God*) *479*
Pisa, Council of *196, 212*
Pisidian Antioch *82*
Pius IV (pope) *238, 240*
Pius IX (pope) *370, 381, 383*
Pius V (pope) *245*
Pius VII (pope) *330, 339, 383*
Pius X (pope) *230*
Pius XI (pope) *427, 433*
Pius XII (pope) *455*
Plato *107, 166*
Pliny the Younger (governor) *102*
Polycarp (bishop of Smyrna) *102–105, 144*
Pontius Pilate (Roman governor of Judea) *77–78*
Potiphar (Egyptian captain of the palace guard) *5–6*
Presbyterian Church in America *472*
Presbyterians *268, 270, 286, 294, 358*

Princeton Evangelical Fellowship   427
Princeton Theological Seminary   338,
   371, 396, 421, 424
Princeton University   294, 307, 310,
   395–396, 427
Priscilla   85–86
Prison Fellowship   473, 476
Promise Keepers   483
Providence, Rhode Island   267
Ptolemy (Roman general, ruler of Egypt
   and Palestine)   55, 59
Ptolemy I Soter   56–57
Pumbeditha (Jewish academy)   108,
   162
Puritanism   267, 276
Puritans   232, 247, 255, 262, 265,
   270–272, 282, 286–287, 289

Q

Qarqar, battle of   31
Quakers (also known as Society of
   Friends)   273, 277, 284
Quauhtlatoatzin (Juan Diego)   225
Queen Victoria (queen of England)   361

R

Rabin, Yitzhak (Israeli prime
   minister)   483–484
Rabina bar Huma   134
Rachel (wife of Jacob, mother to
   Joseph)   4–7
Radewijns, Florentius   193
Raikes, Robert (founder of Sunday school
   movement)   318
Raphael (Italian painter)   213
Ras Shamara Tablets   426
Rashi (also known as Rabbi Solomon bar
   Isaac)   165
Ratislav (prince of Moravia)   154
Rav. See Abba Arika   108
Rayburn, James Jr. (founder of Young
   Life)   441
Rebekah (wife of Isaac, mother to Jacob
   and Esau)   4
Recared (Visigoth king)   146
Redwald (ruled East Anglia)   141

Reform Judaism   335, 342, 348, 358, 384,
   455
Reformation, the   129, 176, 179, 191,
   205, 212, 215–221, 223–225, 227–229,
   231, 233–235, 239, 243, 245, 247–248,
   251, 255, 259, 265, 267, 273, 285
Rehoboam (Solomon's son, king of
   Israel)   22–23
Rembrandt van Rijn (Dutch
   painter)   281
Renaissance, Byzantine   154
Renaissance, the   201, 212, 214, 219
Reuben (son of Jacob)   5, 15
Reubeni, David (Jew burned as a heretic
   in Spain)   218, 226
Rhode Island   267–268, 317
Ricci, Matteo (Roman Catholic
   missionary to China)   248, 291
Richard I (king of England)   178
Ridley, Nicolas (English bishop)   233,
   236
Robe, James (Scottish revivalist)   361
Robert the Bruce (king of Scotland)   190
Roberts, Oral (American
   televangelist)   482
Roe v. Wade (Supreme Court decision
   regarding abortion)   471–472
Rogers, Adrian (Southern Baptist
   pastor)   479
Rogers, John. See Matthew, Thomas   229
Rokycana (archbishop)   202
Roman Catholic Church   30, 122, 124,
   129, 144, 152, 156, 163–164, 173, 177,
   183, 205, 216–219, 224, 226, 234, 237,
   243, 254, 266, 272, 311, 339, 366, 381,
   383–384, 455
Rome   30, 65–67, 86–88, 90–97, 99,
   101–105, 108–111, 117, 120, 124–125,
   128–129, 131–133, 136, 139–141,
   145–147, 149, 153–155, 158, 163–164,
   172, 177, 179–181, 189, 193–194,
   196, 199–201, 208, 211–213, 234,
   427, 433
Romulus Augustulus   133
Rosen, Moishe (founder of Jews for
   Jesus)   472

Rothschild, Lionel de (first Jewish member of Parliament) 374
Russell, Charles Taze (founder of Jehovah's Witnesses) 389
Russian Orthodox Church 160, 250, 290, 293

S

Saadia ben Joseph 157
Sadat, Anwar (president of Egypt) 477
Saint, Nate (missionary martyr) 459, 461
Saint, Rachel (sister of Nate Saint) 459, 461
Saladin (caliph) 177–178
Salome Alexandra (widow of Aristobulus) 64
Salvation Army 390
Samoset (American Indian) 258, 260
Samson (judge in ancient Israel) 16, 18
Samuel the Nagid (courtier-rabbi) 164–165
Samuel, the prophet 17, 19–20, 53, 108
Sang-yum, Suh (Korean evangelist) 321
Sanhedrin 64, 74, 78–80, 89, 106–108, 130, 333
Sankey, Ira (song leader with D. L. Moody) 370, 385, 387
Sanquhar Declaration 284
Sara (Jewish academy) 162
Sarah/Sarai (wife of Abraham, mother to Isaac) 2–4
Saskatoon Revival 471
Sattler, Michael (Anabaptist leader) 221–222
Saul (first king of Israel) 19–20, 50
Saul of Tarsus. See Paul, the apostle
Savonarola, Girolamo (Dominican friar) 203, 208–209
Schaeffer, Francis (founder of L'Abri Fellowship) 456
Schleiermacher, Frederick Ernst Daniel (author of On Religion) 325, 346
Schmucker, Samuel Simon (proponent of the Definite Synodical Platform) 370

Schneersohn, Joseph Isaac (Orthodox Jewish rabbi) 438
Schneersohn, Menachem Mendel (Orthodox Jewish rabbi) 438
Scholasticism 179
Schweitzer, Albert 408
Scofield, C. I. 409
Scopes, John T. (defendant in Scopes Monkey Trial) 424–425
Scott, Peter Cameron (founder of Africa Inland Mission) 398
Second Vatican Council 464
Seleucus (Roman general, ruler of Syria, king) 55, 57, 59
Seleucus IV Philopater (Seleucid king) 59
Selim the Grim (ruler of the Ottoman Empire) 230
Seljuk Turks 166, 168–170
Sens, Council of 172
Septimius Severus (emperor) 106
Serra, Junípero (Spanish priest, founder of California missions) 311
Seung-hoon, Lee (introduced Catholicism to Korea) 321
Seventh-Day Adventist Church 364, 366, 376
Seymour, William J. (African American preacher) 405
Shallum (king of Israel) 30
Shalmaneser III (Assyrian emperor) 31
Shamgar (judge in ancient Israel) 16
Sharon, Ariel (Israeli general and prime minister of Israel) 481, 484
Shem (son of Noah) 2
Sheshbazzar (governor of Judah) 47
Sigebert (king of East Anglia) 141
Sigismund (German king) 196–197
Silas (missionary with Paul) 84
Simeon the Stylite 130
Simon ben Kosiba (known as Bar Kokhba) 103
Simon Maccabeus 63
Simon Magus 98
Simpson, A. B. (founded Christian and Missionary Alliance) 400

"Sinners in the Hands of an Angry God" 302–304

Six Day War 468–469, 472

Sixtus IV (pope) 203, 210, 226

Slessor, Mary (missionary to Nigeria) 389

Smith, Chuck (founder of Calvary Chapel) 464

Smith, Joseph, Jr. (founder of Mormon Church) 352–353

Smith, William A. (established Boys' Brigade in Scotland) 394

Smyth, Egbert C. (professor at Andover Seminary) 395

Smyth, John (founder of first Baptist church in Amsterdam) 254–255

Solomon (son of King David) 20–22, 29, 44, 47, 49, 53, 64, 73–74

Solomon bar Isaac (also known as Rashi) 165

Solomon ibn Gabirol (Jewish poet and philosopher) 166

Sophronius (patriarch of Jerusalem) 142

Soubrious, Bernadette 374

Southern Baptist Convention 365–366, 386, 479

Spanish Inquisition 203–204, 207, 210, 226

Spener, Philipp Jakob 281, 288

Speyer, Diet of 223

Spinoza, Benedict de 278

Spurgeon, Charles Haddon 369, 375, 434

Squanto 258–259

St. Bartholomew's Day Massacre 246

Stanley, Henry (newspaperman who found David Livingstone) 361, 363

Stephen (first Christian martyr) 79–81, 89, 93

Stephen II (pope) 149

Stewart, Lyman (editor of The Fundamentals) 410

Stoddard, Solomon (grandfather of Jonathan Edwards) 308

Stott, John R. W. (English evangelical pastor) 446, 474

Stowe, Calvin (husband of Harriet Beecher Stowe) 369

Stowe, Harriet Beecher (author of Uncle Tom's Cabin) 367

Student Volunteer Movement 395

Sudan Interior Mission 397

Suleiman the Magnificent 214, 230

Sunday, Billy (American evangelist) 390, 398, 432

Sutera, Lou (revival leader in Canada) 471

Sutera, Ralph (revival leader in Canada) 471

Sviatoslav (Russian ruler) 158

Swaggart, Jimmy (American televangelist) 482

Sylvester I (pope) 149

Sylvester II (pope) 161

Synod of Hieria 149

T

Taborites (radical followers of Jan Hus) 198–199

Talmud, the 107, 126, 134, 161, 165, 184, 187, 234, 298, 314

Tarif (Muslim Berber chief) 146

Taylor, Hudson (missionary to China) 361, 368–369, 382, 457

Taylor, Kenneth (founder of Tyndale House Publishers) 456

Taylor, Nathaniel (successor to Jonathan Edwards) 308

Teignmouth, Lord (governor-general of India) 326

Temple, the 3, 18, 20–21, 23, 27, 29, 32–34, 36, 40–49, 51–54, 59–62, 65–67, 72, 74, 76, 88, 93–94, 96–97, 106, 123, 126, 145, 207, 230, 449, 469

Templeton, Chuck (evangelist with Billy Graham) 443

Tennent, William (Presbyterian minister) 294, 307

Terah (Abraham's father) 2

Teresa of Avila (Carmelite nun, author of *The Way of Perfection*) 243
Tertullian (church father) 101, 105–106
The Fundamentals 410
Theodora (wife of Justinian I) 135, 137
Theodosius I (emperor) 126
Theodosius II (emperor) 131
Theological Education by Extension (TEE) 463
Thessalonica 85, 154
Third Lateran Council 163, 177
Thirty Years' War 252, 256, 259, 265, 281
Thirty-Nine Articles 242, 320, 374
Tholuck, Friedrich August Gottreu (German Protestant theologian) 350
Thomas à Kempis 193, 198
Thomas Aquinas 179, 186
Thornton, Henry (English abolitionist) 326
Tiridates III (king of Armenia) 112
Titus Livius (historian) 30
Torquemada, Tomas de 203, 210
Torrey, Reuben (R. A.) (first president of Moody Bible Institute) 405, 410
Townsend, Cameron (founder of Wycliffe Bible Translators) 429, 431
Trajan (emperor) 102
Treaty of Nanking 363
Trent, Council of 128–129, 231, 238, 240
Trotman, Dawson (founder of the Navigators) 407, 428
Trotter, Mel 390, 401
Tsu Hsi (empress of China) 403
Tyndale, William (translator of English Bible) 214, 221, 224, 227, 229, 239

U

Ulphilas (bishop of Constantiople) 122
United Nations 444, 447–452, 468
University of Oxford 174
University of Paris 174, 191
Urban (bishop of Paris) 108
Urban II (pope) 168–169
Urban VI (pope) 193–194
Ursinus (candidate for pope) 124

Ursinus, Zacharias (German minister) 240
Uzziah (king of Judah) 29, 32, 178

V

Valens (emperor) 128
Valentinian (emperor) 124, 127
Valentinian III (emperor of the western Roman Empire) 132–133
Venn, John (rector in Clapham, England) 326
Vespasian (Roman emperor) 62, 97–99
Vienne, Council of 189
Vietnam War 475
Vikings 153
Visigoths 128, 133, 145–146
Vladimir (prince of Kiev) 158
Voltaire (Francois-Marie Arouet, French writer) 311
von Zinzendorf, Count Nikolaus Ludwig (founder of the Moravian church) 202, 293, 295–296

W

Waldenses 176
Waldo, Peter 176
Ware, Henry (professor of divinity at Harvard University) 334
Warfield, Benjamin Breckinridge (theologian) 396, 410
Wars of Religion 240, 251, 285
Warsaw Ghetto Uprising (World War II) 442
Washington, George 314
Watt, James (inventor of the steam engine) 308, 311
Watts, Isaac (hymn writer) 291–292
Weizmann, Chaim (Zionist and first president of Israel) 415–416, 423
Welsh Revival 405
Wesley, Charles 296, 299–301
Wesley, John 197, 299–302, 312, 315, 319–320, 329, 387, 480
Westminster Confession of Faith 273, 472
Westminster Seminary 424, 435

Westphalia, Peace of   236
Wheaton, Warren (founder of Wheaton, Illinois)   367
White, Ellen Gould (leader of Seventh Day Adventists)   376
Whitefield, George   294, 297–302, 480
Whittingham, William (translator)   239
Wilberforce, Samuel (English bishop)   376
Wilberforce, William (English abolitionist and member of Parliament)   321, 326, 334, 354–355
Wilder, Robert   395
Wilfrid (bishop of York)   145
Willard, Frances   391
Willard, Frances (president of National Woman's Christian Temperance Union)   391
William I (emperor of Germany)   383
William I (of Normandy, William the Conquerer)   165–166
William II (king of England)   167–168
William of Holland (king)   183
William of Ockham (monk)   191
William of Orange (Protestant king of England)   286–287
William the Pious (founder of Cluny monastery)   156
Williams, Roger (founder of Providence, Rhode Island)   267
Willow Creek Community Church   475
Wilson, George (secretary-treasurer of the Billy Graham Evangelistic Association)   453
Wilson, Woodrow   415
Wimber, Carol (wife of John Wimber)   474
Wimber, John (founder of the Association of Vineyard Churches)   474
Winthrop, John (Massachusetts governor)   263, 268
Wise, Isaac Mayer (American Reform Jewish rabbi)   384
Wittenberg, Germany   212, 216, 219, 224
Women's Union Missionary Society   378
World Council of Churches   410, 421, 451, 470

World War I   414–417, 449
World War II   214, 436, 439, 441–445, 449, 463
Worms (Talmudic academy)   165
Worms, Concordat of   167, 171–172
Worms, Diet of   216, 218–219
Worms, Edict of   223
Wycliffe Bible Translators. See Cameron Townsend   407, 429, 430–431
Wycliffe, John (Bible translator)   197, 429
Wycliffe, John (translator of first English Bible)   194–195, 198, 431

X
Xavier, Francis (missionary)   230, 232, 248, 268
Xerxes (king of Persia also known as Ahusuerus)   49–50

Y
Yale University   291, 307
Yale, Elihu   290
Williams, George (founder of Young Men's Christian Association)   366
YMCA. See George Williams   366, 370, 398
Youderian, Roger (martyred missionary)   459, 461
Young Life   441
Youth for Christ   443, 453

Z
Zacharias (pope)   150
Zalman, Elijah ben Solomon (leader of the yeshiva of Vilna, Lithuania)   314
Zechariah, the prophet   47–49, 74
Zedekiah (king of Judah)   37, 40, 42–43
Zephaniah, the prophet   36
Zevi, Shabbetai   280
Zimri (king of Israel)   24
Zizka, John (military Taborite leader)   199
Zwingli, Ulrich (Swiss reformer)   217–218, 220, 223

ABOUT THE AUTHORS

Mike and Sharon Rusten have been successful as marriage, parenting, and business partners, and as coauthors. Mike has a B.A. from Princeton, and M.A. from the University of Minnesota, an M.Div. from Westminster Theological Seminary (Philadelphia), a Th.M. from Trinity Evangelical Divinity School, and a Ph.D. from New York University. Sharon attended Beaver College (Pennsylvania) and Lake Forest College (Illinois) and received a B.A. from the University of Minnesota. Together, Mike and Sharon also attended the American Institute of Holy Land Studies, now Jerusalem University College. The Rustens have two grown children and live in Minnetonka, Minnesota.

Books in The Complete Book Popular Reference Series

 The Complete Book of Bible Trivia contains more than 4500 questions and answers about the Bible. *ISBN 0-8423-0421-5*

 The Complete Book of Christian Heroes is an in-depth popular reference about those who have suffered for the cause of Christ throughout the world. *ISBN 0-8423-3485-8 Coming Spring 2005*

 **The Complete Book of When and Where in the Bible and throughout History** focuses on more than 1000 dates that illustrate how God has worked throughout history to do extraordinary things through ordinary people. *ISBN 0-8423-5508-1*

 The Complete Book of Zingers is an alphabetized collection of one-sentence sermons. *ISBN 0-8423-0467-3 Coming Spring 2005*

 The Complete Book of Who's Who in the Bible is your ultimate resource for learning about the people of the Bible. *ISBN 0-8423-8369-7 Coming Spring 2005*

 The Complete Book of Bible Basics identifies and defines the names, phrases, events, stories, and terms from the Bible and church history that are familiar to most Christians. *ISBN 1-4143-0169-3 Coming Summer 2005*

 In **The Complete Book of Bible Secrets and Mysteries** Stephen Lang, an expert in the Bible, serves up secrets and mysteries of the Bible in a fun, entertaining way. *ISBN 1-4143-0168-5 Coming Spring 2005*

The Complete Book of Bible Trivia: Bad Guys Edition, an extension of Stephen Lang's best-selling book *The Complete Book of Bible Trivia*, focuses on facts about the "bad guys" in the Bible. *ISBN 1-4143-0379-3 Coming Summer 2005*